Humanae vitae, 50 Years Later

Humanae vitae, 50 Years Later

Embracing God's Vision for Marriage, Love, and Life

A COMPENDIUM

* * *

Edited by Theresa Notare

Preface by Most Rev. Charles J. Chaput, OFM Cap.

The Catholic University of America Press
Washington, D.C.

The paper used in this publication meets the minimum requirements of American National Standards for Information Science—Permanence of Paper for Printed Library Materials, ANSI Z39.48-1984.
∞

Library of Congress Cataloging-in-Publication Data
Names: Notare, Theresa, date- editor. | Chaput, Charles J., author of preface.
Title: Humanae vitae, 50 years later : embracing God's vision for marriage, love, and life : a compendium / edited by Theresa Notare ; preface by Most Rev. Charles J. Chaput, OFM Cap.
Other titles: Humanae vitae, fifty years later
Description: Washington, DC : The Catholic University of America Press, [2019] | Includes bibliographical references.
Identifiers: LCCN 2019009975 (print) | LCCN 2019016442 (ebook) | ISBN 9780813232171 (PDF ebook) | ISBN 9780813232164 (pbk. : alk. paper)
Subjects: LCSH: Catholic Church. Pope (1963-1978 : Paul VI). Humanae vitae. | Birth control—Religious aspects—Catholic Church. | Marriage—Religious aspects—Catholic Church. | Sex—Religious aspects—Catholic Church. | Family planning—Religious aspects—Catholic Church.
Classification: LCC HQ766.3 (ebook) | LCC HQ766.3 .H812 2019 (print) | DDC 205/.663—dc23
LC record available at https://lccn.loc.gov/2019009975

DEDICATION

To St. Paul VI.

For having the wisdom and courage to promulgate *Humanae vitae*, whose treasures the Church continues to discover.

Contents

III
Natural Family Planning

IV
Health and Love: Examining Distortions Introduced by the Contraceptive Mentality from Medical, Psychological, and Legal Perspectives

V
Humanae vitae—Contemporary Challenges

VI
Signs of Growth and Healing

List of Tables

Acknowledgments

A VOLUME SUCH AS THIS STANDS on the work of many people. Those who shared in this endeavor did so with the desire to help readers deepen their understanding of Catholic teaching that is articulated in the papal encyclical, *Humanae vitae,* on its fiftieth anniversary year (2018). They should not only be acknowledged, but commended for their vision, hard work, and generosity.

The first group of collaborators include the episcopal members of the American bishops' Committee for Laity, Marriage, Family Life and Youth (2016–2018), their consultants, and staff of the Secretariat of Laity, Marriage, Family Life and Youth (LMFLY). The essays were to form a segment of a larger *Humanae vitae* anniversary project that was approved by the bishops' committee in 2016. The comprehensive project included: an academic symposium (with various co-sponsors), a website page, and various pastoral resources of the United States Conference of Catholic Bishops (USCCB). It is, therefore, with deep gratitude that this group of clergy and laity should be thanked. Notably, one of the consultants, Dr. John Grabowski (The Catholic University of America), was pivotal in steering the initial discussions to the specific event of the academic symposium from which scholarship could be generated and published. These insightful leaders tasked Theresa Notare (Assistant Director, NFP Program, USCCB) with the responsibility of administration of the project.

As the symposium moved forward, a steering committee of Catholic scholars helped to identify the authors featured in this volume. Appreciation is extended to:

- Andy Lichtenwalner, PhD, former Executive Director, Secretariat of LMFLY, USCCB
- Theresa Notare, PhD, Assistant Director, NFP Program, Secretariat of LMFLY, USCCB
- John S. Grabowski, PhD, Associate Professor, School of Theology and Religious Studies, The Catholic University of America
- Richard J. Fehring, PhD, RN, FAAN, Professor Emeritus, and Director, The Institute for Natural Family Planning, Marquette University, College of Nursing
- Very Rev. Thomas Petri, OP, STD, Vice President and Academic Dean, Assistant Professor, Moral Theology and Pastoral Studies, the Pontifical Faculty of the Immaculate Conception at the Dominican House of Studies, Washington, D.C.
- David S. Crawford, PhD, Associate Dean for Academic Affairs, and Associate Professor of Moral Theology and Family Law, Pontifical John Paul II Institute for Studies on Marriage and Family at The Catholic University of America, Washington, D.C.
- Janet E. Smith, PhD, Fr. Michael J. McGivney Chair of Life Ethics, Sacred Heart Major Seminary, Archdiocese of Detroit.

Once the authors were selected, they worked diligently to produce the essays in this compendium. We are grateful for their willingness to be part of this project. Their expertise and insights are rich with love of God's truth.

Gratitude is extended to the staff of The Catholic University of America Press, notably the acquisitions editor, John Martino, and to copy editor, Maria Caulfield. Both are gifted professionals and more than knowledgeable about the content in this volume. Their painstaking work helped to refine the text. In addition, appreciation is extended to Madeline Watkins, USCCB/LMFLY staff, who assisted in the compilation of the sources cited in the bibliography.

Finally, the collaborators are indebted to Our Sunday Visitor Institute whose generous grant funded the authors' contribution to this compendium. The Catholic Church in the United States is fortunate to have so loyal a benefactor!

Preface

Humanae vitae, *Fifty Years Later (1968–2018)*

Most Rev. Charles J. Chaput, OFM Cap.

✸ THIRTY YEARS AGO, IN REMARKS to brother bishops, Joseph Ratzinger noted that life in the modern Church comes with a recurring litany of complaints. The complaints are familiar. They never vary. They target the Catholic teachings on contraception, sexual morality, and the nature of conscience and freedom. And each individual complaint rests upon a commonly shared desire for a "much more far-reaching change of 'paradigms' [about] the basic ideas of being and of human obligation."[1]

As a result, and over time, said Ratzinger, some key elements of the Catholic faith "have witnessed a certain kind of reduction . . . a reduction [in confidence and zeal] which has been gradually preparing the way for another 'paradigm.'" It's a new and quite different paradigm that would "confer the aura of morality upon changed norms of behavior" more accurately labeled "as a surrender of moral integrity."[2]

Not much has changed in thirty years, or in the fifty years since *Humanae vitae.* Neither has the truth changed about the dignity of human life, the nature of the human person, the beauty of marriage, and the purpose of human sexuality. The fiftieth anniversary of *Humanae vitae*, therefore, provides an opportunity to celebrate the Catholic proclamation that truth, goodness, and beauty go together. And, they are experienced with the greatest joy and freedom in obedience to the word of God and the enduring wisdom of the Church. This is the paradigm for the believing Christian. And it is the only paradigm that matters.

Men and women fall in love with each other because they see a reflection of God's beauty and goodness in each other—body, mind, and soul. God is a Communion of Persons united in a love so fruitful that it overflows into the created world. That world gives glory to God and reflects his attributes, especially that crown of creation, human beings. We're uniquely created in the image and likeness of God. God has, therefore, made our love fruitful, like his own, and called us to take part in the creation of new life.

Many otherwise good and decent people today are blind to this good news. Remembering a few simple facts is important.

In 1960, the Food and Drug Administration (FDA) approved the first birth control pill for release to the public. Supporters argued that the pill would strengthen

1 Joseph Ratzinger, "Difficulties Confronting the Faith in Europe Today," *Communio: International Catholic Review* 38 (Winter 2011): 728–737, cited at 731.

2 Ratzinger, "Difficulties Confronting the Faith in Europe Today."

marriages by allowing couples to rationally space their children. Children would be enriched by more attention and love from their parents. Financial strains would ease. Families would flourish. Demand for the new pill was heavy and immediate.

Pope John XXIII set up a birth control commission to advise him on whether the historical Christian rejection of contraceptives would apply to the new contraceptive technology. Pope Paul VI expanded that commission and awaited their conclusions. After study and discussion, the commission advised that it would not. In other words, most members found the pill to be morally legitimate. A few commission voices disagreed. They included Karol Wojtyła, the cardinal archbishop of Kraków. But they were in the minority.

What happened next is very well known. In his 1968 encyclical, *Humanae vitae,* Paul VI taught that the pill *was,* in fact, a form of prohibited birth control. As a result, many Catholic clergy, scholars, and laypersons simply refused to accept the decision. That resistance continues in our own day.

Humanae vitae revealed deep wounds in the Church about our understanding of the human person, the nature of sexuality, and marriage as created by God. We still seek the cure for those wounds. But, thanks to the witness of Popes John Paul II, Benedict XVI, Francis, and many other faithful shepherds, the Church has continued to preach the truth of Jesus Christ about who we are and what God desires for us. People willing to open their eyes and their hearts to the truth will see the hope that Catholic teaching represents and the power that comes when that truth makes us free.

With the above in mind, it is useful to focus on three things. First, I want to look at the emergence of Christianity in Rome and how the Gospel changed pagan society's view of the human person. Second, I want to examine the signs of our own times. We're living in a new kind of pagan society. We need to understand our culture's topography so the Church can fruitfully respond to it. And third, I want to consider *Humanae vitae's* teaching and prophecies, the ways in which Paul VI called us to lives of self-giving and self-denial, and his predictions if our society refused to take up that call.

Many people today dismiss the Catholic view of sexuality as an oddity, or worse. It is an unhealthy thorn in the side of enlightened culture. We are often scolded, even by critics within the Church, that we focus too much on the "pelvic issues." The battles over sex compete with and obscure more urgent parts of the Gospel, like care for the poor—or so the argument goes.

As a bishop for thirty years, I can testify that in every diocese I have served, the Church has put far more money, time, and personnel into the care and education of the underprivileged than into programs related to sex. And it's not that critics don't know this. Many do not *want* to know it because the facts interfere with their erroneous storyline that the Church is a sexually repressed, body-denying institution locked in the past.

My point is, the Church believes what she believes about human sexuality because of what she believes about the meaning and dignity of the human person *as a whole*. We care for the poor and work against injustices like human trafficking for the same reasons we believe that sexual love is reserved for marriage between one man and one woman who are open to children.

For proof, we can look to some contrasts from the world in which Christianity arose. I will draw on the work of Kyle Harper, a professor of classics and letters and provost at the University of Oklahoma. In ancient Greece and Rome, society divided into men and women of status who had honor and those who had none. Aristocratic women were told to preserve their chastity for marriage. Aristocratic men were expected to have sex as they pleased, ideally in moderation and discreetly.

Slaves and prostitutes existed to meet the needs of their masters and clients. Harper writes that the austere classical philosophers and more promiscuous Romans both "presumed that sex was just sex, one instinctual need among others, to be channeled in certain fundamental ways."[3] Prostitutes and slaves were safety valves. They were a way to release pent-up energies for free-born men. This isn't so alien to the way many think about sex and pornography in our own society. The fifth-century bishop Salvian summed up Roman sexual policy as forbidding adulteries but building brothels.[4]

This regime rested on exploiting the weak, a fact that Romans couldn't see because Rome lacked any sense of the innate dignity in all human beings. Harper notes that: "None of the classical political regimes, nor any of the classical philosophical schools, regarded human beings as universally free and incomparably worthy creatures. Classical civilization, in short, lacked the concept of human dignity."[5]

This changed drastically with the rise of Christianity. Christians welcomed all new life as something holy and a blessing. They argued that *all* human beings—Jew and Greek, slave and free, men and women—are made in the image and likeness of God. The new faith held that men and women are not simply souls trapped in bodies. We are a *unity* of body and soul—ensouled bodies and embodied souls.

In other words, your human body is not just a bag of flesh—or in today's much more cynical terms, "animated meat" or "wetware." It's more than just raw material for your own uses or those of others. Your body is part of who you are and the expression of your being.

Christians preached that the world is *not* subject to the course of the planets. It *doesn't* depend on the whims of fate. Rather, God has given all women and men free will, the power to act in accord with God's commands or against them. Christianity embedded that notion of free will in human culture for the first time.[6] Christian

3 Kyle Harper, "The First Sexual Revolution," *First Things* 279 (January 2018): 42.

4 Kyle Harper, *From Shame to Sin: The Christian Transformation of Sexual Morality in Late Antiquity* (Cambridge, Mass.: Harvard University Press, 2013), 47. See also Salvian, *De Gubernatione Dei*, 7.22.

5 Kyle Harper, "Christianity and the Roots of Human Dignity in Late Antiquity," in *Christianity and Freedom: Volume I: Historical Perspectives*, eds., Timothy Samuel Shah and Allen D. Hertzke (Cambridge, Mass.: Cambridge University Press, 2016), 127.

6 Harper, *From Shame to Sin*, 4.

sexual morality was a key part of this understanding of free will.[7] The body was "a consecrated space" in which we could choose or reject God.[8]

Christians therefore demanded care for the vulnerable *bodies* of society. The first recorded opposition to slavery as an institution in history comes from Gregory of Nyssa.[9] Christianity likewise created the category of "the poor" as a group of people whose material poverty contradicts their dignity as human beings. And Christians preached that the bodies of slaves and prostitutes did not exist for the sexual gratification of masters and paying clients.

In other words, early Christians saw their faith, including its understanding of sexuality, as a message of freedom and new life in Jesus Christ, not repression. "Sexual morality was part of the proclamation of a half-hidden story of God's restoration of the created cosmos," Harper concludes.[10] It was and remains "integral to the Christian vision of redemption" because it is the logical outgrowth of that vision, not a tumor we can safely excise.[11]

One part of that early Christian understanding of sex was contraception. As with abortion, the early Church rejected contraception. The fact that Christians did not use contraception or expose unwanted children to the elements to die set them apart from their fellow Romans.

Christian opposition to contraception was universal throughout the Middle Ages and Reformation era. It remained so until 1930. In that year, the Lambeth Conference of Anglican bishops wrote that while the preferred method of limiting births should be abstinence, "nevertheless in those cases where there is such a clearly felt moral obligation to limit or avoid parenthood, and where there is a morally sound reason for avoiding complete abstinence, the Conference agrees that other methods may be used, provided that this is done in the light of the same Christian principles."[12]

The Lambeth bishops went on to note their "strong condemnation of the use of any methods of conception control from motives of selfishness, luxury, or mere convenience" or as a means of population control.[13] They condemned "the sinful practice of abortion" and sex outside marriage.[14] They also urged restrictions on the purchase of contraceptives.[15]

7 Harper, *From Shame to Sin*, 13.

8 Harper, *From Shame to Sin*, 92.

9 Harper, "Christianity and the Roots of Human Dignity in Late Antiquity," 132.

10 Harper, "The First Sexual Revolution," 43.

11 Harper, "The First Sexual Revolution," 45.

12 *The Lambeth Conference 1930. Encyclical Letter from the Bishops with Resolutions and Reports* (London: Society for Promoting Christian Knowledge, 1930), 43.

13 "Resolution 15 - The Life and Witness of the Christian Community - Marriage," Lambeth Conference 1930, Anglican Communion, http://www.anglicancommunion.org/resources/document-library/lambeth-conference/1930/resolution-15-the-life-and-witness-of-the-christian-community-marriage.

14 "Resolution 16 - The Life and Witness of the Christian Community - Marriage," Lambeth Conference 1930, Anglican Communion, http://www.anglicancommunion.org/resources/document-library/lambeth-conference/1930/resolution-16-the-life-and-witness-of-the-christian-community-marriage.

15 "Resolution 18 - The Life and Witness of the Christian Community - Marriage," Lambeth Conference 1930, Anglican Communion,

The Anglican bishops at Lambeth thought they could remove one seemingly small part of Christian teaching to accommodate modern culture, while keeping the rest of it intact. History shows they were wrong. Their minor tweak gradually turned into a full reversal on the issue of contraception. Other Christian leaders followed suit.

Today, this leaves the Catholic Church almost alone as a body of Christian believers whose leaders still maintain the historical Christian teaching on contraception. The Church can thus look stubborn and out of touch for not adjusting her beliefs to the prevailing culture. But, she's simply remaining true to the faith she received from the apostles.

Since Lambeth, developed society has moved sharply away from Christian faith and morals, without shedding them completely. To borrow a thought from G. K. Chesterton, we are surrounded by fragments of Christian ideas removed from their original framework and used in strange new ways. Human dignity and rights are still popular concepts—just don't ask what their foundation is, or whether human rights have any solid content beyond sentiment or personal preference.

Our culture isn't reverting to the paganism of the past. It's creating a new religion to replace Christianity. It's vital that we understand that today's new sexual mores are part of this larger change. As Professor Harper notes, "In our secular age, just as in the early years of Christianity, differences in sexual morality are really about the clash between different pictures of the universe and the place of the individual within it."[16]

Much of the moral conflict, broken family life, social unraveling, and gender confusion that seems so common today stems—directly or more subtly—from our disordered attitudes toward creation and our appetite to master, reshape, and even deform nature to our wills. We want the freedom to decide what reality is. And we insist on the power to make it so.

Humans have a very long and imaginative record when it comes to sins of the flesh. But our most recent dysfunctions about sex began with treating human fertility as a disease. They live on in the tragedy of children whose sex is altered by a cocktail of hormones and scalpels. For Christians, this modern hatred of the body—because hatred is exactly what it is—and the desire to master and transcend the body's limitations attack the heart of our humanity.

The irony of critics who dismiss Christian sexual morality as repressive is this: beneath all of today's enlightened talk about liberating human sexual behavior is a contempt for the weakness and inefficiency of the flesh. The body is a defective machine. It gets fat. It gets old. It gets sick. Then it dies. It can't do what my will demands of it. The body is a prison that needs to be smashed and rebuilt to new designs. The result is familiar. It is history's latest episode of Gnosticism with a new script, new cast, and better sets. However, the story is always the same. It is a story of a hatred of the limits imposed by mortal flesh and blood.

---

http://www.anglicancommunion.org/resources/document-library/lambeth-conference/1930/resolution-18-the-life-and-witness-of-the-christian-community-marriage.

16 Harper, "The First Sexual Revolution," 46.

Therein lies a key contrast. As the Congregation for the Doctrine of the Faith (speaking for Pope Francis) stressed in *Placuit Deo:*

> Gnosticism . . . associates itself with a negative view of the created order, which is understood as a limitation on the absolute freedom of the human spirit. Consequently, salvation is understood as freedom from the body and from the concrete relationships in which a person lives . . . [but] true salvation, contrary to being a liberation from the body, also includes its sanctification (cf. Rom 12:1). The human body was shaped by God, who inscribed within it a language that invites the human person to recognize the gifts of the Creator and to live in communion with one's brothers and sisters.[17]

Respect for the human body and the purpose of its sexual expression is *fundamental* to the Christian worldview. Unlike the Gnostics (ancient and modern), we believe that God created us male and female for a good and holy reason. Ordering ourselves to that purpose leads us to joy. And God became incarnate in the person of Jesus to redeem us, body and soul.

Pope Francis warns that our desire for mastery and autonomy has created a human crisis similar to the crisis of our natural environment. "In our day," he says, "marriage and the family are in crisis. We now live in a culture of the temporary, in which more and more people are simply giving up on marriage as a public commitment. This revolution in manners and morals has often flown the flag of freedom, but in fact it has brought spiritual and material devastation to countless human beings, especially the poorest and most vulnerable."[18]

Francis also notes how this seemingly "progressive" culture functions religiously. He warns against the "ideological colonization" of Third World countries and the "polite persecution" that Christians in the First World face when they dissent from the new sexual orthodoxies.[19]

As Francis has made clear, we need to resist these new orthodoxies if we want to be faithful to Jesus Christ. And that brings us back to *Humanae vitae,* the first sharp challenge by the Church to what was then called "the new morality." *Humanae vitae* is remembered for the great "No" that Paul VI uttered, and rightly so. But we often forget that his "No" came only after an even more powerful "Yes" to the beauty of marital love.

Paul VI begins *Humanae vitae* by noting four key elements of married love. Married love is *human.* It's an act of the free will by which a man and woman are joined, body and soul, in a communion of life. It's also *total,* a gift of one's whole life and self. It is *faithful,* a gift made exclusively to one person until death. And

17 Congregation for the Doctrine of the Faith, Letter *Placuit Deo, To the Bishops of the Catholic Church on Certain Aspects of Christian Salvation* (February 22, 2018), 14.

18 Pope Francis, "Not Just Good, but Beautiful," in *Not Just Good, but Beautiful: The Complementary Relationship between Man and Woman* (Walden, NY: Plough Publishing House, 2015), 3–4.

19 Inés San Martín, "Pope Francis: Ideological colonization a 'blasphemy against God,'" *Crux,* November 21, 2017, https://cruxnow.com/vatican/2017/11/21/pope-francis-ideological-colonization-blasphemy-god/. See also Junno Arocho Esteves, "Pope: Beware of 'polite persecution' disguised as culture, progress," *Catholic News Service,* April 12, 2016, http://www.catholicnews.com/services/englishnews/2016/pope-beware-of-polite-persecution-disguised-as-culture-progress.cfm.

finally, marriage is *fruitful,* overflowing to new life like the love of the God in whose image we are made.

Paul VI argues that marriage is not just a social convention we have inherited but the design of God Himself. Christian couples are called to welcome the sacrifices that God's design requires so they can enter into the joy it offers.[20] This means that while husbands and wives may take advantage of periods of natural infertility to regulate the birth of their children, they can't actively intervene to stamp out the fertility that is natural to sexual love.

Paul VI saw that the Church's teaching often hadn't been followed in the years prior to *Humanae vitae.* So, he offered four predictions of the future if that trend continued. Each of his warnings has come true, in ways more tragic than he could imagine.

First, Paul VI said that the widespread use of contraception would lead to "conjugal infidelity and the general lowering of morality." Obviously, the pill isn't the only factor in creating our current sexual confusions. But clearly, it has had a massive effect (indeed all contraceptives have their role to play). One only has to view the contemporary world. Our young people are drowning in pornography. Sexually transmitted infections and family breakdown are not only on the rise, they are seen as the collateral cost of having true freedom.

Second, Paul VI warned that men would lose respect for women, viewing them as instruments of selfish enjoyment and no longer as revered and beloved companions. Turn on the radio or television and see how this has played out. Look at the growing list of men who fall from the peak of their careers because of decades of sexual predation.

Popular culture glorifies sexual coercion and physical abuse in a way unthinkable just a few decades ago. Read the studies of today's sexual relationships and accounts of the hook-up culture in our cities and on our college campuses.[21] As I wrote in a pastoral letter on *Humanae vitae* twenty years ago,

> [A]ccording to [Pope Paul], contraception might be marketed as liberating for women, but the real 'beneficiaries' of birth control pills and devices would be men.... Many feminists have attacked the Catholic Church for her alleged disregard of women, but the Church in *Humanae vitae* identified and rejected sexual exploitation of women years before that message entered the cultural mainstream.[22]

In other words, Paul VI was right.

Third, Paul VI warned that widespread use of contraception would license public authorities to advocate and implement birth control as a form of

20 Clement of Alexandria was even more blunt than Paul VI: "Sex not intended to produce children is a rape of nature." Quoted in Harper, *From Shame to Sin*, 2013, 111; see also Clement, *Paidogogos* 2.10.95.

21 For three examples of a growing trend in scholarship, see Mark Regnerus, *Cheap Sex: The Transformation of Men, Marriage, and Monogamy* (New York: Oxford University Press, 2017); Mark Regnerus and Jeremy Uecker, *Premarital Sex in America: How Young Americans Meet, Mate, and Think about Marrying* (New York: Oxford University Press, 2011); and Donna Freitas, *The End of Sex: How Hookup Culture Is Leaving a Generation Unhappy, Sexually Unfulfilled, and Confused About Intimacy* (New York: Basic Books, 2013).

22 Much of this section is drawn from that pastoral letter. The letter can be found in full at: https://www.ewtn.com/library/bishops/chaputhv.htm.

population policy. This is precisely what's happened. As my brother bishops in the developing world can confirm, Western countries often tie their aid money to contraceptives, abortion, and sterilization. As Pope Francis said, this is a kind of "ideological colonization," and a way to keep the wrong people from having more babies.

Fourth, Paul VI worried that contraception would mislead human beings into thinking they had unlimited dominion over their own bodies, relentlessly turning the human person into the object of his or her own intrusive power. Our current obsession with transgender issues simply proves his point. As a result, a deep confusion drives much of our thinking about human life today.

A friend of mine, a wife and mother with an impish sense of humor, refers to the pill as America's chemical corset. It's a curious thought. My own sister (I suspect like a lot of modern women), would look back on corsets as an annoying museum piece: uncomfortable, antiquated, and, quite literally, restrictive. They were a way to control and reshape women's bodies to fit the expectations of society, especially men.

Contraception works in much the same way. First, it presupposes that a woman's body should work like a man's in order for a woman to flourish and be free. Second, because a woman's body does *not* work like a man's, it says that her fertility and biological rhythms are problems and weaknesses; in effect, a disease that needs to be managed, like cancer or a chemical imbalance. Thus, we get a paradox. Millions of women make sure they avoid meat with hormones and take care to use plastics sparingly. Many of those same women *also* fill themselves with hormones and insert plastic coils inside their bodies to thwart their natural fertility.

And yet it's the Church—not the pharmaceutical industry with its profits and manufactured infertility, or the doctors who deal with the pill's collateral health damage, or the abortion industry that cashes in lavishly on the failures of contraception, but *the* Church—that gets criticized as abnormal and intrusive. Nothing speaks more nakedly to the doublethink we now accept as the rhythm of our daily lives.

The boomer generation (my own cohort that came of age at the time of *Humanae vitae*) inherited a moral framework that gave us a sense of order and meaning even as we rejected it. Liberated sex was seen as life-giving, organic and a source for more generous, less confining love. *Humanae vitae* was seen as just one more effort to bottle up the energy and freedom of young people. As late as the 1980s, much of our popular entertainment still showed casual sex as affectionate, healthy and fun, with few if any consequences.

Today's film and television dramas are very different. They are far more wounded and vastly more cynical. Lena Dunham's cable series "Girls," and the short story "Cat Person" published by *New Yorker* magazine and the media uproar it created, are just two of the most obvious examples.[23] The #MeToo movement, emotional wreckage, sexual disease, and date rape are the realities we've inherited from the sexual revolution. Paul VI would not be surprised.

23 Kristen Roupenian, "Cat Person," *New Yorker*, December 11, 2017, https://www.newyorker.com/magazine/2017/12/11/cat-person.

Half a century after *Humanae vitae*, the Church in the United States is at a very difficult but also very promising moment. *Difficult*, because the language of Catholic moral wisdom is alien to many young people, who often leave the Church without ever really encountering her. *Promising*, because the most awake of those same young people want something better and more enduring than the emptiness and noise they now have. Our mission now, as always, is not to surrender to the world as it is but to feed and ennoble the deepest yearnings of the world—and thereby to lead it to Jesus Christ and his true freedom and joy.

Introduction

Embracing God's Vision for Marriage, Love, and Life

RATHER THAN DISCUSS THE THREE-YEAR GENESIS of this volume which involved a committee of bishops and a planning group of content experts, I would like to begin with a reflection about the marriage of my parents. My mother and father met in their neighborhood in the 1940s as teenagers. Dad often reminisced that he knew he would marry her when he saw her at a distance. It took my mother longer to decide if she shared my father's feelings, but decide she did. Being faithful Roman Catholics, they chastely dated after high school, became engaged just before dad was drafted into the US Army, and married when he returned from the Korean War—but only after he obtained her father's blessing. Like most Catholics at that time, my parents quickly had several children. As we grew into adolescence, and much to my mother's embarrassment, my father liked to have philosophical "birds and bees" conversations with my siblings and me. Dad would wax eloquent about the nature of men, women, and sex—he never went into biological detail, he would focus on love and chastity as the name of the game and emphasized that sex was for marriage where babies could be properly cared for—no matter how much one wanted to do otherwise when dating and "in love."

In his discourses, usually with a cup of coffee in one hand and a cigarette in the other (it was the 1960s after all and he was not perfect), he spoke poetically about the lifelong, even into eternity, spousal love he had for my mother. "That is how marriage is," he concluded. "A man should be able to die for his wife, and she for him."

Related to Dad's talks on marriage, he candidly liked to boast that he and mother were virgins when they married and that they "followed the Church's teaching on birth control." After one of his teachings, Dad would typically add another important element to his narrative—that there was only one choice in life, especially when it came to sex—to follow God's will and commandments. "It wasn't always easy," he would admit, "but it was always the best." My father was not theologically sophisticated, yet instinctively, he understood and embraced God's design for love and marriage.

As I edited the essays in this volume, I often paused to mentally reflect on various aspects of my parents' marriage. Their marriage, and my father's graced insights, I believe, witness to the truth expressed in these essays and, of course, to Catholic teaching found in Pope Paul VI's encyclical *Humanae vitae* (July 25, 1968). That encyclical, which was widely maligned at the time of its promulgation and subsequently ignored by many, represents a great "Yes" to God's design for married love and the gift of life.

Humanae vitae is a treasure, an unknown treasure for many Catholics (and indeed, for the world). In the life of the Catholic Church, its content represents a deepening of theological and spiritual understanding regarding the nature of married love and the transmission of life. The teachings, if embraced by men and women, can help heal the wounds of a world broken by sin but redeemed by Christ. The authors of the essays in this volume would agree. They have studied the damaging effects of the modern sexual revolution, each according to their discipline. And what have they seen? That revolution, which began in the nineteenth century and swelled to dizzying heights in the 1960s, tricked men and women into rejecting God's truth while slyly appealing to what men and women want—freedom, self-fulfillment, joy, and loving relationships. The messages of the modern sexual revolution have twisted these goods by first insisting that there is no absolute truth—only "personal truth." And, secondly, by over prioritizing personal desires at the expense of mutuality, which is the foundation of all friendships—especially that of the spousal union. With this as its basis, the modern sexual revolution has extracted the conjugal embrace from the permanent and faithful bond of marriage, reducing it to a meaningless activity. It has delinked procreation from sex by promoting contraception and, consequently, rendered meaningless the bonding nature of sexual intercourse. Its creed challenges the very nature of being made male and female.

The negative outcomes of the modern sexual revolution are legion. There is a rise of non-marital sexual activity in most developed nations; this has led to epidemic levels of sexually transmitted infections and diseases. Depression, especially among women who have multiple sexual partners, has risen. More children are born without the benefit of their parents being married, which brings another set of negative outcomes, including high rates of single women and children living in poverty. Abortion has been legalized in nations which accept unlimited contraceptive practices. Divorce rates are high. Many have attempted to redefine marriage to include same-sex couples. Cohabitation rates have risen in most developed nations with an accompanying rejection of marriage itself. And most developed nations are experiencing a demographic winter due to men and women opting not to become parents. Finally, the rejection of the human person as being created male or female and the insistence that a person can choose his or her sex is among the most extreme of the negative outcomes of the modern sexual revolution. To this sexual chaos, the teachings of the Catholic Church enter with healing balm—God's truth for authentic freedom, self-fulfillment, joy, and love. In *Humanae vitae*, which rests upon the whole of revelation about how God made men, women, and marriage, our loving God invites His children to share in His life as men and women made in His image.

Church teaching in *Humanae vitae* stands upon this central belief—that God made men and women in His image. To be made in God's image speaks of God's desire to love us, His invitation to share in His life, and the inherent gifts that He gives to each man and woman. And what are these gifts? Foremost is the capacity to love just like God. To be able to be faithful, trustworthy, merciful, compassionate, and forgiving are just a sampling of an endless list of attributes.

Saying it more simply, to have the capacity to love like God is the foundation of life and all human relationships.[1] Each man and woman is called by God to love Him and to form loving relationships with friends, neighbors, coworkers, people in need, and so forth—to create small communions of persons—relationships that imitate God's Trinitarian nature.

Among the many ways that we can form loving relationships is the unique union of a man and a woman in marriage. Scripture and Catholic Sacred Tradition reveal that marriage "is not . . . the effect of chance or the product of evolution of unconscious natural forces, it is the wise institution of the Creator to realize in mankind His design of love."[2] In the divine plan, God willed that marriage be a lifelong union between a man and a woman marked by fidelity, permanence, and fruitfulness.[3] He oriented marriage "toward the begetting and education of children."[4] And, for Christian spouses, God willed that through His Son, a special sacrament would be available by which husband and wife would be fortified "and receive a kind of consecration in the duties and dignity of their state."[5]

Marriage, therefore, is a radical call to love like God in such a way that it joins husband and wife in the "one flesh union"[6] and includes stewardship over the powers of procreation. Sexual intercourse is by God's design both unitive and procreative. Its dignity exists in the integrity of its design—to realize the marital one flesh union *with* its potential to bring new life into the world. Procreation is the invitation by the Lord of Life to share in the wonder of new life—children who will have their own vocations and eternal lives. This is why the Church teaches that children are the supreme gift in marriage.[7] This is also why the Church teaches that "when married couples deliberately act to suppress fertility . . . by using contraception" they deny "part of the inherent meaning of married sexuality" and actually do harm to their unity.[8] This may seem like a hard saying in today's world, so influenced by the messages of the modern sexual revolution, but the burden is lifted when we realize that God is the one who has given the gifts and He does not leave His children alone. In addition, since the methods of Natural Family Planning respect God's design, husband and wife can rely on them to both attempt a pregnancy or avoid one in their marriage.

In this volume, Catholic teachings on the nature of human sexuality, marriage, married love, and the gift of life are explored. They are anchored in the view that,

1 See Vatican Council II, *Gaudium et spes* (December 7, 1965), 24, http://www.vatican.va/archive/hist_councils/ii_vatican_council/documents/vat-ii_cons_19651207_gaudium-et-spes_en.html.

2 Pope Paul VI, Encyclical Letter *Humanae vitae* (July 25, 1968), 8, http://w2.vatican.va/content/paul-vi/en/encyclicals.index.html.

3 See *The Code of Canon Law*, §1055; Pope Paul VI, *Humanae vitae*, 9.

4 *Gaudium et spes*, 50.

5 *Gaudium et spes*, 48.

6 See Gn 2:24.

7 See *Gaudium et spes*, 50.

8 United States Conference of Catholic Bishops, *Married Love and the Gift of Life* (Washington, D.C.: USCCB Publishing, 2006).

in and through Christ's work of redemption, God's original vision of the person, human sexuality, and marriage grounds human relationships and, after the Fall, heals them. These essays were commissioned to explore the teachings as articulated in *Humanae vitae* upon its fiftieth anniversary (1968–2018). The essays were first presented in an abbreviated form at a symposium held at The Catholic University of American (April 4–6, 2018). The event was generously funded, in part, by Our Sunday Visitor Institute and cosponsored by the:

- Committee on Laity, Marriage, Family Life and Youth, United States Conference of Catholic Bishops
- School of Theology and Religious Studies at The Catholic University of America
- Institute for Natural Family Planning, Marquette University, College of Nursing
- National Catholic Bioethics Center
- Pontifical Faculty of the Immaculate Conception at the Dominican House of Studies, Washington, D.C.
- Pontifical John Paul II Institute for Studies on Marriage and Family at The Catholic University of America, Washington, D.C.
- Witherspoon Institute

The intention of the above cosponsors in commissioning these fine essays is to spark deeper reflection on the timeless truths that *Humanae vitae* presents and to inspire further scholarly thinking to help the faithful embrace more fully what God has given in marriage and the gifts of love and life.

Returning to thoughts of my parents' marriage, Dad once admitted to me that sometimes he had to go to his room, shut the door, pray, and remember why he loved my mother. Life has its difficulties, and even our loved ones can make us angry or lead us to disappointment. "Doing the right thing, even with someone you deeply love, is not always easy," Dad said. Both he and my mother lived their joint vocation of married love, sometimes easily, and sometimes with raw determination. My siblings and I knew that we were the beneficiaries of their good efforts. We were not materially rich, but we had treasure beyond measure in the love that our parents shared with us.

In the last years of his life, my mother nursed my father through a long illness. My father died at home in mother's arms. His last words to her were that she was "the love of his life." Their love was easy and passionate. At times it was hard and sacrificial. They chose the best way, they embraced each other and God's gift of married love and life. Keep this in mind as you read the following essays. And, remember the marriages of others who have done likewise. They are living witnesses of God's original gifts. Through their examples may we be inspired to teach God's truths with the compassion and clarity that Paul VI so eloquently presents in *Humanae vitae*.

Theresa Notare, PhD
Assistant Director, Natural Family Planning Program
United States Conference of Catholic Bishops

July 25, 2018

PART I

A World Afflicted

1

The Legacy of Humanae vitae

Donald T. Critchlow

✷ IN 1966, THE ROCK GROUP Buffalo Springfield sang "There's something happening here/What it is ain't exactly clear." The song was about the Vietnam War, but the lyrics could very well have described the culture of the 1960s. Something was happening here, the beginnings of a transformative sexual revolution.[1] The deep consequences of this revolution were not fully clear at the time but over the next half century, it became obvious that fundamental changes had occurred in sexual mores, gender relations, and the traditional family structure.

This sexual revolution was never complete and came with resistance. Sexual politics entered into the mainstream of American political life as a cultural war over social issues was unleashed. Issues such as reproductive rights, homosexual rights, and same-sex marriage divided the two major political parties, Republican and Democratic, the electorate, families, and generations. Rhetoric on these social issues was often inflammatory and extremists emerged on both sides. By the first decades of the twenty-first century, however, the social consequences of this sexual revolution had become clear to most people, wherever they stood on the social issues. For most informed observers, this revolution while "liberating" women and giving them greater control of their bodies, brought increasing and destructive high rates of out-of-wedlock births, higher numbers of impoverished women, and often abasement of men and women in sexual relations.

In the midst of this sexual revolution, Pope Paul VI's encyclical *Humanae vitae*, released on July 25, 1968, stands as a profound and affirmative expression of traditional values concerning God's love for human life, the divine gift of life, responsible parenthood and marriage, and the dignity of women in an age of great and rapid change. His affirmation of the family to the preservation of a healthy social order was deeply rooted in classical philosophy and long-standing Church teachings and practice. Of equal importance, although given less attention by the media and many commentators at the time were the encyclical's warnings about dangers of morally unrestrained state power in regulating human life

1 It should be noted that the modern sexual revolution of the 1960s has its beginnings in the late 19th and early 20th centuries. See a summary discussion of this in Theresa Notare's "Changing Human Behavior. How Culture, Contraception, and Religion Combined in the Early 20th Century to Create the Modern Sexual Revolution," in *Science, Faith, & Human Fertility. The Third Conference on Ethical Fertility Health Management*, ed. Richard Fehring and Theresa Notare (Milwaukee: Marquette University Press, 2012): 347–372.

and death and the consequences of a breakdown in moral order for civilization itself. This warning is worth quoting in full:

> Everything therefore in the modern means of social communication which arouses men's baser passions and encourages low moral standards, as well as every obscenity in the written word and every form of indecency on the stage and screen, should be condemned publicly and unanimously by all those who have at heart the advance of civilization and the safeguarding of the outstanding values of the human spirit.[2]

In effect, the encyclical presented a jeremiad warning of the consequences of human arrogance.

Humanae vitae proved controversial in its drafting and later release. The Church's opposition to artificial contraception (sterilization and abortion) had important political and policy implications for the Roman Catholic Church in the United States, especially the National Conference of Catholic Bishops[3] and Catholic welfare organizations.

Americans on the drafting commission and its subcommittees were major proponents for changing the Church's opposition to artificial contraception. Dissent within the Church in America continued to rumble after the encyclical's release in 1968. Furthermore, Catholic Church leaders and those involved in social welfare and medical institutions confronted delicate issues of accepting public monies while resisting government family planning policies. Fifty years later, these issues of church-state relations have not been resolved; indeed, they may be even more complex given advances in reproductive technology, the growth of government, court interpretation of civil rights for people with same-sex attraction, and what many see as social decay caused or coinciding with the breakdown of the family.

Any full assessment of *Humanae vitae* needs to be placed within the political and policy context of the post-Second World War period, changing federal policies about family planning, public comment on the encyclical following its release, and the social consequences of the corresponding breakdown of the family revealed in social science literature today.

This essay explores the historical context of *Humanae vitae* through an examination of the modern population movement promoted by philanthropic foundations, feminists, and American elites; the drafting of the encyclical; its release and reaction; the politics of abortion as it emerged in the 1970s; and the state of the American family today.

Controlling Population after the Second World War

Witnessing the horrors of a second global war in the twentieth century, many American leaders in business, philanthropic foundations, and academia

2 Pope Paul VI, Encyclical Letter *Humanae vitae* (July 25, 1968), 22, http://w2.vatican.va/content/paul-vi/en/encyclicals.index.html.

3 Now called the United States Conference of Catholic Bishops (or USCCB).

concluded that future wars could be prevented by population control. This neo-Malthusian world view took deep root in American and global elites. The obsession with global and national population control as the panacea for addressing the problems of the world cannot be overemphasized. Population control manifested itself in policy initiatives internationally and domestically, as well as funding efforts to develop better contraceptive methods. This belief in the necessity of population control manifested itself in developing birth control programs and centers in Asia, Western Europe, Africa, the Middle East, and Latin America, as well as supporting scientific and technological research for better artificial contraceptives, including oral contraception ("the pill").[4]

The development of domestic- and international-supported family planning occurred in three overlapping stages. The first stage, occurring in the immediate aftermath of the Second World War, was initiated by philanthropic foundations, led by the Population Council, to support the establishment of family planning clinics and programs in countries outside the United States. In the second stage, as these programs were established, lobbying efforts were undertaken to commit the federal government to family planning within the United States. These lobbying efforts proved successful in President Lyndon Johnson's Great Society programs to eliminate poverty. Federal family planning programs targeting inner-city populations and Native Americans on reservations. President Richard Nixon's administration extended federal efforts and funding for family planning programs. This second stage occurred within a context of growing fears of a population explosion that was going to lead to world famine, wars, and social conflict. These fears were articulated in books such as Paul Ehrlich's *Population Bomb* (1968), numerous magazine articles, science fiction novels, and popular movies projecting a dystopian future for humankind unless the rate of population growth was controlled.

The third stage came in response to reactions against federally supported family planning, specifically publicly funded sterilization and abortion. This domestic reaction coincided with revelations of widespread abuses of population control programs abroad funded by the United Nations (UN) and the US, especially in Southeast Asia and India. Feminists were especially outraged by the draconian nature of population control programs in India, which included forced sterilization of thousands of rural villagers. The history of federal and international family planning is detailed in my study, *Intended Consequences: Birth Control, Abortion and the Federal Government in Modern America* and Matthew Connelly's *Fatal Misconception: The Struggle to Control World Population*.[5] Connelly's withering critique of international family planning programs, written from a perspective of

4 Two useful histories of the development of oral contraception are Bernard Asbell, *The Pill: A Biography of the Drug that Changed the World* (New York: Random House, 1995) and Elizabeth Siegel Watkins, *On the Pill: A Social History of Oral Contraceptives, 1950–1970* (Baltimore: Johns Hopkins University Press, 1998).

5 Donald T. Critchlow, *Intended Consequences: Birth Control, Abortion, and the Federal Government in Modern America* (New York: Oxford University Press, 1999) and Matthew Connelly, *Fatal Misconception: The Struggle to Control World Population* (Cambridge, Mass.: Harvard University Press, 2008).

a supporter of abortion, makes for shocking reading as to the travesties—indeed, horrors—committed in the name of social justice through population control.

In response to the growing anti-abortion movement, the Republican Party shifted its favorable positions on abortion and federally supported family planning. At the same time, under criticism from some feminist critics, advocates of population control movement within the federal government, the UN, and the philanthropic community responded strategically. Governmental agencies and philanthropic foundations, such as the Ford Foundation, involved in population control, incorporated into their family planning programs an emphasis on economic development and health care, giving particular attention to women. Programs were implemented to support women work collectives and education of women. The underlying assumption was that if women gained greater economic independence and pursued university degrees, marriage would occur later in their lives, resulting in fewer children.

Within the United States, population control advocates, working through various organizations, shifted their focus to the environmental movement, sex education, rights for people with same-sex attraction, and reproductive rights for women. In doing so, less attention was given to explicit population control.

Before a brief summary of the emergence of the postwar population control movement which set the context for *Humanae vitae*, a few general points should be made. The population control movement, while involving prominent elites in business, politics, education, and philanthropy was not a cabal or a conspiracy. Key leaders involved in the population control endeavors shared a neo-Malthusian perspective on the necessity to reduce the rate of population growth, but the movement itself was a loosely organized movement that brought together diverse groups and individuals, including birth control advocates, eugenicists, and feminists. These groups and organizations brought different perspectives to the movement. The birth control movement, for example, had emerged in the early twentieth century, led by Margaret Sanger and other feminists, who organized Planned Parenthood of America. From the outset, Sanger and many of her supporters, such as Katherine Dexter McCormick, who financed the development of the oral contraceptive pill, saw contraception as an instrument for liberation and social control. Better contraception offered a means of liberating women from the burdens of too many children, poverty, and social advancement. At the same time, Sanger and others viewed contraception as a means of racial advancement. Sanger did not mince words when she wrote McCormick in 1950 her views on race betterment. "I consider that the world and almost our civilization for the next twenty-five years, is going to depend upon a simple, cheap, safe contraceptive to be used in poverty-stricken slums, jungles, and among the most ignorant people."[6] Continuing without pause, she added, "I believe that now, immediately, there should be national sterilization for certain dysgenic types of our population who are being encouraged to breed and would die out were the government not feeding them."[7]

6 Quoted in Asbell, *The Pill*, 9.

7 Asbell, *The Pill*, 9.

Sanger, who entered politics as a left-wing socialist in the early 1900s, became a committed neo-Malthusian under the influence of Charles V. Drysdale, a leader of the Malthusian League in England. Under the tutelage of Havelock Ellis, the acknowledged "father" of the modern sexual revolution and author of the seven-volume, *Studies in the Psychology of Sex*, she became committed to human selective breeding through eugenics.[8]

Sanger and other supporters of Planned Parenthood saw family planning primarily in terms of individual freedom and the right of women to determine the spacing of their children. Leaders of Planned Parenthood voiced concerns about overpopulation, but their focus remained on the rights of women and families to control reproduction through contraception. The emergence of the black civil rights movement and the feminist movement gave impetus to the rights aspect to the cause of federal family planning as it emerged in the second stage, the implementation of federal family planning in the 1960s. As a result, the fight over artificial contraception, federal support for contraception, and abortion became more of a rights issue than just population control per se.

Sanger used eugenics arguments to promote birth control, especially in her writings in the 1920s and 1930s. John D. Rockefeller III, a key figure in the post-World War II population control movement, also used eugenic arguments in his philanthropic work. He wanted initially to call his newly established Population Council, the Eugenics Council.[9] Similarly, the euthanasia movement in the first half of the 20th century espoused eugenics, but in the latter half, it evolved into the assisted suicide movement which emphasized individual rights, not eugenics.[10] In this way, family planning organizations in their multiple manifestations brought together advocates for eugenics, euthanasia, abortion rights, population control, immigration restriction, and environmentalism. They shared a faith in massive social engineering, even while espousing individual rights. Freedom entailed social control over the living and the dying. Control was to be exerted by the enlightened in the name of humanity.

The Emergence of the Postwar Population Control Movement

In the postwar period, philanthropists, military leaders, wealthy industrialists, and scientific experts joined together to undertake one of the most massive efforts at social engineering seen in history—the control of global population growth.

8 See for example, Phyllis Grosskurth, *Havelock Ellis: A Biography* (London: Quartet, 1981), xv. Regarding modern sexual liberalism, Grosskurth sees Ellis as "one of the seminal figures responsible for the creation of a modern sensibility." David M. Kennedy, *Birth Control in America: The Career of Margaret Sanger* (New Haven: Yale University Press, 1970) remains an important biography of Sanger, but also important for the understanding of the history of the birth control movement in modern America is James W. Reed, *The Birth Control Movement and American Society: From Private Vice to Public Virtue* (Princeton: Princeton University Press, 1993).

9 It should be noted that the eugenics movement stood as a distinct group from birth control advocates.

10 See Ian Dowbiggin, *A Merciful End: The Euthanasia Movement in Modern America* (New York: Oxford University Press, 2007); see also Dowbiggin, *A Concise History of Euthanasia: Life, Death, God, and Medicine* (Lanham: Rowman and Littlefield, 2007).

Giving voice to the need for global population control, Rockefeller established the Population Council in 1952. The first draft of the council's charter spoke of the need to control overpopulation and creating conditions in which "parents who are above average in intelligence, quality of personality" produce "larger than average families."[11] The eugenics language was dropped in the final version of the charter, although the belief that population control was for the masses and not for the elite remained an understood assumption as the Population Council launched efforts to organize and fund birth control clinics in Hong Kong, Japan, Korea, Pakistan, Taiwan, Thailand, Malaysia, Ceylon, Tunisia, and Egypt.

The Population Council represented the American elite. Serving on the council's board were high government officials, former military generals, university presidents, and key figures from the world of philanthropy. Other organizations entered the field of population control as well. The Ford Foundation poured millions of dollars into population control programs. In the early 1960s, the UN, at the prompting of American and world leaders, got involved in a worldwide effort to reduce population growth. Others joining the cause were Planned Parenthood of America and the Population Crisis Committee, funded by Hugh Moore, the founder of the Dixie Cup Company. Moore was vociferous in his commitment to population control and played a key role in establishing International Planned Parenthood, whose primary mission was population control. He and others in International Planned Parenthood were critical in organizing the First International Conference on Voluntary Sterilization in 1964. These efforts at population control were supported by an array of philanthropic institutions, including the Rockefeller Brothers Fund, the Milbank Memorial Fund, the Scaife Foundation, and the Avalon Foundation. These organizations funded birth control programs throughout the world in an attempt to control the rate of population growth.

These philanthropic foundations and individuals within the movement also funded scientific research projects to produce better contraception, including new intrauterine devices (IUDs) and oral contraception. The Population Council, among many other foundations, helped develop an oral contraceptive ("the pill"), that hit the market in 1960.[12]

These early efforts at international family planning were conducted through private American organizations working with host nations. John F. Kennedy's election in 1960 provided the first major opportunity for population control advocates to increase federal involvement. Moore took out a full-page ad in the *Wall Street Journal* in August 1963 imploring the federal government to address what he described as the "population explosion." Behind the scenes, influential New York publisher Cass Canfield and General William H. Draper began lobbying the Kennedy State Department to send experts to developing nations to assist family planning programs.[13] Further opportunity for advancement came

11 Thomas Parran to John D. Rockefeller III, October 28, 1952, RG 2, Box 45, RA, cited in Critchlow, *Intended Consequences*, 23.

12 Later Population Council funding was provided to develop the "morning-after pill."

13 Moore's attitude toward the Kennedy administration and his campaign to arouse elite and public opinion is found in his correspondence with William Draper. See Hugh Moore to William Draper, April

under Lyndon Johnson's Great Society. Population control advocates began to promote federal family planning as a means to reduce poverty in the United States.[14] The argument put forward was simple: if the poor had fewer children, poverty would be reduced. This lobbying effort was done behind the scenes with the conscious intent not to arouse Roman Catholic bishops in the United States. In 1965, these lobbyists working with presidential aide Bill Moyers, were able to insert into Johnson's State of the Union message a single sentence, "I will seek new ways to use our knowledge to deal with the explosion in world population, and the growing scarcity of world resources." Leaders of the population control movement were jubilant that they had gotten this one sentence into the address.

The Johnson administration moved into federally supported family planning in a big way. The Public Health Service began directing funds for family planning pilot projects in community health programs. Interior Secretary Stewart Udall instructed the Public Health Service to make family planning services available to Native Americans on Indian reservations. The Department of Defense issued a policy directive allowing family planning services for military personnel on army bases. The United States Agency for International Development (USAID) launched family planning projects on a global basis. The head of the agency's Office of Population, Reimert Ravenholt, a population control fanatic, had his business cards printed on condoms.

The federal government's involvement in domestic and international family planning in this period drew bipartisan support in Congress. In 1965, eight family planning bills were introduced in Congress. By 1966, more than thirty states provided family planning services. The Office of Economic Opportunity under the Johnson administration launched forty-five family planning projects, located in public housing projects, churches and community centers. These centers provided counseling and services. The Children's Bureau established a program to provide grants to states for family planning, while the Office of Education funded 645 programs to develop family planning. Medicaid became a primary source for furthering federal family planning.

Under Richard Nixon's administration, these programs were enlarged through the Family Planning Services and Population Research Act in 1970. The legislation provided $382 million for services, research, and training in family planning. Title X of this legislation provided the second major source of funding for federal family planning next to Medicaid. Rockefeller, Moore, and Draper actively lobbied Congress for the passage of the Family Planning Services and Population Research Act.

26, 1962; Hugh Moore to William Draper, May 21, 1962; and William Draper to Hugh Moore, May 31, 1962; and William Draper to Moore, June 1, 1962; Moore Papers, Box 3, Princeton University, cited in Critchlow, *Intended Consequences*, 42.

14 This strategy was not unique. Both the Malthusians of the early 19th century and, later, Margaret Sanger, especially after World War I, said that the practice of birth control would end poverty. See for example, "What We Stand For, Principles and Aims of the American Birth Control League, Inc.," *Birth Control Review* 8 (September 1924): 256.

Meanwhile, the message that a global and domestic population explosion had brought the world to the verge of catastrophe found its way into the popular culture. Popular magazines were full of reports of a population explosion. Movies and science fiction books, such as *Logan's Run* which was published in 1967 and later adapted as a film, depicted the disastrous effects of a society that did not control population growth. Paul Ehrlich, author of *Population Bomb*, became a featured speaker at conferences, college campuses, and late-night television talk shows. Distributed by the Sierra Club, a leading conservation organization, *Population Bomb* became a main selection of the Book of the Month Club, allowing it to remain on the best seller list for two years. Public anxiety about uncontrolled population growth reached a fever pitch as people worried about mass starvation, destruction of the environment, and world war. Ehrlich called for zero population growth and urged Congress to undertake coercive measures to enforce Americans from having more than two children. Americans were urged to delay marriage and have childless relations. He recommended that government award grants to encourage male sterilization.

Calls for more coercive measures to curb population growth came from other quarters. In 1967, Kingsley Davis, a leading demographer at the University of California, published an article in *Science*, "Population Policy: Will Current Progress Succeed?" warning that voluntary family planning might not be enough. He observed that advocates of zero population growth might necessitate indirect measures such as tax credits for having fewer children, but if this failed, zero population advocates might be required to undertake more extreme measures. The tone of his article was neutral, and it was not clear that he supported such measures. No matter, more alarmist population control advocates were already critical of voluntary family planning, whether through birth control devices, the pill, or sterilization. Just a year after the release of *Humanae vitae,* Richard Bowers, a founding member of Zero Population Growth, a breakaway organization from the Sierra Club, declared, "Voluntarism is a farce." He urged that elected officials consider licenses for couples to have children, sterilization of welfare recipients, and new laws enforcing population limits, including forced sterilization for parents with more than five children. He gained the support of Cordelia Scaife May, heir to the Mellon banking fortune. Bowers and Zero Population Growth represented the extreme wing of the movement. Rockefeller refused to meet with representatives of Zero Population Growth, but fears of the population explosion had reached a frenzied point at the time of the release of *Humanae vitae* in 1968.[15]

Catholic Church in America Responds

Throughout the advancement of federal family planning, proponents worried about arousing Catholic Church opposition. American bishops were aware of

15 See Terry Sollom, Rachel Benson Gold, Rebekah Saul, and Adam Sonfield, "Public Funding for Contraceptive, Sterilization and Abortion Services, 1994," *Family Planning Perspectives* 28, no. 4 (July/August 1996): 166–173; Donald T. Critchlow and W. J. Rorabaugh, *Takeover: How the Left's Quest for Social Justice Corrupted Liberalism* (Wilmington, Del.: Intercollegiate Studies Institute), 101–132.

lobbying efforts by the population control lobby to advance its agenda. In 1959, an internal memorandum circulated in the National Catholic Welfare Conference (NCWC)[16] warning of "systematic concerted effort to convince United States national agencies, as well as international bodies, to provide public funds, support, and assistance in promoting artificial prevention."[17] The memorandum declared that the Catholic Church's opposition to artificial birth control was based on long-held principles of natural law, but the Church believed also that "economic development and progress are best promoted by creating conditions favorable to development."[18]

In an effort to counter lobbying efforts at the UN to promote greater family planning assistance programs, the apostolic delegate representing the Vatican in the United States instructed Rev. Paul Tanner at the NCWC to "propagandize by every legitimate means the Catholic view of the matter." Tanner arranged a meeting with Richard Gardner, the assistant secretary of state for international organizations to discuss the Catholic Church's position on family planning in the UN. At the meeting, Gardner assured him that the United States would oppose any such measures.[19]

The Church hierarchy became further alarmed by other family planning proposals emerging in the nation's capital. In 1962, a National Institutes of Health (NIH) report called for more research on the physiology and control of human reproduction, which under Church pressure, revised its call for federal family planning. In 1963, Senator J. William Fulbright proposed an amendment that would have allowed the use of federal funds for international population control programs. William Consedine, an NCWC staff member, warned in a report to the conference that the only barrier to the acceptance of federal support for birth control programs domestically was "the wide recognition of the implacable opposition of the Church to such programs." He noted that Catholics were a minority in the country, but an increasingly effective and articulate one. He observed that Catholic pressure had forced the NIH to retreat and that the Fulbright amendment had been revised under Catholic pressure. Still, he warned that this was not the end of the battle. The District of Columbia was about to open its first birth control center using federal funds and other efforts were under way to extend family planning. He concluded, "These federal developments in the birth control picture show a progressive theme of increasing acceptance of permanent programs by responsible officials in our government despite

16 The NCWC changed names several times and is now called United States Conference of Catholic Bishops (USCCB).

17 Bishops of the United States, "Explosion or Backfire" (1959), Box 86, NCWC. Also see "Digest of Memorandum," January 28, 1958, which expressed concern that "birth control advocates are carrying on an unremitting effort to popularize their cause" Box 85, NCWC, cited in Critchlow, *Intended Consequences*, 119.

18 Critchlow, *Intended Consequences*, 119.

19 Most Rev. Egidio Vagnozzi to Msgr. Paul Tanner, September 23, 1961; Rev. Paul Tanner to Most Rev. Egidio Vagnozzi, September 29, 1961; and Harmon Burns Jr. to Msgr. P. Tanner, September 27, 1961, Box 86, NCWC, cited in Critchlow, *Intended Consequences*, 119.

the doctrine of the Church. But absent that restraint it takes no imagination to visualize the probability of future activity."[20]

Consedine proved prescient in his predictions. In the spring of 1965, the US Supreme Court ruled in *Griswold v. Connecticut* that the criminalization of contraceptive counseling was unconstitutional. The ruling was based on an interpretation of the Fourteenth Amendment protecting the right to privacy. Catholic authorities accepted this decision without protest, not realizing that the privacy doctrine opened legal arguments for the constitutional right to abortion and same-sex marriage. Within the next three years of Consedine's warnings, the federal government had moved steadily into family planning assistance.

The entrance of the federal government into family planning placed Catholic bishops into a quandary of principle. Catholic social services and hospitals counted on federal funds, but now, the federal government was insisting these agencies and hospitals provide family planning counseling and services. The dilemma was not easily resolved. Divisions were apparent in the NCWC itself over the issue. These divisions became apparent in the response to testimony offered before Congress by William H. Ball, general counsel of the Pennsylvania Catholic Welfare Committee. Appearing before Congress in late August 1965, Ball took a strong stance against federally supported family planning. He based his argument on defending individual civil rights and the importance of choice. While he supported the right of the federal government to undertake population research, he opposed federally supported family planning because it imposed "serious dangers to civil liberty, while offering no genuine prospect of relieving problems of poverty, crowding and disease." He warned that government involvement in family planning would be naturally coercive, in that "if the power and prestige of government is placed behind programs in providing birth control service to the poor, coercion necessarily results and violations of human privacy become inevitable."[21]

He turned to a full-throated criticism of trying to address the problems of poverty and other social problems through a simple fix such as family planning. He declared, "It is easy indeed to be mesmerized by concepts of social planning just as it is natural to want the least and shortest steps to solve the worst and most complex of our problems. We must remember that the planning of family is a thing radically different from the planning of highways. And government control of birth may come close to being government control of life. We think this is no place for the government." He concluded that after federal support for family planning would come abortion.[22]

20 Mr. William Consedine to Msgr. Francis Hurley, March 19, 1964, Box 86, NCWC. For an overview of Catholic involvement in American politics, see Mary T. Hanna, *Catholics and American Politics* (Cambridge, Mass.: Harvard University Press, 1979). A traditionalist critique of the Catholic Church in America and birth control, as well as liberal culture is found in E. Michael Jones, *John Cardinal Krol and the Cultural Revolution* (South Bend, Ind.: Fidelity Press, 1995), especially 227–301, cited in Critchlow, *Intended Consequences*, 120.

21 Critchlow, *Intended Consequences*, 120–121.

22 For an earlier example of the feminist critique of population control and the failure of family planners to place the use of "the pill" in a larger perspective of women's health, see Barbara Seaman, *The*

Ball's testimony did not go over well with everyone within the bishops' conference. Monsignor Tanner, later bishop of St. Augustine, Florida, said that while Ball's testimony was good, it did not represent the view of the NCWC because, "We as Catholics have no right to impose our views on these people. This is quite a new issue that we will have to resolve carefully."[23] Monsignor Tanner later said he was misquoted by the press, but it was clear there was division within the bishop's conference as to its stance on federally funded family planning.

This division became apparent over proposed guidelines on family planning by the Office of Economic Opportunity (OEO). In late 1965, Ball and Consedine, representing the bishops' conference, met with agency Director Sargent Shriver (President Kennedy's brother-in-law and a practicing Catholic), to discuss OEO proposed guidelines. Shriver candidly told Ball and Consedine he was under pressure from Planned Parenthood for OEO to finance abortion and sterilization, which he opposed. Meanwhile, the bishops had begun working on a public statement on OEO guidelines. Many on the conference did not want the bishops to go too far out on the issue. At an informal meeting to discuss the NCWC's position, Msgr. Francis Hurley, then on the NCWC staff and later to become archbishop of Anchorage, raised a rhetorical question, "Is not the situation similar to what we said thirty or forty years ago about education not being the federal government's concern? Is there something intrinsically dangerous in government's involvement in family planning? Are we in a position to say that Planned Parenthood has not a right to be in involvement in the poverty program."[24] A number of NCWC staff concurred that no public statement should be issued.

At the same time, Patrick O'Boyle, archbishop of Washington, D.C., reported that a careful analysis of the Economic Opportunity Act of 1964 by attorney Paul Connolly made Ball's legal opposition to the act untenable and that the statute offered "bountiful opportunities" to Catholic welfare agencies to receive federal funding. Connolly recommended,

> Rather than to attack the use of public funds for birth control, it would seem to me advisable to participate with all proper agencies in the community seeking a solution to the problem of parental irresponsibility short of

Doctor's Case Against the Pill (Alameda: Peter Wyden, 1969). For later examples of feminist critiques of population control, see Claudia Dreifus, *Seizing Our Bodies: The Politics of Women's Health* (New York: Viking, 1977) and Betsy Hartmann, *Reproduction Rights and Wrongs: The Global Politics of Population* (New York: Harper Collins, 1987). On the history of the birth control movement, Linda Gordon, *Woman's Body, Woman's Right: Birth Control in America* (New York: Viking, 1976), offers a nuanced, dialectical feminist/Marxist analysis that sharply differentiates birth control as a woman's right from contraceptives as an instrument of birth control. Gordon later developed her critique of Malthusianism and birth control; see Linda Gordon, "Malthusianism, Socialism, and Feminism in the United States," *Journal of European Ideas* 4, no. 2 (1983): 203–214. Also of interest is a feminist critique of oral contraceptives in Selig Greenberg, "The Pill," *The Progressive* 33 (February 1969): 34–37. An important reply to the feminist critique of population control is Ruth Dixon-Mueller, *Population Policy and Women's Rights: Transforming Reproductive Choice* (Westport: Praeger Publishers, 1993), cited in Critchlow, *Intended Consequences*, 113.

23 Critchlow, *Intended Consequences*, 122.

24 Critchlow, *Intended Consequences*, 124.

> advocating the generalized use of contraceptives. I think the general sense of the community is to take positive action to limit childbearing, especially among those who cannot care for their offspring and whose children become public charges.[25]

He warned the Church not to appear "intransigent" and to "cooperate as far as it can within its principles toward alleviating this obvious social evil."[26]

The bishops felt compelled to draft a public statement on federal family planning. Here was the hitch, though: they could not agree on what to say. The first draft of a statement prepared in early 1965, "Family Planning and Public Policy," proposed a moderate statement declaring family planning was "commendable," when "motivated by consideration of health and welfare of mothers and children," and while the majority of Americans "generally agree that family planning is morally justifiable," the Church endorsed only continence which takes advantage of infertile periods. The statement declared that poverty was best alleviated through education, training, and opportunity for gainful work at good wages. Nonetheless, the statement accepted that "where a consensus exists as to the need for public assistance in family planning, the government may respond to the request of its citizens for such assistance." This assistance should be qualified, however, with the understanding that the government not advocate birth control and that funding should not include abortion or sterilization."[27] Even this draft met resistance within the NCWC staff and among many bishops because it seemed to go too far in opposing artificial birth control.

Ball's position in opposition came under open attack. In late 1965, Father Dexter Hanley, Georgetown University theologian, criticized Ball's position on privacy as "not honest." Furthermore, the Church in America needed to acknowledge that "the population is at this moment too heavily concentrated for the economy to support. We also need to acknowledge," he said, "at this moment, some families have more children than their means or physical health will allow them to raise and educate properly." [28] He added for good measure, that Ball's accusation of government coercion was specious because "coercion is virtually implicit in government birth control programs; choice is illusionary, especially for the largely illiterate poor and Negroes."[29]

Others joined in the attack on Ball. Cardinal James Francis McIntyre, archbishop of Los Angeles, wrote Archbishop O'Boyle in Washington, D.C. that Ball should be replaced because "on the question of birth control, I feel there are

25 Paul Connolly to Patrick A. O'Boyle, March 8, 1965, Box 93, NCWC, cited in Critchlow, *Intended Consequences*, 123.

26 Critchlow, *Intended Consequences*, 123.

27 Draft Statement, "Family Planning and Public Policy," March 19, 1965, Box 95, NCWC, cited in Critchlow, *Intended Consequences*, 125.

28 Birth Control Notes, November 3, 1966, Box 93, NCWC, cited in Critchlow, *Intended Consequences*, 125–126.

29 Critchlow, *Intended Consequences*, 125–126.

others of comparable ability."[30] Father John Courtney Murray, SJ, maintained that "contraception today has become an issue of private, not public morality." It was a subject "that went beyond what Saint Thomas had faced." As a result, the Church needed to "reconsider our premises."[31]

It had become clear that given divisions over birth control itself and federally funded family planning, the majority of bishops decided it was best not to issue a statement. Led by Cardinal Lawrence Shehan, archbishop of Baltimore, and Cardinal Joseph Ritter, archbishop of St. Louis, the bishops' conference decided not to issue a public statement.[32] This left individual bishops on their own as to the birth control issue. Most bishops decided to avoid the issue. Others took stronger stances. In Milwaukee, Archbishop William E. Cousins came out in strong support of Dr. John J. Brennan, an active member of the Milwaukee Catholic Physicians Guild, in opposing the participation of Planned Parenthood in a community program. Archbishop John Krol in Philadelphia supported Cecil H. Moore, head of the local chapter of the National Association for the Advancement of Colored People, in attacking a Planned Parenthood proposal for a birth control program as "racial suicide."[33]

These were isolated instances, however. Division over federally funded family planning—and artificial birth control—within the Catholic Church in America remained before *Humanae vitae* was released in 1968. The question for the NCWC was how the bishops should respond to federal family planning policy. As NCWC counsel Consedine asked, "By condoning what is happening? Or, by a fight of total opposition?"[34] He personally believed that the NCWC and the bishops could be "more effective" by avoiding direct opposition.[35] The answer to

30 James Francis Cardinal McIntyre to Archbishop O'Boyle, November 30, 1965, Box 93, NCWC, cited in Critchlow, *Intended Consequences*, 126.

31 Critchlow, *Intended Consequences*, 126. Similarly, Father Richard A. McCormick, SJ, another leading theologian, told the bishops that he felt the statement did not make very clear the principles that allowed the Church to support the expenditure of public funds for something the Church held immoral. The idea of civil religious division as constituting a reason for exception, as maintained in the draft, appeared to him as hypocritical. Francis J. Connell at Holy Redeemer College wondered how much weight should be given to majority opinion. For example, he noted, "Many people in the South today disagree with us on the matter of equality of Negroes. Our protests are certainly leading to civil division in our country, but . . . are we going to give up without a struggle and say that we don't wish to impose our views on those who differ from us?" Still, he could not come up with a reasonable principle for the Church condemning contraception while at the same time, in effect, accepting federally supported family planning. John Courtney Murray to Francis Hurley, March 27, 1965, Box 95, NCWC; Richard A. McCormick, SJ, to Francis Hurley, March 27, 1965, Box 95, NCWC; and Francis J. Connell to Msgr. Hurley, March 23, 1965, Box 95, NCWC. Also see Francis Canavan, SJ, to Msgr. Hurley, March 25, 1965, Box 95; Richard McCormick to Francis Hurley, March 25, 1965, Box 95, NCWC, cited in Critchlow, *Intended Consequences*, 127.

32 Cardinal Lawrence Shehan to Archbishop O'Boyle, September 3, 1965, Box 86, NCWC; Archbishop O'Boyle to Egidio Vagnozzi, September 4, 1965, Box 86, NCWC; and Francis Hurley to Rev. Geno Baroni, May 14, 1965, Box 95, NCWC, cited in Critchlow, *Intended Consequences. Consequences*, 127.

33 "Racial Motive Is Discounted in Birth Control," *Philadelphia Inquirer*, January 7, 1966, Box 93, NCWC, cited in Critchlow, *Intended Consequences*, 127.

34 NCWC, Minutes of the Staff Meeting, February 4, 1966, Box 93, NCWC, cited in Critchlow, *Intended Consequences*, 127.

35 Critchlow, *Intended Consequences*, 127.

these questions rested in Rome where a select commission on birth control had been meeting since 1963.

Humanae vitae Constructed and Released

Pope John XXIII convened a small commission of theologians, social scientists, and physicians in October 1963 to prepare a Vatican statement on the population question. The commission agreed at its first meeting that it should move beyond demographic questions and address the Church's message on marriage and birth control. An expanded commission was formed in March 1964 to include thirty-four laypersons, nine members of the clergy, and twelve members of religious orders, under the direction of seventy-five-year old Italian prelate, Cardinal Alfredo Ottaviani. The commission included several American delegates, including two physicians, André Hellegers and John Cavanagh, and Patrick and Patricia Crowley, founders of the Christian Family Movement. The commission opened a year later in Rome in March 1965 with a lecture by legal scholar John T. Noonan providing a history of the Church's position of contraception. Noonan spoke for two hours, concluding that "The matter is open enough to deserve the attentive study of the Church in light of new scientific, social, and historical understanding."[36] His message was clear: the Church's position on contraception had changed over time and should be reconsidered in light of recent history.

With this opening lecture, the commission debated contraception for the next two years. Conservatives on the commission argued that that the Church's tradition of opposition against contraception should remain. Father John Ford, a Jesuit theologian, articulated the conservative position by maintaining that

> Contraception (that is contra-conception) involves a will which is turned against new life. . . . It is against this life, in advance, that is, against its coming to being. Your conception is your very origins, your link to the community of living persons before you, the first of all gifts, received from your parents, your first relationship with God as he stretched out his finger to touch you. To attack it is to attack fundamental human good, to intrude on God's domain.[37]

Those pushing for an articulation of a new position for the Church argued for a new relationship between married couples, free from the burden of conception. They maintained that acceptance of contraception would result in the strengthening of Christian marriage and great care of children conceived in marriage. In Spring 1967, the commission recommended acceptance of contraception.

36 Quoted in Robert Blair Kaiser, *The Politics of Sex and Religion: A Case History in the Development of Doctrine, 1962–1984* (Kansas City, Mo.: Leaven Press (Sheed and Ward), 1985), 80, cited in Critchlow, *Intended Consequences*, 129.

37 Cited in Critchlow, *Intended Consequences*, 129.

This majority report was leaked to the press and was picked up by the Catholic weekly, *National Catholic Reporter*, on April 15. The report made headlines on both sides of the Atlantic.[38]

The tenor of commission meetings set the stage for reception of the majority report and the subsequent encyclical. Noonan, who had played a critical role in documenting what he saw as inconsistencies and mutable Church positions on contraception, captured tensions within the commission when he noted that John Ford's "resistance to any development of doctrine on contraception" was "fueled by the conviction that major mutations in moral theology could not occur."[39] In his book, *A Church That Can and Cannot Change*, which is based on lectures at the University of Notre Dame, Noonan sought to eviscerate Father Ford and Gerald Kelly's two-volume treatise on moral theology, particularly in what Noonan saw as its apology for Church doctrine on slavery. In a footnote, Noonan describes an encounter with a "Christian bigot," whom he does not identify other than to say he was a theologian, small in stature and a "thinness suggestive of ascetic consumption of food." Not a canonist, Noonan writes, this person carried with him a copy of the 1917 *Code of Canon Law*, which he referred to constantly on questions of usury and contraception. Noonan concludes, "I was convinced after an hour of one-on-one debate with him that he would cheerfully have lit the fire if I were at the stake, at the same time assuring me with complete sincerity that he was acting for my good and that by an act of contrition I could still save my immortal soul, although not my mortal skin."[40] Discourse on artificial contraception had become personal and positions seemingly incommensurable.

In the midst of this controversial report, the board of trustees at The Catholic University of America denied Charles Curran, a leading advocate for artificial contraception, tenure in the Theology Department, overturning the faculty's unanimous recommendation for tenure. In support of Curran, 2,000 students, joined by the much of the faculty, went on strike in protest of the decision. Under pressure, the board backed down and granted tenure to Curran.[41]

A year later, Pope Paul VI issued *Humanae vitae*. The encyclical reaffirmed the Catholic Church's opposition to contraception and specifically addressed fundamental issues of human sexuality, the family, and modern social relations. The encyclical concluded by calling for "an atmosphere favorable to education in chastity, that is to the triumph of liberty over license by means

38 Robert G. Hoyt, *The Birth Control Debate* (Kansas City, Mo.: National Catholic Reporter, 1968); see also Kaiser, *The Politics of Sex and Religion*, 182, cited in Critchlow, *Intended Consequences*, 129.

39 John T. Noonan, Jr., *A Church That Can and Cannot Change* (Notre Dame, Ind.: University of Notre Dame Press, 2005), 127–128. For discussion of Vatican Council theological discussion see, Noonan, 283.

40 Noonan, *A Church That Can and Cannot Change*, 117, and for the description of the Commission debate, see 282.

41 The Curran issue is discussed by Philip Gleason, *Contending with Modernity: Catholic Higher Education in the Twentieth Century* (New York: Oxford University Press, 1995), 312–313. For a critical perspective on the Curran controversy, see George A. Kelly, *The Battle for the American Church* (Garden City, N.Y.: Doubleday, 1979), 57–99, cited in Critchlow, *Intended Consequences*, 129–130.

of respect to moral order."[42] American critics of *Humanae vitae* overlooked the social gospel message embodied in the encyclical by focusing on artificial contraception.

The response to the encyclical in the American press was hostile. Major newspapers and magazines reported that the pope's pronouncement had created a "crisis of authority" within the Church. Adding fuel to the fire, Hugh Moore organized a petition signed by 2,600 scientists criticizing *Humanae vitae*. The petition was published in the *New York Times, Wall Street Journal,* and *Commonweal*. It was translated into Spanish and French and sent to every American bishop.[43]

Opposition to the encyclical came from within the Church itself. The Los Angeles Association of Laymen publicly declared its opposition to the encyclical. Noonan and other Americans on the Vatican commission announced in a news conference that the encyclical was not infallible, and that Catholics should follow their own consciences.[44] After signing a petition against the encyclical, twenty-six professors of theology at The Catholic University of America in Washington, D.C., and twenty-six parish priests of the Archdiocese of Washington were suspended by Cardinal O'Boyle. Within months, many of these suspended priests left the priesthood. Other priests joined them, including an auxiliary bishop of St. Paul-Minneapolis.

For many lay Catholics, *Humanae vitae* conveyed a church still living in the Middle Ages and "out of touch" with modern life. This portrait of a church out of touch with modern marriage found expression in magazine articles, op-eds, and books.[45] The stage for opposition to the Catholic Church's position on oral contraception had been set earlier by liberal Catholics. John Rock, one of the pioneers of oral contraception, gained wide press attention for his book, *The Time Has Come: A Catholic Doctor's Proposals to End the Battle Over Birth Control*, published in 1963. In 1964, Michael Novak, who was beginning his writing career as a liberal Roman Catholic before he became a defender of orthodoxy,

42 The encyclical *Humanae vitae* was reprinted in full in *Catholic Almanac* (New York: Sunday Visitor Press, 1969), 97–105.

43 "The Catholic Church and Birth Control," *U.S. News and World Report* (August 12, 1968): 38–39, cited in Critchlow, *Intended Consequences*, 131.

44 John T. Noonan, Jr. took a leading role in articulating the theological argument against the Church's position on artificial birth control, even before *Humanae vitae* was issued. See "Authority, Usury and Contraception," *Cross Currents* 16 (Winter 1966): 71–75. See also Noonan, "Natural Law, the Teaching of the Church and Contraception," *American Journal of Jurisprudence* 25, no. 1 (1980): 16–37. *Humanae vitae* was defended in John C. Ford, SJ, and Germain Grisez, "Contraception and the Infallibility of the Ordinary Magisterium," *Theological Studies* 39, no. 2 (1978): 258–312. For a response to Noonan, see Joseph Boyle, "Human Action, Natural Rhythms, and Contraception: A Response to Noonan," *American Journal of Jurisprudence* 26, no. 1 (1981): 32–46, cited in Critchlow, *Intended Consequences*, 131.

45 Historical assessment of dissent over *Humanae vitae*, often from sympathetic perspectives, is found in Roger Van Allen, "John Cogley's Dissent from *Humanae vitae*," *US Catholic Historian* 26 (Summer 2008): 69–83; Daniel Callahan, "Contraception and Abortion: American Catholic Responses," *The Annals of the Academy of Political and Social Science* 387 (January 1970): 109–117; and Richard A. McCormick, "*Humanae Vitae* 25 Years Later: From July 17, 1993," *America* (July 17, 1993), https://www.americamagazine.org/issue/100/humanae-vitae-25-years-later.

published *The Experience of Marriage,* an edited collection of thirteen anonymous American Catholic couples.[46]

With the release of *Humanae vitae,* Noonan and six other dissenting American members of the commission gathered in Washington, D.C., for a news conference that drew national attention. Noonan, speaking for the group, expressed dismay that the pope had ignored his own commission. He was quoted as declaring that "The new document is not an infallible statement. It is a fallible document written by a fallible man in the fallible exercise of his office."[47] This full-throated criticism of *Humanae vitae* found its way throughout the American popular press. Writing under the pseudonym, Xavier Rynne, Father Francis X. Murphy wrote in *The New Yorker* that the encyclical reflected the minority views of five or six hardline reactionary cardinals to which the pope was being held captive.[48]

Headlines of the popular press captured the rift within the Church over *Humanae vitae* and the attention it drew from mainstream media. The press, especially the *New York Times,* gave special attention to dissent within the Church. For example, Deirdre Carmody reported in the *Times* on July 31, 1968, under the headline, "Catholic Experts in Strong Dissent on Edict by Pope," that 87 Catholic theologians issued a statement that the encyclical was not binding on Catholics. The dissent proclamation was reprinted in full.[49] This was just one of many articles appearing in the press. In November, the *New York Times* ran a twelve-page story by Thomas J. Fleming under the headline, "Confrontation in Washington: The Cardinal vs. the Dissenters."[50] The article recounted the confrontation between Cardinal O'Boyle and theological opponents of *Humanae vitae,* including the Association of Washington Priests that issued a statement in support of theologians at The Catholic University of America who rejected the infallibility of the papal encyclical. Fleming described Cardinal O'Boyle as finally losing patience with the dissenters when Rev. T. Joseph O'Donoghue at St. Francis de Sales parish added editorial comments to the pastoral letter written by Cardinal O'Boyle in support of *Humanae vitae.* Fleming described Cardinal O'Boyle's reaction to the priest's letter as setting off a temper tantrum, much "like a Zeus Nike missile" going off. The article quoted James Gibbons, one of the two leading figures of the dissenting laymen, telling Cardinal O'Boyle when he made reference to the marriage act, instead of sexual intercourse, as "Doesn't this suggest any thing to you? Are you willing even to consider that maybe you've got a sick, twisted Irish celibate's view towards sex?" The essay ended quoting one dissident as saying that the repression of dissenters within the Church was

46 John Rock, *The Time Has Come* (New York: Alfred Knopf, 1963) and Michael Novak, *The Experience of Marriage* (New York: MacMillan, 1964).

47 Asbell, *The Pill,* 201.

48 Xavier Rynne, "Letter from Vatican City," *The New Yorker* (November 2, 1968), at https://www.newyorker.com/magazine/1968/11/02/letter-from-vatican-city-13.

49 Deirdre Carmody, "Catholic Experts in Strong Dissent on Edict by Pope," *New York Times* (July 31, 1968).

50 Thomas J. Fleming, "Confrontation in Washington: The Cardinal vs. Dissenters," *New York Times* (November 24, 1968).

"the thing that had made me realize for the first time that the whole system is basically un-American." [51]

The tenor of multiple articles in American and foreign newspapers depicted the Catholic Church in America in disarray—priests confronting an intransigent out-of-touch hierarchy and lay Catholics deserting the Church in droves. The tone of these articles was evident in the headlines, "Theologians Gain Support in Dissent on Birth Control," "Vatican's Credibility Gap," "Rebellion from Within," "Rebel Priest 'Picked Off and Silenced, One by One," "Tyranny in Transfer," "Catholic Doctors' Group Balks at Backing Pope's Birth Edict," and "Young Rebels Want Pope to Resign."[52] Press reports depicted American dissent as part of a larger movement in Britain and Western Europe. The press depicted bishops as at first taking a strong stance to quell and punish dissenters within the clergy, and then backing down under pressure.

Many American lay Catholics appeared to concur with opposition to the encyclical. A Gallup poll a month after the encyclical was released found that 54 percent of American Catholics opposed the encyclical, while only 28 percent favored it. Eighteen percent had expressed no opinion.[53]

Parish numbers appeared to fall as many people left the Church. Critics of *Humanae vitae* blamed the encyclical for declining church attendance, although church attendance numbers in liberal Protestant and mainline churches were also in decline. Sociologist and Catholic priest, Andrew Greeley reported that after *Humanae vitae*, Catholic Church attendance fell dramatically. His 1974 findings showed that weekly attendees of Mass fell from 70 percent to 50 percent. His study found that before the encyclical, 70 percent of those American Catholics polled held that the pope drew his authority from Jesus; by 1974 fewer than half of Catholics agreed with this.[54] What was evident though was that the encyclical did not change American Catholic women's use of contraception. By

51 Fleming, "Confrontation in Washington: The Cardinal vs. Dissenters," (1968).

52 David R. Jones, "Theologians Gain Support in Dissent on Birth Control," *New York Times* (August 2, 1968); "The Vatican's Credibility Gap," *The Guardian* (August 1, 1968); Richard D. Lyons, "Catholic Doctors' Group Balks Pope's Birth Edict," *New York Times* (December 2, 1968); Norman Crossland, "Young Rebels Want Pope to Resign," *The Guardian* (September 7, 1968); William McSweeney, "Rebellion from Within," *The Guardian* (August 2, 1968); Campbell Page, "Dissident Priests Remain Defiant," *The Guardian* (October 25, 1968); Rev. P. Sharkey, "Tyranny in Transfer" Letter to the Editor, *New York Times* (October 14, 1968); "Pope Paul Stresses Need for Authority," *New York Times* (September 12, 1968); Ivan Yates, "Rebel Priests 'Picked Off and Silenced, One by One, *The Observer* (November 3, 1968); Edward B. Fiske, "40 Priest Reject Appeal to Mediate on Birth Control," *New York Times* (November 13, 1968); "Cardinal O'Boyle's Mistake," *New York Times* (October 1, 1968); Edward B. Fiske, "A Visit to Archbishop Cooke's Domain," *New York Times* (October 13, 1968); "Discipline for Priests on Birth Control," *New York Times* (September 12, 1968); Edward B. Fiske, "British Catholics Widening Protest," *New York Times* (August 18, 1968); "Another Opinion, For Birth Control," *New York Times* (August 4, 1968); Edward B Fiske, "Catholic Bishops Will Act on Birth Control and War: Conference Hints at a Softer Stand on Papal Encyclical," *New York Times* (November 12, 1968); Edward B. Fiske, "Bishops In Accord on Birth Doctrine," *New York Times* (November 15, 1968); Edward B. Fiske, "Catholic Bishops Temper Curbs on Birth Control," *New York Times* (November 16, 1968).

53 Quoted in Asbell, *The Pill*, 200.

54 Asbell, *The Pill*, 297.

1970, an estimated 68 percent of Catholic women used contraception. Rates of use of artificial contraception remained higher on average for women identifying themselves as Catholic than non-Catholic women. In separate studies, Princeton University's Charles Westoff and Elsie Jones estimated that less than 9.5 percent of white married Catholic women, aged eighteen to thirty-nine, conformed with Catholic teaching on birth control.[55]

Controversy over the pill, however, was far from over. In the late 1960s, feminists began to raise concerns about the health effects of oral contraception. In 1969, Barbara Seaman published *The Doctor's Case Against the Pill.* As reports of strokes, breast cancer, and other negative effects of women taking the pill began to circulate, Senator Gaylord Nelson (D-Wisconsin) held public hearings on the pill's side effects. Critics claimed that the pill had not been properly tested before being put on the market by Searle and other drug companies. Reports that the pill had been tested in Puerto Rico on a few hundred poor women placed the pharmaceutical industry in a bad light. The pharmaceutical industry responded to this criticism with a full-blown, counter-media attack advertising the pill as a drug of liberation. In 1988, the three drug companies still manufacturing high-dose estrogen oral contraceptives voluntarily withdrew from the market all remaining products containing over 50 micrograms of estrogen.[56]

The Abortion Issue Erupts

In 1968, the Catholic Church in America appeared in turmoil over the contraception issue and growing secularization in society. The eruption of the abortion issue that began with efforts on the state level to liberalize abortion laws and the Supreme Court's decision in *Roe v. Wade* in 1973 subsumed the contraception debate. *Humanae vitae* spoke directly to contraception, but its message concerning sexual relations between couples, marriage, and family informed Catholic opposition to abortion and laid the foundation for subsequent encyclicals concerning life and social mores. As a result, any discussion of the legacy of *Humanae vitae* needs to include the fierce public debate over abortion.

In the 1940s and 1950s, abortion advocates undertook a deliberate campaign to appeal to doctors and lawyers on the need to liberalize abortion laws. The American Law Institute drafted a model abortion law in 1959 that was taken to state legislatures to enact reform of existing abortion laws. Contrary to a narrative that abortion was illegal before *Roe v. Wade*, abortion was legal in most states.[57]

55 Charles F. Westoff and Elsie F. Jones, "The Secularization of U.S. Catholic Birth Control Practices," *Family Planning Perspectives* 9, no. 5 (September/October 1977): 203–207, cited in Critchlow, *Intended Consequences*, 132.

56 Asbell, *The Pill*, 308.

57 James C. Mohr, *Abortion in America: The Origins of National Policy, 1800–1900* (New York: Oxford University Press, 1978); also, Leslie Reagan, relying heavily on court records in Illinois, provides a detailed account of the enforcement of abortion laws in her *When Abortion was Against the Law: Women, Medicine and the Law, 1867–1973* (Berkeley: University of California Press,1996). Reagan maintains that most abortions remained a relatively safe operation performed by doctors in clinical settings until late 1950s, when they were driven underground by the enforcement of state anti-abortion laws. Cited in Critchlow, *Intended Consequences*, 133–134.

These laws were restrictive, usually allowing physicians to perform abortions in order to save the life of the mother. Support for reforming abortion law gained momentum when the effects of the pregnancy drug thalidomide became known and an epidemic of rubella measles swept across America in the 1950s. Both the drug and the disease caused fetal deformity, fueling the call for more liberalized abortion laws. Fears of overpopulation also fueled abortion law reform.

Although the Catholic Church's opposition to abortion was long-standing, many public officials and the general American public did not fully understand the issue or the social ramifications of legalized abortion. In 1967, California Governor Ronald Reagan signed at that time the nation's most liberal abortion law, the Therapeutic Abortion Act. In an hour-long meeting in the governor's office Cardinal McIntyre of Los Angeles tried to dissuade Reagan from signing the legislation, and Reagan seriously considered vetoing the act, but the legislation had passed with bipartisan support and he did not want to leave Republican legislators out on a political limb.[58] Later critics—both left and right—attacked him for signing this piece of legislation. Years later, Reagan would also claim that at the time, he did not have a full grasp of the abortion issue and, once he understood it better, he became a firm opponent of abortion.[59]

Nelson Rockefeller, governor of New York, revealed similar confusion as to the arguments over abortion. Although he was decidedly pro-abortion, his ignorance about the arguments for and against abortion was remarkable. In the late 1960s, when Governor Rockefeller was grappling with the moral complexities of the abortion question, he instructed an aide to arrange a meeting with the eminent theologian Thomas Aquinas, whom he had seen quoted in an editorial. Rockefeller laughed at himself when he learned that Aquinas had died in the thirteenth century.[60] Rockefeller was not any more shallow than other politicians of his age then or later.

The debate over abortion was framed by both sides as a rights issue: the right to life for a fetus and the right to reproduction freedom for women.[61] Those supporting the legal right of a woman to have an abortion claimed this was a right for a woman to control her own body. The Supreme Court in *Roe v. Wade* upheld this right, albeit parsed into a trimester scheme, by interpreting the US Constitution, specifically the Fourteenth Amendment, as embodying the right to privacy. Noonan noted that within these narrow legal definitions of the right to privacy, there remained a larger cultural perception that "every law restricting sexual behavior as an arbitrary imposition of another's will on the sacred sphere

58 Lou Cannon, *Governor Reagan* (Washington, D.C.: Public Affairs Press, 2003), 186.

59 Reagan, *When Abortion Was Against the Law*, 5–6. This discussion of abortion law and practice before 1960 is drawn from Leslie Reagan's on abortion law before *Roe v. Wade*, research cited in Critchlow, *Intended Consequences*, 133.

60 Richard Norton Smith, *On His Own Terms: A Life of Nelson Rockefeller* (New York: Random House, 2014), 619.

61 Daniel K. Williams, *Defenders of the Unborn: The Pro-Life Movement before Roe v. Wade* (New York: Oxford University Press, 2016).

of personal liberty."[62] Such laws restricting sexual behavior were denounced as antiquated impositions of a male dominated society. As a result, "the existence of laws exacting the possibility of uninterrupted pregnancy as the price of natural intercourse appeared as an unbelievable anachronism."[63]

As a consequence of the controversy over abortion being framed as a rights issue by both sides, the debate over population control remained within the background for the pro-choice side. In 1968, Planned Parenthood-World Population formally changed its stand and endorsed abortion as a means of population control. Pro-abortion activists concluded that the best way to achieve their agenda was to file rights cases in the federal courts. Their hopes were raised when the Supreme Court decided to review restrictive state abortion laws in Texas and Georgia. Sarah Weddington represented the plaintiff in the Texas case *Roe v. Wade*. Working with public interest lawyers such as Bea Durden, Roy Lucas, and Harriet Pilpel of Planned Parenthood, Weddington developed a pro-abortion brief based on a more finely tuned privacy argument for abortion based on the First, Fourth, Fifth, Ninth, and Fourteenth Amendments.[64] Pilpel was not the only addition to the legal team that saw abortion as a necessary means of population control. They were joined by Nick Danforth, a population control advocate, who became director of the Population Law Center and later went to work for the United States Agency for International Development. Another member of the team was Yale law student David Tundermann, who studied the links between environmental problems and world population. Weddington and her husband were strong population control advocates in Austin, Texas.

Until 1970 or so, population control remained a bipartisan issue. This began to change with the abortion issue and the rise of what became social conservatism within the Republican Party. This shift within the Republican Party became apparent when Richard Nixon rejected the findings of his National Commission on Population Growth and America's Future, chaired by John D. Rockefeller III. The commission divided on a number of issues, including calls for "abortion on request" and immigration restriction. The commission's report warned that population growth in the United States should be restrained and observed that "We are impressed that induced abortion has a demographic effect whenever legalized."[65] The commission qualified its support for abortion by declaring that abortion should be "only a back-up measure in cases of contraceptive failure." The report added, "To the moral poignancy involved in [abortion] must be balanced by the moral poignancy of a woman giving birth to an unwanted child and even more, the moral poignancy of the child's prosperous life."[66]

62 Quoted in John T. Noonan, Jr., "Introduction," and "An Almost Absolute Value in History," in *The Morality of Abortion: Legal and Historical Perspectives* (Cambridge, Mass.: Harvard University Press, 1970), xv.

63 Noonan, *The Morality of Abortion* (1970), xvi.

64 For a sympathetic account of the movement to overturn abortion law, see David Garrow, *Liberty and Sexuality: The Right to Privacy and the Making of Roe v. Wade* (New York: Macmillan, 1998).

65 Critchlow, *Intended Consequences*, 161–172.

66 Full a full discussion of the Nixon response to the report and dissenting opinion within the commission, see Critchlow, *Intended Consequences,* 161–173.

In 1972, the report was submitted to Nixon who rejected its recommendations. Anxious to win the Roman Catholic vote in the upcoming election, Nixon had begun to cultivate these voters by calling for state support of parochial schools, while beginning to distance himself from federal funding of sterilization. Stunned by Nixon's rejection of the report, Rockefeller saw Nixon as playing political calculus to win Catholic voters, but moreover he felt that an intransigent and unenlightened American public was the major obstacle to advancing abortion.

Through a carefully calculated strategy, Rockefeller, the Population Council, and Rockefeller-associated foundations decided to undertake a campaign to advance the liberalization of American cultural mores. He extended his financial support for the National Abortion Rights Action League (NARAL), Planned Parenthood, the American Civil Liberties Union (ACLU), Reproduction Freedom Project, the Center for Constitutional Rights, the Alan Guttmacher Institute, Zero Population Growth, and Catholics for Choice, a pro-abortion group organized to counter the Catholic Church's position on abortion. As part of this campaign, Rockefeller increased funding for organizations promoting sex education such as Dr. Mary Calderone's Sex Information and Education Council of the United States (SIECUS), including a $50,000 grant to fund a SIECUS program in New York to make students aware of their sexual identities and to overcome any guilt feelings about self-exploration, masturbation, or the exploration of the genitals of other children. He provided major funding for a New York public television documentary, "Who Are We?" that focused on eight homosexuals from all walks of life to provide role models for young homosexuals and lesbians.[67] Rockefeller and his staff arranged meetings with major magazine editors, journalists, and television producers to promote liberal sexual values.

The Modern Sexual Revolution and the Crisis of the Family

The modern sexual revolution in post-World War II America began before the introduction of oral contraception (the pill). While critics of *Humanae vitae* focused on the Church's opposition to the pill, little attention was given by its critics of a sexual revolution. Any assessment of the legacy of *Humanae vitae* should lead to two fundamental conclusions:

(1) *Humanae vitae* proved correct in warning about the social consequences of the sexual revolution and presaged the repercussion of what Pope John Paul II described as the culture of death in a secularized world, a culture addressed in other important encyclicals.

(2) Elite opinion-makers and philanthropists such as Rockefeller encouraged a sexual revolution that was already occurring without their efforts. The

67 In 1970, the Ford Foundation provided a $500,000 grant to SIECUS. In addition, John D. Rockefeller contributed $50,000 to SIECUS, followed by annual contributions of $25,000 in subsequent years, as well as a $50,000 gift in 1970. See John D. Rockefeller III to Mary S. Calderone, February 26, 1970, Box 2; Undated memorandum, "Contributions 1970, John D. Rockefeller III," Joan Dunlop Papers, Box 3, and David K. Lelewer to John D. Rockefeller III, June 9, 1972, Box 3, Joan Dunlop Papers, RA. Contributions to the PPFA project in New York City are recorded in an undated memorandum, "JDR Giving," Joan Dunlop Papers, Box 3, RA, cited in Critchlow, *Intended Consequences*, 175–183.

liberalization of sexual mores in America and Western societies—and advanced industrial nations—is a complex phenomenon that cannot be attributed to any single social, economic, or cultural cause, whether it be hyper-individualism, urbanization, or classical liberalism. The breakdown of the traditional family and the depersonalization of sexual relations that occurred with this sexual revolution have created profound social problems in the United States and post-industrial societies. *Humanae vitae* warned of the profound consequences of the breakdown of the two-parent family and the depersonalization of sexual relations that was manifested in the sexual revolution. By focusing on the Catholic Church's opposition to oral contraception, critics of *Humanae vitae* ignored the larger intent of the encyclical, that is, the social consequences of a secular culture that narrowly defined liberation as freedom of personal choice and individual consent.

Viewed within the larger context of subsequent encyclicals, *Humanae vitae* needs to be seen in a broader perspective, one which upholds a morality founded on "the human person made in God's image," as eloquently observed by William E. May.[68] The Catholic Church's opposition to the culture of death, articulated in John Paul II's encyclical *Evangelium vitae*, challenged a secularized culture that accepted abortion, euthanasia, and embryo stem-cell research, as well as population control, as components of enlightened progress and technical instruments to address serious social issues of poverty, out-of-wedlock births, rising medical costs, and human suffering.[69]

Once embattled over oral contraception, the Church has strengthened its argument by framing issues of life within a larger and deeper Judeo-Christian tradition of justice. By challenging social injustice and policies that dehumanize and frustrate the human striving for fulfillment, the Church appeals to a larger public audience beyond the confines of a subculture of traditional Catholics. John Paul II's *Evangelium vitae* placed contraception, abortion, laboratory reproduction, euthanasia, and the death penalty within a larger framework of the culture of death. He acknowledged that contraception and abortion were two different "moral evils," the former preventing the possibility of conception and the latter destroying life already conceived. He maintains that the contraceptive society reinforces a narrow and ultimately destructive self-centered concept of freedom.

The power of this message, as well as scientific discovery of embryonic development, helped shift public opinion on abortion. Although induced abortions in America remain high with approximately 926,200 performed in 2017, public opinion on abortion has shifted against abortion-on-demand.[70] Although polling on

68 William E. May, "Contraception, Gateway to the Culture of Death," http://www.christendom-awake.org/pages/may/contraception.htm.

69 Raymond Dennehy, "Liberal Democracy as a Culture of Death: Why John Paul II Was Right," *Telos* no. 134 (Spring 2006): 31–63.

70 See Rachel K. Jones and Jenna Jerman, "Abortion Incidence and Service Availability in the United States, 2014," *Perspectives on Sexual and Reproductive Health* 49 (March 2017): 17–27; see also "Induced Abortion in the United States," *Guttmacher Institute* (January 2017), https://www.guttmacher.org/news-release/2017/us-abortion-rate-continues-decline-hits-historic-low.

abortion can be tricky based on how questions are framed by pollsters, surveys show that support for broadly legalized abortion has declined since 1975. Moreover, support for making abortion broadly illegal appears to be growing fastest among young adults, ages 18–25.[71] Gallup found that in 1995 only 33 percent of Americans identified themselves as "pro-life;" today 46 percent identify themselves as "pro-life."[72]

However one deciphers these surveys on American opinion on abortion, what is evident is that the pro-life position has gained traction in the larger public. At the same time, the warnings in *Humanae vitae* about the consequences of the breakdown of the traditional family, the depersonalization of sexual relations, and the ripping apart of the social fabric resonate with more meaning today than perhaps they did in 1968 in the midst of the sexual revolution. Social scientists have repeatedly reported negative outcomes such as how children raised in single-parent families experience high rates of drug and alcohol addiction, unemployment, and incarceration. These studies have awakened the American public to the social destruction being caused by the breakdown of traditional American families in our society.

In 1964, when President Johnson declared a war on poverty, promising to end poverty in the United States within a generation, only 30 percent of poor families with children were headed by single mothers.[73] By the end of the 1970s this figure had risen to 60 percent. Out-of-wedlock births have dropped slightly in recent years, especially among teenagers, but continue to be extraordinarily high in inner cities, where the rates of children being raised by single mothers reach 70+ percent for African-Americans. Out-of-wedlock birth rates have continued to rise among Hispanics and lower-income whites as well. Although there has been a slight decline in the rate of out-of-wedlock births among teenagers, the out-of-wedlock birth rate has risen for women in the 25- to 34-year-old age bracket. Teenagers in the United States are more likely to have children out-of-wedlock than any other nation in the industrialized world.

One of the key problems of out-of-wedlock births is cultural and goes against the progressive feminist narrative that males do not matter. The greatest problem is the lack of a male role model. This is especially destructive for young boys. Fathers provide discipline and control over adolescent boys in a way that mothers often cannot. Study after study shows that boys growing up with both biological parents perform better in school, graduate at higher rates, attend college more, and are more likely to be employed as young men than boys who have grown up with a single parent or a single parent with a stepparent. Boys with stepfathers, it should be noted, do better in life than boys without any fathers.

As Harvard University sociologist Robert D. Putnam shows in *Our Kids: The American Dream in Crisis* (2016), access to contraception and abortion has

71 "Generational Difference on Abortion Narrow: Support for Making Abortion Broadly Illegal Growing Fastest Among Young Adults," *Gallup* (March 12, 2010). For contrary polling, see "Public Polling on Abortion," *Pew Research Institute* (July 7, 2017).

72 "Abortion," *Gallup*, at http://news.gallup.com/poll/1576/abortion.aspx.

73 See David T. Ellwood and Christopher Jencks, "The Spread of Single-Parent Families in the United States since 1960," *Faculty Research Papers* (February 2004): 1.

nothing to do with out-of-wedlock births.[74] Women having children out of wedlock have access to these services. Putnam's argument is supported by an array of other studies, including one by Melissa S. Kearney and Phillip B. Levine, who after studying teen birth rates in the United States conclude that "no silver bullet such as expanding access to contraception or abstinence education will solve this particular social problem."[75]

As noted by social scientists George Akerlof, Janet Yellen, and Michael Katz, the introduction of new contraceptive technologies and legalized abortion dramatically changed sexual relations between unmarried couples.[76] Prior to the 1960s, premarital sexual relations between a couple implied a commitment to marry if the woman became pregnant, backed by strong social pressure (hence the shorthand phrase "shotgun wedding"). The introduction of the pill and legalized abortion encouraged women and men to participate in premarital sex on the assumption that pregnancy need not discourage them in their behavior. The sexual revolution that came with new contraceptive technologies and legalized abortion meant that women could no longer hold males to the standards of the previous age. In this new sexually liberated culture, women who insist on marriage before sexual relations or any resulting pregnancy are considered old-fashioned and find it more difficult to compete successfully for boyfriends. As a result, the link between marriage and childbearing is profoundly weakened by a sexually liberated culture. Couples engaged in premarital sex in this new culture assume that they have greater control over pregnancy, an assumption that often proves false. These changing sexual mores encourage sexual activity and cohabitation, while demeaning the importance of marriage.

Within this new culture of sexual liberation, a greater emphasis is placed on individual fulfillment without regard to social responsibility toward children. One of the great ironies of this sexual liberation is that college-educated and upper-class men and women have higher rates of marriage, albeit delayed, and far lower rates of out-of-wedlock births. The higher one goes in income levels. the lower the rate of out-of-wedlock births. For all the talk of sexual liberation and marriage as enforced patriarchal values, more highly educated and higher-income groups maintain the values of previous generations—the "old-fashioned" generation—while lower-income, less-educated people suffer the consequences of a sexually liberated culture. Poor and uneducated women who bear out-of-wedlock children are relegated to a cycle of poverty for themselves and their children.

74 Robert D. Putnam, *Our Kids: The Dream in Crisis* (New York: Simon & Schuster, 2016).

75 Melissa S. Kearney and Phillip B. Levine, "Why is the Teen Birth Rate in the United States So High and Why Does It Matter?" *The Journal of Economic Perspectives* 26 (Spring 2012): 142.

76 George A. Akerlof, Janet L. Yellen, and Michael L. Katz, "An Analysis of Out-of-Wedlock Childbearing in the United States," *Brookings Policy Brief* (August 1996): 2–6; Ellwood and Christopher Jencks, "The Spread of Single-Parent Families in the United States since 1960," *Faculty Research Working Paper Series* (February 2004), https://papers.ssrn.com/sol3/Papers.cfm?abstract_id=517662.

Conclusion: The Importance of Religion

Over the last decade, out-of-wedlock births have declined for teenagers (including minorities), falling by approximately 20 percent. So why do we have more single parents and out-of-wedlock births than ever before? The answer is this: while teenage out-of-wedlock births have fallen, unwed mothers between the ages of 25–34 have soared by 70 percent. These unwed mothers are getting pregnant unintentionally or "semi-intentionally" even if they have contraceptive resources available. Those advocates, such as Planned Parenthood and feminists who maintain that the unavailability of contraceptives is creating poverty, have been proved wrong. Women with poor educational attainments are having more children out-of-wedlock than are those women with college education. The difference is not availability of contraception, but, as Putnam explains, this class discrepancy which is about "the mother's ambivalence about pregnancy, the erosion of personal efficacy by low education, and economic distress."[77] He adds that it might be differing attitudes toward abortion, but this is conjecture.

Whatever the explanation, nonmarital births to college-educated women are less than 10 percent, having risen only slightly since the 1970s, while those to high school-educated women have risen sharply over the last 30 years and now make up about 65 percent of births in this group. Nonmarital births to black college graduates are about 25 percent and have fallen by a third over the last twenty years. In the same period, it has nearly quadrupled for only high school-educated whites, accounting for nearly 50 percent of the birthrate for this group.

Children born to unwed mothers, whether white or black, often enter dysfunctional communities. They don't have adults supervising them, providing support networks, watching out for them, or advising them how to advance themselves socially or economically. They don't develop cognitively and fail to develop what Putnam describes as noncognitive skills, "grit, social sensitivity, optimism, self-control, conscientiousness, and emotional stability."[78]

Community matters, as William Julius Wilson pointed out, twenty-five years ago in his *The Truly Disadvantaged* (1990).[79] Essential to community cohesiveness are churches and other religious institutions. The single factor in helping the poor better their lives is religion. Religion is important for the rich and the poor. Compared to their non-church peers, youth who are involved in religious organizations take more challenging courses in high-school and get higher grades and test scores. Putnam concludes that kids involved in religious organization are less likely to drop out of high school. "Controlling for many other characteristics of the child, her family, and her schooling," he writes, "a child whose parents actually attend church regularly is 40 to 50 percent more likely to go

77 Putnam, *Our Kids*, 65.

78 Putnam, *Our Kids*, 224.

79 William Julius Wilson, *The Truly Disadvantaged: The Inner City, the Underclass, and Public Policy* (Chicago: University of Chicago, 1987; 2012).

on to college than a matched child of non-attenders."[80] More college-educated parents are attending church than their noncollege-educated counterparts. But the poor who are going to church are finding a support system of caring congregations, ministers, priests, and pastoral counselors that provide the kind of community that enables them to improve their lives emotionally, socially, and economically.

Social science studies affirm *Humanae vitae's* warnings as to the moral and social consequences of false liberation. As a consequence, *Humanae vitae* offers profound relevance in our contemporary world, which too readily dismisses the importance of the traditional family to maintaining the well-being of our children, religion as critical to moral order, and God's relationship to humankind as a gift of life. For whatever controversy *Humanae vitae* created when it was released in 1968, fifty years later, the warnings have all proved truly correct. The encyclical warned of the devastating result that would occur with the breakdown of the traditional family and when sexual relations lack moral obligation, real intimacy, or constraint. The lessons of the Judeo-Christian understanding of history is that too often when jeremiads are ignored, chaos ensues. We now find ourselves in such a crisis forewarned in *Humanae vitae.* This suggests—in fact, demands—a rereading of this encyclical that will enable us to understand what has occurred in American society in the last fifty years. More importantly, such a rereading allows an opportunity to begin to address this social crisis as Christians and citizens of our nation.

80 Wilson, *The Truly Disadvantaged*, 204.

2

The Vindication of Humanae vitae, *Continued*

Mary Eberstadt

✷ THE MAJORITY OF ESSAYS in this volume explore the teachings in Pope Paul VI's encyclical *Humanae vitae*. They do this with the concern to consider the question of truth—what it looks like and how we know it when we see it. Unlike most of the essays' authors, I am not a theologian or philosopher. And that, in a way, is exactly the point of my reflection. For reasons examined below, it is precisely in leaving aside these accustomed tools for measuring the truth of Catholic teaching, and in picking up new, secular tools, that the beauty of *Humanae vitae* shines forth in a new and continuously illuminating way. If the truths of Church teaching are so luminous that they can be discerned even without the aid of theology and philosophy, what does that tell us? Surely it tells us that *Humanae vitae*, and the two thousand years of teaching it represents, remains true in ways that all reasonable people can discern, if only they are supplied with the relevant evidence.

Delivering some of that ledger is my intention here. For quite a while now, it has been apparent that the modern sexual revolution, which reached an explosive peak in the 1960s,[1] bids fair to become one of the most formative disruptions in human history. It is having massive repercussions across the world—microcosmic, macrocosmic, moral, religious, political, and otherwise. This ongoing fallout is one of the greatest intellectual puzzles of our time, and alongside other observers, I have been trying here and there to put some of its pieces together. Ten years ago, upon being asked to write an essay for what was then the fortieth anniversary of *Humanae vitae*, I researched evidence from a wide variety of sources about the predictions in that document to see how they mapped onto reality at that time. Citing evidence from sociology, psychology, history, and contemporary women's literature, I concluded then:

> Four decades later, not only have the document's signature predictions been ratified in empirical force, but they have been ratified as few

1 See Donald Critchlow's chapter 1 in this volume (especially note 1), for further discussion of the modern sexual revolution which began in the nineteenth century and saw a second phase in the 1920s, with the third phase occurring in the 1960s.

> predictions ever are: in ways its authors could not possibly have foreseen, including by information that did not exist when the document was written, by scholars and others with no interest whatever in its teaching, and indeed even inadvertently, and in more ways than one, by many proud public adversaries of the Church.[2]

Here I will revisit that foregoing analysis with new evidence from the past ten years alone.

One recurring theme in Pope Francis's teaching is that human realities trump scholarly abstractions: "*La realidad es superior a la idea.*"[3] His signature phrase about pastors who have the "smell of the sheep" is the folk version of this maxim. Cautions about "rigidity," "empty rhetoric," and getting "stuck in pure ideas" appear often in his work, and in that of his inner circle, too. What matters most are "the realities people face in their daily lives," as Cardinal Blase Cupich said in a speech at Cambridge.[4]

This attention to "reality" is especially fitting on this fiftieth anniversary year of the famous and infamous encyclical reiterating Church teaching about sexual morality. To say that proof abounds in support of *Humanae vitae*'s veracity is not to say that a valid argument falls always and everywhere on happy ears—not fifty years ago, not ten years ago, and not today. The reasons for resistance to the teaching are obvious. The promise of sex on demand, unencumbered by constraint, may be the strongest collective temptation humanity has ever encountered. That's why, since the invention of the birth control pill, resistance to the traditional Christian code has been unremittingly ferocious and why so many in the laity and clergy wish that this "rule"—among others—were less taxing. As the disciples of Jesus complained upon hearing his teaching about marriage, "it is better not to marry" (Mt 19:10), since these lessons are hard.

Even so, to confuse "hard" with "wrong" is a fundamental error. If we are truly to lean into reality, as Pope Francis asks of us, there is only one conclusion to be drawn from the mass of current empirical evidence. It is the same conclusion that was visible ten years ago, and that will remain visible ten, one hundred, or two hundred years from now. It is simply this: the most globally reviled and widely misunderstood Catholic document of the last half century is also the most prophetic and explanatory of our time.

Leaving aside theology, philosophy, ideology, and other abstractions, let us count up the new realities vindicating the teachings in *Humanae vitae,* one by one.

2 Mary Eberstadt, "The Vindication of *Humanae Vitae,*" *First Things* (August/September 2008), https://www.firstthings.com/article/2008/08/002-the-vindication-of-ihumanae-vitaei.

3 Pope Francis, Apostolic Exhortation *Evangelii gaudium* (November 24, 2013), Spanish translation, 233, http://www.vatican.va/evangelii-gaudium/sp/files/assets/basic-html/page177.html.

4 Cardinal Blase Cupich, "'Pope Francis's Revolution of Mercy: *Amoris Laetitia* as a New Paradigm of Catholicity," The Annual Von Hügel Lecture, video, 1:19:05, February 9, 2018, Cambridge University, https://www.youtube.com/watch?v=AxbgtpUYk0Q.

Contraceptive Use and Abortion

The first empirical reality is this: if individual intentions are set aside and nothing but uncontroversial facts are assessed, it is transparently clear that the increased use of contraception has also increased abortion. Fifty years ago, when contraception became commonplace, many people of good will defended it precisely for the reason that they thought it would render abortion obsolete. Reliable birth control, they reasoned, would prevent abortion. The statistical record since the 1960s, however, shows this commonly held logic to be wrong. Many studies have emanated from the social sciences during the past decades trying to explain what secular wisdom regards as a puzzling fact. Far from preventing abortion and unplanned pregnancies, contraception's effects after the invention of the pill ran quite the other way: rates of contraception usage, abortion, and out-of-wedlock births all exploded *simultaneously*.

Writing in the *Quarterly Journal of Economics* twenty-two years ago, economists George Akerlof, Janet Yellen, and Michael Katz summarized these unexpected connections:

> Before the sexual revolution, women had less freedom, but men were expected to assume responsibility for their welfare. Today women are more free to choose, but men have afforded themselves the comparable option. "If she is not willing to have an abortion or use contraception," the man can reason, "why should I sacrifice myself to get married?" By making the birth of the child the physical choice of the mother, the sexual revolution has made marriage and child support a social choice of the father.[5]

In other words, contraception has led to more pregnancies and more abortions because it eroded the idea that men had equal responsibility with women in case of an unplanned pregnancy. Contraception, as these economists explain, sharply reduced the incentive for men to marry—including to marry their pregnant girlfriends. In the new, post-pill order, pregnancy became the woman's responsibility—and if birth control "failed," that was not the man's problem. This analysis by perfectly secular scholars is manifestly sound. Among other subsidiary proofs, it explains why the phrase "shotgun wedding" is now antiquarian.

Then there is the fact that contraception and abortion are bound together juridically. As The Catholic University of America's Michael Pakaluk, among other scholars, has indicated:

> As regards jurisprudence, the fruit of contraception is abortion. Until the 1960s, Comstock Act laws were on the books in many states, making the sale of contraceptives illegal even to married couples. These laws were overturned in 1965 by the Supreme Court's muddled *Griswold* decision. But

5 George A. Akerlof, Janet L. Yellen, and Michael L. Katz, "An Analysis of Out-of- Wedlock Childbearing in the United States," *Quarterly Journal of Economics* 111, no. 2 (May 1996): 277–317.

by 1973—only eight years later—the Supreme Court in *Roe v. Wade* had inferred from the right to contraception a right to abortion.[6]

Putting that point differently: legal reasoning justifying freedom to contracept has been used to justify freedom to abort—a linkage that undermines the claim that a hard-and-fast line can be drawn between the two. Or, we might say, freedom to contracept was not enough. People needed the added freedom to terminate a product of failed contraception.

History connects the same causal dots. The push to liberalize abortion laws in countries around the world did not begin until the first third of the twentieth century, as birth control devices came into wider circulation, and American states did not start liberalizing abortion laws until after the federal approval of the birth control pill in 1960.[7] *Roe v. Wade* comes after the pill, not before. As a matter of historical fact, the mass use of contraception called forth the demand for more abortion.

Writing in the *National Catholic Bioethics Quarterly* in 2015, another researcher, Scott Lloyd likewise concluded that contraception leads to abortion—not inevitably in individual cases, of course, but repeatedly and reliably as twinned social phenomena: "Because the lower risk perceived with contraceptives enables sexual encounters and relationships that would not occur otherwise, it invites pregnancies that occur in situations where women do not feel ready to become pregnant."[8]

As we review the record, mercy and forgiveness are patently in order—that is, toward the postwar generation that championed contraception. Who, back then, could have anticipated that contraception would lead to abortion on a scale never before seen? If all critics in the past could have known what social science has demonstrated since, would there have been an uproar over *Humanae vitae*? Might not some of those dissenting Catholics—and others—who publicly rebuked the Church have acted differently if they'd realized that embracing contraception would open the way to vastly more abortion? It is plain in hindsight that the "lowering of moral standards"[9] foreseen by *Humanae vitae* would come to include disrespect not only for women, but for the human fetus, too.

6 Michael Pakaluk, "The Link between Contraception and Abortion," *First Things* (January 23, 2018), https://www.firstthings.com/web-exclusives/2018/01/the-link-between-contraception-and-abortion.

7 See, for example, the timeline in Marge Berer, "Abortion Law and Policy Around the World," *Health and Human Rights Journal* 19, no. 1 (June 2017): 13–27. As noted, "[t]he first country to reform its abortion law was the Soviet Union" in 1920. See also the timeline of Supreme Court cases concerning "reproductive freedom" compiled by the American Civil Liberties Union at https://www.aclu.org/other/timeline-important-reproductive-freedom-cases-decided-supreme-court. In 1965, *Griswold v. Connecticut* strikes down state proscriptions against the sale and use of contraceptives for married couples. Seven years later, in *Eisenstadt v. Baird*, the Court establishes the right of unmarried couples to contraceptive use. One year later, *Roe v. Wade* establishes the right to abortion on demand. Plainly, abortion was not liberalized and then legalized *independent* of the increasing circulation and destigmatization of contraceptives. The timeline of US jurisprudence alone suggests a causal chain.

8 Scott Lloyd, "Can We Be Pro-Life and Pro-Contraception?" *National Catholic Bioethics Quarterly* 15, no. 2 (Summer 2015): 231–239.

9 Pope Paul VI, Encyclical Letter *Humanae vitae* (July 25, 1968), 17, http://w2.vatican.va/content/paul-vi/en/encyclicals.index.html#encyclicals.

Two conclusions from this review of economic analysis would seem especially pertinent to Catholic leaders from here on out. First, we cannot pretend that we do not know these things, as if fifty years of social science doesn't exist. Second, and as a corollary, from now on, anyone inside or outside the Church who cooperates in expanding the use of contraception needs also to explain why it is permissible to increase abortion. Reality since 1968 has made it impossible to pretend that contraception has not played a decisive role in the scourge of abortion. Pope Francis himself has called abortion a "very grave sin" and a "horrendous crime."[10] The old defense of birth control as the alternative to abortion has been overruled by facts. The reality that it is an accelerant to abortion has been confirmed by time.

Improved Ecumenical Relations

In part because fifty years of experience have established reality number one, a second reality has become evident: people outside the Catholic Church—including some leading Protestants—have come to see *Humanae vitae* in a new and more favorable light.

One of the least reported religious stories of our time, this potent trend may reconfigure Christianity, replacing disunity over birth control with a new unity. Observing what the sexual revolution has wrought, more and more Protestant voices now question yesterday's nonchalance about contraception. This reconsideration is far from a majority view, but it manifests what any minority view must have in order to win over others: evidence and moral energy. Consider the following examples from the last ten years:

"Protestants have done themselves a disservice by ignoring *Humanae Vitae*'s substantial statement on human anthropology and sexuality. . . . Protestants would be well-served to study Paul VI's encyclical and take heed of its warnings."

Evan Lenow, professor at Southwestern Baptist Theological Seminary[11]

> "Many evangelicals are joining the discussion about birth control and its meaning. Evangelicals arrived late to the issue of abortion, and we have arrived late to the issue of birth control, but we are here now."
> R. Albert Mohler Jr., president, Southern Baptist Theological Seminary[12]

10 Pope Francis used these words in a 2016 interview with the Italian Catholic media outlets TV2000 and Blu Radio. See Inés San Martin, "Pope Francis Calls Abortion 'Horrendous Crime' and 'Very Grave Sin,'" *Crux* (November 20, 2016), https://cruxnow.com/vatican/2016/11/20/pope-francis-calls-abortion-horrendous-crime-grave-sin.

11 Evan Lenow, "Protestants and Contraception," *First Things* (January 2018), https://www.firstthings.com/article/2018/01/protestants-and-contraception

12 R. Albert Mohler, Jr., "The Pill Turns 50–TIME Considers the Contraceptive Revolution," *albertmohler.com* (April 26, 2010), https://albertmohler.com/2010/04/26/the-pill-turns-50-time-considers-the-contraceptive-revolution.

> "For evangelicals, an anti-contraception position is not seen as exclusively Roman Catholic, as it would have been in the past."
> Jenell Paris, professor of anthropology, Messiah College[13]

> "Whenever current events touch on life issues, evangelicals like me become increasingly uncomfortable with the contraception culture. We realize we have much more in common with Catholics, who revere life, than the radical feminists who revere the rights of women above all else."
> Julie Roys, evangelical author and blogger[14]

> "Many Evangelicals See Something to Admire in Candidates' Broods"
> *New York Times*, headline (2012)[15]

These second thoughts among Protestants and other non-Catholics are less a radical break from Christian tradition than a return to it. Church teaching on contraception, including Protestant teaching, followed an unbroken line through the centuries. Not until the Anglican Communion made the first exception to the prohibition at the Lambeth Conference of 1930 did Catholics and Protestants divide on this moral teaching. The famous Resolution 15 was intended for married couples only, and in carefully delineated circumstances; but it ushered in contraception for convenience. Its language matches the terminology deployed by would-be Catholic "reformers" today:

> In those cases where there is such a clearly felt moral obligation to limit or avoid parenthood, and where there is a morally sound reason for avoiding complete abstinence, the Conference agrees that other methods may be used, provided that this is done in the light of the same Christian principles.[16]

Then as now, Protestants who were not at ease with abandoning traditional Christian teaching turned to Rome for authority. Charles Gore, then-retired bishop of Oxford, objected to Resolution 15. He had "manifold reason to believe that in the case of Birth Prevention the 'very strong tradition in the Catholic Church' has been in the right, and has divine sanction." [17] The move by some

13 Quoted in Mark Oppenheimer, "Many Evangelicals See Something to Admire in Candidates' Broods," *The New York Times,* January 20, 2012, http://www.nytimes.com/2012/01/21/us/more-protestants-oppose-birth-control.html.

14 Julie Roys, "Christians and the Contraception Culture," *Engaging Issues. Seeking Truth.* (blog), March 1, 2012, http://julieroys.com/rethinking-contraception.

15 Oppenheimer, "Many Evangelicals See Something to Admire in Candidates' Broods."

16 Anglican Communion, http://www.anglicancommunion.org/resources/document-library/lambeth-conference/1930/resolution-15-the-life-and-witness-of-the-christian-community-marriage?year=1930.

17 Charles Gore, "Lambeth on Contraceptives" (1930), http://anglicanhistory.org/gore/contra1930.html.

Protestants toward *Humanae vitae* today is, in part, a tacit declaration that Gore's insight might have been the right one.

In Africa, both Protestants and Catholics lean toward traditionalism in Christian moral teaching. Here as elsewhere in history, the maxim delivered by sociologist Laurence R. Iannaccone holds: "Strict churches are strong"—and concomitantly, lax churches are weak.[18] It is in tradition-minded Africa that Christianity has grown explosively in the years since *Humanae vitae*—as opposed to those nations whose Christian leaders have struggled (and struggle still), to change the rulebook.

As the Pew Research Center noted in a report, "Africans [are] among the most morally opposed to contraception."[19] Substantial numbers of people in Kenya, Uganda, and other sub-Saharan countries—Catholic and otherwise—agree with the proposition that contraception use is "morally unacceptable"; in Ghana and Nigeria, it is more than half the population. Despite decades of secular proselytizing, many in Africa have resisted the attempts of reformers to bring them into line with the secular Western sexual program—which includes, of course, diminishing the number of Africans.

Nigerian-born writer and speaker Obianuju Ekeocha, author of *Target Africa: Ideological Neocolonialism in the Twenty-first Century*, wrote an open letter to Melinda Gates, whose foundation dedicates impressive resources to spreading birth control among Africans:

> I see this $4.6 billion buying us misery. I see it buying us unfaithful husbands. I see it buying us streets devoid of the innocent chatter of children. . . . I see it buying us a retirement without the tender loving care of our children.[20]

Africans are not the only intended beneficiaries of campaigns to expand the contraceptive *Weltanschauung*. Nor are they alone in abjuring the idea that the world would be better off with fewer of them. As one notable Indian targeted with the same message some years back put it, "It is futile to hope that the use of contraceptives will be restricted to the mere regulation of progeny. There is hope for a decent life only so long as the sexual act is definitely related to the conception of precious life."[21] The author of this quote is not moral philosopher Elizabeth Anscombe, whose famous 1972 essay "Contraception and Chastity" defended

18 Laurence R. Iannaccone, "Why Strict Churches are Strong," *American Journal of Sociology* 99, no. 5 (March 1994): 1180–1211, https://www.journals.uchicago.edu/doi/abs/10.1086/230409.

19 Michael Lipka, "Many Africans See Contraception as Immoral," *Pew Research Center FactTank: News in the Numbers*, April 16, 2014, http://www.pewresearch.org/fact-tank/2014/04/16/africans-among-the-most-morally-opposed-to-contraception.

20 Obianuju Ekeocha, *Target Africa: Ideological Neocolonialism in the Twenty-first Century* (San Francisco: Ignatius Press, 2018), 200

21 M. K. Gandhi, *Self-Restraint vs. Self-Indulgence* (Ahmedabad, India: Navajivan Publishing House, 1947), 149.

Humanae vitae with this same logic.[22] It is instead Mahatma Gandhi—one more non-Catholic to affirm the reasoning behind Christian moral teaching.

Or, consider one more endorsement from another quarter outside the Catholic Church, written by a Mormon doctor ten years ago: "...[c]ontraception is a heavy part of the fuel behind the sexual revolution and many of the problems in society we are facing. I think '*Humanae Vitae*' is...a prophetic statement."[23]

Governmental Abuse

Just as the truth of the encyclical is acknowledged here and there around the world outside St. Peter's Square, so has history vindicated another particular concern that it cited: the enduring fear that "public authorities" might "impose" these technologies on the citizenry—as *Humanae vitae* also warned.[24] This has happened, of course, in China, via its long-standing, barbaric "one child" policy, replete with forced abortions and involuntary sterilizations. A softer kind of coercion has appeared in the United States and other Western nations where efforts have been made to link desired outcomes with mandatory birth control. In the 1990s and beyond, for example, some US judges backed state-imposed implantation of long-term contraceptives on women convicted of crimes. Such implied force has provoked criticism by (among others) the American Civil Liberties Union. "The recent attempts to coerce women to use Norplant represent a reversion to an era of overt racism and eugenics," the ACLU explained.[25]

The Modern Woman

Reality number three concerns the state of modern women. Contraception, it was and is perennially asserted, will make them happier and freer than ever before. Has it? Evidence points to the contrary—from social science suggesting that female happiness across the United States and Europe has been declining over time, to the dolorous notes so often struck in academic and popular feminism, to the growing worry among secular women that marriage has become impossible and it is time to go it alone.[26] A decade after I documented what social science and other sources were showing about those trends, there is much more that could be added to the record. *Humanae vitae* was surely right to spy an impending increase in divisiveness between the sexes and a diminution of respect for women.[27]

22 Elizabeth Anscombe, "Contraception and Chastity," first published in 1972 and reprinted in *Why* Humanae Vitae *Was Right*, ed., Janet E. Smith (San Francisco: Ignatius Press, 1993).

23 Robert Conkling, "A Mormon Physician on *Humanae Vitae*," *Zenit* (September 25, 2008), https://www.catholic.org/news/international/europe/story.php?id=29615.

24 See Pope Paul VI, *Humanae vitae*, 17.

25 American Civil Liberties Union "Norplant: A New Contraceptive with the Potential for Abuse," press release, https://www.aclu.org/other/norplant-new-contraceptive-potential-abuse.

26 Eberstadt, "The Vindication of *Humanae Vitae*."

27 See Pope Paul VI, *Humanae vitae*, 17.

Consider in particular, the continuing secular sex scandals of 2017 and 2018, and the #MeToo movement. What do these ongoing revelations about sexual harassment in one realm after another tell us? They mean that the revolution licensed predation. That is not a theological judgment, but an empirical one—foreseen in part, by social scientist Francis Fukuyama. His 1999 book *The Great Disruption* made a point that echoes in *Humanae vitae*, though based on a thoroughly secular analysis:

> One of the greatest frauds perpetrated during the Great Disruption was the notion that the sexual revolution was gender-neutral, benefiting women and men equally. . . . In fact, the sexual revolution served the interests of men, and in the end put sharp limits on the gains that women might otherwise have expected from their liberation from traditional roles.[28]

Almost twenty years later, that point is irrefutable. The abuse scandals show that the revolution democratized sexual harassment. No longer does a man have to be a king or a master of the universe to abuse or prey upon women in unrelenting, serial fashion, and for a long time, with no punishment. One needs only a world in which women are assumed to use contraception, assumed to be sexually available at all times. All one needs is the world we have had since the 1960s, the world that *Humanae vitae* foresaw. This brings us to still another reality: fifty years into the sexual revolution, one of the most pressing, and growing, issues for researchers is not overpopulation, but its opposite: *under-population.*

The Demographic Winter and Loneliness

A great many people, especially in the increasingly barren and graying West, are suffering from what experts in those stricken societies call an "epidemic" of loneliness. This finding would not surprise Pope Francis, who in an interview with *La Repubblica* in 2013 called the "loneliness of the old" one of the worst "evils" in today's world.[29] Fifty years after the embrace of the pill—undeniably, *because* of the embrace of the pill—loneliness is spreading across the materially better-off countries of the planet. Toward the end of last year, the *New York Times* published a harrowing story about what the birth dearth looks like from the other end of time's telescope: "4,000 lonely deaths a week. . . . Each year, some of [Japan's elderly] died without anyone knowing, only to be discovered after their neighbors caught the smell."[30] The story goes on to note, "The extreme isolation of elderly Japanese is so common that an entire industry has emerged around it,

28 Francis Fukuyama, *The Great Disruption: Human Nature and the Reconstitution of Social Order* (New York: Free Press, 1999), 121–122.

29 Pope Francis, "The Pope: How the Church Will Change," interview by Eugenio Scalfari, *La Repubblica* (October 1, 2013), http://www.repubblica.it/cultura/2013/10/01/news/pope_s_conversation_with_scalfari_english-67643118.

30 Norimitsu Onishi, "A Generation in Japan Faces a Lonely Death," *New York Times* (November 30, 2017), https://www.nytimes.com/2017/11/30/world/asia/japan-lonely-deaths-the-end.html.

specializing in cleaning out apartments where decomposing remains are found." According to another recent report in *The Independent*, cleanup firms are burgeoning and insurance companies offer policies to protect landlords in case a "lonely death" happens on their property.[31]

Japan is just one country facing post-pill demographic change. "Loneliness is becoming a common phenomenon in France," *Le Figaro* reported several years ago.[32] Citing a study on the "new solitudes" by the Fondation de France, the article names the prime driver of this loneliness: "family rupture," especially divorce. In similar vein, a 2014 study on "Socio-Demographic Predictors of Loneliness Across the Adult Life Span in Portugal" agreed that divorce increases the likelihood of loneliness—though it did not ask whether having children in the picture might ameliorate the problem.[33] Oddly, one can read through many "loneliness studies" without seeing reference to children.

The secular culture reflects this same somber demographic reality. In Sweden, a 2015 documentary on *The Swedish Theory of Love* also told harrowing tales of lonely deaths and questioned the dominance of "independence" in that country as an ideal.[34] And then there's Germany. In an article in *Der Spiegel* titled "Alone by the Millions: Isolation Crisis Threatens German Seniors," the German Centre of Gerontology reports that "One in four [Germans over 70] receives a visit less than once a month from friends and acquaintances, and nearly one in 10 is not visited by anyone anymore.[35]

Such human poverty abounds in societies awash in material wealth. This ironic juxtaposition, too, was not foreseen by those who argued for and against *Humanae vitae* in 1968. Yet without doubt, what unites these tragic portraits is the sexual revolution, which by the 1970s was operating at full throttle in Western nations, driving up divorce rates, driving down marriage rates, and emptying cradles. It does not take a demographer to connect the dots. As one elderly German poignantly summarized in *Der Spiegel*: her husband didn't want any children. "I should have insisted on it," says the former cook, "and then I perhaps wouldn't be so lonely today."[36]

31 Anna Fifield, "Japan's Lonely Deaths: A Growing Industry is Now Devoted to Cleaning Up after Japanese People Dying Alone," *The Independent* (January 30, 2018), https://www.independent.co.uk/news/long_reads/lonely-deaths-japan-die-alone-clean-apartments-japanese-industry-next-homes-clear-a8182861.html.

32 Michael Cosgrove, "Loneliness is Becoming a Common Phenomenon in France," *Le Figaro* (February 7, 2010), http://plus.lefigaro.fr/note/loneliness-is-becoming-a-common-phenomena-in-france-20100702–236888.

33 Félix Neto, "Socio-Demographic Predictors of Loneliness Across the Adult Life Span in Portugal," *Interpersona* 8 (2014), https://interpersona.psychopen.eu/article/ view/171/html.

34 See Influence Film Club, "The Swedish Theory of Love," (2015), directed by Erik Gandini, http://influencefilmclub.com/film/the-swedish-theory-of-love.

35 Guido Kleinhubbert and Antje Windmann, "Isolation Crisis Threatens German Seniors," *Der Spiegel* (January 10, 2013), http://www.spiegel.de/international/germany/germany-faces-epidemic-of-lonely-and-isolated-seniors-a-876635.html.

36 Kleinhubbert and Windmann, "Isolation Crisis Threatens German Seniors."

Additional Challenges

In addition to its destructive force at the beginning and end of the human lifespan, the sexual revolution also continues to generate permutations of sexuality unheard of in history. There are the scores of "gender identities" that have achieved sacrosanct status—and the ongoing accommodations of law and custom to such radical ideas. So unexpected and pervasive are these new transformations that several books outlining the new sexual cartography have appeared within the last year alone. I recommend three of these especially for the light they shed on the current day: Ashley McGuire's *Sex Scandal: The Drive to Abolish Male and Female,*[37] about the social and political enforcement of androgyny; Mark Regnerus's *Cheap Sex: The Transformation of Men, Marriage, and Monogamy,*[38] an economic analysis of how the modern sexual revolution, and especially pornography, have radically changed incentives for marriage; and Ryan T. Anderson's groundbreaking examination in *When Harry Became Sally: Responding to the Transgender Moment.*[39] The shifting boundaries mapped by these and other new analyses of the fallout from the modern sexual revolution are no mere abstractions but poignant facts for many millions of manifestly confused and suffering human beings.

A further reality to ponder is historical and worth reiterating at a time when hope burns eternal in some precincts that the Catholic Church will cease its intransigent insistence on supposedly retrograde points of doctrine. The churches that have accommodated themselves to the sexual revolution have imploded from within. As a headline in *The Guardian* put it simply in 2016, on the eve of a contentious conference at Lambeth Palace where African representatives of the Anglican Communion dissented once more from changing moral teaching, "The Anglican schism over sexuality marks the end of a global church."[40]

In 1930, people would have been shocked if told that the doctrinal war over sex would shatter the Anglican Communion; that parts of the Communion would go to legal war over churches and jurisdictions as well as doctrine; and that the separation of North and South, Episcopal and Anglican, Africa and Europe, would yield divisions and subdivisions, sorrow and acrimony, on a global scale.

In 1998, Bishop John Shelby Spong of Newark, New Jersey, a leader of the Episcopalian Church, urged an embrace of the sexual revolution. He published his radical ideas in a book called *Why Christianity Must Change or Die*, agitating for still more dismantling of Church teaching.[41] The Christianity of which he

37 Ashley McGuire, *Sex Scandal: The Drive to Abolish Male and Female* (Washington, D.C.: Regnery Publishing, 2017).

38 Mark Regnerus, *Cheap Sex: The Transformation of Men, Marriage, and Monogamy* (New York: Oxford University Press, 2017).

39 Ryan T. Anderson, *When Harry Became Sally: Responding to the Transgender Moment* (New York: Encounter Books, 2018).

40 Andrew Brown, "The Anglican schism over sexuality marks the end of a global church," *The Guardian* (January 8, 2016), https://www.theguardian.com/commentisfree/2016/jan/08/anglican-schism-sexuality-end-global-church-conservative-african-leaders-canterbury.

41 John Shelby Spong, *Why Christianity Must Change or Die: A Bishop Speaks to Believers in Exile* (San Francisco: HarperCollins Publishers, 1998).

spoke *did* change, exactly as he and others hoped. And now the retooled version they fought for is dying. As one study demonstrated:

> Around 2000 serious decline set in [in Sunday attendance]. . . . Average Sunday attendance dropped by nearly one third between 2000 and 2015. . . . "The rate of baptism has been cut almost in half over a thirty-year period." . . .The most dramatic data is for marriages. . . . In 2015 the Episcopal Church married less than a quarter of the number it married in 1980.[42]

The facts of religious history make their own case in favor of Paul VI's prophetic stance. Disaster descended on the Anglican Communion for doing exactly what dissenters from *Humanae vitae* want the Catholic Church to do: make exceptions to teaching (truth) that people find difficult. Surely anyone urging Rome to follow Lambeth's lead today must first explain how Catholicism's fate will be different.

In this moment of watchfulness inside and outside the Church, a global fellowship knows the truths of *Humanae vitae* and related teachings *as* truths, however unwanted or hard. They are among the latest pilgrims in a line stretching two thousand years back. They have sacrificed to stand where they do, and they sacrifice still—including by relinquishing the good opinion of a mocking world.

Conclusion

It is fitting to close on a hopeful note—because hope does abound in this modern sexual revolutionary fog, including for reasons that would have been less visible in 1968. To review the record of the last fifty years is not to engage in a dirge. It is the opposite: to empower the rest of us going forward with knowledge that people fifty years ago did not have.

It is not a secret that the years since *Humanae vitae* was issued have been challenging for the Catholic Church. How could it be otherwise? The modern sexual revolution is now locked in mortal combat with two millennia of Catholic teaching that harks straight back to Jesus. That is the bad news.

At the same time, increasing numbers of people outside the Catholic Church are concluding from that same increasingly well-documented wreckage, that Catholic moral teaching has called many things right—not only with *Humanae vitae*, but for the preceding millennia of consistent teaching. The tough but beautiful consistency of that moral code has drawn in converts ever since it was mocked by the pagans of Rome, and by pagans in every era to follow. It has made St. Augustines out of sinners in every age. That code embodies a story about God and his people that to this day brings converts to the Church—people who seek truth and can find it nowhere else, especially in an age of secularist materialism that takes the modern sexual revolution as its cornerstone. With every

42 David Goodhew, "Facing Episcopal Church Decline," *Covenant:* the weblog of *The Living Church* (July 24, 2017), summarizing Jeremy Bonner, "United States of America," in *Growth and Decline in the Anglican Communion: 1980 to the Present*, ed. David Goodhew, 227–248 (New York: Routledge, 2016), cited at 236–237.

year, more evidence accumulates about the record of that materialism versus the record of truth.

In sum, to discern the record of the last half century is to see that the Catholic Church was right to stand as a sign of contradiction to the devastation the modern sexual revolution would wreak; that accommodating to that revolution has been an epic failure for the churches that have tried it; and that the truths of *Humanae vitae* and related documents burn all the more brightly against the shadowy toll of the destruction. Mocked and rejected though it may be in some precincts, the Church via that encyclical and related teachings, was correct in one of the biggest warnings issued in history—and those teachings continue to be vindicated over and over by scholars and others with no connection to Rome, seeking only to document and analyze the record of our times. Surely that consistent and inadvertent underlining of the encyclical's reiteration of long-standing doctrine, across half a century, tells us something about truth and how we know it when we see it.

3

Humanae vitae *and the Technological Conquest of Humanity*

Michael Hanby

THE CONTROVERSY SURROUNDING THE promulgation of *Humanae vitae* in 1968 is often treated by both sides as a question of moral theology, narrowly conceived. That this is partly true is evidenced by the fact that opposition to this encyclical subsequently generated whole schools of moral theology designed to circumvent its teaching, eventually eliciting the response of *Veritatis splendor*. Yet analysis of the circumstances surrounding the 1968 debate, as well as subsequent magisterial teaching which sought to deepen the encyclical's teaching, show that *Humanae vitae* has a still more comprehensive concern: the "technologization" of modern life and the human being and its threat to the human future, a crucial if often unwitting factor in the opposition to the encyclical then and now.

This essay will recast the debate surrounding this encyclical against this more comprehensive horizon, arguing with Pope John Paul II that its "anthropological vision" is indispensable to defending the humanum against the anti-human tendencies of technological society.

The Signs of the Times and the Spirit of the Age

When viewing the early debate surrounding *Humanae vitae* through the lens of the question concerning technology, one is immediately struck by two things. The first is just how deeply the debate was determined by this very question and shaped by the contending parties' attitudes toward the overwhelming power of technological progress in twentieth-century modernity. The Papal Commission Final Report, for example, justified its reform proposals in advance of the encyclical partly on grounds that "man's tremendous progress in control of matter by technical means, and the universal and total 'intercommunication' that has been achieved correspond perfectly to the divine decrees."[1] *Gaudium et spes* generally sounds a more ambivalent note, one which would resound with increasing clarity through the remainder of Pope Paul VI's pontificate.[2]

1 Robert G. Hoyt, ed., *The Birth Control Debate* (Kansas City, Mo.: National Catholic Reporter, 1968), 79.

2 See Pope Paul VI, Apostolic Letter *Octogesima adveniens* (May 14, 1971), 29, 38, http://w2.vatican.va/content/paul-vi/en/apost_letters.index.3.html.

At the very outset, *Gaudium et spes* declares that "the human race is involved in a new stage of history . . . triggered by the intelligence and creative energies of man."[3] These energies "recoil upon him, upon his decisions and desires, both individual and collective, and upon his manner of thinking and acting with respect to things and people."[4] The "spiritual agitation and changing conditions of life" in this new era have their root in modern science and technology, which have transformed both the theoretical and the practical orders.[5]

Humanae vitae would later echo this ambivalence, citing man's astonishing technical conquest of nature as the occasion for a deepened reflection on the traditional teaching. Indeed, the most remarkable of all these revolutionary social developments, Paul VI writes,

> . . . is to be seen in man's stupendous progress in the domination and rational organization of the forces of nature to the point that he is endeavoring to extend this control over every aspect of his own life—over his body, over his mind and emotions, over his social life, and even over the laws that regulate the transmission of life.[6]

Yet, despite the Council's expressed desire to discern the "signs of the times" and the Church's supposedly newfound willingness to "learn from the world," antagonists of *Humanae vitae* then and now exhibit a striking *lack* of historical consciousness and a stunning failure to learn the lessons of the first half of the twentieth century, which were mostly forgotten between the discovery of the concentration camps and the discovery of the double helix.[7] This is the second thing one notices. Though modern man's technical dominion was the acknowledged occasion for this new reflection, the debate shows little interest in the meaning of this dominion or what is truly novel in it. The disputants show no interest in the difference between modern technology and ancient *techne*. Little thought was given to technology as a social *system* or as a regime of necessity. There was no attempt to situate the advent of the contraceptive pill within the larger scientific and social history, nor any real analysis of the massive social and economic transformations that impelled great masses of people toward contraception in the first place.[8]

3 Vatican Council II, *Gaudium et spes* (December 7, 1965), 4, http://www.vatican.va/archive/hist_councils/ii_vatican_council/index.htm.

4 *Gaudium et spes*, 4.

5 See *Gaudium et spes*, 4–5.

6 Pope Paul VI, Encyclical Letter *Humanae vitae* (July 25, 1968), 2, http://w2.vatican.va/content/paul-vi/en/encyclicals.index.html.

7 When "eugenics" was discredited in the aftermath of the Second World War, "cultural" explanations of human behavior (nurture) gained temporary ascendency over explanations from "nature," while "at the same time the science of genetics—and with it, confidence in the genetic determination of everything but human behavior—could prosper." See Evelyn Fox Keller, "Nature, Nurture, and the Human Genome Project," in *The Code of Codes: Scientific and Social Issues in the Human Genome Project*, eds. D. Kevles and L. Hood (Cambridge: Harvard University Press, 1992), 281–299.

8 The eugenics movements of the late nineteenth and twentieth centuries, which had formed the backdrop to Pope Pius XI's encyclical letter, *Casti connubii*, and whose influence is much greater than we

Gaudium et spes had marveled that "technology is now transforming the face of the earth."[9] Yet, the initial debate surrounding *Humanae vitae* exhibits little awareness of how technology had already changed us, transforming our way of life and our most basic notions of being, nature, reason, and truth. And so, it exhibits little *self*-awareness of how the transformations wrought by technology had already shaped the terms of the controversy. The controversy is thus marked both by historical amnesia about atrocities just committed and naivete about the brave new world that lay just over the horizon.

Signs of the Times

About the same time that the report of the Papal Commission was leaked to the world, another report was issued, this one from the National Academy of Sciences, entitled *Biology and the Future of Man*. Enthralled with dramatic advances in molecular biology over the previous two decades, its authors conclude by contemplating possibilities for "intervening in the biological processes of nature" that had not been uttered aloud in polite society since the 1940s. Its final paragraph reads thus:

> *Homo sapiens* has overcome the limitations of his origin. He controls the vast energies of the atomic nucleus, moves across his planet at speeds barely below escape velocity, and can escape when he so wills. He communicates with his fellows at the speed of light, extends the powers of his brain with those of the digital computer, and influences the numbers and genetic constitution of virtually all other living species. Now he can guide his own evolution. In him, Nature has reached beyond the hard regularities of physical phenomena. *Homo sapiens*, the creature of Nature, has transcended her. From a product of circumstances, he has risen to responsibility. At last, he is Man. May he behave so![10]

It is astonishing in retrospect that supporters of the Papal Commission could speak so self-assuredly about mature and responsible collaboration "with men of learning and of science" to control matter and to intervene "in the biological processes of nature" at the very moment when eminent "men of learning and science,"

typically understand, is an ineliminable dimension of this history. At the risk of vast oversimplification, "eugenics" a term coined by Darwin's cousin Francis Galton, was made possible by the conflation of Darwinian biology, with its emphases on breeding and heredity, with the statistical analysis of populations pioneered by the social sciences. On the relationship between eugenics and Darwinian evolution, see Daniel Kevles, *In the Name of Eugenics: Genetics and the Uses of Human Heredity* (New York: Knopf, 1985); Richard Hofstadter, *Social Darwinism in American Thought* (New York: Braziller, 1959); David J. Depew and Bruce H. Weber, *Darwinism Evolving: Systems Dynamics and the Genealogy of Natural Selection* (Cambridge: MIT Press, 1997), 193–242.

9 *Gaudium et spes*, 5.

10 Philip Handler, ed., *Biology and the Future of Man* (Oxford: Oxford University Press, 1970), 926, quoted in Keller, "Nature, Nurture, and the Human Genome Project," 288. See also Daniel J. Kevles, *In the Name of* Eugenics, 251–268.

like the prominent molecular biologist Robert Sinsheimer, were unashamedly contemplating a "new eugenics," more powerful but less obviously authoritarian than the old.[11] More astonishing still is that the concepts of human dominion and biological nature presupposed and advanced by each of these documents are all but indistinguishable. It is as if there had been no Nazi medical experiments, no International Eugenics Congress, no Cold Spring Harbor Laboratory, no *Buck v. Bell*, no Birth Control Leagues, no Social Hygiene movement.[12] It is as if Chesterton and Lewis and Huxley had never issued their warnings about the shape of things to come. It is as if there were no Crick and Watson lurking in the shadows and no Robert Edwards and Patrick Steptoe waiting just over the horizon. It is as if *Casti connubii* and *Humanae vitae* pertained merely to the private choices of individual couples and were not integrally related to Catholic social teaching—a lasting misconception corrected by Pope Benedict XVI in *Caritas in veritate*—or as if the social forces commending universal contraception were not the same forces that preoccupied the Church's social magisterium.[13]

The scientific and technological revolution may have ushered in a new era of human history and recoiled upon our manner of thinking and acting, but somehow it left the essential question unchanged from when Bouvier sought guidance for confessors from the Penitentiary in 1842. In other words, it is as if man's technological dominion had only given us the pill and some new moral dilemmas and had not also put the truth of the human person—and his future *as human*—radically into question.[14]

In his magisterial albeit tendentious volume on contraception, John Noonan traces how the Church's teaching from the high-water mark of scholasticism to the promulgation of *Casti connubii* in 1930, developed principally through the manuals and the Penitentiary and in response to a pastoral emergency—the

11 Hoyt, *The Birth Control Debate*, 88; Robert Sinsheimer, "The Prospect of Designed Genetic Change," *Engineering and Science* 32, no. 7 (1969): 8–13; cited in Keller, "Nature, Nurture, and the Human Genome Project," 289.

12 In 1919 Margaret Sanger declared, "More children for the fit, less from the unfit—that is the chief issue of birth control." The historical relationship between the birth control movement and early twentieth century eugenics is indisputable, though many conservatives or so-called "positive eugenicists" were opposed to contraception. Cited in Kevles, *In the Name of Eugenics*, 90. See also Havelock Ellis, "Birth-Control and Eugenics," *Eugenics Review* 9, no. 1 (April, 1917): 32–41. For analyses of the profound influence of eugenics on American culture and the conflation of eugenics, progressivism and American Protestantism, see Amy Laura Hall, *Conceiving Parenthood: American Protestantism and the Spirit of Reproduction* (Grand Rapids, Mich.: Eerdmans, 2007); Christine Rosen, *Preaching Eugenics: Religious Leaders and the American Eugenics Movement* (Oxford: Oxford University Press, 2004).

13 "*Humanae vitae* indicates the strong links between life ethics and social ethics, ushering in a new area of magisterial teaching that has gradually been articulated in a series of documents, most recently, John Paul II's encyclical *Evangelium vitae*." See Pope Benedict XVI, Encyclical Letter *Caritas in veritate* (June 29, 2009), 15, http://w2.vatican.va/content/benedict-xvi/en/encyclicals.index.html.

14 And yet, as Cardinal Carlo Caffarra reminded us, "It is well known that the problem for which Paul VI meant to offer a solution was not the licitness or illicitness of contraception. More exactly, it was the licitness or illicitness of a *particular* method of contraception: chemical contraception." See Carlo Caffarra, "Who is Like the Lord, Our God?" in *Why* Humanae Vitae *was Right: A Reader*, ed. Janet E. Smith (San Francisco: Ignatius Press, 1993), 255–256.

widespread adoption of contraceptive methods by European Catholics in the nineteenth and early 20th century. Perhaps, then, contraception was destined to come down to us principally as a question of moral and pastoral theology: "Are all contraceptive acts intrinsically evil, and how should pastors and confessors counsel those of their flock whom they suspect to be taking recourse to them?" This history presumably forms the backdrop of Pope Francis's demand that the confessional not become a torture chamber. And if, as is rumored, the "ideal" of *Humanae vitae*, no. 12, is to be transformed from an ontological reality to a lofty aspiration and subordinated to the principle of discernment, it will be because the question has been interpreted through these lenses.

I do not wish to deny, of course, that contraception and related issues raise grave moral and pastoral concerns, much less to relativize the Church's teaching on intrinsically evil acts, which is indispensable to the defense of the very humanity of the human person and the preservation of his reason and freedom.[15] Nevertheless, the questions themselves do not exhaust all that is at stake in upholding these teachings.

In the name of pastoral encounter, we are encouraged these days to set aside abstract truths and look with compassion on the realities of life in all their concrete circumstances. A salutary directive, but what does it mean? After all, Pope Francis teaches us emphatically that "everything is interconnected."[16] So it seems an oddly abstract notion of concreteness that would isolate the moral decisions of couples from all the historical, social, and ideological conditions that give them these specific choices, give those choices their meaning, and make their choosing compulsory. Separating moral questions from their ontological and anthropological bases results then in a kind of ahistorical presentism and an abstract and atomistic empiricism for which the only relevant data are the couple's feelings and self-understanding at a particular moment in time.[17] Such abstract concreteness is finally just another species of moralism that separates moral questions from their ontological and anthropological bases *and* from their historical circumstances as they actually are.

There is more to fear these days from a moralism of the left parading about in pastoral guise, it seems, but a moralism of the right would be no less impotent in the face of our historical moment. A moralistic interpretation of *Humanae vitae* in whatever form is abstract in that it fails—or willfully refuses—to see and think about the interconnections between these pastoral situations and the dominant socio-political forces of our time. It abstracts these situations from the history which produced them, in this case abstracting the sexual revolution from

15 See Caffarra, "Who is Like the Lord, Our God?", 264–271.

16 Pope Francis, Encyclical Letter *Laudato si'* (May 24, 2015), 70, http://w2.vatican.va/content/francesco/en/encyclicals.index.html.

17 This is precisely what Father James Martin does in treating "LGBT" identities as ahistorical and unquestionable givens, as if the notion of "identity" and the appropriation of these terms did not entail and conceal a theory of human nature in conflict with a Catholic theological anthropology and the doctrine of creation. See James Martin, SJ, *Building a Bridge: How the Catholic Church and the LGBT Community Can Enter into a Relationship of Respect, Compassion, and Sensitivity* (New York: HarperOne, 2018), 36ff.

the technological revolution of which it is the supreme expression. The sexual revolution is then reduced merely to a progressive revision of sexual morality instead of what it truly is: a revolution in fundamental ontology and our archetypal self-understanding and an interminable war against the human person as a creature of God, and therefore *as human*. We thus treat "concrete situations" abstractly when we reduce them to so many discrete moral decisions, and we fail to grasp the full depth of "the new area of magisterial teaching" inaugurated by *Humanae vitae* or to appreciate the dangers in compromising it.

Biotechnocracy

Fifty years on, the danger should be still more obvious. Every social ill prophesied by *Humanae vitae* has come to pass, and some which the encyclical did not foresee. We are witnessing in our time not only the abolition of man, but of woman also. The technological disassembly of the one act of conjugal love into discrete unitive and procreative dimensions has now made it possible to manufacture children for whom the once natural question "Who is my mother?" has no obvious natural answer. If the predictions of Stanford law and genetics professor Henry Greely are correct, it will soon be possible to manufacture children begotten from *no* adults who have ever lived, but from embryos created for the purpose of harvesting their gametes.[18] Contraception, abortion, same-sex marriage, artificial reproduction, surrogacy, genetic screening, germ-line manipulation, defective "research" embryos, human-animal hybrids, gender theory and gender reassignment, each belongs to different and perhaps novel moral species, and careful discernment is undoubtedly needed to determine which. But they spring from the same ontological and anthropological root and perpetuate the same ontological and anthropological lie; moreover, they are not just the discrete moral acts of individuals and couples. Increasingly, they are mutually reinforcing elements of a complex adaptive social *system*—an evolving *biotechnocracy*, if you will—whose dynamic exigencies govern us more deeply and comprehensively than the rule of law.

This system is technological in at least two senses. Mundanely, the technological conquest of human biology is the practical precondition for all these phenomena. Same-sex marriage would have remained permanently unimaginable without the possibility of giving same-sex couples children by technological means, a requirement for so-called "marriage equality."[19] We could never have imagined that a man might "really" be a woman if we did not also imagine that it were technologically possible for us to transform him into one. Yet these phenomena also suggest, more deeply, that technology has entered into the heart of our fundamental ontology and our very self-understanding—into the way we conceive of nature, knowledge, and truth. "There is a strong, and, it seems, almost

18 Henry T. Greely, *The End of Sex and the Future of Human Reproduction* (Cambridge: Harvard University Press, 2016), 124–135.

19 See Michael Hanby, "The Brave New World of Same Sex Marriage," *The Federalist* (February 19, 2014), http://thefederalist.com/2014/02/19/the-brave-new-world-of-same-sex-marriage.

irresistible tendency in the human mind," writes Hans Jonas, "to interpret human functions in terms of the artifacts that take their place, and artifacts in terms of the replaced human functions."[20] If technology is indeed the ontology of the age, as philosopher George Grant once said, then a moral critique of technology which merely evaluates its uses will not suffice, for it fails to grasp what technology has become for us.[21] Technology is not just a collection of tools, external and subservient to us, that we can then use badly or well. It must be approached as a system—a regime of necessity—that shapes our perspectives and limits our imaginations, even in relation to our very being, and sets the conditions of our action.

The "new area of magisterial teaching" inaugurated with *Humanae vitae* develops against the backdrop of a deepening awareness of this problem. Paul VI worried that the opening which the 1960s seemed to offer to Christian transcendence might in reality be the "more accentuated sliding towards a new positivism: universalized technology as the dominant form of activity, as the overwhelming pattern of existence, even as a language, without the question of its meaning being really asked."[22] John Paul II observed in *Redemptor hominis*, that "the man of today seems ever to be under threat from what he produces," and this, the pope says, "seems to make up the main chapter of the drama of present-day human existence in its broadest and universal dimension."[23] Benedict XVI explains that "technology is never merely technology" because "technology is the objective side of human action whose origin and *raison d'etre* is found in the subjective element . . . . It reveals man and his aspiration towards development."[24] It thus tends "to become an ideological power that threatens to confine us within an *a priori* that holds us back from encountering being and truth. Were that to happen, we would all know, evaluate and make decisions about our life situations from within a technocratic cultural perspective to which we would belong structurally, without ever being able to discover a meaning that is not of our own making."[25]

Pope Francis seems convinced that this confinement has already come to pass, at least judging from *Laudato si'*.[26] He laments "the way that humanity has taken up technology and its development according to an undifferentiated and one-dimensional paradigm. This paradigm exalts the concept of a subject who, using logical and rational procedures, progressively approaches and gains control over an external object. This subject makes every effort to establish the scientific and

20 Hans Jonas, *The Phenomenon of Life: Toward a Philosophical Biology* (Evanston, Ill.: Northwestern University Press, 2001), 110.

21 George Grant, *Technology and Justice* (Toronto: Anansi, 1986), 32.

22 *Octogesima adveniens*, 29.

23 Pope John Paul II, Encyclical Letter *Redemptor hominis* (March 4, 1979), 15, http://w2.vatican.va/content/john-paul-ii/en/encyclicals.index.html.

24 Pope Benedict XVI, *Caritas in veritate*, 14, 69.

25 Pope Benedict XVI, *Caritas in veritate*, 70.

26 For a more extended engagement with this encyclical, see Michael Hanby, "The Gospel of Creation and the Technocratic Paradigm: Reflections on a Central Teaching of *Laudato Si'*," in *Communio: International Catholic Review* 42, no. 4 (Winter 2015): 724–747.

experimental method, *which in itself is already a technique of possession, mastery and transformation.*"[27] Pope Francis calls this the "technocratic paradigm," and follows Romano Guardini, saying "the technological mind sees nature as an insensate order, as a cold body of facts, as a mere 'given,' as an object of utility, as raw material to be hammered into useful shape."[28] So powerful is it that "the idea of promoting a different cultural paradigm and employing technology as a mere instrument is nowadays inconceivable. The technocratic paradigm has become so dominant that it would be difficult to do without its resources and even more difficult to utilize them without being dominated by their internal logic."[29]

St. Augustine recognized, along with the best of ancient wisdom, that those who lust for domination end up dominated by it. Hans Jonas helps us to better understand this tragic irony with respect to our technical dominion, where our servants become our masters. "Control," he explains,

> by making ever more things available for more kinds of uses, enmeshes the user's life in ever more dependencies on external objects. There is no other way of exercising the power than by making oneself available to the use of the things as they become available. . . . Tasks for theory are set by the practical results of its preceding use, their solutions to be turned again to use, and so on.[30]

As these products and their exigencies succeed each other and accumulate, Jonas says, "the situation for later subjects and their choices of action will be progressively different from that of the initial agent and ever more the fated product of what was done before."[31]

To glimpse the power of this fate over our thought and action, one need only look to any of a thousand bioethical dilemmas, where indeed "the tasks for theory are set by the practical results of its preceding use." The need to identify and isolate an analytically discrete "moment of conception," accurate to the fraction of a second, from a continuum of events that begins with conjugal embrace of man and woman and concludes with the birth of a child would not commend itself to us with such urgency were it not for our ability to dissociate, analyze, intervene, and manipulate the various stages of that process. Never mind whether life—the being of living things, Aristotle says—fully submits to this sort

27 Pope Francis, *Laudato si'*, 106, emphasis mine.

28 Pope Francis, *Laudato si'*, 115, citing Romano Guardini, *The End of the Modern World* (Wilmington, Del.: Intercollegiate Studies Institute, 1998), 55.

29 Pope Francis, *Laudato si'*, 108.

30 Jonas, *The Phenomenon of Life*, 193, 209. C. S. Lewis echoes this same idea. "The last men, far from being the heirs of power, will be of all men most subject to the dead hand of the great planners and conditioners and will themselves least exercise power upon the future." I trust, that in referring to the "last men," the echoes of Nietzsche are more than fortuitous. See C. S. Lewis, *The Abolition of Man* (New York: HarperCollins, 2001), 57–58. See also Friedrich Nietzsche, *Thus Spoke Zarathustra* (New York: Viking, 1966), 5.

31 Hans Jonas, *The Imperative of Responsibility: In Search of an Ethics for the Technological Age* (Chicago: University of Chicago Press, 1984), 7.

of analysis, or what other forms of thought may be needed to think properly about it.[32] Similarly, the need to precisely define and identify death within an instant of its occurring would not be so urgent were it not for our ability to prolong life artificially and to harvest organs, and if extraordinary cost did not accompany extraordinary measures. This *mysterium tremendum* need not yield to our methods of analysis, but technical reason has robbed us of every other form of rationality, and we need knowledge we can do something with.[33] The conditions for thinking "speculatively"" about the truth of human nature are thus dictated by the practical and moral emergencies generated by our technology.[34]

We can perhaps see better why Jonas considers this dynamic a fate if we carry this foregoing line of analysis into the realm of human moral action. We remain free, within certain parameters, to choose whether to avail ourselves of the available technological possibilities, but none of us is free from *having to choose*, from having to take up a stance with respect to these technologies in the face of powerful but subtle forms of systematic social coercion that shape our choices. A woman who wishes to succeed in the workforce will have to choose whether to contracept, but her choices are powerfully framed by the availability of chemical contraceptives as a standard part of the regime of so-called "reproductive health" and the market's expectation that she will use them. These expectations are more coercive than we usually perceive, for they operate internally as well as externally. They redefine the archetypal relationship between every woman and her own body, irrespective of the choice of any particular woman, representing that relation as a field of technical possibilities subject to individual choices that, in reality, are anything but. This representation, it is important to see, defines the collective imaginary in a way that shapes a woman's self-experience prior to her conscious choice.

Similarly, an expectant couple is still free to choose whether to submit their developing child to amniocentesis and genetic analysis, but choose they must. The very necessity of choosing makes the archetypal meaning of the parent-child relationship despotic, and woe to this particular couple if they should get a negative result. The weighted expectations of the entire medical industrial complex are against them in that event, and it would take nothing more spectacular than a slight adjustment to the schedule of insurance benefits to make their "free choice" for abortion all but compulsory. It is for reasons such as these that Greely thinks that the development of what he calls "easy PGD"—for easy preimplantation genetic diagnosis—will make natural procreation obsolete within a generation or so.[35]

32 Aristotle, *De Anima*, 415 b13, in Richard McKeon, trans., *The Basic Works of Aristotle* (New York: Random House, 1941), 559.

33 For a discussion of the kind of metaphysical considerations needed to think through the question of "origins," see D. C. Schindler, "Historical Intelligibility: On Creation and Causality," *Anthropotes: Rivista di Studi sulla Persona e la Famiglia* 36, no. 1 (2010): 15–44; Hanby, *No God, No Science?: Theology, Cosmology, Biology* (Malden, Mass.: Wiley Blackwell, 2017): 262–284.

34 See Michael Hanby, "Re-Conceiving the Organism: Why American Catholic Bioethics Needs a Better Theory of Human Life," in *Communio: International Catholic Review* 41 (Fall 2014): 615–631.

35 "Easy PGD" involves a combination of improved genomic mapping and a capacity to produce or

Whether science or science fiction, such examples show the "human underside" of a social system, "organized for collective inquiry" in John Dewey's words, that more nearly resembles Francis Bacon's *New Atlantis* than John Locke's *Second Treatise*.[36] It is an open-ended system that "attacks nature collectively"—and therefore progressively—by introducing new processes into history, where work in one branch of the sciences like in vitro fertilization (IVF) technology contributes to unforeseeable and uncontrollable achievements in a second field like genetics. Of course, this is too simple. The cause-and-effect trains set in motion by technocratic processes do not follow a linear chain reaction but multiply "virally" in multiple directions at once.[37] Our technocracy is thus really a *biotechnocracy*, both because it takes on a life of its own as a complex adaptive system whose ensemble behavior is irreducible to and uncontrollable by the human beings who initiate it and because human beings are not simply the subject of its irreversible processes but its object as well.[38] Its rule is *post-political*, for technology does not wait on politics, and its dynamic exigencies perpetually exceed the scope of human governance, and it is *absolutist*, irrespective of the political system in which it unfolds, because it knows no limits save the limit of possibility.[39] Biotechnocracy thus puts a new twist on the old adage "art imitates nature," mimicking nature as metabolic process and fulfilling more perfectly than Hobbes's *Leviathan* the foundational technological aspiration of modern political order, to create and submit ourselves to the rule of an artificial man—an automaton "that moves . . . by springs and wheels as doth a watch."[40] Which is why technology has become our fate.

Re-reading the Signs: The Triumph of Art Over Nature

Where did this brave new world come from? According to Benedict XVI this "new era" is grounded in the very foundation of the modern age, in "the new

procure female gametes without the difficulties presently associated with egg retrieval. This could possibly be achieved by a variety of methods already in use or in development.

36 John Dewey, *Reconstruction in Philosophy* (London: Forgotten Books: 2012), 37.

37 Or as biotech entrepreneur Gregory Stock puts it, "The coming possibilities will be the inadvertent spinoff of mainstream research that virtually everyone supports . . . Researchers and clinicians working on in vitro fertilization (IVF) don't think much about future human evolution, but nonetheless are building a foundation of expertise in conceiving, handling, testing, and implanting human embryos, and this will one day be the basis for the manipulation of the human species." Gregory Stock, *Redesigning Humans: Our Inevitable Genetic Future* (New York: Houghton Mifflin, 2002), 5.

38 I owe the inspiration for this insight to Hannah Arendt's profound treatment of labor in distinction from work and action. "The natural processes on which [technology] feeds increasingly relate to the biological process itself, so that the apparatuses we once handled freely begin to look as though they were shells belonging to the human body as the shell belongs to the body of a turtle.' Seen from the vantage point of this development, technology in fact no longer appears 'as the product of a conscious human effort to enlarge material power, but rather like a biological development of mankind in which the innate structures of the human organism are transplanted into an ever-increasing measure into the environment of man.'" Hannah Arendt, *The Human Condition*, 2nd ed. (Chicago: University of Chicago Press, 1958), 152–153, citing Werner Heisenberg, *Das Naturbild der heutigen Physik* (1955), 14–15.

39 Arendt, *The Human Condition*, 231.

40 Arendt, *The Human Condition*, 299; Thomas Hobbes, *Leviathan* (London: Penguin, 1985), 81.

correlation of experiment and method that enables man to arrive at an interpretation of nature in conformity with its laws and thus finally to achieve 'the triumph of art over nature.'"[41] Our modern word "technology," which fuses *techne* and *logos*, making and knowing, expresses this correlation. Technology is first a way of apprehending the world before it is a collection of instruments. This is presumably why Pope Francis calls the technocratic paradigm an *epistemological* paradigm.[42] The new technological manner of knowing is a knowing-by-doing that "takes experience apart and analyzes it," in Francis Bacon's words, abstracting the intelligible wholes that present themselves to our experience from the totality to which they actually belong, breaking them down so as to reduce them to their simplest components, and reconstructing them as the sum of those abstracted components and their interactions. This is the meaning of the famous Baconian maxim, "knowledge is power." It is not simply that we now know the phenomena of nature *for the sake of controlling them*; it is rather that we know natural phenomena *by means of* controlling them. Hence, Bacon says that truth and usefulness come to the same thing,[43] and Benedict XVI says that "truth has come to be seen as coinciding with the possible": because the "truth" of this kind of knowledge is precisely *identical* to our power, to our *success* in replicating experimental results, producing new experiments, and manipulating these phenomena to our own ends.[44] It is also why the "technocratic paradigm" sets in motion an interminable and systematic war against all forms of antecedent order, including that represented by our own nature. With the conflation of knowledge and power, truth, and utility, truth is essentially whatever is technically possible, but the ultimate limits of possibility can only be discovered by perpetually transgressing the present limits of possibility.

The triumph of art over nature, then, is the triumph of a new kind of practical reason, novel both in its "scale, objects, and consequences," and, as we shall see, in the ontological vision which it presupposes and perpetuates.[45] This triumph now determines what it means for us to think. It makes traditional theoretical and contemplative reason obsolete, both because it deprives contemplation of its objects and because the new conflation of truth and possibility makes such speculation superfluous.[46] Reason instead becomes formal, algebraic, and func-

41 Pope Benedict XVI, Encyclical Letter, *Spe salvi* (November 30, 2007), 16, http://w2.vatican.va/content/benedict-xvi/en/encyclicals.index.html, citing Francis Bacon, *Novum Organum* I, 117. According to historian Stephen Gaukroger, the culture of scientific modernity is characterized, by "the gradual assimilation of all cognitive values to scientific ones." For Gaukroger, "This is not merely a distinctive feature of Western scientific practice, it is a distinctive feature of Western modernity: a particular image of the role and aims of scientific understanding is tied up in a fundamental fashion with the self-image of modernity." Stephen Gaukroger, *The Emergence of a Scientific Culture: Science and the Shaping of Modernity 1210–1685* (Oxford: Oxford University Press, 2006), 11.

42 See Pope Francis, *Laudato si'*, 107.

43 Francis Bacon, *The New Organon*, Lisa Jardine and Michael Silverthorne, ed. (Cambridge: Cambridge University Press, 2000), I.124.

44 See Pope Benedict XVI, *Caritas in veritate*, 70.

45 Jonas, *The Imperative of Responsibility*, 6.

46 See Arendt, *The Human Condition*, 289–294 and Jonas, *The Phenomenon of Life*, 188–210.

tionalist, *enacting* the conflation of truth and utility in its very exercise. If by manipulating variable *x*, I can produce or inhibit result *y*, and if y then enables me to proceed to experiment *z*, it is pointless to ask what a cause or knowledge, or truth or entity is, or even what *x*, *y*, and *z are*. As Dewey says, "They are what they can do and what can be done with them."[47]

Notice that this insinuates a disincentive to understanding, an inducement to thoughtlessness, into the heart of our prevailing form of reason, which is why there is no such thing as a profound question in American public life. And, it helps us understand *Gaudium et spes* no. 36 more deeply, which says that "when God is forgotten, the creature itself grows unintelligible." It is not just that in a pluralist society we cannot agree on the answer to the questions "who is God?" and "what is man?" It is rather that questions in the "what is?" form cannot even be intelligibly posed within the dominant form of rationality underlying our alleged pluralism. We have a crisis of faith because we have a crisis of thought. We have a moral crisis, in part, because we have an intellectual crisis that cannot be overcome by appeal to the authority of science.

The "triumph of art over nature" presupposes the conflation of art *and* nature, which means that the technocratic paradigm is not merely epistemological, but ontological as well.[48] The seventeenth and eighteenth centuries conceived of this reduction principally in terms of *natura naturata*, the finished artifacts issuing forth from the gracious hand of a "contriving" God who imposes laws on inert matter, already a truncated, mechanistic understanding of God and creation.[49] In the Romantic reaction of the nineteenth century, the hand of God is replaced by the gracious hand of history or natural selection, thereby shifting the accent to *natura naturans* and nature as a dynamic process. There is less here than meets the eye, however, as the conflation of nature and art terminates logically in the conflation of being and history, specifically, history conceived *as* a history of construction, the linear series of causes and effects that produce the present.[50]

For Aristotle and the tradition, the maxim that "art imitates nature" had both a positive and negative sense. Positively, what art and nature have in common, and what distinguishes both from chance and necessity, is that the end, the perfected product, if you will, is the reason for the steps that produce it. The last end is a first cause in both instances. Art and nature are therefore correlative concepts, as Robert Spaemann explains, and their similarity undoubtedly helps explain that "irresistible tendency" to interpret human functions and artifacts

47 Dewey, *Reconstruction in Philosophy*, 115.

48 "The analytical method," writes Hans Jonas, "implies a primary ontological reduction of nature, and this precedes mathematics or other symbolism in its application to nature." See Jonas, *The Phenomenon of Life*, 129.

49 See Hanby, *No God, No Science?*, 107–185.

50 "The shift from the 'why' and the 'what' to the 'how' implies that the actual objects of knowledge can no longer be things or eternal motions but must be processes, and that the object of science therefore is no longer nature or the universe but the history, the story of the coming into being, of nature or life or the universe." Arendt, *The Human Condition*, 296. See Hanby, *No God, No Science?*, 107–249.

in terms of each other.[51] Yet the fact that art is said merely to *imitate* nature means, negatively speaking, that a thing existing by nature possesses something that an artifact lacks, or better, *is something* that an artifact is not. From the very beginning, a thing existing by nature *(physei)* has its own "reason" within it as the principle and source of its unfolding and therefore has a unity and interiority that an artifact lacks. It has, or rather *is*, its own project, though the "shape" of this project is given with its being and thus *ontologically* precedes its unfolding in time. Aristotle and the scholastics called this interior principle substantial form. The form of an artifact, by contrast, does not precede its production except in the mind of its maker, who imposes it from without. Its unity is not given with its existence, but rather comes about as the end-result of its piece by piece assembly. It is therefore not a whole, except in an analogous sense, but a humanly contrived aggregate. And, its project is not its own, but its maker's. "*We* are the end of artificial things," says St. Thomas Aquinas.[52] The distinction between nature and art is thus ultimately a distinction between two different ways of being a thing.

The scientific revolution which commenced in the seventeenth century (and has not ended) is a revolution against any metaphysics that would place form, mind, *logos*, or meaning at the foundation of reality and any concept of nature that made "wholeness an autonomous cause with respect to its component parts."[53] At the root of this revolution was a new notion of matter, liberated from form and conceived, albeit with variations, as some sort of dimensive and hence measurable quantity—the "insensate order" of Pope Francis's analysis.[54] The abolition of substantial form effectively eliminated the distinction between ontological and temporal orders, thereby paving the way for the conflation of being and history. But it also evacuated natural things of just that indivisible *a priori* unity, interiority, and intrinsic intelligibility which heretofore distinguished them from artifacts, qualities that would henceforth be invisible to the eyes of science.[55] Natural things became artificial, and therefore plastic, limited in their functions and transformations only by "the bounds of the possible" which science perpetually transgresses.[56] For according to Francis Bacon, "the task and purpose of human power is to generate and superinduce on a given body a new nature or natures" within those bounds.[57] As nature becomes a machine, so the knowledge of nature becomes engineering.

51 Robert Spaemann, "What Does it Mean to Say that 'Art Imitates Nature?'" in *A Robert Spaemann Reader: Philosophical Essays on Nature, God, and the Human Person*, eds. D. C. Schindler and Jeanne Heffernan Schindler (Oxford: Oxford University Press, 2015), 192–210.

52 Thomas Aquinas, *Commentary on the Aristotle's Physics*, trans. Richard J. Blackwell, Richard J. Spath, and W. Edmund Thirlkel (South Bend, Ind.: Dumb Ox Books, 1999), Bk. 2, lect. 4, 173.

53 Jonas, *The Phenomenon of Life*, 201.

54 Whether the unit of measurement be extension, mass, corpuscles, or energy is largely a matter of indifference.

55 Spaemann, "What Does it Mean to Say that 'Art Imitates Nature?'", 197.

56 Bacon, *The New Organon*, II.1.

57 Bacon, *The New Organon*, II.1.

This way of imagining and looking at the world has given us enormous control over nature, or at least the illusion of control, since the systematic processes introduced into the stream of history by our power "recoil" upon every facet of our lives and elude our control by their very nature *as* processes. Nevertheless, this alleged control *over* nature has come at the price of a profound bifurcation insinuated into the very heart of nature and indeed into the very heart of man himself. The original exemplar of this tendency is Descartes's famous dualism of thinking and extended substance, now universally denied in theory but practically affirmed in every reductive analysis, as the analyst temporarily exempts himself from his own reduction and retreats to an Archimedean point outside of nature in the very moment of his theorizing.[58] Yet Descartes's is simply the first of a seemingly endless series of dualisms to issue from this technological ontology, many of which remain with us to the present day: dualisms between primary and secondary qualities, nature and nurture, scientific biology and folk biology; between replicators and vehicles,[59] DNA "software" and cellular "hardware,"[60] between the sexually differentiated body and its "orientation," and of course, most recently, between a merely biological "sex" and any number of socially constructed genders.[61] All of these phenomena are made possible by a technological ontology which seemingly makes all things possible except two: the thought of the true Creator God, radically transcendent and therefore radically immanent, who knows and loves the world into being from nothing and endows it with meaning, and the human person as a *per se* unity of body and soul: *corpore et anima unus*, who in his very being is the image and participant in this creative knowledge and love.[62]

Humanae vitae and the Technocratic Paradigm

The teaching of *Humanae vitae*, enriched and deepened during the pontificate of John Paul II, stands in sharp contrast to the technocratic paradigm in both its objective dimensions as a philosophy of nature—the ontological paradigm—and its subjective dimensions as a way of apprehending reality—the epistemological paradigm of which Pope Francis speaks. Against this backdrop, the teaching of

58 "In the experiment man realized his newly won freedom from the shackles of earth-bound experience; he placed nature under the conditions of his own mind, that is, under conditions won from a universal, astrophysical viewpoint, a cosmic standpoint outside nature itself." Arendt, *The Human Condition*, 265.

59 See Conor Cunningham, "Trying My Very Best to Believe Darwin, or, The Supernaturalistic Fallacy: From Is to Nought," in P. M. Candler and C. Cunningham, eds., *Belief and Metaphysics* (London: SCM, 2007), 100–141.

60 See J. Craig Venter, *Life at the Speed of Light: From the Double Helix to the Dawn of Digital Life* (New York: Viking, 2013).

61 See David S. Crawford, "Mechanism, Public Reason, and the Anthropology of Orientation," in *Humanum Review: Issues in Family, Culture, and Science* (Fall 2012), http://humanumreview.com/issues/same-sex-unions and Crawford, "Liberal Androgyny: 'Gay Marriage' and the Meaning of Sexuality for Our Time," *Communio: International Catholic Review*, 33, no. 2 (Summer, 2006): 239–265.

62 See *Gaudium et spes*, 14 and Pope John Paul II, Encyclical Letter *Veritatis splendor* (August 6, 1993), 48 http://w2.vatican.va/content/john-paul-ii/en/encyclicals.index.html.

Humanae vitae, no. 12 on the "inseparable connection between the unitive and the procreative significance of the marriage act" appears as a defense of the reality of the human person as a *per se* unity of body and soul against his ontological bifurcation into biological and affective dimensions, and against the absolutization of "partial perspectives" that accompany this thinking, "be they of the biological or psychological, the demographic or sociological orders."[63] Without the full "truth about man"—the premise of *Humanae vitae*, according to Karol Wojtyła—"the relevant principles of morality would not be fully founded and, even more, would in a certain way be suspended in the air."[64] Yet, Wojtyła wondered whether "the men of our day are truly prepared to comprehend the teaching that the encyclical contains."[65] Clearly he was right to do so. Ironically, it was a dualist understanding of the body and its subhuman "biological laws and rhythms" that led early critics to charge the encyclical with biologism, and the same tendency persists today in thinkers like Todd Salzman and Michael Lawler who wish to liberate affectivity from the meaning of the sexually differentiated body.[66]

Karol Wojtyła was a strong defender of the encyclical's anthropological vision and a sharp critic of the sufficiency of these "partial perspectives" even before he became pope, and these were to be enduring themes of his pontificate. In *Love and Responsibility*, he wrote, "The expression 'order of nature' cannot be confused nor identified with the expression 'biological order,' as the latter, even though also signifying the order of nature, denotes it only inasmuch as it is accessible for the empirical-descriptive methods of natural sciences."[67]

However, the "'biological order' as a work of the human mind separating some elements of this order from what really exists, has man as its immediate author." The "order of nature," by contrast "constitutes a group of cosmic relations that occur among beings that really exist. It is thus the order of existence and the whole order present in existence finds its basis in the one who is the unceasing source of this existence, in God the Creator."[68] He would echo these thoughts as pope in his 1996 message on evolution to the Pontifical Academy of Sciences, insisting that with man "we find ourselves facing a different ontological order—an ontological leap, we could say."[69] For the "passage into the spiritual realm," he continues, "is not something that can be observed in this way."[70]

63 Pope Paul VI, *Humanae vitae*, 7.

64 Karol Wojtyła, "The Anthropological Vision of *Humanae Vitae*," trans. William May, *Nova et Vetera* (English edition) 7, no. 3 (2009): 732.

65 Wojtyła, "The Anthropological Vision of *Humanae Vitae*," 741.

66 For the first, see Bernard Häring, "The Inseparability of the Unitive-Procreative Functions of the Marital Act," in *Contraception: Authority and Dissent*, ed, C. Curran (New York: Herder, 1969), 176–192. For a defense of the "naked facticity" of nature, see Todd Salzman and Michael Lawler, *The Sexual Person: Toward a Renewed Catholic Anthropology* (Washington, D.C.: Georgetown University Press), 48–49.

67 Karol Wojtyła, *Love and Responsibility* (Boston: Pauline Books and Media, 2013), 40.

68 Wojtyła, *Love and Responsibility*, 41.

69 Pope John Paul II, *Message to the Pontifical Academy of Sciences: On Evolution* (October 22, 1996), https://www.ewtn.com/library/papaldoc/jp961022.htm.

70 Pope John Paul II, *Message to the Pontifical Academy of Sciences: On Evolution.*

These passages illuminate the meaning of "partiality" in those perspectives alluded to in *Humanae vitae*, no. 7. "Partial" or "limited" will not just mean incomplete, but abstract, reductive, and superficial, unless they can be incorporated into a more comprehensive metaphysical and theological horizon. This integration is not impossible, but it is extraordinarily difficult given the ontology that we have already seen to be inscribed into them. For to admit the "spiritual realm" is to acknowledge more things in heaven and on earth than are dreamt of in "biology, psychology, demography or sociology," things, in fact, which cannot be apprehended by these two-dimensional thought forms. Joe Sachs puts the point perfectly in his introduction to Aristotle's *De Anima*. "That inward depth of life that opens in perception cannot be found on or between the extended surfaces of bodies, and when we cut bodies open, all we find on *their* insides are more outsides."[71] Nor can one recover this "inward depth" simply by adding the "spiritual realm" to the biological, but only by recognizing that "the spiritual" is the full *truth* of the body, of which modern biology is but the selective, technocratically conceived representation.

This becomes clear in Wojtyła's 1978 article on the anthropological vision of *Humanae vitae*. In it, he contrasts the encyclical's "integral vision of man" with these partial perspectives, correlating them with a form of reductionism that is all too familiar. He writes,

> This is particularly important in the present field in which there is such a great tendency to consider everything in the light of definite biological processes. . . . Precisely here is the field of the problematic directed at *Humanae vitae*. The vision of man under different partial aspects is the indirect fruit of particular sciences that, in order to know the same object, because of his complexity (therefore also become of his sovereign richness)—use different methods. With these methods we can surely succeed in reaching a richer knowledge, but indirectly this leads to the dividing and destruction of what is in itself the supreme unity of man... In particular, there seems to weigh on the modern mentality the division of a Cartesian type that opposes in man his understanding, his consciousness, and his body. As a result of this division it is too easy to examine everything regarding the body as exclusively and solely in the light of somatic processes that, as the process of medical science shows, can be directed and dominated artificially. It is precisely here, among other things that the problem of the practice and technique of contraception is situated.[72]

Notice it is the integral vision of man that is concrete, the partial perspectives that are abstract. From the concrete perspective afforded by the full truth of the human person, we can begin to grasp why any act which violates the principle

71 Joe Sachs, trans., *Aristotle's On the Soul and on Memory and Recollection* (Chelsea: Green Lion Press, 2004), 5.

72 Sachs, *Aristotle's On the Soul and on Memory and Recollection*, 748.

of inseparability in *Humanae vitae* no. 12, should be regarded as intrinsically evil. Although the forms of this violation can differ in species and gravity, and a child may even happen to issue from some of them (as in the case of IVF), each of these acts is the practical expression of an ontological lie—and thus an act of violence against being and reason, harming and blinding both those who commit them and the society which countenances them. Each proceeds *as if* the body were not an intelligible *sign*, but merely a "brute fact" void of intrinsic and specifically human meaning. Contraception—the separation of sexuality from procreation—does violence to the couple and their love, undermining the "reciprocal indwelling of the unitive and procreative meanings" that, according to Cardinal Caffarra, places the realization of the unitive meaning as such precisely at the heart of the procreative and vice versa.[73] Lose one, and you lose both. Lose both, and you lose the truth. Lose the truth, and only power ultimately remains. Assisted reproductive technologies—the separation of procreation from sexuality—compound the violence by two additional assaults on the child, who in the very act of his conception is treated *as if* he were not a person, "the incommunicably proper existence of a spiritual nature" and the fruit of his parents' love, but were merely an object to be tested, selected and worked upon.[74] We lament that this regime often leads to experimentation *on* embryos, but we lament too late, because the very conditions under which the embryo is produced, and the fact that it is impossible to collect longitudinal data on it beforehand, dooms him to live *as* an experiment of a system of collective violence against nature that, unlike the embryo's parents, is unburdened either by love or responsibility.[75]

It is therefore not just a historical accident that questions concerning sex and fertility have assumed such a central place in Catholic moral reflection, for Cardinal Caffarra states, "what is at stake is the cause of God and man." And "when the truth taught by H.V. became obscured in the conscience of contemporary man," he continues, "this could not fail to bring about, inevitably, a profound crisis in his understanding of the relationship of man to God the Creator: a relationship that is the heart, at one and the same time, of metaphysical reflection, of ethical reflection, and of religious experience."[76]

It is important to stress that *Humanae vitae* doesn't require us to refuse the union of knowing and making *simpliciter*, but only to reject the technocratic attempt to reconstruct such union on terms set by art divorced from nature. Put positively,

73 Caffarra, "Who is Like the Lord, Our God?", 70.

74 I follow Joseph Ratzinger in preferring Richard of St. Victor's "existential" formulation over the "essentialist" definition of Boethius and St. Thomas, though Spaemann seems correct in saying that the two are complementary and that the former comprehends the latter. See Ratzinger, "Concerning the Notion of Person in Theology," *Communio: International Catholic Review* 17 (Fall, 1990): 439–454 and Robert Spaemann, *Persons: The Difference Between 'Someone' and 'Something'* (Oxford: Oxford University Press, 2007), 29–30.

75 For more, see Michael Hanby, "When Art Replaces Nature," *Humanum Review: Issues in Family, Culture, and Science* 2 (2014), http://humanumreview.com/articles/when-art-replaces-nature.

76 Caffarra, "Who is Like the Lord, Our God?", 261.

Humanae vitae holds up the fruitful conjugal embrace as the original, *paradigmatic* union of knowing and making, which anchors the creative love of spouses in both nature and the creative love of God.[77] By the same token, it valorizes childhood in its ontological meaning as a visible expression of creation *ex nihilo*.[78] For with the birth of each child, there appears a new world where once there was nothing, a new subject of being who occupies a perspective within the cosmos never to be repeated, and whose interior depths are transparent only to God.

"The exercise of conjugal sexuality, when it is fertile," Caffarra says, "constitutes the mysterious tangential point between the created universe of being *and* God's creative love; it is even the point at which this creative love comes within the created universe of being, with a view to the new term of its potency." Hence, "the fertility inherent in the conjugal act is not merely a biological fact. It brings the spouses, objectively, into a real relationship with God the creator, whether or not they are conscious of the fact."[79] Of course, consciousness of [this] fact remains necessary, for when man loses sight of the comprehensive horizon of creation, he loses sight of the interior horizon of his humanity, and comes to view all circumstances within a narrow and abstract frame that drains them of their full, human meaning. Inevitably, then, "ethical man" is subordinated to "economic" or "technical man," who in the name of the premises of that same "progress in the dominion and organization of the forces of nature would like to take a position with respect to himself, to his own humanity, not foreseeing that a position of this could include in itself a certain alienation from what is decisive for his very being."[80]

Conclusion

The meaning of the technocratic paradigm in which we now live, move, and have our being cannot be apprehended by the forms of knowledge which this paradigm has produced. This is especially important to recall in our time of pastoral conversions and paradigm shifts, lest "pastoral" become a synonym for "thoughtless" and we fail to recognize which paradigm we are really shifting into. It was the same pope who promulgated *Gaudium et spes*, after all, who also said, "the world is in trouble because of the lack of thinking."[81] Nothing could be more disastrous right now than for the Church to give up on thinking, to renounce her inherent "Platonism" and replace philosophy and theology with the partial—and

77 For a deeper development of this point, see David L. Schindler, "The Meaning of the Human in a Technological Age: *Homo faber, Homo sapiens, Homo amans*," *Anthropotes: Rivista di Studi sulla Persona e la Famiglia* 15, no.1 (1999): 31–51.

78 The phenomenon of being a child, which is the same thing as my being at all, is, as Hans Urs von Balthasar remarked, "astonishing beyond measure." And it's a wonder, he says, how little the enigma of reproduction has concerned philosophers. See Hans Urs von Balthasar, *The Glory of the Lord V: The Realm of Metaphysics in the Modern Age* (San Francisco: Ignatius Press, 1991), 615.

79 Caffarra, "Who is Like the Lord, Our God?," 257.

80 Wojtyła, "The Anthropological Vision of *Humanae vitae*," 733.

81 Pope Paul VI, Encyclical Letter *Populorum progressio* (March 26, 1967), 85, http://w2.vatican.va/content/paul-vi/en/encyclicals.index.html. See also, Pope Benedict XVI, *Caritas in veritate*, 53.

superficial—perspectives of a biology, sociology, psychology, political science, and economics generated from within the technological mind. To do so would be to surrender the world to its technological fate and so to betray the commission of the Good Shepherd by abandoning his flock to the wolves.

Truth is the intelligible face of being. It is not abstract. Indeed, we have seen that truth is the *most* concrete thing, that only *the truth* about God and the human person grounds us fully in reality and thus saves us from the reductive machinations of our biotechnocracy. To neglect the truth of this encyclical is not only to acquiesce in an ontological lie, but to become an unwitting accomplice in the triumph of the technocratic paradigm. To adhere to this truth, however, to contemplate, proclaim, and defend it, is to recall the teaching of another great encyclical that is celebrating an important anniversary this year: Truth is the condition of freedom.[82]

82 Pope John Paul II, *Veritatis splendor*, 86–87.

PART II

A Deeper Understanding of the Doctrinal Principles in *Humanae vitae*

4

Thomas Aquinas on Marriage, Fruitfulness, and Faithful Love

J. Budziszewski

✷ In this essay, I wish to present Thomas Aquinas's teachings about love and matrimony as a background for the teachings of *Humanae vitae.* First, though, let us consider why this is necessary, and to this end, let us review the current status of matrimony in the popular culture.

What the Popular Culture Thinks of Matrimony

According to a widely held view, the love of a man and a woman is not a commitment of the will to the true good of another person, but a feeling or an emotion. Although couples may still employ the traditional marriage vows, the promise to love each other is scarcely taken seriously, because no one can promise to have a feeling. Although marriage is still viewed as requiring mutual consent, divorce is not; each party is deemed to have a unilateral right to spousal repudiation. Some people insist that the words "until death do us part" refer to the death of the relationship, not the death of the parties. In any case, what the partners really intend is that they will stay married "until things shall stop working out." Even now, married persons sometimes describe themselves as bonded, but they seem to be thinking less of a weld, which makes two pieces of metal into one, and more of Velcro.

Essentially, then, what the culture calls matrimony is cohabitation with formalities. Like cohabiting couples—or cohabiting threesomes or what have you—a married couple may speak of having a committed relationship, but commitment in the traditional sense is just what they do not have. Although they may use the language of sharing of lives, they mean no more than living in the same household and having sexual intercourse. Typical is the reaction of a young woman to a talk which I gave at a nominally Christian college. Among the points I had emphasized was that in matrimony, the husband and wife give themselves mutually to each other. She raised her hand during the discussion to say, "If that's what marriage really is, you're pushing me away from it more and more." I don't think the young woman meant that she had a call to consecrated celibacy. What she meant was that she owned herself utterly and intended to go on doing so.

In her opinion, marriage was no more than an arrangement of convenience between two autonomous individuals.

Although in most cases—not all—sexual intercourse is still expected in matrimony, the parties would consider the idea that their bodies are no longer their own as absurd. Moreover, the view that intercourse may have a purpose beyond feelings of pleasure and excitement is viewed as too obvious for discussion. A Valentine's Day greeting card which I came across in a stationery store illustrated this view of things by featuring a photograph of bare buttocks with coarse sayings sprayed across them in red paint. Sexual intercourse is not viewed as suggestive of the possibility of new life; neither is having children viewed as requiring intercourse, because these days there are labs for that. Though even in this day of plummeting birth rates, children may still be desired, adults tend to view them as a lifestyle enhancement, something like a home entertainment center, but more expensive. And, of course the enhancement is available to singles and unmarried couples too, although they are more likely to choose abortion.

Though having a few children may still be regarded favorably, having more than a few is commonly looked upon as strange because children consume resources, use up disposable income, and require a great deal of care. Increasing these costs is the fact that although parents do not think they owe it to their children to stay together, or to guard and nourish the children's virtues, they do think they owe it to them to provide them with entertainment. Thus, they might decline to have a second child if it would prevent them from taking a family trip to Disney World. Many couples decline to have any children at all, considering what is sometimes called the "childfree" lifestyle superior because it leaves them more at liberty to engage in activities which they consider worthwhile. A puzzled writer who is not quite so extreme as to condemn all childbearing says nevertheless, "I don't have the answer to the origin of the longing for children that many experience. It's almost certainly due to a complex mixture of biological and social factors. It might even be an evolutionary trick."[1]

How Pope Paul VI Responds

In *Humanae vitae*,[2] Pope Paul VI presents a view of matrimony, its purpose, and its meaning which is very much at odds with the views we have just considered. Although marital nihilism was not nearly so far advanced at the time he writes as it is now, he perceives the direction in which things are going. He also seems to be aware of a certain caricature of the traditional Catholic view, which makes this view difficult to defend. As I read the encyclical, he is reaching for a better way to explain and defend the doctrine, which has always been held, and perhaps develop certain aspects of it more fully. As in most papal encyclicals, its

1 Bernadette Young, "Parenthood and Effective Altruism," *Effective Altruism Forum* 14 (April 2014), http://effective-altruism.com/ea/66/parenthood_and_effective_altruism.

2 Pope Paul VI, Encyclical Letter *Humanae vitae* (July 25, 1968), http://w2.vatican.va/content/paul-vi/en/encyclicals.index.html.

language is stiff and ponderous, not readily accessible to most readers. Yet, its insights are not stiff at all.

Paul VI emphasizes that the love between the husband and wife is not primarily a matter of instinct or emotion but an act of free will by which the spouses give themselves to each other mutually, totally, indissolubly, and exclusively. Each spouse loves the other for the other's own sake. Through this gift, they attain genuinely human fulfillment. Although they respect their bodies, they are not reduced to them; although they render to each other their mutual duties, they are not reduced to transactors "paying up."

From this, one might think that their love would be angelic and non-bodily, limited to their tenderness and sharing with each other. On the contrary, their love is fruitful, for it strives to bring about new life: to give birth to children, to raise them, and to bring them up. In fact, this marital project of bearing fruit is not something distinct from their tenderness and sharing. On the contrary, opening themselves to such a possibility is the most beautiful way that they do give themselves to each other, and the very basis of their love. This partnership in procreation is not just a subjective idea they may or may not have, for it pertains to the objective meaning and purpose of matrimony. Its meaning and purpose are not a mere product of their will but a matter of natural law, for they arise from the ground plan of the human person, who is a body-soul unity. And yet, the spouses' wills are crucial too, because they must freely and deliberately align themselves *with* their design, taking this design in both the biological and spiritual sense.

Certain things follow from these premises. First, the procreative and unitive meanings of the matrimonial act cannot be severed. It is not just that they should not be severed; they *cannot* be severed. On one hand, the loving union of the spouses is *naturally directed* to offspring, even if the procreative partners do not care to procreate. On the other hand, the good of the offspring *naturally requires* the loving union of their parents, even if they neglect their parental responsibilities. To miss these points is to misunderstand their shared life in a radical way, for conjugal love is *precisely this kind* of love. An association just for sex is not matrimony. Neither is an association just for companionship with no sex. Matrimony is a friendship built around the possibility of a great good, which is new life.

A second thing which follows from Paul VI's premises is that by honoring the laws of our biological functions, we, in no way, dehumanize, depersonalize, or diminish ourselves. True, we are more than the other animals, for we are rational and spiritual. Yet, to say that we are rational and spiritual does not give us a reason to imagine that we are *not* animals, for we are animals with a rational and spiritual difference. The angels are disembodied persons, but we are embodied persons, and our embodiment has *personal* meaning because it is an aspect of who and what we are. So, when we say that the sexual powers have a procreative purpose, we are not treating ourselves as mere means to impersonal ends and denying that we are ends in ourselves. Rather, we acknowledge *what kinds of ends in ourselves we are.* We are beings whose biological functions are not shackles but constitutive properties of our embodied personhood. They are inheritances, not encumbrances; enrichments, not impoverishments. They are not things to be struggled against but things to be cherished as gifts. Since the laws of our bodies are aspects of our being, we do not diminish ourselves by honoring them. We would alienate ourselves by *not* honoring them.

The third thing that follows from the premises is that there are no excuses for violating these laws, for example, by using contraception. As Paul VI knows, some thinkers had argued that it would be permissible to use contraception sometimes, so long as we did not use the totality of the time—or even that we could use contraception *all* the time, so long as it somehow made life better as a whole. Their excuse was what Pius XII had called the "principle of totality,"[3] according to which, just to the degree that something is a part of a greater whole, the whole, in its own interest, can dispose of the part. Paul VI showed that although the principle of totality is true, these thinkers were gravely misinterpreting it. It is as though they had pretended that there is no difference between extracting diseased teeth, which can no longer perform their function, and extracting perfectly healthy teeth, just because we would rather draw our food through straws. The former respects our totality. The latter violates and insults it.

Where Is St. Thomas Aquinas in All of This?

Where is St. Thomas Aquinas in all of this? I do not suppose that anyone would be surprised by the suggestion that some of the seeds of Paul VI's doctrine are present in the doctrine of St. Thomas Aquinas. To make that sort of suggestion, it would be enough to collate each of Paul VI's principal claims with some corresponding claim in St. Thomas, pointing out that both St. Thomas and Paul VI say P, that both St. Thomas and Paul VI say Q, and so on.

But I want to say more than that. It seems to me that Paul VI's themes are all present in St. Thomas's doctrine, either explicitly or implicitly. Some might consider this suggestion extreme. To show why it is not, I must present the thought of St. Thomas more fully and systematically, concluding with a correction of some of the common misunderstandings and caricatures of his thought.

3 See Pope Pius XII, *The Moral Limits of Medical Research and Treatment: Address to the First International Congress on the Histopathology of the Nervous System* (September 14, 1952), Section 13, http://www.papalencyclicals.net/pius12/p12psych.htm. The full quote is: "As for the patient, he is not absolute master of himself, of his body or of his soul. He cannot, therefore, freely dispose of himself as he pleases. Even the reason for which he acts is of itself neither sufficient nor determining. The patient is bound to the immanent teleology laid down by nature. He has the right of use, limited by natural finality, of the faculties and powers of his human nature. Because he is a user and not a proprietor, he does not have unlimited power to destroy or mutilate his body and its functions. Nevertheless, by virtue of the principle of totality, by virtue of his right to use the services of his organism as a whole, the patient can allow individual parts to be destroyed or mutilated when and to the extent necessary for the good of his being as a whole. He may do so to ensure his being's existence and to avoid or, naturally, to repair serious and lasting damage which cannot otherwise be avoided or repaired." Pius XII also notes: "The principle of totality itself affirms only this: where the relationship of a whole to its part holds good, and in the exact measure it holds good, the part is subordinated to the whole and the whole, in its own interest, can dispose of the part. Too often, unfortunately, in invoking the principle of totality, people leave these considerations aside, not only in the field of theoretical study and the field of application of law, sociology, physics, biology and medicine, but also of logic, psychology and metaphysics." Section 35.

Setting aside a few details of canon law, the greatest differences between St. Thomas and Paul VI concern neither the content of the doctrine of matrimony nor its foundations in natural law, but *how it is explained.* And it is primarily because of these differences in the mode of explanation that a discussion like this one is necessary.

Briefly, St. Thomas always begins with procreation and explains marital union in the context of the procreative partnership. He is also very practical, considering the significance of matrimony for all sorts of other things too, such as inheritance. Paul VI leaves out some of these practical considerations, and sometimes, his explanations move in the other direction. What I mean is that here and there, instead of explaining marital union in a procreative light, he explains marital procreation in a unitive light—a path which John Paul II was later to follow still more vigorously.

But this is an expository difference, not a theoretical difference. Anyone who seeks to explain difficult points must begin with his best guess about "where people are," about what the people whom we are trying to persuade find easier to grasp. Even today, when what people call "matrimony" seems to have so little to do with unity, people feel its absence as a lack. Even as they act against unity, they long for it. The unitive may sometimes be first in the order of discovery, and in these cases, it should be first in the order of explanation. But Paul VI does not deny that the procreative good is first in essence. Without the procreative good, the marital kind of unity would not even exist (although other kinds would). And so, what Paul VI hints at, and what John Paul II develops more fully, is that the procreative good is implicit in the natural meaning of the unitive good—something St. Thomas also thoroughly believes—and that therefore, one may be able to lead resistant people to the procreative good by beginning the discussion with the unitive good.

The upshot is that, rather than turning St. Thomas on his head, as some people might think, these twentieth-century popes really are Thomist, just as they claimed. St. Thomas may not explain things quite as they do, but he thinks of things exactly as they do.

To show how this is true, let us consider some of the themes of St. Thomas's writings on matrimony.

What Matrimony Is

Although we carelessly use the terms "marriage" and "matrimony" as synonyms, they are not the same thing. Matrimony is the union itself—what civil law calls a "status." Marriage is the *act of entering into* this union ("getting married").

To understand what marriage is according to St. Thomas, we must consider its cause, its essence, and its effect. Its *cause* is the *lawful consent* of two persons to be joined in the matrimonial kind of partnership. Its *essence* is the *indissoluble union* between them for the sake of its purpose, which is procreation. Its *effect* is a *common life* in family matters, because of which it must be regulated by Divine and human laws.[4]

4 Thomas Aquinas, *Summa theologiae*, hereafter ST, trans. Dominican Fathers, *Supplementum*, q. 44, art. 3, http://www.newadvent.org/summa/. It should be noted that the Supplementum is a text that was pre-

"In matrimony there is a joining in respect of which we speak of husband and wife; and this joining, through being directed to some one thing [procreation], *is* matrimony; while the joining together of bodies and minds is a *result* of matrimony."[5] We see in this passage four different aspects of the matrimonial union. Their union in having and raising children, and their union in a shared family life, have to do with the *essential character* of matrimony. Their union in the joining of their bodies, and their union in the joining of their minds, are things that result *from* its essential character.

One of the complications of understanding all this is that marriage is directed not only by natural law, but also by religious law and civil law. Another is that, as always, even the natural law must be considered in the context of salvation history: creation, the Fall, and redemption. Our nature does not change. However, the condition in which we find our nature does change.

Natural law *as such* shapes matrimony in matters concerned with having and raising children. Natural law *after the Fall* shapes matrimony so that its natural purposes are not unraveled by the wound of sin, which tempts people to engage in intercourse in ways that forestall the formation of families and undermine their good order. The law of Moses, which St. Thomas calls the "Old Law," shapes matrimony by spelling out who can be married and who is ineligible; these are *applications*[6] of the general principles of the natural law to concrete situations. The law of the Gospel, which St. Thomas calls the "New Law," shapes matrimony so that the union of husband and wife can represent and make present the mystery of Christ's union with the Church. Finally, the civil law shapes matrimony with respect to "other advantages resulting from matrimony, such as the friendship and mutual service which husband and wife render one another." Examples of such regulations might be those concerned with inheritance and spousal support.

We can say, then, that natural law institutes marriage in one way, religious law institutes it in another, and civil law institutes it in still another. These various "institutions" or origins "are not of the same thing in the same respect" according to St. Thomas.[7] However, they are all linked. Thus, for the civil law to treat marriage as something contrary to what it is by nature would be profoundly wrong; any such so-called civil marriage would not be marriage at all.

The Three Marital Goods

According to St. Thomas, matrimony is directed to three different goods, two of them natural, one of them supernatural. The first of these goods, he says, is

pared by St. Thomas after his death by one or more members of his religious orders, compiling materials that Thomas had written previously into the format of the *Summa*. Nevertheless, we will treat the teaching on marriage of the Supplementum as essentially that of Thomas for the purposes of this essay.

5 *ST, Supp.*, q. 44, art. 1, emphasis added.

6 *determinatio*

7 *ST, Supp.*, q. 42, art. 2 and ad 3.

"the birth of children and the educating of them to the worship of God."[8] If I ask my students to identify the purpose of the sexual powers, they usually reply "pleasure." If, on the other hand, I focus their attention on our natural teleology by asking them to identify the purpose of the eye, the purpose of the ear, the purpose of the capacity for anger, and so on, and *then* ask them to identify the purpose of the sexual powers, they say, instead, "reproduction," which is not bad. However, procreation means much more. Reproduction merely means turning out new humans by one means or another. If this were the only purpose of the sexual powers, there wouldn't matter whether the partners were united. In fact, it wouldn't matter if there were any partners. We could dispense with parents altogether, gestating children in flasks and raising them in state-run institutions, as they do in Huxley's *Brave New World*. Procreation, by contrast, is the loving act by which posterity is generated. It means conceiving children in the embrace of their father and mother; it means not only having them together but nurturing them together, so that they can become virtuous adults; and it means forming families, thereby forging new links between dimmest antiquity and remotest futurity. Any guppy can reproduce. We have the privilege of procreating.

Just now, I spoke of nurturing the children so that they can become virtuous adults. Instead, St. Thomas speaks of educating them "to the worship of God." That may seem narrower, but as he often does, he is using the figure of speech called metonymy, in which a part represents a whole. The statement that parents educate children to the worship of God does not mean that they educate them *only* to the worship of God, any more than the commandment against bearing false witness forbids *only* lying while giving legal testimony. Rather, just as the gravest sort of lie is used as a placeholder for all lying, so the gravest responsibility of educating children is used as a placeholder for their entire upbringing. If parents teach their children reading, writing, arithmetic, good manners, the art of conversation, and how to sing, well and good, but even with all this, if they do not teach them to worship God, they have failed. In saying this, by the way, we are still within the realm of natural law. According to St. Thomas, even the pagans knew that deity is to be worshipped, and paying God the reverence that is due to him is an aspect of the natural virtue of justice.

The second matrimonial good, he says, is the *mutual faithfulness* of husband and wife—"that fidelity which one must render to the other."[9] This is another metonymy. He does not express his thought by saying that the second matrimonial good is union; rather he uses the most important aspect of their union to represent everything about their union. Faithfulness is the most important because if they are not faithful to each other, then they cannot be faithful to their duties of parental love and care. Now just insofar as matrimony is a union, it resembles other forms of union, such as the union of friends. Indeed, St. Thomas does say that the spouses are friends. But matrimony is not just any

8 Thomas Aquinas, *De articulis fidei* (*Explanation of the Faith*), hereafter *AF*, Part 2, trans. Joseph Collins, http://dhspriory.org/thomas/english/DeArticulisFidei.htm.

9 Thomas Aquinas, *AF*, Part 2.

friendship. It is a *particular* kind of friendship, which derives all of its special characteristics from its procreative purpose. According to St. Thomas, "the entire communion of works" in which matrimonial unity consists is directed to having and raising children, should God so bless the spouses in this way. So important is this fact that if we view procreation and unity as *entirely distinct* goods of matrimony, we are making a profound mistake. Rather, the "principal end" of marriage is offspring, but this end "includes" the education of the offspring, and their education *requires* a special kind of friendship between the parents, which becomes a second good of matrimony.[10]

We will return to this point. For now, suffice it to say that in our day, the point is denied. Far from viewing the matrimonial union as deriving its meaning from the possibility of new life, sometimes, people even say that it will be enhanced by *preventing* possibility of new life. Even among people who do intend to have children, one often hears the remark, "We are putting off children so that we can enjoy each other first." This view is contradicted by experience. According to the inherited wisdom of the human race, if we seek to enhance matrimonial unity by refusing the gift of children, we merely turn a pair of selfish *ME*s into a single selfish *US*. Insofar as it can confirm or disconfirm this sort of thing, sociology concurs. For example, new children do not reduce matrimonial stability; on the contrary, each new child reduces a married couple's risk of divorce by twenty percent.[11] If you are ready for marriage, you are ready for children. If you are not ready for children, you are not ready for marriage.

The third good of matrimony is sacramental: "In other words," St. Thomas says, "the indivisibility of matrimony which shows forth the indivisible union of Christ and His Church."[12] Notice here how the unitive and the sacramental good are connected, for it is *because* of the indivisible union of the husband and wife that God can use it to represent and make present the indivisible union of Christ and His Church. As the man and woman are espoused, so Christ and the Church are espoused. And as the union of their bodies makes the spouses biologically fruitful, so the sacrament makes their union spiritually fruitful, for they pass on their faith to their children and display it to the world.

In this article, I focus primarily on the procreative and unitive goods of marriage rather than the sacramental good. These three goods of marriage, however, are tightly linked. Among humans, biological fruitfulness requires faithful union; God makes use of faithful union to manifest the sacrament; and the sacrament is spiritually fruitful, for the husband and wife are bound by the same love which binds Christ with the Church, and they raise their own children in the faith. According to St. Thomas, procreation pertains to marriage insofar as man is an animal; faithfulness pertains to marriage insofar as he is a man; and the sacrament pertains to marriage insofar as he is a believer. This is because all animals procreate; humans,

10 *ST*, *Supp.*, q. 49, art. 2, ad 1.

11 Hillard S. Kaplan, Jane B. Lancaster, and Kermyt G. Anderson, "Human Parental Investment and Fertility: The Life Histories of Men in Albuquerque," in *Men in Families,* ed. Alan Booth and Ann Crouter (Mahwah, N.J.: Lawrence Erlbaum Press, 1998).

12 Thomas Aquinas, *AF*, Part 2.

who are *rational* animals, procreate in a rational and indivisible partnership; and believers enjoy the supernatural elevation of this partnership by grace.[13]

The Procreative Good Considered in Itself

Considering our nature alone, what is so special about the marital union? For example, why is it indissoluble, and why should it be between one man and woman? In reply, St. Thomas distinguishes among three categories of animal. Among some of the beasts, the female is capable not only of giving birth to the offspring but also of training them without help from the male. In such species, intercourse is "random and indiscriminate." Among other beasts, the female needs assistance, so the male cooperates with the female in caring for them. This requires that he recognize the offspring, that he possess a natural inclination to care for them, and that a definite male be joined to a definite female. In such species, the male and female cooperate until the children are grown. "But above all in the human species," St. Thomas says—above all in *rational* animals—"the male is required for the education of the offspring, which are attended to not only regarding bodily nourishment, but to a greater degree regarding the nourishment of the soul." He reminds us of Hebrews 12:9, which says, "We have had earthly fathers to discipline us and we respected them."[14] This is from his *Commentary on St. Paul's First Letter to the Corinthians,* but he develops the argument even more fully in the *Summa Contra Gentiles,* where he writes,

> [W]e must consider that in the human species offspring require not only nourishment for the body, as in the case of other animals, but also education for the soul. For other animals naturally possess their own kinds of prudence whereby they are enabled to take care of themselves. But a man lives by reason, which he must develop by lengthy temporal experience so that he may achieve prudence. Hence, children must be instructed by parents who are already experienced people. Nor are they able to receive such instruction as soon as they are born, but after a long time, and especially after they have reached the age of discretion. Moreover, a long time is needed for this instruction.[15]

He adds, "Then, too, because of the impulsion of the passions, through which prudent judgment is vitiated, they require not merely instruction but correction," and the father, he deems, is more suited to correction than the mother.[16]

13 *ST, Supp.*, q. 65, art. 1.

14 Thomas Aquinas, *Commentary on St. Paul's First Letter to the Corinthians,* chap. 7, lecture 1, referring to 1 Cor 7:1–9, trans. Fabian Larcher, http://dhspriory.org/thomas/english/SS1Cor.htm; quote appears at https://dhspriory.org/thomas/english/SS1Cor.htm#71.

15 Thomas Aquinas, *Summa Contra Gentiles*, III, chap. 122, https://dhspriory.org/thomas/ContraGentiles3b.htm#122. Hereafter *SCG*.

16 Thomas Aquinas, *SCG*, III, chap. 122; quote appears at https://dhspriory.org/thomas/ContraGentiles3b.htm#122.

Today, anyone who says that a child needs both a mother and a father is likely to be roundly criticized. I was surprised one semester by the intensity of a classroom full of law students who thought that giving preference in adoption to couples over singles violates a basic human right. What they wanted to protect was the so-called autonomous decision of an adult to adopt a child if he wants to. By contrast, St. Thomas is thinking of the natural right of the child to be well raised. The child is not just a feature of someone else's life; the child *is* a life. There is no right to act against the well-being of children.

Indeed, sociological research shows that family structure is the strongest predictor—an even stronger indicator than poverty—of whether a child will have behavioral, psychological, or health problems.[17] One social scientist comments that "Reams of social science and medical research convincingly show that children who are raised by their married, biological parents enjoy better physical, cognitive, and emotional outcomes, on average, than children who are raised in other circumstances."[18] For example, children raised in fractured families are much more likely to drop out of high school,[19] to get into trouble with the law,[20] to be physically or sexually abused,[21] to have out-of-wedlock children,[22]

17 Sara McLanahan, "Parent Absence or Poverty: Which Matters More?" in *Consequences of Growing Up Poor*, ed. Greg Duncan and Jeanne Brooks-Gunn (New York: Russell Sage Foundation, 1997).

18 David C. Ribar, "Why Marriage Matters for Child Wellbeing," in *The Future of Children: Marriage and Child Wellbeing Revisited*, ed. Sara McLanahan and Isabel Sawhill, special issue, 25, no. 2 (Fall 2015): 22. Recent comprehensive reviews of the research on this subject include Paul Amato, "The Impact of Family Formation Change on the Cognitive, Social, and Emotional Well-Being of the Next Generation," *Future of Children* 15, no. 2 (2005): 75–96; Susan Brown, "Marriage and Child Well-Being: Research and Policy Perspectives," *Journal of Marriage and Family* 72, no. 5 (2010): 1059–1077; Sara McLanahan, Laura Tach, and Daniel Schneider, "The Causal Effects of Father Absence," *Annual Review of Sociology* 39 (2013): 399–427; David C. Ribar, "What Do Social Scientists Know about the Benefits of Marriage? A Review of Quantitative Methodologies," IZA Discussion Paper 998 (January 2004); Linda Waite and Maggie Gallagher, *The Case for Marriage: Why Married People Are Happier, Healthier, and Better Off Financially* (New York: Broadway Books, 2000); and W. Bradford Wilcox, Jared R. Anderson, William Doherty, David Eggbeen, Christopher G. Ellison, William Galston, Neil Gilbert, John Gottman, and Ron Haskins, more… *Why Marriage Matters, Third Edition: Thirty Conclusions from the Social Sciences* (New York: Institute for American Values, 2011).

19 "Living in a single-parent family doubles the risk that a child will become a high-school dropout." Waite and Gallagher, *The Case for Marriage*, 133.

20 "Both divorced and unwed parenting dramatically increase the risk that a child will get into trouble with the law. Even after researchers control for factors such as neighborhood characteristics, race, mother's education, and cognitive ability, boys raised in single-parent homes are twice as likely (and boys raised in stepfamilies, three times as likely) to have committed a crime that leads to incarceration by the time they reach their early thirties." Waite and Gallagher, *The Case for Marriage*, 134.

21 "Living without both parents not only increases the risk that a child will commit a crime, but it increases the likelihood he or she will be the victim of a crime as well, especially the devastating crime of being abused in your own home.... Stepfathers and mothers' boyfriends are disproportionately likely to sexually and otherwise abuse children." Indeed, a large body of research confirmed that as Martin Daly and Margo Wilson put it, "[S]tepchildren constituted an enormously higher proportion of child abuse victims in the United States than their numbers in the population-at-large would warrant." Waite and Gallagher, *The Case for Marriage*, 135.

22 "Young women whose parents divorced ... were more than three times as likely to have an out-of-wedlock child as were women whose parents stayed married." Waite and Gallagher, *The Case for Marriage*, 136.

and, interestingly, to get divorced themselves.[23] Through interviews with adults whose parents divorced, one writer concludes that the pain of parental divorce continues into adulthood even when the divorce was amicable.[24]

The care of not just the mother but both parents is not a temporary but a permanent need according to St. Thomas: "The child requires the father's direction for a long time."[25] In the first place, the education and development of the child continue "until it reach[es] the perfect state of man as man, and that is the state of virtue."[26] In the second place, even after the children attain maturity and virtue, their parents are needed to help them to establish their own new families. Thus:

> By the intention of nature marriage is directed to the rearing of the offspring, *not merely for a time, but throughout its whole life*. Hence it is of natural law that parents should lay up for their children, and that children should be their parents' heirs. Therefore, since the offspring is the common good of husband and wife, the dictate of the natural law requires the latter to live together for ever *inseparably*: and so the indissolubility of marriage is of natural law.[27]

Someone might object that in some cases the child might *not* need a mother and father. For example, the mother might be so wealthy that she can "outsource" the paternal contribution to the child's education and discipline. We may well doubt whether this is really true; a father is not the same thing as a paid tutor. But suppose that in some case it really were true. This would not matter, because according to St. Thomas, the precepts of the natural law are not based on exceptions. He explains, "Nor, indeed, is the fact that a woman may be able by means of her own wealth to care for the child by herself an obstacle to this argument. For natural rectitude in human acts is not dependent on things accidentally possible in the case of one individual, but, rather, on those conditions which accompany the entire species."[28] Paul VI agrees. "[T]here are certain limits, beyond which it is wrong to go, to the power of man over his own body and its natural functions—limits, let it be said, which no one, whether as a private individual or as a public authority, can lawfully exceed."[29] Yes, the natural law steers us away from bad consequences, but this does not permit us to make exceptions to the provisions of nature just because we think we have found some other way to prevent

23 All studies agree about the increased risk; one study calculates it as 60% for women and 35% for men. Norval D. Glen and Beth Ann Shelton, "Pre-Adult Background Variables and Divorce: A Note of Caution about Overreliance on Explained Variance," *Journal of Marriage and the Family* 45, no. 2 (1983): 405–410.

24 Leila Miller, *Primal Loss: The Now-Adult Children of Divorce Speak* (Phoenix: LCB Publishing, 2017).

25 Thomas Aquinas, *SCG*, chap. 123.

26 *ST*, *Supp.*, q. 41, art. 1.

27 *ST*, *Supp.*, q. 67, art. 1, emphasis added.

28 Thomas Aquinas, *SCG*, III, chap. 122.

29 Pope Paul VI, *Humanae vitae*, 17.

bad consequences. Only the creator and enactor of nature could do that, as when God tolerated polygamy among the patriarchs.[30]

The same principle applies in the case of contraception. Some argue that chastity is no longer required, because now, even the unchaste can prevent births. All children will have mothers and fathers, because in cases where there would not be mothers and fathers, children will not come into being. What this argument overlooks is that nuptial partnership is the law of our design, and we are not free to invent another arrangement for ourselves. In fact, even the attempt to outwit natural consequences has natural consequences. Although contraception was commonly expected to abolish unwed motherhood, it led to such far-reaching changes in sexual behavior that unwed motherhood has soared.

The Unitive Good Considered in Itself

St. Thomas teaches that the union of the husband and wife is threefold. The first aspect of their union, he says, "is through the devotion of their love," which is so strong that they both leave their parents behind. "[T]his is natural," he says, "for natural desires fit in harmoniously with actions that must be performed." The second aspect of their union is the sharing of their life. Here he quotes the book of Sirach, "With three things my spirit is pleased, which are approved before God and men: the concord of brethren, and the love of neighbors, and man and wife that agree well together." The third aspect of marital union is the bodily joining of the husband and wife: "They shall be two in one flesh, that is, in their carnal intercourse . . . . the male and female become . . . . only one and the same body" with respect to the function of bringing about new life.[31] "After an injury inflicted upon a man in his own person," St. Thomas says, "none is so grave as that which is inflicted upon a person with whom one is joined." This is why the Decalogue prohibits adultery immediately after it prohibits murder.[32]

It is most interesting that even though cooperation in procreation underlies all three aspects of union, St. Thomas lists the "devotion of the love" of the husband and wife before listing the sharing of their life and even before their joining in one flesh. Much of what St. Thomas teaches about the devotion of love of the husband and wife emerges not from his discussion of marriage itself but from his discussion of the love of God or the love of friends. Needless to say, each of these loves has its own characteristics. However, whatever St. Thomas says about

30 "Now the law prescribing the one wife was framed not by man but by God, nor was it ever given by word or in writing, but was imprinted on the heart, like other things belonging in any way to the natural law. Consequently, a dispensation in this matter could be granted by God alone, through an inward inspiration, vouchsafed originally to the holy patriarchs, and by their example continued to others, at a time when it behooved the aforesaid precept not to be observed, in order to ensure the multiplication of the offspring to be brought up in the worship of God." *ST*, *Supp.*, q. 65, art. 2.

31 Thomas Aquinas, *Commentary on St. Paul's Letter to the Ephesians*, trans. Matthew D. Lamb, chap. 5, lecture 10, referring to Eph. 5:31, http://dhspriory.org/thomas/english/ Eph5.htm. The internal reference is to Sir (Eccl) 25:1–2 (DRA).

32 Thomas Aquinas, *Collationes de decem praeceptis* (*Explanation of the Ten Commandments*), hereafter *CDP*, trans. Joseph Collins, http://dhspriory.org/thomas/ english/TenCommandments.htm.

all love is necessarily true of each particular love, including marital love. From his discussion of the love of God, for example, we find that all love whatsoever is an act of the will, which is intrinsically directed to another person—in the case of marital love, this means the love of the husband for the wife, and the love of the wife for the husband.

We often say we love something when we mean only we desire it. Considered closely, however, love is far more than desire. To desire something is to will some good to ourselves, but to love someone is to will good to the beloved. St. Thomas distinguishes a number of features of this will to love:

- As we have seen, the lover wills the good of the beloved.
- Moreover, he wills the good of the beloved *as his own* good. St. Thomas writes that this is why someone whom we love is called "another self" and why St. Augustine says, "Well did one say to his friend: Thou half of my soul."[33]
- He wills the beloved's good this way because it is the good of someone *with whom he is united.*
- He seeks the *perfection, or completion*, of this union.
- The more closely he approaches union, and the more complete his union becomes once it is attained, the more intense his love becomes.[34]

"Indeed," St. Thomas writes, "a person is loved in himself when the lover wishes the good for him, even if the lover may receive nothing from him."[35] Normally, of course, the spouses receive a great deal from each other.

> We have spoken of three aspects of union, but there are also three kinds of union.
>
> The first is the kind of union which *causes* love. For example, because the lover is already one with himself, he loves himself. The second is the kind of union which *is the same thing* as love. For example, because the lover has a bond of affection with the beloved, he comes to have the same relation to her that he has to himself. But finally, there is the kind of union which *is caused* by love. For example, the bond of affection causes the lover and beloved to seek the real union of matrimony. After getting married they live together, speak together, share the life of their household, share the joining of their bodies, and work together in bringing up their children.[36]

Although feelings by themselves are not love, strong feelings result from love. As St. Thomas puts it, "in the hearts of those who love there are four feelings that

33 *ST*, I-II, q. 28, art. 1.

34 Thomas Aquinas, *SCG*, I, chap. 91.

35 Thomas Aquinas, *SCG*, III, chap. 153.

36 *ST*, I-II, q. 28, art. 1, ad 2.

usually arise from the good works which the lovers accomplish," four that normally result from the lovers' freely willed partnership in a good life.

- The lovers experience *confidence* that what has begun well will get better.
- They experience *glory* because each one glories in the good of the other.
- They are *consoled* because through delight in the good they share, each one possesses a remedy against sadness.
- They experience *exuberant joy* because not only is sadness absorbed, but their exuberance "overcomes every tribulation."[37]

In a cynical age like ours, such thoughts may seem naïve and excessively idealistic. On the contrary, St. Thomas never loses sight of down-to-earth realities of marital union, including its difficulties and temptations. For example, rather than arguing that the husband and wife stay together because they are so much in love, he argues that they love each other more *precisely because they stay together*:

> For thus, when they know that they are indivisibly united, the love of one spouse for the other will be more faithful. Also, both will be more solicitous in their care for domestic possessions when they keep in mind that they will remain continually in possession of these same things. As a result of this, the sources of disagreements which would have to come up between a man and his wife's relatives, if he could put away his wife, are removed, and a more solid affection is established among the relatives. Removed, also, are the occasions for adultery which are presented when a man is permitted to send away his wife, or the converse. In fact, by this practice an easier way of arranging marriage with those outside the family circle is provided.[38]

Again, rather than saying that if the husband and wife are good friends, then the husband will be content with one wife and she with one husband, St. Thomas argues in the other direction: If the husband does content himself with one wife and she with one husband, *then they will be better friends*:

> Strong friendship is not possible in regard to many people. . . . Therefore, if a wife has but one husband, but the husband has several wives, the friendship will not be equal on both sides. So, the friendship will not be free, but servile in some way. The status of the wife should not be like that of a servant.[39]

In the same passage, notice the emphasis on the *equality* of this friendship. St. Thomas does not believe the wife and husband are equal in all respects. In any compound made up of different elements, one element must set the direction; two persons cannot settle disagreements by voting. Thus, although the wife rules

37 Thomas Aquinas, *Commentary on St. Paul's Second Letter to the Corinthians*, chap. 7, lecture 1, referring to 2 Cor 7:4, trans. Fabian Larcher, http://dhspriory.org/thomas/english/ SS2Cor.htm.

38 Thomas Aquinas, *SCG*, III, chap. 123.

39 Thomas Aquinas, *SCG*, III, chap. 123.

the household, the husband rules the wife. Considered as friends, on the other hand, the wife and husband are equal. She is not his servant, and St. Thomas makes plain, as St. Paul made plain before him, that he is to exercise his presidency for his wife's sake, with care and tenderness, rather than for himself. Therefore, even though she submits herself to his governance, he submits himself to her needs.

Although St. Thomas never overlooks the inequality of husband and wife regarding rulership, neither does he overlook their equality regarding friendship. For example, he has no patience with the double standard: offenses against purity and faithfulness are equally wrong regardless of which spouse is at fault. Consider St. Thomas's discussion of the Decalogue. First, he speaks of an unfaithful wife, remarking that an adulteress is triply guilty. She is guilty of sacrilege, because she violates God's command; of treachery, because she betrays her husband; and of theft, because she expends her heredity upon children that are not his. One can imagine husbands nodding as they read these lines. But, then, St. Thomas brings husbands up short: "Husbands, however, do not sin any less than wives, *although they sometimes may salve themselves to the contrary*."[40] In contemporary language, male infidelity is equally wicked, *although some husbands comfort themselves by pretending otherwise.*

Another aspect of the equality of the marital friendship is that the husband and wife have equal rights with respect to sexual intercourse. With due consideration for his wife's feelings, the husband may request it, but with due consideration for her husband's feelings, so may the wife request it. The fact that they are "one flesh" means more than that they have intercourse with each other. It means that they are really one. Each spouse belongs equally to the other and acquires equal privileges and duties as a result. Yes, consideration includes not suggesting intercourse when one's spouse is not feeling well. Apparently, though, it also includes not refusing the suggestion for intercourse just because one doesn't care for it much. In fact, according to St. Thomas intimacy may be requested in two ways: "First, explicitly, as when they ask one another by words; secondly, implicitly, when namely the husband knows by certain signs that the wife would wish [intercourse], but is silent through shame. And so even though she does not ask for [intercourse] explicitly in words, the husband is bound to [offer] it, whenever his wife shows signs of wishing him to do so."[41]

One of the interesting things about marital unity is that it balances the other kinds of unity in society. Today, it is widely assumed that the only reason for the prohibition of incest is that inbreeding concentrates genetic abnormalities. St. Thomas gives a fascinating but entirely different reason, for "in human society it is most necessary that there be friendship among many people. But, friendship is increased among men when unrelated persons are bound together by matrimony. Therefore, it was proper for it to be prescribed by laws that matrimony

40 Thomas Aquinas, *CDP*, emphasis added.

41 *ST*, *Supp.*, q. 64, art. 2. These are references to the marital "debt," the explicit discussion of which is deferred until later in the essay. Here, I am avoiding the term just to avoid distraction.

should be contracted with persons outside one's family and not with relatives."[42] For any form of association produces temptations to reject all friendship with persons who do not belong to the association. In blood relationships, the temptation is so strong that the noun "clan" has given rise to the pejorative adjective "clannish," meaning insular and unfriendly to outsiders. Yet, we see much the same sort of insularity in married couples who are so focused on each other that they have no other friends. But just because marriage must be outside the clan, relation by marriage and relation by blood balance each other, each moderating the other's cliquishness.

Concerning this point, notice how great a contrast there is between St. Thomas and some utopians. Both he and they want human friendship to extend broadly. The utopians think the way to broaden friendship is to ban all particularistic relationships; they want the entire community to be one big family and one big marriage. Unfortunately, rather than extending friendship, this strategy abolishes it, for to say that everyone is family is really to say that there is no family, and to say that everyone is married to everyone else is really to say that no one is married to anyone. By contrast, St. Thomas thinks the way to extend human friendship more broadly is to *multiply* particularistic relationships. Marriage outside the clan keeps people related by blood from walling themselves off; the extended family keeps married persons from walling themselves off.

It is quite amazing how far St. Thomas is willing to go in describing the quality of loving union. He says, for example, that the lover and the beloved mutually indwell each other. "The beloved is contained in the lover, by being impressed on his heart" and becoming the object of his affections; the lover, in turn, "is contained in the beloved, inasmuch as the lover penetrates, so to speak, into the beloved." Or, take the idea that the lover "loves to love." In our day, we associate such language with soupy sentimentalism and the lavish use of emojis, but St. Thomas gives diamond-hard meaning to it. The power of will, he explains, is directed to the good. Love is a spontaneous act of the will, directed to the good of the beloved. But, since to will is itself a good, man can will himself to will. For this reason, love, by its own nature, "is capable of reflecting on itself." "Wherefore," says the Angelic Doctor, "from the moment a man loves, he loves himself to love."[43] This does not mean that he is infatuated with his feelings. It means that with all his heart, he *concurs* with the direction of his will. His attitude toward the beloved might be expressed, "I exult that you exist in this world, I seek all good for you, *and I know it is good that I do.*"

Yet, we must never think that we can genuinely have such loving unity by shutting ourselves off from what makes marriage possible. For joining in marriage is not like joining in the writing of a book, the starting of a business, or the enjoyment of a garden. Only marriage is joining in the hope of new life. Another way to explain is to say that marriage is true only if it is complete in both form and purpose. Thus, not only has marriage the form of an "inseparable

42 Thomas Aquinas, *SCG*, III, chap. 125.

43 *ST*, II-II, q. 25, art. 2.

union of souls, by which husband and wife are pledged by a bond of mutual affection that cannot be sundered" but it has the purpose of having and bringing up offspring.[44] Does this imply that a husband and wife are not truly married, if through no act of their own, they are unable to conceive children? Not at all. What it does imply is that the rock from which the meaning of marriage rises is in their willingness to cherish and rear the children whom God does offer them.

Caricature and Misunderstanding

St. Thomas Aquinas's doctrine of marriage, fruitfulness, and faithful love is often caricatured. According to this distortion, he considers matrimony merely a necessary evil, a reluctant concession to the sinfulness of human beings, and the need to continue the human race. Pleasure is bad too. It is something to be endured, not enjoyed. One version of the burlesque has it that the only justification for the spouses to have sexual intercourse is that they are trying to make babies. Another has it that there is a second justification as well, for a wife should submit grimly to intercourse just so that her husband will not be tempted to seek sex elsewhere. Neither of these two views allows love to be a part of the picture.

The caricature is seductive, because sometimes, it borrows sentences and phrases from St. Thomas's own writing, for example, when he speaks of things which "excuse" marriage (as though it were something shameful!), of marriage as a "remedy for sin" (as though it were nothing more!), and of "paying the marriage debt" (as though sexual intercourse was merely something given to the mortgage holder to avoid being foreclosed upon!).

Yet, all of this is dreadfully mistaken. In this article, I am not concerned with how the parody came about, but I do want to show how radically it distorts St. Thomas's actual teachings.

Just by discussing St. Thomas's doctrine of marital union, we have already dispelled part of the caricature. Love is very much part of his picture of matrimony. Although he considers procreation to *underlie* the marital union as its end, or natural purpose, the love of the husband and wife which is the *form* of this union is profoundly important in its own right—and surprisingly, he says far more about union than about procreation itself. True, much of what he says about union comes in the context of his discussion of other kinds of love, as we have seen (the love of God, the love among friends, etc.). But each of his observations about love in general applies equally to the loving union of the husband and wife, although matrimony has additional characteristics.

As to the idea that blessings are necessary to "excuse" marriage, we must remember that he is *replying to objections*, and that he is defending *both* marriage *and* consecrated celibacy against their detractors. Just as some people thought nothing could excuse celibacy because the human race needs to continue, some people thought nothing could excuse marriage because consecrated celibacy is better. In reply to the objectors, St. Thomas uses their language. Celibacy is

44 *ST*, III, q. 29, art. 2.

allowable because, in order for the human race to continue, *not everyone* needs to turn the wheel of the generations, and marriage is allowable because, even though undistracted devotion to God is better, *some* need to turn the wheel of the generations. The fact that consecrated celibacy is better does not make marriage bad. Each state of life is very good for those who are called to it.[45]

As to whether marital intercourse is wrong unless the husband and wife are trying to make babies, St. Thomas does say that intercourse is wrong if it is not *rightly related* to its procreative purpose, but there is a difference between saying that it must be rightly related to procreation and saying that the motive must always be procreation. How so? We can understand the matter better by comparing temperance in sex with temperance in food.

We eat because food is necessary. However, St. Thomas points out that necessity can mean two different things. In the first sense, food is necessary because we require it for life and health. In this sense food is necessary to all animals. But, in the second sense, he says, food is necessary because without it we cannot live *becomingly.* The beasts know nothing of this, but we rational animals do. The reason we eat and drink more on festive occasions than at other times is not simply to live and be healthy, but to live *becomingly.* Obviously, God endorses this motive, after all, at the wedding feast in Cana, Jesus turned water into wine. Even at feasts, eating and drinking must still be rightly ordered to life and health, but right order does not require that we eat and drink just for life and health. Rather, it allows us to enjoy the blessings of food and drink "so long as they are not prejudicial" to life and health."[46] It would of course be prejudicial to life and health if we ate as much as we could and then purged so that we could eat still more, but it is not prejudicial to life and health to toast the married couple with wine.

The distinction between the two senses of necessity applies to sexual intercourse too. Remember that the husband and wife are joined in a procreative partnership. In the first sense of necessity, then, sexual intercourse is necessary simply so that they may be fruitful. In this sense, sexual intercourse is necessary to all animals. But in the second sense, sexual intercourse is necessary so that the husband and wife may enjoy their procreative partnership *becomingly*, so that they may *celebrate* it. Even celebratory intercourse must still be rightly ordered to procreation, but right order does not require that the spouses enjoy intercourse just for making babies. Rather, it allows them to enjoy intercourse so long as they do nothing to *thwart* the procreative possibility of their action. For example, just as they may fast from food for a time, so they may fast from sexual intercourse for a time. However, just as they may not insult the nutritive order of their bodies

45 Concerning the mistaken condemnation of consecrated celibacy, see esp. Thomas Aquinas, *SCG*, III, chap. 136–137, as well as *De perfectione spiritualis vitaem* (*On the Perfection of the Spiritual Life*). Concerning the mistaken condemnation of marriage, see esp. *ST*, *Supp.*, q. 49, art. 1, as well as *Commentary on St. Paul's First Letter to the Corinthians*, chap. 7, lecture 1, ibid. St. Thomas remarks, "it should be noted that in their dislike for fornication, against which [St. Paul] had just spoken, some, whose zeal for God was not accompanied by wisdom, arrived at a point where they even condemned marriage. Hence, it says in 1 Tm (4:2–3): 'Through the hypocrisy of liars who forbid marriage.'"

46 *ST*, II-II, q. 141, art. 6 and ad 2.

by deliberately purging during meals, so they may not violate the procreative order of their bodies by depriving coition of its fertility.

By clearing up the two senses of necessity, we clear up another point too. What does St. Thomas mean using the Pauline language of requesting the "payment" of the "marriage debt"?[47] It means just this: that one spouse proposes sexual intercourse to the other, just for the enjoyment of their union. Yes, they must always honor the procreative possibility of the act, after all, their union is a *procreative* partnership. Yet, procreation need not be their motive at the time.

The payment of the marriage debt is not an aspect of the husband's authority. Indeed, St. Thomas insists that in proposing sexual intercourse, the husband and wife are utterly equal; either may propose intercourse to the other.[48] Neither does proposing it mean disregarding the feelings or well-being of the other spouse; St. Thomas always reminds husbands to be considerate to their wives.[49] Why on earth then does St. Thomas use the language of a "debt" at all? For that matter, why does St. Paul? If to us, this language seems to diminish the loving unity of marriage, reducing intercourse to a cold transaction, we are missing the point. The point is to *emphasize* its loving unity and *deny* that it is a cold transaction. Do we really believe that the husband and wife become one? Do we really believe that in marriage, they give themselves to each other? Then we must believe that they are *not* coldly separate, autonomous beings, who merely happen to have worked out an arrangement of convenience. *With respect to the joining of their bodies, they are one.* Just because they really are united, each spouse owes it to the other to act as though they are united. This is a real duty, a real owing, a real debt. To force oneself upon one's spouse is wrong—but so is to withhold intercourse out of spite or indifference.

From this point of view, the mutual debt which the spouses owe to each other is like the duty of loving care which each person owes to himself, a point which St. Paul also emphasizes when he says, "Even so husbands should love their wives as their own bodies. He who loves his wife loves himself."[50] St. Thomas comments on this verse, "Just as a man sins against nature in hating himself, so does he who hates his wife.[51] *They should be enjoying each other.*

What then of St. Thomas's language of marriage as a "remedy" for sin?[52] This description is merely realistic. Marriage would have existed even had

47 *ST*, *Supp.*, q. 64.

48 *ST*, *Supp.*, q. 64, art. 5.

49 For example, in explaining 1 Thes 4:4–6, where St. Paul instructs men "that each one of you know how to take a wife for himself in holiness and honor, not in the passion of lust like heathen who do not know God," St. Thomas quotes 1 Pt 3:7, "Likewise you husbands, live considerately with your wives, bestowing honor on the woman as the weaker sex, since you are joint heirs of the grace of life, in order that your prayers may not be hindered." *Commentary on St. Paul's First Letter to the Thessalonians*, chap. 4, lecture 1, trans. Michael Duffy, http://dhspriory.org/thomas/english/SS1Thes.htm.

50 Eph 5:28 (RSV-CE).

51 Thomas Aquinas, *Commentary on St. Paul's Letter to the Ephesians*, chap. 5, lecture 9, trans. Duffy.

52 *ST*, *Supp.*, q. 42, art. 1.

there been no need for a remedy (even if there had never been a Fall).[53] After the Fall, though, the procreative and unitive significance of marriage are colored by the fact that our desires are disordered. Sexual desire is good in itself; God provided it to direct us into a procreative partnership. However, in our fallen condition the desire become so strong that we are tempted to indulge it in ways which are detrimental to the procreative partnership. The results are all too clear: to mention but one, fatherless and motherless children who are passed from stepparent, to stepparent, to stepparent. Although marriage makes sexual desire even stronger (for any impulse which is exercised becomes stronger), marriage now takes on a second significance it would not have had before the Fall, for it provides a way for the desire to be satisfied without sin.

But marriage is not *only,* or even *primarily,* a remedy for sin. There is a difference between saying that conjugal intercourse remedies the temptation to sin, which is obviously true, and saying that one may request intercourse only because otherwise, one might sin. In fact, there *should* always be more to the desire for sexual intercourse than that: if a husband proposed coition to his wife in the same spirit in which he would propose it to a concubine or a prostitute, something would be wrong.[54]

This brings us to the final misunderstanding. Does St. Thomas think that pleasure in marital intercourse is bad? Not at all. His true view is that "since the desires of good actions are good, and of evil actions, evil; much more are the pleasures of good actions good, and those of evil actions evil."[55] As to the pleasure of sexual intercourse itself, the Author of nature *made* it pleasurable so that there would be a motive to engage in it: "the end which nature intends in sexual union is the begetting and rearing of the offspring. *And that this good might be sought after, it attached pleasure to the union.*"[56] Indeed, God has made everything which should sometimes be done pleasurable. Sometimes I need more oxygen, and it is pleasurable to yawn. Sometimes I should eat, and it is pleasurable to have a meal. Sometimes I need to stretch my muscles, and it is pleasurable to take a walk. Knowledge, friendship, worship, all these good things are also delightful.

St. Thomas even argues that had it not been for the Fall, the pleasure of sexual intercourse would have been *greater than it is now*. Beasts, he points out, cannot reason. A man who cannot use his reason to regulate his sexual desire becomes like them. However,

53 *ST*, *Supp.*, q. 42, art. 2.

54 "Accordingly to make use of sexual intercourse on account of its inherent pleasure, without reference to the end for which nature intended it, is to act against nature, as also is it if the intercourse be not such as may fittingly be directed to that end .... [T]he name of concubine is expressive of that union where sexual intercourse is sought after for its own sake." *ST*, *Supp.*, q. 65, art. 3. See also below, concerning the four possible motives for marital intercourse.

55 *ST*, I-II, q. 34, art. 1.

56 *ST*, *Supp.*, q. 65, art. 3, emphasis added.

> In the state of innocence nothing of this kind would have happened that was not regulated by reason, not because delight of sense was *less*, as some say (rather indeed would sensible delight have been the *greater* in proportion to the greater purity of nature and the greater sensibility of the body), but because the force of concupiscence would not have so inordinately thrown itself into such pleasure, being curbed by reason.[57]

The office of reason, he says, is "not to lessen sensual pleasure," but to prevent the force of desire from clinging to pleasure unreasonably. A sober person does not take less pleasure in food than a glutton, and in the same way, a temperate person does not take less pleasure in sexual intercourse than a lustful one. However, one's desire does not "linger" in such pleasures.[58] Reason masters them.

If we had not fallen, then, our pleasures would have been even stronger, but they would not have disordered our thinking. Our minds would obey God, and our passions and desires would obey our minds. Today it is different. Unregulated sexual desire not only obstructs the mind in itself, but it also disorders the will, which is mind-guided desire.[59] St. Thomas distinguishes eight ways in which this happens, calling them the "daughters of lust." As to the mind in itself, lust first obstructs simple understanding that an act is good, then it obstructs the counsel, judgment, and command of reason about what is to be done for the sake of the good. As to the will, lust works by disordering the desire for our ultimate purpose: first through self-love, because we desire pleasure too much; then through hatred of God, because He forbids the desired pleasure; then through love of this world, because it contains the desire pleasure; and finally, through abhorrence or despair of the future world, because we come to consider spiritual pleasure distasteful.[60] It is as though we were ignitable, filled with combustible material which tends to go up in flames at the least spark. St. Thomas calls this ignitability the *fomes* of sin, using the Latin word which refers to tinder or kindling wood.[61]

Yet, St. Thomas teaches that just as it is possible for a person to desire sexual pleasure too much, *so it is possible to desire it too little*: "And so, to abstain from all sexual pleasures, without a reason [such as consecrated celibacy], is called the vice of insensibility."[62] Husbands and wives *should* enjoy sexual pleasure properly.

Ah, but what is it to enjoy it properly? Finally, we come to one of the most commonly misunderstood elements of St. Thomas's teaching.

In at least four places, St. Thomas distinguishes among four possible motives which may lead the husband and wife to join their bodies in sexual intercourse.

57 *ST*, I, q. 98, art. 2, ad 3, emphasis added.

58 *ST*, I, q. 98, art. 2, ad 3.

59 "The will is a rational appetite." *ST*, I-II, q. 8, art. 1.

60 *ST*, II-II, q. 153, art. 5.

61 See esp. *ST*, I-II, q. 74, art. 3, ad 2, and q. 91, art. 6. One wonders whether the developers of the Tinder sexual hookup app knew Latin.

62 Thomas Aquinas, *SCG*, III, chap. 136.

For simplicity, let us speak in terms of the husband's motivation, although all this applies equally to the wife's. First are two good and innocent motives: he might approach her for the sake of having children, or he might approach her because of the "marital debt." Next are two bad and impure motives: he may seek pleasure with his wife merely for pleasure, but with such an attitude that he would not turn to anyone else for it, or he may seek pleasure with her merely for pleasure, but with such an attitude that any woman might do[63]—perhaps even with such an attitude that another woman might do even better.[64] Of the two impure motives, the first is a venial sin, the second is mortal.

The passages in which St. Thomas calls attention to these motives are often mistakenly viewed as though he were saying (1) that the only pure motives for agreeing to sexual intercourse are either to have children or to comply with a cold demand, and (2) that it is categorically wrong for the husband and wife to desire sexual pleasure. This view could not be correct, because as we have seen, St. Thomas says that God made sexual intercourse pleasurable *precisely to give* the two spouses a motive to engage in it. But where does the error lie?

Actually, there are two errors. In the first place, bearing in mind what we said above about the so-called debt, to honor the marital debt is to agree to sexual intercourse not as compliance with a cold demand but precisely as an expression of the spouses' loving unity. Thus, it is good and pure for the two procreative partners to join their bodies to enjoy either the procreative *or the unitive* aspect of their marital friendship, and this is the correct interpretation of the two licit motives for marital intercourse.

Just now, I spoke of "enjoying" these aspects of their marital friendship, and I use this language advisedly. It is *right* to enjoy them; the spouses may, and should, seek pleasure in them. But when they do so, they should seek it *precisely as* the enjoyment of fruitfulness or loving union. To enjoy pleasure in procreation or in love, and to enjoy pleasure for its own sake, are entirely different things. If all the husband wants in his wife is genital stimulation leading to release, then he is not enjoying her, but merely making carnal use of her, and, likewise, if that is all she seeks in her husband.

What St. Thomas is really criticizing, then, is not the interest in sexual pleasure, but the hedonistic error about it. We may think about the matter like this. The husband ought to cherish his union with his wife as good in itself; but just because it *is* good in itself, it is also pleasurable, for pleasure, says St. Thomas, is the *repose* of the soul in the good. Notice that pleasure is not the main thing, but the enjoyment of the main thing. It is not the good itself, but the delight of experiencing the good.[65]

63 *ST*, *Supp.*, q. 49, art. 6; see also *ST*, *Supp.*, q. 65, art. 3, *De malo*, q. 15, art. 2, and *Commentary on St. Paul's First Letter to the Thessalonians*.

64 "But when this takes place outside the bonds of marriage, the action becomes a mortal sin; and this happens when he would perform the action, even if she were not his wife, *and more willingly* with another woman." Thomas Aquinas, *Commentary on St. Paul's First Letter to the Thessalonians*.

65 See *ST*, I-II, q. 31, art. 8; q. 33, art. 4; q. 34, art.1; and q. 38, art. 1.

Hedonists get this backward. Rather than viewing pleasure as repose in whatever is good, they view pleasure itself as the good, as the only good there is. From this point of view, one does not really cherish one's wife for her own sake; he cherishes only the resulting pleasure. It follows from this theory that if there were a way to have the pleasure of one's wife without one's wife, then that would be just as good, or even better. Never mind marriage—let us just arrange to have electrodes implanted, to stimulate the pleasure centers of our brains. Why experience pleasure indirectly, when one can experience it directly?

St. Thomas is pointing out that I should not treat my wife as that electrode. *She herself* is what I should cherish, experiencing the pleasure of that cherishing. What she and I enjoy, in both the procreative and unitive aspects of our marital friendship, is delightful. It is delightful to rest in the hope of new life; it is delightful to rest in our mutual love, as partners in this hope. But if I say "never mind our hope of children, never mind our mutual love, I just want pleasure," then I am missing the point. I understand neither children, nor love, nor delight.

Conclusion

St. Thomas and Paul VI are on the very same trajectory. Their doctrinal conclusions are identical, and they have compatible views of natural law. However, the two thinkers differ in the objections to which they responded, in the framework they use for explanation, and finally, in where they placed their theoretical emphasis. The last difference suggests new and interesting lines of development which St. Thomas did not explore.

Differences in Objections

Among the objections to which St. Thomas is forced to respond are that no one at all should marry, that *everyone* should marry, and that sexual intercourse is permissible outside marriage. In each case, his replies take for granted marriage concerns procreation. For him, this is not so much a conclusion as an obvious premise. To my knowledge, none of his hypothetical objectors seriously maintains that the sexual powers may be used without regard to procreation.

By contrast, Paul VI is concerned precisely with the anti-procreative objection. The dissenters reason as though somehow the invention of chemical contraception had repealed those precepts of natural law which have to do with sexuality. These dissidents believe that the procreative and unitive goods of marriage have been severed. Openness to new life, they think, is optional. Unity no longer refers to the procreative partnership of husband and wife but only to their mutual enjoyment of sexual pleasure. Not only does Paul VI seek to reply, but in his warnings about the decline of moral standards, he hints that new objections are coming up over the horizon. Why should this be? Because the dissidents' view opens the possibility that marriage itself is optional. For if sexual intercourse can be non-procreative, then why shouldn't anyone enjoy sexual pleasure? Why not casual friends? Why not strangers? Why must there be only two of them, and why must they be of opposite and complementary sex?

Although Paul VI does not respond to these possible future objections, he does respond to another actual objection: that the Church's traditional emphasis on procreation is obsessed with the body and reduces persons to biological organisms. Having insisted that human beings are body-soul unities so that every human act is done *jointly* by body and soul, St. Thomas would have found this protest ridiculous. Thus, even though the objection itself is novel, the elements of the reply are not novel. When Paul VI argues that the procreative union has not only biological but also spiritual significance, he is following in St. Thomas's footsteps.

Differences in Mode of Explanation

The most obvious point of difference between the modes of explanation used by St. Thomas and Paul VI is that St. Thomas employs Aristotle's fourfold framework of "causes": everything that comes into being has a material, formal, final, and efficient cause. Today, since the term "cause" is usually used only for efficient causes, we might instead call these the four necessary aspects of explaining why a thing is the thing it is. The material cause is what it consists of; the formal cause is its pattern; the final cause is its underlying purpose; and the efficient cause is that which brings it into being and maintains it in being. Thus, marriage consists of the husband and wife, each of them a composite of body and soul; its pattern is their lifelong union; its underlying purpose is procreation; and what brings it into being and maintains it in being is their love.

Although Paul VI does not explicitly use this fourfold explanatory framework, obviously he accepts all four propositions. For this reason, I take this difference between the two thinkers as purely expository and implying no theoretical disagreement. It makes sense for St. Thomas to use the fourfold framework of explanation, because in his day everyone used it. Even though it remains in the background of Paul VI's thought too, it may be prudent for Paul VI not to dwell upon it, because in his day even many specialists in this area are unfamiliar with this kind of explanation.

Theoretical Emphases and Possibilities of Development

Finally, St. Thomas and Paul VI differ in theoretical emphasis. The difference lies in how they describe the marital union. I do not wish to overstate this difference, for both thinkers view the marital union as not only objective but also subjective. It is objective in that it is a feature of real existence, not just in the eye of the beholder. It is subjective, not in the sense that "what's true for you is not true for me," but in the sense that it is experienced by human persons—and they experience it not just in their outward relations, but in the interior of their being. Persons are aware of their own essential reality; they can reflect on themselves and know that they are reflecting. A fly is not aware that he has an interior, or even that he is a being. A person is.[66]

66 "'Person' signifies what is most perfect in all nature—that is, a subsistent individual of a rational nature." *ST*, I, q. 29, art. 3.

St. Thomas and Paul VI also agree that the personal, subjective experience of the marital union has a certain intrinsic structure, intrinsic in the sense that it is natural to us. As we have seen, St. Thomas has a great deal to say about this structure. For example, he says that the lover loves the beloved for the beloved's sake, that he regards the beloved's good as his own, and that the lover and the beloved are "contained" in each other, in the sense that the beloved is impressed on the lover's heart, and the lover penetrates into the beloved's.

Paul VI uses very similar language, but there is a difference. He places such features of union in the context of what he calls the mutual gift of self. As he explains, "husband and wife, through that mutual gift of themselves, which is specific and exclusive to them alone, develop that union of two persons in which they perfect one another, cooperating with God in the generation and rearing of new lives."[67] Again, he remarks that "[w]hoever really loves his partner loves not only for what he receives, but loves that partner for the partner's own sake, content to be able to enrich the other with the gift of himself."[68]

This difference is subtle, but it matters. It is not that St. Thomas says nothing about gifts. For example, he speaks of marriage itself as a gift; he speaks of grace as a gift which makes marital faithfulness possible; and he speaks of husband and wife giving their bodies to each other. Since both of them are body-soul unities, the mutual gift of their bodies certainly *implies* a mutual gift of their persons or selves. However, St. Thomas never speaks of the gift of self *per se.*

A related difference of emphasis—this one even more subtle—is that although St. Thomas often refers to the underlying procreative "purpose" of marriage to the reason why God intended it, Paul VI joins this word "purpose" with the word "meaning": as he writes, "to use this divine gift while depriving it, even if only partially, of its *meaning and purpose*, is equally repugnant to the nature of man and of woman, and is consequently in opposition to the plan of God and His holy will."[69]

This pairing makes a difference, because purpose and meaning are not the same thing. One of them concerns the outward or objective character of a thing; the other, its inward or subjective character. A purpose is what something is *for*, its proper work. A meaning is what a thing *signifies* to a rational being. Ideally, purposes in things and meanings in minds are correlated. For example, the purpose of the eyes is to see, and there is something wrong if the only thing they mean to us is sensitive spots on our heads. But, although meaning is *properly correlated* with purpose, it is more than just the recognition of purpose, because it *builds* on purpose. Thus, eyes signify more to us than seeing: indeed, we think of them as windows of the soul. One reason is that they are so expressive. Another is that they are portals by which the truth of external things reveals itself to the mind.

It is the same way with the sexual organs. Again, purpose and meaning are correlated, for their purpose is procreation, and there is something wrong if we

67 Pope Paul VI, *Humanae vitae*, 8.

68 Pope Paul VI, *Humanae vitae*, 9.

69 Pope Paul VI, *Humanae vitae*, 13, emphasis added.

view them only as sources of interesting sensations. Yet, they signify more than procreation. For example, because one organ enters the other, they speak to us of how the beloved is impressed on the lover's heart and the lover penetrates into the beloved's. Because their joining in one flesh makes new life possible, it speaks to us of how the creator of all invites us to imitate and join in His work.

Although Paul VI does not explore the possibilities of this line of thought, they are already latent in his pairing of purpose with meaning. As we now know, John Paul II later takes up the invitation and runs with it. He continues Paul VI's argument by pointing out that the meaning of union is inseparably bonded to the powers which bring union about. We join ourselves by means of what? By means of an act which is intrinsically open to the possibility of new life. Therefore, whenever we give ourselves sexually, we are doing something that *cannot help but mean* that happy chance. If we deny that meaning and attempt to overwrite it with other meanings, *then we are not truly giving ourselves to each other.*

Do these differences of language and emphasis between St. Thomas and Paul VI reflect doctrinal differences? No. Do they signal incompatibilities in theory? Certainly not. But do they point to the possibility of a further unfolding of doctrine, an organic development of our understanding of these things? Yes. We are seeing it now.

Paul VI's argument against contraception is straightforwardly teleological: by rendering infertile an act which could otherwise be fertile, contraception violates the procreative good of marriage. St. Thomas plainly agrees: "That the emission of semen under conditions in which offspring cannot follow is illicit is quite clear," he says, not only from Scripture, but also from nature. "Hence, after the sin of homicide whereby a human nature already in existence is destroyed, this type of sin appears to take next place, for by it the generation of human nature is precluded."[70]

Paul VI, however, goes one step further, showing that although contraception is directly contrary only to the procreative good, it is indirectly contrary to the unitive good as well. How so? The methods of Natural Family Planning require a degree of restraint because for at least several days of the month the partners must abstain from intercourse. By contrast, contraception encourages the attitude that even this moderate degree of restraint is too much to expect of mere flesh and blood. But how could it be too much, unless we view the passions as irresistible forces, burning monsters, which demand to be fed at the least movement of impulse? And if we do view them this way, then how is it possible for the spouses to show respect for each other? Such an attitude is especially injurious for women, because just as Paul VI predicted, not only do men in our day see no reason for restraint whatsoever, but they demand that their wives have essentially male patterns of sexual response. If their wives are less than eager to leap into bed at any time, they consider themselves unjustly deprived. From this point of view, far from departing from St. Thomas's thought, Paul VI deepens and extends it.

70 Thomas Aquinas, *SCG*, III, chap. 122.

What then should we think of contraception? By now, the answer should be plain. Not only does contraception throw sand in the axle on which the great wheel of the generations turns, but it also discredits temperance, restraint, and the mutual reverence and tenderness of the spouses. By resisting the natural goods of marriage, it cannot help but resist its supernatural good as well. The sacrament of marriage declares that Christ and His Church are espoused in the same way as a faithful husband and wife. Do we really wish to compare the union of Christ and the Church with a marriage which frustrates and defies the purposes for which marriage was created? Surely, our Creator and Redeemer intends for us a greater joy than that.

5

In Defense of Humanae vitae

Dietrich von Hildebrand on Human Generation as the "Superabundant End" of the Conjugal Act

Maria Fedoryka

Initial Explanation of the Principle of Superabundance

The concept of "superabundant finality" was introduced by Dietrich von Hildebrand in his writings on marriage and sexuality to capture theoretically the relationship of the conception of new human life to the spousal act.[1] The traditional formulation, represented and articulated most fully by Thomas Aquinas and his followers, framed this relationship as one of finality, simply: the child is the *finis operis* ("end of the act") of the conjugal union of the spouses.[2] By adding the concept of superabundance to the concept of finality, in denominating the child as the "superabundant end" of the conjugal act, von Hildebrand was in no way departing from the perennial Catholic position on the inseparable and primary ordination of the spousal act to the possible generation of new human life. Rather, his aim was to bring more precision to the ancient "final cause" as applied to procreation, that it might capture more exactly the complex structure of human generation in relation to the act at its origin. As a human act, von Hildebrand maintained, the act is one of personal union between the spouses—and this unitive character of the act then metaphysically grounds

* This essay was originally published in a longer form as "'*Finis* superabundant *operis*': Refining an Ancient Cause for Explaining the Conjugal Act," *American Catholic Philosophical Quarterly* 90, no. 3 (Summer 2016): 477–498. It has been edited to fit the interests of this volume and is used with permission.

1 See Dietrich von Hildebrand, *Purity: The Mystery of Christian Sexuality* (Steubenville, Ohio: Franciscan University Press, 1989); *Marriage: The Mystery of Faithful Love* (Manchester, N.H.: Sophia Institute Press, 1991); *Man, Woman, and the Meaning of Love* (Manchester, N.H.: Sophia Institute Press, 2002); and *The Encyclical* Humanae Vitae: *A Sign of Contradiction* (Chicago: Franciscan Herald Press, 1969). The first was originally published in English in 1927, the second in 1942, the third in 1966, the fourth in 1968.

2 I have not actually found this concept of *finis operis* used by Thomas Aquinas himself with reference to the spousal act in relation to the child. Aquinas speaks only of offspring as the "principal end." See his *Summa theologiae* III, *Supplementum* q. 65, art. 1. All quotations taken from *The Summa Theologiæ of St. Thomas Aquinas,* second and revised edition, 1920, literally translated by the Fathers of the English Dominican Province, online edition 2017 at http://www.newadvent.org/summa/. But Aquinas's concept of *finis operis* has taken on a technical status, such that its eventual application to this relation by his followers can meaningfully be traced back to him.

(and thereby secures as inseparable) its additional "superabundant" ordering toward generative fecundity. This essay seeks to make clear von Hildebrand's idea of superabundant finality, via an analysis of two important dimensions of von Hildebrand's thought deeply linked to, and therefore illuminative of, the concept, namely, the essential constitution of love by the dual aspects of union and fecundity, and the love-embodying nature of sexuality. In the process of these reflections, it will become clear that von Hildebrand's position provides a powerful defense of the Church's teaching on the impermissibility of contraception.

Von Hildebrand explains what he means by the "principle of superabundance" in some detail in his late work *The Encyclical* Humanae Vitae*: A Sign of Contradiction.*[3] He introduces the principle by showing how it applies to the reality of knowledge: knowledge has the important role of enabling the person to undertake action, and more importantly still, the work of moral perfection and sanctification. In this sense, it functions as a means for achieving some end. But, prior to this end-achieving function that it is able to take on, knowledge possesses a nature, and therefore a meaning and value, of its own, as the act in which the human person apprehends reality as it is in itself. Its *raison d'être*, as von Hildebrand writes, is not determined exclusively by its service to the achievement of some end; its existence is "justified" already by virtue of the value of its intrinsic nature. When it additionally functions as serving the realization of some end, this role can be said to stand in a superabundant relationship to its intrinsically-constituted nature and meaning.[4]

Von Hildebrand contrasts this situation with one of instrumental finality. In this latter case, something has its nature, meaning and value (which in turn grounds its *raison d'être*) only in virtue of the end it serves to bring about. He gives the example of a knife: the end of cutting determines the nature of the knife; it has its only reason for existence insofar as it serves that end; apart from this function of cutting, it has no meaning or value (qua knife). It is, in short, merely a means to an end, its nature and meaning not intelligible apart from reference to its instrumental function.[5]

Von Hildebrand applies the principle of superabundance to the spousal act. He does this in light of his analysis of marriage as a bond having love as its inner soul, and of the spousal act as a unique expression and completion of spousal love and its culmination in the bond of marriage. Thus, for von Hildebrand, the conjugal act possesses a meaning already as a realization of conjugal love existing between the spouses. When one discovers its service to the end of the creation of new human persons, this end, he writes, is related to the spousal act (as an act of spousal union) in a superabundant manner:

3 Von Hildebrand, *The Encyclical* Humanae Vitae, 29–34. Von Hildebrand deals with this on pages 74–80 in his much earlier *Man, Woman, and the Meaning of Love*, and discusses the issue in slightly different terms in *Purity*, 10–14.

4 Von Hildebrand, *The Encyclical* Humanae Vitae, 30.

5 Von Hildebrand, *The Encyclical* Humanae Vitae, 30–31.

> … the intrinsic meaning and value of marriage consists in its being the deepest and closest love union. We saw that in its mutual self-donation and in its constitution of a matchless union, the conjugal act has the meaning of a unique fulfillment of spousal love. But to that high good, which has a meaning and value in itself, has been entrusted procreation. The same act, which in its meaning is the constitution of the union, has been superabundantly made the source of procreation; thus, we must speak of procreation as the end—but not in the sense of mere instrumental finality. Though we may consider the sexual instinct in animals as a mere means for the continuation of the species, as an end in the sense of an instrumental finality, this is patently impossible with respect to the love between man and woman or to their union in marriage.[6]

By introducing the concept of superabundance, von Hildebrand sought to accommodate theoretically a newly emerging insight into the conjugal act: the spousal embrace is not only an act with two separate dimensions or aspects (as held by Aquinas, and reflected in the teaching of the Church up to that time), each having its own proper "end," one "primary"—the generation of new life—and the other "secondary"—"*fides*" (expressed by Aquinas as "the mutual services which married persons render one another in household matters,"[7] which includes among them the Pauline "rendering the debt to one another"[8]). While this traditional view may be true as a partial description, the insight brought to the issue by von Hildebrand was that the act in its inner constitution possesses an essential unity, by virtue of which the two dimensions of the act are not simply juxtaposed, but are organically united.[9] What binds them together is the *nature of love itself*, as possessing the dual aspects of union and fecundity.[10] According to von Hildebrand, the act possesses an interior metaphysical dimension fashioned to be animated by love (to be discussed in detail below) and it is therefore that the act is at once unitive and procreative:

6 Von Hildebrand, *The Encyclical* Humanae Vitae, 31.

7 *ST*, *Supp.* q. 41, art. 1. It should be noted that the Supplementum is a text that was prepared by St. Thomas after his death by one or more members of his religious orders, compiling materials that Thomas had written previously into the format of the *Summa*. Nevertheless, we will treat the teaching on marriage of the Supplementum as essentially that of Thomas for the purposes of this essay.

For Aquinas, the fact that the male and the female contribute different but essential elements to the proper functioning of the household ("since one is not self-sufficient in all things concerning life": *ST*, *Supp.* q. 41, art. 1) is the secondary reason for the natural inclination to marriage.

8 *ST*, *Supp.* q. 49, art. 2 ad. 3.

9 This insight is found in the writings of Pope Pius XII; in Vatican II's *Gaudium et spes*; in the papal encyclical, *Humanae vitae*; and in the work of Karol Wojtyła. It is widely acknowledged that von Hildebrand was one of the major inspirations of this approach to spousal love and marriage.

10 This idea of the organic and therefore inseparable unity of the two dimensions of the spousal act is at the heart of *Humanae vitae's* defense of the Church's teaching on contraception. Paul VI uses the term "meaning" to refer to both the unitive and fecund dimensions of the conjugal act. Pope Paul VI, Encyclical Letter *Humanae vitae* (July 25, 1968), 13. In Latin, *significationem*. http://w2.vatican.va/content/paul-vi/en/encyclicals.index.html.

> It is no chance that God has invested that act with this creative significance. As God's love is the creative principle in the universe, so love is everywhere creation, and there is a profound significance in the nexus—at once symbol and reality—whereby from the creative act—in which two become one flesh from love and in love—the new human being proceeds.[11]

No mere "instrument" of the coming to be of new human life, the conjugal act as unitive rather gives rise from its own depth, from the heart of its intrinsic meaning, to this fruit: for the union of love is necessarily fecund.

This indicates that the principle of superabundance as it operates in the case of the spousal act in fact has a two-fold application: there is here not only a structural superabundance—as in the case of knowledge—but a content-ful one. In the case of knowledge, there is no meaningful, material connection between the act of knowledge in its specific nature as knowledge, and the content of the task it makes possible by a superabundant addition. There is only a superabundance structurally or formally, where superabundance refers only to the fact that knowledge has a second (and therefore "superabundant") meaning and function in addition to its own intrinsic meaning. In the case of the spousal act, the superabundance refers to this structural moment; but the concept of superabundance also captures the content-ful, meaningful relation that subsists between the union of the spouses and the coming into being of the child as the *fruit of that union*. That is, superabundance also captures the truth about the intrinsic essence of love itself, according to von Hildebrand, that it is constituted of two inseparable dimensions: union and the "overflow" or fecundity of that union.[12] Speaking of the child as the superabundant end of the act thus not only tells us that the act has a second meaning, apart from the end it brings about in the creation of the child, but also that the creation of a child is organically and inseparably (at least in concept or meaning) related to the union between the spouses, as "embodying"[13] the fruitfulness of the union of love. Thus, the spousal act as unitive can in no way be understood as standing in an instrumental relation to human generation.[14]

Those who misread von Hildebrand's position as entailing the moral liceity of separating the aspect of sex as unitive and sex as procreative miss precisely the specific meaning of superabundance that is implied in the case of the spousal

11 Von Hildebrand, *Purity*, 14–15.

12 "The fact that the closest communion of love between two people produces a new human being mysteriously reflects the fruitfulness of love as such." See von Hildebrand, *Marriage*, 30. Kevin Schemenauer writes of this dimension of superabundance in von Hildebrand, though he does not indicate that it is different from what I call structural superabundance. See his *Conjugal Love and Procreation: Dietrich von Hildebrand's Superabundant Integration* (Lanham, Md.: Lexington Books, 2011), 139ff.

13 The term "embodiment" is not used by von Hildebrand but is everywhere implied. An exact account of it will play a central role in the course of this essay.

14 Von Hildebrand does not himself clarify this point, but it would seem that because only the first structural sense of superabundance applies to knowledge, it stands in a merely instrumental relation to the end that it brings about.

act.[15] In fact, von Hildebrand's vision brings metaphysical grounding to the equation: It is only when we understand that this bodily act is intrinsically structured to be the embodiment of the spiritual act of spousal love (even if it is not always lived in this way[16]), that we can make sense of the fact that precisely it, and not some other act, should be ordained to be at the origin of new human life.[17] The child proceeds from this act because it is an embodiment and specific realization of the essential "diffusivity" (or "superabundance") flowing from the union of love—and as such, cannot be separated from it without violation of the act as an act of love.[18] "The God-given, essential link between love of man and woman and its fulfillment in the marital union, on the one hand, and the creation of a new person, on the other hand, has precisely the character of superabundance, which is a much deeper connection than would be one of merely instrumental finality."[19] Were the act to achieve its essence only from its function of bringing about new life, or were the act as procreative simply juxtaposed to the act in its unitive meaning, the creation of the child would remain in some significant sense external to the love between the spouses.

Now, if it is to be maintained that the act is procreative in virtue of the unitive dimension of the act, as its organic outflow, the act already as a physical act would have to be unitive not merely by the addition of the subjective factor of the spouses engaging in it "lovingly," but would have to have a unique metaphysical constitution which would make it inherently unitive: it would in its intrinsic

15 Von Hildebrand himself writes in a late work: "It was occasionally said that by affirming that the marital act retains a meaning and high value even when—through no intervention of ours—conception cannot occur, I was opening the door to a justification of artificial birth control But, this approach showed a misapprehension of my position, for I had emphatically stated in many articles and books that artificial birth control cannot be allowed. It was precisely my intention to call attention to the great mystery of God's having entrusted the generation of a new human being to the most intimate union of love. The dignity and beauty of the marital act as an irrevocable mutual self-donation in which the two spouses become 'one flesh' cause the mysterious link between this act and the birth of a new human being to shine forth in all nobility and grandeur." *The Encyclical* Humanae Vitae, xi. See Schemenauer's review of von Hildebrand's critics on this issue in his *Conjugal Love and Procreation*, Chapter 4, Section D. Since I will not address the issue in this essay, I will add that Schemenauer here also points the reader to the passages in von Hildebrand's works where he affirms the Church's position that the child is the "primary end" of marriage.

16 See von Hildebrand's comment on this in *The Encyclical* Humanae Vitae, 42–44.

17 " . . . we can do justice to the significance of this mysterious process [of the procreativity of this particular physical act] only if we take the union of love into full account. It is possible to gauge in its fullness and depth the sublimity of the connection between sex and the origin of a new human being, or to recognize all that is implied by the fact that it is no mere living thing, but a man, who comes into existence, only if we already understand the peculiar relationship which subsists between physical sex and wedded love." See von Hildebrand, *Purity*, 15.

18 This argument against the direct separation on the part of the spouses of the conjugal act from the possibility of conception is not the main one featured in von Hildebrand's writings. He puts more emphasis on the divinely appointed character of the connection between union and procreation, and on their separation as therefore an act against *religio*. See William Marra's "Human Love and the Sacredness of Sex," *International Review of Natural Family Planning* IV, no. 4, (1980): 334–344, for a reflection on this dimension on von Hildebrand's thought. See for example his *Man, Woman, and the Meaning of Love*, 80.

19 Von Hildebrand, *The Encyclical* Humanae Vitae, 34–35.

structure have to be fashioned to be incorporated into the personal act of love. Von Hildebrand's position on sexuality provides just such a vision of the spousal act: it is by its nature a kind of "incarnation" of love, "embodying" the two dimensions of union and fruitfulness.[20] We now turn to considering this part of von Hildebrand's view of sexuality in its intrinsic relation to love.

The Conjugal Act as "Embodiment" of Love

As stated, von Hildebrand's position on the superabundant relation between the spousal act as unitive and the spousal act as procreative rests on his conviction of the absolute centrality of spousal love to marriage and to the spousal act in its intrinsic structure. The inseparability (at least in meaning) of the two within the spousal act, then, rests on the inseparability of union and fruit within the unitary essence of love itself, which the conjugal act must embody in a concrete way.

In his work *Marriage, the Mystery of Faithful Love*, von Hildebrand writes about the essential connection that exists between love and fruitfulness:

> The fact that the closest communion of love between two people produces a new human being mysteriously reflects the fruitfulness of love as such. For we must not forget that every true love possesses an intrinsic spiritual fruitfulness and that conjugal love harbors this spiritual fruitfulness of love quite independently of procreation. This fruitfulness expresses itself in an élan of the soul, which is implied in love, in a new awakening of the soul which stimulates it to spiritual growth and a higher moral life. It expresses itself in the influence which the spouses unconsciously exert on one another, in the spiritual elevation of one another which their mutual understanding makes possible.[21]

While the unitive and the fruitful dimensions of love are distinct in their *rationes*, they can in no way be separated, as both together making up the constitutive essence of love. In considering this, we must avoid thinking abstractly of the union of love, but focus on it as an essentially personal reality: the particular character of the union of persons proper to love, achieved by the free acts in which each spouse makes a sincere gift of himself/herself to the other, realizes a kind of intensity of being that from its very roots entails a growth, an expansion, an overflow, that fills up the souls of those so united,[22] and then has a tendency to move beyond them towards others. Love's proverbial generosity is one specific

20 Besides the metaphysical weakness of the position that posits the link between the procreative dimension of the act and the love of the spouses simply in the subjective enactment of a loving attitude when entering into the act, von Hildebrand writes that "it is incompatible with the very nature of the person to consider the deepest human spiritual experiences as mere subjective aspects of something which, in God's eyes, is a means for an extrinsic end." See von Hildebrand, *Man, Woman, and the Meaning of Love*, 79.

21 Von Hildebrand, *Marriage*, 30.

22 Perhaps the "finding of self" in the "sincere gift of self" spoken of in the passage so often quoted by John Paul II from *Gaudium et spes* exemplifies this fruitfulness.

articulation of this expansiveness proper to love.[23] Insofar as it is love itself that is thus constituted, we must resist thinking of the fruitfulness as a "result" of love. Rather, the fruit proceeds organically out of the union, and is integral to it, always already leavening it in its inner constitution.[24]

Further, while each fruit of love has a being of its own, that which "overflows" is not something which has its complete meaning in itself but bears the "stamp" of the union that is at its origin; as fruit, included in its nature and meaning is a qualitative echo of the union that is its source.

Here we must note two things that are implicit in the above reflection: first, the grounding character of union in relation to the fruit. And second, while both dimensions of union and fecundity belong to love, each has its own, distinct intelligible structure, and the two are not to be conflated. One difference that concerns us here is the fact that the union of love is freely established by the persons, while the fruit of the union arises as a gift.

This distinction between, and the inseparability of the two dimensions of love is one cornerstone of von Hildebrand's idea of superabundant finality as applied to the spousal act. In effect, each dimension will have its own "trajectory" within the exercise of the spousal act, with a definitely determined order between them. Superabundant finality will line up with the act's relation to the generation of new human life, as an "outflow" of the union between the spouses established through the mutual gift of self.

The second cornerstone of von Hildebrand's principle of superabundance is the nature of embodiment, and more specifically, of the conjugal act as an embodiment of love. To begin with, the body is "always already" personal. The union between the human soul and the human body is such that the human body participates in personhood, itself taking on a personal character. In the human being we find, as it were, one single reality existing in two dimensions: the spiritual-personal, and the material-bodily–with the personal giving metaphysical form to the unity, rendering the bodily wholly personal in character.[25] In short, the personal soul is "embodied"[26] and the body is "ensouled."

23 If "the good is diffusive of itself," this is true *a fortiori* of love. Beginning from the reality of the gift, Aquinas also argues for the connection between love and generosity: "Now, the reason of donation being gratuitous is love; since therefore do we give something to anyone gratuitously forasmuch as we wish him well. So, what we first give him is the love whereby we wish him well. Hence it is manifest that love has the nature of a first gift through which all free gifts are given." *ST* I, q. 38, art. 2.

24 Fruitfulness is so integral to the union of love that it is not always easy to isolate it conceptually. But it is an unmistakably new factor, beyond the dimension of union.

25 Ann-Therese Gardner makes the interesting observation that von Hildebrand's theory of the body-soul unity is driven by his deep insight into the way in which love interiorly defines bodily spousal union. See her "The Phenomenology of Body and Self in Dietrich von Hildebrand and Edmund Husserl," *Quaestiones Disputatae* 3, no. 2 (Spring 2013): 28–36. The body's role in the living of spousal love implies a metaphysics according to which the body is deeply related to personal interiority, able "to participate in the interior realms of affectivity and acts of will"; the body is "somehow part of [the Ego], though mysteriously so" (33).

26 This is a term used by John Paul II in his discussion of this crucial issue in his *Letter to Families* (February 2, 1994), 19, http://w2.vatican.va/content/john-paul-ii/en/letters/1994.index.3.html. I would like to see the term take on a technical status, to delimit clearly the wholly *sui generis* way in which the personal

But the mutual "indwelling" of body and soul that constitutes the incarnate person's way of being is not all that underlies the transmission of self in the case of the spousal act. In fact, the contact between body and soul is constituted by depth-dimensions. That is, while the person is one single substance in "two dimensions," we could say that in some way, there is a hierarchy in the degree of intensity to the contact between body and soul. According to von Hildebrand, there is a unique intersection between body and soul in the sexual sphere, in virtue of which the bodily experience of sex is essentially and organically connected with spiritual and psychological experiences in the human person.[27] We find that the sphere of sex occupies a most deep and intimate place within the person. "When [sex] speaks," writes von Hildebrand, "it is no mere *obiter dictum* [casual expression], but a voice from the depth, the utterance of something central and of the utmost significance."[28] Sex, according to von Hildebrand, contains the "secret" of the person, as it "belongs to his inmost being."[29] Von Hildebrand points out that sex is originally fashioned to "speak" the central word of a radical self-donation in the depths of the person's being, whereby the person comes to truly belong to the other, and thereby simultaneously achieves a genuine self-possession. But it can alternatively entail a radical flinging away of oneself, when it is employed in the pursuit of pleasure; because of its centrality to the human personality, its misuses involve a correspondingly deep wound and loss of self.[30]

Finally, the spousal act as a physical act is wholly unique among physical acts in that it has an *intrinsic* ordination to containing a *particular* spiritual content. There are very few bodily actions of this kind; the kiss and the embrace are two such others. In virtue of this intrinsic ordination, these acts have proper to them one and only one meaning, even if these meanings may contain shadings. Compare these with other bodily actions—such as, for example, a wave of the hand—in which, while it is truly the person acting, the meaning of these bodily actions is not intrinsic to them, but is assigned to them "from without," by convention.[31] The meaning of the bodily act of sex, by contrast, is not given to it from without; rather, it is intrinsically structured to contain one and only one meaning: the spiritual reality by which its interiority is structured to be animated is *spousal love*.[32]

---

body and certain personal acts exist, namely, as possessing an interior metaphysical space, ordained to rendering bodily spiritual realities. See Damian Fedoryka's article on this topic, "Proportionalism: Some of Its Presuppositions and the Consequence for Ethics," *Anthropotes* 1 (1993): 69–102.

27 Von Hildebrand, *Purity*, 5.

28 Von Hildebrand, *Purity*, 5.

29 Von Hildebrand, *Purity*, 5.

30 See von Hildebrand, *Purity*, 15.

31 Damian Fedoryka writes that the latter kinds of acts are "instrumental acts," while the former are "embodying acts." See his "Proportionalism: Some of its Presuppositions and the Consequence for Ethics," 69–102.

32 Von Hildebrand writes: "We cannot grasp the mystery embodied in this sphere until we grasp that its deepest meaning consists in being a unique fulfillment of spousal love and its desire for union. We must realize that this sphere is essentially ordained toward the constitution of a lasting, irrevocable union, the union to which spousal love aspires, and which is sanctioned by God; only

More particularly, firstly, sex in the various dimensions of its psychological and bodily features, in the gestures and in its "dynamism," *already as bodily* is fashioned as an *objective analogy* of the character of spousal love; thus, the experiences and gestures, both psychological and physical, and, most importantly in the present context, the procreative function (which as such is not a gesture or behavior or even, indeed, a rational activity), do not stand in an arbitrary relation to spousal love, but repeat, as it were, in their qualitative character and in their physical structure the characteristics of spousal love.[33] Secondly, the bodily aspect of the spousal act possesses an interior "metaphysical space," ordained to be "animated" by the spiritual reality of mutual self-donation in its highest instance, as the consummation of spousal love. Thus, in the spousal act, the body and spirit are destined to form one single reality, now existing in two dimensions.[34]

We can here briefly review these characteristics of love which the bodily conjugal act expresses: In love, one is drawn towards the other—the "dynamism" of sexuality[35] "incarnates" this tendency; the one who loves makes a gift of himself—which is "repeated," as it were, in the bodily sphere in the inherent structure of sexuality as an experienced bodily transmission of self to the other; the

---

then can we grasp the real sinfulness of every isolation of the satisfaction of sexual desire from the constitution of this God-sanctioned union. Only when we understand that the sexual act implies a mutual, irrevocable self-donation and is by its very nature called and destined to constitute an indissoluble union, can we see the desecration involved in sexual satisfaction outside of marriage." See von Hildebrand, *The Encyclical* Humanae Vitae, 7.

33 Using the language of "organic unity" rather than analogy, von Hildebrand emphasizes this point in *Purity*: "There exists . . . a profound relation of quality between the bodily union and that psychological and spiritual factor of specifically matrimonial love formulated under the terms *mutuum adjutorium* (mutual assistance), and *fides* (fidelity) as one of the three ends [of marriage]. We have here to do with an organic unity, deeply rooted in the attributes of wedded love on the one hand and of sex on the other." More particularly, "In virtue of its profound centrality and intimacy, as also of its mystery, sex is capable of a particular relationship with love, the most spiritual and the deepest of all experiences" (*Purity*, 7); when lived properly, the quality of sex possesses "a blend of intimacy, centrality, mystery and tenderness, which gives expression to a unique liberating surrender and unites in a fashion beyond words to describe" (*Purity*, 16).

34 While it is beyond the scope of this essay to develop this further, it is important to see the distinction of the second point from the first, and even more, to see what the second adds to the first. It is well known that Paul M. Quay recognizes the importance of the capacity of the material to be fashioned on the analogy of the spiritual, thus becoming a "symbol" for it, for the sphere of sexuality; but as far as I can tell, he stops short of a real *prise de conscience* of the factor of embodiment in sexuality: " . . . the material sign that we call a symbol has a sign-value not only by some sort of convention or by material similarity but by the fact that its material form, structure, action, or appearance is similar to or like the immaterial or spiritual thing it signifies. Hence, once we know that something is a symbol, it can lead us by itself to knowledge of its significance and meaning." See Paul M. Quay, *The Christian Meaning of Human Sexuality* (San Francisco: Ignatius Press, 1985), 16. My position here is that the spousal act does more than by its form point to the spiritual reality of spousal love; it actually forms one "thing" with it, in virtue of its interior metaphysical space, and thus, forms a "second dimension" with the act of love, even while adding its own perfection to the love.

35 What Roger Scruton calls "sexual desire," emphasizing that it is an intentional response to the beloved. See his *Sexual Desire* (New York: The Free Press, 1986). In this connection it is interesting to note that in the *Theology of the Body*, John Paul II repeatedly denies that the sexual dynamism is instinctual, but suggests that it is an "irradiation" of the emotions in the bodily dimension.

experienced union of love as found in affectivity is embodied in the specifically intimate quality of sex as articulated above; the attendant happiness of the union is embodied in the bodily pleasure. Finally, love is fruitful; it is fruitful in virtue of the fecundation that is effected by mutual self-giving and receiving. Sex, then, also embodies this fruitfulness, and that in a supreme way: in the possible coming to be of new human life as a gift intended by God to both child and parents, that flows from the bodily union of the spouses and is received by them as a gift.

We can say that in the sphere of sex what is true of the body generally is true in a more intensive sense: the body can be a co-subject with the soul in personal bodily activity in an elevated and intensified way. This unity of the body with the soul in the spousal exchange is the reason that John Paul II can speak of the "language of the body."[36] The bodily conjugal exchange now speaks on the behalf of the spirit—actually "amplifying" its word, expanding its scope. This expansion of scope is particularly conspicuous in the case of generative fruitfulness: without the body, the spouses as contingent could never bring a new being into existence. For as finite beings, they cannot create out of nothing; nor can they communicate their own souls to a new being; but in and through their body, a body incorporated into the selfhood of the spouses in the way articulated above, they are able to transmit themselves to the child generated by their act of mutual self-giving.[37]

But I anticipate somewhat. In putting together our reflections on love with our reflections on embodiment, we can draw out the intelligible connection between spousal union and human generation. In the spousal act, body and soul constitute two dimensions, as it were, of a single personal act, namely, a unique kind of self-donation which is specifically spousal. At the same time that the deepest and most complete mutual self-giving in love proper to human existence takes place, the highest kind of fruitfulness flowing from spousal union reveals itself: the coming to be of a new human person. Thus, both dimensions of spousal love have their highest and most proper instance of embodiment in the spousal act as unitive-generative.

While there are many other spiritual dimensions of fecundity proper to the conjugal act, once we discover it, we see that the possible generation of a new human person corresponds most directly to the kind of union that takes place between the spouses. In this connection it is worth quoting in full one of Karol Wojtyła's reflections on the astonishing depth of this union:

36 The body (in the spousal act) is able to speak the language of spousal love in unison with the soul-person—even, as he says, on the person's behalf: " . . . man—male or female—does not merely speak with the language of the body. But in a certain sense he permits the body to speak 'for him' and 'on his behalf,' I would say, in his name and with his personal authority." See Pope John Paul II, *Man and Woman He Created Them: A Theology of the Body*, trans. Michael Waldstein (Boston: Pauline Books and Media, 2006), 106–111.

37 Pope Benedict XVI wrote of this mutual ennobling of body and soul through their union: "Christian faith . . . has always considered man a unity in duality, a reality in which spirit and matter compenetrate, and in which each is brought to a new nobility." See Pope Benedict XVI, Encyclical Letter *Deus caritas est* (December 25, 2005), 5, http://w2.vatican.va/content/benedict-xvi/en/encyclicals.index.html. It is striking to consider that the angelic being cannot co-create—cannot participate in God's fatherhood, as can the human person.

> By its nature, because it is what it is, the person is its own master (*sui juris*), and cannot be ceded to another or supplanted by another in any context where it must exercise its will or make a commitment affecting its freedom. (It is *alteri incommunicabilis*.) But love forcibly detaches the person, so to speak, from this natural inviolability and inalienability. It makes the person want to do just that—surrender itself to another, to the one it loves. The person no longer wishes to be its own exclusive property, but instead to become the property of that other. This means the renunciation of its autonomy and its inalienability. Love proceeds by way of this renunciation, guided by the profound conviction that it does not diminish and impoverish, but quite the contrary, enlarges and enriches the existence of the person. What might be called the law of *ekstasis* seems to operate here: the lover 'goes outside' the self to find a fuller existence in another.[38]

Von Hildebrand writes that in giving of self proper to spousal love "the giving is literally complete and ultimate. Not only the heart but the entire personality is given up to the other."[39]

We might say that to the great "potency" of this particular, spousal union of persons corresponds the astonishing possibility that new human life be generated as its fruit. Though we could not have anticipated it, and though the connection is not a necessary but a contingent one, once we see it, we recognize the deep intelligible correlation between this profound mutual self-donation of love marked by its fecundity in the interiority of the spouses and the creation of a new human person, who will be a new agent of love entering into and expanding the circle of love founded by the spouses.

Here emerges with more clarity the point mentioned at the beginning of this essay: the fact that the child stands in the relation of a superabundant end to the act does not entail the liceity of directly separating the spousal act from the possible coming to be of a child. On the contrary: if love is in its essence constituted by union and fruitfulness, and the spousal act is a concrete embodiment of spousal love in its two dimensions, we must conclude that to directly divorce the fruitfulness from the union is in a real way to make a strike against the love.[40] This is why Paul VI writes in *Humanae vitae* that the *prohibition* against the separation of the unitive and procreative meanings of the spousal act is grounded in the *impossibility* of their being separated.[41] If the spouses willfully close off the possibility of this fruitfulness, then they alter what happens in the conjugal act

38 Karol Wojtyła, *Love and Responsibility*, trans. H. T. Willetts (San Francisco: Ignatius Press, 1981), 125–126. We see at the end of this quote a reference also to the fruitfulness essential to love.

39 Von Hildebrand, *Marriage*, 8.

40 Another angle from which to make this point is to say that the biological intervention entailed by contraception is never merely biological. As the conjugal act is intrinsically fashioned to contain the spiritual reality of love, one cannot tamper with it physically without tampering with the act of the spirit.

41 "That teaching, often set forth by the magisterium, is founded upon the inseparable connection, willed by God and unable to be broken by man on his own initiative, between the two meanings of the conjugal act: the unitive meaning and the procreative meaning." Pope Paul VI, *Humanae vitae*, 12.

itself, insofar as it is so deeply and intelligibly related to that spousal mutuality of self-giving, as articulated above. If the spouses do effect this separation, the conjugal act is not "filled out" with the "interior soul" which it is metaphysically fashioned to embody; for if it were, the spouses would be open to the fruit to which it is organically related, whether or not the fruit comes into being. The act then ceases to be an act of love. A violation of the objective structure of the act then occurs. The body becomes an "instrument," no longer an "embodiment" of something spiritual, no longer participating in the subjectivity of the spouses; it becomes rather a means to some end other than union (usually pleasure in the generic sense of satisfaction).

The Child as the Finis Superabundant *Operis* of the Spousal Act

Having explored the foundations of von Hildebrand's position, we can now return to his idea of superabundant finality, briefly comparing it with the Scholastic view, and seeing what it adds to it, even while retaining its essential structure. According to Thomas Aquinas, the general principle of human acts states that certain actions have a *per se* end and are determined in their nature by this end. Aquinas states that "the object [of the act] . . . stands in relation to the act as its form, as it were, through giving it its species."[42] This end of the act is referred to by Aquinas as the "*finis operis*,"[43] which he distinguishes from the aim of the agent, the "*finis operantis*." This analysis is a theoretical account of the fact that certain acts have a nature proper to them, such that the nature is not in these cases determined by what the agent's motive may happen to be.

Not denying that finality structures the relationship between the act and the coming to be of the child, von Hildebrand sought to capture the complexity present in the spousal act as an act of love encompassing the two dimensions of union and fruitfulness. The act does have the possible coming into existence as its end, and this end does indeed define the nature of the act as procreative; but this end, and in turn, this procreative nature, is embedded, as it were, and grounded in the act's metaphysically prior ordination to uniting the spouses in love. In the case of animals, it would be accurate to say that the coming into existence of progeny is the end of the act, simply. This is because the generative act in this case has only one function, and thus only one dimension: the continuation of the species. In the case of the act at the source of human generation however, we find another element which entirely changes the metaphysical nature of the case: the child is a *fruit* of *the act of a mutual exchange between the spouses*, with all that this implies as articulated above. As soon as we recognize that this is the case, we must create a theoretical space for the unitive dimension which is the source of this fruit, as a distinct dimension of the act, with its own relative

42 *ST* I-II, q. 18, a. 2, ad. 2. The full response reads, "The object is not the matter 'of which' (a thing is made), but the matter, 'about which' (something is done); and stands in relation to the act as its form, as it were, through giving it its species."

43 The term *finis operis* is variously translated as "end of the external act," or "the proximate end of the act," or "moral object."

integrity. This dimension is constituted by the self-giving of persons, who mutually give and receive their very selves—which yields the manifest presence of a purpose and meaning distinct from (even if essentially related to) that constituted by the act's capacity to be at the source of new life. The act is constituted as unitive by the fact that it is objectively formed to be an embodiment, and not, as we have seen, merely an expression, of the mutual love between the spouses, which is concretely realized in the directedness of the spouses to each other as ends. Their mutual self-giving is what then organically gives rise to the act's possible generative fecundity.

We thereby discover two "finalities"[44] structuring the act, but each in its own proper way, the one corresponding to the unitive dimension of love, the other to the fecundity of love. In short, the child is, if we may put it this way, the "*finis* superabundant *operis*" of the spousal act. The end of union is one at which the spouses aim directly, insofar as their sincere mutual self-giving is willed as the direct end of their activity, while the coming to be of the child, while organically related to the union, is received by the spouses as a gift.

Conclusion

By way of summary, I would like to mention that von Hildebrand's view is particularly well-suited to countering the oft-repeated criticism of the Church's position on contraception as biologistic—that is, as holding that the moral prohibition against contraception is derived from biological facts. I believe that the teaching itself is not biologistic, but I do believe that many defenses of it are vulnerable to this charge. One instance of this is found in the position that distinguishes the order of nature and the order of persons, and then assigns each of the two ends of marriage to each order, respectively, the child belonging to the order of nature, the union of the spouses to the order of persons.[45] On this view, one may not licitly separate the possibility of conception from the spousal act because this would disrupt the structure of the act in the order of nature.[46] On von Hildebrand's account both ends belong to the order of *love*—and thereby to the order of persons. The possible coming into existence of new human life has its metaphysical roots in the structure of love, which the body is then

44 The rather abstract concept of finality ought here to be filled out in its particular meaning with reference to the case at hand: since the spousal act is itself actually an embodiment of love, the union achieved between the spouses in its exercise is not an "effect" or "result" achieved external to the act, but is rather already "lived" in the very act itself. The coming to be of the child should be similarly viewed: as organically flowing from the union itself, fruitfulness is in some sense "internal" to the act, at least in its meaning; the marriage expands into "family," a "unit" of separate individuals metaphysically bound together by the bond of love. The latter point is the central element underlying John Paul II's reflection on the family in his *Letter to Families*.

45 This is the approach that Wojtyła takes in *Love and Responsibility*. See also the work of Paul Gondreau, such as "The 'Inseparable Connection' between Procreation and Unitive Love (*Humanae vitae*, no. 12) and Thomistic Hylemorphic Anthropology," *Nova et Vetera* (English edition) 6, no. 4 (2008): 731–764.

46 Adding that the order of nature is created by God would not be a way of getting around the biologistic element of this position, as some authors have attempted to do.

metaphysically fashioned to embody. On this account, while the coming to be of the child is made possible by the workings of nature, it is ultimately secured as an end that may not be licitly separated from the act *because the law of love forbids it.*[47] We may say that von Hildebrand's view provides the necessary metaphysical bridge, as it were, that renders the order of nature morally relevant in the case of persons. While the God-given structure of nature reveals to us the particular form that fruitfulness will take on in this particular concretization of spousal love, it is not the natural/physiological end of the act as such that gives rise to the prohibition against contraception but the law of love according to which the two dimensions of union and fecundity must be respected in their absolute inseparability.

47 As mentioned earlier in this essay, this is not to say that there may not be other kinds of defense of the Church's teaching, such as the one von Hildebrand tends to use: that directly rendering the act infertile goes against the virtue of *religio*. But I believe that von Hildebrand provides a framework for the strongest argument that reasons from the structure of the act itself.

6

The New Natural Law Theory, Basic Goods, and Contraception

Patrick Lee

✷ THE TEACHING OF THE CHURCH on contraception, reiterated by Pope Paul VI in *Humanae vitae,* that contraception is intrinsically immoral, is often presented as based on the idea that the natural or biological teleologies within human nature are themselves moral laws. According to this depiction of the teaching, contraception is wrong because it interferes with the natural finality of the sexual act, and acting contrary to the natural finality of a basic power or act (the procreative power or the sexual act) is unnatural and therefore morally wrong.[1]

That argument does not seem sound. It does not seem to be always immoral to act contrary to the natural finality of a single power or act. Moreover, I do not think the basic moral criterion is human nature itself, or the natural teleologies that are parts of human nature (though I think the moral criterion is grounded in human nature).

The natural law theory of Germain Grisez, Joseph Boyle, and John Finnis suggests a distinct approach to these issues. Their approach—often called the "New Natural Law theory," (NNL theory)—does not base moral conclusions on patterns found within human nature as given. Rather, on the NNL theory, the basic goods themselves, such as life, health, knowledge, and friendship, provide a criterion for whether an act is morally right or not.[2] Early in the debate pre-

1 See, for example, Charles Curran writes, "What is the primary reason for rejecting the papal teaching condemning all artificial contraception for married couples? The primary objection of most dissenting theologians centers on the papal insistence that the biological structure of the marital act is normative, and human beings must always respect its God-given finality and structure. This approach has been called physicalism." Charles Curran, *Ongoing Revision in Moral Theology* (Notre Dame, Ind.: Fides/Claretian Publishers, 1975), 31. And more recently, in a joint statement on *Humanae vitae* from theologians in the Wijngaards Institute for Catholic Research: "Secondly, it is mistaken to derive a moral prescription directly from a factual description, i.e., a judgment of value (about what morally ought to be) directly from a judgement of fact (about what is). However, this is what *Humanae vitae* does when it infers that people engaging in sexual intercourse must always be open to the possibility of procreation from the (incorrect) fact that each and every act of sexual intercourse has a procreative finality." "Catholic Scholars' Statement on the Ethics of Using Contraceptive 2016," *Wijngaards Institute for Catholic Research,* http://www.wijngaardsinstitute.com/statement-on-contraceptives.

2 For expositions of this natural law theory see: Germain Grisez and Russell Shaw, *Beyond the New Morality: The Responsibilities of Freedom,* 3rd ed. (Notre Dame, Ind.: University of Notre Dame Press, 1988); John Finnis, *Natural Law and Natural Rights* (New York: Oxford University Press, 1980); Germain Grisez,

ceding *Humanae vitae,* Germain Grisez contended that the argument referred to above was inadequate and advanced a new argument based on the basic moral principle requiring respect and openness to basic human goods.[3] In subsequent years, Grisez and colleagues refined this argument in various places.[4]

Given the ongoing problem of confusion and dissent among many Catholics regarding the Church's moral teaching on married love and respect for human life, the New Natural Law theory offers an incisive way of understanding the truth of Church teaching from the standpoint of basic human goods. What follows is a discussion of two arguments advanced by the New Natural Law in defense of the Church's teachings as revealed in *Humanae vitae.*

The New Natural Law Theory and the Immorality of Contraception

According to the NNL theory, there are two reasons why contraception is intrinsically wrong, that is, why every sexual act must be open to procreation. These reasons correspond to the two principal goods that sexual acts are able to realize, namely, the procreative good and marital communion. NNL theory argues that contraception violates both.

On the NNL theory, the criterion for determining whether a kind of act is right or wrong is how in this kind of act one's will is related to the intrinsic goods of human persons. On this approach, the moral norm is not itself human nature or the teleologies inherent in a human being just by themselves but the intrinsic goods of human persons. Acts that are respectful of all of the basic, intrinsic goods of persons, both in oneself and in others, are morally right, while acts that either repudiate or are unduly neglectful of any intrinsic goods of a person are morally wrong. That is, the focus on this approach is not directly on the teleologies themselves in human beings, but on the basic goods to which these natural teleologies are oriented. In particular, a kind of act in which the content of the choice—what is chosen—includes the diminishing or impeding of an intrinsic good of a human person is intrinsically morally wrong. One need not intend procreation, but to be respectful of the human goods at stake in sexual acts, those acts must be open to procreation: that is, the will must be open to procreation, and the act chosen must be the kind of act that could procreate if conditions outside one's conduct obtained.

Among the intrinsic, basic goods of the human person are: life, health, knowledge, friendship, and marriage itself. To choose contrary to one or more of these goods is to set oneself against the flourishing of a person and thus to act contrary to love of God and neighbor.

Joseph Boyle, and John Finnis, "Practical Principles, Moral Truth, and Ultimate Ends," *American Journal of Jurisprudence* 32, no. 1 (1987): 99–151.

3 Germain Grisez, *Contraception and the Natural Moral Law* (Milwaukee: Bruce, 1964).

4 See, for example, John C. Ford, Germain Grisez, Joseph Boyle, John Finnis, and William E. May, *The Teaching of Humanae Vitae, A Defense* (San Francisco: Ignatius Press, 1988); Germain Grisez, *The Way of the Lord Jesus,* vol. 2, *Living a Christian Life* (Quincy: Franciscan Press, 1993), 506–519; John Finnis, "On Retranslating *Humanae Vitae,*" in John Finnis, *Collected Essays of John Finnis: Religion and Public Reasons* (Oxford: Oxford University Press, 2011), 344–367.

The key moral question is: "How is the will related to the relevant basic goods in the choice to contracept?"

What is the content of the choice to contracept? There are, of course, various devices and methods used for contraception: withdrawal, the use of devices such as condoms, the use of hormones that prevent ovulation, and so on. But these devices or methods are ways of contracepting only if they are used as ways of preventing conception. Contraception is a choice to do something precisely to prevent conception. It is not a choice to undo conception, or a choice to kill what has been conceived (that is abortion). Nor is every choice to do something that causes prevention of conception a choice to contracept, since such a prevention of conception—or causing of infertility—could be a side effect of what one chooses to do, rather than what one chooses. The key text in *Humanae vitae* that defines contraception is the following: "Similarly excluded is any action which, either before, during, or after sexual intercourse, is specifically intended to impede procreation—whether as an end or as a means."[5] Contraception is a choice to deprive a sexual act of its potential to procreate, a choice to impede procreation. As its name indicates, contraception is a choice directly *against* the coming to be of new human life. However, human life itself is a basic human good, an intrinsic good of a person. It is morally wrong, therefore, to act against, that is, to direct one's will against an intrinsic good of a person.

Now, just as it is possible to direct one's will *toward* goods that do not yet exist—by willing to bring them into being—so too it is possible to direct one's will *against* a good that does not yet exist—namely, by choosing to ensure that it does not come to be. Thus, one reason why contraception is wrong is that it is an anti-life act, it is a directing of one's will against the coming to be of new life, a closing of will to new life.[6]

Contraception and Marital Union

Catholic theologians or philosophers who hold that contraception is morally permissible typically argue that a married couple may impede procreation and yet have sexual intercourse for the purpose of fostering their marital union. This position presupposes that the choice to contracept is compatible with sexual intercourse's capacity to foster the spouses' marital union. But the second argument of NNL theorists against contraception shows that that is a mistake. This second argument concerns the relationship between the sexual act and the marital unity it is meant to express. The sexual act should express marital love and commitment, that is, the marital union between the spouses. But it can truly express marital love and commitment only if it actualizes a real bodily union, only if the man and woman become one flesh. And contraception makes that impossible.

The first step in this argument is to see the distinctive nature of marriage, that is, marriage as a natural community. Instances of the following type of

5 Pope Paul VI, Encyclical letter *Humanae vitae* (July 25, 1968), 14, my translation of the Latin, online at https://w2.vatican.va/content/paul-vi/la/encyclicals.index.html.

6 This argument is developed in much more detail in the works cited above in notes 3 and 4.

community can be observed in every society: a man and a woman committed to sharing their lives on all levels of their humanity (bodily, emotionally, and spiritually) in the kind of relationship that would be fulfilled by their conceiving and rearing children together (though not reaching that fruition in every case). This type of relationship is marriage.

What marriage is can be clarified by seeing how the need for this kind of relationship often comes to be recognized. A young man and woman fall in love and long to be one with each other. They spend time together, talk, play games, share meals, and so on. They eventually desire to unite sexually. They desire this sexual union not merely for gratification but as an expression or embodiment of their love for each other. These sexual acts involve a very thorough bodily union and also could lead to children. Hence, they come to realize that this act would be appropriate only as part of a more encompassing and enduring personal union. They see that what they long for—to form an all-encompassing personal union—would be both good in itself and provide a home for any children they might conceive. The purpose of this union is to build up that comprehensive union, a union that, if all goes well, will enlarge into a family. That is marriage in the traditional sense.[7]

Two points about the nature of marriage are especially important here. First it is a bodily, as well as an emotional and spiritual, union. In marriage the man and the woman are committed to sharing their lives, on the bodily, emotional, and spiritual levels of their being. Second, their union would be fulfilled by conceiving and rearing children together.[8]

There are, of course other relationships *similar* in some ways to marriage. For example, men and women may cohabit, regularly have sex together, and view the possibility of having children as a possibly attractive optional "extra," or perhaps, instead, as a burden to be avoided. This is quite different from marriage: in marriage, their comprehensive union—bodily, emotional and spiritual—is prolonged and enriched by their having and raising children together. By contrast, in the latter type of community, if a child does come to be from their sexual acts, the members in this relationship must then decide whether they will or will not form a new kind of union, one especially apt for and fulfilled by procreation.

7 Though no doubt occurring less frequently, the need for the union could arise through a couple first desiring to have children. They would then see that the children would need the love and care of both their mother and their father, and that they could provide such a loving environment for their children only if they love each other and are committed to an all-encompassing union together. The two basic ends of marriage—procreation and the union of the spouses—mutually imply each other.

8 It is important to distinguish between the bond of marriage and the fuller union the marriage is meant to realize. The commitment that initiates marriage—marital consent—is a commitment to do things in order to form the marital union in its fullness. The mutual commitment or marital consent creates a moral bond—a set of rights and obligations to each other—and initiates the marital community. This bond is the minimum, the core of marriage—what exists even if the spouses are emotionally estranged and perhaps live in different cities. Although the marital *communion* may become weakened, the marital *bond*—the marital rights and obligations—continues—the couple remains married. For the commitment of marriage to be valid it must be an undertaking to do what is reasonable to build up the sort of community that marriage is meant to be.

Another type of relationship similar to marriage but fundamentally distinct from it is an alliance formed directly for the purpose of raising children. For example, two or more individuals may agree to cooperate for the sake of raising children—two widowed sisters, for example, or several celibate religious men or women. Though these relationships are, like marriage, oriented toward raising children, the way they are oriented toward that purpose is quite different. In marriage the spouses form a bodily, emotional, and spiritual union, and procreation and child-rearing are the fruition of their union. But, in this latter relationship the union of the members of the community is a consequence of their decision to cooperate in the rearing of children. These unions need not involve sexual relations. Such communities are, of course, not marriages, nor does anyone think they are. Marriage is both a comprehensive union between the spouses and is intrinsically oriented to procreation.

In marriage, procreation is not merely accidental to the nature of the marital relationship. Marriage is intrinsically oriented to procreation and that orientation colors all of the other aspects of the spouses' relationship to each other. For conceiving and rearing of children together extends and intrinsically fulfills their bodily, emotional, and spiritual union. The man and the woman who are in love naturally see their becoming mother and father with each other as the prolongation, enrichment, and fulfillment of the total union with each other that they long for. And the child himself or herself is a concrete embodiment of their love and union.

On the other hand, procreation is not the sole end to which marriage is merely instrumental. Rather, the union of the spouses is in itself good, not a mere means in relation to procreation. Their being specifically fulfilled by marriage begins from the time they consent and from the time they begin mutually to build their marital union. And, if a married couple discover they cannot have children, they are still married, and their marriage is in itself worthwhile.

Paradoxically, if the spouses' union *were* viewed as merely instrumental in relation to having children, then it would *not* be a suitable environment for children. What children need above all is a loving environment, and so to prepare a suitable environment for children, the parents, or potential parents, must be committed to each other for their own sakes, not just as a means in relation to getting some job done.[9]

Germain Grisez helpfully compared the relationship between marriage and procreation to the relationship between the crypt of a church and the upper church built upon it:

9 G. K. Chesterton made this point, vividly explaining that children need a secure home, referring to it as a feeling of home, and went on to say: "But they cannot keep [that] feeling for ten minutes, if there is an assumption that Papa is only waiting for Tommy's twenty-first birthday to carry the typist off to Trouville; or that the chauffeur actually has the car at the door, that Mrs. Brown may go off the moment Miss Brown has 'come out.'" G. K. Chesterton, *Brave New Family: G. K. Chesterton on Men and Women, Children, Sex, Divorce, Marriage, and the Family,* ed. Alvaro de Silva (San Francisco: Ignatius Press, 1990), 33–34.

> Sometimes a crypt is built and used as a church in the expectation that eventually it will be the foundation for a grander, upper church. Still, the eventual upper church is not an extrinsic end to which the crypt is only instrumental; rather, the upper church will complete the structure of which the crypt is the first and basic part. But even though the plan for the upper church determines the plan for the crypt, if the upper church never is built, the crypt can serve as, and really be, an entirely adequate church for those who worship in it.[10]

Thus, the marital union of the spouses in its fullness is an intrinsically good part of an intrinsically good whole, the family. The union of the spouses is both good in itself, and intrinsically oriented to enlarging into family.[11]

How, then, can an act of sexual intercourse foster marital union? This is key to understanding the relationship between contraception and marital union. What is it about sexual intercourse that enables it to actualize or cultivate marital union? Some people say that sexual intercourse *signifies* or symbolizes—as an extrinsic sign—the spouses' mutual love. On this view, what makes sexual intercourse distinctive is its relation to something other than itself, namely, its signification of an emotional or spiritual union. Indeed, this view has at times been proposed as a way of exalting marriage: proponents of this view might emphasize that marriage is a *spiritual* union, much deeper than mere bodily realities, and that sexual intercourse is an apt sign or symbol.[12] On this view, while the sexual acts are bodily, what they signify, and thus marriage itself, is purely spiritual.

This position is mistaken. It is true that sexual intercourse is a sign or a symbol. But, if that were its central reality, then one could fairly easily change what it signifies, perhaps by stipulation, to suit different situations. The meaning of a kiss or a hug, for example, can vary considerably from one situation to another.

Moreover, make-believe kissing, for example in acting in a play or a movie (that is, engaging in the act but only pretending to convey what it might otherwise signify), does not seem to be necessarily morally wrong, even though it may be awkward or embarrassing for the actors. Sexual intercourse, on the other hand, during make-believe, as in a play or a movie, cannot keep from being more than make-believe, whether the something more be good or bad. The reason for this difference seems to be that the central importance of sexual intercourse does not come from a separable relation to something extrinsic, but in its basic reality.

Again, there is a world of difference between being forced to kiss someone and being forced to have sex with someone. And kissing an unconscious person without that person's consent does not seem necessarily wrong—or at least

10 Grisez, *The Way of the Lord Jesus*, vol. 2, *Living a Christian Life*, 569.

11 See also Patrick Lee and Robert P. George, *Conjugal Union: What Marriage Is and Why It Matters* (New York: Cambridge University Press, 2014), Chapter 3; John Finnis, "Marriage: A Basic and Exigent Good," in *Collected Essays of John Finnis: Human Rights and Common Good*, 317–333.

12 Some contemporary "personalized" wedding vows emphasize that one's bride or groom is not just one's spouse, but one's *soul mate*. Of course, marriage does involve a union of souls, but what marriage is—the essence of marriage—includes bodily union as well.

not seriously wrong—whereas having sex with an unconscious person without that person's consent is a grave violation. But if sexual acts derived their central importance from their signifying something extrinsic, then that relation would be separable from the sexual act. And, it would be difficult to see in that case how sexual acts could be so strikingly different in the ways mentioned above.

Another view of how sexual acts are important is that they can foster personal union insofar as they are gifts of pleasure, thus intensifying mutual affection. On this view, when two people engage in a sexual act, they become united because they exchange pleasure, and that mutual gift—the gift of a unique pleasure—is the source of the bonding power of sexual acts.

However, this cannot be the central source of sexual activity's power to unite. Pleasure in general is not just by itself a genuine good. Pleasure can be a good, but only if it is an aspect of a condition or activity that is *already* genuinely fulfilling. And this point is also true of sexual pleasure. Hence, sexual pleasure by itself does not constitute a fitting gift. To be a genuine good, it must be part of a sexual act that already realizes a genuine good.[13]

These points indicate that what is most important in sexual acts is not what they signify or what they cause, but what they actually are prior to those extrinsic relations. Sexual intercourse *is* a sign or a symbol, and it is pleasurable, but these aspects of it are not sufficient to explain how it can have the importance it obviously has, nor how it can contribute to marital communion. Indeed, the sign-value and the distinctiveness of the pleasurable aspects of sexual intercourse are due to the distinctive reality that a sexual act is. It has a sign-value, and is often a powerful experience, precisely because of what it is *in reality*, before being a sign.

Now, the reality of sexual acts is not difficult to determine. Sexual intercourse is a biological act jointly performed by a male and female that is defined by its being a reproductive act. Moreover, when a man and a woman have sexual intercourse, they become biologically united. With respect to most biological systems (the nervous system, the circulatory system, and so on), each individual man or woman is complete. But with respect to the reproductive system the male and the female human beings (like other mammals), are *in*complete. No human being has a complete reproductive system: each of us has only one half, either male or female. And so no human being can perform the biological function of reproduction by himself or herself. Rather, in the reproductive act the male and the female complete each other to become a single subject of a single biological function.[14]

Just as an individual's different bodily parts (e.g., heart, lungs, and arteries) are incomplete and can function only in cooperation with other bodily parts (e.g., circulation of oxygenated blood) and so are biologically united to these others as parts of a whole individual, so too in sexual intercourse, the sexual organs of the male and those of the female participate in a single biological function

13 See Patrick Lee and Robert P. George, *Body-Self Dualism in Contemporary Ethics and Politics* (New York: Cambridge University Press, 2008), 185–194; Alexander Pruss, *One Body: An Essay in Christian Sexual Ethics* (Notre Dame, Ind.: University of Notre Dame Press, 2013), 115–127.

14 See Grisez, *The Way of the Lord Jesus, Volume 2, Living a Christian Life*, 570 ff.; Pruss, *One Body, An Essay in Christian Sexual Ethics*, Chapter 5.

performed by the couple as a unit. Sexual intercourse, therefore, establishes a real organic or biological union with respect to this function; although, with respect to other functions (e.g., respiration and digestion), the male and female remain fully distinct.[15]

Human beings are bodily beings, not just spiritual subjects, or sets of conscious experiences, that inhabit or supervene upon bodies. The human body is part of the personal reality of the human being. As Pope John Paul II explains, the body *expresses the person* rather than being a mere extrinsic instrument of a conscious and desiring subject.[16] The biological unity realized in sexual intercourse can be a truly personal unity and a part—the bodily component—of the more encompassing, personal union that marriage distinctively is.

Thus, what is distinctive of sexual activity, and what makes it so powerfully significant, is precisely what makes it sexual to begin with, namely, that in sexual intercourse a man and a woman become bodily one in a reproductive-type act—realizing the most thoroughgoing bodily union two people can bring about. Moreover, it is a joint act that disposes them to become mother and father together, and so it tends to unite their lives together into the indefinite future.

But this comprehensive personal union, in body, mind, and heart, is realized only if their bodies, minds, and hearts are integrated with their commitment to each other. Of course, it is possible for two people to become biologically united without actualizing a personal union between them. St. Paul refers to this fact when he says that it is gravely wrong to become one body with a prostitute.[17] It is even possible for two spouses to become biologically united without actualizing their marital union—if for example, one spouse forces sexual intercourse on the other, or if the spouses engage in sexual intercourse for the pleasure alone, as opposed to taking pleasure in the act as an embodiment of their marital union. Thus, in sexual acts the bodily and the spiritual aspects of the person are not necessarily integrated, and so it is possible for someone to use his body and that of his partner as if these bodies were mere extrinsic instruments. But it also is possible to have sexual intercourse in an integrated way, as *embodying* and *actualizing* the multileveled union that is the marriage of those spouses.

How, then, do sexual acts contribute to marital union? Not as extrinsic signs, nor merely as means of producing intense pleasure, but as being *part of* that marital union. Loving marital intercourse *actualizes or embodies* the total marital

15 Of course, not every instance of two entities sharing in an action are instances of two entities becoming biologically one. In this case, however, the potentiality for a specific type of act, reproduction, can be actualized only in cooperation with an individual of the opposite sex of the species, and the reproductive bodily parts are internally oriented toward actuation together with the bodily parts of an individual of the opposite sex. Note also that, strictly speaking, men and women engaging in sexual acts do not choose to reproduce; what they can choose and do is to perform reproductive-type acts, some of which may (they may or may not hope) reproduce.

16 Pope John Paul II, *Man and Woman He Created Them—A Theology of the Body*, trans. Michael Waldstein (Boston: Pauline Books and Media, 2006), 183. Compare also Pruss, *One Body: An Essay in Christian Sexual Ethics*, 197–201; Lee and George, *Body-Self Dualism in Contemporary Ethics and Politics*, Chapter 1.

17 See 1 Cor 6:15–16.

union. Moreover, the bodily union realized in sexual intercourse modifies or shapes all of the other ends of the marital union. These points are implicit in the traditional teaching, both in secular and ecclesiastical law, that the first act of sexual intercourse consummates marriage. Because the marital communion is bodily as well as emotional and spiritual, it is not fully established or completed until the spouses have become one at the biological level ("one flesh"). Subsequent acts of sexual intercourse, then, renew and embody their multileveled marital union.

If these points on what marriage is and how sexual acts can contribute to marital union are true, it follows that contraception violates marital union. In contraception, the spouses choose to prevent their act (or rather their acts), from procreating. But in doing this, they cannot be performing a procreative-type act, and so are not becoming one flesh. The spouses' sexual act can embody or actualize their marital union only if they truly do become one body. And they become one body only if, together, they become the subject of a single biological act, that is, only if, together, they perform a reproductive-type act—the kind of act that would procreate if conditions outside their conduct obtained.[18]

As *Humanae vitae* expressed it, repeating traditional Catholic teaching, the marital act must be "essentially oriented to procreation" [*per se destinatus ad procreationem*].[19] For only if that is so, do they become one body. If, on the contrary, they do not become biologically united, then their acts are not part of their marital union. Such acts can only provide an illusory experience of union without real union. In short, the use of contraception renders their sexual acts nonmarital, and nonmarital sexual acts are immoral.

Nonmarital sexual acts, in whatever variety, are immoral because they involve a disintegration of the sexuality of the persons involved. If, for example, a man and a woman become one in their bodies but not one on other levels of their lives—for example, they are not married, or they perform the act in an unloving or in a manipulative manner—then their acts only mimic and distort the marital union that a sexual act is capable of realizing. In that case, they treat their sexuality as *separate* from the other aspects of themselves, and so use their bodies as mere extrinsic instruments for the attainment of enjoyable but illusory experience of union.[20]

In a similar way, sexual acts that do not make the actors biologically one (such as masturbation, oral sex to completion, or sex with contraception), involve using each other's bodies as instruments for having an illusory experience of union without actualizing real union on any level. Enjoyable experiences do not just of themselves make people one or enhance their personal unions. Marital intercourse integrated with the spouses' marital commitment embodies and is

18 As Robert George and I express it in our book, *Conjugal Union, What Marriage is and Why it Matters* (New York: Cambridge University Press, 2014), it is a marital act only if the spouses perform the behavioral conditions for procreation.

19 Pope Paul VI, *Humanae vitae*, 11.

20 See Pope John Paul II, Apostolic Exhortation *Familiaris consortio* (November 22, 1981), 11, http://w2.vatican.va/content/john-paul-ii/en/apost_exhortations.index.html.

part of the spouses' sharing their lives on all levels. But to pursue the illusory experience of that, without its reality—whether this be because the participants lack a marital union to embody, or because they do not become one body—is to violate the marital good.

It is precisely by willingly and lovingly performing a procreative-type act that a husband and wife embody their procreative-type union. They need not intend to procreate. But, deliberately to negate the procreative capacity of a sexual act is to render this sexual act (or sexual acts) not unitive. Contraception prevents the two from becoming one body, and so contracepted sexual acts are not marital.

Furthermore, contraception involves a violation of marital union in a second way. It involves a choice by the spouses precisely to impede what would be the culmination of their marital unity. As indicated above, the child is the culmination or crowning point of the spouses' unity. The child is the fruit of their marital union or the concrete and personal continuation of their union. And so, to choose to prevent the coming to be of a child is to choose to impede the culmination of their marital unity, to direct their wills against that culmination. Contraception is different from a choice not to pursue that union or child (as in Natural Family Planning); rather, it is a choice to ensure that this culmination does not occur. The contraceptive choice is, therefore, contrary to marital union.

In sum, the marital unity of spouses is not incidentally related to the procreative dimension of the union. The specific type of community they have is a procreative-type community. What consummates their union is a procreative-type act. The marital unity of the spouses—bodily, emotional, and spiritual—is extended and naturally fulfilled by procreating and rearing children together. The child is the concrete fruit and expression of their marital commitment and their love for one another. Thus, in acting against conception, the spouses render their sexual acts nonmarital, and close their wills to the culmination of their marital union.

This understanding supports Paul VI's teaching in *Humanae vitae*: "The Church teaches that each and every marital act must remain *per se* oriented to the procreation of human life." [*Ecclesia, . . . docet necessarium esse, ut quilibet matrimonii usus ad vitam humanam procreandam per se destinatus permaneat*].[21] In other words, marital intercourse has a unitive meaning (its character as expressing love and marital union) and a procreative meaning (its suitability for procreation), and these two meanings are necessarily intertwined. They must not be—in a way, *cannot* be—separated.

Objection: Contraception and NFP

Various objections could be raised to the arguments just presented. The most frequent objection to any account of why contraception is immoral is the claim that it is not significantly different morally from the methods of Natural Family Planning (NFP). "Isn't contraception the same as NFP?" it is often objected. "Isn't

21 Pope Paul VI, *Humanae vitae*, 11.

the couple using NFP trying to avoid conception?" And, "What difference does it make whether one avoids conception by avoiding intercourse when one knows ovulation is occurring and conception would likely occur, or avoids conception by directly preventing it?"

In the first place, it is important to note that the two types of choices are clearly different (whether that difference is *morally* significant will be considered in a moment). The basic difference is between *choosing to prevent* something (which happens with contraception), and a choice *not to do* what might cause a good because of the difficulties consequent to or concomitant with that good (as with NFP). You can't choose to prevent something unless you are in a situation (or think you are in a situation) in which something is about to come to be—or in which it is (or you think it is) likely that unless you act this thing will come to be. In contraception, one is in a situation in which a baby might come to be, and one chooses to do something to make sure—or make more likely—that a baby will *not* come to be. Hence, the content of one's choice, or the proximate object of one's choice, is the not-coming-to-be of a baby.

By contrast, with an NFP method (which makes use of periodic sexual abstinence to avoid a pregnancy), one chooses not to do what might cause a baby, because of the difficulties that would accompany the coming to be of a baby at this time. In this type of choice, the content of one's choice is: not to do what would cause a baby—in other words, not to have sexual intercourse, in order to avoid the difficulties that would accompany the coming to be of a baby. The not-coming-to-be of the baby is not the content of one's choice. In a morally upright choice of periodic sexual abstinence, one chooses not to do what might cause a baby, because causing (procreating) a baby now would bring responsibilities to that baby, and it seems that those responsibilities are incompatible with other responsibilities one has. Put otherwise: one chooses not to do what might cause a baby, because having a baby now would detract from the pursuit of other goods one has a responsibility to pursue.

Is the difference between the two types of choice morally significant? Or, is the type of choice made in periodic sexual abstinence, though technically different, morally speaking in the same category? The difference is indeed morally significant. In a choice to prevent the coming to be of a baby (as with contraception), one's will is directed against the procreative good. This is wrong for (at least) two reasons. First, one's will is closed to new life, one's will is related to the intrinsic good of life negatively. Second, by choosing contrary to the coming to be of a baby, one makes one's sexual act different from a procreative-type act and chooses contrary to the culmination of marital union. In such acts, the man and the woman do not become one body and they act against the fullness of their union, and so the act is not a marital act.[22]

22 Someone might object that the sexual acts of infertile couples are not procreative and so the account I have given is mistaken to tie marriage and marital acts so strongly on procreation. However, procreation is not something that a couple directly *does;* procreation is not directly part of their voluntary conduct. All that a couple can do (even if they know that the woman is ovulating) is jointly perform the act that will procreate, or would procreate, if conditions outside their conduct obtain. All that any couple can jointly

It is worth noting that the difference between choosing to prevent a good and choosing not to cause a good, applies in many other cases as well. There are numerous instances where in a perfectly morally upright way, I may decide not to do what would cause a good, in order to avoid the difficulties concomitant to that good. For example, I may choose not to begin writing a book this summer because doing so would take me away from other responsibilities I have (perhaps it would mean I was unable to go on a vacation with children or grandchildren). In such acts I have not acted *against* the good I have chosen not to cause or pursue. Choosing not to pursue a good is quite different from choosing to impede or prevent the coming to be of a good: for example, I would act against a basic good if I intentionally prevented my child from learning to ensure that he stayed at home. A choice not to pursue a good at a particular time, is compatible with openness to that good; a direct choice to prevent the coming to be of a good is not.

Conclusion

Some who dissent from *Humanae vitae* usually claim that the Church's teaching on contraception could be abandoned and the rest of the Church's teaching on sex and marriage retained. The Church has traditionally taught that sexual acts have a profound meaning precisely because they can express and embody the two-in-one flesh union that is marriage. But if sexual acts need not be open to procreation, then sexual acts could have a nonmarital and yet morally upright meaning, perhaps because of their intense pleasure.

The teaching of *Humanae vitae* is that the procreative significance of sexual acts must be respected. Sexual pleasure is good but only if it is the enjoyment of an act that embodies and actualizes a marital union. The experience of intimacy is good but only insofar as it is a veridical experience, an experience of one's marriage. A sexual act contributes to marital union by expressing and embodying that union. It fosters martial union only if the husband and the wife truly become one flesh. If one says, on the contrary, that sex acquires its value by being a sign, or by being a gift of pleasure—the alternatives to saying its meaning comes from its being a one-flesh union oriented to procreation—then it is hard to see why such acts must only be within marriage, even within a stable relationship. Indeed, it would be hard to see why sexual acts would have a profound inherent meaning at all. The question to ask, then, is whether this line of thinking

do in this regard is to provide the behavioral conditions for procreation. Sexual intercourse is the first part (and the only part over which the couple has direct voluntary control) of the procreative process, not the whole of it—other parts of it are natural, nonvoluntary acts or conditions. The man and the woman mate—become bodily one—if they perform the first part of the reproductive process, the only part over which they have direct voluntary control. Spouses become one body if, but only if, they jointly perform the behavioral conditions of procreation. And so, the sexual acts of fertile couples and of infertile couples are the same in kind—provided they are choosing to embody their marriage, are actually mating, and their wills are open to procreation. What the spouses *do*—their voluntary conduct—provided they do not contracept—is the same whether the nonbehavioral conditions of procreation obtain or not (and whether they know that or not).

and acting could be in line with a love of and respect for the flourishing of the human person. Unfortunately, current society provides a stark response in the sexual chaos where hook-up sex, soaring rates of sexually transmitted infections, high rates of divorce, abortion on demand, a booming pornography industry, and lower rates of men and women entering marriage exist. Clearly all of that is not good for men and women. But the teaching of the Church on married love and respect for human life is a beacon of hope. That teaching, beautifully explained in *Humanae vitae*, is no mere arbitrary "ban," but is based on the logical demands of love and respect for the intrinsic goods of every human person.

7

Humanae vitae *and the "Un-engendering" of Gender*

Margaret Harper McCarthy

✷ IN *THE ABOLITION OF MAN*, C. S. Lewis listed contraception as one of the several novel inventions that had given us unprecedented power over our nature. But, as Lewis noted, the possession of this very power required that whole generations also be *subjects* to it.

> As regards contraceptives, there is a paradoxical, negative sense in which all possible future generations are the patients or subjects of a power wielded by those already alive. By contraception simply, they are denied existence; by contraception used as a means of selective breeding, they are, without their concurring voice, made to be what one generation, for its own reasons, may choose to prefer.[1]

Looking ahead to what he thought was the inevitable implication of separating the "inseparable meanings" of the conjugal act, Lewis predicted the "man-molding" by "conditioners" who would be about the business of cutting out their posterity "in what shape they please."[2] Now with much water under the bridge, there is little question about the accuracy of his prediction. But to that prediction, we can now add something equally disturbing about the other "meaning" of sex—the ostensible beneficiary of contraception—an observation about how much the human couple has become subject to a power they thought *they* were wielding. I will leave it to others to document what we all can see before our naked eyes: the difficulty for the married to stay in marriage and the miserable "approach" to it that we have left for our children: encounters that can barely even be called such, so little do the parties actually meet each another, and armed as they are with all the contractual "protections" if they do.[3] It would be hard to deny how

1 C. S. Lewis, *The Abolition of Man* (New York: HarperCollins Publishers, 2001), 55.

2 Lewis, *Abolition of Man*, 60.

3 On the relationship between contraception and divorce, see Fehring, Richard J. "The Influence of Contraception, Abortion and Natural Family Planning on Divorce Rates as Found in the 2006–2010 National Survey of Family Growth," *The Linacre Quarterly* 82, no. 3 (2015): 273–282. For a literary description of current "courtship practice," see Tom Wolfe, *I am Charlotte Simmons* (New York: Farrar, Straus & Giroux, 2004). See also Kay Hymowitz on the male "Darwinian" adaptation to the "brutal sexual

much the union of man and woman itself has been changed, even to the point of near extinction, by "their" new power, notwithstanding the once-noble goals of improving the state of their union by focusing on it more "single-mindedly," so to speak. All, by the way, predicted by *Humanae vitae*.[4]

We are brought right to the heart of the new idea of "gender." Gender, in its new coinage, at one and the same time dissociates sex from children and the sexes from each other. Un-*engendering* gender, it un-genders (real) *gender*, separating the sexes, from each other, they being no longer indispensable to each other. This, in turn, separates the next *generation* from the two genders, they being no longer indispensable to it (since assisted-reproductive technologies, or ARTs, necessarily follow from contraception). For the new generation, it is now no longer *engendered*. The (broken) circle is now complete. What God has joined has been put asunder at every level.

In the following, I look at the question of the "inseparability" of the two "meanings" of sex, as *Humanae vitae* puts it. I do this by looking first at the *separation* of the inseparable meanings at the heart of the new "gender." Beginning here, we can see what is at stake in that separation. We can also see what are the motivations for undermining each of them, in putting them asunder. I then turn positively to the "inseparability" doctrine in *Humanae vitae*, to look at the sense in which the two "meanings" stand or fall together, while taking up the challenge for which "gender" proports to be the "solution."

(Real) Gender

Let us begin by noting what is implied in the Latin root of the English word "gender," *gener-*, *genus*. According to its origins, the word implies being caught up in the rhythm of *generations*. Generation puts the individual in a *genus* (a "breed" a "stock")—with a *genealogy*—through the activity of *generation* (begetting, conceiving, giving birth), by which it comes into the world as *engendered*, and prepared, in turn, for the same act of *generosity*, by virtue of being *gendered*, capable, that is, of union with the opposite sex.[5] According to its own roots, the word "gender" indicates a three-fold relation: first, with one's forebears (I am *engendered*); second, with the opposite sex (I am *gendered*); and, finally, with

ecosystem" absent of any clear "script," in "Love in the Time of Darwinism," *City Journal* (Autumn 2008), https://www.city-journal.org/html/love-time-darwinism-13124.html.

4 Pope Paul VI, Encyclical Letter *Humanae vitae* (July 25, 1968), 17, http://w2.vatican.va/content/paul-vi/en/encyclicals.index.html. See also chapter 2 of this book, "The Vindication of *Humanae Vitae*, Continued," by Mary Eberstadt, which discusses the most recent phenomena owing to the widespread use of contraception.

5 The English term "gender" derives from the Latin *gener-*, *genus* meaning "kind," "sort," "class," "race," or "breed," as suggested in related terms such as "genus." These nouns are tied to the verbs "to engender," "to beget," or "to produce" (offspring). The terms "genealogy," "generation," and "generosity" are related. See "Gender," in *The Oxford English Dictionary* (Oxford: Oxford University Press, 1971). As Prudence Allen notes, the root of the term is consistently used to designate something tied to *generation*, both in ancient Greek philosophy and in the Old and New Testaments. See Prudence Allen, "Gender Reality vs. Gender Ideology," *Solidarity: The Journal of Catholic Social Thought and Secular Ethics* 4, no. 1, art. 1 (2014): 25–26.

one's potential progeny (I am capable of *generating*). Here, we are interested in the second and third of these two relations—the two "meanings"—but, of course, these two, and their inseparability, depend upon the first, which should be clear today from all the talk of "assignment." (And, of course, the first depends on the second and the third.)

Let us say a brief word on the original relation. By the simple fact of *being sexual,* we are the kinds of beings that are brought into existence through the sexual process. "Every human being who comes into being owes his existence to a sexual process; he has been begotten and born."[6] The fact that our attempt to circumvent the sexual process goes hand-in-hand with the attempt to overcome our being sexual does not contradict this. It only confirms it. The fact that we come to be through sexual generation means that we are caught up in a cycle of birth and death.[7] Sexual difference brings to light the most basic difference between us and God: we are finite creatures. As sexual beings, our conception marks the beginning of our parents' deaths and is the beginning of ours too (in the more distant future). There are, of course, *asexual* organisms that come into being and are quickly replaced by new individuals of their species through asexual reproduction (e.g., yeast budding or one-celled organisms).[8] Sexuality is not, therefore, *identical* with finitude. What the sexual process makes more visible is the deeper logic of finitude: namely, the fact that we exist by virtue of and for the sake of a communion, a co-unity. The sexual process shows the positive side of finitude, so to speak. To state the obvious, the sexual process gives rise to a progeny, which is the fruit of the unity of *one sex with another,* a unity of two in difference. What is more, in the hierarchy of organisms, going from simple to more complex, this unity-of-two at the origin of new individuals becomes progressively more a unity of two. As for the two,[9] sexual difference at the lowest end of life is found within the same individual (as in the case of monoecious, hermaphroditic organisms). In higher forms of life however, it occurs *between* two distinct (dioecious) individuals with different reproductive organs, activities, and contributions, in which case, sexual difference becomes a full-fledged relation to an outside, to another. As for unity, reproduction in sexual

6 Hans Urs von Balthasar, *Theo-Drama, Theological Dramatic Theory,* vol. II: *The Dramatis Personae: Man in God,* trans. Graham Harrison (San Francisco: Ignatius Press, 1990), 369.

7 See von Balthasar, *Theo-Drama Vol. II*, 374–376. Von Balthasar traces the history of thought on the reciprocity of generation and death, including the Patristic discussion about sex in Paradise. See also Von Balthasar's *The Christian State of Life*, trans. M. F. McCarthy (San Francisco: Ignatius Press, 1983), 92–103. Von Balthasar himself does not simply tie sexuality to death, as many of the Greek Fathers did, but holds it to be profoundly marked by death, and so agrees with the underlying point of the Greek Fathers, namely that in the original state, virginity and procreation would have been united, as it is in Mary. See von Balthasar, *The Christian State of Life,* 102–103.

8 There is also parthenogenesis, which is sexual in the sense that there is a "female' organism with female organs that produces eggs that duplicate their own genetic material.

9 Etymologically, the word "sex" is of uncertain origin, but is thought to be connected to the Latin *seco-, secare,* meaning "to cut," or "to divide," from which we get the English words "section," "segment," "intersect," among others. See "Sex (n)" in *The Online Etymology Dictionary* at http://www.etymonline.com. For its part, *secare* has its root in the Proto-Indo-European *sek,* which gives rise to the English *scythe, saw, sickle* and *sword,* see http://realenglishschool.eu/en/res-blog/latin-roots-5-seco-secare-secui-sectum-to-cut-2.

beings at the lowest levels of life occurs generally outside the body, involving the least amount of parental unity and care of progeny; whereas at the highest levels of life, reproduction takes place inside the body, involving the highest degree of parental unity and care and education of progeny, well beyond birth, where the inside is even extended to a home where children are educated within the community of their parents.[10]

At the beginning of her famous tome, Simone de Beauvoir noted this direct relation between higher organisms and their relation to and dependence on the outside, be it between the sexes (the two parents) or be it between the generations (the parents and their progeny). The implications for the female, she considered, are most problematic: "the more the female becomes a separate individual, the more imperiously the living continuity is affirmed beyond any separation. The fish or the bird that expels the virgin ovum or the fertilized egg is less prey to its offspring than the female mammal."[11] As for the human female, "[S]he is the most deeply alienated of all the female mammals, and she is the one that refuses this alienation the most violently; in no other is the subordination of the organism to the reproductive function more imperious nor accepted with greater difficulty . . . [H]er destiny appears even more fraught the more she rebels against it by affirming herself as an individual." [12]

The alternative to this way of interpreting the phenomenon is to look at it positively, as did Hans Jonas who noted the "dialectical" nature of organisms in their the ascent up the ladder of organic life, namely that as their relation to the "outside" increases progressively so does their individuality or "in-itselfness."[13] When we get finally to the human being, this coincidence of extremes—extreme relation to the outside and extreme individuality—is manifest in the person, who

10 See the metaphysical discussion of this movement in organic being as it concerns the question of the relation between the universal (species) and the particular in D. C. Schindler, "Perfect Difference: Gender and the Analogy of Being," *Communio: International Catholic Review* 43 (Summer 2016): 212–215.

11 Simone de Beauvoir, *The Second Sex,* trans. Constance Borde and Sheila Malovany-Chevallier (New York: Vintage Books, 2011), 36.

12 De Beauvoir, *The Second Sex,* 44. In her first chapter, "Biological Data," de Beauvoir concludes that the human female, compared to all other females in the animal world, is the one most absorbed by maternity since no other progeny takes longer to stand on its own two feet than the human child. Indeed, the human female body is the most problematic for de Beauvoir because the demands that the human child makes on its mother are altogether at odds with the fact that she belongs to the species at the top of a chain in which individual members have acquired *the most* individuality, being the least subordinated to species (31, 34). For de Beauvoir, since maternity has "no individual benefit to the woman," (42) the human female, *at the biological level itself,* long before the effects of social influence, is a contradiction in terms (21–48).

13 Hans Jonas, *The Phenomenon of Life* (New York: Dell Publishing Co., 2001), 99–107. In his examination of metabolism and the move from plant to animal life, Jonas refers to the "double-edged sword" dialectic between increasing "self-hood" (or individualization)—marked by greater perception, locomotion, and emotion—and greater dependence on (and exposure to) the environment. We could also add to the side of greater individuality: quicker messages from the senses to the brain, more memory, more ability to learn and change behavior. See also Susan Waldstein, "Reading Natural Hierarchy in a Trinitarian Key," *Communio: International Catholic Review* 42 (Winter 2015): 652–692 and her "Sexual Reproduction is not a Cosmic Accident," *Humanum* 2016, no. 4 (2016), at http://humanumreview.com/articles/convergent-evolution-and-the-theology-of-the-body.

is at once a "someone," unique or "incommunicable" (beyond just being an individual of the species), and deeply situated within a field of relations, having both a proper name and a family name.[14] Indeed, at this point, human beings do not simply replace their forebears. (And they too will not be replaced.) Death is not natural for them.[15] It is dramatic. They mourn their dead and "keep them alive" through the memory of inter-generational bonds, even going so far as to hope to see them one day "in the flesh."[16] In sum, at the height of sexual life, we find that *being engendered* means: (1) we owe ourselves to a unity of the most extreme kind; (2) that our unity with that unity is of the most extreme kind; (3) and finally, that both unities are unities in difference of the most extreme kind. They are communities of *persons* where the members are the most distinct as individuals and the most deeply united with the other members. This is especially as the "horizontal" communion opens up vertically, and becomes an ultimate reality, within the community of the saints, where our finitude is taken up into Infinitude.[17]

"Gender"

Today's "gender" calls into question (or "troubles"), the most basic fact of our being, the fact of our being born. The very term itself is set up alongside the term "sex" to suggest that it is something else—thus, hiding or neutralizing the latter, and with it, the whole inheritance we receive by virtue of it. We should not be distracted by rare disorders of the genetic or hormonal kind, originating at some point *in utero*,[18] or by psychosomatic disorders such as "dysphoria" or

14 See Robert Spaemann, *Persons: The Difference between 'Someone' and 'Something'* (Oxford: Oxford University Press, 2006), 67–69; 184–186.

15 Wis 1:13 says "God did not make death" (*The New American Bible*).

16 Jb 19:26.

17 See Cardinal Joseph Ratzinger's discussion of the novelty of the Biblical God, who, precisely *as* a "Thou," inviting man into a communion, makes of the human person an ultimate reality, not that is a penultimate one, on the way to an undifferentiated unity. See *Truth and Tolerance*, trans. H. Taylor (San Francisco: Ignatius Press, 2004), 34. Indeed, as Spaemann says, the very idea of the "person" owes itself to Christianity: "Without Christian theology we would have had no name for what we now call 'persons'. . . . That is not to say that we can only speak intelligibly of persons on explicitly theological suppositions, though it is conceivable that the disappearance of the theological dimension of the idea could in the long run bring about the disappearance of the idea itself," *Persons*, 17–18. On this point, von Balthasar contrasts the novelty with the ancients: "For Heraclitus, the divine was 'that which rests still in change,' at once embracing and transcending the contrary pairs. Plotinus perfects this by removing the 'One' which knows no opposite term above the 'spirit' that has its life in the tension between thinking and being thought, between loving and being loved, between 'I' and 'Thou.' The 'One,' source of all love and insight, cannot itself be a loving 'Thou.' A final point is the necessary consequence of this: thirdly, the divine absolute, which cannot cease to be the object and the goal of all of man's religious striving, disappears into the realm of that which cannot be uttered, that which lacks a 'Thou': it is that which is loved, that to which all goodness must be attributed, but since it remains severed impersonally from all dialogue between 'I' and 'Thou,' it can be attained only by the one who leaves his personal being as a limitation behind him and penetrates through to that which is devoid of contraries." Hans Urs von Balthasar, *Explorations in Theology*, III: *Creator Spirit* (San Francisco: Ignatius Press, 1993), 26.

18 We refer to physiological conditions of hermaphroditism (now called "intersex") resulting from chromosomal and/or hormonal (Turner's Syndrome, Klinefelter's Syndrome, Androgen Insensitivity Syndrome)

"autogynephilia."[19] These are neither undramatic nor unimportant. The point is that gender in its current usage does not ultimately require any of this, even if it makes use of it for purposes of public argument and persuasion, especially in the Catholic world so used is it to the "natural law arguments" about "the way one is born." The idea of gender means to release us precisely from *the way we are born*.[20] "Gender" is the attempt to eliminate any *pre-existing ground* to open up the way for our own *re-conception*.[21] Judith Butler, who is on the avant-guard of all of this, insists on this point when she rejects all metaphysical nouns—being, substance, subject, and sex—even the popular "gender identity," things we might call "givens." Gender, for her is a verb, or "performance," which makes all of these. She is quite consciously translating, at the level of sex, Nietzsche's claim that "there is no 'being' behind doing, effecting, becoming . . . the deed is everything."[22] "Gender" is this groundless deed "performed" on ourselves, a sort of creation *ex nihilo*. It is the ultimate expression of modernity's stalemate between "nature" and "person," where person means pure indeterminacy (pure will) standing over and against nature.[23] Pope Benedict XVI spoke to this essential core of today's gender:

---

or from abnormal prenatal conditions (progesterone effect). For a description of these states, see R. J. Stoller, *Presentations of Gender* (New Haven: Yale University Press, 1985), 22–23 and John Money and Anke E. Erhardt, *Man & Woman, Boy & Girl* (Baltimore: Johns Hopkins University Press, 1972). We note, here, however, that both Money and Stoller refer to these as *disorders*. See Stoller, *Presentations of Gender*, 18–24.

19 In addition to the cases of infants born with ambiguous genitalia, Paul R. McHugh discusses the cases of "dysphoria" in adult men as a result of either guilt over their homosexuality or on account of being more sexually aroused *"being"* the sex to which they were attracted (autogynephilia). He refers to the research of psychiatrist and psychoanalyst John Meyer who found that most men who had undergone some kind of surgical sex alteration as a solution to various emotional difficulties found themselves in the same difficulties as before. See McHugh, "Surgical Sex: Why We Stopped Doing Sex Change Operations," *First Things* (November 2004), http://www.firstthings.com/article/2004/11/surgical-sex.

20 Note, for example, in "bathroom-gate" how little it mattered that persons choosing the bathroom for the opposite sex need provide any physiological or other serious reason other than an "inner sense." See the "Dear Colleague Letter on Transgender Students" issued jointly by the US Department of Justice and US Department of Education (Friday, May 13, 2016), at https://www2.ed.gov/about/offices/list/ocr/letters/colleague-201605-title-ix-transgender.pdf.

21 M. L. Di Pietro describes the goal of "gender" theory thus: "a human nature completely artificial, open to mutations, combinations, manipulations," in "Identità sessuata e genere," *Anthropotes*, 20, no. 1 (2004): 83–105, cited at 98.

22 Judith Butler, *Gender Trouble* (New York: Routledge, 1990), 95.

23 See Robert Spaemann who speaks of the "stalemate" between the modern "utopian" conception of "person" as pure indeterminate freedom and its deterministic conception of "nature," Spaemann, "Human Nature," in *Essays in Anthropology: Variations on a Theme* (Eugene: Cascade Books, 2010), 2–8. Looking at modern political theory, Leo Strauss's comment on the "war of all against all" having as its target nature itself is striking: "Man can guarantee the actualization of wisdom, since wisdom is identical with free construction. But wisdom cannot be free construction if the universe is intelligible. Man can guarantee the actualization of wisdom, not in spite of, but because of, the fact that the universe is unintelligible. *Man can be sovereign only because there is no cosmic support for his humanity*. He can be sovereign only because he is absolutely a stranger in the universe. He can be sovereign only because he is forced to be sovereign. Since the universe is unintelligible and since control of nature does not require understanding of nature, there are no knowable limits to his conquest of nature" (italics added). Leo Strauss, *Natural Right and History* (Chicago: University of Chicago Press, 1950), 174–175.

> Man and woman as created realities, as the nature of the human being, no longer exist. Man calls his nature into question. From now on he is merely spirit and will. The manipulation of nature, which we deplore today where our environment is concerned, now becomes man's fundamental choice where he himself is concerned. From now on there is only the abstract human being, who chooses for himself what his nature is to be.[24]

The idea of gender underwent a long incubation period well before it was introduced into the current lexicon with its new definition. It can be traced back to early feminism, then followed through its various waves (equality, radical, post-modern) and alongside the homosexual movement.[25] Gender makes much use of the nature-culture (nurture) distinction which had become a dualism in modernity (along with that between nature and person) such that any evidence of development through upbringing and education became proof of something simply imposed on a nature which, for its part, had lost its (teleological) relation to the "outside" (to parents, educators, the other sex).[26] More to the point, the alleged "imposition" is taken to be the fruit of a nefarious scheme of subjection. This extrinsic and adversarial relation between nature and culture (nurture/education) ran throughout the first real feminist manifesto, written by John Stuart Mill, *On the Subjection of Women*,[27] and it remained in constant play throughout the course of feminism and its eventual gender theory.

It is interesting to note how vehement is the insistence about "gender" as a "social construct," especially in the face of all of the bodily evidence to the contrary, including that provided by Simone de Beauvoir herself.[28] One of the more radical followers of de Beauvoir wrote: "Patriarchy is so powerful, that

24 Pope Benedict XVI, *Address of His Holiness Benedict XVI on the Occasion of Christmas Greetings to the Roman Curia* (December 21, 2012), http://w2.vatican.va/content/benedict-xvi/en/speeches/2012/december.index.html.

25 As Marguerite Peeters notes: "[G]ender historically has a double origin. And today it has a double application: radical feminist and homosexual. These two interpretations are un-separable. Their common element is to consider the male and female identity, the complementarity between man and woman, the nuptial vocation of the human person, marriage between a man and a woman, the family founded on marriage, paternity and maternity, the educative vocation of the father and the mother, childhood, as many social constructions contrary to equality and civil liberty and discriminatory, in particular for women and homosexuals." Peeters, "Tre miti da smascherare," *L'Osservatore Romano* (March 3–4, 2014): 5.

26 See especially Robert Spaemann's essay, "Nature," in *A Robert Spaemann Reader: Philosophical Essays on Nature, God, and the Human Person*, trans. D. C. Schindler (Oxford: Oxford University Press, 2015), 22–29.

27 J. S. Mill's *Subjection of Women*, https://www.earlymoderntexts.com/assets/pdfs/mill1869.pdf. Mill makes it all but impossible to access the nature of a woman, on account of the fact that it is so entangled with the fruits of education, which keep nature in an "unnatural state" (33). One would need, says Mill, to "subtract" whatever *could* be attributed to education in order to do so (13, 40).

28 Notwithstanding the fact that the central thesis of de Beauvoir's *Second Sex* is that "gender," in her case, *woman*, is an imposition of the Hegelian master-slave dialectic on the body, she signals a deep malaise about the body itself and in particular, the female one. See her first "Biological Data," *Second Sex*, 23–27. See also Schindler, "Perfect Difference: Gender and the Analogy of Being."

it has a successful habit of passing itself off as nature."[29] But Butler is the most vehement in her insistence that "there is no 'there' there," when she claims that the very appearance of a given nature (even the "alleged" underlying "sex" earlier feminists had taken for granted) is itself the effect ("construct") of a "discourse" [30] which is so clever that it makes the "alleged" nature *look* original, while really behind it lurks something more original, namely, power or "gender border control."[31] The argument for gender (even sex) as a mere social construct (or "effect") has thus been thoroughly inoculated against any contrary evidence.

In sum, gender exists to hide any trace of a reality lying underneath it. Now the path is clear so that *we* can do the constructing ourselves. As Benedict XVI said:

> [T]he famous saying of Simone de Beauvoir: "one is not born a woman, one becomes so" . . . lay[s] the foundation for what is put forward today under the term "gender" as a new philosophy of sexuality. According to this philosophy, sex is no longer a given element of nature that man has to accept and personally make sense of: it is a social role that we choose for ourselves, while in the past it was chosen for us by society . . . hitherto society did this, now we decide for ourselves.[32]

Even more, though, gender's hiding is a resistance to the reality it hides. Specifically, it resists the three relations implied in the etymology of the very word it takes for itself. Historically, the idea of gender as a social construct was aimed at feminism's dominant concern—then and always—the problem of the child for the woman whose unique part in the labor of having a child (conceiving,

29 Kate Millet, *Sexual Politics* (New York: Doubleday, 1970; reprint, First Illinois Paperback, 2000), 58.

30 Butler writes: "[T]he body is not 'sexed' in any significant sense prior to its determination within a discourse through which it becomes invested with an 'idea' of natural or essential sex. The body gains meaning within discourse only in the context of power relations. Sexuality is an historically specific organization of power, of discourse, of bodies and of affectivity. As such, sexuality is understood by Foucault to produce 'sex' as an artificial concept which effectively extends and disguises the power relations responsible for its genesis." Butler, *Gender Trouble*, 92. Also, "If it is possible to speak of a 'man' with a masculine attribute and to understand that attribute as a happy but accidental feature of that man, then it is also possible to speak of a 'man' with a feminine attribute, whatever that is, but still to maintain the integrity of the gender. But once we dispense with the priority of 'man' and 'woman' as abiding substances, then it is no longer possible to subordinate dissonant gendered features as so many secondary and accidental characteristics of a gender ontology that is fundamentally intact. If the notion of an abiding substance is a fictive construction produced through the compulsory ordering of attributes into coherent gender sequences, then it seems that gender as substance, the viability of *man* and *woman* as nouns, is called into question by the dissonant play of attributes that fail to conform to sequential or causal models of intelligibility," 24.

31 Butler, *Gender Trouble*, 136. Butler also writes: "A political genealogy of gender ontologies, if it successful, will deconstruct the substantive appearance of gender into its constitutive acts and locate and account for those acts within the compulsory frames set by the various forces that police the social appearance of gender," 33.

32 Pope Benedict XVI, *Christmas Address to the Roman Curia* (December 21, 2012).

bearing, birthing, nursing) and raising it was, and still is, considered to be at odds with her humanity and an obstacle to her equality with men who, being less involved concretely in the having and raising of the child have been able to pursue distinctly human interests (such as art, literature, and philosophy), single-mindedly, often in a "room of their own," free from the toil and distraction of the day-to-day care of children, hearth, and home.[33] The woman, said de Beauvoir, is in the "servitude of maternity,"[34] which in itself is already "alienating" and "of no benefit to the woman."[35] What is worse, though, is that this state of affairs puts her in a state of deep dependence on the father of her children who, for his part, is complicit in the grand scheme of alienating the woman, as *his* "other," along the model of Hegel's master-slave dialectic.[36] For de Beauvoir (and her followers), just as the two "servitudes" went hand-in-hand, so too did her independence from the child require her independence from the man.[37] Resisting the one meaning (maternity) meant resisting the other meaning (unity with the man), since as we noted before, it is at the highest point on the ladder of organic life that the relation to one's progeny implies the highest degree of unity in difference between the parents. And in the history that developed, this putting into question of that meaning took the form of either making the sexes interchangeable (as in equality feminism[38]) or setting them apart from one another (post-modern "difference feminism"[39]), or finally, turning them in a different orientation altogether (post-modern multiple difference feminism[40]). In sum, gender frees the mother from her child, and then the woman from the man,

33 Clearly, only one class is in view, here. See J. S. Mill, *On the Subjection of Women* ("Women in the Arts and Sciences"), 40–45; C. P. Gilman, *Women and Economics* (Boston: Small, Maynard & Co., 1898); de Beauvoir, *The Second Sex*, 735–751; Luce Irigaray, *I Love to You* (New York: Routledge, 1996), 20–23; Elisabeth Badinter, *The Conflict: How Modern Motherhood Undermines the Status of Women* (New York: Metropolitan Books, 2012); Sheryl Sandberg, *Lean In: Women, Work, and the Will to Lead* (New York: Alfred A. Knopf, 2013). See G. K. Chesterton who offered an alternative (positive) interpretation of the single-minded focus (of men) and the "being everything" (of women) in "The Emancipation of Domesticity," in *What's Wrong with the World* (San Francisco: Ignatius Press, 2010), 91–95.

34 De Beauvoir, *The Second Sex*, 35.

35 De Beauvoir writes: "Woman experiences an even stronger alienation when the fertilized egg drops into the uterus and develops there; gestation is, of course, a normal phenomenon that is not harmful to the mother if normal conditions of health and nutrition prevail: certain beneficial interactions develop between her and the fetus; however, contrary to an optimistic theory that is so obviously useful socially, gestation is tiring work that offers woman no benefit as an individual," *The Second Sex*, 42.

36 De Beauvoir, *The Second Sex*, 159–167.

37 See de Beauvoir's discussion of abortion and contraception in *The Second Sex*, 524–570, and the "independent woman," 721–751.

38 See for example: de Beauvoir, *The Second Sex*; Kate Millett, *Sexual Politics* (New York: Avon Books, 1969); and Betty Friedan, *The Feminine Mystique* (New York: Dell Publishing Co., 1963).

39 Luce Irigaray is most representative of "difference feminism." See Irigaray, "Equal or Different," in *The Irigaray Reader*, ed. Margaret Whiteford (Oxford: Blackwell Publishers, 1991), 30–33; "Sexual Difference," *The Irigaray* Reader, 165–177; "*An Ethics of Sexual Difference*, trans. C. Burke and G. C. Gill (Ithaca: Cornell University Press, 1993); *I Love to You* (New York: Routledge, 2006); and Elizabeth Grosz, *Space, Time, and Perversion* (New York: Routledge, 1995), 45–57.

40 Judith Butler, "Bodies that Matter," in *Engaging with Irigaray* (New York: Columbia University Press, 1994), 141–173.

since the one thing they cannot have without the other has been jettisoned and made them no longer indispensable to each other.[41]

Now that the two meanings have been separated, the two relations can be resisted in another form. It should come as no surprise that gender brings back the child on new grounds (since there still have to be children for the reproduction of society). Gender is a close ally with artificial reproductive technology, which makes sex no longer indispensable for having children, not only in the sense that it replaces the sexual act, but also in the sense that it tends ever more towards the elimination of the *sexes* altogether, be it through cloning or the coaxing of gametes out of stem cells.[42] ARTs give future parents mastery over their reproductive limits, its timing, its heteronormativity, not to mention its lack of control over results.[43] But they also "free" future children from the burden of being born. Politically speaking, they provide society the "cell" for which it has been waiting[44] new forms of kinship,[45] ones established on the basis of choice

41 We refer, of course, to the conception of a child, the long pregnancy, and nursing of the child (all of which falls to the mother). But we could also add to that first "division of labor" the manner in which that plays itself out postpartum. See Claude Levi-Strauss who observes the universal practice of some sort of division of labor between man and woman, even when not *necessary* (as in the case of conception, birth, and nursing) concluding it has no other purpose than to perpetuate their being *necessary to each other.* Levi-Strauss, "The Family," in *Man, Culture and Society*, ed. H. Shapiro (London: Oxford University Press, 1956), 261–295.

42 See Aldous Huxley, *Brave New World* (New York: Harper and Row Publishers, 1932), 1–3; reference comes from the 5th ed., 1965. Simone de Beauvoir indicated a certain preference for this when in the very chapter describing the *hierarchy* of organisms at the top of which there is the most amount of individuality and the most amount of sexual differentiation and collaboration, insists: "these notions of superiority of one system over another [gonochorism vs. hermaphroditism] involve highly contestable theories concerning evolution. All that can be affirmed with certainty is that these two means of reproduction coexist in nature, that they both perpetuate species, and that the heterogeneity of both gametes and gonad-producing organisms seems to be accidental. The differentiation of individuals into males and females thus occurs as an irreducible and contingent fact," *The Second Sex,* 23.

43 On modernity's usurpation of fruitfulness, see Fabrice Hadjadj, "Rediscovering the Language of Wood," *Humanum* 2015, no. 4 (2015), at http://www.humanumreview.com/articles/rediscovering-the-language-of-wood-why-cant-we-just-substitute-be-fruitful-and-multiply-with-connect-and-download.

44 Speaking to the role of the family in the "reproduction of society," John Rawls writes: "The family is part of the basic structure, the reason being that one of its essential roles is to establish the orderly production and reproduction of society and of its culture from one generation to the next. . . . Reproductive labor is socially necessary." Rawls, *Justice as Fairness: A Restatement* (Cambridge, Mass.: Harvard University Press, 2001), 162. That said, given that the "reproduction of culture" involves not only having children but "ensuring [their] moral development and education into the wider culture . . . [giving them] . . . a sense of justice and the political virtues that support just political and social institutions" (162), and given that "no particular form of the family (monogamous, heterosexual, or otherwise) is so far required by a political conception of justice so long as it is arranged to fulfill these tasks effectively and does not run afoul of other political values," (163), it is hard to imagine that ARTs would not be, indeed, the preferred manner of "reproducing" the kind of (liberal) society Rawls speaks, since they overcome many of the natural family's threats to it, as Rawls see it (166).

45 Though wary of allying new gender "performances" to marriage and family (with the so-called "gay marriage" movement) because it would be "foreclosing the sexual field," leaving out other "minorities" (non-monogamous, etc.), Butler still heralds the legalization of gay marriage and the right to adoption and assisted reproductive technology by gay couples, because these provide a challenge to heterosexuality and its structure of kinship (and culture) established on the basis of carnal bonds. See her *Undoing Gender* (New York: Routledge, 2004), 11, 26, 102–130, esp. 124–127.

and emancipated from "operations of power," however counterintuitive it may be to think of "emancipation" for children who are "deliberately constructed,"[46] *made,* that is, *not begotten.*[47]

This is what gender does for us. It sunders woman from child, man from woman, then child from mother and father. That was chillingly prophesied decades ago, by the Marxist feminist, Shulamith Firestone, when she wrote:

> [[J]ust as to assure elimination of economic classes requires the revolt of the underclass (the proletariat) and . . . their seizure of the means of *production,* so] to assure the elimination of sexual classes requires the revolt of the underclass (women) and the seizure of control of *reproduction*: not only the full restoration to women of ownership of their own bodies, but also their (temporary) seizure of control of human fertility—the new population biology as well as all the social institutions of child-bearing and child-rearing. [And just as the end goal of socialist revolution was not only the elimination of the economic class *privilege* but of the economic class *distinction* itself, so] the end goal of feminist revolution must be, unlike that of the first feminist movement, not just the elimination of male *privilege* but of the sex *distinction* itself: genital differences between human beings would no longer matter culturally. . . . The reproduction of the species by one sex for the benefit of both would be replaced by (at least the option of) artificial reproduction: children would be born to both sexes equally, or independently of either, however one chooses to look at it; the dependence of the child on the mother (and vice versa) would give way to a greatly shortened dependence on a small group of others in general and any remaining inferiority to adults in physical strength would be compensated for culturally. [The division of labor would be ended by the elimination of labor altogether (through cybernetics).] The tyranny of the biological family would be broken.[48]

From woman with child, to woman with man, to child with parents, "gender" goes full circle.

Let us note something about the character of "gender's" resistance to the three relations belonging to sexual difference. The resistance does not consist in making them altogether disappear. To the contrary, it makes them very apparent. Indeed, they are all appearance and no substance. This is clear in the extravagant use that gender makes of the leftover packaging, everything that is actually

46 Anthony Giddens, *Modernity and Self-Identity: Self and Society in the Late Modern Age* (Stanford: Stanford University Press, 1991), 220.

47 Apropos of the logic of dominion associated with ARTs, Spaemann observes: "The future is the result of that which future human beings make of what was given to them. To want to have this, too, in our grasp, that is, to want to replace upbringing with breeding . . . would destroy what binds us to our children: the shared naturalness of our genesis," Spaemann, "Begotten not Made," *Communio: International Catholic Review* 2 (Summer 2006): 292.

48 Shulamith Firestone, *The Dialectic of Sex* (New York: William Morrow and Company, Inc., 1970), 11.

*in*essential to sexual difference, even if not immaterial: the much-maligned "stereotypes" such as preference for lipstick, maxi-skirts, and the like, which now, detached as they are from the essence of sexual difference, really are stereotypes. Men, of course, have worn "skirts" in the past, and currently in other cultures, and put on "make-up," before going into battle. But now a man declares himself to be a "woman" precisely on account of such things, regardless of the fact that he is, in principle, able to do the kinds of things with a woman that would make him a father and so, also, regardless of the fact that he cannot in principle do the things that would make him a mother. Let us note too that the reason gender resists what is essential to sexual difference is that being born of a mother and father, being capable of a "one flesh" union with the opposite sex, and being capable, thereby, of begetting children binds us to each other in a given order of things, *prior to our choosing*, (though of course, in the exercise of the latter two relations our consent is necessary). But, again, the relations are not simply put away; they are brought back in, and on new terms. First, they are vehemently declared *not* to be natural, or "prior" (against all appearances). Indeed, they have been banished from the (not so) newly invented "state of nature." Then they are declared to be mere "choices," or "options" available to the indeterminate will; and they are, thus, under its control and management in their new contractual form.[49] Having a child is a mere "choice," with a built-in "returns policy" in the event that the promises are not delivered in a satisfactory way. Unions are merely "voluntary."[50] Even the child's relation to his parents is reconceived, along contractual lines, he, being a "putative adult" with whom the parents are "in negotiation."[51] And of course, our own relation to our very selves, our gender, is a renegotiable choice. It may well be that the majority of people still happen to choose according to the "alleged" evidence of their bodies. They may still get married to the opposite sex, conceive their children the "old fashioned way," and identify themselves as the "gender" that happens to line up with the way their

49 D. C. Schindler shows Locke's subversion of the natural familial relations in his re-description of them as essentially contractual in *Freedom from Reality: The Diabolical Character of Modern Liberty* (Notre Dame, Ind.: University of Notre Dame Press, 2017), 182–185.

50 Jay Fliegelman notes the enthusiasm of early Americans about marriage for the express reason that, in contrast to the paternal-filial bond, it was a *voluntary* (contractual) union. See Fliegelman, *Prodigals and Pilgrims: The American Revolution Against Patriarchal Authority, 1750–1800* (Cambridge: Cambridge University Press, 1982), 123–153.

51 The contemporary English sociologist, Anthony Giddens, who considered the family to be the avant-garde of the project of democratization, says the following about the new conception of the parent-child relation: "Can a relationship between a parent and young child be democratic? It can, and should be, in exactly the same sense as is true of a democratic political order. It is a right of the child, in other words, to be treated as a putative equal of the adult. Actions which cannot be negotiated directly with a child, because he or she is too young to grasp what is entailed, should be capable of counterfactual justification. The presumption is that agreement could be reached, and trust sustained, if the child were sufficiently autonomous to be able to deploy arguments on an equal basis to the adult." Anthony Giddens, *Transformation of Intimacy: Sexuality, Love, and Eroticism in Modern Societies* (Cambridge, UK: Polity Press, 1992), 191–192. See also Fliegelman, who discusses the early American sources for this rethinking of the nature of the child-parent relation, *Prodigals and Pilgrims*, 9–35.

bodies were originally configured ("cis-gender"); but the key is that they do these things, not because they are consenting to some prior arrangement, to a given order of things, but simply because they have *chosen* it. Nevertheless, the more emphatically the newly chosen relation contravenes the original form, substituting it with another option—intentional childlessness, homosexual practice, or the manufacture of children—the more it demonstrates successful resistance to the idea that we are constituted, *prior to our choice,* in the three relations. This is why the old aberration will be the new norm,[52] and the old norm will become ever more suspect, the stubborn resistance of reality to our free resistance. It is in this precise sense of resistance that gender can be said to be diabolical in the deepest sense as that which separates (διαβάλλω) things that belong together, and then reunites them, transformed, and on its own terms.[53] We can see how much the forced separation of inseparable things necessarily changes those things. They stand and fall together.

Why do we do this? We have already hinted at the reason. To be in a *given order,* which places us in a *prior* relation to *another* strikes us a *negative, confining.*[54] In being born, we arrive on the scene caught up in a set of arrangements we did not "sign up for." We find ourselves already facing a certain direction, standing as we do at a "gender-border control." And our futures are not simply in our hands, or dreams. Turning to the "inseparable meanings," it is clear how demanding fruitfulness is on the unity between the sexes. As we said, it entails a unity of the greatest kind where the division of labor between the sexes make them necessary to each other, and not only in the very beginning, in the conception of the child, but well beyond birth (given the child's extended period of dependence on his parents). And it is clear how demanding the unity of the sexes is on fruitfulness, both for the parents (the fruit bearers) who are not in control of the future, the kind of child they will have, or not, and for the children (the fruit) who cannot think of themselves as fashioned out of their own

52 It is clear that with the passing of legislation making "same-sex marriage" legal, that such unions must set new terms for what marriage is—for what qualifies as a "spouse" and as a mother or father, in order to be included under the term "marriage." Instead of being a newly discovered species under the old genus, it becomes the genus. Naomi Wolf had already looked forward to this when she said: "We need a heterosexual vision of the marriage that gay and lesbian activists are seeking: a commitment untainted by centuries of inequality; a ritual that invites the community to rejoice in the making of a new, freely chosen family," Wolf, "Radical Heterosexuality . . . or How to Love a Man and Save Your Feminist Soul," in *Transforming a Rape Culture,* ed. E. Buchwald, P. R. Fletcher, and M. Roth (Minneapolis: Milkweed Editions, 1993), 361.

53 I am indebted here to David C. Schindler for his discussion of the character of the "diabolical" in his treatment of the modern conception of liberty. See his *Freedom from Reality,* 151–192.

54 Pierre Manent notes that in the modern "state of nature" the "natural" is "not the independent individual as such, it is the war of all against all that gives him birth. In other words, the individual exists only through a kind of negative sociability, that of war," Manent, *Intellectual History of Liberalism,* trans. R. Balinski (Princeton: Princeton University Press, 1994), 40. Also, concerning the "diabolical" character of modern freedom, Schindler notes that the priority of the given is negated on the grounds of the perceived antagonism, which is then perpetuated either through mutual exclusion or respectful indifference. See Schindler, *Freedom from Reality,* 160–161.

ribs, heirs to nothing.[55] We think of these aspects of the given order as negative, because they are limitations on our freedom of movement, or worse, "operations of power,"[56] and therefore fundamentally "unsafe," not, that is, only because of the occasional, even frequent, abuse, but by definition. They are the fronts of the "war of all against all." We may avoid the "war" altogether, as some feminist "pacifists" have urged us to do when they say that sex is by definition "rape."[57] We may turn in another orientation altogether, turning our backs on that war. Or, we may enter the fray and simply "stay protected," containing the war by observing by the "rules of engagement."[58] In any event, even where there is no apparent antagonism in the three relations, the antagonism is assumed. This is why they have been banished from the "state of nature," and brought back in on "safer," contractual, ground.[59]

Essentially, this perception of antagonism is tied to the dominant conception of freedom, according to which freedom is no longer in a *prior* relation to the objective good, by way of the desire for happiness prior, that is, to any deliberation or action (even if, at the normative level, we accept the need for practical limits on that freedom).[60] We have already noted how this came to expression in the person-nature stalemate where the person, now a pure, undetermined will, stands over and against (or indifferently to) his nature.[61] To this, we could add that the person, instead of being defined by relation in which that same nature catches him up, stands over and against (or indifferently to) it. With an eye to that dimension, Joseph Ratzinger wrote, "[T]he radical demand for freedom, which has proved itself more and more clearly to be the outcome of the historical course of the Enlightenment . . . and which today largely shapes the public mentality, *prefers to have neither a whence nor a whither, to be neither from*

55 We note the last of Nietzsche's three metamorphoses of the spirit: the "child" who "starts over," the first being the camel that kneels down to receives the load of tradition (and its values, beliefs, imperatives), and the second being the lion that roars and laughs at the inheritance, casting it off. See "Thus Spoke Zarathustra: A Book for All and None," in *The Portable Nietzsche*, ed. and trans. Walter Kaufmann (New York: Penguin Books, 1976), 137–139.

56 Michel Foucault, *The History of Sexuality, vol. 1: An Introduction*, trans. R. Hurley (New York: Pantheon Books, 1978), 135–157.

57 This is the thesis of Andrea Dworkin in "I Want a Twenty-Four Hour Truce During Which there is No Rape," in *Transforming a Rape Culture*, ed. Buchwald, et al., 11–22.

58 For feminists who have not declared sex to be "rape" by definition (see note 57, above), there is much talk about educating women in the rules of consent. See for example, Melanie Ann Beres, "Rethinking the Concept of Consent for Anti-sexual Violence Activism and Education," *Feminism & Psychology* 24 (June 2014): 373–389.

59 On this point, Schindler writes: "although Locke insists on a clear difference between the state of nature and the state of war, the latter not only turns out to reveal the *inner truth* of the former, but it is also the indispensable cause of political community," where the "antagonism is not overcome . . . but simply driven underground," *Freedom from Reality*, 183.

60 See Schindler's discussion of Locke's "re-conception" of freedom through his re-definition of the good, which is now deprived of objectivity and content, and made a mere function of pleasure, *Freedom from Reality*, 13–62.

61 See note 23, above.

nor for, but to be wholly at liberty."[62] It is hard not to see how much freedom so conceived is at odds with the older understanding and especially at odds with the relations that betoken it. Ratzinger continues:

> The child in the mother's womb is the very example which brings out the basic figure of human freedom and makes clear what is typically human about it. . . . The being of another person is so closely interwoven with the being of this person . . . to be oneself in this way is to be radically from and through another. Conversely, this being-with compels the being of the other—that is, the mother—to become a being-for, which contradicts her own desire to be an independent self and is thus experienced as the antithesis of her own freedom. [We must now add that even once the child is born and the outer form of its being-from and—with changes, it remains just as dependent on, and at the mercy of, a being-for...] The child in the mother's womb is simply a very graphic depiction of the essence of human existence in general.[63]

It is clear that the dominant conception of freedom cannot coexist easily with the reality that betokened the older conception of freedom.

> [The radical demand for freedom] regards what is actually the fundamental figure of human existence itself as an attack on freedom which assails it before any individual has a chance to live and act. The radical cry for freedom demands man's liberation from his very essence as man. . . . In the new society, the dependencies which restrict the I and the necessity of self-giving would no longer have the right to exist.[64]

Wariness about the relations in which "the fundamental figure of human existence" is caught up is understandable. We do abuse each other. And we always have, as the ancient myths attest, filled as they are with brutal fathers, devouring mothers, patricidal sons, and fratricidal brothers. But what is new here is that we have made this abuse the first, last, and most definitive word about our relations to each other. They are by definition "unsafe." It is not good to be together: a son, a daughter, a man, a woman, a mother, a father. Returning to the "diabolical," we could say that this factor goes to the heart of the first temptation as it is described by Genesis, where the Tempter cast doubt on the goodness of God by distorting the details of the divine command, exaggerating it to include the abundance already at hand: "did He say not to eat of *any* of the trees?" (Gn 3:1). John Paul II put it this way:

62 Joseph Cardinal Ratzinger, "Truth and Freedom," *Communio: International Catholic Review* 23 (Spring 1996): 27–28, emphasis added.

63 Ratzinger, "Truth and Freedom," 27.

64 Ratzinger, "Truth and Freedom," 27–28.

> *Original sin attempts . . . to abolish fatherhood,* destroying its rays which permeate the created world, placing in doubt the truth about God who is Love and leaving man only with a sense of the master-slave relationship. As a result, the Lord appears jealous of his power over the world and over man; and consequently, man feels goaded to do battle against God. No differently than in any epoch of history, the enslaved man is driven to take sides against the master who kept him enslaved.[65]

What, then, we might ask, is so new about our resistance? Is it that we take this description of things as an account of what is *original* instead of original *sin*?

Returning to the reason why we seek to jettison the natural human relations, we might wonder whether, in doing so, we actually succeed in securing more freedom and greater individuality for ourselves. Recall that it is because there is always a relation behind or inside every substance (or sex)—or the appearance of it—that Butler wants to jettison substance and sex altogether because to be anything would mean to be entrapped in a relation that is, by definition, an "operation of power." To deny the one is to deny the other. Butler puts words like "I," "subject," and "self," between her post-modern scare quotes because those terms only exist for her as products of operations of power. Absent those, there is no subject, no self.[66] There is only "fluidity."[67] No relation. No substance. No self. De Beauvoir, in her way, had already gone down this path when in her [nervous] account of biology—well before her account of social influences—she suggested a preference for forms of reproduction where there is the least amount of relation (asexual, hermaphroditic, fertilization outside the female body) even though these occurred at the level of biological life where, as it happens, there is

65 Pope John Paul II, *Crossing the Threshold of Hope* (New York: Alfred A. Knopf, Inc., 1994), 228. We could mention how human fatherhood too had been interpreted inside this same dialectic as expressed famously by Jean-Paul Sartre: "There are no good fathers: this is a rule. We bear no grudge against men, but against the bond of fatherhood, which is rotten." See *Les mots* (Paris: Gallimard, 1964), 11.

66 For Butler there is no "pre-discursive" subject, which stands neutrally outside relations of power. Thus, the "subject" (her scare quotes) is always constituted in the interplay of both *having been constituted* and the rejection of that constitution. As she says: "My position is mine to the extent that 'I' . . . replay and re-signify the theoretical positions that have constituted me, working the possibilities of their convergence, and trying to take account of the possibilities that they systematically exclude. But it is clearly not the case that 'I' preside over the positions that have constituted me, shuffling through them instrumentally, casting some aside, incorporating others, although some of my activity may take that form. The 'I' who would select between them is always already constituted by them. The 'I' is the transfer point of that replay, but it is simply not a strong enough claim to say that the 'I' is situated; the 'I,' this 'I,' is constituted by these positions, and these 'positions' are not merely theoretical products, but fully embedded organizing principles of material practices and institutional arrangements, those matrices of power and discourse that produce me as a viable 'subject.' Indeed, this 'I' would not be a thinking, speaking 'I' if it were not for the very positions that I oppose, for those positions, the ones that claim that the subject must be given in advance, that discourse is an instrument or reflection of that subject, are already part of what constitutes me." See "Contingent Foundations: Feminism and the Question of 'Postmodernism,'" in *Feminists Theorize the Political,* ed. J. Butler and J. W. Scott (New York: Routledge, 1992), 9. See also Butler, *Bodies that Matter: On the Discursive Limits of "Sex"* (New York: Routledge, 1993), 124 and *Gender Trouble,* 148–149.

67 The idea of "gender fluidity" comes to us from Judith Butler, above all through her book *Gender Trouble.*

the least of all individuality (bacteria, protozoa, annelid worms, mollusks, fish, toads and frogs).[68] The dissolution of the self is even evident at the level of pronouns. The lesbian poet Eileen Myles, speaking about the use of the plural "they" for a single subject, says, "[I]'m obsessed with that part in the Bible when Jesus is given the opportunity to cure a person possessed by demons, and Jesus says, 'What is your name?' And the person replies, 'My name is legion.' Whatever is not normative is many. . . Part of it is just the fiction of being alive. Every step, you're making up who you are."[69]

One can see here the traces of the "Devil's bargain" where "having the whole world" by circumventing the "limits" of the natural relations marked on and in our sexually distinct bodies really does come at the cost of "one's very soul," of being *anyone* in particular.[70]

Humanae vitae

We have just seen in the discussion of the gender project, how much it is dominated by separation: separation of woman from the child, man from woman, and child from parents, the latter being secured through the separation of ourselves from our own bodies. All of this, of course, is only possible because of the separation of the two meanings of the sexual act, without which men and woman would be indispensable to each other and they to their children. This is a negative illustration of *Humanae vitae's* central point, that the two meanings stand and fall together. According to the encyclical, they are "inseparably connected" so much so that if they are separated, each of the meanings is degraded. Openness to procreation is the condition of a true conjugal unity—and conjugal unity is the condition of true parenthood, what the encyclical calls "responsible parenthood,"[71] a point taken up explicitly in the later document from the Congregation for the Doctrine of the Faith, *Donum vitae.* Let me say a word about the two meanings and their inseparability, paying special attention to the chief concerns in those in favor of separation.

The Procreative Dimension Necessary to Conjugal Love: "True Mutual Love"

It is well-known that before the Second Vatican Council, some charged that the teaching of the Church on the "end of marriage," (the procreation and education of children), appeared to instrumentalize marriage and the act belonging to it. This charge, of course, assumes a notion of "end" which is extrinsic to an action,

68 De Beauvoir notes: "the phenomena of asexual multiplication and parthenogenesis are neither more nor less fundamental than those of sexual reproduction," *The Second Sex,* 26. See also note 42 above. We are reminded that the process of *bokanovskification* in the Fertilizing Rooms of *Brave New World* where scores of identical individuals are produced through the budding of one fertilized ova.

69 Eileen Myles quoted by Ariel Levy in "Dolls and Feelings," *New Yorker* (December 14, 2015), http://www.newyorker.com/magazine/2015/12/14/dolls-and-feelings.

70 The element of self-subversion as belonging to the "diabolical" is discussed in Schindler's *Freedom from Reality,* 167–169.

71 Pope Paul VI, *Humanae vitae,* 12.

not the end belonging to the tradition, the teleological end which coincides with the fullness of an action, the marriage act in this case.[72] That said, from the side of the theology of marriage, it was possible to ask just where conjugal love *was*. As the historian of the theology of marriage, García de Haro, notes: "[b]efore the Council, the Magisterium had not clearly and unequivocally pronounced on the nature of the marriage contract."[73] On the one hand, marriage, in the constant theological tradition, was a "consent to the union, exclusive and indissoluble, between a man and a woman, with the end of procreating and educating children."[74] On the other, in the canonical doctrine, it was the "consent to the yielding of the mutual right to the body."[75] At most it was said that love was one of the duties of marriage (not part of its nature).[76] Tied to this was the general theological view that marriage *as such* was not ordered to the perfection of love.[77] In many ways, the development of the theology of marriage before and during the Council with its increasing emphasis on the sacredness and dignity of marriage, its status as a state of life, and therefore, its specific contribution to the universal call to love, was the necessary response to the perception of instrumentalization.[78] Moreover, it was precisely the manner in which the theology of marriage was developed that procreation was not placed next to love,[79] but included in it, thus deepening, both conjugal love and its "end."[80] Building on *Casti connubii*, *Gaudium et spes* introduced the language of "mutual giving"[81] which in turn, became the premise for the wrongfulness of contraception, which would render

72 See Francis Slade, "Ends and Purposes" in *Final Causality in Nature and Human Affairs*, ed. R. F. Hassing, Studies in Philosophy and the History of Philosophy 30 (Washington, D.C.: The Catholic University of America Press, 1997), 83–85.

73 Ramón García de Haro, *Marriage and the Family in the Documents of the Magisterium—A Course in the Theology of Marriage*, trans. William E. May (San Francisco: Ignatius Press, 1993), 200.

74 García de Haro, *Marriage and the Family*, 200.

75 *Codex Iuris Canonici* (1917), can. 1081, par. 2. The 1917 code can be found in English and Latin at https://www.iuscangreg.it/cic1917.php?lang=EN.

76 This was the content of Ottaviani's response to those who noted the absence of marital love in the draft on "Chastity, Virginity, Marriage, Family" submitted by the Theological Commission (of which he was head) in preparation for the council. *Acta Concilio Oecumenico Vaticano II Apparando*, series II (*Praeparatio*), vol. 2, pars. 3, 977–978; cited in *What is Marriage*? Theodore Mackin (New York: Paulist Press, 1982), 256–257.

77 For example, Garrigou-Lagrange, representing a fairly traditional view, writes: "holy virginity is immediately ordered to the good of the soul, to the contemplative life and union with God, whereas marriage is ordered to the conservation of the human species and the active life," *The Love of God and the Cross of Jesus*, vol. 1, trans. Sr. Jeanne Marie, OP (St. Louis: B. Herder Book Co., 1947), 348.

78 David Crawford develops this point in "*Humanae Vitae* and the Perfection of Love," *Communio: International Catholic Review* 25 (Fall 1998):414–438.

79 Vatican Council II, *Gaudium et spes* (December 7, 1965), 51, http://www.vatican.va/archive/hist_councils/ii_vatican_council/index.htm. An early attempt to use the language of love was made by Pope Pius XI in his encyclical letter, *Casti connubii* (December 31, 1930), 9, 24, at https://w2.vatican.va/content/pius-xi/en/encyclicals.index.html.

80 On this point, see especially Nicholas J. Healy, Jr., "Christian Personalism and the Debate over the Nature and Ends of Marriage," *Communio: International Catholic Review* 39 (Spring-Summer 2012): 196.

81 *Gaudium et spes,* 48. *Casti connubii* speaks of the "generous surrender of [one's] own person made to another for the whole of life," 9.

the "total self-gift" partial.[82] But this becomes explicit in *Humanae vitae* when it speaks of fruitfulness as constitutive of conjugal love, and then of the "inseparable connection . . . between the unitive significance and the procreative significance," between, that is, the "uniting [of] husband and wife in the closest intimacy" on the one hand, and the "capacity of generating new life," on the other.[83] John Paul II, for his part, took up this development in his *Catechesis on Human Love* ("Theology of the Body") where he speaks of the "language of the body" and of contraception as a "lie" which "falsifies" (subjectively) an act which "signifies" (objectively) total self-giving.[84] In sum, it was this deepening of the theology of marriage—now called a "community of life and love,"[85] a "partnership of their whole life" [86]—that the procreative end found itself on more secure ground.[87] As a result, it became clearer that far from instrumentalizing conjugal love, the openness to procreation was a condition for conjugal love to *be itself*.[88] This helps to explain why the Church declares null marriages entered into by parties intending always to contracept. It is not just a matter of punishing disobedience but of recognizing that the conjugal act and the marriage it betokens is quite literally not one.[89]

Part of seeing how little the openness to the procreative end instrumentalizes conjugal love is to see how that same openness prevents the instrumentalization

82 Pope Paul VI, *Humanae vitae,* 51. *Casti connubii* had spoken of contraception as "a sin against conjugal faith," 72.

83 Pope Paul VI, *Humanae vitae,* 9, 12. Karol Wojtyła, speaks of a "certain progress" in *Humanae vitae,* 12 with respect to *Gaudium et spes,* 51, where the former assuming the "entire objective dimension" in the idea of "signifies," broadens this by adding the necessity of "faithful interpretation" (via meaning) on the part of the spouses. See Wojtyła, "The Anthropological Vision of *Humanae Vitae,*" trans. William E. May, *Nova et Vetera* (English edition) 7, no. 3 (2009): 742–743.
Pope Paul VI, *Humanae vitae,* 12.

84 See Pope John Paul II, *Man and Woman He Created Them—A Theology of the Body*, trans. M. Waldstein (Boston: Pauline Books & Media, 2006), 618–620, 118:4–6. John Paul II also discusses this in *Familiaris consortio,* 32: "The innate language that expresses the total reciprocal self-giving of husband and wife is overlaid, through contraception, by an objectively contradictory language, namely, that of not giving oneself totally to the other. This leads not only to a positive refusal to be open to life but also to a falsification of the inner truth of conjugal love, which is called upon to give itself in personal totality." Apostolic Exhortation *Familiaris consortio* (November 22, 1981), http://w2.vatican.va/content/john-paul-ii/en/apost_exhortations.index.html.

85 *Gaudium et spes,* 48.

86 *Codex Iuris Canonici* (1983), 1055. The 1983 Code can be found in English at: http://www.vatican.va/archive/ENG1104/_INDEX.HTM.

87 On the relation between conjugal love and its procreative end, García de Haro writes concerning the development of the theology of marriage: "Vatican Council II will be able to locate [conjugal love]—without disturbing but rather developing the Tradition—as the formal, life-giving principle of the conjugal community: a community of life and of love, whose end is the procreation and education of children," García de Haro, *Marriage and The Family,* 200. John Paul II also does not renounce the tradition's use of "end," but rather confirms it as he situates it in a deeper theology of marriage. See *Man and Woman He Created Them,* 642–643, 127:3.

88 On the "personalist" argument for the "inseparability" of the two meanings, see Cormac Burke, "Marriage: A Personalist or an Institutional Understanding?" *Communio: International Catholic Review* 19 (Summer 1992): 293.

89 *Codex Iuris Canonici* (1983), 1101.

of the lovers themselves, conjugal and otherwise. It is hard to deny now that we have lived for decades with the separation of the meanings, how poorly the unity between man and woman has fared. Naïve prophets of an improved marital life could hardly have imagined the level to which we would have descended, habituated as we are now with our transactional encounters, when they aren't merely virtual. And turning to the recent debate about sexual harassment in the public square, could the incidences have risen so high had contraception not made "yes" the default answer?[90] In sum, has not the separation led to the reduction of persons to a means to an (private) end, to persons trapped within "operations of power," the very thing the protection was meant to prevent? To put it in the terms of the contraception debate, where have all the personal values gone?[91]

Looking at things positively, what is it about the openness to procreation that makes conjugal love *love*? The answer is tied to the kind of love which is opposite to instrumentalization ("love of utility" or "love of pleasure"). Love of the other "for one's own sake," wants the good of the beloved, not only an aspect of the beloved relative only to oneself. It wants, in other words, for the beloved to be, to flourish.[92] And this is wanted precisely by a desire to be with the beloved, to interlock one's life with him or her. *Gaudium et spes* ties this love to the Creator's special love for man when it says that "man . . . is the only creature on earth which God willed for itself."[93] God, in other words, wants us *to be*, in the most radical sense, in order to be with us and with us forever.[94] What is striking about this conciliar text is the corollary, that man "cannot fully find himself except through a sincere gift of himself."[95] John Paul II, who quoted this full text in every one of his encyclicals, notes how this "being for oneself," (or "own sake"), and "for another," might be an "apparent contradiction."[96] On the contrary, says he, it is the "magnificent paradox of human existence."[97] "There is a very deep connection

90 On this point see Angela Franks, "Consent is not Enough: Harvey Weinstein, Sex, and Human Flourishing," *Public Discourse* (November 26, 2017), at http://www.thepublicdiscourse.com/2017/11/20563.

91 It might be surprising to note how much this was prophesied outside Catholic ranks. In response to the campaigns to spread contraception in India, Mahatma Gandhi wrote: "It is futile to hope that the use of contraceptives will be restricted to the mere regulation of progeny. There is hope for a decent life only so long as the sexual act is definitely related to the conception of precious life." Elsewhere, he said: "I urge the advocates of artificial methods to consider the consequences. Any large use of the methods is likely to result in the dissolution of the marriage bond and in free love." Cited by Mary Eberstadt, "The Prophetic Power of *Humanae Vitae*," *First Things* (April 2018), at https://www.firstthings.com/article/2018/04/the-prophetic-power-of-humanae-vitae.

92 This distinction is first drawn by Aristotle in the *Nicomachean Ethics,* book VIII, 1156a–1156b.

93 *Gaudium et spes*, 24.

94 On love as the affirmation of the beloved's existence, see Josef Pieper, *On Love* (San Francisco: Ignatius Press, 1997), 163–172.

95 *Gaudium et spes*, 24.

96 See Pope John Paul II, *Letter to Families* (February 2, 1994), 11, at https://w2.vatican.va/content/john-paul-ii/en/letters/1994/documents/hf_jp-ii_let_02021994_families.html.

97 Pope John Paul II, *Letter to Families,* 11. See also Pope John Paul II, "A Meditation on Givenness," *Communio: International Catholic Review* 41 (Winter 2014): 4–5.

between being for oneself and being for others."[98] In the first place, "sincere giving" (being for others) is the welcome of another, a letting be of another as a being "for his or her own sake."[99] It is precisely here, in the *giving welcome*, that one paradoxically finds oneself. In finding the other, one finds oneself. This is so by virtue of the "communional essence of man"[100] which begins, at the most radical level with the vertical relation to the One who gave us our very selves.[101] Now, when the mutual welcome, or self-giving and self-finding takes place in the "one flesh" union of man and woman—this is already written in the objective capacity of that act, which can, in principle, make the two fruitful, both more of themselves and in a manner which expresses their mutual being with,[102] not only because the prospect of children entails a whole life together, an earthly forever,[103] but because they betoken the defiance of death which every love worth its name seeks, as Vladimir Solovyov said.[104] Indeed, it was to the capacity of a man and woman to generate life that Plato turned when he offered his famous definition of love: "giving birth in the Beautiful (the Eternal)." [105] In light of the doctrine of creation, procreation is just this, from above, since God, who is Love is the direct source, the "Father from whom every fatherhood in heaven and on earth is named."[106] To use the language of *Humanae vitae*, the openness to that which betokens the "forever" is simply the other side of the coin of the "unitive meaning," the "uniting [of] husband and wife in the closest intimacy."[107]

We should note, *apropos* of the problem of instrumentalization, that mutual love of the other "for his or her own sake" is not without pleasure or joy. On the contrary, it is the most beatifying, or enjoyable (from *fruor*), a paradox noted all throughout the intellectual tradition.[108] But this, again, depends on a notion of the human being that already includes a relation to the other. Having jettisoned

98 Pope John Paul II, "A Meditation on Givenness," 4–5.

99 Pope John Paul II, *Man and Woman He Created Them,* 178–181, 13:2–4. This begins with Creation itself when the Giver *welcomes* us in the most radical way by giving us being. It is then carried out among us horizontally when we welcome each other.

100 Pope John Paul II, "A Meditation on Givenness," 5.

101 Pope John Paul II, *Man and Woman He Created Them,* 187–188, 15:3. See also his *Letter to Families,* 11, and "A Meditation on Givenness," 5.

102 Cormac Burke aptly shows how the openness to fruitfulness is the expression of the desire of spouse to give themselves totally to each other: "Giving one's seed . . . is conjugal love embodied in a unique and privileged physical action whereby intimacy is expressed ('I give you what I give no one else') and union is achieved. 'Take what I have to give. This will be a new me. United to you, to what you have to give, to your seed, this will be a new you-and-me, fruit of our mutual knowledge and love,'" Cormac Burke, "Marriage and Contraception," in *Creative Love: The Ethics of Human Reproduction*, ed. J. Boyle (Front Royal, Va.: Christendom Press, 1989), 154.

103 On this point, see Janet E. Smith, *Humanae Vitae: A Generation Later* (Washington, D.C.: The Catholic University of America Press, 1991), 114–115.

104 Vladimir Solovyov, *The Meaning of Love*, trans. T. Beyer, Jr. (Hudson: Lindisfarne Press, 1985), 66.

105 Plato, *Symposium,* trans. E. Brann, P. Kalkavage, and E. Salem (Indianapolis: Hackett Publishing Company, 2017), 204a-209c.

106 Pope Paul VI, *Humanae vitae,* 8, 13.

107 Pope Paul VI, *Humanae vitae,* 12.

108 See Pieper, *On Love*, 233–245.

precisely this conception of the human person, Kant could not think of sexual relations between husband and wife as anything other than relations of mutual use, the mutual reduction of the other to a thing, a means to one's individual end.[109] But the connection between the love of another "for his or her own sake" and joy is particularly clear when we bring the procreative meaning of the conjugal act into view since there, we see at one and the same time, a gesture that makes the man and woman capable of welcoming yet another being "for oneself" and the receiving of a great joy (pleasure). It is not for nothing that the child who is the incarnate token of the welcome parents give to each other is called their fruit, their joy.[110] In sum, we can see that openness to the child is the condition both of the non-instrumentalization of the individual lovers and the conjugal love itself.

The Unitive Dimension Necessary for Procreation: "The Exalted Vocation to Parenthood"

Looking at things from the other side of the coin, if the two meanings of the conjugal act are inseparable, then the unity of spouses is necessary to "man's exalted vocation to parenthood," as the encyclical puts it.[111] One of the obvious ways in which we can see that conjugal love is not instrumentalized in the long tradition of opposition to contraception is the Church's injunction against any form of procreation which circumvents the conjugal act or, indeed, of other older methods of procuring children in the event of sterility, which methods circumvented marriage: divorce, polygamy, and concubinage. Going back to Pope Pius XII's *Allocution to Midwives*, where one might say that the promotion of the child is at the heart of the document's concern (in its injunctions against abortion and birth control), we find an injunction against artificial insemination, against that is, the procurement of a child by any means, and the reduction of the couple to a "biological laboratory."[112] It was, of course, the role of *Donum vitae* to address the circumvention of the marriage act in all the variety that had developed by the time of the issuance of the document in 1987.

Essentially, the heart of *Donum vitae's* injunction against the separation of the conjugal act from procreation was that the child would become subject to a dominion characteristic of things made, not begotten. This substitution of the act of begetting belonging to natural things, including human beings, by which they bear fruit, with the technical act of making, says *Donum vitae*, "establishes the domination of technology over the origin and destiny of the human person. Such

109 Immanuel Kant, *Metaphysical Elements of Justice*, part I of the *Metaphysics of Morals*, 2nd ed., trans. John Ladd (Cambridge: Hackett Publishing Company, Inc. 1999), section III, 25, p. 88.

110 *Gaudium et spes*, 50, "Children are really the supreme gift of marriage and contribute very substantially to the welfare of their parents." See also Pope John Paul II, *Letter to Families*, 11.

111 Pope Paul VI, *Humanae vitae*, 12.

112 Pope Pius XII, *Discorso di Sua Santità Pio PP. XII alle Partecipanti al Congresso della Unione Cattolica Italiana Ostetriche* [*Allocution to Midwives*] (October 29, 1951), section IV, https://w2.vatican.va/content/pius-xii/it/speeches/1951.index.1.html (my translation). An English translation of the *Allocution to Midwives* can be found in *Papal Teachings: Matrimony*, trans. M. Byrnes (Boston: St. Paul Editions, 1963), 427 (no. 637). Subsequent citations are taken from this translation.

a relationship of domination is in itself contrary to the dignity and equality that must be common to parents and children."[113] We are reminded of Lewis' "conditioners" who can now cut out their posterity "in what shape they please," designing them and subjecting them inevitably to "quality control."[114] The issue here is about a kind of action which has domination as its very logic, notwithstanding intentions which are often those of well-meaning parents filled with the natural desire for something very good. The futuristic movie *Gattaca* comes to mind. There, the parents of the protagonist are presented with their four embryos on the doctor's computer screen. "Which one do you want?" he asks them. These have already been screened for disease, as well as predisposition to myopia, alcoholism, domestic violence, obesity and the like. So now it is a question of choosing things like sex, eye color, and whatever else would make their child a "compatible candidate." They are bewildered. It doesn't seem right, and not only because the other three have to be eliminated, but because their attitude toward the embryo they will choose will be fundamentally different from that towards their first born, the one they had the "old-fashioned way" in the back of their Pontiac. Their intentions are good, but they are inside a logic which contradicts them. The child is now the direct object of their design. It is an object of an "operation of power."

The Church's injunction against *this* side of the separation is helpful for understanding its injunction against the other side of the separation, especially in the face of the objection that the couple has been made a mere means to the end of the child. For here one can see that the child, not being a means to an end, must also come from an activity which is not simply a means to an end, a "biological laboratory."[115] The German philosopher Robert Spaemann's comment is elucidating, and funny, when he says, as though speaking to his child: "Don't believe I was thinking of *you* when I was with your mother."[116] The child, of course, can be wanted, but only as the fruit (or superabundance), of an act of mutual, gratuitous, and uncalculating self-forgetfulness—the very activity which, as it happens, does not work well under calculating conditions. Here, we can see the precise sense in which procreation is the "end" of the conjugal act, because the fruit is the expression and fullness of the activity itself.

113 Congregation for the Doctrine of the Faith, Instruction *Donum vitae* (February 22, 1987), 30 http://www.vatican.va/roman_curia/congregations/cfaith/doc_doc_index.htm. We note here the basic distinction between a natural end "which exists independently of willing, or prior to it," and a "purpose" which originates in the will. Procreation, being a natural end of the conjugal act, therefore, exists independently of the will of the parents, even if parents eagerly seek and desire the flourishing of the activity they are engaging in. The point is that the child, being a natural end, is not the design of the parents as is the case in the technical act of making. On this point, see Slade, "Ends and Purposes" in *Final Causality in Nature and Human Affairs.*

114 Hans Jonas speaks of a "right of ignorance," a "right of each human life to find its own way and be a surprise to itself." See Jonas, "Biological Engineering," in *Philosophical Essays: from Ancient Creed to Technological Man* (Englewood Cliffs: Prentice-Hall, Inc., 1974), 163.

115 See note 113, above.

116 "Genetic Manipulation of Human Nature in the Context of Human Personality," in *Human Genome, Human Person and the Society of the Future: Proceedings of the Fourth Assembly of the Pontifical Academy for Life: Vatican City, February 23–25, 1998*, eds. Juan de Dios Vial Correa and Elio Sgreccia (Vatican City: Libreria Editrice Vaticana, 1999), 344.

Returning to the child, the injunction against the separation of conjugal union from procreation involves a deepening of just what procreation is, that is, of what children are. As we saw, on the ladder of sexual organic life, the higher the organism, the deeper degree of union there is in the activity of the parents, both in the actual conception and education of the new individual and in that individual's education (according to the dialectical relation between individuality and relation to others, or greater capacity to learn and greater need to be taught). For human beings, unlike lower sexual organisms, children remain with their parents well beyond birth because of their need to be raised and educated.[117] Adolf Portmann speaks of the child's need for a "second uterine year" in the womb of the family, since only in the family does a human child learn to speak, stand upright, and walk.[118] This need, being human, is not only for food and shelter, but for being brought up into the human community, beginning with the first community of one's parents. The insistence on the unity of parents as a constitutive dimension of the child, be it in the child's coming to be or in his or her long education, is simply a recognition of what a child is: a being from, with, and for a unity in difference, a communion of persons. Any relaxing of the unity of the parents, on the contrary, implies a different conception of the child, either by thinking of him or her as the object of domination or the subject of resistance to the fact of givenness.[119] The former is evident in all the myriad of ways in which children have been put to the test, literally, in laboratories, by the conditioners. The latter has been in view for far longer, beginning with the leniency of liberalism towards divorce. When John Locke approved of divorce on the grounds that the end of marriage was procreation, he was not wrong about the end, so much as that in which it consisted.[120] Taking "the procreation and education of children" seriously means to take seriously the love of parents for each other, which is itself "a condition of the sincerest care of the offspring."[121]

Here we can address what is often the most difficult challenge to the teaching of *Humanae vitae,* namely, that most of the time in the life of a married couple

117 Pope Pius XI wrote: "The blessing of offspring . . . is not completed by the mere begetting of [children], but something else must be added, namely the proper education of the offspring . . . . Now it is certain that both by the law of nature and of God this right and duty of educating their offspring belongs in the first place to those who began the work of nature by giving them birth, and they are indeed forbidden to leave unfinished this work and so expose it to certain ruin," *Casti connubii,* 16.

118 Adolf Portmann, "The Special Position of Man in the Realm of the Living," trans. Werner J. Dannhauser, *Commentary* (November 1965): 38–41.

119 Lewis notes the paradox of the "one dominant age" to come "which resists all previous ages most successfully and dominates all subsequent ages most irresistibly, and thus is the real master of the human species," *The Abolition of Man*, 58.

120 John Locke, *The Second Treatise of Government* (Indianapolis: Hackett Publishing Company Inc., 1980), 7:81–83. Thomas Aquinas, too, had linked the question of divorce with the needs of children, but concludes the opposite, on the basis of a different conception of the child. See *Scriptum super Sententiis,* IV, d. 26, q. 1, a. 1 (Parma edition, 1856, 918).

121 Pope Pius XII, *Allocution to Midwives,* 427 (no. 636). This theme is central to the book I edited *Torn Asunder: Children, The Myth of the Good Divorce and the Recovery of Origins* (Grand Rapids, Mich.: Eerdmans Publishing, 2016) where the argument for indissolubility is shown from the point of view of the nature of the child. On this point, see also Smith, Humanae Vitae: *A Generation Later*, 117.

they are infertile, including during their fertile years, and that they, unlike the animals beneath them, are not without sexual interests outside the windows of fertility.[122] Given all of this, how can the Church say that "each and every marital act must of necessity retain its intrinsic relationship to the procreation of human life"?[123] Augustine famously interpreted the procreative end to imply the wrongfulness (venial sin) of a conjugal act that is not consciously and intentionally procreative, or during infertile periods.[124] But the Church does not follow him on this. How, though, can the Church maintain that "each and every marital act must of necessity retain its intrinsic relationship to the procreation of human life" without following Augustine in his practical application of the principle? A frequent way to read the principle is to say that spouses "retain the intrinsic relationship to procreation" if they do not intentionally thwart the procreative end or falsify an act that means total self-giving. This reading is often brought to bear on the difference between contraception and periodic continence; and, in that context it is helpful.[125] Still, it is hard to see how this minimal reading can be used to read the use of infertile times positively as "retaining their intrinsic relationship to procreation."[126] Might it not be better to interpret the principle in a more maximal (and positive) way by looking at infertility as a feature of the kind of procreation and education that belongs to the human couple? And, with respect to the claim that is often made that the general infertility of the human couple shows that spouses are *not only* for procreation, might we not say that, on the contrary, they are *more deeply* for it, since their sexuality takes into account the kind of progeny they are apt for conceiving. *Humanae vitae* teaches that new life is not the result of each and every act of sexual intercourse: "God has wisely ordered laws of nature and the incidence of fertility in such a way that successive births are already naturally spaced through the inherent operation of these laws."[127] Children, in other words, need time with their parents to learn from them many things, chiefly about the communion of persons that put them in being, that marks them now, and that asks to be taken up by them in the future.

122 And of course, there is the dramatic issue of the couple who cannot conceive children at all.

123 Pope Paul VI, *Humanae vitae,* 11; Pope Pius XI, *Casti conubii,* 54, 56; Pope Pius, XII, *Allocution to Midwives,* 414 (no. 613).

124 "*Numquid hoc non est peccatum, amplius quam liberorum procreandorum necessitas cogit, exigere a coniuge debitum? Est quidem peccatum, sed veniale,*" Augustine, *Sermo* 51, c. 13, n. 22 (*Patrologia Latina,* 38, 345); see also *De bono coniugali*, c. 6, n. 6 (PL 40, 378); *De Nuptiis et concupiscentia,* I, c. 14, n. 16 (PL 44, 423); *Contra Julianum Pelagianum,* V, c. 16, n. 63 (PL 44, 819); and *Contra Julianum (opus imperfectum),* I, 68 (PL 45, 1091). It should be noted that Aquinas teaches the same: ST II-II, q. 154, art. 2 ad 6; *Supp.* q. 49, art. 5; cf. q. 41, art. 4. For a more complete understanding of Augustine's view, see Cormac Burke, "Saint Augustine and Conjugal Sexuality," *Communio: International Catholic Review* 17 (Winter 1990): 561–564.

125 This explanation often appears in discussions about the difference between the use of contraception and the practice of periodic continence. See Smith, Humanae Vitae: *A Generation Later,* 118–128.

126 Smith writes: "Although it is clear that spouses having sexual intercourse during the infertile periods are not giving quite as fully of themselves as they are during fertile times, they are not falsifying the act itself. They tell all the truth that is to be told at a given time; they have given all there is to give at the time," Humanae Vitae: *A Generation Later,* 124.

127 Pope Paul VI, *Humanae vitae,* 11.

In this sense, the love of spouses for each other is always a primary education, and always, therefore, "retains its intrinsic relation to the procreation of human life," as the Church, together with Augustine, insists.[128]

In sum, we can see that to insist that procreation be unseparated from conjugal union is to insist that neither child nor parents be a means to an end.

Conclusion

We saw that the un-engendering of gender exists to drive a wedge between the person and his or her nature so as to drive a further wedge between the person and the three fundamental relations of that same nature. We saw, furthermore, that the move of (resistant) separation is driven by the concern for "safety" for the individual and for his freedom (now conceived as over and against those same relations). In light of the dialectical relation between relation and the individual (that sexuality displays along the ladder of organic life), we asked though what success the gender project could have when the very subject of freedom has to be sacrificed to fluidity in order to be free.

Turning to *Humanae vitae*, we looked especially at the doctrine of inseparability with its claim that the two meanings can only stand unseparated. Gender theory already makes this clear, negatively, since there the two meanings must fall together. Detachment from the child means detachment of the man from the woman, the child from them. But what we see with *Humanae vitae* is that inseparability is not only the condition for saving conjugal love but also the condition for keeping man, woman, and child truly safe, as personal subjects in relation—who don't have to sacrifice their very selves, their souls, in order to be free. As John Paul II said:

So-called "safe sex," which is touted by the "civilization of technology," is actually, in view of the overall requirements of the person, radically *not safe*, indeed it is extremely dangerous. It endangers [both] the person [and the family]. And what is this danger? It is *the loss of the truth about one's own self [and about the family]*, together with the risk of a loss of *freedom* and consequently of a loss of *love* itself."[129]

128 Pope Paul VI, *Humanae vitae*, 11.

129 Pope John Paul II, *Letter to Families*, 13.

PART III

Natural Family Planning

8

A Historical Review of the Catholic Scientists Who Answered the Call of Humanae vitae

Richard J. Fehring

FIFTY YEARS AGO, POPE PAUL VI called on scientists to "explain more thoroughly the various conditions favoring a proper regulation of birth" and to study what he called "sufficiently secure" methods of natural fertility regulation, what we refer today as methods of Natural Family Planning (NFP).[1] In today's parlance scientists would interpret the words "secure methods" as "effective methods" of NFP for pregnancy avoidance. Furthermore, scientific standards would dictate the need for scientists to provide an evidence base (i.e., multiple high-level evidence studies) for effective methods of NFP. This challenge also means, from a science perspective, developing and providing "sufficient" evidence for effective NFP methods for women who are experiencing what are called special reproductive situations, such as the postpartum transition to fertility or during the transition to menopause, and for couples wishing to achieve a pregnancy.

Paul VI also called on physicians and health professionals to provide couples with the necessary knowledge to use NFP for their family planning needs.[2] This essay, however, is not about the provision of NFP services or analyzing NFP effectiveness studies. Rather, my focus is on the scientists who responded to Paul VI's call not only to develop NFP methods but also to provide the evidence for their effectiveness, as well as to highlight the Catholic scientists who heard and answered that call.

This essay will follow a historical timeline of the Church's call for scientific research: pre-*Humanae vitae* era, which includes the papacies of Pius XI (1922–1939) and Pius XII (1939–1958), the Papal Birth Control Commission (1963–1966) and writing of *Humanae vitae* (1966–1968); and the post-*Humanae vitae* era (1968–2005). The pre-*Humanae vitae* era will include Catholic scientists' responses to Pope Pius XI's encyclical *Casti connubii* (1930) and the writings of Pope Pius XII on natural birth regulation and contraception. The post-*Humanae vitae* era will end with the pontificate of Pope John Paul II. This essay is essentially an historical overview of the interaction between the Catholic Church, the

1 Pope Paul VI, Encyclical Letter *Humanae vitae* (Boston: Pauline Books, 1968), 24.

2 Pope Paul VI, *Humanae vitae*, 27.

pope's call (and sometimes pleading) for scientific help, and the Catholic scientists' responses.[3]

Before beginning the discussion, however, there is a need to define what a scientist is and identify the characteristics of a Catholic scientist. In this essay, a scientist is one who has the proper education to develop, propose, obtain significant funding, carry out research, and publish findings in peer-reviewed scientific journals. This usually requires a person to have at least a PhD in a discipline of science and/or be a medical doctor (MD) who has research experience and knowledge. Those degrees are a minimum. A scientist is one who also has a consistent track record of research and publications in peer-reviewed journals in an area of research. The most active scientists are usually those who have post-doctoral fellowships, the ability to write successful research grant proposals and obtain significant grant money to carry out research, and the ability to gather and work with a research team. Without these qualifications (unless applying for a graduate training grant), a scientist will not receive significant federal or foundation funding. In today's world, a scientist usually works with a team of scientists that includes a biostatistician who helps to analyze data with sophisticated statistical methods.

If a research scientist develops and wishes to test the effectiveness of a new method of NFP in helping couples avoid an unintended pregnancy, then that scientist will need institutional research human rights approval with yearly updates, reapplication of human rights approval every three years, registration to the federal government for clinical trials with frequent reports, a well-defined data safety plan certified that he or she has met the research design criteria, and yearly federal grant reports. Furthermore, federal grants are usually not provided to individuals but rather to research and academic institutions that have the resources to support such research endeavors.

Another important aspect or characteristic of a scientist is one who feels called to research a significant topic area in science. In other words, a scientist has a passion for an area of research and is consistent in researching that area. This passion could come from personal experience (e.g., suffering from infertility), an idea from a peer or colleague, significant research areas delineated by professional organizations, or for others, a sense of purpose, faith, or personal calling from God guiding one in that direction. For those scientists who are researching methods of NFP, that call, and the subsequent research might also mean suffering in some way. Suffering could come in the form of ridicule by peers, rejected articles for publication, rejected grant proposals for research, failing to be granted tenure, not being promoted, or not receiving pay raises. A passionate researcher, or one who feels called, will accept the rejection but continue to work on his or her area of research and find ways to work with colleagues who are fair-minded.

Although there are other areas of research (besides investigating the effectiveness of NFP methods) that the encyclical *Humanae vitae* lends itself to research,

3 It should be noted that even the post-*Casti connubii* and post-Pius XII NFP scientists were active well into the post-*Humanae vitae* era.

such as the psychological effects of using NFP, the effects of NFP on marital dynamics, and the pursuit of moral methods of managing infertility, this essay will focus on the Church's call to develop and research methods of NFP and provide examples of early scientists who contributed to the science of NFP.

The Church's Call to Scientists Pre-*Humanae vitae* (1930–1966)

Paul VI was not the first pope to call on scientists to develop and research natural methods of birth regulation and not the first pope to condemn the use of the new hormonal birth control pill for family planning purposes. The Catholic Church slowly developed its understanding of what we now refer to as NFP in the modern period. It began with a tentative approval of natural birth regulation methods as an ethical support for marriage. The methods and morality of abstaining from sexual intercourse during the estimated fertile phase of the woman's menstrual cycle to avoid pregnancy was addressed by leaders in the Catholic Church in the late 1800s.[4] However, it was not until Pius XI's promulgation of *Casti connubii* on December 31, 1930, that the Catholic Church formally approved the use of periodic sexual abstinence during the woman's fertile phase.[5]

At that time, there was little support for the development, research, and promotion of natural methods of birth regulation within the medical profession and the Church. There was much skepticism concerning the various theories about the infertile time of the menstrual cycle—many clergy were still advocating inaccurate methods of avoiding the fertile phase of the menstrual cycle.[6] Priests were not encouraged to promote natural methods of birth regulation, but, rather, only to suggest their use in the confessional when there were grave reasons for their use.[7] Furthermore, there was much doubt among Catholic physicians and the National Federation of Catholic Physicians (now called the Catholic Medical Association) whether these methods actually worked and whether they were moral.[8]

NFP Scientists during Pius XI's Papacy (1922–1939)

About the same time of Pius XI's encyclical *Casti connubii*, the first effective calendar-based methods of natural birth regulation were being researched, presented at medical conferences, and made known to the European, Japanese, and

4 Sacred Penitentiary 1853 and 1880, in *Natural Family Planning: Nature's Way—God's Way*, ed., Anthony Zimmerman (Milwaukee: DeRance, Inc., 1980), 228. Note that the methods proposed at that time were not accurate and would lead to unintended pregnancy.

5 Pope Pius XI, Encyclical Letter *Casti connubii*, December 31, 1930 (New York: Paulist Press, 1941).

6 John T. Noonan, Jr., *Contraception: A History of its Treatment by the Catholic Theologians and Canonists* (Cambridge, Mass.: Harvard University Press, 1986), 438–475.

7 Leslie Tentler, *Catholics and Contraception: An American History* (Ithaca, N.Y.: Cornell University Press, 2004). See also John D. Conway, *What They Ask about The Rhythm* (Notre Dame, Ind.: Ave Maria Press, 1956), 3–7.

8 Ethicus, "The Morality of the Use of the Safe Period," *The Linacre Quarterly* 1, no. 2 (March 1933): 23–26.

Unites States populations.[9] Dr. Kyusaku Ogino (Japan) and Dr. Herman Knaus (Austria) are the two individuals who have been credited with the discovery of the first usable and scientific methods of natural birth regulation.[10] They independently (and in very different manners) discovered that ovulation preceded menstruation by about fourteen days.

Ogino was the head of gynecology at Takeyama Hospital in Negata, Japan. As a surgical gynecologist, he observed the ovaries of 118 of his patients during abdominal surgery. Based on the size and condition of the follicle or corpus luteum, he was able to determine roughly when ovulation occurred. He published his results in a Japanese scientific journal in 1923.[11] Knaus, who was the head of an obstetrics and gynecology clinic at the German University in Prague, used a different approach to estimate the time of ovulation during the menstrual cycle. He injected a pituitary extract into women subjects and then recorded the activity of their uterine muscles. He noticed that before ovulation, the pituitary injection would cause uterine contractions but after ovulation, it did not. By conducting this research on a day-to-day basis, he was able to estimate the time of ovulation (based on the last day of uterine contractions) and, like Ogino, observed that ovulation preceded menstruation by about fourteen days. What became known as "Knaus's Law" stated that menstruation would follow ovulation by fourteen days. And, like Ogino, he developed a calendar formula for determining the fertile and infertile times of the woman's menstrual cycle. Knaus published his findings in a German scientific journal in 1932.[12]

Despite the work of Ogino and Knaus, the calendar-based methods of natural birth regulation were actually first developed and popularized in Europe by a Catholic physician from the Netherlands, Dr. John Smulders, and by a Catholic professor of obstetrics and gynecology at Loyola University in Chicago, Dr. Leo Latz. Smulders based his calendar method on the work of Ogino and Dutch gynecologist Dr. Theodoor Hendrik van de Velde.[13] Smulders discussed his method in a book published in 1930 by the Dutch Roman Catholic medical association. Latz, actually studied the Knaus's research and later the Ogino research and developed his calendar method. He published his research and method for natural birth regulation in a 1932 book titled *The Rhythm of Sterility and Fertility in Women*.[14]

9 Kyusaku Ogino, *Conception Period of Women* (Harrisburg: Medical Arts Publishing Company, 1934), 79–80; Herman Knaus, *Periodic Fertility and Sterility in Woman: A Natural Method of Birth Control* (Vienna: Wilhelm Maudrich, Publisher, 1934).

10 Ogino, *Conception Period of Women*, 79–80.

11 Kyusaku Ogino, "Period of Ovulation, Relation Between Corpora Lutea and Cyclical Changes in the Uterine Endometrium; Cyclical Changes in the Uterine Endometrium and Fertile Time," *Japanese Gynecological Journal* 19 (1924): 6.

12 See Herman Knaus, *Periodic Fertility and Sterility in Woman*.

13 Jean Nicolas Joseph Smulders, *Peeriodieke Onthounding in Het Huwelijk. Methode Ogino-Knaus* (Nijmegen-Utrecht: Dekker & Van de Vegt,1930).

14 Leo Latz, *The Rhythm of Sterility and Fertility in Women* (Chicago: Latz Foundation, 1932).

Latz also conducted and published an effectiveness study on the use of the calendar method for avoiding pregnancy.[15] He provided evidence of no pregnancies from over 54,000 acts of intercourse during the infertile times indicated by his method. Over the next twenty years, his foundation (The Leo Latz Foundation) sold more than six-hundred thousand copies of his book, in which he declared that his simple method could be taught by physicians, professional nurses, or social workers in a twelve-minute office session.[16] The title of Latz's book most likely supplied the title "Rhythm Method" for calendar-based methods, a term still commonly (and erroneously) used for all NFP methods by health professionals and the lay public. Another famous (or infamous) Catholic physician from Harvard University, Dr. John Rock, founded the first Rhythm Clinic in the United States in the 1930s to teach Catholic couples.[17] Unfortunately, Rock was later responsible (along with another physician from Puerto Rico), for obtaining Food and Drug Administration approval for the first hormonal birth control pill (Enovid) in the United States in 1960.

During the 1930s through the mid-1950s, the Rhythm Method was one of the most popular methods of family planning among US women and Catholic women in particular. Upward of 30 percent of women of reproductive age, and 55 percent of Catholic women used calendar-based methods well into the 1950s.[18] With the advent of the hormonal birth control pill, that statistic changed dramatically. The ease of use of birth control pills, coupled with anecdotal evidence of couples unintentionally becoming pregnant with the Rhythm Method, led to a decline in use of calendar-based methods. Interestingly, more women of reproductive age in the United States currently use "Rhythm" than the so-called modern methods of NFP, which rely on cervical mucus and basal body temperature.[19] Furthermore, efforts have been renewed to investigate calendar-based methods using a careful scientific approach.[20]

15 Leo J. Latz and E. Reiner, "Natural Conception Control," *Journal of the American Medical Association* 105, no. 16 (October 19, 1935): 1241.

16 For his work on natural birth regulation, Dr. Latz was dismissed from his position at Loyola University and his book lost its imprimatur from Chicago Cardinal George Mundelein. It was considered scandalous that married couples should have the information that his book provided. Latz continued teaching about his work and NFP at three Catholic nursing programs in Chicago.

17 John Rock, *The Time Has Come* (New York: Avon Books, 1963).

18 Charles F. Westoff and N. R. Ryder, "Conception Control among American Catholics," in *Catholics/U.S.A.; Perspectives on Social Change*, eds. W. T. Liu and N. J. Pallone (New York: John Wiley & Sons, 1970), 257–268.

19 K. Daniels, J. Daugherty, and J. Jones, "Current Contraceptive Status Among Women Aged 15–44: United States, 2011–2013," *NCHS Data Brief* 173 (December 2014): 1–7.

20 Researchers at Georgetown University's Institute for Reproductive Health have developed a fixed-day, calendar-based method of NFP bead system and mobile phone app used to help couples track fertility. The Institute for Reproductive Health researchers found this method of natural birth regulation to be comparable in efficacy to barrier methods of contraception. These researchers are currently investigating the effectiveness of a new calendar-based method of NFP based on day specific probabilities of pregnancy and the use of a cell phone app called Dynamic Optional Timing or DOT. See D. Li, L. Heyer, V. H. Jennings, C. A. Smith, and D. B. Dunson, "Personalised Estimation of a Women's Most Fertile Days," *The European Journal of Contraception & Reproductive Health Care* 21, no. 4 (2016): 323–328.

In 1935, a Catholic parish priest in Germany by the name of Father Wilhelm Hillebrand was teaching his married parishioners the Knaus Calendar method of NFP.[21] A number of the couples he taught became pregnant although that was not their intention (i.e., supposedly they only had intercourse during what the Knaus formula indicated was the infertile time). This disturbed Hillebrand and he sought help from his two physician brothers. One of his brothers was familiar with the early temperature work by Van de Velde and shared this information with him. Hillebrand devised a method in which the couple would use basal body temperature readings (the first morning measurement of body temperature before rising and activity), along with the calendar formulas to determine the fertile and infertile times of the menstrual cycle. Hillebrand is credited as the first person to develop the use of basal body temperature (BBT) along with the calendar methods as a natural means of birth regulation. In 1959, he was awarded an honorary doctorate for his work with body temperature as applied to family planning from the University of Berlin, Germany. Later, in 1977, Dr. Rudolf Vollman would credit Hillebrand as the first person to use the term "Natural Family Planning" in his writings.[22]

The beauty of the Rhythm or calendar-based methods is that they are simple to use and teach. As noted above, it was not until the introduction of hormonal contraceptives in late 1950s that the Rhythm Method of family planning fell into disfavor. In fact, in 1936, Dr. Carl Hartman,[23] a renowned obstetrician and gynecologist from Johns Hopkins Medical School Department of Embryology, stated that the calendar-rhythm methods of family planning were as effective as any available contraceptive at that time.[24]

NFP Scientists during Pius XII's Papacy (1939–1958)

It was not until 1951 when Pius XII gave an address to the Italian Catholic Union of Obstetrical Nurses that the use of NFP was elevated to something more than a topic to be mentioned quietly in the confessional.[25] Pius XII provided a mandate to these nurses: they should not only understand and provide natural methods of birth regulation but also know and defend the moral law. In the same address,

21 Rudolf Vollman, "Foreword," in *Natural Family Planning: Introduction to the Methods*, ed. Clara R. Ross (Washington, D.C.: The Human Life Foundation, 1977), 1–5.

22 Vollman, "Foreword," in *Natural Family Planning: Introduction to the Methods*, 1–5.

23 C. G. Hartman, *Time of Ovulation in Women* (Baltimore: The Williams & Wilkins Co., 1936).

24 It is commonly expressed that the newer methods of NFP (mucus only and mucus plus temperature, etc.) are more effective than the Calendar Rhythm Method. However, in the 1990s, Robert Kambic, a Catholic scientist at the time from Johns Hopkins University involved with NFP science for many years, conducted a meta-analysis of the Rhythm Method studies and found that the typical-use effectiveness of the method was around 15 unintended pregnancies per 100 over twelve months of use. This unintended pregnancy rate is well within the unintended pregnancy rates found with many of the studies conducted with the more modern methods of NFP. See Robert T. Kambic and Virginia Lamprecht, "Calendar Rhythm Efficacy: A Review," *Advances in Contraception* 12, no. 2 (1996):123–128.

25 Pope Pius XII, *Address to Italian Catholic Union of Midwives* (October 29, 1951) in *Natural Family Planning: Nature's Way—God's Way*, ed. Zimmerman, 229–230.

he stated that these methods are to be used for serious reasons only, but that these reasons could include the woman's health (body and mind) and economic reasons. He even said there could be serious reasons why married couples could use natural birth regulation methods for the entirety of their reproductive lives.

Pius XII gave an address that same year to a congress on large families. At the congress, he stated that he hoped scientists would provide a secure base for the natural methods of birth regulation, that Catholic scientists should "bend their backs" to this problem, and that Catholic medical and research faculties should do all they can to meet this need and, in doing so, be eager to serve the Lord.[26] In response to the development of the new anovulant progestational pill (i.e., hormonal birth control pill), Pius XII stated in a 1958 address to the Italian Congress of Hematologists that the use of such pills would be against the natural law and would be illicit.[27] He did note, however, that it would be licit to use these drugs to treat serious organic disorders. Physicians began using the new progestational pill to treat menstrual cycle irregularity but also realized that it suppressed ovulation and could be used as a hormonal contraceptive.

A number of scientists were stimulated by their faith and the pleadings of Pius XII and Catholic bishops for the need for better methods of natural birth regulation. Notable were the Catholic physician/scientists who researched and developed basal body temperature (BBT) as a method of NFP. Drs. Vollman (Switzerland and subsequently the United States), Peter J. Bartzen (United States), Gerhard Döring (Germany), and John Marshall (England) are notable for their work on the BBT.[28] Vollman developed a charting system where he had women record not only temperature but also abdominal (ovulation) pain and changes in cervical mucus. He also studied the lengths and characteristics of the woman's menstrual cycle through phases of life.[29] Marshall (1968), a neurologist, is credited with conducting the first prospective field trial of the effectiveness of BBT in avoiding pregnancy.[30]

Like Vollman, other physicians began independently to combine various biological indicators to aid women in the self-determination of the fertile and

26 Pope Pius XII, *Address to the National Congress of the Family Front and the Association of Large Families* (November 26, 1951), in *Natural Family Planning: Nature's Way—Gods Way*, ed. Zimmerman, 231.

27 Pope Pius XII, *Address to Hematologists*, in *Natural Family Planning: Nature's Way—God's Way*, ed. Zimmerman, 228.

28 P. J. Bartzen, "Effectiveness of the Temperature Rhythm System of Contraception," *Fertility and Sterility* 18, no. 5 (1967): 694–706; Gerhard K. Döring, "Detection of Ovulation by the Basal Body Temperature Method," in *Proceedings of a Research Conference on Natural Family Planning*, eds. William A. Uricchio and Mary Kay Williams (Washington, D.C.: The Human Life Foundation, 1972), 171–180: Gerhard K. Döring, "Uber die zuverlassigkeit der temperaturmethode zur empfangnisverhutung" [*Reliability of the Temperature Method as a Means of Contraception*], *Deutsche Medizinische Wochenschrift* 92, no. 23 (1967): 1055–1061. [English abstract: *The Yearbook of Obstetrics and Gynecology*, (Yearbook Medical Publisher), 354–355]; Rudolf. F. Vollman, "Assessment of the Fertile and Sterile Phases of the Menstrual Cycle," *International Review of Natural Family Planning* 1 (1977): 40–47; John Marshall, "A Field Trial of the Basal-Body Temperature Method of Regulating Births," *Lancet* 292, no. 7558 (July 6, 1968): 6–10.

29 Vollman, "Foreword" in *Natural Family Planning: Introduction to the Methods*, 1–5.

30 Marshall, "A Field Trial of the Basal-Body Temperature Method of Regulating Births," 6–10.

infertile times of their menstrual cycles.[31] Drs. Edward Keefe (United States) and Josef Rötzer (Austria) are considered early developers of the multiple indexed methods. In the United States, these are called the Sympto-Thermal Methods (STM).[32] Keefe asked his women patients to check for temperature, cervical mucus elasticity, and internal cervix changes. He is noteworthy for developing the Ovulindex Thermometer that is specifically used for BBT. The thermometer is calibrated in tenths of a degree and thus more sensitive to detecting small changes in body temperature. In a short biography published by the NFP Program of the United States Conference of Catholic Bishops (USCCB), Keefe mentioned that as a Catholic physician, he was inspired by the pleadings of Pius XII to develop and research methods of NFP.[33] Rötzer is known for developing the rule for identifying the full thermal shift (i.e., three higher basal body temperature readings than the preceding six).The World Health Organization adapted this rule as the standard means of determining the BBT shift.[34] It is important to note that Rötzer's research influenced other physicians who would impact NFP education in the United States. Notably, Dr. Konald Prem, the department chair of obstetrics and gynecology at the University of Minnesota, was instrumental in helping John and Shiela Kippley develop the STM system based on Rötzer's work for the Couple to Couple League.[35]

Husband and wife team, Drs. John and Evelyn Billings (Australia) are considered the developers of the single fertility (mucus only) indicator model of NFP called the Ovulation Method or the Billings Ovulation Method® (also referred to as OM or BOM®).[36] In the 1950s, John Billings was asked by the archbishop of Melbourne to help improve the Rhythm Method. He studied the calendar method and BBT but also read some early studies on cervical mucus. Billings at first combined BBT with cervical mucus changes. When his wife, Evelyn, became actively involved with the development of the Ovulation Method in the 1960s, she realized that women were able to effectively track their fertile and infertile times of the cycle by the changes in their cervical mucus alone. Dr. James Brown, an endocrinologist, and Dr. Henry Burger, (Distinguished Scientist, Hudson Institute, Australia), helped to validate the method

31 Rudolf Vollman, *The Menstrual Cycle* (Philadelphia: W. B. Saunders, 1977).

32 Edward F. Keefe, "Self-Examination of the Cervix as a Guide in Fertility Control," *International Review of Natural Family Planning* 10, no. 4 (Winter 1986): 333–338; Josef Rötzer, "Further Evolution of the Sympto-Thermal Methods," *International Review of Natural Family Planning* 1, no. 2 (Summer 1977): 139–150.

33 Edward Keefe with Theresa Notare, "NFP Pioneers, a Lifetime of Service," in *NFP-Diocesan Activity Report* 4 (1993): 4–5.

34 Josef Rötzer, *Family Planning the Natural Way: A Complete Guide to the Symptom-Thermal Method—Including Questionnaires, Charts, and Reliable Procedures* (Old Tappan, N.J.: Fleming H. Revell Co., 1981).

35 John Kippley, "The Couple to Couple League, Progress Through Teamwork." *International Review of Natural Family Planning* 1 (1977): 90–92.

36 Evelyn Billings and Ann Westmore, *The Billings Method* (New York: Ballantine, 2003); John J. Billings and Evelyn L. Billings, "Determination of Fertile and Infertile Days by the Mucus Pattern: Development of the Ovulation Method," in *Proceedings of a Research Conference on Natural Family Planning*, ed. Uricchio and Williams, 35–148.

by conducting correlational studies with female reproductive hormones and the peak in cervical mucus.[37] Meanwhile, Dr. Eric Odeblad, a Swedish physician and scientist, was conducting research and classifying cervical mucus apart from the work of the Billings. Eventually, he joined with the Billingses to help provide a scientific foundation for the ovulation method and, in particular, the functions of cervical mucus in reproduction.[38]

In the mid-1960s, Dr. Gabriele Bonomi (Italy) also developed and published a mucus-only method of NFP. His method was little known outside of Italy due to the lack of promotion.[39] Bonomi was inspired by the document *Humanae vitae* and founded the "*Humanae vitae* Movement" in Italy to educate youth and couples about the value of conjugal love lived according to a natural order designed by God for the good of men and women.

The Papal Birth Control Commission and the Influence of an Inaccurate "Study" (1963–1966)

After Pius XII died in 1958, the new pope, John XXIII, called the Second Vatican Council to address the concerns of the modern world. Originally, one of the topics to be addressed in the general sessions of the council was that of the transmission of human life.[40] Archbishop (later Cardinal) Leo Joseph Suenens of Belgium persuaded the Holy Father to take the topic out of the general council and appoint a special commission of theologians and scientists to discuss the issue. John XXIII did not live to see the work of the commission completed. That would be the task of his successor, Paul VI (1963–1978).

The Papal Birth Control Commission met from 1963 to 1966 and grew from six to over seventy-five members.[41] In 1966, they completed their task by submitting a majority and a minority report to Paul VI. The majority report recommended that the Church change its teaching on contraception.[42] The report was not to be shared with others outside of the commission and was meant only for use by the pope. As is now known, some members of the commission leaked the report to the press.[43] As a result, many expected the Church to change its moral

37 E. L. Billings, J. J. Billings, J. B. Brown, and H. G. Burger, "Symptoms and Hormonal Changes Accompanying Ovulation," *The Lancet* 299, no 7745 (February 5, 1972): 282–284.

38 Erik Odeblad, "The Discovery of Different Types of Cervical Mucus and the Billings Ovulation Method," *Bulletin of the Natural Family Planning Council of Victoria* 21, no. 3 (1994): 3–34; Erik Odeblad, "Cervical Mucus and Their Functions," *Journal of the Irish Colleges of Physicians and Surgeons* 26, no. 1 (1997): 27–32.

39 Gabriele Bonomi, *Nuovo Metodo Natural per il Controlle delle Nascite: D'uovo* (Brescia: Bailetti, La Chiara, 1968).

40 Robert McClory, *Turning Point* (New York: Crossroad Publishing Co., 1995), 39–41.

41 McClory, *Turning Point*, 188–190.

42 Majority Report of the Birth Control Commission, "Responsible Parenthood," in McClory, *Turning Point*, 171–187.

43 Bernardo Colombo, email communication to author, 1994. Colombo was a professor of biostatistics and sociology at the University of Padua, Italy, and a member of the Birth Control Commission, appointed for the second meeting in 1964.

teachings on contraception. In the end, as is well known, Paul VI rejected the majority report and promulgated *Humanae vitae* in 1968.

Despite the majority report, it is interesting to note that among the three married couples appointed to the commission, two of them included Catholic scientists who had contributed to NFP research. These scientists were Drs. Charles Rendu (France) and Laurent Potvin (Canada). Rendu, along with his wife, Elizabeth, was very active in promoting NFP in France and in French-speaking African countries. Potvin, also with his wife, Colette, promoted NFP in Canada. Both couples rejected the majority report and signed the minority report. The third married couple on the commission, Patrick and Patricia Crowley (United States), sided with the majority report. In fact, many of the commission members who signed the majority report were influenced by a flawed survey that the Crowleys had conducted and provided.[44]

The Crowleys, along with Donald Barrett, a professor from the University of Notre Dame, were the cofounders of the Christian Family Movement (CFM). Reporting on the CFM survey to the Commission, Patricia Crowley said that the use of the Rhythm Method was harmful to married life. One of the concerns of the Papal Birth Control Commission was whether the use of natural birth regulation might be harmful to marital relationships.[45] The Crowley study was not only biased but also flawed scientifically. It provided anecdotal information based on questions which were skewed toward a negative perception of Catholic teaching and the Rhythm Method. While anecdotal experiences by users of the Rhythm Method can provide some understanding of how Rhythm affected the marital bond, anecdotes and biased surveys are often misleading and can give a false perspective.[46] When done correctly, large scientifically studied populations can provide a broader picture of reality and give a person more confidence in proclaiming both benefits and deficits. In any case, the Crowley study was not a valid scientific report.

One of the first serious academic studies on how NFP affects marital relationships was conducted and published in 1970 by Drs. John Marshal and Beverley Rowe.[47] Marshall was one of the original members of the Papal Birth Control Commission. He and Rowe were concerned that the practice of NFP (i.e., in the form of BBT) and the required amount of abstinence for pregnancy avoidance might have a negative effect on marriage. Their study showed that of the 502 couples who responded to their detailed psychological questionnaire, 75 percent

44 See McClory, *Turning Point*, 86–108. The Crowley study was a central influence on the commission's majority report urging a change in the teaching. See also P. Crowley and P. Crowley, "Report to the Papal Birth Control Commission," (1965/1966), University of Notre Dame Archives.

45 See McClory, *Turning Point*, 72–74.

46 Richard J. Fehring and Elizabeth McGraw, "Spiritual Responses to the Regulation of Birth: A Historical Comparison," *Life and Learning* 12 (December 2003): 265–283; Richard J. Fehring, "An Analysis of the Majority Report 'Responsible Parenthood' and its Recommendations on Abortion, Sterilization, and Contraception," *Life and Learning* 13 (2003): 121–146.

47 J. Marshall and B. Rowe, "Psychological Aspects of the Basal Body Temperature Method of Regulating Births," *Fertility and Sterility* 21 (1970): 9, 14–19.

of the wives and 66 percent of the husbands felt their overall use of BBT was satisfactory, and 75 percent of the wives and 74 percent of the husbands felt that the use of BBT was helpful to their marriage. However, 48 percent of the husbands and wives felt that the practice of periodic sexual abstinence was somehow harmful to their marriage.

As mentioned, Marshall also conducted the first effectiveness studies of the combined Rhythm and BBT method of NFP. He showed the total failure rate in those confining coitus to the postovulatory phase of the cycle as 6.6 pregnancies per 100 women-years, while the failure rate of those engaging in coitus in both the preovulatory and postovulatory phases was 19.3.[48] Marshall and a statistician colleague are also known for developing a formula for calculating the day-specific probabilities of pregnancy and defining the biological fertile window.[49]

Another very early member of the Birth Control Commission was Bernardo Colombo from the University of Padua.[50] His brother Carlo was a bishop and personal theologian to Paul VI and a later member of the commission. Colombo was involved with multiple studies of NFP throughout his academic career, including studies on the Ovulation Method, comparisons of days of abstinence, day-specific probabilities of pregnancy, and developing a large data set of menstrual cycles that is being used to this day.[51] Colombo was distraught with the political nature of the Birth Control Commission and that members released the majority report to the press rather than keeping it secret (as they promised) until it was given to the pope.[52]

About the same time as the Birth Control Commission was meeting, another commission was created in the United States. It was called the Commission on Rhythm.[53] This commission was called after an International Symposium on Rhythm was held in Washington, D.C., in 1964. This symposium was cosponsored by the Family Life Bureau of the National Catholic Welfare Conference.[54] It was organized at the urging of the Rt. Rev. Msgr. John C. Knott, director of the Family Life Bureau, and the president of the National Federation of Catholic Physicians Guilds, Dr. Clement P. Cunningham. After this symposium, a number

48 Marshall, "A Field Trial of the Basal-Body-Temperature Method of Regulating Births," 8.

49 J. C. Barrett and J. Marshall, "The Risk of Conception on Different Days of the Menstrual Cycle," *Population Studies* 23, no. 3 (1969): 455–461.

50 McClory, *Turning Point*, 47–48.

51 B. Colombo, G. Masarotto, and G. Daily, "Fecundability: First Results from a New Data Base," *Demographic Research* 3 (2000): 5; B. Colombo, A. Mion, K. Passarin, and B. Scarpa, "Cervical Mucus Symptom and Daily Fecundability: First Result of a New Database," *Statistical Methods in Medical Research* 15, no. 2 (April 2006): 161–180.

52 Carrying on the work of Colombo at the University of Padua is the Catholic biostatistician Dr. Bruno Scarpa. He has participated (and continues to do so) in many NFP studies and conferences. In addition to Scarpa, the biostatistician Dr. Rene Ecochard from the University of Lyon, France, has made significant contributions as well. Ecochard has a consistent record in NFP research and publishing. In addition, he and his wife have been active in promoting NFP in France and other countries.

53 Herbert Ratner, "Commission on Rhythm: Origin of the Commission," *The Linacre Quarterly* 32, no. 4 (1965): 356–357.

54 Now called United States Conference of Catholic Bishops.

of physicians met in Chicago to continue discussions on the topic of Rhythm and Church teaching and to plan future meetings on the subject. Cunningham also had a personal meeting about the issue with Paul VI in Rome.

The second International Symposium on Rhythm met in Kansas City in 1965 and included a scientific program for physicians. Among the speakers and topics presented were: Dr. Konald Prem (University of Minnesota), speaking on "The Basal Temperature Method of the Practice of Rhythm"; Dr. Max Levin (New York Medical School), on "Sexual Fulfillment in the Couple Practicing Rhythm"; and Dr. Daniel McSweeney (Tufts University School of Medicine), on "The Cervical Mucus Test for the Determination of Ovulation."[55] Over 300 participants attended the symposium.

Dr. Herbert Ratner (Chicago) reported on the international symposiums in the journal of the National Federation of Catholic Physician Guilds, *The Linacre Quarterly*. The continued meetings of this planning commission included a mixture of priests and physicians, including department heads of medical schools. The 4th International Symposium on Abortion, Rhythm and Life was held in 1969 in Chicago.[56] As indicated by the title, the commission took on a broader role that included the rising issue of abortion and other threats to family life and marriage. Of significance is that this commission initiated a new journal *Child and Health* with Ratner as chief editor. The journal included articles on Rhythm, pro-life subjects, and family topics.

Post-*Humanae vitae* NFP Scientists (1968–2005)

By the time *Humanae vitae* was promulgated, most of the major systems of NFP were already developed and studied.[57] In fact, twenty years later in 1988, Dr. Claude Lanctot, a Catholic physician scientist from Canada, indicated at an international NFP conference in Hong Kong that the NFP pioneer phase was already completed. He noted that during the years 1955–1970, the modern methods of NFP were developed.[58] The next phase, covering the years 1970–1988, was what he called the "popularization phase" or what could be referred to as the program development, marketing, and scaling-up phase.

Soon after *Humanae vitae* was promulgated, the Catholic bishops in the United States provided funds for the development of The Human Life Foundation (later called the Human Life and Natural Family Planning Foundation), which was to be an independent, nonsectarian organization dedicated to pursue research essential

55 Herbert Ratner, "Commission on Rhythm: The 2nd International Symposium on Rhythm," *The Linacre Quarterly* 33, no. 1 (1966): 310.

56 Herbert Ratner, "National Commission on Human Life Reproduction and Rhythm," *The Linacre Quarterly* 36, no. 1 (1969): 77–78.

57 The methods are the calendar methods, Sympto-Thermal methods, and the newer cervical mucus-only methods.

58 Claude Lanctot, "Historical Background of Natural Family Planning," in *Proceedings of the International Seminar on Natural Family Planning and Family Life Education*, eds. Ramon C. Ruiz, John Russell, and Irene Osmund Ruiz (Hong Kong: Hong Kong University Press, 1988), 1–10.

to the improvement of NFP.[59] The first Scientific Advisory Committee of this foundation included six scientists with doctorate degrees and ten physicians who were either full professors at a university or department chairs of medicine. One of the first projects for this group was to organize and present an international conference on NFP, commonly referred to as the Arlie House Conference.[60] Of significance is that this might have been the first major conference that used the term "Natural Family Planning." A physician scientist from the National Institutes of Health (NIH) suggested using the term "Natural Family Planning." The conference was partially funded by the NIH Center for Population Research and National Institute of Child Health and Human Development.[61] The proceedings were published and included nineteen papers and discussion from fifty-nine conferees who came from eight countries. There were presentations on three of the newer NFP methods, namely, BBT, STM, and the Ovulation Method. Of note was the presentation of papers on psychological and sociological implications of family planning as well.

Among the participants at this conference were Drs. Gerard Döring and John Marshall, developers of the temperature method (BBT); John and Evelyn Billings, developers of the new Ovulation Method; and Lanctot, one of the researchers and promoters of the STM in Canada and the United States.[62] In 1972, what became known as the Billings Ovulation Method® (BOM®) was just being introduced in the United States. The sense at the conference was that this method had a lot of potential for a simple approach that provided a natural indicator for the beginning, peak, and end of the fertile phase. Although as mentioned, another Catholic physician, Bonomi, developed a single mucus indictor method in the 1960s and published a book in Italian, it seems that the BOM is the one that took off and generated the most optimism at that time, probably because it was introduced to the United States, Canada, and other developed English-speaking countries around the world. In addition, the BOM received federal and international funding for large multi-country studies.

After the 1972 Arlie House conference, a number of effectiveness studies of the BOM were conducted and published, including one in the United States that was led by Sr./Dr. Hanna Klaus at Saint Louis University School of Medicine.[63] Klaus, a Catholic physician, obstetrician, and gynecologist as well as a religious missionary sister, dedicated her life to promoting NFP. Her study is the first effectiveness study of the Billings Ovulation Method® in the United States.[64]

59 Larry Kane, "NFP Pioneers: Human Life and NFP Foundation," *NFP-Diocesan-Activity-Report* 5, no. 4 (1994): 6–7.

60 See Uricchio and Williams, eds., *Proceedings of a Research Conference on Natural Family Planning*, xvii–xviii.

61 Kane, "NFP Pioneers: Human Life and NFP Foundation," 6–7.

62 Uricchio and Williams, eds. *Proceedings of a Research Conference on Natural Family Planning*, xxiii–xxv.

63 H. Klaus, J. M. Goebel, B. Muraski, M. T. Egizio, D. Weitzel, R. S. Taylor, M. U. Fagan K. Ek, and K. Hobday, "Use Effectiveness and Client Satisfaction in Six Centers Teaching the Billings Ovulation Method," *Contraception* 19, no. 6 (1978): 613–629.

64 Later, at the request of the Billingses, Klaus also turned her attention to investigate and develop programs that integrate fertility knowledge with chastity education for adolescents. She eventually developed

In the 1970s, interest in the Billings Ovulation Method® and the Sympto-Thermal Method stimulated federal funding for two randomized comparison studies in Columbia and the United States.[65] Dr. William A. Uricchio, a Catholic scientist and past president of the Human Life Foundation, was one of the main organizers of the comparison study conducted in the United States. At this time, and probably the most famous research of the Billings Ovulation Method® is the five-country effectiveness study that was funded by the World Health Organization (WHO) and the United States Aid to International Development (USAID).[66]

The STM was promoted and studied by Lanctot along with Dr. Suzanne Parenteau-Carreau, also a Catholic physician from Canada.[67] The STM became a standard method and program of NFP through an organization called SERENA. The SERENA program began in the 1950s based on the CLER program in France that was developed and led by Rendu, the Catholic scientist and gynecologist who was a member of the Papal Birth Control Commission, and with the early pioneers and promoters of NFP, Drs. Michele and Francois Guy from Grenoble, France. Parenteau-Carreau is a long-time medical patron, consultant, researcher, and scientist associated with SERENA.[68]

Over the years, there emerged a number of variants of the Billings Ovulation Method®. In the early 1970s, Klaus and a young Catholic physician obstetrician gynecologist, Dr. Thomas Hilgers, worked at the University of Saint Louis School of Medicine. Klaus was involved with an NFP federal grant proposal that was written to study the BOM®. It eventually was funded with Hilgers as the principal investigator. Hilgers conducted a number of studies on cervical mucus and other indicators of fertility. From his work, along with contributions from his wife, Susan, and two Catholic professional nurses, Diane Daly and Ann Prebil,[69] he developed a cervical mucus-based system

---

the TeenSTAR (Sexuality Teaching in the context of Adult Responsibility) program, which was studied and then promoted worldwide. See H. Klaus, "Abstinence and Abstinence-only Education," *Journal of Adolescent Health* 39, no. 2 (2006): 151–154 and H. Klaus, L. M. Bryan, M. L. Bryant, U. Fagan, M. B. Harrigan, F. Kearns, "Fertility awareness/natural family planning for adolescents and their families: report of multisite pilot project," *International Journal of Adolescent Medical Health* 3, no. 2 (1987): 101–119.

65 M. E. Wade, P. McCarthy, J. R., Abernathy, G. S., Harris, H. S. Danzer, and W. A. Uricchio, "A Randomized Prospective Study of the Use-Effectiveness of Two Methods of Natural Family Planning: An Interim Report," *American Journal of Obstetrics and Gynecology* 134, no. 6 (1979): 628–631; M. E. Wade, P. McCarthy, G. D., Barunstein, J. R. Abernathy, C. M. Suchindran, G. S. Harris, H. C. Danzer, and W. A. Uricchio, "A Randomized Prospective Study of the Use Effectiveness of Two Methods of Natural Family Planning," *American Journal of Obstetrics and Gynecology* 141, no. 4 (1981): 368–376; J. E. Medina, A. Cifuentes, J. R. Abernathy, J. M. Spieler, and M. E. Wade, "Comparative Evaluation of Two Methods of Natural Family Planning in Columbia," *American Journal of Obstetrics and Gynecology* 138, no. 8 (1980): 1142–1147.

66 World Health Organization, "A Prospective Multicentre Trial of the Ovulation Method of Natural Family Planning, II: The Effectiveness Phase," *Fertility and Sterility* 36, no. 5 (November 1981): 591–598.

67 F. J. Rice, C. A. Lanctot, and D. Garcia-Devesa, "Effectiveness of the Sympto-Thermal Method of Natural Family Planning: An International Study," *International Journal of Fertility* 26, no. 3 (1981): 222–230; Suzanne Parenteau-Carreau, "The Sympto-Thermal Methods," *International Journal of Fertility* 26, no. 3 (1981): 170–181.

68 Suzanne Parenteau-Carreau, *Planning Your Family the S-T Way* (Ottawa: SERENA Canada, 1977).

69 T. W. Hilgers, G. E. Abraham, and D. Cavanagh, "Natural Family Planning I. The Peak Symptom and Estimated Time of Ovulation," *Obstetrics and Gynecology* 52, no. 5 (November 1, 1978): 575–582; T. W. Hilgers, K. D. Daly, A. M. Prebil, and S. K. Hilgers, "Cumulative Pregnancy Rates in Patients

of NFP that is now called the Creighton Model Fertility*Care*™ system, or the Creighton Model.

The Creighton Model is a form of the Ovulation Method that uses a standardized mucus rating, couple teaching program, menstrual cycle charting, follow-up, and pregnancy evaluation. Hilgers moved to Creighton University School of Medicine in Omaha, Nebraska, where he was an associate professor of medicine and founder of the Creighton University Natural Family Planning Education and Research Center. He and his wife eventually started their own independent institute named after and dedicated to Paul VI.[70] Hilgers is also known for the development of what is called NaProTECHNOLOGY,™ a system of woman's health care that integrates the use of the Creighton Model (CrM) into medical treatment protocols.[71]

An additional example of an NFP method that is based on the work of the Billingses can be seen in the Modified Mucus Method, developed by Dr. Kathleen Dorairaj, a Catholic physician from India. This simplified form of the Ovulation Method was specifically designed for the indigent population in India.[72]

The Human Life and Natural Family Planning Foundation was instrumental in promoting and facilitating NFP in the United States. One of the members of the foundation was Mary Catherine Martin, who received her doctorate in nursing from The Catholic University of American in Washington, D.C. Martin's doctoral dissertation treated the development of an NFP teacher training program and teaching materials.[73] Through her efforts and the funding of the Human Life and NFP Foundation, booklets were published on NFP including reproductive graphics that were used in many diocesan and regional NFP teaching programs. These materials also became the bases for the NFP materials used in the WHO multicountry study of the BOM®.[74]

In 1974, the president of the United States National Federation of Catholic Physician Guilds was Dr. John Brennan, an obstetrician and gynecologist from Milwaukee. Brennan wrote a letter to every member of the federation and provided each with a Billings booklet.[75] He encouraged the members to

With Apparently Normal Fertility and Fertility-Focused Intercourse," *Journal of Reproductive Medicine* 37, no. 10 (1992): 864–866; see also T. W. Hilgers and J. B. Stanford, "Creighton Model NaProEducation Technology for Avoiding Pregnancy: Use Effectiveness," *The Journal of Reproductive Medicine* 43, no. 6 (June 1998): 495–502.

70 The Pope Paul VI Institute for the Study of Human Reproduction.

71 Thomas W. Hilgers, *The Medical Applications of Natural Family Planning* (Omaha: Pope Paul VI Institute Press, 1991); Thomas W. Hilgers, *The Scientific Foundations of the Ovulation Method* (Omaha: Pope Paul VI Institute Press, 1995); Thomas W. Hilgers, *The Creighton Model NaProEducation System* (Omaha: Pope Paul VI Institute Press, 1996).

72 Kathleen Dorairaj, "The Modified Mucus Method," in *Proceedings of the International Seminar on Natural Family Planning and Family Life Education*, ed. Ramon C. Ruiz, John Russell, and Irene Osmund Ruiz, (Hong Kong: Hong Kong University Press, 1988), 53–60.

73 Mary Katherine Martin, "NFP Pioneers: NFP Teacher Training and Service Development Efforts–1974–1985," *NFP-Diocesan-Activity-Report* 6, no. 1 (1995): 10–11.

74 Martin, "NFP Pioneers" 10–11.

75 John Brennan, "What Can the Doctor Do?" in *A Reader in Natural Family Planning. Report on International Conferences*, ed. Anthony Zimmerman (Collegeville, Minn.: The Human Life Center), 59.

have copies of the booklet for their patients (at that time it cost only 20 cents). Brennan was also an officer of the Human Life and Natural Family Planning Foundation and member of the World Organization of the Ovulation Method Billings (WOOMB).

About the same time that Brennan was encouraging the use of NFP among Catholic physicians in the United States, Paul VI continued to plead for research and scholarship on natural methods of birth regulation. In a speech given in 1974 to the 25th General Assembly of Pharmacology, the Holy Father again invited health professionals to deepen and broaden their knowledge about the Church's teaching on the grave question which, at the deepest level, concerns the "concept of man."[76] Towards the end of his pontificate in 1977, in an allocution to the Congress of the International Federation of Family Life Promotion, Paul VI stated the importance of the knowledge of the biological laws of human fertility which can enhance a healthy regulation of births by natural methods. He stressed the need for more scientific research in NFP by stating that "scientific research be intensified in this area."[77] He also said that the scientific work should be coordinated and supported with funds which are proportionate to the issue in question and to the services rendered. Paul VI died in 1978.

NFP Scientists During John Paul II's Papacy (1978–2005)

John Paul II greatly expanded the Church's reflection on the understanding of human sexuality as designed by God and the methods of NFP as ethical support for married couples. He did this in many ways, notably through the development of the Theology of the Body;[78] addresses to promoters of NFP and nurse midwives; the apostolic exhortation *Familiaris consortio*;[79] and in particular, through the encyclical *Evangelium vitae*.[80] Early in his pontificate (November 3, 1979), he provided encouragement to the growing number of physicians and scientists addressing NFP "since at stake is the welfare of families and of societies in their legitimate concern to harmonize human fertility with their capabilities."[81] A few months later, on January 26, 1980, he addressed midwives, emphasizing the important contribution they make

76 Pope Paul VI, *To Participants in the Twenty Fifth General Assembly of Pharmacology, September 7, 1974*, in *Natural Family Planning: Nature's Way–God's Way*, ed. Zimmerman, 257.

77 "Letter of Cardinal Villot in the name of Pope Paul VI to the Congress of the International Federation for Family Life Promotion, June 1977," in *Natural Family Planning: Nature's Way–God's Way*, ed. Zimmerman, 257–258.

78 See http://www.usccb.org/nfp/catholic-teaching/theology-of-the-body.cfm.

79 See Pope John Paul II, Apostolic Exhortation *Familiaris consortio* (November 22, 1981), http://w2.vatican.va/content/john-paul-ii/en/apost_exhortations.index.html.

80 Pope John Paul II, Encyclical Letter *Evangelium vitae* (March 25, 1995), http://w2.vatican.va/content/john-paul-ii/en/encyclicals.index.html.

81 Pope John Paul II, *Address to Promoters of Natural Family Planning* (January 26, 1980), in *Natural Family Planning: Nature's Way—God's Way*, ed. Zimmerman, 258–259.

in providing advice and practical guidance to couples wishing to carry out responsible procreation.[82]

In *Familiaris consortio*, John Paul II asked that scholars explain the moral and anthropologic differences between contraception and natural birth regulation.[83] In *Evangelium vitae,* he notes that the moral law obliges couples "in every case to control the impulse of instinct and passion, and to respect the biological laws inscribed in their person."[84] John Paul II said that "[i]t is precisely this respect which makes legitimate, at the service of responsible procreation, the use of natural methods of regulating fertility."[85] He also mentioned the effectiveness of NFP methods when he stated that an "honest appraisal of their effectiveness should dispel certain prejudices which are still widely held, and should convince married couples, as well as health care and social workers, of the importance of proper training in this area.[86] A main concern in this encyclical is the desire to build, what John Paul II calls, a "Culture of Life." It involves the implementation of long-term practical projects and initiatives inspired by the Gospel. John Paul II gives direction to this effort by saying, "At the first stage of life, centres for natural methods of regulating fertility should be promoted as a valuable help to responsible parenthood, in which all individuals, and in the first place the child, are recognized and respected in their own right.[87]

The Holy Father continues and notes that a unique responsibility belongs to health-care personnel—doctors, pharmacists, nurses, chaplains, men and women religious, administrators and volunteers. He sees that the work of education in the service of life involves the training of married couples in responsible procreation.[88] John Paul II especially calls upon intellectuals to build a new culture, with a specific challenge to Catholics, "who are called to be present and active in the leading centres where culture is formed, in schools and universities, in places of scientific and technological research, of artistic creativity and of the study of man."[89] Appropriate contributions should come from universities, particularly from Catholic universities, centers and institutes.[90]

University-Based NFP Scientists

Georgetown University: In the mid-1980s, Dr. John Queenan, a Catholic professor of obstetrics and gynecology and chair of the Department of Obstetrics and Gynecology at Georgetown University School of Medicine, was instrumental

82 Pope John Paul II, *Address to Midwives* (1980), in *Natural Family Planning: Nature's Way—God's Way*, ed. Zimmerman, 259–260.

83 Pope John Paul II, *Familiaris consortio*, 32.

84 Pope John Paul II, *Evangelium vitae*, 97.

85 Pope John Paul II, *Evangelium vitae*, 97.

86 Pope John Paul II, *Evangelium vitae*, 97.

87 Pope John Paul II, *Evangelium vitae*, 88.

88 Pope John Paul II, *Evangelium vitae*, 89.

89 Pope John Paul II, *Evangelium vitae*, 98.

90 See Pope John Paul II, *Evangelium vitae*, 98.

in obtaining a multimillion-dollar grant from USAID and WHO to start the Institute for International Studies in Natural Family Planning[91] at Georgetown University, which was associated with the department of obstetrics and gynecology.[92] From its inception, Georgetown's NFP institute would be secular in nature despite being associated with a Catholic university.[93] This approach was due to the requirements of the USAID grant. In addition, its mandate was to research the natural methods and provide programming in developing nations. Dr. Victoria Jennings, a non-Catholic and specialist in Public Health, was named the executive director.

The staff from Georgetown's Institute for International Studies in NFP became involved in a significant project in 1988. They met with experts on breastfeeding and fertility in Bellagio, Italy. The group of experts developed a consensus report on fertility and breastfeeding. Based on the research, they agreed on several principles for effective pregnancy avoidance when a woman breastfeeds: total breastfeeding, has no menstrual bleeding, and is within the first six months of the birth of her child. If a postpartum and breastfeeding woman meets the three criteria, then she has a less than 2 percent chance of pregnancy when engaging in intercourse. This became known as the Bellagio Consensus. The method it produced is called the Lactational Amenorrhea Method (or LAM).[94]

In 1990, Georgetown's NFP institute sponsored a large international conference at the university. The proceedings were published in two parts: the first as a supplement to the *American Journal of Obstetrics and Gynecology*[95] and the second

91 The Institute was founded in 1985. It was renamed the Institute for Reproductive Health in the 1990s.

92 John T. Queenan, "Welcoming Remarks by John T. Queenan," in *Natural Family Planning: Current Knowledge and New Strategies for the 1990s. Proceedings of a Conference, Part II, Georgetown University, Washington, DC, December 10–14, 1990*, ed. John T. Queenan, Victoria H. Jennings, Jeffery M Spieler, and Helena von Hertzen (Washington, D.C.: Georgetown University Institute for International Studies in Natural Family Planning, 1991), 4. This conference was cosponsored by Georgetown's Institute for International Studies in Natural Family Planning, the United States Agency for International Development, and the World Health Organization.

93 Over the years, the scientists at Georgetown's institute have adhered to family planning research regulations, such that they followed that discipline's definitions of fertility awareness-based methods (FABMs), effectiveness rates, and recommendations for avoidance of sexually transmitted infections by referring to "unprotected" sexual intercourse in their materials. At the same time, they have made contributions to the viability of natural methods, notably, their attempts to simplify the methods with their Standard Days and Two-Day methods. Unfortunately, in recent years, they also included the option of condom-use during the fertile phase of the menstrual cycle if clients choose that behavior. That was not part of their original mandate when they were founded. It also places their methods into the category of "combined methods"—those natural methods which also make use of barriers—rather than authentic NFP methods.

94 World Health Organization Task Force, "The World Health Organization Multinational Study of Breast-feeding and Lactational Amenorrhea. III. Pregnancy during breast-feeding," *Fertility and Sterility* 72 (September 1999): 431–439.

95 John T. Queenan, Victoria H. Jennings, Jeffery M Spieler, and Helena von Hertzen, eds., *Natural Family Planning: Current Knowledge and New Strategies for the 1990s. Proceedings of a Conference, Part I*, "Supplement," *American Journal of Obstetrics and Gynecology* (St Louis: Mosby-Year Book, Inc., 1991).

published by the institute itself.[96] The conference included a "Who's Who" in NFP, including representatives from NFP programs from thirty-one countries and five continents. The conference focused on the scientific experts in the physiology of reproduction, NFP method updates and effectiveness, and the breastfeeding transition to fertility and the use of NFP. At this conference, a number of scientific papers were presented on the lactational amenorrhea method and the use of NFP during the postpartum breastfeeding transition to fertility.

Marquette University: In the early 1980s, Brennan approached Dr. Richard Fehring, a young Catholic scientist and assistant professor at Marquette University who received his doctorate in nursing science at The Catholic University of America, to start an NFP training program at Marquette University College of Nursing. Fehring explored a number of existing NFP teacher training programs and eventually attended the Creighton University program under the direction of Hilgers. In 1985, Fehring and other faculty at Marquette started providing NFP services through the College of Nursing and at the Catholic Hospitals in Milwaukee. Fehring became the president of the American Academy of Natural Family Planning (AAFNP)[97] in 1990 and published one of the first effectiveness studies of the Creighton Model.[98]

In 1998, Dr. Fehring started what is now called the Marquette University Institute of NFP and, with other Catholic professional nurses (in particular Mary Schneider and Susana Crespo), and Catholic physicians, developed a new system of NFP that integrates hormonal monitoring technology. They named the new system the Marquette Model (MM) of NFP.[99] In 2000, a for-credit NFP teacher training program for health professionals was approved and launched at Marquette University and in 2001 it became an all-online access program.

Fehring became a member of the National NFP Advisory Board of the USCCB and writer-editor of *Current Medical Research in NFP* published by the USCCB. In cooperation with Dr. Theresa Notare, assistant director of the Natural Family Planning Program at the USCCB, Fehring and others at the Marquette University Institute for NFP developed, presented, and published proceedings of three national scholarly conferences on NFP.[100]

96 Queenan, et al., ed., *Natural Family Planning: Current Knowledge and New Strategies for the 1990s. Proceedings of a Conference, Part II.*

97 The accrediting and certification association of Creighton Model education centers and teachers. The AANFP later changed its name to the American Association of Fertility*Care*™ Professionals.

98 R. J. Fehring, D. Lawrence, and C. Philpot, "Use-Effectiveness of the Creighton Model Ovulation Method of Natural Family Planning," *Journal of Obstetric, Gynecologic, and Neonatal Nursing* 23, no. 4 (1994): 303–309.

99 R. J. Fehring, M. Schneider, and K. Raviele, "Efficacy of Hormonal Fertility Monitoring as a Method of Natural Family Planning," *Journal of Obstetric, Gynecologic, and Neonatal Nursing* 36, no. 2 (2007): 152–160.

100 Richard J. Fehring and Theresa Notare, eds., *Integrating Faith and Science Through Natural Family Planning* (Milwaukee: Marquette University Press, 2004); Richard J. Fehring and Theresa Notare, eds., *Human Fertility: Where Faith and Science Meet* (Milwaukee: Marquette University Press, 2008); Richard J. Fehring and Theresa Notare, eds., *Science, Faith, and Human Fertility: The Third Conference on Ethical Fertility Health Management* (Milwaukee: Marquette University Press, 2012).

Dr. Mary Lee Barron, a Catholic professor and advanced practice nurse at Saint Louis University School of Nursing, was one of the early developers of the MM. She collaborated in research studies on the MM and, in particular, the MM studies on the breastfeeding transition.[101] Barron also developed an NFP education clinic at Saint Louis University. Another significant Catholic physician that was involved with the early development of the MM is Dr. Kathleen Raviele.[102] More recently, Dr. Thomas Bouchard, a family medicine physician associated with the University of Calgary and past president of the Canadian Federation of Catholic Physicians, is an MM provider and has conducted a number of MM effectiveness studies with other scientists at the Marquette University NFP Institute.[103]

Germany: During the 1980s in Germany, the development of NFP was based on followers of Rötzer and a group of German scientists and promoters of NFP who started the NFP *Arbeitsgruppe* (work group) for the collection of data for NFP projects and the development of NFP teachers and programs.[104] In 1985, the group received funding from the German Federal Ministry for Youth, Family, Women and Health for further studies in NFP and for development of NFP programs. The scientific part of this group was situated, at first, at the University of Dusseldorf and then in 2007 at the University of Heidelberg. The scientific leader of this group was professor Dr. Guenter Freundl, a retired professor of the Department of Obstetrics and Gynecology at the University Düsseldorf. Freundl is a dedicated Catholic scientist and principal investigator for many research projects on NFP since 1984.[105] The current section leader for NFP research is Dr. Petra Frank-Herrmann, a Catholic physician and lecturer at the University of Heidelberg.[106] The German work group on NFP and its scientific arm is one

101 Mary Lee Barron and Richard J. Fehring, "Basal Body Temperature Recording: A Useful Recommendation to Couples Seeking Pregnancy?" *Journal of Maternal Child Nursing* 30, no. 5 (2005): 290–296 and Richard J. Fehring, Mary Schneider, and Mary Lee Barron, "Protocol for Determining Fertility while Breastfeeding," *Fertility and Sterility* 84, no. 3 (2005): 805–807. Dr. Raviele was also the first female president of the Catholic Medical Association.

102 Some of her publications include: Fehring, Schneider, and Raviele, "Efficacy of Hormonal Fertility Monitoring"; Richard J. Fehring, Mary Schneider, and Kathleen Raviele, "Pilot Evaluation of an Internet-based Natural Family Planning Education and Service Program," *Journal of Obstetric, Gynecologic, and Neonatal Nursing* 40 (2011): 281–291; Richard J. Fehring, Mary Schneider, Kathleen Raviele, Dana Rodriguez, and Jessica E. Pruszynski, "Randomized Comparison of Two Internet-Supported Fertility Awareness Based Methods of Family Planning," *Contraception* 88, no. 1 (July 2013): 24–30.

103 Thomas P. Bouchard, Mary Schneider, and Richard J. Fehring, "Efficacy of a New Postpartum Transition Protocol for Avoiding Pregnancy," *Journal of the American Board of Family Medicine* 26, no. 1 (2013): 35–44; Thomas P. Bouchard, Richard J. Fehring, and Mary M. Schneider, "Achieving Pregnancy Using Primary Care Interventions to Identify the Fertile Window," *Frontiers in Medicine* 4, art. 250 (January 9, 2018): 1–7.

104 Elizabeth Raith-Paula, Petra Frank-Herrmann, Günter Freundl, and Thomas Strowitzki. *Natürliche Familienplanung heute* (*Natural Family Planning Today*), 4th Edition (Heidelberg, Germany: Springer, 2008), 13.

105 G. Freundel, A. Flynn, P. Frank-Herrmann, and C. Gnoth, "European Multicenter Study of Natural Family Planning (1989–1995): Efficacy and Drop-Out," The European Natural Family Planning Study Groups, *Advances in Contraception* 15, no. 1 (1999): 69–83.

106 P. Frank-Herrmann, J. Heil, C. Gnoth, E. Toledo, S. Baur, C. Pyper, E. Jenetzky, T. Strowitzki, and G. Freundl, "The Effectiveness of a Fertility Awareness-Based Method to Avoid Pregnancy in Relation to a

of the most prolific and consistent research teams in the world. Both Freundl and Frank-Herrmann are noted for their effectiveness studies on the European Double Check Method of NFP, investigating the accuracy of fertility monitors, and integrating NFP with women's health.

Italy: In 1988, three Rome-based medical universities and two pontifical universities presented a conference dedicated to the scientific developments for the twentieth anniversary of *Humanae vitae.*[107] This conference had scientists from England, Europe, German, Italy, and Australia, and it included a number of articles on breastfeeding and fertility, demographics of family planning, and also development of new technology in determining the fertile period of the menstrual cycle.

Fertility Monitors

In 1990, Carl Djerassi, one of the developers of the early progesterone hormonal birth control pill in the United States, predicted that women would be able to monitor their own hormones in order to determine the fertile and infertile times of their menstrual cycles. He called this new method "Jet Age" Natural Family Planning.[108] In the late 1990s, Djerassi's "prediction" seemed to be realized with the introduction of two electronic fertility hormonal monitors.

The first hormonal monitor was produced by Unipath Ltd. (Bedford, England). Called the "Persona," the monitor's purpose was to help women determine their window of fertility in order to avoid pregnancy. The second monitor that was developed was the Clearplan Easy Fertility Monitor (now called the Clearblue® Fertility Monitor, or CBFM). Clearplan Easy Fertility Monitor was developed for couples choosing to achieve a pregnancy.[109]

A number of Catholic scientists conducted a study on the effectiveness of the Persona, including Drs. Freundl at the University of Dusseldorf, John Bonner from Trinity University in Ireland, and Anna Flynn from England.[110] The results from that study enabled Unipath to incorporate a new algorithm for the current Persona that is sold in Europe and Canada.

Regarding the second monitor, health professionals and researchers at Marquette University have incorporated use of the CBFM with other markers of fertility (i.e., cervical mucus and BBT) as an aid to learning and using NFP.[111] The CBFM is currently used on its own along with a calendar algorithm for women

Couple's Sexual Behavior during the Fertile Time: A Prospective Longitudinal Study," *Human Reproduction* 22, no. 5 (2007): 1310–1319.

107 P. F. A. Van Look and S. Mancuso, "Natural Fertility Regulation Today," *International Journal of Gynecology and Obstetrics*, Supplement 1 (1989).

108 C. Djerassi, "Fertility Awareness: Jet-Age Rhythm Method?" *Science* 248 (June 1, 1990): 1061–1062.

109 K. May, "Home Monitoring with the ClearPlan Easy Fertility Monitor for Fertility Awareness," *Journal of International Medical Research* 29 (Suppl 1) (2001): 14A–20A.

110 J. Bonnar, A. Flynn, G. Freundl, R. Kirkman, R. Royston, and R. Snowden, "Personal Hormone Monitoring for Contraception," *British Journal of Family Planning* 24, no. 4 (1999): 128–134.

111 Fehring, Schneider, and Raviele, "Efficacy of Hormonal Fertility Monitoring."

and couples who want a simple, fast, objective, and accurate means to determine the fertile and infertile phases of the menstrual cycle.

In addition to the above, in the early 1990s, Brown (Australia) developed an ovarian monitor for the purpose of having a home use device that measured hormonal profiles of estrogen and progesterone throughout the menstrual cycle.[112] The monitor utilizes a timed three-hour urine collection that is diluted to 150 ml. Samples of the urine are placed in pre-coated assay tubes and then read by the monitor. The monitor is based on homogenous enzyme immunoassay principles and is designed to measure estrone glucuronide (E1G) and pregnanediol glucuronide (PdG) levels.

The home use Ovarian Monitor has been in development for over twenty years primarily under the influence of Drs. Brown and Len Blackwell (New Zealand). The Ovarian Monitor is designed to measure urinary assays of estrone glucuronide (E1G) and pregnanediol glucuronide (PdG) as measures of ovarian activity during a woman's menstrual cycle. Researchers from New Zealand, Australia, and Chile[113] continue to research, develop, and study the accuracy and reliability of the Ovarian monitor in comparison to those found in a laboratory.[114] Fertility monitors are among the innovative approaches to NFP education and hold the promise of providing more precise information to a woman about her window of fertility.

NFP Scientists during the Papacies of Benedict XVI and Pope Francis (2005–2018)

When John Paul II died in 2005, it was an uncertain time for those who felt his presence and support for NFP science. There was great anticipation for the new pope and his direction for the future of life issues and NFP. The NFP science community was grateful that Pope Benedict XVI supported their work. When he retired, he expressed gratitude to NFP researchers working on ways to combat sterility and said scientists "are to be encouraged to continue their research with the aim of preventing the causes of sterility and of being able to remedy them, so that sterile couples will be able to procreate in full respect for their own personal dignity and that of the child to be born."[115]

112 J. B. Brown, J. Holmes, and G. Barker, "Use of the Home Ovarian Monitor in Pregnancy Avoidance," *American Journal of Obstetrics and Gynecology* 165, no. 6 (1991): 2008–2011.

113 In particular, two Catholic scientists, Len Blackwell from Massy University in New Zealand and Dr. Pilar Vigil from Chile.

114 L. F. Blackwell, P. Vigil, M. E. Alliende, S. Brown, M. Festin, and D. G. Cooke, "Monitoring of Ovarian Activity by Measurement of Urinary Excretion Rates Using the Ovarian Monitor, Part IV: The Relationship of the Pregnanediol Glucuronide Threshold to Basal Body Temperature and Cervical Mucus as Markers for the Beginning of the Postovulatory Infertile Period," *Human Reproduction* 31, no. 2 (February 2016):445–453.

115 Pope Benedict XVI, *Message of His Holiness Benedict XVI on the Occasion of the 40th Anniversary of Paul VI's Encyclical* Humanae vitae, given on October 2, 2008 at the International Congress at the Catholic University of the Sacred Heart, Rome, https://w2.vatican.va/content/benedict-xvi/en/messages/pont-messages/2008.index.html.

In his recent apostolic exhortation *Amoris laetitia*, Pope Francis reiterated the teachings of *Humanae vitae*, saying that "the use of methods based on the 'laws of nature and the incidence of fertility' (*Humanae vitae*, 11) are to be promoted, since 'these methods respect the bodies of the spouses, encourage tenderness between them and favour the education of an authentic freedom' (*Catechism of the Catholic Church*, no. 2370)."[116]

Conclusion: Looking Forward

The Church continues to call for work on the science of NFP and related topics. Many of the current NFP scientists from the post-*Humanae vitae* era and, in particular, the John Paul II era, are still engaged in NFP research—they are an inspiration. There is also cause for hope in the presence of non-Catholic scientists who have answered that call and recognize the value of the natural methods of NFP and the truth of Catholic teaching expressed in *Humanae vitae*. One such scientist is Dr. Joseph Stanford, professor of Family Medicine at the University of Utah. Stanford is a man of faith (Latter-Day Saints) and a friend of Catholic teaching on married love, responsible parenthood, and the encyclical *Humanae vitae*. He is one of the most consistent and active NFP researchers in the world today. He also has presented a number of times at conferences sponsored by the USCCB's NFP Program and the Catholic Medical Association.[117] It is more than encouraging that a scientist of his caliber has taken up the call of Paul VI to "men of science."

Over the years, there have been hundreds of scientists, Catholic and non-Catholic, who have been involved with the work of understanding human reproduction, discovering natural indicators of fertility, developing new methods of NFP, investigating the effectiveness of these methods, integrating NFP methods with women's health care, and explaining the effects of using these methods on the marital bond. It is impossible to mention each one in this essay.[118] Yet, this essay is an attempt to pay some small homage to these noble efforts.

Looking ahead, current and future NFP scientists continue to take up the work begun by Knaus, Latz, Smulders, and others in the early 1900s. Some of that work is already promising in the form of new technology for monitoring reproductive hormones, the integration of internet technology and mobile cell phone applications, and the understanding of how the menstrual cycle is a vital sign for women's health. But that is the subject of another essay. For now, it is enough to tell the story of the NFP scientists to encourage and inspire young scientists to take up the task called for in *Humanae vitae*.

116 Pope Francis, Apostolic Exhortation *Amoris laetitia* (March 19, 2016), 222, http://w2.vatican.va/content/francesco/en/apost_exhortations.index.html.

117 Joseph B. Stanford, "The Role of Randomized Control Trials in NFP Studies," in *Human Fertility: Where Faith and Science Meet*, ed. Fehring and Notare, 185–196.

118 For those interested in further reading on these pioneers, see the book by Jan Mucharski, *History of the Biological Control of Human Fertility* (Oak Ridge, N.J.: Married Life Information, 1982).

9

The Current State of Science in Natural Family Planning

Joseph B. Stanford

✷ IN *HUMANAE VITAE* (and quoting *Gaudiem et spes*), Paul VI states that men and women of all branches of science can "considerably advance the welfare of marriage and the family and also peace of conscience, if by pooling their efforts they strive to elucidate more thoroughly the conditions favorable to a proper regulation of births."[1] Many scientists of the Roman Catholic and other faiths have helped to develop the scientific evidence to support the use of Natural Family Planning (NFP). The purpose of this essay is to give an overview of the current evidence for the use of NFP, its effectiveness to avoid pregnancy, its effectiveness to conceive, its application for subfertility (infertility), its applications for women's health, and its impact on marital relationships, and to consider the future of NFP research.

Current Use of NFP

In the United States, about 2% of women in the reproductive age range currently use some form of NFP.[2] It should be noted here that NFP is, by definition, used by a couple, not just by a woman alone, but the statistics available are reported for women. The majority of these report they use "Rhythm," which is less likely to be understood or used as effectively as other methods.[3] Compared to women who have never used NFP, women who use NFP in the United States are more likely to be married (69% vs. 35%), Hispanic (29% vs. 22%), Catholic (37% vs. 25%); are more likely to state that religion is very important in their life (68% vs. 56%); and would be pleased if they got pregnant right now (57% vs. 41%).[4]

1 Pope Paul VI, Encyclical Letter *Humanae vitae* (July 25, 1968), 24, quoting *Gaudium et spes*, 52, w2.vatican.va/content/paul-vi/en/encyclicals.index.html.

2 A. M. Bertotti and S. M. Christensen, "Comparing Current, Former, and Never Users of Natural Family Planning: An Analysis of Demographic, Socioeconomic, and Attitudinal Variables," *The Linacre Quarterly* 79, no. 4 (2012): 474–486.

3 Michael D. Manhart, Marguerite Duane, April Lind, Irit Sinai, and Jean Golden-Tevald, "Fertility Awareness-Based Methods of Family Planning: A Review of Effectiveness for Avoiding Pregnancy Using SORT," *Osteopathic Family Physician* 5, no. 1 (2013): 2–8.

4 Bertotti and Christensen, "Comparing Current, Former, and Never Users of Natural Family Planning."

Internationally, 2.6% of women of reproductive age use some form of "Rhythm," with very few countries rising above 10% of reproductive-age women using it (e.g., Congo, Libya, Korea, Sri Lanka, Lebanon, Romania, Bolivia, and Peru).[5]

A recent major trend related to NFP is the explosion in the availability and use of mobile app software for tracking menstrual cycle data. Currently, a large majority of women worldwide have access to a smartphone with hundreds of apps available to track their menstrual cycle and, sometimes, ovulation, yet almost none of these have any published data as to their accuracy. Much more research is needed to validate mobile applications, and there is a strong need for women to have access to independent evaluation and evidence.[6]

There is some evidence of a shift in reasons for learning NFP from avoiding pregnancy towards conceiving. For example, a multicenter study of the Creighton Model Fertility*Care*™ system in the United States of new users in 1996–2000 found that 65% of couples/women were learning NFP with the initial purpose to avoid pregnancy, and 18% with the initial purpose to conceive (the remainder were learning it for health reasons).[7] Just over a decade later, a similar multicenter study of new users in 2009–2011 found 42% learning NFP with the initial purpose to avoid pregnancy, and 41% of women learning with the initial purpose to conceive.[8]

Effectiveness of NFP to Avoid Pregnancy

Within the literature on contraception and family planning, the currently accepted metrics for effectiveness to avoid pregnancy are typical use and perfect use pregnancy rates, usually calculated for 100 women (couples) in the first year of use.[9] Typical use pregnancy rate calculations include all cycles (or months) and associated pregnancies where the prospectively assessed intention is to avoid pregnancy; any pregnancies that occur without a prior assessment of an intent to conceive are called unintended pregnancies. Perfect use pregnancy rate calculations include all cycles (or months) and associated pregnancies where the method studied was used correctly and consistently for avoiding pregnancy. For comparability with other family planning studies, I report here data according to these measures. Because NFP can be used to avoid pregnancy or to conceive,

5 Ann Biddlecom, Vladimíra Kantorová, Stephen Kisambira, Petra Nahmias, and Hantamalala Rafalimanana, *Trends in Contraceptive Use Worldwide* (New York: United Nations, 2015).

6 D. A. Epstein, J. H. Kang, E. Agapie, J. Schroeder, L. R. Pina, J. Fogarty, J. A. Kientz, and S. A. Munson, "Examining Menstrual Tracking to Inform the Design of Personal Informatics Tools," *Proceedings of the SIGCHI Conference on Human Factors in Computing Systems. CHI Conference* (New York: Association of Computing Machinery, 2017): 6876–6888.

7 J. B. Stanford and K. R. Smith, "Characteristics of Women Associated with Continuing Instruction in the Creighton Model Fertility Care System," *Contraception* 61, no. 2 (2000): 121–129.

8 J. B. Stanford and C. A. Porucznik, "Enrollment, Childbearing Motivations, and Intentions of Couples in the Creighton Model Effectiveness, Intentions, and Behaviors Assessment (CEIBA) Study," *Frontiers in Medicine (Lausanne)* 4 (2017): 147.

9 J. Trussell, R. A. Hatcher, W. Cates Jr., F. H. Stewart, and K. Kost, "A Guide to Interpreting Contraceptive Efficacy Studies," *Obstetrics & Gynecology* (3 Pt 2) 76 (September 1, 1990): 558–567.

the prospective assessment of intention of use is a key issue, one that I address further below in a brief critique of the concept of unintended pregnancy.[10]

Michael Manhart et al. reviewed 29 studies of NFP to avoid pregnancy in a systematic review published in 2013. They reported typical use pregnancy rates ranging from 1.6 to 22 per 100 women in the first year of use and perfect use pregnancy rates ranging from 0.4 to 4.8.[11]

More recently, a systematic review of 51 published reports was conducted by Rachel Peragallo Urrutia and colleagues (including myself) and is currently under review. The pregnancy rates we reported are of very similar range to those reported by Manhart et al. In this review, we also developed a set of 13 quality criteria that we used to rate studies as having high, moderate, or low quality. We found no reports that met all high-quality criteria, 21 reports that met at least moderate quality on all criteria, and 30 reports that had one or more criteria rated as low. The quality criteria most often not met by studies (i.e., reported as "low" quality), were systematic detection of pregnancy, use of appropriate statistical methods (lifetable or one-year Pearl Rate), comparable duration of study (first year of use), adequate description of the study population for generalizability, and assessment of unintended pregnancy according to the criteria described above. This indicates room for future improvement of quality in conducting and reporting NFP effectiveness studies.

The moderate quality studies with the lowest pregnancy rates among new users were a study of Sensiplan® (a German multi-indexed method or "Symp-to-Thermal Method"), in Germany, with a typical use pregnancy rate of 1.8 and perfect use pregnancy rate 0.4 per 100 women;[12] and a study of the Marquette Method (fertility monitor only), with a typical use pregnancy rate of 6.8 and perfect use pregnancy rate 0 per 100 women, albeit with only 41% of women continuing to one year.[13] Both of these studies were based on women with regular menstrual cycles.

In assessing the literature for NFP and other family planning methods which reports unintended pregnancy rates during typical use and perfect use, it is necessary to critically examine the conceptual foundations of the standard forms of analysis. There are two key points, one related to the variability of typical use pregnancy rates according to user characteristics, and the other to the concept of unintended pregnancy.

10 V. Lamprecht and J. Trussell, "Natural Family Planning Effectiveness: Evaluating Published Reports," *Advances in Contraception* 13, nos. 2–3 (1997): 155–165.

11 Manhart et al., "Fertility Awareness-Based Methods of Family Planning."

12 P. Frank-Herrmann, J. Heil, C. Gnoth, E. Toledo, S. Baur, C. Pyper, E. Jenetzky, T. Strowitzki, and G. Freundl, "The Effectiveness of a Fertility Awareness Based Method to Avoid Pregnancy in Relation to a Couple's Sexual Behaviour during the Fertile Time: A Prospective Longitudinal Study," *Human Reproduction* 22, no. 5 (2007): 1310–1319.

13 Riuhard J. Fehring, Mary Schneider, Kathleen Raviele, Dana Rodriguez, and Jessica E. Pruszynski, "Randomized Comparison of Two Internet-Supported Fertility Awareness Based Methods of Family Planning," *Contraception* 88, no. 1 (July 2013): 24–30.

TABLE 9–1—Pregnancy Rates per 100 Women-Years (Pearl rates) in Couples Using the Basal Body Temperature Method of NFP, London area, Stratified by Woman's Age[1]

Age, years	Women	Cycles	Pearl rate
20–24	20	212	**28.3**
25–29	95	1105	**11.9**
30–34	129	1944	**5.5**
35–39	77	1488	**0.8**

1. Marshall and Rowe, "The effect of personal factors."

Impact of Characteristics of NFP Users on Pregnancy Rates

Typical use unintended pregnancy rates are a range across different populations, in contrast to perfect use pregnancy rates, which are designed to assess underlying biological characteristics of a method, and which should be fairly consistent across most populations. In contrast, typical use pregnancy rates are highly impacted by population characteristics and motivations, probably more so than by which NFP method is being studied. As one example, consider an early study of the Basal Body Temperature Method of NFP (postovulatory intercourse only), a biologically highly effective method of NFP that theoretically should have extremely low perfect use pregnancy rates (although these have never been adequately evaluated).[14] In an early study in London, the typical use pregnancy rates were stratified by woman's age, as shown in Table 9–1. There is a monotonic, consistent decrease in pregnancy rates from the youngest age group (20–24 years) at 28.3 per 100 woman-years to the oldest age group (35–39 years), at 0.8; a magnitude of difference more than 30-fold.[15] This difference cannot be attributed primarily to biological fecundity, but rather, must be related to the underlying motivation of the users affecting the level of consistent and correct use of the method.

Critique of Concept of Unintended Pregnancy

The measurement of unintended pregnancy itself is a heterogeneous concept. It is based on simply asking women (occasionally also men) to declare whether they intend(ed) to get pregnant, or to avoid pregnancy. In contraceptive or

14 C. Tietze and S. Lewit, "Statistical Evaluation of Contraceptive Methods: Use-effectiveness and Extended Use-effectiveness," *Demography* 5, no. 2 (1968): 931–940.

15 J. Marshall and B. Rowe, "The Effect of Personal Factors on the Use of the Basal Body Temperature Method of Regulating Births," *Fertility and Sterility* 23, no. 6 (1972): 417–421.

family planning studies, the standard is for it to be determined prospectively.[16] Many "unintended" pregnancies are nevertheless wanted and valued.[17] In a qualitative study, we identified a spectrum of possible underlying attitudes and circumstances that were all considered "mistimed" pregnancies (a subcategory of unintended pregnancy), as demonstrated by the following quotes, each from a different woman with a mistimed/unintended pregnancy:

- "We planned it, we weren't expecting it quite so soon, but we were hoping for it, so it came as a very pleasant surprise, we were very excited."
- "I have mixed emotions, we had tried, and so I guess in a way it was planned . . . I would just say to him, 'I want a baby, I want a baby.'"
- "We were shocked at first . . . I just thought the birth control would work."
- "It isn't really wanted, so I am getting rid of it."

Gaps in Data on NFP Effectiveness to Avoid Pregnancy

Finally, it should be noted that a number of gaps remain in the studies of NFP to avoid pregnancy. Manhart and colleagues noted the need for more data about the effectiveness of NFP during fertility transitions, such as the postpartum period, premenopause, or right after discontinuing long-acting contraceptives.[18] Based on my own work and collaboration with colleagues, I would add that we need more research on factors related to continuation or discontinuation of use of NFP, the effective use of NFP in women with irregular ovulation and cycles (including in women with Polycystic Ovary Syndrome or PCOS), and the impact of different types of instruction of NFP such as online instruction or instruction through mobile apps. Further, as noted above, we need more explicit investigation of the impact of couple characteristics and context on NFP use and effectiveness, and the development of reproducible and objective approaches to understand and broaden the traditional measures of effectiveness beyond solely the somewhat subjective measurement of unintended pregnancy.

Effectiveness of NFP to Conceive

Many women and men are interested in using NFP to conceive, as much as to avoid.[19] This also seems to be true for fertility awareness methods, websites, and

16 Lamprecht and Trussell, "Natural Family Planning Effectiveness."

17 J. Trussell, B. Vaughan, and J. B. Stanford, "Are All Contraceptive Failures Unintended Pregnancies? Evidence from the 1995 National Survey of Family Growth," *Family Planning Perspectives* 31, no. 5 (1999): 246–247, 260.

18 Manhart et al., "Fertility Awareness-Based Methods of Family Planning."

19 J. B. Stanford, J. C. Lemaire, and P. B. Thurman, "Women's Interest in Natural Family Planning," *The Journal of Family Practice* 46, no. 1 (January 1998): 65–71; J. B. Stanford, A. G. Hutchinson, and J. G. Payne, "Utah Couples' Potential Use of Natural Family Planning," *Utah's Health: An Annual Review* 9, no. 1 (2003): 40–45; and C. J. Leonard, W. Chavira, D. V. Coonrod, K. W. Hart, and R. C. Bay, "Survey of Attitudes Regarding Natural Family Planning in an Urban Hispanic Population," *Contraception* 74, no. 4 (October 2006): 313–317.

apps, although systematic data are lacking to date.[20] A number of observational studies have found increased fecundability, meaning a shorter time to pregnancy, among women and couples trying to conceive.[21] Over 75% of couples can conceive within six months using NFP or fertility awareness techniques.[22] However, randomized trials have had mixed results and have not yet clearly demonstrated the benefit of NFP to conceive.[23] This is an area where further research is needed, with attention to design to avoid some of the limitations of prior studies.

Application of NFP to Subfertility

Subfertility, or what is clinically called infertility, is the inability of a couple to conceive a child for a year or more.[24] In developed countries, it is experienced by about 1 out of 6 couples over their reproductive lifetimes.[25] From the couple's point of view, the immediate impact and concern of subfertility is the desire to have a child as soon as possible; however, subfertility is also an indicator of underlying health issues that impact not just the reproductive system, but

20 Toni Weschler, *Taking Charge of Your Fertility: The Definitive Guide to Natural Birth Control, Pregnancy Achievement, and Reproductive Health*, 20th anniversary edition, ed. (New York: Harper Collins, 2015), 560.

21 Emily Evans-Hoeker, David A. Pritchard, D. Leann Long, Amy H. Herring, Joseph B. Stanford, and Anne Z. Steiner, "Cervical Mucus Monitoring Prevalence and Associated Fecundability in Women Trying to Conceive," *Fertility and Sterility* 100, no. 4 (2013): 1033–1038; and C. Gnoth, D. Godehardt, E. Godehardt, P. Frank-Hermann, and G. Freundl, "Time to Pregnancy: Results of the German Prospective Study and Impact on the Management of Infertility," *Human Reproduction* 18, no. 9 (September 2003): 1959–1966.

22 C. Gnoth et al., "Time to Pregnancy"; Qivan Mu and R. J. Fehring, "Efficacy of Achieving Pregnancy with Fertility-Focused Intercourse," *MCN: The American Journal of Maternal Child Nursing* 39, no. 1 (2014): 35–40; T. W. Hilgers, K. D. Daly, A. M. Prebil, and S. K. Hilgers, "Cumulative Pregnancy Rates in Patients with Apparently Normal Fertility and Fertility-focused Intercourse," *The Journal of Reproductive Medicine* 37, no. 10 (October 1992): 864–866; and J. B. Stanford, Ken R. Smith, and Michael W. Varner, "Impact of Instruction in the Creighton Model Fertility*Care*™ System on Time to Pregnancy in Couples of Proven Fecundity: Results of a Randomized Trial," *Paediatric and Perinatal Epidemiology* 28, no. 5 (September 2014): 391–399.

23 Stanford et al., "Impact of Instruction in the Creighton Model FertilityCare System"; and M. Manders, L. McLindon, B. Schulze, M. M. Beckmann, J. A. Kremer, and C. Farquhar, "Timed Intercourse for Couples Trying to Conceive," *The Cochrane Database of Systematic Reviews* 3 (March 17, 2015): Cd011345.

24 E. Greenhall and M. Vessey, "The Prevalence of Subfertility: A Review of the Current Confusion and a Report of Two New Studies" [see comments], *Fertility and Sterility* 54, no. 6 (1990): 978–983; and J. L. Evers, "Female Subfertility," *The Lancet* 360, no. 9327 (2002): 151–159.

25 M. E. Thoma, A. C. McLain, J. F. Louis, R. B. King, A. C. Trumble, R. Sundaram, and G. M. Buck Louis, "Prevalence of Infertility in the United States as Estimated by the Current Duration Approach and a Traditional Constructed Approach," *Fertility and Sterility* 99, no. 5 (2013): 1324–1331; J. F. Louis, M. E. Thoma, D. N. Sørensen, A. C. McLain, R. B. King, R. Sundaram, N. Keiding, and G. M. Buck Louis, "The Prevalence of Couple Infertility in the United States from a Male Perspective: Evidence from a Nationally Representative Sample," *Andrology* 1, no. 5 (2013): 741–748; J. Datta, M. J. Palmer, C. Tanton, L. J. Gibson, K. G. Jones, W. Mcdowall, A. Glasier, P. Sonnenberg, N. Field, C. H. Mercer, A. M. Johnson, and K. Wellings, "Prevalence of Infertility and Help Seeking among 15,000 Women and Men," *Human Reproduction* 31, no. 9 (September 2016): 2108–2118; and R. Slama, O. K. H. Hansen, B. Ducot, A. Bohet, D. Sorensen, L. Giorgis Allemand, M. J. Eijkemans, L. Rosetta, J. C. Thalabard, N. Keiding, and J. Bouyer, "Estimation of the Frequency of Involuntary Infertility on a Nation-wide Basis," *Human Reproduction* 27, no. 5 (May 2012): 1489–1498.

general health. A growing body of research links subfertility to the reduced health of the woman, the man, the child, and potentially future generations.[26] Hence, the most valuable approach to subfertility would be to correct the underlying pathology and restore the normal state of health, which includes normal reproductive capacity for women and men. Commonly used and most widely promoted conventional fertility treatments do nothing to accomplish this goal. Superovulation, intrauterine insemination, and in vitro fertilization (IVF), with or without intracytoplasmic sperm injection, are all designed to bypass the normal physiologic reproductive process to one extent or another. The available evidence suggests they do nothing to mitigate the impact of underlying pathology of subfertility on the offspring.[27]

In contrast, the integration of NFP into the evaluation and treatment of subfertility can accomplish several important things: (1) insight into abnormal functioning of the woman's reproductive menstrual cycle, (2) increased accuracy in the timing and interpretation of medical tests (such as women's hormone levels), (3) the empowerment of women and couples as equal partners in the evaluation and treatment process, including key lifestyle factors, (4) a means to evaluate whether treatments are restoring normal reproductive function, and (5) a foundation for a fully restorative approach to reproductive medicine, which is discussed next.

Restorative Reproductive Medicine

Restorative Reproductive Medicine (RRM) broadly designates medical approaches that seek to diagnose and correct underlying pathology of the reproductive system, whether the purpose is to conceive or to address other health issues. It is fundamentally based on insights from NFP methods that have enabled a deeper understanding of normal reproductive physiology, and the equal partnership of the woman or couple in addressing their own health. Medical treatments including medication and surgery are applied in a way to diagnose and treat, with the goal to restore optimal functioning of the human reproductive system. The most advanced and studied system of RRM to date is called NaProTECHNOLOGY™ (from natural procreative technology). It was developed by Dr. Thomas W. Hilgers and colleagues, based on the Creighton Model Fertility*Care*™ System.[28]

26 N. E. Skakkebaek, E. Rajpert-De Meyts, and K. M. Main, "Testicular Dysgenesis Syndrome: An Increasingly Common Developmental Disorder with Environmental Aspects," *Human Reproduction* 16, no. 5 (May 2001): 972–978; and G. M. Buck Louis, M. A. Cooney, and C. M. Peterson, "The Ovarian Dysgenesis Syndrome," *Journal of Developmental Origins of Health and Disease* 2, no. 1 (February 23, 2011): 25–35.

27 J. B. Stanford, S. E. Simonsen, and L. Baksh, "Fertility Treatments and Adverse Perinatal Outcomes in a Population-based Sampling of Births in Florida, Maryland, and Utah: A Cross-Sectional Study," *British Journal of Obstetrics and Gynecology* 123, no. 5 (2016): 718–729.

28 T. W. Hilgers, *The Medical and Surgical Practice of NaProTECHNOLOGY* (Omaha, Neb: Paul VI Institute Press, 2004), 1244; and T. W. Hilgers, "The New Women's Health Science of NaProTECHNOLOGY," *Archives of Perinatal Medicine* 17, no. 4 (2011): 191–198, https://www.restorative-reproductive-medicine.com/wp-content/uploads/2013/05/APM174-2-Hilgers.pdf.

Table 9–2 displays patient characteristics and pregnancy outcomes from three different studies with an RRM approach for subfertile couples: two studies of NaProTECHNOLOGY™, and one from Sensiplan®.[29] These studies all included significantly subfertile couples, with a mean prior time attempting to conceive of 3.2–5.6 years, and a mean woman's age about 35 years. Considering the time frame, the pregnancy rate in the Sensiplan® study from treatment of up to eight months may be comparable to that of the other studies, which reported live birth rates from up to two years' treatment. There are limitations in comparing these results with results from studies of IVF, because of identified and unidentified differences in the couples being studied. Nevertheless, these live birth rates are similar to those of IVF studies that include up to several cycles of IVF over 1–1.5 years in the Netherlands, United Kingdom, and the United States.[30] However, these RRM studies have much lower rates of low birth weight, primarily due to lower rates of multiple gestation pregnancies (twins or higher order multiples).[31] This is extremely significant, because twins and higher order multiple pregnancies pose much higher risks for both mothers and the babies.[32]

Application of NFP to Women's Health

Most of the considerations described above regarding the key contribution of NFP charting and insights for subfertility, also apply to women's health in general. NFP charting enables: (1) insight into normal and abnormal functioning of the woman's menstrual cycle, (2) accuracy in the timing and interpretation of medical tests (such as women's hormone levels), (3) the empowerment of women to understand their own health and physiology, (4) a means to evaluate whether treatments are supporting normal functioning of a woman's body, and

29 J. B. Stanford, T. A. Parnell, and P. C. Boyle, "Outcomes from Treatment of Infertility with Natural Procreative Technology in an Irish General Practice," *Journal of the American Board of Family Medicine* 21, no. 5 (November–December 2008): 375–384; E. Tham, K. Schliep and J. Stanford, "Natural Procreative Technology for Infertility and Recurrent Miscarriage: Outcomes in a Canadian Family Practice," Canadian Family Physician 58, no. 5 (May 2012): e267–274; and P. Frank-Herrmann, P. C. Jacobs, E. Jenetzky, C. Gnoth, C. Pyper, S. Baur, G. Freundl, M. Goechkenjan, and I. Strowitzki, "Natural Conception Rates in Subfertile Couples Following Fertility Awareness Training," *Archives of Gynecology and Obstetrics* 295, no. 4 (April 2017): 1015–1024.

30 A. M. Lintsen, M. J. Eijkemans, C. C. Hunault, C. A. Bouwmans, L. Hakkaart, J. D. Habbema, and D. D. Braat, "Predicting Ongoing Pregnancy Chances after IVF and ICSI: a National Prospective Study," *Human Reproduction* 22, no. 9 (September 2007): 2455–2462; D. J. McLernon, A. Maheshwari, A. J. Lee, and S. Bhattacharya, "Cumulative Live Birth Rates after One or More Complete Cycles of IVF: A Population-based Study of Linked Cycle Data from 178,898 Women," *Human Reproduction* 31, no. 3 (2016): 572–581; and B. Luke, M. B. Brown, E. Wantman, A. Lederman, W. Gibbons, G. L. Schattman, R. A. Lobo, R. E. Leach, and J. E. Stern, "Cumulative Birth Rates with Linked Assisted Reproductive Technology Cycles," *New England Journal of Medicine* 366, no. 26 (2012): 2483–2491.

31 S. Sunderam, D. M. Kissin, L. Flowers, J. E. Anderson, S. G. Folger, D. J. Jamieson, W. D. Barfield; Centers for Disease Control and Prevention (CDC), "Assisted Reproductive Technology Surveillance—United States, 2009," *Morbidity and Mortality Weekly Report, Surveilance Summaries* 61, no. 7 (November 2012): 1–23.

32 The ESHRE (European Society of Human Reproduction and Embryology) Capri Workshop Group, "Multiple Gestation Pregnancy," *Human Reproduction* 15, no. 8 (August 2000): 1856–1864.

TABLE 9-2—Patient Characteristics and Outcomes in Three Studies Using an RRM Approach to Subfertility[1]

Location	Galway, Ireland	Toronto, Canada	Heidelberg, Germany
Year	2009	2012	2017
Method	NaProTECHNOLOGY™	NaProTECHNOLOGY™	Sensiplan®
Number of couples	1072	108	187
Time frame	2 yrs	2 yrs	8 mo
Mean age woman (years)	35.8	35.4	34.7
Mean years trying	5.6	3.2	3.5
Adjusted live birth rate	53%	66%	NR
Adjusted pregnancy rate	65%	73%	38%
Low birth weight (%)	6%	15%	NR

1 Stanford et al., "Outcomes from treatment of infertility"; Tham et al., "Natural procreative technology for infertility and recurrent miscarriage"; and Frank-Herrmann et al., "Natural conception rates in subfertile couples following fertility awareness training."

(5) a foundation for a fully restorative approach to reproductive medicine, which can be applied to women's health conditions beyond fertility alone.

Types of Ovarian Activity

One of the most important contributions to understanding women's health is the conception of the ovarian continuum, or the continuum of ovarian activity, developed by Dr. James Brown and colleagues. Brown worked closely with Drs. John and Evelyn Billings, and developed the Ovarian Monitor, which enabled accurate daily assessment of progesterone and estrogen metabolites in urine. He and his colleague followed and evaluated women of all ages and reproductive situations with the Ovarian Monitor and the Billings Ovulation Method® over many decades. His integrated summary of this work has been published posthumously.[33]

33 J. B. Brown, "Types of Ovarian Activity in Women and Their Significance: The Continuum (a Reinterpretation of Early Findings)," *Human Reproduction Update* 17, no. 2 (2011): 141–158.

Women's ovarian activity passes through a continuum over her lifetime: (1) no ovarian activity, (2) estrogenic activity alone, (3) transient rises of progesterone, (4) menstrual cycles with deficient luteal phases, and (5) fertile ovulatory cycles. A woman will likely pass through each of these phases of ovarian activity multiple times during her reproductive lifetime: from menarche to pregnancies and breastfeeding, and ultimately, menopause. The phases do not necessarily always occur in sequence, but they define a spectrum of possible ovarian function that impacts all facets of a woman's life, as well as her fertility.

From the fundamental understanding of the spectrum of ovarian function, a whole variety of women's health conditions can be evaluated and treated, with the goal to address underlying causes, and correct them to the extent possible, based on the general principles of RRM, as previously described. This is a much better foundation for enhancing women's health than suppression of ovarian activity by exogenous steroids, such as occurs with hormonal contraception. The applications include endocrine disorders (including polycystic ovarian syndrome, thyroid disorders, and others), disorders of ovulation, reproductive infections, inflammatory conditions, anatomic abnormalities, autoimmune disease, and endometriosis. Again, the most developed approach for medical and surgical RRM is NaProTECHNOLOGY™. Other important work for RRM and women's health comes from clinicians and investigators working with other NFP systems.[34]

Having outlined this compelling underlying rationale for RRM, it should also be recognized that rigorous evidence for the outcomes of the RRM approach to these women's health conditions is largely lacking. To put this in perspective, there is also minimal evidence for the outcomes of using hormonal contraception for most women's health conditions. There are wide opportunities for research for NFP and the spectrum of women's health.

Impact of NFP Use on The Marital Relationship

Anecdotally, NFP has been heralded as a godsend to improve communication and harmony in marriage, with impact well beyond the domains of sex and fertility. NFP has also been anecdotally faulted for causing stress and difficulties in marriage. What is the empiric evidence? First, there are relatively few systematic studies of this aspect of NFP use. Most of the studies have suffered from methodological limitations, especially selection bias.[35] However, there are some studies that indicate benefits of NFP for most couples using it.[36]

34 Pilar Vigil, Leonard F. Blackwell, and Manuel E. Cortés, "The Importance of Fertility Awareness in the Assessment of a Woman's Health: A Review," *The Linacre Quarterly* 79, no. 4 (2012): 426–450.

35 M. A. Wilson, "The Practice of Natural Family Planning versus the Use of Artificial Birth Control: Family, Moral and Sexual Issues," *The Catholic Social Science Review* 7 (2002): 185–211, https://www.pdcnet.org/cssr/content/cssr_2002_0007_0185_0211.

36 J. Marshall and B. Rowe, "Psychologic Aspects of the Basal Body Temperature Method of Regulating Births," *Fertility and Sterility* 21, no. 1 (1970): 14–19; L. Vande Vusse, L. Hanson, R. J. Fehring, A. Newman, and J. Fox, "Couples' Views of the Effects of Natural Family Planning on Marital Dynamics," *Journal of Nursing Scholarship* 35, no. 2 (April 2003): 171–176; and Richard J. Fehring and Donna M. Lawrence, "Spiritual Well-Being, Self-Esteem and Intimacy among Couples Using Natural Family Planning," *The Linacre Quarterly* 61, no. 3 (1994): 18–29.

Fehring and colleagues examined data from the U.S. National Survey of Family Growth (a representative national sample). Among couples that had ever used NFP (including Rhythm methods), they found 9.6% who had been divorced, compared to 14.4% divorced among couples who had never used NFP, with an odds ratio of 0.7. The odds for divorce were also lower for regular church attendance, which is also more likely among those using NFP. Use of oral contraception had increased odds of divorce (1.3), as did sterilization (2.1), and having had an abortion (2.0).[37]

Future Horizons for Research in NFP

In April 2018, I conducted a search of the medical literature that is indexed by the U.S. National Library of Medicine (also known as PubMed). The number of scientific publications found for various search terms is shown in Table 9–3:

These results indicate clearly a need for more research in NFP and related areas for RRM.

There are many areas ripe for future NFP research, including areas where NFP research can make key contributions to the broader disciplines of biomedical and social science. We need research that helps clinicians and users understand the relationship of motivations, intentions, and behaviors during NFP use to the rates of pregnancy, whether intended or unintended. We need research to understand the impact of communication and relationship characteristics on NFP use, and vice versa. We need additional research to understand how diet, lifestyle, and environmental factors impact woman's ovarian function and, thus, her cycle and the use of NFP. We need further development of simple methods of NFP for wide dissemination and meeting the needs of many new potential users.[38] We need further development of detailed methods that have the flexibility and power to address women with all different reproductive situations, including breastfeeding, and the women's health conditions described earlier.[39] As the delivery of NFP instruction continues to shift towards online and mobile computing (app) platforms, we need research about how most effectively to teach women and couples the methods with the new platforms. A variety of methods, platforms, and service delivery systems will be needed to meet the needs of women and couples in all different circumstances worldwide. We need research

37 R. J. Fehring, "The Influence of Contraception, Abortion, and Natural Family Planning on Divorce Rates as Found in the 2006–2010 National Survey of Family Growth," *The Linacre Quarterly* 82, no. 3 (July 1, 2015): 273–282.

38 See R. G. Simmons, D.C. Shattuck, and V. H. Jennings, "Assessing the Efficacy of an App-based Method of Family Planning: the Dot Study Protocol," *JMIR Research Protocols* 6, no. 1 (2017): e5; and D. Li, L. Heyer, V. H. Jennings, C. A. Smith, and D. B. Dunson, "Personalised Estimation of a Woman's Most Fertile Days," *The European Journal of Contraception and Reproductive Health Care* 21, no. 4 (August 2016): 323–228.

39 See Hilgers, "The New Women's Health Science of NaProTECHNOLOGY"; Vigil et al., "The Importance of Fertility Awareness"; and R. J. Fehring, M. Schneider, and T. Bouchard, "Effectiveness of an Online Natural Family Planning Program for Breastfeeding Women," *Journal of Obstetric, Gynecologic, and Neonatal Nursing* 46, no. 4 (2017): e129–137.

TABLE 9-3—Count of Results in PubMed for Various Search Terms (April 2018)

Natural Family Planning	484
Natural Procreative	23 (with about half unrelated)
Cooperative Reproductive	29 (with about half unrelated)
Restorative Reproductive	1
Contraceptive Agents (female)	36,917
Contraceptives (oral)	27,060
In Vitro Fertilization	32,947

documenting and improving the algorithms and outcomes for integrating medical support for women's health with NFP.[40] We need research that addresses the full spectrum of women's reproductive function, not just the general mean or normal experience.[41] We need research that assesses the long-term impact of optimizing a woman's ovarian function and cycle health over her lifetime.[42] This may reduce her future risk of chronic diseases and cancer.[43] Last, but not least, the new and rapidly developing areas of medical science known as the 'omics (genomics, proteomics, metabolomics) and the microbiome open up new opportunities to dig another layer deeper in our understanding of reproductive physiology, including ovulation, fertilization, implantation, and maintenance of pregnancy.[44]

40 See Hilgers, *The Medical and Surgical Practice of NaProTechnology*; Hilgers, "The New Women's Health Science of NaProTECHNOLOGY"; Vigil et al., "The Importance of Fertility Awareness."

41 See M. E. Alliende, "Mean versus Individual Hormonal Profiles in the Menstrual Cycle," *Fertility and Sterility* 78, no. 1 (2002): 90–95.

42 See S. A. Treloar, T. A. Bell, C. M. Nagle, D. M. Purdie, and A. C. Green, "Early Menstrual Characteristics Associated with Subsequent Diagnosis of Endometriosis," *American Journal of Obstetrics and Gynecology* 202, no. 6 (June 2009): 534.e1-6.

43 See E. A. Whelan, D. P. Sandler, J. L. Root, K. R. Smith, and C. R. Weinberg, "Menstrual Cycle Patterns and Risk of Breast Cancer," *American Journal of Epidemiology* 140, no. 12 (December 15, 1994): 1081–1090; C. G. Solomon, F. B. Hu, A. Dunaif, J. Rich-Edwards, W. C. Willett, D. J. Hunter, G. A. Colditz, F. E. Speizer, and J. E. Manson, "Long or Highly Irregular Menstrual Cycles as a Marker for Risk of Type 2 Diabetes Mellitus," *Journal of the American Medical Association* 286, no. 19 (November 2001): 2421–2426; and D. W. Cramer, "The Epidemiology of Endometrial and Ovarian Cancer," *Hematology/Oncology Clinics of North America* 26, no. 1 (February 2012): 1–12.

44 See S. M. Wolf, W. Burke, and B. A. Koenig, "Mapping the Ethics of Translational Genomics: Situating Return of Results and Navigating the Research-Clinical Divide," *The Journal of Law, Medicine, and Ethics* 43, no. 3 (Fall 2015): 486–501; S. Li, A. L. Dunlop, D. P. Jones, E. J. Corwin, "High-Resolution Metabolomics: Review of the Field and Implications for Nursing Science and the Study of Preterm Birth," *Biological Research for Nursing* 18, no. 1 (January 2016): 12–22; J. A. Garcia-Velasco, M. Menabrito, and I. B. Catalan, "What Fertility Specialists Should Know about the Vaginal Microbiome: A Review," *Reproductive Biomedicine Online*, 35, no. 1 (July 2017): 103–112; and I. Moreno and J. M. Franasiak, "Endometrial Microbiota–New Player in Town," *Fertility and Sterility* 108, no. 1 (2017): 32–39.

Conclusions

Millions of couples worldwide have benefited from the scientific work done to develop the understanding of the "study of natural rhythms" of human fertility. These investigations have established NFP as a healthy and scientifically, medically, and socially viable family planning method that is accessible for couples across a variety of methods that can meet the needs of couples with different social circumstances, resources, and preferences. NFP is equally relevant for spacing pregnancy and conceiving, has a critical salutary role to play for subfertile (infertile) couples, is foundational to understanding and improving women's health, and has a positive impact on marital relationships. When considering what remains to be investigated, however, it is clear that the current evidence can become the foundation for much more impactful research and greater understanding to come.

10

Natural Family Planning and Ethical Women's Health Care

Kathleen M. Raviele

✷ SINCE ORAL CONTRACEPTIVES BECAME available on the market in 1960, their use has expanded to treat almost all female illnesses from acne, to cramps, to abnormal bleeding, and pelvic pain, while playing a key role in contraception. A health-care professional's knowledge of the modern methods of Natural Family Planning (NFP) is invaluable in managing a woman's reproductive issues because these methods do not interfere with her fertility while assisting couples to either achieve or avoid a pregnancy. Even those who have gone through residency in obstetrics and gynecology with a fellowship in reproductive medicine can acquire valuable tools for managing gynecologic issues by learning the various methods of NFP. In addition, there are ethical solutions to all gynecologic and reproductive problems, including irregular cycles, abnormal bleeding, pelvic pain, dysmenorrhea, a desire to space children or to avoid pregnancy indefinitely, and infertility. Learning one of the modern methods of NFP also provides a woman with invaluable insight into her health since a normal menstrual cycle is a reflection of the woman's health and hormonal well-being.

In this essay, I will discuss the value of charting the menstrual cycle and a woman's signs of fertility as the foundation for ethical women's health care. I will provide examples of the medical applications in a clinical setting that allow both the woman and her physician to live out the teachings of *Humanae vitae.* Here, I will discuss abnormal uterine bleeding, endometriosis, the importance of identification of the day of ovulation, polycystic ovary syndrome and infertility. In each case, I will briefly describe each condition, followed by a description of the medical response, both ethical and nonethical. By way of conclusion, I will offer a brief reflection on changes the medical profession ought to make to not only provide quality women's health care but to do so within the rubrics of respect for human life and God's gifts to humanity.

The Value of Charting the Menstrual Cycle

The components of the NFP method's charting that are extremely valuable are: the menses itself (or "period," which is the woman's bleeding), with any symptoms leading up to the period, its length, the amount of bleeding, associated pain or intestinal symptoms, and any unusual bleeding, either during the menstrual flow or at other times in the cycle; the identification of the six-day fertile window when couples can conceive, including the five days leading up to the day of ovulation and the day of ovulation—which is critical for couples wishing to avoid pregnancy as well as for couples experiencing infertility; and lastly, an accurate determination of the day of ovulation and the length of the post-ovulatory luteal phase, or the days after ovulation before the start of the next menses. Charting the signs that are used to identify these days provides a reliable record of the events during that cycle. It is important to understand that current NFP programs use different signs and charting, but with these components identified, all can be used to assess a woman's reproductive health. In addition, after decades of paper and calendar charting, modern e-charting has become a preferred choice for women in identifying their period of fertility. This deserves a few words.

The free menstrual-cycle tracking applications for smartphones (available through the Apple iTunes store), have taken over as the preferred method of charting for young women, at least for the days of the woman's menstrual flow. The usual recall of the first day of the last menstrual period (LMP) when visiting the doctor tends to be overestimated the further away from the date the woman is. In a group of 385 women aged 35–49 in a cohort study in Washington, D.C., more than half of the women (56%) accurately recalled their LMP date; 74% were within one day, and 81% were within two days.[1] A period-tracking app on the smartphone puts this information at a young woman's fingertips. A recent analysis of twenty accurate, free menstrual-cycle apps revealed that 80% provided information on achieving a pregnancy and 50% for avoiding a pregnancy.[2] Yet, very few were created by health-care professionals. Their study showed that the top three apps were Clue, Glow, and Pink Pad Period Tracker Pro.

One of the current NFP programs developed an app for the iPhone as an evidence-based fertility monitoring application that includes the ability to track multiple natural indicators of fertility, including an electronic urinary hormonal monitor. This application is based on 15-plus years of university-based development and research in fertility-awareness-based methods with over 3,000 women using their online fertility monitoring system.[3] A Sympto-Thermal NFP program also has an app to chart the fertility signs associated with their NFP method, including menstruation, temperature, mucus sensations and characteristics, and the cervix sign. It also allows for recording the Luteinizing Hormone (LH) ovulation test results, fertility monitor readings, weight, notes, and other events.[4]

1 Ganesa Wegienka and Donna Day Baird, "A Comparison of Recalled Date of Last Menstrual Period with Prospectively Recorded Dates," *Journal of Women's Health* 14, no. 3 (April 2005): 248–252.

2 Michelle L. Moglia, Henry V. Nguyen, Kathy Chyjek, Katherine T. Chen, Paula M. Castaño, "Evaluation of Smartphone Menstrual Cycle Tracking Applications Using an Adapted APPLICATIONS Scoring System," *Obstetrics and Gynecology* 127, no. 6 (June 2016): 1153–1160.

3 *Marquette Fertility* (Richard Fehring, 2017), iOS 8.0 or later, compatible with iPhone, iPad, and iPod touch, available at https://itunes.apple.com/us/app/marquette-fertility/id1059216926?mt=8.

4 *CycleProGo* (Clocking Edge, LLC, 2018), iOS 8.0 or later, compatible with iPhone, iPad, and iPod touch, available at https://itunes.apple.com/us/app/cycleprogo/id615146496?mt=8.

Characteristics of the menstrual period are very significant in a woman's medical history. The duration of the period, its frequency, and the amount of bleeding may signal a gynecologic problem. A normal menstrual flow lasts from three to seven days, with five days being the norm, and it should begin every twenty-one to thirty-five days. In younger women, abnormal bleeding accounts for one-third of visits to a doctor; and for women in the peri- and post-menopause, it accounts for 70% of visits.[5] If the patient is changing a menstrual sanitary pad more often than every two hours, is anemic, passing clots, or bleeding for more than seven days or in between periods, an evaluation should be carried out. Her history should be obtained including exposure to any hormones, pain associated with the bleeding, other medical history, and previous surgery. Evaluation includes a pelvic exam, Pap smear, cervical cultures if infection is suspected, a pregnancy test, a complete blood count (CBC), and a thyroid screen. A pelvic ultrasound will identify leiomyomata (fibroids) or adenomyosis (an enlarged uterus due to endometriosis in the wall of the uterus), and a sonohysterogram will identify endometrial polyps. Other hormonal conditions will be discussed later. If the woman is forty-five years of age or older, an endometrial biopsy should be performed to rule out endometrial cancer. A young woman with a very heavy menstrual flow may have a coagulopathy, and this is best evaluated by a hematologist. This is the standard medical workup, but often women are simply placed on oral contraceptives without an evaluation.

Examples of Ethical Medical Applications

Abnormal Uterine Bleeding

Abnormal uterine bleeding is quite simply that—any bleeding outside of the normal menstrual flow. A common treatment for abnormal uterine bleeding, particularly in young women, is to cycle them on oral contraceptives (OCs). The woman experiences a lighter, regular period; but this interferes with her fertility, and these drugs have significant side effects. It is not uncommon in young teenagers who are within two years of menarche to experience anovulatory cycles that result in prolonged or skipped menses. After a workup with a complete blood count (CBC) and thyroid screen, they can be cycled on progesterone for ten days each month to establish a regular pattern. After six months to one year, the progesterone can be stopped and the cycles observed.

In older women with a heavy menstrual flow, there are three nonhormonal drugs that decrease bleeding by about 50%. These include mefenamic acid and meclofenamate sodium, which are nonsteroidal anti-inflammatories, as well as tranexamic acid, a synthetic derivative of the amino acid lysine that exerts its antifibrinolytic effect through the reversible blockade of lysine binding sites on plasminogen molecules.[6] Often, even with structural problems, such as

5 C. P. Spencer and M. I. Whitehead, "Endometrial Assessment Revisited," *British Journal of Obstetrics & Gynaecology* 106, no. 7 (1999): 623–632.

6 C. J. Dunn and K. L. Goa, "Tranexamic Acid: A Review of Its Use in Surgery and Other Indications," *Drugs* 57, no. 6 (June 1999): 1005–1032.

leiomyomata and adenomyosis, these drugs will make the periods manageable. However, if the patient has leiomyomata, she may need surgical removal of the fibroids or a hysterectomy; and if she has endometrial polyps, a hysteroscopy and dilation and curettage of the endometrium to remove the polyps is warranted.

Often, medical recommendations call for the treatment of these conditions with a levonorgestrel intrauterine device (LNG-IUD) or an endometrial ablation. The locally released levonorgestrel hormone in the IUD leads to endometrial concentrations that are 200–800 times those found after daily oral use and a plasma level that is lower than with other forms of levonorgestrel-containing contraception. The contraceptive effect of the LNG-IUD "is achieved mainly through its local suppressive effect on the endometrium, leading to endometrial thinning, glandular atrophy, and stromal decidualization without affecting ovulation."[7] In other words, the LNG-IUD prevents a clinical pregnancy by making the endometrium thin and inhospitable to the blastocyst, thus preventing successful implantation. Regardless of the benefits to a woman with heavy periods, or other gynecologic conditions, the potential loss of human life with this device would make its use unethical.

Endometrial ablation has also been recommended in the treatment of heavy periods. Endometrial ablation destroys a thin layer of the lining of the uterus. Menstrual bleeding may cease altogether even though the ovaries are still ovulating, or it is reduced to normal or lighter levels. According to an FAQ sheet of the American College of Obstetrics and Gynecology, there are several techniques for doing an endometrial ablation: applying radiofrequency energy to the endometrium for ninety seconds; freezing the endometrium under ultrasound guidance; inserting heated fluid through a hysteroscope for ten minutes; insertion of a heated balloon; applying microwave energy through a probe, and inserting a resectoscope with an electrical wire loop, roller-ball, or spiked-ball tip to destroy the endometrium.[8]

Pregnancy can still occur after an endometrial ablation. If it does, the risks of miscarriage and other problems are greatly increased because of diminished endometrium for implantation. Therefore, this is not a technique that can be used in a woman still capable of becoming pregnant, even if she is using NFP. A couple would not be justified in having a sterilization procedure, either, to accommodate an endometrial ablation. Another treatment to manage the heavy periods would need to be done.

Endometriosis

Symptoms associated with a period may also point to another condition, such as endometriosis, an estrogen-dependent inflammatory disease of the pelvis.

7 Abdelhamid M. Attia, Magdy M. Ibrahim, and Ahmed M. Abou-Setta, "Role of the Levonorgestrel Intrauterine System in Effective Contraception," *Patient Preference and Adherence* 7 (August 9, 2013): 777–785.

8 "Endometrial Ablation," American College of Obstetricians and Gynecologists, July 2017, https://www.acog.org/Patients/FAQs/Endometrial-Ablation.

Approximately 10% of women and menstruating girls have this condition, characterized by pain with intercourse, during ovulation, or in the days leading up to a period, and significant, often debilitating pain with a period. There is a prevalence of 38% in women experiencing infertility and a seven-to-tenfold increased risk in women with a first-degree relative with endometriosis. The inheritance pattern is that of a polygenic-multifactorial mechanism.[9]

The etiology is thought to be related to retrograde menstruation with transplantation of endometrial glands and stroma through the fallopian tubes. However, although 90% of women have retrograde menstruation with periods, only 10% of women develop endometriosis. In the sites where the endometrial tissue has implanted, including the peritoneal surfaces, uterus, ovaries, bowel, and bladder, there is a local overproduction of prostaglandins by an increase of cyclooxygenase-2 (COX-2) activity and overproduction of local estrogen by increased aromatase activity.[10]

As endometriosis can be found without menses, there is a coelomic metaplasia theory to explain the formation of endometriomas in the ovary and in the recto-vaginal septum. Changes occur in the peritoneal mesothelial cells, transforming them into endometrial glandular cells. Lastly, research has proposed that endometriosis can be caused by small defects of embryogenesis, where endometrial tissue appears outside the uterus during organogenesis, as seen in deceased fetuses.[11] This would give credence to the hypothesis that complete excision would be curative.

Although the diagnosis may be suspected from the history or the appearance of a possible endometrioma in the ovary by ultrasound, the diagnosis can only be definitively made by laparoscopy and biopsy. The surgery is best performed by a minimally invasive, subspecialty-trained gynecologic surgeon with the goal to excise or ablate all the endometriosis. The more advanced the endometriosis, the more likely complete excision will relieve pain symptoms and laparoscopic presacral neurectomy will relieve midline pain. Suppressing periods and ovulation with OCs, low-dose norethindrone acetate, or GnRH agonists for six months to a year after surgery does not improve pregnancy rates, but it does improve pain in the short-term after surgery. In addition, GnRH agonists are expensive and cause bone loss, so they cannot be used for a long time. The intention is not to prevent pregnancy with these drugs but to relieve pain symptoms; however, care should be taken to avoid harm to an unborn child, and they should not be used for a long period of time. If the woman has an ovarian endometrioma, excision is recommended both for pain relief and for fertility, but it can reduce her ovarian reserve and contribute to pelvic adhesions.[12]

9 ACOG, "Management of Endometriosis," *Practice Bulletin* no. 114 (July 2010).

10 S. E. Bulun, D. Monsavais, M. E. Pavone, M. Dyson, Q. Xue, E. Attar, H. Tokunaga, and E. J. Su, "Role of Estrogen Receptor-β in Endometriosis," *Seminars in Reproductive Medicine* 30, no. 1 (2012): 39–45.

11 Pietro G. Signorile and Alfonso Baldi, "Endometriosis: New Concepts in the Pathogenesis," *The International Journal of Biochemistry & Cell Biology* 42, no. 6 (2010): 778–780.

12 Patrick P. Yeung, James Shwayder, and Resad P. Pasic, "Laparoscopic Management of Endometriosis: Comprehensive Review of Best Evidence," *The Journal of Minimally Invasive Gynecology* 16, no. 3 (May–June 2009): 269–281.

Some of the most difficult endometriosis to treat is recurrent deeply infiltrating endometriosis, particularly in the recto-vaginal septum, which can recur even after a total hysterectomy and bilateral salpingo-oophorectomy (removal of both fallopian tubes and ovaries) has been performed. There is also a major risk of complications from its excision. Danazol has been used in the medical treatment of endometriosis and heavy menstrual bleeding for more than forty years. This medication has both central antigonadotropic actions and direct atrophic effects on endometriotic tissue. The associated side effects include weight gain, acne, oily skin, hepatic dysfunction, mild hirsutism, hot flashes, and voice change, which may take the form of hoarseness or deepening of pitch and may occur and persist after cessation of the drug. Investigators have found that patients treated with low-dose Danazol (200 mg/dose), compounded in a methylcellulose capsule and administered vaginally nightly for a year experienced significant relief of pain symptoms within three months, no pain by six months and persistence of pain relief through the twelve months of therapy. Ultrasound showed a reduction in the nodularity from the endometriosis in the recto-vaginal septum by six months, and there were no metabolic or systemic side effects.[13]

There are some lifestyle changes that can be recommended by health-care professionals and NFP teachers. Endometriosis has been shown to be a condition of oxidative stress with higher concentrations of lipid peroxidation markers in the serum and peritoneal fluid of these women. This milieu favors inflammation with activation of peritoneal macrophages, releasing free radicals and disrupting the balance between oxidants and antioxidants. Research has shown that women consuming a diet with increased omega-3 polyunsaturated fats have a lower incidence of endometriosis,[14] and a high antioxidant diet (fruits and vegetables providing vitamins A, C, and E) improves peripheral antioxidant markers in women with endometriosis.[15] Even vitamin supplementation with vitamin E (1200 IU) and vitamin C (1000 mg) taken daily was shown, in a group of fifty-nine women, aged 19–41 with known endometriosis and randomized to placebo or vitamin treatment, to reduce chronic pelvic pain in 43% of treated patients, decreased dysmenorrhea in 37%, and reduced dyspareunia in 24% of patients as compared with controls. There also was a significant decrease in peritoneal fluid inflammatory markers in the treated patients.[16] This, along with at

13 Sandro Razzi, Stefano Luisi, Francesco Calonaci, Aldo Altomare, Caterina Bocchi, and Felice Petraglia, "Efficacy of Vaginal Danazol Treatment in Women with Recurrent Deeply Infiltrating Endometriosis," *Fertility and Sterility* 88, no. 4 (2007): 789–794.

14 Matthias L. Laschke and Michael D. Menger, "The Gut Microbiota: A Puppet Master in the Pathogenesis of Endometriosis," *American Journal of Obstetrics and Gynecology* 215, no. 1 (2016): 68–70.

15 Jennifer Mier-Cabrera, Tania Aburto-Soto, Soraya Burrola-Méndez, Luis Jiménez-Zamudio, Mari C Tolentino, Esther Casanueva, and César Hernández-Guerrero, "Women with Endometriosis Improved Their Peripheral Antioxidant Markers After the Application of a High Antioxidant Diet," *Reproductive Biology and Endocrinology* 7 (2009): 1–11.

16 Nalini Santanem, Nino Kavtaradze, Ana Murphy, Celia Dominguez, and Sampath Parthasarathy, "Antioxidant Supplementation Reduces Endometriosis Related Pelvic Pain in Humans," *Translational Research* 161, no. 3 (2013): 189–195.

least four hours of exercise per week, are interventions that a provider of NFP can recommend to a client who exhibits significant pain symptoms.

Identification of the Day of Ovulation

The next valuable tool for ethical women's health care is the identification of the day of ovulation. Ovulation occurs in a specific day of the cycle after a series of hormonal events occur between the pituitary gland, hypothalamus, and ovary. The gold standard for this is a pelvic ultrasound, and perhaps someday the technology will be such that this will be available to the consumer. However, all the NFP methods identify as closely as possible the actual day of ovulation by identifying any or all of the following: the Peak Day of the cervical mucus, the shift in basal body temperature (BBT), and the day of the luteinizing hormone (LH) surge. If women have confusing signs, they should use an additional sign to confirm when ovulation is occurring or have timed hormonal studies.

There is a lot of variability in the length of the normal menstrual cycle and the actual day of ovulation, with 46% of women varying by seven or more days in cycle length and anovulatory cycles occurring in up to 12% of normal women.[17] In a prospective study of normally menstruating women without any known infertility or subfertility, a total of forty women, aged 18–40, were tracked through one menstrual cycle with daily urine collections, blood samples and transvaginal ultrasound measuring serum LH, estradiol and progesterone and urinary LH, estrone-3-gluceronide and pregnanediol-3-gluceronide (P3G) and follicular development by ultrasound.[18] The day of objective ovulation was determined as the day before the disappearance of the dominant follicle. The study showed excellent correlation between urinary and serum hormone levels, with the rise in estrogen and LH always occurring before ovulation and the rise in progesterone always occurring after ovulation. There was also much variability in the hormone profiles among the participants. The beginning of the surge of LH, both in serum and in urine, was an excellent predictor of ovulation, and the rise in progesterone and P3G above baseline, signaling the end of fertility, confirmed ovulation. The researchers found that measuring progesterone on day 7 and day 9 was sufficient to assess the function of the corpus luteum. Daily follicular monitoring by high-resolution, modern ultrasound equipment and correlating it with modern laboratory assays for the serum and urinary hormones gave a precise relationship of these levels to the actual day of ovulation.

The range of cycle lengths was 22–37 days (median 27 days), and the day of ovulation ranged from day 8 to day 26 (median day 14.5). The luteal phase length was constant at 12.26 +/- 2.49 days. This would surprise many physicians who

17 Mitchell D. Creinin, Sharon Keverline, and Leslie A. Meyn, "How Regular Is Regular? An Analysis of Menstrual Cycle Regularity," *Contraception* 70, no. 4 (2004): 289–292.

18 J. Roos, Sarah Weddell, Erhard Godehardt, Julia Schiffner, Günter Freundl, and Christian Gnoth, "Monitoring the Menstrual Cycle: Comparison of Urinary and Serum Reproductive Hormones Referenced to True Ovulation," *The European Journal of Contraception and Reproductive Health Care* 20, no. 6 (2015): 438–450.

assume that ovulation occurs on day 14 and women with a short cycle have a defect in the luteal phase and women with a long cycle are probably not ovulating at all. This also can lead to diagnosing patients as overdue in pregnancy when they may not have ovulated until day 21 or later. A pregnant woman charting using one of the NFP methods can show her physician when she ovulated and get an accurate due date.

Polycystic Ovary Syndrome and Associated Complications

Some women have ovulatory problems and irregular cycles, making the practice of NFP more challenging. The most common condition is polycystic ovary syndrome (PCOS), characterized by oligo/anovulation; signs of androgen excess with hirsutism, acne, or elevated free testosterone; and polycystic ovaries by ultrasound. The Rotterdam criteria for PCOS require two out of three of these signs to make a positive diagnosis.[19] This condition affects 7% of women, and the cause is unknown. Obesity, insulin resistance, hypertension, and hyperlipidemia often accompany this disorder but are not part of the diagnosis. Evaluation includes, in addition to the menstrual record, vital signs, BMI (25–30 is overweight, over 30 is obese), waist circumference (greater than 35 inches is abnormal), physical exam, free testosterone, dehydroepiandrosterone sulfate (DHEAS), fasting prolactin, thyroid stimulating hormone, fasting 17-hydroxyprogesterone (to rule out non-classical congenital adrenal hyperplasia), a two-hour glucose tolerance test, fasting lipid profile, and pelvic ultrasound (12 or more follicles measuring 2–9 mm in diameter or an ovarian volume greater than 12 cm constitute polycystic ovaries).

This is a condition for which women are frequently placed on oral contraceptives, but an ethical approach would be to cycle them on progesterone, beginning days 16–19 of the cycle daily for ten days to bring on a period monthly. It is unknown whether this helps protect against endometrial cancer, for which these patients are at high risk; but it gives the woman a regular period, and she avoids abnormal uterine bleeding. Acne can be treated with spironolactone 100 mg/day, as well as a topical retinoid, such as retinoid acid, adapalene, or tazarotene, and washing the face with benzoyl peroxide daily. Avoiding dairy products is helpful. Spironolactone also improves hirsutism, which also can be managed with electrolysis. In women who are obese, there are lifestyle changes that will improve the condition. A whole-food diet, low in carbohydrates and high in protein, to achieve at least a 5% reduction in weight improves the woman's metabolic state.[20] Regular vigorous exercise also helps with weight management. If the woman has glucose intolerance, she should be started on an insulin sensitizing agent, such

19 Rotterdam ESHRE/ASRM-Sponsored PCOS Consensus Workshop Group, "Revised 2003 Consensus on Diagnostic Criteria and Long-Term Health Risks Related to Polycystic Ovary Syndrome," *Fertility and Sterility* 81, no. 1 (2004): 19–25.

20 D. S. Kiddy, D. Hamilton-Fairley, A. Bush, F. Short, V. Anyaoku, M. J. Reed, and S. Franks, "Improvement in Endocrine and Ovarian Function During Dietary Treatment of Obese Women with Polycystic Ovary Syndrome," *Clinical Endocrinology* 36, no. 1 (1992): 105–111.

as metformin in doses of 1500 to 2000 mg/day. Metformin lowers the fasting insulin level but does not cause significant changes in the patient's BMI. There is no advantage to taking both metformin and an ovulation-inducing drug unless the woman has a BMI greater than 35 kg/m2, nor is there an improvement in miscarriage rates in the first trimester.[21]

A consensus was reached by a group of experts on PCOS in 2007 on the best treatments for infertility in these patients.[22] Infertility due to anovulation is frequent with PCOS and the first-line treatment is the anti-estrogen clomiphene citrate (CC), starting at 50 mg/day for five days starting days 2–5 of the cycle. Doses should not exceed 150 mg/day. It is reasonably priced, has few side effects, results in a 3%–8% chance of multiple birth, does not require extensive monitoring, and is safe to take for up to six cycles. An ultrasound should be performed at the start of therapy, and a progesterone level drawn a week after ovulation. Human chorionic gonadotropin (hCG) given mid-cycle does not improve the chances of conception. Approximately 75%–80% of women ovulate with CC, and there is a conception rate of 22% per cycle. The aromatase inhibitor letrazole appears to be equally as effective as CC, but this is off-label use. If ovulation cannot be induced with CC, the patient should be referred to a reproductive endocrinologist for gonadotrophin administration, because of the need for close ovarian monitoring to prevent ovarian hyperstimulation syndrome.

If neither CC nor gonadotropins are successful in inducing ovulation, then laparoscopic ovarian surgery (LOS) should be performed.[23] LOS reduces the chance of ovarian hyperstimulation syndrome in these patients as well as multiple births. Surgical ovarian wedge resection was established to help with ovulation in the past before medical ovulation induction was introduced but is no longer performed because of the risk of adhesion formation and a greater risk of premature ovarian failure. LOS has the advantage of assessing the pelvis for other pathology and being minimally invasive. Four to ten punctures with either laser or monopolar cautery are carried out on the ovaries, with few side effects, although adhesion formation and premature menopause can also occur. After twelve weeks, if ovulation does not occur, CC is restarted, and after six months, gonadotropins are resumed. It would not be ethical to resort to an assisted reproductive technology (ART), such as intrauterine insemination or in vitro fertilization (IVF).

Although not part of the Rotterdam criteria for diagnosing PCOS, insulin resistance and hyperinsulinemia occur in half of patients with PCOS. In obese

21 R. S. Legro, H. X. Barnhart, W. D. Schlaff, B. R. Carr, M. P. Diamond, S. A. Carson, M. P. Steinkampf, C. Coutifaris, P. G. McGovern, N. A. Cataldo, G. G. Gosman, J. E. Nestler, L. C. Giudice, P. C. Leppert, and E. R. Myers, "Clomiphene, Metformin, or Both for Infertility in the Polycystic Ovary Syndrome," *New England Journal of Medicine* 356, no. 6 (February 8, 2007): 551–566.

22 The Thessaloniki ESHRE/ASRM-Sponsored PCOS Consensus Workshop Group, "Consensus on Infertility Treatment Related to Polycystic Ovary Syndrome," *Human Reproduction* 23, no. 3 (2008): 462–477.

23 Cindy Farquhar, Julie Brown, and Jane Marjoribanks, "Laparoscopic Drilling by Diathermy or Laser for Ovulation Induction in Anovulatory Polycystic Ovary Syndrome," *Cochrane Database of Systematic Reviews* Issue 6 (2012), Art. No.: CD001122.

patients, it is present in as many as 80% of patients.[24] As mentioned previously, diet and exercise with weight loss can improve this condition. The elevated insulin disrupts normal ovarian function but the etiology of this is unknown. Several studies included in a critical review have shown the effectiveness of the two stereoisomers of inositol, myo-inositol, and D-chiro-inositol in improving ovarian function, restoring ovulation, and improving fertility in women with PCOS.[25] In the ovary, D-chiro-inositol plays a role in insulin-mediated androgen synthesis, and myo-inositol mediates glucose uptake and follicle-stimulating hormone (FSH) signaling. An imbalance of these two inositols in the ovary appears to lead to PCOS. When administered orally in a 40:1 ratio of myo- to D-chiro-inositol, the endocrine profile and insulin resistance improves, with enhanced oocyte follicular development and oocyte maturation, without side effects. These supplements are available over the counter and have become a standard therapeutic recommendation for women with PCOS and insulin resistance.

Infertility

The next area in which NFP can assist in ethical women's health care is infertility. Charting helps identify the days in which hormone studies should be done, depending on when ovulation appears to be occurring, or whether it is occurring at all. Couples using NFP assume that as soon as they stop avoiding pregnancy, they will be able to conceive in the first month that they try to get pregnant. Therefore, after three cycles of trying to achieve a pregnancy, they seek medical help to find out why they are not getting pregnant.

There are some preliminary recommendations that can be made without undertaking an extensive evaluation at that point. A careful medical history on the woman should be taken for prescription medications, over-the-counter medications and supplements, medical problems, and whether vaccinations are up to date, as well as indications of harmful habits such as alcohol, excessive caffeine intake, smoking, and drug use. Women with significant health problems, such as diabetes, hypertension, renal disease, autoimmune disorders, or psychiatric disorders, should be optimized as far as medications and the underlying condition are concerned so that pregnancy is entered into under the best conditions for mother and child. All potentially harmful habits to the developing baby should be stopped, and any potentially teratogenic prescription drugs should be exchanged for safer alternatives before undertaking a pregnancy. A valuable online resource for determining if a medication is safe in pregnancy is REPROTOX.[26]

Folic acid supplementation reduces the risk of a neural tube defect, so it is recommended women take 0.4 mg of folic acid, which is in a standard woman's

24 John E. Nestler, "Role of Hyperinsulinemia in the Pathogenesis of the Polycystic Ovary Syndrome, and Its Clinical Implications," *Seminars in Reproductive Endocrinology* 15, no. 2 (1997): 111–122.

25 Vittorio Unfer, John E. Nestler, Zdravko A. Kamenov, Nikos Prapas, and Fabio Facchinetti, "Effects of Inositol(s) in Women with PCOS: A Systematic Review of Randomized Controlled Trials," *International Journal of Endocrinology* 2016, article ID 1849162.

26 See https://reprotox.org/.

multivitamin. The woman should be as close to ideal body weight as possible, as being either overweight or underweight contributes to infertility and pregnancy-related problems.

The best diet for achieving a pregnancy was identified by a group of Harvard scientists in the Nurses' Health Study which followed women with no known infertility issues for eight years.[27] They found that a higher consumption of monounsaturated fats, vegetable rather than animal protein, low glycemic carbohydrates, high-fat dairy, and iron from plants and multivitamins reduced the risk of ovulatory disorder infertility. These dietary recommendations can be made in the preconception counseling, and it is also a healthy diet to continue through pregnancy.

So, when should a couple be evaluated for possible infertility? An infertility evaluation is time-consuming, expensive, and in some cases painful, so it is important not to start too early and cause overtreatment or delay too long and miss the opportunity to help the couple.

The age of the woman plays a role in deciding when the evaluation should begin. The number of oocytes in the ovaries decreases as the woman ages. The greatest attrition occurs even before birth. At 20 weeks of gestation, the female fetus has 6–7 million oocytes, and at birth the number drops to 1–2 million. With menarche, oocytes decrease further to 300,000–500,000; by age 37, the number is 25,000; and at menopause, on average age 51, only 1,000 remain.[28] Fecundity, or the ability to conceive, is greatest in a woman in the third decade of life, with a significant decline beginning at age 32, accelerating at age 37, due to a decrease in egg quality, rising FSH levels, and decreases in antimullerian hormone (AMH) and inhibin B levels. Measuring the FSH on day 3 of the cycle and an AMH level, done any time in the cycle, can be helpful in determining whether treatment for infertility should be undertaken or continue. The decline in egg quality leads to increased rates of aneuploidy and spontaneous miscarriage. In addition, the older the woman is, the more likely she will have other anatomic defects affecting conception, such as tubal blockage, endometriosis, or leiomyomata. Therefore, women older than 35 years of age should have a workup after six months of attempting a pregnancy, and women who reach 40 should begin an evaluation immediately. It is very helpful to alert couples to these statistics when they are learning NFP so they do not delay childbearing for a long period in their marriage in the hopes of having everything in their lives perfect before they start a family.

Fifteen percent of couples will not be able to achieve a pregnancy in twelve months of having random intercourse. In 40% of cases, there will be a male factor preventing conception, in 40%, a female issue, some of which we have already discussed, and in 20% each partner will have an issue potentially

27 J. E. Chavarro, J. W. Rich-Edwards, B. A. Rosner, and W. C. Willett, "Diet and Lifestyle in the Prevention of Ovulatory Disorder Infertility," *Obstetrics and Gynecology* 110, no. 5 (2007): 1050–1058.

28 The American College of Obstetricians and Gynecologists Committee on Gynecologic Practice and the Practice Committee of the American Society for Reproductive Medicine. "Female Age-Related Fertility Decline," Committee Opinion Number 589 (March 2014).

impairing conception. The man can be medically evaluated first by history: an undescended testicle as a child, mumps in childhood, age over 40, use of saunas or hot tubs, cigarette smoking, and alcohol or drug abuse, any of which can lower the sperm count. In a surprising meta-analysis of 185 studies including 42,935 men who provided semen samples, investigators found that the sperm count in men in Western countries has declined by 52.4% from 1973 to 2011.[29] The cause of this is unknown but could pose a significant public-health problem as there is little that can be done to boost sperm counts when a male factor is the cause of infertility. The standard way semen is obtained for sperm counts in infertility evaluations is to have the man masturbate in the office. It would be unethical to tell a man to masturbate, but the sample can be obtained by having the husband wear a special collection sheath during intercourse, similar to a condom but having nothing in it that is spermicidal. Several pinprick holes are made in the sheath to allow some sperm to exit during the marital act, removing the contraceptive purpose of the condom and making collection licit, and the specimen is brought to the lab in a sterile container within one hour to be processed. Three factors are analyzed: the count, the motility, and the morphology. If any of these parameters are abnormal on two separate samples, taken a month apart, the patient should be referred to a urologist for an evaluation and exam. If the man has azoospermia (no sperm present), a karyotype should be performed as Klinefelter syndrome (47, XXY) accounts for up to 14.5% of azoospermic men. If the woman is normal and the man has oligospermia (fewer than 20 million sperm/ml), the couple may still achieve a pregnancy. If nothing can be done to improve the sperm count, morphology, or motility, couples are medically encouraged to resort to the immoral practice of ART, such as intrauterine insemination, IVF, or intracytoplasmic sperm injection (ICSI). All of these techniques remove the conception from occurring during marital intercourse and place it in the hands of the physicians and lab technicians and are illicit.

The evaluation of the woman can be carried out in one cycle. She calls with the first day of her menses, and on day 3, blood is drawn to determine FSH, LH, and estradiol levels. A hysterosalpingogram (HSG) to assess tubal patency and a pelvic ultrasound looking for structural abnormalities are done days 8–10 of the cycle, before ovulation and after the bleeding has stopped. There is an increased chance of pregnancy in the six months after an HSG. If there is a tubal blockage, the woman should be treated with seven days of doxycline 100 mg twice a day to avoid a flare of a pelvic infection.

A post-coital test is performed shortly before ovulation (days 12–14) on a woman with a regular cycle 28 to 30 days apart. The couple has relations, and the woman is examined within two to twelve hours, and cervical mucus is obtained. Under the microscope, if her mucus shows 5–10 forward motile sperm, the stretch of the mucus (spinnbarkeit) is 8 cm or greater, and when the mucus dries ferning is seen, these are good indications that her mucus is not a factor in

29 H. Levine, N. Jørgensen, A. Martino-Andrade, J. Mendiola, D. Weksler-Derri, I. Mindlis, R. Pinotti, and S. H. Swan, "Temporal Trends in Sperm Count: A Systematic Review and Meta-Regression Analysis," *Human Reproduction Update* 23, no. 6 (2017): 646–659.

their infertility. The day of ovulation is identified with the Peak Day of cervical mucus, the first day of temperature rise (BBT), or the day after the LH surge; and a serum progesterone, thyroid stimulating hormone, AMH, and prolactin are drawn on day 7 or day 9 after ovulation. If there is a history suggestive for endometriosis, or the hysterosalpingogram suggests a tubal factor, a laparoscopy should be scheduled after the next period with a gynecologist skilled in laparoscopy and the treatment of endometriosis.

After all the test results are in, the physician should sit down with the couple to go over the results and form a treatment plan. If the woman's tubes are blocked, there is little hope that the couple will be able to achieve a pregnancy by licit means. If leiomyomata are present, a discussion regarding possible removal should be carried out. If she has a thyroid disorder or an elevated prolactin level, these conditions should be treated. If poor cervical mucus is a factor, treatment with guaifenesin and oral antibiotics in the fertile window may improve the mucus.

In cases of anovulation or oligoovulation, the woman's testing should fall into one of the three classes established by the World Health Organization (WHO): Class I, hypogonadotropic hypogonadism (low FSH, LH, and estradiol); Class II, normogonadotropic normal estrogen anovulation (PCOS); and Class III, hypergonadotropic, hypoestrogenic anovulation (premature ovarian failure or menopause). If the woman has low FSH and estradiol levels, often associated with excessive exercise and weight loss, this should be corrected with behavioral interventions. If she has PCOS, as previously discussed, CC is very effective at restoring ovulation. If she has premature ovarian failure or menopause, there is no drug that will help her ovulate. These patients will be encouraged to have the illicit practice of ART with IVF and donor eggs, but adoption is the best moral alternative in these cases.

Is there evidence that tracking with NFP helps a couple achieve a pregnancy earlier than random acts of intercourse? In an observational study of 340 women attempting a pregnancy using the fertile phase, the cumulative probabilities of conception were, at one (38%), three (68%), six (81%), and 12 (92%) cycles.[30] The researchers concluded that as most of the women using NFP under 30 years of age had conceived by six months, this group also should be evaluated for infertility after six months of trying.

In a study of highly educated, noninfertile women aged 30 to 44 trying to conceive, even informal instruction on cervical mucus observations to identify the fertile window and consistent use of this sign, reduced the time to pregnancy (TTP) over women using a calendar calculation.[31] In another prospective randomized study of 143 women of proven fertility aged 18 to 35, formal education in the Creighton Model Fertility*Care*™ System (CrMS) did not shorten the TTP

30 C. Gnoth, E. Godehardt, P. Frank-Herrmann, K. Friol, J. Tigges, and G. Freundl, "Definition and Prevalence of Subfertility and Infertility," *Human Reproduction* 20, no. 5 (2005): 1144–1147.

31 Emily Evans-Hoeker, David A. Pritchard, D. Leann Long, Amy H. Herring, Joseph B. Stanford, and Anne Z. Steiner, "Cervical Mucus Monitoring Prevalence and Associated Fecundability in Women Trying to Conceive," *Fertility and Sterility* 100, no. 4 (2013): 1033–1038.

over random acts of intercourse.[32] Lastly, in a prospective study of 256 women of unknown fertility, with a mean age of 29.22 years and an age range of 20–43, who were trying to achieve a pregnancy, the women charted online urinary estrone and LH using the Clearblue® Fertility Monitor (CBFM, Swiss Precision Diagnostics, Geneva, Switzerland), mucus observations, or both. The cumulative probabilities of conception were three (58%), six (73%), nine (75%), 12 (78%), and 24 (86) cycles of use. For women who already had at least one living child, the cumulative probabilities of conception were three (66%), six (82%), nine (82%), 12 (86%), and 24 (90%) cycles. The highest pregnancy rates were in those who used NFP incorporating the fertility monitor alone versus mucus alone to identify the fertile window and the day of ovulation.[33]

NFP can assist couples experiencing infertility and give them some control over the process without resorting to illicit methods of ART. A study involving 1,072 women in an Irish general practice office, trying to get pregnant for at least a year were trained in the CrMS of NFP and evaluated for the cause of infertility according to the protocol for Natural Procreative Technology (NPT or NaProTECHNOLOGY™).[34] They then underwent ethical, mainstream medical treatments for the underlying cause of their infertility. The average age of the initial group was 35.8 years (range 25–48), 24% had a previous live birth (representing secondary infertility), and they had been attempting pregnancy for a mean length of time of 5.6 years. By twelve months, 44.6% of couples had withdrawn from the study, and by twenty-four months, 62.7% had withdrawn. Those remaining couples had a cumulative proportion of live births of 27.1 per 100 couples for those treated up to twelve months, and 52.8 per 100 couples for those treated up to twenty-four months. Through an infertility evaluation as set by the protocols for NPT, which are not explained in the study, it was determined that more than half the women had luteal phase defects, 25% had limited cervical mucus, 10% had PCOS, 24% had endometriosis, and 13.6% had a male factor issue. It was not clear how endometriosis was diagnosed, as there was no surgery described, and no one appeared to have a tubal factor. Clomiphene citrate was given to 75.3% of the women, hCG injections to 67%, progesterone to 18%, and cervical mucus enhancers to 71%. Five percent of women achieved pregnancy without any treatment. These are all treatments that are ethical and done in gynecological practices. Major weaknesses of the study were not revealing the reasons for withdrawal from the study and not separating out subgroups by the cause of their infertility, length of their infertility,

32 Joseph B. Stanford, Ken R. Smith, and Michael W. Varner, "Impact of Instruction in the Creighton Model Fertility*Care*™ System on Time to Pregnancy in Couples of Proven Fecundity: Results of a Randomized Trial," *Paediatric Perinatal Epidemiology* 28, no. 5 (2014): 391–399.

33 Thomas P. Bouchard, Richard J. Fehring, and Mary M. Schneider. "Achieving Pregnancy Using Primary Care Interventions to Identify the Fertile Window," *Frontiers in Medicine* 4, art. 250 (January 9, 2018): 1–7.

34 Joseph B. Stanford, Tracey A. Parnell, and Phil C. Boyle, "Outcomes from Treatment with Natural Procreative Technology in an Irish General Practice," *Journal of the American Board of Family Medicine* 21, no. 5 (November–December 2008): 375–384.

and which treatments succeeded. The age of the woman is very important, as previously discussed, and there was no mention of testing ovarian reserve. A cohort treatment study based on outcome, without randomization or blinding is a low level of evidence.

In a retrospective cohort study, a general practice group in Canada reviewed all patients they saw for NPT services for infertility or recurrent miscarriage from August 2000 to July 2006.[35] They included 108 patients with two previous miscarriages (secondary infertility), or who were infertile for one year with random acts of intercourse or six months of CrMS-focused intercourse with no pregnancy. A total of 44% of the women had had a previous pregnancy, the average age was 35.4 years, and 25% of the women had been trying to get pregnant for less than one year. After evaluation, they found 12% had a male factor, 14% had endometriosis, 6% had PCOS, 9% had deficient cervical mucus, 14% had anovulation, and 50–62% had low estrogen before and after ovulation or low progesterone in the luteal phase. Of the women who conceived, 43% received medications to improve cervical mucus, 41% were given CC, 47% received progesterone in the luteal phase, 41% were given hCG injections after ovulation, and 8% had a surgical procedure done. By twenty-four months, there were 51 clinically detected pregnancies, and 24% achieved pregnancy with CrMS instruction alone. The weaknesses of this study include: that it was retrospective; there was no randomization; and there was a high percentage of women who had been pregnant before (so one would expect that they would achieve another pregnancy). Again, this study has a low level of evidence for NPT techniques being superior to standard ethical infertility treatments that do not allow for ART.

Lastly, recurrent miscarriage (two or more) and infertility issues have been attributed to a short luteal phase (fewer than nine days). However, even in women with normal cycles, there is a great deal of variability in the LH surge and hormone levels. In a study of 107 normally fertile women, aged 19–44 (median 32.6), over 283 cycles, subjects recorded daily basal body temperature, cervical mucus, and collected daily morning urines to measure estrone-3-gluceronide (E3G), pregnanediol-3α-gluceronide (PDG), FSH, and LH by time-resolved fluorometric immunosorbent assays (Delfia).[36] Serial vaginal ultrasounds were performed every other day until a follicle reached 16 mm and then daily until ovulation. The mean cycle length was 28.1 days (range 22–44 days), mean time to ovulation was 14.8 days (range 9–33 days), and the mean length of the luteal phase was 13.3 days (range 7–17 days). This study showed a great deal of variability in hormone levels over the course of a cycle, with 52% of cycles deviating from the classic mean hormone curves. In an

35 Elizabeth Tham, Karen Schliep, and Joseph B. Stanford, "Natural Procreative Technology for Infertility and Recurrent Miscarriage: Outcomes in a Canadian Family Practice," *Canadian Family Physician* 58, no. 5 (2012): e267–274.

36 Ana Direito, Sébastien Bailly, Aude Mariani, and René Ecochard, "Relationships Between the Luteinizing Hormone Surge and the Other Characteristics of the Menstrual Cycle in Normally Ovulating Women," *Fertility and Sterility* 99, no. 1 (January 2013): 279–285.e3.

earlier study of 107 normal women, deviations from the classic mean curves occurred in 56% of normal cycles.[37]

Progesterone is secreted by the corpus luteum in a pulsatile fashion and peaks 6–8 days after ovulation. If implantation occurs, continued progesterone secretion is controlled by rising hCG levels. If pregnancy does not occur or is defective, progesterone levels fall and bleeding occurs. Ovulation induction, supplementation with progesterone or hCG in the luteal phase will correct a luteal phase defect. Progesterone supplementation can be done orally, vaginally, or intramuscularly (IM), with no difference in the route of administration. Luteal supplementation with hCG increases the risk of ovarian hyperstimulation syndrome. There appears to be no benefit, once bleeding occurs, in administering progesterone in a pregnant patient. More research is needed to determine if progesterone improves pregnancy outcome in normal, unstimulated cycles when given in the luteal phase.[38] The diagnosis of a luteal phase defect cannot be reliably made based on lab tests, even done repeatedly through the cycle, as progesterone levels can fluctuate in a 90-minute period from 2.3 to 40.1 pg/mL. Good clinical judgment, however, is to treat women with unexplained infertility or recurrent miscarriage and a short luteal phase with progesterone.[39]

Conclusion

In summary, NFP education and use empowers women to better understand their fertility and respect their reproductive system. The documentation of the quality of the period, timing of ovulation and length of the post-ovulatory phase assists a woman and her physician in identifying potential health problems that can interfere with her fertility or her health and well-being. The vast amount of research on NFP over the past fifty years has enhanced our ability to provide ethical and effective treatments for women's gynecological conditions, many of which are already standard medical treatments, without the use of hormonal contraceptives, sterilization, or ART. Catholic physicians and all physicians of good will are able to provide excellent, evidence-based health care for women which respects their dignity, upholds the dignity of marriage, protects human life, and honors God's creation.

37 Maria Elena Alliende, "Mean Versus Individual Hormonal Profiles in the Menstrual Cycle," *Fertility and Sterility* 78, no. 1 (2002): 90–96.

38 Practice Committee of the American Society for Reproductive Medicine, "Current Clinical Irrelevance of Luteal Phase Deficiency: A Committee Opinion," *Fertility and Sterility* 103, no.4 (2015): e27–32.

39 Tolga B. Mesen and Steven L. Young, "Progesterone and the Luteal Phase: A Requisite to Reproduction," *Obstetrics and Gynecology Clinics of North America* 42, no. 1 (2015): 135–151.

11

The State of Fertility Awareness Based Method Education for Medical Professionals

Marguerite R. Duane and Erin Adams

✷ In one of the last sections of his encyclical *Humanae vitae*, Pope Paul VI issues a challenging plea to physicians and medical personnel:

> [T]hey should regard it as an essential part of their skill to make themselves fully proficient in this difficult field of medical knowledge [natural regulation of birth]. For then, when married couples ask for their advice, they may be in a position to give them right counsel and to point them in the proper direction.[1]

Paul VI recognizes that "It is supremely desirable . . . that medical science should by the study of natural rhythms succeed in determining a sufficiently secure basis for the chaste limitation of offspring."[2] Yet, despite advances in the science supporting natural means of monitoring and regulating fertility and the growing interest in fertility awareness among women, men, and medical students alike, very little effort has been invested in educating medical professionals about the science of Natural Family Planning (NFP).

The terms NFP and Fertility Awareness-Based Methods (FABMs)[3] both refer to the "means by which a couple uses the daily observations of signs and symptoms of the fertile and infertile phases of the menstrual cycle to guide the timing of intercourse according to their desire to achieve or avoid pregnancy."[4] The term NFP highlights that these methods are based on observations of natural signs and specifically excludes the use of artificial barriers or chemicals; whereas the term FABM highlights that these methods can be used for monitoring a

1 Pope Paul VI, Encyclical Letter *Humanae vitae* (July 25, 1968), 27, http://w2.vatican.va/content/paul-vi/en/encyclicals.index.html.

2 Pope Paul VI, *Humanae vitae*, 24.

3 In this essay we use the terms NFP, FABMs, and FAB Methods interchangeably to reflect the terms used in the research cited or most prevalent in use at the time.

4 William Andrew Uricchio and Mary Kay Williams, eds., *Proceedings of a Research Conference on Natural Family Planning* (Washington, D.C.: Human Life Foundation and the Center for Population Research, National Institute of Child Health and Human Development, 1973). The conference was convened at Airlie House, Warrenton, Virginia, on January 23–26, 1972.

woman's reproductive health as well as for family planning.[5] Although the term FABM does not explicitly exclude the use of methods of contraception, when couples use their knowledge of fertility awareness in combination with barriers, chemicals, or withdrawal, it is more accurate to refer to this as a Fertility Awareness Combined approach. It is important to note that almost all of the research done on the effectiveness of NFP or FAB methods have been done when couples choose to avoid sexual contact when they are fertile.[6]

The failure of the medical education system to adequately prepare physicians and other medical professionals to discuss NFP or FAB methods with patients neglects those who need or desire family planning methods that are free from medical side effects, safe for the environment, and morally acceptable to people of many different faiths. Perhaps it is precisely because these methods are seen primarily as a faith-based matter and not a medical one that the health-care system has not adequately studied or supported their use more broadly. Nonetheless, NFP or FABMs are based on solid scientific research which shows these methods are safe and effective, both for achieving and avoiding pregnancy, as well as for addressing common women's health concerns.[7] In this essay, it is our interest to highlight the deficit in the NFP education of medical professionals and offer innovative solutions to address this need.

A Brief History of the Major Scientific Advances and Development of NFP Methods

To understand the inadequate state of medical education today as it pertains to FABMs, it is important to consider the history of the research that led to their development. In this volume, a thorough review of the last 150 years of NFP scientific history is provided by Richard J. Fehring in chapter 8, "A Historical Review of the Catholic Scientists Who Answered the Call of *Humanae vitae*." Fehring discusses scientific advancements, effectiveness studies, and shifting attention within the Catholic Church toward support of NFP by highlighting the contributions of Catholic scientists. Here, we add to that history with an overview of key scientific advances, methodological detail, and current technologies in development.

The most significant scientific discovery that led to the development of modern FABMs was made independently and in two different parts of the world by Dr. Kyusaku Ogino (Japan) and Dr. Herman Knaus (Austria). In the 1920s,

5 Stephen R. Pallone and George R. Bergus, "Fertility Awareness-Based Methods: Another Option for Family Planning," *Journal of the American Board of Family Medicine* 22, no. 2 (2009): 147–157.

6 See Michael D. Manhart, Marguerite Duane, April Lind, Irit Sinai, and Jean Golden-Tevald, "Fertility Awareness-Based Methods of Family Planning: A Review of Effectiveness for Avoiding Pregnancy Using SORT," *Osteopathic Family Physician* 5, no. 1 (2013): 2–8. The average effectiveness rates for FABMs are 95%–99% with correct use, 86%–98% with typical use.

7 See Kathleen Raviele's chapter (10) in this volume, "Natural Family Planning and Ethical Women's Health Care." See also Manhart et al., "Fertility Awareness-Based Methods of Family Planning," 2–8 and Thomas W. Hilgers, "The New Women's Health Science of NaProTECHNOLOGY," *Archives of Perinatal Medicine* 17, no. 4 (2011): 191–198, http://www.ptmp.com.pl/archives/apm/17-4/APM174-2-Hilgers.pdf.

Ogino and Knaus found in their separate research that ovulation occurs on average fourteen days before the first day of the menses.[8] Using this information, Dr. Leo Latz, an obstetrician-gynecologist, published *The Rhythm of Sterility and Fertility in Women* in 1932. Latz described formulas a woman can use to predict the fertile time in her menstrual cycle based on her previous cycles. Eventually called the Calendar Rhythm Method (or Rhythm Method), it was one of the most effective forms of family planning available at the time.

Research in the 1950s and 60s led to the discovery of cervical mucus as a viable biomarker for tracking ovulation in women.[9] Further investigation led to the development of the ovulation method as it was proven that women were able to effectively track their fertile and infertile times of the cycle by the changes in cervical mucus alone.[10] By the end of the 1970s, the Billings Ovulation Method®, Creighton Model *FertilityCare*™, and Family of the Americas methods had been developed and were being used to help couples avoid pregnancy with correct use rates greater than 99%.[11] Additionally, in the 1980s, Dr. Thomas Hilgers developed Natural Procreative Technology, or NaProTECHNOLOGY ™, which integrates the use of the Creighton Model *FertilityCare*™ chart to aid in the targeted diagnosis, management and treatment of a myriad of gynecologic problems.[12]

The Sympto-Thermal Method (STM) was also developed in the 1950s in response to improvements in basal body temperature (BBT) tracking and the inclusion of cervical mucus as a biomarker.[13] Though BBT as a biomarker had been discovered as an accurate indicator of ovulation in the 1930s, research found that including cervical mucus monitoring increased efficacy.[14] Since the

8 Leo J. Latz, *The Rhythm of Sterility and Fertility in Women: A Discussion of the Physiological, Practical, and Ethical Aspects of the Discoveries of Drs. K. Ogino (Japan) and H. Knaus (Austria) regarding the Periods when Conception is Impossible and when Possible* (Chicago: Latz Foundation, 1932), 35.

9 Kyusaku Ogino, *Conception Period of Women* (Harrisburg, Pa.: Medical Arts Publishing Company, 1934), 79–80 and Herman Knaus, *Periodic Fertility and Sterility in Woman: A Natural Method of Birth Control* (Vienna: Wilhelm Maudrich, 1934).

10 Hanna Klaus, "Natural Family Planning: A Review," *Obstetrical & Gynecological Survey* 37 (February 1982): 128–150.

11 See for example H. J. Bhargava, C. Bhatia, L. Ramachandran, P. Rohatgi, and A. Sinha, "Field Trial of Billings Ovulation Method of Natural Family Planning," *Contraception* 53 (February 1996): 69–74; M. P. Howard, and J. B. Stanford, "Pregnancy Probabilities during Use of the Creighton Model Fertility*Care* System," *Archives of Family Medicine* 8 (September–October, 1999): 391–402; and Thomas W. Hilgers and Joseph B. Stanford, "Creighton Model NaProEducation Technology for Avoiding Pregnancy: Use Effectiveness," *The Journal of Reproductive Medicine* 43, no. 6 (June 1998): 495–502.

12 Hilgers, "The New Women's Health Science of NaProTECHNOLOGY," 191–198. Hilgers also established the Pope Paul VI Institute for the Study of Human Reproduction in Omaha, Nebraska where his medical practice and educational programs are offered among other related work.

13 Richard J. Fehring, "Under the Microscope: A Brief History of Natural Family Planning," *Natural Family Planning Current Medical Research* 25, nos. 3 and 4 (Summer/Fall 2014): 16, http://www.usccb.org/issues-and-action/marriage-and-family/natural-family-planning/medical-research/index.cfm.

14 See Margaret Nofziger, *Signs of Fertility: The Personal Science of Natural Birth Control* (Deatsville, Ala.: MND Publishing, Inc, 1998), 39–40; G. K. Döring, "Regarding the Reliability of the Temperature Method for the Prevention of Conception," German Medical Weekly [*Deutsche Medizinische Wochenschrift*] 92 (June 9, 1967), trans. Dr. Don Heinrich, http://www.nfpandmore.org/Doering-1967-100315.pdf; and Fehring, "A Brief History of Natural Family Planning," 16.

late 1990s, two high-quality studies conducted in Germany found the correct use effectiveness rates of STM to be 99.5% and typical use to be 98%.[15]

The combination of multiple biomarkers to increase efficacy has also been influenced by the increased availability of medical devices for hormone monitoring at home.[16] For example, in the 1990s at Marquette University, Fehring developed the Marquette Model, a Sympto-Hormonal Method, which uses cervical mucus observations as well as hormone readings from the Clearblueâ Fertility Monitor to determine the time of ovulation.[17] Research has shown that with typical use, the effectiveness rate for the electronic fertility monitor plus algorithm was 98%, and for the monitor plus mucus observations, the method was 93% effective.[18] In the last decade, we have seen the introduction of Fertility Education and Medical Management Model (FEMM), which combines careful observations of cervical mucus with readings from a luteinizing hormone (LH) strip to confirm the fertile window.[19] The primary focus of FEMM is to teach women to monitor their cycle so they may better understand and manage their health. To date, there have been no studies conducted to evaluate the effectiveness of FEMM to avoid pregnancy.

There has been a movement toward simplification of fertility tracking. The advantage of these methods is that they are easy to teach and use. A criticism is that they are not flexible enough to follow the menstrual cycle variability which some women experience. Researchers and clinicians at Georgetown University's Institute for Reproductive Health (IRH) have developed simplified forms of both the cervical mucus and algorithm-based methods. The simplified cervical mucus method is called the TwoDay Method. It is based on a woman's observation of

15 Fehring, "A Brief History of Natural Family Planning," 16; P. Frank-Herrmann, G. Freundl, C. Gnoth, E. Godehardt, J. Kunert, S. Baur, and U. Sottong, "Natural Family Planning with and without Barrier Method Use in the Fertile Phase: Efficacy in Relation to Sexual Behavior: A German Prospective Long-Term Study," *Advances in Contraception: The Official Journal of the Society for the Advancement of Contraception* 13 (June–September 1997): 179–189; and P. Frank-Herrmann, J. Heil, C. Gnoth, E. Toledo, S. Baur, C. Pyper, E. Jenetzky, T. Strowitzki, and G. Freundl, "The Effectiveness of a Fertility Awareness Based Method to Avoid Pregnancy in Relation to a Couple's Sexual Behaviour during the Fertile Time: A Prospective Longitudinal Study," *Human Reproduction* 22, no. 5 (May 2007): 1310–1319.

16 On this point, see Fehring's chapter 20 in this volume, "Signs of Growth and Healing: Health Care and Science."

17 Richard J. Fehring, Mary Schneider, Kathleen Raviele, and Mary Lee Barron, "Efficacy of Cervical Mucus Observations Plus Electronic Hormonal Fertility Monitoring as a Method of Natural Family Planning," *Journal of Obstetric, Gynecologic, and Neonatal Nursing* 36 (March–April 2007): 152–160; Richard J. Fehring, Mary Schneider, Kathleen Raviele, Dana Rodriguez, and Jessica E. Pruszynski, "Randomized Comparison of Two Internet-Supported Fertility Awareness Based Methods of Family Planning," *Contraception* 88, no. 1 (July 2013): 24–30; Richard J. Fehring, Mary Schneider, and Thomas Bouchard, "Effectiveness of an Online Natural Family Planning Program for Breastfeeding Women," *Journal of Obstetric, Gynecologic, and Neonatal Nursing* 46, no. 4 (July–August 2017): e129–137; and Richard J. Fehring and Mary Schneider, "Effectiveness of a Natural Family Planning Service Program," *MCN: The American Journal of Maternal Child Nursing* 42 (January–February 2017): 43–49.

18 Fehring et al., "Effectiveness of an Online Natural Family Planning Program for Breastfeeding Women," 129.

19 Meghan Grizzle Fischer and Pilar Vigil, "White Paper: The Case for FEMM," FEMM, https://femmhealth.org/wp-content/uploads/2016/02/FEMM-white-paper_2015.pdf.

whether cervical secretions are present or absent to identify potential days of fertility. This method does not require interpretations of the quality of the secretions. With correct use, the TwoDay method is 96% effective and with typical use it is 86% effective.[20] Also developed at Georgetown, the algorithm-based Standard Days Method (SDM) identifies a fixed fertile window. The SDM estimates the six-day fertile phase of the menstrual cycle as falling within days 8–19—a formula based on computer analysis of 7,500 menstrual cycles. An efficacy trial found that the SDM was more than 95% effective with correct use and more than 88% with typical use among women who reported regular recent cycles of 26–32 days.[21]

Another simplified method is the Lactation Amenorrhea Method (LAM), which was also developed by the IRH. This method may be used by a woman for the first six months after delivery if she is exclusively breastfeeding her baby and does not have a return of her menses.[22] Effectiveness rates for LAM are very high, greater than 98%, with both typical and correct use.[23]

In a field that prides itself on promoting the most current, evidence-based forms of medical care, it begs the question as to why medical professionals do not routinely learn about and provide modern fertility awareness based methods to their patients. Medical research in this field has been a long-standing practice and essential to the development, and improvement of the calendar-based methods, cervical mucus methods, Sympto-Thermal Method, Sympto-Hormonal Method, and simplified methods. Also, as discussed in this essay, both patients and medical students express interest in learning about these natural methods. The lack of education for students neglects the needs of both the medical professionals to be competent in their field and the patients whom they serve.

Patient Interest

At the core of all medical advances and decisions is the patient. The patient is who we, as physicians, serve. For this reason, it is important to understand the patient's desire and interest in fertility awareness-based methods before moving forward.

Patient interest in FABMs has been demonstrated in several studies. A 1999 study of 747 women of reproductive age in Missouri showed that although only 2.8% were currently using a FABM, 22.5% would be interested in using NFP to avoid pregnancy and 37.4% would use a natural method to become pregnant.[24]

20 M. Arevalo, V. Jennings, and I. Sinai, "Efficacy of a New Method of Family Planning: The Standard Days Method," *Contraception* 65 (May 2002): 333–338.

21 Arevalo, et al., "Efficacy of a New Method of Family Planning: The Standard Days Method," 333–338.

22 M. Labbok, V. Hight-Laukaran, A. Peterson, V. Fletcher, H. von Hertzen, and P. Van Look, "Multicenter study of the Lactational Amenorrhea Method (LAM): I. Efficacy, duration, and implications for clinical application," *Contraception* 55, no. 6 (June 1997): 327–336.

23 A. Peterson, R. Peŕez-Escamilla, M. Labbok, V. Hight-Laukaran, H. von Hertzen, and P. Van Look, "Multicenter Study of the Lactational Amenorrhea Method (LAM) III: Effectiveness, Duration, and Satisfaction with Reduced Client-Provider Contact," *Contraception* 62 no. 5 (November 2000): 221–230.

24 J. B. Stanford, J. C. Lemaire, and P. B. Thurman, "Women's Interest in Natural Family Planning," *The Journal of Family Practice* 46, no. 1 (January 1998): 65–71.

This shows a significant increase in interest when compared to the percent of women in the study already using NFP (2.8%). In particular, there is an association between women who had previously had difficulty achieving pregnancy and an interest in NFP.[25] Seven years later, a cross-sectional study by C. J. Leonard and associates of reproductive-aged women in Phoenix, Arizona, demonstrated even greater interest, with 61% of patients indicating they would be interested in using NFP to avoid pregnancy and 50% to achieve pregnancy.[26] Of these patients, young age and a desire for future pregnancy were predictive of NFP use to achieve pregnancy. In addition, this study looked at low-income women, illustrating NFP is an important option to include in this population. Both of these studies show that there is a significant and demonstrable interest among women within the United States to learn more and potentially use FABMs in the future. However, without knowledgeable physicians, women may not be informed and/or supported in their use of these important and effective options for family planning and women's health.

The Popularity of Fertility Apps

Another indicator of patient interest in FABMs is reflected by the increasing number of available fertility tracking apps for women (with the corresponding implication of profit for the manufacturers). As of 2015, one study showed 95 fertility tracking apps on the market, the majority of which were not founded on evidence-based FABMs and/or included a disclaimer that they were not intended for use to avoid pregnancy.[27] Nonetheless, these apps are popular with millions of women accessing them. For example, Clue reports 5 million active users, Kindara has 1.5 million downloads, and the Natural Cycles app, which has been officially approved as a contraceptive method in Europe and now in the United States, has 600,000 active users.[28] Supporting this popularity is the amount of money being invested into the industry. Since 2009, 1.26 billion dollars has poured into female technology, or femtech, start-ups, which include fertility awareness apps and tracking devices.[29] With increasing competition, it is important that efficacy be advocated as a measure of quality.

Before discussing the motivating factors that spark interest in FABMs, a common misconception must first be addressed. It is often assumed that the majority

25 Stanford et al., "Women's Interest in Natural Family Planning," 65–71.

26 C. J. Leonard, W. Chavira, D. V. Coonrod, K. W. Hart, and R. C. Bay, "Survey of Attitudes regarding Natural Family Planning in an Urban Hispanic Population," *Contraception* 74 (October 2006): 313–317.

27 Marguerite Duane, Alison Contreras, Elizabeth T. Jensen, and Amina White, "The Performance of Fertility Awareness-Based Method Apps Marketed to Avoid Pregnancy," *The Journal of the American Board of Family Medicine* 29 (July 1, 2016): 508–511.

28 Suzanne Bearne, "My fertility app made me too stressed to conceive," *BBC News* online, April 6, 2017, http://www.bbc.com/news/business-39503947; Rosie Spinks, "Instagram Influencers are Inspiring Women to Stop Taking the Pill," *Quartzy*, March 1, 2018, https://qz.com/quartzy/1218004/birth-control-pill-versus-fertility-tracking-natural-cycles-instagram-campaign-pushes-the-ideal-of-hormone-free/; and Tia Newcomer, email message to author (Duane), March 1, 2018.

29 Bearne, "My fertility app."

of patients are motivated to use a FABM for religious reasons. This is not accurate as analysis of several different studies by James N. Gribble and associates showed that in 12 of 14 studies, religion was the reason for using natural methods for only 0.5–7.4% of women.[30]

Motivating Factors for Use of FABMs

Fertility awareness-based methods provide a wide range of benefits compared to contraceptives. Women can use some methods to monitor their health and manage common reproductive health concerns, and couples can use these methods to help achieve or avoid pregnancy. One study found that couples who had used an NFP method previously were most likely to be interested in future use of FABMs, including the majority of women in this sample who used contraceptives to avoid pregnancy. This study also found that interest in FABMs was independent of religious affiliation, education level, or income.[31] Below, we discuss additional factors that make FABMs an appealing option for women and couples.

No Harmful Side-Effects

FABMs provide an effective way for couples to avoid pregnancy that does not expose women to artificial hormones, or their side effects.[32] There is a growing population of patients interested in leading a more natural, healthy, organic lifestyle by eliminating artificial hormones from their food and their medicine. This group includes women who want to use FABMs as a way to limit their exposure to artificial hormones or chemicals. This is highlighted by an expert consensus opinion, which stated that there are certain lifestyle habits that can affect fertility, such as smoking, alcohol use, caffeine, seafood consumption, and nutritional supplements.[33] These lifestyle habits affect not only fertility but health in general. For these patients, the movement from hormonal suppression of their fertility to natural, medication-free methods, like FABMs, is appealing.[34] If physicians were to start a conversation with their patients about FABMs, it would intuitively lead to a discussion about healthy lifestyle habits, from which all patients could benefit.

30 J. N. Gribble, R. I. Lundgren, C. Velasquez, and E. E. Anastasi, "Being Strategic about Contraceptive Introduction: The Experience of the Standard Days Method," *Contraception* 77 (March 2008): 147–154.

31 Stanford et al., "Women's Interest in Natural Family Planning," 65–71.

32 Mario Philip R. Festin, James Kiarie, Julie Solo, Jeffrey Spieler, Shawn Malarcher, Paul F. A. Van Look, and Marleen Temmerman, "Moving Towards the Goals of FP2020—Classifying Contraceptives," *Contraception* 94 (May 30, 2016): 289–294.

33 Samantha Pfeifer, Samantha Butts, Gregory Fossum, Claris Gracia, Andrew La Barbera, Jennifer Mersereau, Randall Odem, Richard Paulson, Alan Penzias, Margareta Pisarska, Robert Rebar, Richard Reindollar, Mitchell Rosen, Jay Sandlow, and Michael Vernon, "Optimizing Natural Fertility: A Committee Opinion," *Fertility and Sterility* 107 (January 2017): 52–58, https://doi.org/10.1016/j.fertnstert.2016.09.029.

34 Spinks, "Instagram Influencers Inspiring Women to Stop Taking the Pill."

Economical

While most FABMs require couples to invest time to learn the methods up front, all are either cost-free or relatively inexpensive, as well as immediately reversible. This is an important motivating factor that was demonstrated in the Leonard study, where low-income women without access to other methods were eager to learn more.[35] Another advantage of FABMs is that they encourage open communication and participation by both partners. In a 2017 survey of more than 2,500 people, 74% of men and 64% of women expressed that using FABMs had helped to improve their relationship.[36] These findings were similar to the results from an earlier study where couples most commonly reported that FABMs "deepened the relationship" and "improved communication."[37]

Versatile

FABMs are unique in that they can be used to either achieve or avoid pregnancy. Therefore, FABMs are beneficial for couples who may need to avoid pregnancy temporarily but desire to achieve pregnancy in the future. Even if a woman is not currently interested in pregnancy, if she learns how to track her menstrual cycle, she will later know how to use the same method to become pregnant.[38] This understanding will allow for a smooth and easy transition when a patient moves between phases of life. Moreover, when used correctly for avoiding pregnancy, FAB methods have unintended pregnancy rates of <5 per 100 women-years. With typical use, these methods are 86%–98% effective.[39]

Assistance in Maintaining Women's Health

Another important reason why people may be interested in learning about FABMs is to monitor ovulation since the presence of ovulation is a sign of good health.[40] For this reason, giving a woman the knowledge to understand her body and the signs that indicate good reproductive health will empower her not only to plan pregnancy but also to better manage her reproductive and overall health. For example, women with disorders of ovulation may detect significantly decreased cervical mucus;[41] therefore, by learning how to identify the presence or absence of ovulation each month, a woman can keep track of her overall health status. In a 2017 survey of almost 2,000 women, 95% of them stated that

35 Leonard et al., "Survey of Attitudes regarding Natural Family Planning in an Urban Hispanic Population," 313–317.

36 Matthias Unseld, Elisabeth Rötzer, Roman Weigl, Eva K. Masel, and Michael D. Manhart, "Use of Natural Family Planning (NFP) and Its Effect on Couple Relationships and Sexual Satisfaction: A Multi-Country Survey of NFP Users from US and Europe," *Frontiers in Public Health* 5 (2017): 42, https://doi.org/10.3389/fpubh.2017.00042.

37 L. Vande Vusse, L. Hanson, R. J. Fehring, A. Newman, and J. Fox, "Couples' Views of the Effects of Natural Family Planning on Marital Dynamics," *Journal of Nursing Scholarship* 35, no. 2 (2003): 171–176.

38 Pfeifer et al., "Optimizing Natural Fertility" 5–58.

39 Manhart et al., "Fertility Awareness-Based Methods of Family Planning," 2–8.

40 Pilar Vigil, Leonard F. Blackwell, and Manuel E. Cortés, "The Importance of Fertility Awareness in the Assessment of a Woman's Health: A Review," *The Linacre Quarterly* 79, no. 4 (2012): 426–450.

41 Hilgers, "The New Women's Health Science of NaProTECHNOLOGY," 194.

the use of NFP allowed them to understand their body better.[42] This knowledge has been deemed so important that in 2015, the American College of Obstetricians and Gynecologists (ACOG) released a statement that was also endorsed by the Academy of Pediatrics.[43] In this statement, ACOG recommended that physicians discuss with adolescents what they should expect in a normal menstrual cycle and that physicians ask about menstrual pattern at every visit. ACOG also stated that the identification of abnormal menstrual patterns in adolescence may improve early identification of health concerns in adulthood.[44] This recognition of the importance of physician understanding of the cycle, as well as education of the patient, is an important step and acknowledgment that women should be observing the pattern of their menstrual cycle as an indication of their overall health.[45]

Meeting Patient Needs

FABMs provide an array of options for a woman or a couple to find a method that will work best with their lifestyle as well as the woman's ability and comfort level in making observations. With cervical fluid methods (e.g., Billings Ovulation Method®, Creighton Model Fertility*Care*™, TwoDay method, etc.), women observe cervical secretions and may chart what they sense and/or see. These observations of cervical secretions can be paired with at-home testing of basal body temperature or urinary hormone metabolite levels as recommended by the Sympto-Thermal methods (e.g., Couple to Couple League, Rötzer Method) and Sympto-Hormonal methods (e.g., Marquette and FEMM methods), respectively.[46] Calendar-based (e.g., Rhythm Method) or algorithm-based (e.g., Standard Days Method), methods do not require women to observe any biological fertility signs, but simply to keep track of the days of their cycle. However, this limits who can use algorithm-based methods. For example, the Standard Days Method is limited to women with regular cycles between 26–32 days in length. Also, the Lactational Amenorrhea Method (LAM) may only be used by post-partum women for the first six months after giving birth if they have not experienced a return of menses and are exclusively breastfeeding.

Nonetheless, there are a variety of evidence-based FABMs available, which may appeal to a great majority of people. Therefore, it is imperative that accurate,

42 Unseld et al., "Use of Natural Family Planning and Its Effect on Couple Relationships and Sexual Satisfaction," 42.

43 "ACOG Committee Opinion No. 651: Menstruation in Girls and Adolescents: Using the Menstrual Cycle as a Vital Sign," *The American College of Obstetricians and Gynecologists*, https://www.acog.org/Clinical-Guidance-and-Publications/Committee-Opinions; Vaishali Popat, Tamara Prodanov, Karim Calis, and Lawrence Nelson, "The Menstrual Cycle: A Biological Marker of General Health in Adolescents," *Annals of the New York Academy of Sciences* 1135 (2008): 43–51.

44 "ACOG Committee Opinion No. 651: Menstruation in Girls and Adolescents: Using the Menstrual Cycle as a Vital Sign."

45 Pilar Vigil, Francisco Ceric, Manuel Cortés, and Hanna Klaus, "Usefulness of Monitoring Fertility from Menarche," *Journal of Pediatric and Adolescent Gynecology* 19, no. 3 (2018): 173–179; Popat et al., "The Menstrual Cycle," 43–51.

46 Manhart et al., "Fertility Awareness-Based Methods of Family Planning," 2–8.

evidence-based information be made available to all future physicians and health-care professionals so that they can provide these as viable options for family planning and more comprehensive women's health care. As such, it is also important to acknowledge and address misinformation that may be perpetuated about the use and effectiveness of FABMs.

Correcting Misinformation

A critical reason why physicians do not inform patients about FABMs is related to an incorrect effectiveness rate for pregnancy avoidance published by the Centers for Disease Control (CDC). Currently, the CDC quotes a single typical use failure rate of 24% for all FABMs.[47] The statistic is derived from the 1995 and 2002 National Surveys for Family Growth—retrospective surveys based on patient recall and corrected for underreporting of abortion.[48] Furthermore, fully 86% of the users surveyed reported using the Calendar Rhythm Method as their primary form of family planning, not a modern method of NFP. This single statistic masks important differences in effectiveness among the variety of modern FABMs, a fact acknowledged by the author of this estimate.[49] Given that modern FABMs differ significantly in the signs observed and the rules guiding use for avoidance of pregnancy, it is misleading to quote one overall statistic for all methods.

In this context, the lack of accurate education about FABMs not only hinders medical professionals in their practice of medicine but also prohibits patients from receiving information about the full range of reproductive health care options that may be available to them.

Medical Student Interest

Despite the lack of FABM education in medical schools, research indicates that medical students desire to learn about them. In a 2014 survey of 145 second-year medical students at the Medical College of Wisconsin, 80%–90% of students agreed with the two statements that physicians should have adequate knowledge to inform patients about fertility awareness-based options and they should be able to answer questions about FABMs.[50] Yet, 65% of these students did not feel medical school had prepared them well to discuss FABMs with patients and 40% of students would like to learn more.[51]

47 Centers for Disease Control and Prevention, "Contraception: How Effective Are Birth Control Methods?", https://www.cdc.gov/reproductivehealth/contraception/index.htm.

48 J. Trussell, "Contraceptive Failure in the United States." *Contraception* 83 no. 5 (2011): 397–404.

49 M. Duane, R. Motley, and M. Manhart, "Letters to the Editor: Physicians Need More Education About Natural Family Planning," American Family Physician 88 (August 2013): 158–159, https://www.aafp.org/afp/2013/0801/p158.html.

50 C. Jojola, L. Weasler, and L. Simonds, "Student Interest in Learning about Fertility Awareness-Based Methods: An Unaddressed Competency in the Medical School Curriculum" (unpublished paper, Family Medicine Education Consortium Northeast Region Meeting, Arlington, Va., October 24–26, 2014).

51 Jojola et al., "Student Interest in Learning about Fertility Awareness-Based Methods."

Similarly, in a survey of about 650 medical students from seven different medical schools, 85% of students agree that physicians should have adequate knowledge about FABMs to offer them to patients.[52] However, 80%–90% of these students were not familiar with any of the modern evidence-based FABMs. Interestingly, the method students reported being the most familiar with was the Calendar Rhythm Method.[53] More importantly, 60%–70% of students, an even higher percentage than in the previous study, want to learn about modern FABMs with two-thirds of those students expressing interest in online learning opportunities.[54] The evidence demonstrates an unmet need in this critical group who provide direct health services to the patient population. A strategy to provide FABM education to medical students must be developed if patients are to have accurate and ready access to this helpful information.

Education of Medical Professionals: A Review of the Literature

Students and residents most likely do not learn about FABMs because physicians are largely uninformed about them. In 2010, Dr. Patrick Beeman undertook a review of the literature to examine the breadth, depth, and content of NFP education in medical and nursing programs.[55] The author conducted an English language literature search of major medical and nursing research databases for the previous ten years dating back to the beginning of the year 2000. This initial search uncovered 166 relevant articles, only two of which were related to health professionals' or students' knowledge or attitudes towards NFP. Therefore, Dr. Beeman extended the search timeline to 1982, uncovering an additional six articles that specifically addressed the topic of medical professionals' education and familiarity with NFP. Finally, an additional study which looked at sexual and reproductive health topics included in the pre-clinical medical education curriculum was added since it mentioned Rhythm/NFP.[56] Sadly, over a 28-year period, only nine published research articles reported on NFP education in the medical setting.

In general, these early studies showed that the majority of medical professionals learned about NFP outside of their basic educational programs and/or via written materials.[57] For medical professionals who did learn about these

52 Lucy Guevera and Marguerite Duane, "Survey of Student Interest in Learning about Fertility Awareness Based Methods" (unpublished paper, Family Medicine Education Consortium Meeting, Danvers, Mass., October 31, 2015).

53 Guevera and Duane, "Survey of Student Interest in Learning about Fertility Awareness-Based Methods."

54 Guevera and Duane, "Survey of Student Interest in Learning about Fertility Awareness-Based Methods."

55 Patrick Beeman, "Natural Family Planning in Education and Practice: A Narrative Review of the Literature," *The Linacre Quarterly* 77, no. 4 (November 2010): 399–414.

56 F. J. Steinauer, F. LaRochelle, M. Rowh, L. Backus, Y. Sandahl, and A. Foster, "First Impressions: What are Preclinical Medical Students in the US and Canada Learning about Sexual and Reproductive Health?" *Contraception* 80, no. 1 (July 2009): 74–80.

57 S. Girotto, F. Delzotti, M. Baruchello, G. Gottardi, M. Valente, A. Battaggia, B. Rosa, P. Fedrizzi, M. Campanella, M. Zumerle, and F. Bressan, "The Behavior of Italian Family Planning Physicians Regarding the Health Problems of Women and, in Particular, Family Planning (Both Contraceptive and NFP),"

methods in their program, they reported that there was less than one hour of instruction devoted to the topic. This same study was the only one that found that 4% of physicians and 1% of nurses were formally trained to teach NFP.[58] When specifically asked about their level of knowledge, less than half reported they knew NFP sufficiently well.[59] Other studies, however, found that physicians overestimated their knowledge of these methods and underestimated the effectiveness rates.[60] In the earliest studies, physicians reported that they were most familiar with or likely to recommend the Calendar Rhythm Method, rather than any of the more modern evidence-based methods.[61] It is not surprising that the majority of medical professionals would not mention NFP as a viable option for most patients, with 53%–65% rarely recommending these methods on a regular basis.[62]

In preparation of this essay, another search was conducted of all the same major medical and nursing research databases since 2010 (except for the Health Source Nursing/Academic databases which was not available to the author). A total of 197 articles pertinent to natural or the Fertility Awareness Based Methods were identified, including eight that specifically addressed the topic of medical professionals and students' knowledge of NFP and fertility awareness. Additionally, there were two letters to the editor calling for family physicians and general practitioners to learn more about these natural methods.[63]

Findings from these studies published since 2010, as well as data from studies presented by Dr. Duane at medical conferences in 2015 and 2017, show similar results regarding medical professionals' lack of education or inadequate knowledge of NFP/FAB methods. For example, a 2010 study of obstetrician-gynecologists and family physicians in Canada showed only 3%–6% of them had correct knowledge of the effectiveness of the Billings Ovulation Method®, the basal body temperature (BBT), Standard Days, and Lactation Amenorrhea methods.[64] Furthermore, 50% of these physicians do not mention NFP as an

---

Advances in Contraception 13, no. 2–3 (1997): 283–293; Richard J. Fehring, "Physician and Nurses' Knowledge and Use of Natural Family Planning," *The Linacre Quarterly* 62 (November 1995): 22–28.

58 Fehring, "Physician and Nurses' Knowledge and Use of Natural Family Planning," 22–28.

59 Girotto et al., "The Behavior of Italian Family Planning Physicians," 283–293.

60 Beeman, "Natural Planning in Education and Practice: A Narrative Review of the Literature," 399–414; see also R. Snowden, Kathy I. Kennedy, Federico Leon, Virginia C. Orense, Harin W. Perera, Rodney Phillips, Ian Askew, Anna Flynn, and Lawrence J. Severy, "Physicians' Views of Periodic Abstinence Methods: A Study in Four Countries," *Studies in Family Planning* 19 (July–August 1988): 215–226.

61 Girotto et al., "The Behavior of Italian Family Planning Physicians," 283–293 and Snowden et al., "Physicians' Views of Periodic Abstinence Methods," 215–226.

62 J. B. Stanford, P. B. Thurman, and J. C. Lemaire, "Physicians' Knowledge and Practices regarding Natural Family Planning," *Obstetrics and Gynecology* 94 (November 1999): 672–678; Fehring, "Physician and Nurses' Knowledge and Use of Natural Family Planning," 22–28; Girotto et al., "The Behavior of Italian Family Planning Physicians," 283–293.

63 Duane et al., "Letters to the Editor: Physicians Need More Education About Natural Family Planning," 158–159; J. V. Turner, "Fertility-Awareness Practice and Education in General Practice," Australian Journal of Primary Health 22 (November 2016): 375–376.

64 J. Choi, S. Chan, and E. Wiebe, "Natural Family Planning: Physicians' Knowledge, Attitudes, and Practice," *Journal of Obstetrics and Gynaecology Canada: JOGC* 32 (July 2010): 673–678.

option when patients ask them for contraceptive advice, and another 24% only mention them with reservation. In another survey of clinicians from Title X clinics, researchers found that there was considerable variability in their understanding of what NFP is and how the methods may be used in the clinical setting.[65] Again, this may reflect a lack of education about these methods, both in medical school and residency programs. For example, a preliminary survey of family medicine residency programs in 2012 revealed that only 5%–10% of the women's health curriculum is devoted to discussing FABMs compared to 30% for oral contraceptives.[66] More importantly, 25% of programs do not provide any education in FABMs. Further, more than half of faculty members do not feel confident in presenting information on FABMs accurately and the method they report being most familiar with is the Calendar Rhythm Method. Another 2012 survey of obstetrics and gynecology residents found that very few (9%) had experience counseling patients about the use of Cycle Beads and less than half had ever counseled patients about other methods of NFP.[67]

In a 2016 study of the barriers to fertility awareness education in general practice, female general practitioners reported they only had enough knowledge to provide basic instruction in fertility awareness; whereas, all but one male physician felt unqualified to educate patients.[68] In this study, physicians and nurses both agreed that the single most important factor for providing fertility awareness education is the presence of nurses specifically trained in this area. Furthermore, respondents believed it would be best if these nurses could be trained via an online certification program. Another study of natural fertility and infertility treatments demonstrated significant knowledge gaps among obstetrics and gynecology residents and medical students.[69] Although this study did not specifically evaluate their knowledge of NFP or FAB methods, it did examine their awareness of lifestyle factors impacting natural fertility, risk factors for infertility, and success of assisted reproductive technologies. Of note, there was no mention of NaProTECHNOLOGY™ or other natural methods that may be used by couples to help them conceive. Although fertility knowledge does increase with

65 P. J. Kelly, J. Wit, K. McEvers, M. Enriquez, P. Abshier, M. Vasquez, and E. McGee, "Clinician Perceptions of Providing Natural Family Planning Methods in Title X Funded Clinics," *Journal of Midwifery & Women's Health* 57, no. 1 (January–February 2012): 35–42.

66 L. Gordon, R. J. Motley, and Marguerite Duane, "Survey of Fertility Awareness Methods Incorporated into Women's Health Curricula in Family Medicine Residency Programs," (unpublished paper, Family Medicine Education Consortium Northeast Region Meeting, Cleveland, Ohio, September 27–30, 2012).

67 A. Y. Miklavcic and C. R. Isaacs, "Obstetric-Gynecology Resident Education regarding Barrier and Over-the-Counter Contraceptives: A National Study," *Journal of Women's Health* 21 (November 2012): 1196–1200.

68 K. D. Hampton, J. M. Newton, R. Parker, and D. Mazza, "A Qualitative Study of the Barriers and Enablers to Fertility-Awareness Education in General Practice," *Journal of Advanced Nursing* 72 (July 2016): 1541–1551.

69 R. Kudesia, E. Chernyak, and B. McAvey, "Low Fertility Awareness in United States Reproductive-Aged Women and Medical Trainees: Creation and Validation of the Fertility & Infertility Treatment Knowledge Score (FIT-KS)," *Fertility and Sterility* 108 (October 2017): 711–717.

training, the majority of those students and residents surveyed overestimated success rates for in vitro fertilization, or IVF, and underestimated complication rates. The authors do recognize the importance of routine fertility counseling beginning in adolescence to empower women with knowledge about their body, but again they make no mention of the use of FABMs.[70]

Finally, in 2017, Peter Danis and colleagues published a study that specifically examined medical students' knowledge of FABMs for family planning and their confidence in using that knowledge to counsel patients.[71] At the beginning of their third-year rotation in obstetrics and gynecology, students completed an assessment to measure their baseline knowledge of fertility awareness and then attended two lectures on FABMs and their applications for women's health, before completing a post-test. They found that even a brief educational intervention can increase medicals students' knowledge of FABMs and confidence in counseling patients on these methods. Similarly, a study of first-year medical students who completed an eight-week elective on FABMs found that there was a significant increase in students' knowledge of these methods, whether they completed the course in-person or on-line.[72] Furthermore, a follow-up study of these students 6–7 years after they completed the elective found those students who completed the FABM elective demonstrated greater knowledge of FABMs and were significantly more confident in their ability to discuss FABMs with women.[73]

Education of Medical Professionals: Current and Future Opportunities

As seen in the literature, medical professionals learn very little about NFP or FAB methods in traditional educational programs. Fortunately, in the United States some NFP and FABM teacher training programs have developed educational opportunities specifically for health-care professionals, in addition to the many other non-medical people trained to teach women or couples how to use their method.

The Creighton Model FertlityCare™ Medical Consultant Program

The earliest program developed specifically for doctors is the Creighton Medical Consultant program, founded by Hilgers and his colleagues in

70 Rashmi Kudesia, Hina J. Talib, and Staci E. Pollack, "Fertility Awareness Counseling for Adolescent Girls; Guiding Conception: The Right Time, Right Weight, and Right Way," *Journal of Pediatric and Adolescent Gynecology* 30 (February 2017): 9–17, https://doi.org/10.1016/j.jpag.2016.07.004.

71 P. G. Danis, S. A. Kurz, and L. M. Covert, "Medical Students' Knowledge of Fertility Awareness-Based Methods of Family Planning," *Frontiers in Medicine* 4 (June 1, 2017): 65.

72 Erin Adams and Marguerite Duane, "Comparison of an Online vs. Live Course on Fertility Awareness Based Methods," unpublished paper, Family Medicine Education Consortium Meeting (Danvers, Mass.: October 31, 2015).

73 Sajel Nuwamanya, Colleen Hamm, and Marguerite Duane, "An Educational Intervention to Improve Understanding of FABMs in Medical School," (unpublished paper, Family Medical Education Consortium Meeting, Cleveland, Ohio, November 11, 2017).

1981.[74] In 2006, Hilgers also launched the St John Paul the Great Fellowship in Medical and Surgical NaProTECHNOLOGY ™ which is designed

> [T]o provide an opportunity for obstetrician-gynecologists who have completed their residency to acquire additional skills in approaches to the treatment of women's health problem[s] which are designed to cooperate with the menstrual and fertility cycle.[75]

To date, 22 physicians have completed the fellowship program.[76]

Institute for Natural Family Planning, College of Nursing, Marquette University

In 2001–2002, the Marquette University College of Nursing introduced the first professional online program designed for health-care professionals to learn to teach the Marquette Method.[77] Initially, it was offered sequentially as two three-credit semester-long courses until about 2013. The first course covered NFP history, anatomy and physiology, scientific foundations, fertility indicators, sexual ethics, and other topics. The second course served as a supervised practicum during which students were required to teach 10 clients and use a case study approach to understand the application of these methods. During this time, approximately, 125 health-care professionals completed their training. In 2014, Marquette went to a continuing education format for their three online courses and since then they have had 75 physicians, advanced practice nurses, physician assistants, and professional nurses complete the training.[78]

Fertility Education Medical Management

Fertility Education and Medical Management (FEMM)[79] offers training for health-care professionals to provide targeted evaluation and ethical management of medical conditions in their patients when they arise. In addition, the FEMM Teacher Training course educates health-care professionals to provide their method of NFP and to help patients understand their fertility and facilitate their active participation in the long-term management of their health and fertility.[80] To date, there have been 190 medical students, 22 residents, 12 nursing

74 Thomas Hilgers, "The Medical and Surgical Practice of *NaProTECHNOLOGY*," (Omaha: Pope Paul VI Institute Press, 2004), 184. The training is provided in two one-week in-person sessions, usually over the course of a year.

75 St. John Paul the Great Fellowship in Medical and Surgical NaProTECHNOLOGY, Pope Paul VI Institute, at http://popepaulvi.com/fellowship.php.

76 Christine Hemphill, email message to author (Duane) (March 2, 2018).

77 R. J. Fehring, "The Future of Professional Education in Natural Family Planning," *Journal of Obstetric, Gynecologic, and Neonatal Nursing* 33 (January–February 2004): 34–43.

78 Richard Fehring, email message to author (Duane) (March 2, 2018).

79 FEMM, https://femmhealth.org.

80 FEMM teacher education is also offered to non-health care professionals. See https://femmhealth.org/education/learn-to-teach/become-femm-teacher.

students, and 2 other students that have completed the medical management training; whereas, a total of 18 health-care professional students and residents have completed their teacher training.[81]

Secular and Catholic Diocesan NFP Education Providers

It is important to acknowledge that the major NFP secular organizations and many Catholic diocesan NFP programs have provided education to health-care professionals and medical students through seminars, workshops, conferences, and in their specific method teacher training programs. This has been part of their ongoing outreach education since the 1980s.[82]

FACTS: Teaching Medical Professionals About All Evidence-Based FABMs

In 2010, a collaborative approach to teach the science and basic methodology of all FABMs to medical and other health-care professionals and students was founded by Dr. Marguerite Duane and family medicine physician, Robert Motley. Called the Fertility Appreciation Collaborative to Teach the Science (FACTS), its mission is "to educate future health-care professionals about evidence-based fertility awareness methods (FABMs), so they may empower and engage patients to care for their reproductive health."[83]

FACTS is a project of the Family Medicine Education Consortium, Inc. (FMEC), a northeast regional 501(c)(3) organization that is committed to strengthening Family Medicine/ primary care services and medical education. FACTS is committed to educating physicians, students, and other health-care professionals about how FABMs work, their effectiveness for family planning, and the positive impact they can have on women's reproductive health.

The catalyst that led to the formation of FACTS was feedback from medical students who had completed an introductory course on natural or the Fertility Awareness Based Methods at Georgetown University School of Medicine as part of the Introduction to Health Care course. This course, "The Fertility Awareness Methods In the Learning Years (FAMILY) Planning" selective, was unique in that many of the lectures were delivered by the researchers who had developed each of the methods. Feedback from that initial cohort highlighted the need and

81 [81] Based on the research of endocrinologist Pilar Vigil, the FEMM Medical Management Course provides information to allow "medical professionals to accurately diagnose and treat infertility, menopause, thyroid dysfunction, migraines, depression, weight gain, fatigue, pain, PMS [premenstrual syndrome], PCOS, endometriosis, and acne. The FEMM Medical Protocols assess over 10 hormones, a woman's clinical history, and cycle data, in order to diagnose and treat the underlying causes of symptoms." See https://femmhealth.org/femm-medical-management/; Gabrielle Jastrebski. email message to author (Duane), March 1, 2018.

82 Theresa Notare, PhD, Assistant Director, NFP Program, United States Conference of Catholic Bishops, communication to author (Duane) (April 2018).

83 See www.factsaboutfertility.org.

importance of offering this course to a wider medical student audience, as well as to other health-care professional students:

> "This selective has had the most impact on me out of the entire first year curriculum. The students who had the opportunity to take this class are, in my opinion, at a huge advantage to their peers. We will have future patients who may be interested in this as a form of family planning, and it would be a true disservice if we did NOT have the expertise to counsel them regarding these effective methods."[84]

> "This selective gives my medical education renewed purpose. It amazes me every day how spending a few short minutes to teach these non-invasive, simple, inexpensive methods can make an infinitely greater difference in the lives of our patients, more than any sort of medical procedure or exam."[85]

> "This was, by far, the best class I have taken at Georgetown. The guest speakers were phenomenal. I strongly believe that EVERY medical student should at least have an introduction to NFP. Thank you so much for this course!"[86]

With the above confirmation, FACTS focused its efforts on developing educational programs and content that can be more easily conveyed to future medical professionals.

In 2013, FACTS created a one-hour Continuing Medical Education (CME) presentation to provide an introduction to the science supporting FABMs and their effectiveness rates for family planning. The following year, FACTS developed a speaker training program to prepare fellow medical professionals and NFP/fertility awareness educators to deliver educational presentations.[87] In 2015, FACTS created an online version of the CME course.

Similarly, in 2014, FACTS developed an online version of the Georgetown selective course that is now available to medical and other health-care professional students nationwide. The course, entitled *Fertility Awareness Based Methods for Women's Health and Family Planning*, is the next step in addressing the critical knowledge gap about FABMs among health-care professionals.

To ensure the effectiveness of the online educational course, a study was performed comparing the knowledge retention and experiences of students completing the course online versus in-person education. The results of the study concluded that the online course was as effective as in-person lectures in teaching

84 Marguerite Duane, "Fertility Awareness Methods In the Learning Years: The FAMILY Planning Selective." (unpublished paper, Jesuit Schools of Medicine Conference Washington, D.C., February 25, 2013).

85 Marguerite Duane, "Fertility Awareness Methods In the Learning Years: The FAMILY Planning Selective."

86 Marguerite Duane, "Fertility Awareness Methods In the Learning Years: The FAMILY Planning Selective."

87 Since then FACTS staff have trained 85 speakers.

these methods, thereby providing a strong base for offering this course to more students outside of Georgetown University.[88] The course, which is approved for medical school elective credit through Georgetown University's School of Medicine, is now available through the Visiting Student Application Service (VSAS), for all fourth-year medical students in the United States who are interested in learning about FABMs. Although there are currently 23 family planning and 41 women's health electives listed on the VSAS website, the Fertility Awareness Based Methods for Women's Health and Family Planning elective is the only course available that provides education in FABMs.

Finally, FACTS developed a Student Ambassador program, specifically designed to identify and support medical and health-care professional students who are interested in learning more about FABMs and sharing this information with their classmates and colleagues.[89] FACTS Student Ambassadors have the opportunity to engage in research, present papers at medical conferences, and receive support to be trained in one of the aforementioned FABMs.

Next Steps

Now that we have demonstrated the desire of patients and students to learn more about Fertility Awareness-Based Methods and described opportunities for medical professionals to learn about these methods, it is critical to more clearly define the current state of education about FABMs in medical school and to describe how medical professionals' knowledge, or lack thereof, impacts the patients' experience. Sharing empirical evidence about the lack of FABM education available to medical professionals and describing the potential impact this may have on patients, will hopefully allow for more funding and educational opportunities. Given the mission of FACTS, it is noteworthy to report that FACTS leaders are currently conducting two critical research studies that will hopefully contribute to creating a strategy to address the lack of FABM information in medical education.

The first study, "An Evaluation of the Current Curricula Regarding Reproductive Health Topics and Methods of Family Planning at United States Medical Schools," will examine the current curricula at US medical schools pertinent to sexual and reproductive health, including FABMs. The study is an in-depth analysis of syllabi and lecture materials and will show the degree to which students are exposed to FABMs as compared to other family planning methods and reproductive health topics. This study is currently in progress and will demonstrate where there may be deficits in reproductive health and family planning education.

Additionally, FACTS is conducting a second study entitled, "Characterizing the Patient Experience in Conversing with Clinicians about Fertility Awareness

88 Erin Adams and Marguerite Duane, "Comparison of an Online vs. Live Course on Fertility Awareness Based Methods" (unpublished paper, Family Medicine Education Consortium Meeting, Danvers, Mass., October 31, 2015).

89 "Become a Student Ambassador!", FACTS, at https://www.factsaboutfertility.org/learn-more/student-ambassadors.

Based Methods." The study is designed to assess women's experiences using FABMs and how they perceive their interactions with medical professionals regarding their use of these methods. The goal is to use the findings from this study to provide feedback to medical professionals to help guide future interactions with patients who desire to use FABMs.

Conclusion

There is much to be done to improve the education in FABMs among medical students, health-care professionals, and patients. The existence of NFP and FABM organizations that have developed educational programs for health-care professionals is more than a beginning—it is encouraging and needed.[90]

As discussed in this essay, the validity of FABM science and medicine is evidence-based, of use for both physicians and patients, and of interest to medical students and patients. This represents an unmet need that must be addressed by the medical community.

The contributions of general and method specific courses such as those offered through the Pope Paul VI Institute for the Study of Human Reproduction and Marquette University College of Nursing's Institute for NFP, demonstrate that fertility literacy can be achieved through FABM education. And, the positive response to broad outreach education by organizations such as FACTS, reveals that medical students and physicians are ready to receive FABM training. With the advent of new FABM organizations such as FEMM, a more diverse group of medical professionals can also be reached.

The collective efforts of the NFP/FABM leaders contribute to removing the systemic ignorance about FABM science and methodology in the medical community. Ultimately, it is the patient who should be at the center of our concern. If more medical professionals become knowledgeable about the viability of FABMs and provide this information to their patients, the patients and society as a whole will benefit.

90 Not discussed in this essay but treated in Fehring's "Signs of Growth and Healing" (chapter 20 in this volume) is the contribution of the International Institute for Restorative Reproductive Medicine (IIRRM), which brings together FABM scientists from various nations to share their research, collaborate when appropriate, and strategize on effective ways to educate widely on these methods, see https://restorative-reproductive-medicine.com.

PART IV

Health and Love

Examining Distortions Introduced by the Contraceptive Mentality from Medical, Psychological, and Legal Perspectives

12

Medical Consequences of Hormonal Contraception

William V. Williams

✷ HORMONAL CONTRACEPTIVES THAT are taken by mouth were developed for women and have been on the market in the United States as a contraceptive since 1960 when Enovid was approved by the Food and Drug Administration (FDA).[1] Their history, however, has an earlier beginning. They can be traced to Margaret Sanger in 1951. Sanger conceived of the idea in collaboration with Gregory Pincus of G. D. Searle & Company. She also funded the research leading to the approval of hormonal contraceptives. Part of Sanger's motivation lay in her belief that contraceptives were essential for women to ensure their rights while improving their lives since they bear the responsibility of carrying pregnancies and are primarily tasked with the nurture of children. Interestingly, Sanger's concern for women also includes a more sinister agenda: eugenics. As some have noted, "the eugenics movement, which encouraged reproduction by particular individuals and discouraged reproduction by others, was also very influential on Sanger and the development of the pill."[2]

The first marketed hormonal contraceptive, Enovid, was comprised of mestranol, a synthetic estrogen, and noretynodrel, a synthetic progestin. The initial clinical studies suffered from a high drop-out rate due to side effects seen, but eventually a pivotal study was performed centered in Puerto Rico. Enovid was approved in spite of 17 percent of participants having suffered from side effects such as nausea, dizziness, headaches, stomach pain, and vomiting. There were three fatalities during the study but the cause of death was never established. Soon, several other companies entered the market, including Syntex, Ortho, Wyeth, and Parke-Davis.[3] Most used norethindrone for the progestin and a variety of synthetic estrogens were employed. It soon became apparent that there were several additional side effects from use of the pill, including increased risk

1 Hormonal contraceptives include birth control pills (popularly referred to as "the pill"), also called oral contraceptives (OCs). In addition, hormonal contraceptives come in other methods of delivery, including injection or dispersal via a patch worn on the woman's skin or a cervical ring.

2 Aliya Buttar and Sheraden Seward, "Enovid: The First Hormonal Birth Control Pill," *Embryo Project Encyclopedia* (January 20, 2009); ISSN: 1940–5030 at http://embryo.asu.edu/handle/10776/1956.

3 See "Oral Contraceptive Pill," Case Western Reserve University, https://case.edu/affil/skuyhistcontraception/online-2012/pill.html.

of blood clots. Eventually the dose of estrogen was lowered and the first-generation pills were taken off the market in the 1980s to be replaced by the "low-dose" pill. But the side effects persisted and many more have come to light over time.

I begin this essay with the above brief history of hormonal contraceptives because of the persistent and troubling issues which are part and parcel of this class of drugs. Hormonal contraceptives appear to respond to the perceived need, as their developers insisted, of effective fertility control. And, also as their developers claimed, hormonal contraception would provide women with freedom from their cycles of fertility—they would be essentially "good" for women, even "healthy." Yet, as discussed above, serious negative side effects have been present from the inception of hormonal contraceptives. These negative side effects are not commonly known by women who use hormonal contraception more frequently than other methods of birth control.[4] This is troubling both for the health-care professionals who are charged to "do no harm" and their patients who ought to have informed consent before taking any medication.

A thorough investigation of the negative outcomes of hormonal contraceptive use should include a study of the biological effects on a woman's body. In addition, evaluations of the psychological effects of the drugs on the patient are important. And researchers ought not neglect the sociological and demographic effects of hormonal contraceptive use in a society. Only through such well-rounded investigation can health-care providers understand whether this class of drugs should continue to be prescribed to patients. In order to begin this investigation, members of the Catholic Medical Association have begun to perform a series of comprehensive literature surveys. Some of these surveys are complete and some are ongoing. Some deal with well-known side effects and others with less known ones. To date, the discussion below is the fruit of this work. As will be demonstrated, hormonal contraceptives carry serious risks and ultimately do more to harm women than set them free. This class of drugs fulfill Pope Paul VI's warnings about the negative outcomes of acceptance of contraception—especially in terms of women's health.[5]

Common Side Effects

There are over eighty hormonal contraceptives on the market with prescribing information available. The prescribing information for common side effects is an instructive way to evaluate the most frequently prescribed contraceptives, beginning with Yaz®.

Yaz® is a combination of drospirenone and ethinyl estradiol. In the Yaz® prescribing information,[6] some common side effects are highlighted. These include fluid retention, emotional disorders (especially depression), and visual changes in contact lens users. In addition to these (which are very common), the adverse reactions listed

4 See "Contraceptive Use in the United States," Guttmacher Institute, July 2018, https://www.guttmacher.org/fact-sheet/contraceptive-use-united-states.

5 Pope Paul VI, Encyclical Letter *Humanae vitae* (July 25, 1968), 17, http://w2.vatican.va/content/paul-vi/en/encyclicals.index.html.

6 From https: www.accessdata.fda.gov/drugsatfda_docs/label/2010/021676s009lbl.pdf.

TABLE 12–1—Adverse Reactions Reported in Patients Receiving Oral Contraceptives Believed to Be Drug-Related (from the Yaz® Prescribing Information)

1. Nausea
2. Vomiting
3. Gastrointestinal symptoms (such as abdominal cramps and bloating)
4. Breakthrough bleeding
5. Spotting
6. Change in menstrual flow
7. Amenorrhea
8. Temporary infertility after discontinuation of treatment
9. Edema
10. Melasma which may persist
11. Breast changes: tenderness, enlargement, secretion
12. Change in weight or appetite (increase or decrease)
13. Change in cervical ectropion and secretion
14. Possible diminution in lactation when given immediately postpartum
15. Cholestatic jaundice
16. Migraine
17. Rash (allergic)
18. Mood changes, including depression
19. Reduced tolerance to carbohydrates
20. Vaginitis, including candidiasis
21. Change in corneal curvature (steepening)
22. Intolerance to contact lenses
23. Decrease in serum folate levels
24. Exacerbation of systemic lupus erythematosus
25. Exacerbation of porphyria
26. Exacerbation of chorea
27. Aggravation of varicose veins
28. Anaphylactic/anaphylactoid reactions, including urticaria, angioedema, and severe reactions with respiratory and circulatory symptoms

in Table 12–1 from the Yaz® prescribing information are believed to be drug-related.

Table 12–2 lists those adverse reactions where relationship to the drug is neither confirmed nor denied by the available data. These listed 28 related and 17 potentially related adverse reactions are likely shared with most combined hormonal contraceptives.[7] The prescribing information does not provide frequency information in the label, which is problematic, since this information

7 Since the chemical constituents of most combined oral contraceptives are similar, similar side effects have been noted and they have "class labeling" from the FDA regarding certain side effects.

TABLE 12-2—Adverse Reactions Reported in Users of Oral Contraceptives where a Causal Association Has Been Neither Confirmed nor Refuted

1. Acne
2. Budd-Chiari syndrome
3. Cataracts
4. Changes in libido
5. Colitis
6. Cystitis-like syndrome Dizziness
7. Dysmenorrhea
8. Erythema multiforme Erythema nodosum
9. Headache
10. Hemolytic uremic syndrome
11. Hemorrhagic eruption
12. Hirsutism
13. Impaired renal function
14. Loss of scalp hair
15. Nervousness
16. Optic neuritis, which may lead to partial or complete loss of vision Pancreatitis
17. Premenstrual syndrome

is typically provided in the prescribing information for most drugs. Some of the published papers on this combined contraceptive show that the incidence of many of these side effects is substantial. In one study,[8] comparing various dosing regimens over a two-year period in a total of 1,067 women aged 18–35 years, at least one adverse event was seen in 64.6%–71.8% of patients, depending on the dosing regimen. Adverse events that were thought to be treatment-related occurred in 20.7%–34.0% of patients and 2.5%–4.8% of patients withdrew from the study due to adverse events. In a related study where these patients were followed for an additional year, 56.3% of women experienced ≥1 adverse event in the safety extension phase.[9] A total of 9.8% of subjects who participated in the safety extension phase had an adverse event that was deemed by the examining physician to be possibly, probably, or definitely related to study medication. This incidence is noteworthy as the patients who were in the extension

8 C. Klipping, I. Duijkers, M. P. Fortier, J. Marr, D. Trummer, and J. Elliesen, "Contraceptive Efficacy and Tolerability of Ethinylestradiol 20 µg/Drospirenone 3 mg in a Flexible Extended Regimen: An Open-Label, Multicentre, Randomised, Controlled Study," *Journal of Family Planning and Reproductive Health Care* 38, no. 2 (April 2012): 73–83.

9 C. Klipping, I. Duijkers, M. P. Fortier, J. Marr, D. Trummer, and J. Elliesen, "Long-Term Tolerability of Ethinylestradiol 20 µg/Drospirenone 3 mg in a Flexible Extended Regimen: Results from a Randomised, Controlled, Multicentre Study," *Journal of Family Planning and reproductive Health* 38, no. 2 (April 2012): 84–93.

TABLE 12–3—Menstrual Complaints Reported by More than 1.0% of Subjects during the First Year of Jadelle® Use

Menstrual Condition	Year 1	Years 1-5
	%	%
Menorrhagia (increased duration)	13.4	25.9
Amenorrhea	9.8	13.9
Menometrorrhagia	9.6	20.5
Oligomenorrhea	9.5	12.8
Long spotting duration or length unclear	8.9	15.1
Dysmenorrhea	3.5[a]	8.0[a]
Polymenorrhea	2.7	5.0
Premenstrual syndrome	1.8[a]	5.8[a]
Menorrhagia (increased amount)	1.6	4.5
Hypomenorrhea	1.5	2.9

[a]Excludes women with condition reported at admission, prior to initiation of Jadelle® implants. Dysmenorrhea and premenstrual syndrome were reported at admission into the studies by 7.8% and 4.9% of the subjects, respectively.

phase had already tolerated the ethinylestradiol-drospirenone combination for a year prior to entering the extension phase. Also, typically adverse events that are ongoing are not counted a second time, which may account for the lower rates of total adverse events and treatment-related adverse events in the second year of study. Serious adverse events during the safety extension phase were seen in 2.7% of the patients.

There are also available progesterone-only contraceptives, such as Norplant®II/Jadelle® (Levonorgestrel Implants),[10] Implanon™ (etonogestrel implant),[11] or Depo-Provera (medroxyprogesterone acetate injectable suspension).[12] These report a long list of adverse events. Prominent among these are menstrual changes, including irregular menstrual bleeding, prolonged episodes of bleeding and spotting, heavy bleeding, intermenstrual spotting, and amenorrhea (see Table 12–3 for Jadelle®).

10 Prescribing information available at https://www.accessdata.fda.gov/drugsatfda_docs/label/2002/20544se2-003_jadelle_lbl.pdf.

11 Prescribing information available at https://www.accessdata.fda.gov/drugsatfda_docs/label/2009/021529s004lbl.pdf.

12 Prescribing information available at https://www.accessdata.fda.gov/drugsatfda_docs/label/2003/20246scs019_Depo-provera_lbl.pdf.

TABLE 12–4—Adverse Events Reported in More than 5% of Subjects in Clinical Trials of Implanon™

Adverse Event	Proportion of Patients
Headache	24.9%
Vaginitis	14.5%
Weight increase	13.7%
Acne	13.5%
Breast pain	12.8%
Upper Respiratory Tract Infection	12.6%
Abdominal pain	10.9%
Pharyngitis	10.5%
Leukorrhoea	9.6%
Influenza-like symptoms	7.6%
Dizziness	7.2%
Dysmenorrhoea	7.2%
Back pain	6.8%
Emotional lability	6.5%
Nausea	6.4%
Pain	5.6%
Nervousness	5.6%
Sinusitis	5.6%
Depression	5.5%
Insertion site pain	5.2%

Also reported as noteworthy (and very common) are weight gain (in clinical trials of Jadelle® use, the average weight change over five years of use was a gain of about nine pounds), fluid retention, emotional disorders, visual changes in contact lens wearers, and ovarian cysts. With Implanon™, it is noted that discontinuation of treatment follows adverse reactions, including bleeding irregularities in 11.0% of patients, emotional lability in 2.3%, weight increase in 2.3%, headache in 1.6%, acne in 1.3% and depression in 1.0%. The most common adverse events seen (without regard to relationship to drug) are shown in Table 12–4.

The overall frequency with which adverse events are encountered is not provided, nor is there a control group to help distinguish which adverse events are more frequent with the implant. One study, which compared etonogestrel- and levonorgestrel-releasing contraceptive implants, with nonrandomized matched copper-intrauterine device, controls showed a higher rate of several common adverse events for the implant users, including acne (18.0 events per 100 patient-years vs. 13.1 per 100 patient-years for the IUD users), amenorrhea (16.9 vs. 2.7), irregular bleeding (48.5 vs. 13.66) and prolonged bleeding (22.3 vs. 19.0).[13] Discontinuation of use from adverse events seems common.

While many of these adverse reactions are not of a serious nature and would be tolerated for many drugs, it is important to keep in mind that contraceptives do not treat a disease, as most drugs do, and do not address any pathology or disorder. In fact, they cause dysfunction of the female reproductive system. Thus, the tolerance for adverse reactions should be extremely low.

More Serious, Less Common, Side Effects

Cardiovascular Effects and Mortality

It is well established and acknowledged in the prescribing information that hormonal contraceptives increase the risk of thrombotic events such as deep vein thrombosis (DVT), pulmonary embolism (PE), myocardial infarction (MI), and stroke as well as high blood pressure. Cigarette smoking compounds these risks. Two recent reviews have been published on venous thrombosis and hormonal contraceptives.[14] Both publications focused on DVT and PE and noted an increased relative risk of 3.5 (95% confidence interval 2.9 to 4.3). They noted that combined oral contraceptives containing levonorgestrel had a lower risk than those using other progestins, but there was still an increased risk.

The increase in risk for MI and stroke has also been the subject of recent review and meta-analyses for combined oral contraceptives.[15] The overall increased relative risk was similar for MI (1.6, 95% CI 1.2 to 2.1) and ischemic stroke (1.7, 95% CI 1.5 to 1.9). This appeared to be independent of the progestin used and was highest for pills with > 50 microgram estrogen.

13 L. Bahamondes, V. Brache, O. Meirik, M. Ali, N. Habib, and S. Landoulsi, "WHO Study Group on Contraceptive Implants for Women. A 3-Year Multicentre Randomized Controlled Trial of Etonogestrel- and Levonorgestrel-Releasing Contraceptive Implants, with Non-Randomized Matched Copper-Intrauterine Device Controls," *Human Reproduction*, 30, no. 11 (November 2015): 2527–2538.

14 B. H. Stegeman, M. de Bastos, F. R. Rosendaal, A. van Hylckama Vlieg, F. M. Helmerhorst, T. Stijnen, and O. M. Dekkers, "Different Combined Oral Contraceptives and the Risk of Venous Thrombosis: Systematic Review and Network Meta-Analysis," *British Medical Journal* (September 12, 2013): 347: f5298 and M. de Bastos, B. H. Stegeman, F. R. Rosendaal, A. Van Hylckama Vlieg, F. M. Helmerhorst, T. Stijnen, and O. M. Dekkers, "Combined Oral Contraceptives: Venous Thrombosis," *The Cochrane Database of Systematic Reviews* 3 (March 3, 2014): CD010813.

15 R. E. Roach, F. M. Helmerhorst, W. M. Lijfering, T. Stijnen, A. Algra, and O. M. Dekkers, "Combined Oral Contraceptives: The Risk of Myocardial Infarction and Ischemic Stroke," *The Cochrane Database of Systematic Reviews* 8 (August 27, 2015): CD011054.

Since MI, PE, and stroke are often fatal events, it is interesting to note that the Yaz® prescribing information documents an increase in cardiovascular mortality for individuals on oral contraceptives which increases with age and increases markedly with smoking (Table 12–5).

This data was taken from a study published in 1981.[16] It is an analysis of Oral Contraception Study of the Royal College of General Practitioners, originally published in 1977, which followed over 23,000 women taking oral contraceptives and an equal number of controls.[17] The study notes that ever-users of oral contraceptives had a 40% higher overall mortality rate than the controls with an excess risk of 23.3 per 100,000 woman-years. The higher death rate was almost entirely due to cardiovascular events. They stated, "Ever-users of oral contraceptives in this study had a mortality rate from circulatory diseases 4.7 times greater than that of controls."[18] However, while the authors did call for restricting use of combined oral contraceptives to nonsmokers and women under 45, they felt use could be justified in other groups, although the reasons were not stated. They did postulate that lower estrogen and progestin doses could further lower the risk.

It is worth commenting on the mindset of the medical community regarding hormonal contraceptive use. Several early studies pointed out an increased mortality rate among users versus nonusers, but nowhere was there an outcry or a call to remove these from the market. Compare this with the situation with Avandia® (rosiglitazone from GlaxoSmithKline), which was approved and found effective in the control of type 2 diabetes.[19] A reanalysis of GSK's data suggested an increase in mortality from MIs. GSK published data from a large study showing no increase in mortality but an increase in congestive heart failure. This resulted in a black box warning being added to the label. Later, the FDA restricted use of Avandia® to those already taking it and to new patients who cannot control their type 2 diabetes with other medications. They pulled it from retail pharmacies and further restricted its availability. Yet, the drug was effective in the treatment of type 2 diabetes, and more recent studies suggest that its use decreases overall cardiovascular mortality.[20] On the other hand, hormonal contraceptives treat no disease but remained on the market in spite of several studies indicating that they may increase mortality.

16 Peter M. Layde, Valerie Beral, and Clifford R. Kay, "Further Analyses of Morality in Oral Contraceptive Users: Royal College of General Practitioners' Oral Contraception Study," *Lancet* 317, no. 8219 (March 7, 1981): 541–546, https://doi.org/10.1016/S0140-6736(81)92872-5.

17 V. Beral, "Mortality among Oral-Contraceptive Users: Royal College of General Practitioners' Oral Contraception Study," *Lancet* 310, no. 8041 (October 8, 1977): 727–731.

18 V. Beral, "Mortality among Oral-Contraceptive Users," 728.

19 See https://www.drugwatch.com/avandia.

20 H. Florez, P. D. Reaven, G. Bahn, T. Moritz, S. Warren, J. Marks, D. Reda, W. Duckworth, C. Abraira, R. Hayward, N. Emanuele, "Rosiglitazone Treatment and Cardiovascular Disease in the Veterans Affairs Diabetes Trial," *Diabetes, Obesity, & Metabolism* 17, no. 10 (October 2015): 949–955; J. C. Stone, L. Furuya-Kanamori, J. J. Barendregt, and S. A. Doi, "Was There Really Any Evidence that Rosiglitazone Increased the Risk of Myocardial Infarction or Death from Cardiovascular Causes?" *Pharmacoepidemiology and Drug Safety* 24, no. 3 (March 2015): 223–227.

TABLE 12–5—Circulatory Disease Mortality Rates per 100,000 Woman-Years

Age	Ever-Users Nonsmokers	Ever-Users Smokers	Controls Nonsmokers	Controls Smokers
15–24	0	10.5	0	0
25–34	4.4	14.2	2.7	4.2
35–44	21.5	63.4	6.4	15.2
45+	52.4	206.7	11.4	27.9

Of interest in the Yaz® label is a table derived from a study published in 1983.[21] Based on the researchers' analyses (Table 12–6), use of oral contraceptives in nonsmokers is safe and can be justified in particular compared with childbirth. But there are multiple biases apparent in how these researchers performed their calculations. They inflated the death rates from childbirth by 33% to "account for well-documented underreporting."[22] Yet, they ignored that mortality associated with use of contraceptives also may be underreported, as the physician may not make the association at the time of death. They adjusted the death rate from cardiovascular events using only two-thirds of the deaths from the cardiovascular International Classification of Diseases based on a study in the United Kingdom, which they assume also applies to the population in the United States (with no data to support that). They further used abortion-related mortality rates only for first trimester abortions (when they are least risky). They also added to their estimates a decreased risk of ovarian and endometrial cancer while ignoring the increased risk of the much more prevalent breast cancer. And finally, the only natural method they considered was "periodic abstinence" or the Rhythm Method—clearly the least effective of the natural methods available. In spite of these obvious manipulations, it is noteworthy that periodic abstinence still appears safer for women over 20 compared with smokers who use oral contraceptives, and periodic abstinence is safer compared with nonsmokers over 30 years of age who use the pill. It is mystifying why a 1983 study, with numerous assumptions leading to mortality estimates that are at best questionable and at worst misleading still appear in the prescribing information of combined oral contraceptives, many of which do not even use the same synthetic steroids used at that time.

21 H. W. Ory, "Mortality Associated with Fertility and Fertility Control: 1983," *Family Planning Perspectives* 15, no. 2 (March–April 1983): 57–63.

22 Ory, "Mortality Associated with Fertility and Fertility Control: 1983," 57.

TABLE 12-6—Annual Number of Birth-Related or Method-Related Deaths Associated with Control of Fertility per 100,000 Nonsterile Women by Fertility Control Method According to Age

Method of Control and Outcome	**15–19 years**	**20–24 years**	**25–29 years**	**30–34 years**	**35–39 years**	**40–44 years**
No fertility control methods \1\	7	7.4	9.1	14.8	25.7	28.2
Oral contraceptives nonsmoker \2\	0.3	0.5	0.9	1.9	13.8	31.6
Oral contraceptives smoker \2\	2.2	3.4	6.6	13.5	51.1	117.2
IUD \2\	0.8	0.8	1	1	1.4	1.4
Condom \1\	1.1	1.6	0.7	0.2	0.3	0.4
Diaphragm/ spermicide \1\	1.9	1.2	1.2	1.3	2.2	2.8
Periodic abstinence \1\	2.5	1.6	1.6	1.7	2.9	3.6

\1\ Deaths are birth-related
\2\ Deaths are method-related

Adapted from H. W. Ory, "Mortality Associated with Fertility and Fertility Control: 1983," *Family Planning Perspectives* 15, no. 2 (March–April 1983): 57–63.

Cancer

Numerous studies indicate an increased risk of certain cancers in patients taking combined oral contraceptives. A systematic review of papers since 2000 included 44 papers on breast cancer, 12 cervical, 11 colorectal, and 9 endometrial cancers studies.[23] A paper in *The Linacre Quarterly* pointed out that the World Health Organization has recognized combined oral contraceptives as Group 1 carcinogens for breast cancer, as well as for cervical and liver cancer.[24] For breast cancer, the risk is said to decrease with time after stopping the

23 J. M. Gierisch, R. R. Coeytaux, R. P. Urrutia, L. J. Havrilesky, P. G. Moorman, W. J. Lowery, M. Dinan, A. J. McBroom, V. Hasselblad, G. D. Sanders, and E. R. Myers, "Oral Contraceptive Use and Risk of Breast, Cervical, Colorectal, and Endometrial Cancers: A Systematic Review," *Cancer Epidemiol Biomarkers & Prevention* 22, no. 11 (November 2013): 1931–1943.

24 A. P. Schneider, C. M. Zainer, C. K. Kubat, N. K. Mullen, and A. K. Windisch, "The Breast Cancer Epidemic: 10 Facts," *The Linacre Quarterly* 81, no. 3 (August 2014): 244–277.

contraceptive, but is also clearly much higher for women who have used these agents prior to their first full-term pregnancy (odds ratio, 1.52, 95% confidence interval (CI) 1.26–1.82).[25] One meta-analysis put the breast cancer overall risk at an odds ratio of 1.08; (CI 1.00–1.17).[26] A recent major study of over 1.7 million cases of breast cancer compared with the population of Denmark confirmed an increased risk of breast cancer with a relative risk of 1.2 (CI (1.14–1.26).[27] There is also known to be a reduction in the risk of colorectal and endometrial cancer. Even though ever-use of oral contraceptives is significantly associated with decreases in colorectal and endometrial cancers, the increase in breast cancer risk, although relatively small, is offset by the high incidence of breast cancer. This means that oral contraceptives may contribute to a substantial number of cancer cases in women overall.

In spite of these analyses, misleading statements remain in the prescribing information for many hormonal contraceptives. For example, the Yaz® prescribing information states,

> Although the risk of having breast cancer diagnosed may be slightly increased among current and recent users of combined oral contraceptives (RR=1.24), this excess risk decreases over time after combination oral contraceptive discontinuation and by 10 years after cessation the increased risk disappears. . . . The subgroup for whom risk has been found to be significantly elevated is women who first used oral contraceptives before age 20, but because breast cancer is so rare at these young ages, the number of cases attributable to this early oral contraceptive use is extremely small.[28]

Clearly, there is a need to revisit the wording and warn women about the overall risk of developing cancer, especially in those who use combined oral contraceptives prior to their first full-term pregnancy.

Effects on Glycemic Regulation (Diabetes and Related Disorders)

The prescribing information for some combined oral contraceptives mentions effects on blood sugar. For example, in the Yaz® prescribing information it is mentioned that,

25 C. Kahlenborn, F. Modugno, D. M. Potter, and W. B. Severs, "Oral Contraceptive Use as a Risk Factor for Premenopausal Breast Cancer: A Meta-Analysis," *Mayo Clinic Proceedings* 81, no. 10 (October 2006): 1290–1302.

26 H. Zhu, X. Lei, J. Feng, and Y. Wang, "Oral Contraceptive Use and Risk of Breast Cancer: A Meta-Analysis of Prospective Cohort Studies," *The European Journal of Contraception and Reproductive Health Care* 17 (Dec. 2012): 402–414.

27 L. S. Mørch, C. W. Skovlund, P. C. Hannaford, L. Iversen, S. Fielding, and Ø. Lidegaard, "Contemporary Hormonal Contraception and the Risk of Breast Cancer," *New England Journal of Medicine* 377 (2017): 2228–2239.

28 Yaz® prescribing information, available at https://www.accessdata.fda.gov/drugsatfda_docs/label/2010/021676s009lbl.

> Oral contraceptives may compound the effects of well-known risk factors, such as hypertension, diabetes, hyperlipidemias, age and obesity. In particular, some progestogens are known to decrease HDL cholesterol and cause glucose intolerance, while estrogens may create a state of hyperinsulinism.[29]

A review of this topic noted that combined oral contraceptives are associated with impaired glucose tolerance and increased insulin resistance.[30] These effects were seen in normal individuals and patients with polycystic ovarian syndrome. These impairments may not be apparent in normal individuals, but they may worsen glycemic control in diabetics and those with metabolic syndrome (a state of insulin resistance associated usually with obesity without frank hyperglycemia). These effects would be expected to worsen cardiovascular risk in users of combined oral contraceptives.

Autoimmune Diseases

One thing often not mentioned in the prescribing information of many hormonal contraceptives is the risk of autoimmune diseases. A recent review showed that there is substantial evidence for an increased risk of several autoimmune diseases, including multiple sclerosis, ulcerative colitis, Crohn's disease, systemic lupus erythematosus, and interstitial cystitis.[31] The evidence is especially convincing for inflammatory bowel disease, particularly Crohn's disease, where one large meta-analysis showed a relative risk of 1.44 for ever-use,[32] while a more recent study showed that for current use, the relative risk was 1.46.[33] The same two meta-analyses showed increased risks for ulcerative colitis as 1.29 for ever use of combined oral contraceptives, while for current use, the relative risk was 1.28. For systemic lupus, the more reliable cohort studies showed relative risks ranging from 1.19 to 2.3, indicating a substantial increase in risk.

Moreover, there appears to be a decrease in the risk for hyperthyroidism but not for hypothyroidism, with combined oral contraceptives. Unfortunately, this information is based on three studies all of which were of moderate to poor quality and all performed more than fifteen years ago. Additional information is needed to confirm these observations. For progesterone-only contraceptives, based on one

29 Yaz® prescribing information, available at https://www.accessdata.fda.gov/drugsatfda_docs/label/2010/021676s009lbl.pdf

30 Manuel E. Cortés and Andrea A. Alfaro, "The Effects of Hormonal Contraceptives on Glycemic Regulation," *The Linacre Quarterly* 81, no. 3 (2014): 209–218.

31 William V. Williams, "Hormonal Contraception and the Development of Autoimmunity: A Review of the Literature," *The Linacre Quarterly* 84, no. 3 (2017): 275–295.

32 P. G. Godet, G. R. May, and L. R. Sutherland, "Meta-Analysis of the Role of Oral Contraceptive Agents in Inflammatory Bowel Disease," *Gut, An International Journal of Gastroenterology and Hepatology* 37, no. 5 (1995): 668–673.

33 J. A. Cornish, E. Tan, C. Simillis, S. K. Clark, J. Teare, and P. P. Tekkis, "The Risk of Oral Contraceptives in the Etiology of Inflammatory Bowel Disease: A Meta-Analysis," *American Journal of Gastroenterology* 103, no. 9 (2008): 2394–2400.

very large cohort study,[34] there is a substantial increase in arthropathies and related disorders, eczema and contact dermatitis, pruritis and related conditions, alopecia, acne, and urticaria. They are also linked to the development of progesterone dermatitis. In spite of this, there are few to no mentions of these risks in the prescribing information of hormonal contraceptives.

Conclusion

It is clear that combined hormonal contraceptives and progestin-only contraceptives have a variety of deleterious effects on users. Some of these are short term and some longer term. It is difficult to understand how use of these agents, which treat no pathology and cure no disease, can be justified by those who follow the Hippocratic maxim, "Above all, do no harm." It is not in accord with the dignity of women for them to be subject to these risks when there are no directly demonstrable benefits. In marked contrast, natural methods of family planning do not have these side effects and modern methods are highly effective. It is also clear that the prescribing information included with these contraceptive agents does not adequately confer these risks. It is time for this to change.

34 T. M. M. Farley and I. Sivin, "Post-Marketing Surveillance of Norplant Contraceptive Implants: II. Non-reproductive Health," *Contraception* 63, no. 4 (April 2001): 187–209.

13

Of Science and Surveillance

An Object Relations View of Affectively Based Side Effects in Hormonal Contraceptive Use

Suzanne Nortier Hollman

Framing Hormonal Contraceptives and Mental Health

According to the World Health Organization, approximately one in four women will experience mood dysregulation in the form of clinical depression at some point in her lifetime, with suicide being a prominent and dangerous feature of this illness.[1] In women who are of reproductive age in the United States, the prevalence of depression is approximately 14%, twice that of men.[2] The prevalence of bipolar disorder in women is between 1% and 2%[3] and one-third of women will meet the criteria for an anxiety disorder during a lifetime.[4] Within this context of the lifetime risk of suffering from a mental health issue, and in concert with women who report mood dysregulation while taking hormonal contraceptives, important questions arise. Which narrative will dominate in the battle of body politics in an area where science is unsettled? Do we dismiss the experience of women who experience psychological side effects at the expense of those who do not, or do we listen, observe, and respond, in an inclusive manner? I posit that the attempt to address these questions necessitates an awareness of the larger political context within which these questions are asked and answered. Science is never value-free.

Philosophers of science, such as Hilary Putnam, argue that scientific investigation is always tied to a particular epistemology.[5] Putnam's work is of particular

1 "Depression," World Health Organization, March 22, 2018, https://www.who.int/en/news-room/fact-sheets/detail/Depression.

2 Sherry L. Farr, Rebecca H. Bitsko, Donald K. Hayes, and Patricia M. Dietz, "Mental Health and Access to Services among US Women of Reproductive Age," *American Journal of Obstetrics and Gynecology* 203, no. 6 (December 2010): 542.e1–9.

3 H. Pamela Pagano, Lauren B. Zapata, Erin N. Berry-Bibee, Kavita Nanda, and Kathryn M. Curtis, "Safety of Hormonal Contraception and Intrauterine Devices among Women with Depressive and Bipolar Disorders: A Systematic Review," *Contraception* 94, no. 6 (December 2016): 641–649.

4 Kathleen Ries Merikangas, Marcy Burstein, and Anja Schmitz, "Anxiety Disorders in Women," in *Women and Health*, Second Edition, ed. Marlene B. Goldman, Rebecca Troisi, and Kathryn M. Rexrode (Academic Press, 2012), 1257–1270.

5 Hilary Putnam, *The Collapse of the Fact/Value Dichotomy and Other Essays*, rev. ed. (Cambridge, Mass.: Harvard University Press, 2004).

relevance to the argument long made by activists, both religious and secular, who point out the disconnect between women who experience side effects from hormonal contraceptives, and those in the medical, pharmaceutical, political, and scientific community who dismiss their experiences as unsubstantiated. He asserts that while there is some utility to making a distinction between what science would classify as truth and fact on one extreme and value judgments and experience on the other extreme, this distinction becomes dangerous when it is viewed as a dichotomy between what is classified as the purely objective and the purely subjective.[6] Thomas Kuhn, in *Structure of Scientific Revolutions*, similarly points out that there is no value-free science.[7] The act of the scientist observing a phenomenon alters it. Translated into the patient-doctor relationship, the way in which a physician may listen to a woman describe particular side effects that she might be experiencing will occur within a theoretical, and I would argue, socio-political framework that will inevitably affect the recommendations made. In this type of interaction, women's bodies become more than physiology, but are politicized as powerful symbolic representations of scientific revolutions, privilege, or oppression. The caution from philosophers of science that experiments and research do not occur within a neutral epistemological environment does not stand in opposition to scientific inquiry. Rather, it serves as a reminder that it is not the only way of knowing.

The Current State of the Science on The Psychological Implications of Oral Contraceptive Use

For the purposes of this essay, the psychological implications connected with hormonal contraceptive use can be delineated into two broad areas: first, the scientific studies that examine the effects on *mood*, and second, the effects of hormonal contraceptive use in women who have been diagnosed with *preexisting mental health issues*. Taken as a whole, it becomes clear that the prevailing politicized narrative that there is no need for women to be concerned about the psychological side effects of oral contraceptives is grossly oversimplified. Conclusions from the literature are much more nuanced, and a thorough reading shows that not all women's bodies are uniform and that there is a myriad of potentially different responses to the same drug.

Effects on Mood

The definition of what constitutes mood within the context of hormonal birth control appears to fall into the subcategories of anxiety, irritability, depression, and mood swings. The biological theories as to how hormonal contraceptives affect mood include estrogen-induced pyridoxine deficiency, or estrogen or

6 Putnam, *The Collapse of the Fact/Value Dichotomy*.

7 Thomas S. Kuhn, *The Structure of Scientific Revolutions*, 3rd ed. (Chicago: University of Chicago Press, 1996).

progestin interaction with the serotonergic system, or noradrenergic systems.[8] A notable feature found in the majority of journal articles on this subject area is the acknowledgement by the authors that the current body of research on the effects of hormonal contraception, either by way of oral contraceptives (OCs) or through the long-acting reversible contraceptives (LARCS) implanted into women, is neither well researched nor well understood. The research in this area is, at most, inconclusive. Some authors conclude that not only are there no adverse mental health effects[9] but that OC use is actually associated with better mood.[10] Elena Toffol and colleagues reached this conclusion after studying cross-sectional, population-based data in Finland from 1991, 2002, and 2007. These authors, however, acknowledge in their conclusion that the association between the length of time that a woman has taken OCs or LARCS and any long-term mental health effects that may be at play, are unclear. In June 2015, a very pro-OC article by Kelli Stidham Hall and colleagues similarly identified gaps in the research. Despite the advocacy tone of the article that suggests that there does not appear to be a link between OC use and psychopathology, these authors nonetheless state that "additional research that uses rigorous prospective, longitudinal, and randomized controlled trial designs is needed to provide a more definitive comment on the null effects of contraception on women's health."[11]

Furthermore, they make the point that women who suffer from depression and anxiety experience an elevated risk for unintended pregnancies, and are more likely to request abortions than women who do not suffer from these conditions.[12] Birgitta Segebladh and colleagues point out that although many women who take OCs do not report side effects that are related to their mental state, depressive symptoms, irritability, and other mood-related side effects are frequently cited by women as one of the main reasons for the discontinuation of OCs.[13] In a 2009 research study, these same authors found depression and anxiety to be common in women who reported side effects from current or past combined oral contraceptive (COC) use. Almost a third of the sample of 118 women

8 See Pagano et al., "Safety among Women with Depressive and Bipolar Disorders."

9 Carolyn L. Westhoff, Stephen Heartwell, Sharon Edwards, Mimi Zieman, Gretchen Stuart, Carrie Cwiak, Anne Davis, Tina Robilotto, Linda Cushman, and Debra Kalmuss, "Oral Contraceptive Discontinuation: Do Side Effects Matter?," *American Journal of Obstetrics and Gynecology* 196 (April 2007): 412.e1–7.

10 Elena Toffol, Oskari Heikinheimo, Päivikki Koponen, Riitta Luoto, and Timo Partonen, "Further Evidence for Lack of Negative Associations between Hormonal Contraception and Mental Health," *Contraception* 86 (November 2012): 470–480.

11 Kelli Stidham Hall, J. R. Steinberg, C. A. Cwiak, R. H. Allen, and S. M. Marcus, "Contraception and Mental Health: A Commentary on the Evidence and Principles for Practice," *American Journal of Obstetrics and Gynecology* 212 (June 2015): 740–746, cited at 741.

12 See Hall et al., "Contraception and Mental Health."

13 Birgitta Segebladh, Anna Borgström, Viveca Odlind, Marie Bixo, and Inger Sundström-Poromaa, "Prevalence of Psychiatric Disorders and Premenstrual Dysphoric Symptoms in Patients with Experience of Adverse Mood during Treatment with Combined Oral Contraceptives," *Contraception* 79, no. 1 (January 2009): 50–55.

who had experienced COC-induced mood side effects met criteria for mood and/or anxiety disorders.[14] A prospective study by Swedish researchers Larsson and colleagues polled 430 women at ages 19, 24, and 29 years old. They found discontinuation rates due to adverse mood symptoms in the range of 14%–21% depending on the age of the respondents.[15] The authors point out that as a result of the cross-sectional research design of their analyses, they were not able to determine whether the mood pathology was preexisting, coexisting, or related to the pharmaceutical properties of the COCs.[16] The authors conclude that, given the high prevalence of women who report depression and anxiety symptoms on COC's, the appropriate course of action is to add antidepressant therapy to the treatment regimen, as opposed to discontinuing the use of COCs.[17] This type of recommendation is not uncommon in the medical field but, within the landscape of feminist body politics that will be discussed later in this essay, it can be viewed as highly contentious.

In November 2016, a paper on the relationship between mood and OC use was published in *Psychoneuroendocrinology*.[18] The study is notable for its methodology in which the authors examined mood changes over the course of three treatment cycles with either placebo (n=94) or COC (n=84). Results were mixed. A small, yet statistically significant mood side effect was identified in the inter-menstrual phase, leading the authors to conclude that there is a clearly identifiable subgroup of women who experience COC-related side effects.[19] This is in line with Poromaa and Segebladh's findings that mood symptoms connected to hormonal contraceptive use is a very real phenomenon for some women.[20] The authors, however, also identified positive mood effects during the premenstrual phase for some women.[21] Once again, the researchers lament the fact that "the amount of research exploring what consequences these compounds may have for . . . mental health and wellbeing is strikingly low."[22] Another research study that examined the use of hormonal contraception in relation to mood disorders also confirmed the complexities involved. Gjertrud Svendal and colleagues' data suggested that the combined contraceptive pill had a protective effect on mood disorders and an opposite

14 Segebladh et al., "Prevalence of Psychiatric Disorders."

15 Gerd Larsson, Febe Blohm, Gunilla Sundell, Björn Andersch, and Ian Milsom, "A Longitudinal Study of Birth Control and Pregnancy Outcome Among Women in a Swedish Population," *Contraception* 56, no. 1 (July 1, 1997): 9–16.

16 Segebladh et al., "Prevalence of Psychiatric Disorders."

17 Segebladh et al., "Prevalence of Psychiatric Disorders."

18 Cecilia Lundin, K. G. Danielsson, M. Bixo, L. Moby, H. Bengtsdotter, I. Jawad, L. Marions, J. Brynhildsen, A. Malmborg, I. Lindh, I. Sundström Poromaa, "Combined Oral Contraceptive Use is Associated with Both Improvement and Worsening of Mood in the Different Phases of the Treatment Cycle—A Double-Blind, Placebo-Controlled Randomized Trial," *Psychoneuroendocrinology* 76 (February 2017): 135–143.

19 Lundin et al., "Combined Oral Contraceptive Use and Mood."

20 Inger Sundström-Poromaa and Birgitta Segebladh, "Adverse Mood Symptoms with Oral Contraceptives," *Acta Obstetricia Et Gynecologica Scandinavica* 91 (April 2012): 420–427.

21 Segebladh et al., "Prevalence of Psychiatric Disorders."

22 Lundin et al., "Combined Oral Contraceptive Use and Mood," 136.

adverse effect regarding compounds that contained only progestin agents. At most, the data on direct causation is not settled, and complicated by differences found in some studies depending on age cohort.[23] In the *Journal of Adolescent Health*, the authors interviewed 354 adolescent girls about mood-related side effects. They found depressed mood in 21% of the sample, reported stress in 19%, increased moodiness in 25% of interviewees, and eating disordered symptoms in 24 of 249 interviewees. The authors do not make a causal link but acknowledge the existence of significant self-reported mood dysregulation.[24] With regard to adolescent females, findings from a large prospective study in Denmark found an association between hormonal contraceptive use among adolescents, and subsequent antidepressant use and first diagnosis of depression within a psychiatric hospital setting. Adolescents in particular seemed more vulnerable than adult women between the ages of 20 and 34 years old.[25]

Jayashri Kulkarni is a psychiatrist who has researched the potential link between hormonal contraception and depression.[26] In a pilot study, Kulkarni found that women who take oral contraceptives are at twice the risk for depression than those who do not, and the author urged for more extensive research studies to elucidate this complicated relationship between mood and synthetic hormones.[27]

During the past decade, researchers have also started to examine the degree to which hormonal contraceptives are associated with neural changes, which in turn, can lead to affective changes. Lisofsky and colleagues point out that "previous neuroimaging research has demonstrated that female gonadal hormones can alter the structure and function of adult women's brains."[28] The authors state that the effects of hormonal contraceptives on the female brain structure is not known because there are no significant longitudinal studies that have examined this phenomenon.[29] In their analysis of twenty-eight young women before and after taking hormonal contraceptives for three months, the researchers found that, compared to the control group, the women experienced

23 Gjertrud Svendal, Michael Berk, Julie A. Pasco, Felice N. Jacka, Anders Lund, and Lana J. Williams, "The Use of Hormonal Contraceptive Agents and Mood Disorders in Women," *Journal of Affective Disorders* 140, no. 1 (September 2012): 92–96.

24 Kelli Stidham Hall, Katherine White, Vaughn I. Rickert, Nancy Reame, and Carolyun Westhoff, "Influence of Depressed Mood, Psychological Stress, and Eating Disordered Symptoms Are Associated with Perceived Oral Contraceptive Side Effects in Minority Adolescents," *Journal of Adolescent Health* 48 (February 1, 2011): S104.

25 Charlotte Wessel Skovlund, Lina Steinrud Mørch, Lars Vedel Kessing, and Øjvind Lidegaard, "Association of Hormonal Contraception with Depression," JAMA Psychiatry 73, no. 11 (2016): 1154–1162, https://jamanetwork.com/journals/jamapsychiatry/fullarticle/2552796.

26 Jayashri Kulkarni, "Depression as a Side Effect of the Contraceptive Pill," *Expert Opinion on Drug Safety* 6 (July 2007): 371–374.

27 Jayashri Kulkarni, Jacynth Liew, and Kathryn A. Garland, "Depression Associated with Combined Oral Contraceptives—a Pilot Study," *Australian Family Physician* 34 (November 2005): 990.

28 Nina Lisofsky, Michaela Riediger, Jürgen Gallinat, Ulman Lindenberger, and Simone Kühn, "Hormonal Contraceptive Use is Associated with Neural and Affective Changes in Healthy Young Women," *NeuroImage* 134, no. 1 (July 1, 2016): 597–606.

29 Lisofsky et al., "Hormonal Contraceptive Use and Affective Changes."

decreases in gray matter volume, which in turn suggests links to changes in mood. The authors concluded that the amygdala, in particular, seems susceptible to hormonal changes, and that the morphology of the amygdala is also susceptible to change. This research study also found that while positive affect did occur in some women, overall there was a decline in mood that was more prominent, and it was unclear as to why this was the case.[30] While the effects on brain physiology is a distinct research area that lies outside the scope of this essay, it is clear that more research is needed. A recent study investigated the hypothesis that oral contraceptives may cause stress-like alterations in the hypothalamic pituitary adrenal (HPA) axis and may also lead to gray matter losses in the hippocampus. The authors advocate strongly for further research in this area.[31] This is the case especially for adolescents where plasticity and endocrine effects within the developing brain are central. In 2011, Pilar Vigil and colleagues very clearly articulate this when they state that "understanding the phenomena linking steroid hormones and adolescent brain organization is crucial in the study of teenage behavior and in later assessment and treatment of anxiety, mood disorders, and depression."[32]

Taken as a whole, there are not enough longitudinal and cross-sectional research studies to establish a firm and direct causal link between altered mood states and the use of hormonal contraceptives for the majority of women. Studies of this type have found either no negative mood changes, increased negative mood changes, or a decrease in negative mood symptoms.[33] What is becoming increasingly clear is the fact that steroid hormones do affect different brains and bodies to different degrees. There is very limited information on the effects on developing brains which is a significant concern given the numbers of adolescent girls being prescribed hormonal contraceptives. The etiology as to why

30 Lisofsky et al., "Hormonal Contraceptive Use and Affective Changes."

31 Johannes Hertel, Johanna König, Georg Homuth, Sandra Van der Auwera, Katharina Wittfeld, Maik Pietzner, Tim Kacprowski, Liliane Pfeiffer, Anja Kretschmer, Melanie Waldenberger, Gabi Kastenmüller, Anna Artati, Karsten Suhre, Jerzy Adamski, Sönke Langner, Uwe Völker, Henry Völzke, Matthias Nauck, Nele Friedrich, and Hans Joergen Grabe, "Evidence for Stress-like Alterations in the HPA-Axis in Women Taking Oral Contraceptives," *Scientific Reports* 7 (October 26, 2017), https://doi.org/10.1038/s41598-017-13927-7.

32 Pilar Vigil, Renán F. Orellana, Manuel E. Cortés, Carmen T. Molina, Barbara E. Switzer, and Hanna Klaus, "Endocrine Modulation of the Adolescent Brain: A Review," *Journal of Pediatric and Adolescent Gynecology* 24, no. 6 (December 2011): 330–337, cited at 330.

33 See Malin Gingnell, Jonas Engman, Andreas Frick, Lena Moby, Johan Wikström, Mats Fredrikson, and Inger Sundström-Poromaa, "Oral Contraceptive Use Changes Brain Activity and Mood in Women with Previous Negative Affect on the Pill—A Double-Blinded, Placebo-Controlled Randomized Trial of a Levonorgestrel-Containing Combined Oral Contraceptive," *Psychoneuroendocrinology* 38, no. 7 (July 2013): 1133–1144. See also J. A. Jarva and K. A. Oinonen, "Do Oral Contraceptives Act as Mood Stabilizers? Evidence of Positive Affect Stabilization," *Archives of Women's Mental Health* 10, no. 5 (October 2007): 225–234; Kirsten A. Oinonen and Dwight Mazmanian, "To What Extent Do Oral Contraceptives Influence Mood and Affect?," *Journal of Affective Disorders* 70, no. 3 (August 2002): 229–240; Michael J. Rosenberg and Michael S. Waugh, "Oral Contraceptive Discontinuation: A Prospective Evaluation of Frequency and Reasons," *American Journal of Obstetrics & Gynecology* 179, no. 3 (September 1998): 577–582, https://doi.org/10.1016/S0002-9378(98)70047-X; and Svendal et al., "The Use of Hormonal Contraceptive Agents and Mood Disorders in Women."

some women with no prior mood disorders appear to be predisposed to affective disorders as a result of hormonal contraceptive use has not been clarified. It is, however, becoming increasingly clear that some women with a history of mood dysregulation seem to be at risk for continued mood side effects while using hormonal contraceptives.

Women Previously Diagnosed with Adverse Mood Conditions

The literature around preexisting psychiatric conditions and contraception is often framed within the context of compliance. Researchers are concerned about side effects, because side effects are cited as the primary reason for the decision to discontinue oral contraceptives.[34] Some researchers believe that women with a prior history of mood disorders, for example, depression and bipolar disorder, are more likely to experience adverse mood reactivity in response to hormonal contraceptive use.[35] Hadine Joffe and colleagues found that a prior history of depression was the only predictor for experiencing adverse mood side effects for women taking oral contraceptives.[36] Malin Gingnell and colleagues conducted a double blind, randomized study to examine a trial of levonorgestrel-containing combined oral contraceptive in thirty-four women with a history of mood deterioration during COC use.[37] They concluded that mood deterioration, including depressed mood, mood swings, and fatigue occurred in women who had previously reported affectively based side effects, and they also found changes in emotional brain reactivity. These authors concluded that this represents a subset of women identified as "COC sensitive women,"[38] and they recommend placebo-controlled Functional Magnetic Resonance Imaging (FMRI) studies to further investigate this link.[39] Another research study by Segebladh and colleagues investigated the prevalence of psychiatric disorders and premenstrual dysphoric symptoms among women using OCs. They found that women who experienced and self-reported ongoing adverse side effects from OC use showed a significant prevalence of mood disorders.[40] In a departure from scientists who argue that those with preexisting affect dysregulation are more prone to continued emotional side effects while taking hormonal contraceptives, a recent review of six published articles examined the safety of hormonal contraception and intrauterine device (IUD) use among women with prior diagnoses of depressive and bipolar disorders. While the authors acknowledge that the evidence is limited, they concluded

34 Poromaa and Segebladh, "Adverse Mood Symptoms with Oral Contraceptives."

35 Hadine Joffe, Lee S. Cohen, and Bernard L. Harlow, "Impact of Oral Contraceptive Pill Use on Premenstrual Mood: Predictors of Improvement and Deterioration," *American Journal of Obstetrics and Gynecology* 189, no. 6 (December 2003): 1523–1530.

36 Joffe et al., "Impact of Oral Contraceptive Pill Use on Premenstrual Mood."

37 Gingnell et al., "Oral Contraceptive Use Changes Brain Activity."

38 Gingnell et al., "Oral Contraceptive Use Changes Brain Activity," 1134.

39 Gingnell et al., "Oral Contraceptive Use Changes Brain Activity," 1134.

40 Segebladh et al., "Prevalence of Psychiatric Disorders."

that OC, levonorgestrel-inducing IUD, and DMPA[41] use in these women was not associated with worse clinical outcomes.[42]

The lack of consensus as to the etiology of emotional side effects reported in women with no prior history of mood dysregulation, or those who do, have found its way into both the scientific and feminist literature. In 2004, the journal *Medical Hypotheses* published an article titled "Do the Emotional Side-Effects of Hormonal Contraceptives Come from Pharmacologic or Psychological Mechanisms?"[43] The authors reviewed the results of seven prior studies and concluded that there are no differences in emotional functioning between women who use oral contraceptives and those who opt for an IUD. While these researchers found that users of hormonal contraceptives had higher rates of anxiety, depression, fatigue, anger, and other neurotic symptoms, they argue that these side effects are not the result of the pharmacological properties of hormonal contraceptives. Instead, Stephen Robinson and colleagues conclude that the majority of the emotional side effects reported by users of hormonal contraception are "a result of a psychological response to the practice of contraception."[44]

These findings are provocative on two levels. First, they stand in opposition to the more nuanced view that there are women who do appear more sensitive to hormonal side effects that are pharmacologically based. More incendiary, however, is the implication that these types of side effects are constructions of women's minds. Given the complexities involved in this area, I would argue that these two views, pharmacological in origin or psychological in etiology, are not mutually exclusive, or even in opposition to each other. Hormonal contraceptives can be distinguished from other types of medication in two important ways. First, the biochemical effects on the body and brain are still poorly understood by science. There is a dearth of longitudinal studies involving FMRI research tracking neural effects, and it is becoming increasingly clear that women's bodies respond in different ways to the pharmacological compounds within the medication. Second, the aim of hormonal contraceptives is first and foremost to prevent pregnancy. That there are so-called psychological side effects is therefore not surprising. Object relations theory within the psychoanalytic school has examined the concept of medication as object—the idea that putting something inside the body has implications well beyond the chemical properties of the substance. In the following section, I examine the object relations view within the context of the feminist narrative.

41 Depomedroxyprogesterone acetate (DMPA), is a reversible injected contraceptive for women. DMPA contains a progestogen and is administered every twelve weeks.

42 Pagano et al., "Safety among Women with Depressive and Bipolar Disorders."

43 Stephen A. Robinson, Matt Dowell, Dominic Pedulla, and Larry McCauley, "Do the Emotional Side-Effects of Hormonal Contraceptives Come from Pharmacologic or Psychological Mechanisms?," *Medical Hypotheses* 63, no. 2 (February 2004): 268–273.

44 Robinson et al., "Do the Emotional Side-Effects of Hormonal Contraceptives?," 268.

Object Relations and the Feminist Narrative and the (Mis)appropriation of Women's Bodies

In her book, *Sweetening the Pill*, Holly Grigg-Spall argues that there has not been adequate consideration of the potential adverse mood-altering impact of interfering with the delicate female hormonal system.[45] The question as to why this is the case can be explored not only from a scientific research perspective but also from the vantage point of gendered body politics within an object relations frame.

From an object relations perspective, medication has meaning beyond that of an inanimate object. There is a relationship between the person and the medication taken that is complicated and fraught with conflict and meaning. Dana Shindel Fain and colleagues argue that an object relations theory perspective on medication serves as "a gateway to one's inner world and the way that he or she perceives authority figures, peers, and oneself."[46] The psychoanalyst Adele Tutter argues that medication is imbued with symbolic meaning that shifts over time, and reveals aspects of the relationship that one has with oneself and with others.[47] In an acknowledgment of the importance for physicians to look beyond the pharmaceutical properties of hormonal contraceptives, the French psychiatrist Marc Louis Bourgeois outlines four levels that prescribing physicians should attend to: first, side effects should not be dismissed; second, the consequences of sterility should be examined as relevant; third, the patient's motivations for choosing hormonal contraception in the context of a prior psychiatric history should be attended to; and fourth, the "subconscious effects on society's view of sexuality and procreation" should be examined.[48] Bourgeois's approach acknowledges the complexities involved in prescribing a drug that stops a normally occurring reproductive process. This goes well beyond the biological. It incorporates the psychological, including motivations that exist outside of human consciousness where we can locate fear, mistrust, and societal messages that affect our view of self and other.

Fain and colleagues urge mental health professionals to treat patients' views on the medications that they take, or are considering, as an essential part of psychotherapy. They lament the fact that therapists and physicians often treat the medication and the patient as two separate entities, as opposed to in relationship with one another.[49] I would argue that this relationship should be considered in the case of contraception even more so than for other types of medication. The decision to use hormonal contraceptives have implications for existential and

45 Holly Grigg-Spall, *Sweetening the Pill* (Alresford, UK: John Hunt Publishing, 2013).

46 Dana Shindel Fain, Amos Sharon, Lucian Moscovici, and Shaul Schreiber, "Psychotropic Medication from an Object Relations Theory Perspective: An Analysis of Vignettes from Group Psychotherapy," *International Journal of Group Psychotherapy* 58, no. 3 (July 2008): 303–326, cited at 303.

47 Adele Tutter, "Medication as Object," *Journal of the American Psychoanalytic Association* 54, no. 3 (2006): 781–804.

48 Bourgeois quoted in Robinson et al., "Do the Emotional Side-Effects of Hormonal Contraceptives?," 270.

49 Fain et al., "Psychotropic Medication from an Object Relations Theory Perspective."

spiritual views on the self, the relationship with God, family, morality, health, and relationships. These discussions are seldom easy, but I argue that for those of us in the helping professions, obligatory. Engaging in this discussion provides a lens through which to view the ways in which any type of medication can enhance or detract from the sense of dignity with which a person is viewed or views the self.

The outcome of using a drug that is designed to prevent pregnancy is not always foreseeable. In my clinical practice, I have seen firsthand the unexpected nonphysiological "side effects" that can occur in response to taking a drug that has an emotional load. Many years ago, I was referred a young Catholic woman with very severe endometriosis for which she had been prescribed oral contraceptives. She had hoped to join a religious order but no longer thought she could apply because after years of excruciating pain and surgery, she decided to try hormonal contraceptives. The ensuing guilt about taking the pill was in such opposition to her strong religious beliefs, that she developed a hatred toward her body which she now viewed as a traitor to her faith. In another instance, a secular young woman who had chosen to have an IUD implanted on the recommendation of her gynecologist, spoke at length about her conflicting feelings around having something "implanted" into her body. While she was initially happy with the device, she experienced excruciating side effects that led to significant and prolonged bleeding. She expressed anger not only at her physician but also towards her partner for what she perceived as being left alone with not only the physical side effects but also the perceived burden of being held solely responsible for her body's reproductive capacity. These brief vignettes illustrate how easily bioethics sneaks into the therapy room, and also how individuals turn against their bodies with serious psychological consequences as a result.

The power dynamic involved here—the patient who is 'being prescribed' to by the physician—sets up a relationship that is by no means egalitarian. The ideal patient is compliant and tolerant of side effects. The fact that the literature on the side effects of hormonal contraception is often framed within the goal of compliance illustrates the degree to which compliant bodies are desirable. The feminist narrative of Emily Martin further shows that the language used to describe women's bodies is often framed negatively, and she argues that women relate to their bodies in a way that is indicative of subjugation.[50] Women have to control their bodies, and by extension, their mind, that is prone to hormonal influences. In this context, the meta message is that if women are unable to do so, they return to their irrational, emotional state. Oral contraceptives have been touted to help alleviate the natural states of premenstrual syndrome (PMS). Grigg-Sprall points out that the language used in the campaign to sell the oral contraceptive Yaz® to women utilized the irrational woman as the starting point. The balloons in the original advertisement, for which Bayer was later fined $20 million for false advertising, features the words "irritability," "moodiness," "feeling anxious,"

50 Emily Martin, *The Woman in the Body: A Cultural Analysis of Reproduction*, rev. ed. (Boston: Beacon Press, 2001).

and "fatigue" among others.[51] The messaging was that Yaz® would even out these emotional states. The aim is the eradication of fluctuating affect. Women have to display restricted and predetermined emotional states wherein entire categories of normal human emotion, the ups and downs, are eliminated or rendered obsolete. Susan Faludi, the Pulitzer prize winning *Wall Street Journal* reporter argues that the ideal woman is feminine, which means she is "forever static and childlike ... silenced, infantilized and frozen."[52]

Biopower and the surveillance of women's bodies are relevant to this discussion because they speak to the politicized narrative surrounding a very complex scientific and also psychological process. The act of putting into a woman's body a substance that prevents a natural process, not only that of pregnancy but also the alteration of menses, the alteration of mood, the hope from the industrial complex for uninterrupted productivity, and the increased predictability and availability of having sex, is fraught with psychological meaning. Not all women take hormonal contraceptives to avoid pregnancy. They do so because of the promise of more even mood states, only to potentially experience an increase in affective disruption. Illustrative of the ways in which women are often unprepared for what to expect from their bodies and their physicians is the case of a very high functioning and accomplished young woman I had been seeing for relationship issues. She had a history of mild depression, but came into my office sobbing one morning, terrified of the persistent bleeding that she was experiencing as a result of an IUD implant. She had scheduled an appointment later that week to have the IUD removed and she was deeply concerned about the procedure. When she returned the following week, she stated that she felt like "a double failure" because the physician dismissed her anxiety about the bleeding as "one of those things that just happens sometimes." Of course, not all women have this type of experience. Minds and bodies are different. It does, however, illustrate the potentially powerful effect of the psychological response to the perception that one's body and mind has failed one, and the violation of trust that she felt toward her doctor. In this particular case, the patient turned against her body first. It was only later that she, of her own accord, when she was able to extricate herself from the power imbalance between prescribing physician and patient, was able to consider turning against the IUD itself. In this instance, the persecutory object was the body itself, not the foreign object with its inconclusive side effect profile which she had been reassured was perfectly safe. The message from the panopticon was that she was an exception, an aberration in a medical world where most bodies respond well. The pathologization of women's bodies and minds who do not respond in the expected ways, that is, with minimal, transient, or no side effects, has been largely dismissed by many within the medical profession and pharmaceutical companies. These minds and bodies disappear into the

51 Natasha Singer, "Bayer Running Ads to Clarify Benefits of Birth Control Pill," *The New York Times* (February 10, 2009), sec. Business Day.

52 Susan Faludi, *Backlash: The Undeclared War Against American Women*. anniversary ed. (New York: Broadway Books, 2006).

unreadable type at the bottom of glossy advertisements in women's magazines, dismissed as outliers. The feminist narrative is extremely useful here. Every body matters. Every experience matters.

Conclusion

While the current state of the science on the psychological side effects of hormonal contraception is not settled, it is nonetheless hopeful that most authors of articles that examine this phenomenon call for additional research in this area. While their motivation for the most part seems to be that of eliminating side effects to enable more women to take hormonal contraceptives, there is a recognition that there are many unsettled questions that call for more research. This is an important validation for the experiences of women who have, for many years, pointed out that their reality includes distressing emotional symptoms which disrupt their lives. While this "Science in the Making" unfolds before us, we have available to us the Catholic Christian view of the human person.[53] Respect for the dignity of every human person, every body, every mind, and every genetic and biochemical fingerprint. This view, by necessity, includes a compassionate stance toward those who are often lost to statistical analyses because they become outliers or minorities in research studies, or because their human experience documented in anecdotal narratives are dismissed.

53 See Bruno Latour, *Science in Action* (Cambridge, Mass.: Harvard University Press, 1988).

14

Against Ideological Colonization

The Teaching of Humanae vitae *and a Humanely Adequate Global Ethic*

Teresa Stanton Collett

✷ THIS IS A STORY ABOUT AN international struggle between hope and despair, equality and bigotry, community and isolation. It is a story of men, women, and institutions emerging from the horrors of two world wars, desperately seeking the path to permanent peace and getting lost in trails of self-interest, quick fixes, and hubris. It is also the story of the Church's stubborn resistance to these siren calls, and the ongoing struggle to persuade our families, friends, neighbors, and leaders that there is a better way—but that way requires placing the human person at the center of public policies, as well the development of self-mastery, prudence, and generosity within each person.

While the title of this essay was provided in my invitation to participate in this collection, it is an excellent road map to the essay's contents. The first (and larger) section examines a long-standing and persistent international campaign to persuade the world that suppressing fertility (almost always women's fertility), will reduce threats to world peace, correct unjust social structures and cultural norms, decrease sexual violence and the number of unwanted children, and protect the natural environment, all while increasing personal prosperity and national economic development.

Many of these claims are belied by the American experience where we have fully embraced contraception and extreme methods of fertility control,[1] yet continue to experience a high percentage of women and children living in poverty,[2] endemic sexual violence and harassment (if reports and studies are to be believed),[3] and a general decline in self-reported well-being of women and children of all socio-economic statuses.[4]

1 Menstrual suppression and egg freezing to preserve fertility after menopause are two examples.

2 United States Census Bureau, "Historical Poverty Tables: People and Families—1959 to 2017," https://www.census.gov/data/tables/time-series/demo/income-poverty/historical-poverty-people.html.

3 See Chai R. Feldblum and Victoria A. Lipnic, "Report of the Co-Chairs of the EEOC Select Task Force on the Study of Harassment in the Workplace," (June 2016), https://www.eeoc.gov/eeoc/task_force/harassment / upload/report.pdf. The report states, "Based on testimony to the Select Task Force and various academic articles, we learned that anywhere from 25% to 85% of women report having experienced sexual harassment in the workplace."

4 Compare Betsey Stevenson and Justin Wolfers, "The Paradox of Declining Female Happiness," *American Economic Journal: Economic Policy* 1, no. 2 (August 2009): 190–225 and Chris M. Herbst, "'Paradoxical'

As researchers Mary and Nicolas Eberstadt, Helen Alvaré, Brad Wilcox, Mark Regnerus, and many more have so carefully documented, widespread availability of contraception and abortion has not resulted in an American utopia. Rather, we have experienced a marked decline in the number of people entering into marriage, a corresponding increase in cohabiting couples, a dramatic increase in the number of children born into fatherless homes, an intensifying dissatisfaction of women (and men) with their lives, general social isolation, and a troubling decline in the well-being of children marked by increasing suicide, violence, and mental illness.[5] In short, there are many indicators that the current experiment in "sexual liberation" premised on women's ability to "control" their fertility is an abject failure. There is little reason to believe that a different result will attend efforts to duplicate our experiment elsewhere.

The second section of this essay explores the question of why the Church's anthropology of the person and the family, embodied in various magisterial documents, including *Humanae vitae*, *Evangelium vitae*, and Pope John Paul II's teachings known collectively as the Theology of the Body, has had so little purchase in recent global discussions of sexual equality, global health, and sustainable development.[6] In other words, the second portion of this essay attempts to identify the reasons why it is so hard to persuade others that the means we use when attempting to control the number, timing, and spacing of children are a matter of grave moral concern. Competing conceptions of communal life and human sexuality will be examined to determine their allure and to identify what actions the Church and its faithful must take to prevail in the current intellectual competition between the contraceptive mentality foreseen by *Humanae vitae* and the Church's understanding of human dignity, sexual equality, and the path toward sustainable human development, economic and otherwise.

Before we review the historical record of global efforts to control population growth and promote contraception, a brief tutorial in international law is in order.

International Law: What it Is and What it Is Not

International law is inherently different from contemporary American law and, while the American founders understood international law to be a species of natural law, that view would have few defenders today. One of the major distinguishing characteristics of international law is the fact that there is no global legislative body and, thus, law is a product of agreement, custom, or "general

Decline? Another Look at the Relative Reduction in Female Happiness," *Journal of Economic Psychology* 32, no. 5 (October 2011): 773–788.

5 Kay S. Hymowitz, *Marriage and Caste in America: Separate and Unequal Families in a Post-Marital Age* (Chicago: Ivan R. Dee, Publisher, 2006) and Charles A. Murray, *Coming Apart: The State of White America, 1960–2010* (New York: Crown Forum, 2012).

6 Pope Paul VI, Encyclical Letter *Humanae vitae* (July 25, 1968), http://w2.vatican.va/content/paul-vi/en/encyclicals.index.html; Pope John Paul II, Encyclical Letter *Evangelium vitae* (March 25, 1995), http://w2.vatican.va/content/john-paul-ii/en/encyclicals.index.html; and Pope John Paul II, *Audiences*, http://w2.vatican.va/content/john-paul-ii/en/audiences.index.html.

principles of law recognized by civilized nations."[7] Agreements between nations, known as conventions or treaties, typically bind only the countries that sign and ratify them.[8] "Customary international law" arises from a general and consistent practice of nations which is followed by those nations from a sense of legal obligation.[9] The United Nations Universal Declaration of Human Rights is an example of a document that, while drafted to be aspirational and not legally binding, has evolved into customary international law.[10] Nations can avoid being subject to a principle of customary international law by persistently objecting to that principle. The third source of international law, "general principles of law recognized by civilized nations," also known as *jus cogens*, are those rules that make it possible to have other rules or agreements. An example of such a principle would be the rule that no man should be the judge of his own case.

It is important to note that while the United Nations, as an international organization, may participate and has done so in drafting some international treaties, it is not a legislative body.[11] Therefore a nation, whether a UN member or not, may ignore or repudiate any proposed agreement by that organization. Similarly the "outcome documents"[12] or "programmes of action"[13] generated by United Nations conferences are not legally binding on any nation, although many commentators characterize

7 Statute of the International Court of Justice, art. 39, art. 38, ¶ 1.

8 Of the nine conventions that the United Nations identifies as core international Human Rights instruments, all have been signed by the United States but only the International Covenant on Civil and Political Rights has been ratified by the Senate. The nine conventions are the International Convention on the Elimination of All Forms of Racial Discrimination; International Covenant on Civil and Political Rights, International Covenant on Economic, Social and Cultural Rights; Convention on the Elimination of All Forms of Discrimination against Women; Convention against Torture and Other Cruel, Inhuman or Degrading Treatment or Punishment Convention on the Rights of the Child; International Convention on the Protection of the Rights of All Migrant Workers and Members of Their Families; International Convention for the Protection of All Persons from Enforced Disappearance; and Convention on the Rights of Persons with Disabilities. The Holy See has been accepted as a signatory to three of the conventions: International Convention on the Elimination of All Forms of Racial Discrimination; Convention against Torture and Other Cruel, Inhuman or Degrading Treatment or Punishment; and the Convention on the Rights of the Child. See "The Core International Human Rights Instruments and Their Monitoring Bodies," United Nations at http://www.ohchr.org/EN/ProfessionalInterest/Pages/CoreInstruments.aspx.

9 Restatement (Third) of the Foreign Relations Law of the United States § 102 (2) (1987).

10 Mary A. Glendon, "Knowing the Universal Declaration of Human Rights," *Notre Dame Law Review* 73, no. 5 (1998): 1153.

11 Austin Ruse, "Radical Social Policy at the United Nations," *National Catholic Bioethics Quarterly* 7, no. 1 (Spring 2007): 25, "Most UN bodies, such as committees, commissions, boards, councils, and conferences, report on their work. These reports include summaries of the work of the body for a given time period or session." See Dag Hammarskjold Library, "UN Documentation: Overview," http://research.un.org/en/docs/reports.

12 The United Nations Terminology Database defines an "outcome document" as "a final written record or report issued at the end of a conference or high-level meeting." See https://unterm.un.org/UNTERM/Display/Record/UNHQ/NA?OriginalId=404a5a733385a69f85257a9c004513e4.

13 The UN Terminology Database has no definition for "programmes of action," but scholars note these documents are not legally binding. "A 'program of action' is a non-traditional type of international legal instrument containing a non-binding, directive text producing limited legal effects." Alexandre Charles Kiss and Mary Frances Dominick, "The International Legal Significance of the Human Rights Provisions of the Helsinki Final Act," *Vanderbilt Journal of Transnational Law* 13 (1980): 293, 314–315.

them as "soft law," arguing that these documents provide interpretative guidance for existing treaties or important guidelines and rules of behavior that are useful in responding to emerging challenges.[14] A variety of UN committees and nongovernment organizations have aggressively attempted to use these documents to create and impose new "human rights" such as a putative "right to abortion" or "right to same-sex marriage" on reluctant governments, with varied degrees of success.[15]

Just as there is no global legislature, there is no global Supreme Court. While international courts such as the International Court of Justice and the International Court of Criminal Justice exist, absent agreement by the plaintiff or defendant nation, these courts have no authority to compel participation in court proceedings, nor do they have independent authority to compel compliance with their rulings.[16] These limitations also exist for various "treaty bodies," committees of elected experts who receive and comment upon reports by signatory countries or others regarding a country's compliance with a particular treaty.

> Their conclusions take the form of non-binding recommendations designed to assist State Parties in the implementation of their treaty obligations. Those conclusions are not judgements nor do they constitute "jurisprudence," in the common law sense of the term. Treaty bodies have no competence to redefine the terms used in the substantive norms of their constitutive treaties, or create new rights or principles. In particular, treaty bodies cannot impose upon State Parties obligations which have not been expressly undertaken by those States when negotiating and ratifying the constituting treaty.[17]

Increasingly, these committees use their reports to advance novel and troubling interpretations of the treaties that, while not legally binding, generate adverse public notoriety both domestically and internationally for the country subject to the report.[18]

14 See, for example, Damilola S. Olawuyi, "Advancing Climate Justice in International Law: An Evaluation of the United Nations Human Rights-Based Approach," *Florida A & M University Law Review* 11, no. 1 (Fall 2015): 103, 125.

15 Douglas A. Sylva and Susan Yoshihara, "Rights by Stealth: The Role of UN Human Rights Treaty Bodies in the Campaign for an International Right to Abortion," *White Paper Series*, no. 8 (Philadelphia: International Organizations Research Group, 2009): 18–20, http://c-fam.org/wp-content/uploads/Rights.By.Stealth.pdf.

16 "The Court can only deal with a dispute when the States concerned have recognized its jurisdiction. No State can therefore be a party to proceedings before the Court unless it has in some manner or other consented thereto." See "Contentious Jurisdiction," International Court of Justice, https://www.icj-cij.org/en/contentious-jurisdiction, referring to Statute of the International Court of Justice, art. 36, ¶ 1.

17 Stefano Gennarini, "The United Nations System," *International Center on Law, Life, Faith and Family*, http://icolf.org/protection-systems/united-nations.

18 The Holy See has repeatedly been subjected to public criticism by United Nations committees based on distorted readings of the treaties. Examples include the *2014 Concluding Observations on the Initial Report of the Holy See*, prepared by the Committee Against Torture at the Convention Against Torture on the Initial Report of the Holy See and the 2014 Convention against Torture and Other Cruel, Inhuman or Degrading Treatment or Punishment, United Nations (June 17, 2014), at https://ccrjustice.org/sites/default/files/attach/2015/09/UNCAT_ConcludingObservationsVatican%28June2014%29.pdf and the

Finally, there is also no global executive officer or head of state. The secretary-general of the United Nations is sometimes portrayed as the spokesman for all member states of the organization and, therefore, spokesman for all or nearly all of the nations of the world,[19] but the Charter of the United Nations identifies him as the "chief administrative officer" of the organization,[20] who acts in that capacity and performs "such other functions as are entrusted" to him by the Security Council, General Assembly, Economic and Social Council, and the now defunct Trusteeship Council.[21] The secretary-general, like the United Nations generally, has no law-making authority.

In addition to the fact that the United Nations as an organization has no law-making authority, the Charter recognizes that membership in the United Nations does not create international jurisdiction over "matters which are essentially within the domestic jurisdiction" of a state.[22] National policies on sexual conduct, procreation, and contraception have historically been understood to be a matter "essentially within the domestic jurisdiction" of a country, and not matters of international concern. This is true even when those domestic policies are inconsistent with provisions of various human rights conventions or the Universal Declaration of Human Rights. Again, this is because international law, as historically understood, is about actions between nations, and not about actions a nation may take in relationship to its citizens. Under this traditional understanding, neither China's one-child policy in effect until recently,[23] nor Ireland's general prohibition of abortion,[24] were matters properly within the jurisdiction

---

Concluding Observations on the *Second Periodic Report* of the Holy See, prepared by the United Nations Committee on the Rights of the Child at the Convention on the Rights of the Child (February 25, 2014), at https://tbinternet.ohchr.org/Treaties/CRC/Shared%20Documents/VAT/CRC_C_VAT_CO_2_16302_E.pdf.

19 The United Nations recognizes 195 countries for membership purposes (193 members and two official observers), but there are additional territories that claim nationhood status. Taiwan is the example most familiar to Americans. "How Many Countries Are There in the World in 2018?" *Political Geography Now*, at http://www.polgeonow.com/2011/04/how-many-countries-are-there-in-world.html.

20 United Nations Charter, art. 97.

21 United Nations Charter, art. 98.

22 Charter of the United Nations, Art. Charter, art. 2, sec. 7. It is important to note that, while this principle has not been amended or altered in any way since the founding of the UN, sovereignty is increasingly understood as subject to a nation's responsibility to protect its population from genocide, war crimes, ethnic cleansing, and crimes against humanity. See "Background Information on the Responsibility to Protect," Outreach Programme on the Rwanda Genocide and the United Nations at http://www.un.org/en/preventgenocide/rwanda/about/bgresponsibility.shtml and the UN General Assembly, Resolution 60/1, 2005 World Summit Outcome, A/RES/60/1, ¶ 138 (October 24, 2005) at http://www.un.org/en/ga/search/view_doc.asp?symbol=A/RES/60/1.

23 Feng Wang, Baochang Gu, and Yong Cai, "The End of China's One-Child Policy," *Studies in Family Planning* 47 (March 30, 2016): 83–86. This piece is republished by the Brookings Institute at https://www.brookings.edu/articles/the-end-of-chinas-one-child-policy.

24 See Sarah Bardon, "Government Sets Out 21 Clauses to Regulate Abortion," *Irish Times* (March 9, 2018). The 2018 Supreme Court of Ireland opinion on abortion can be found at *M (Immigration—Rights of Unborn) v. Minister of Justice and equality & ORS*, [2018 IESC 14 [2017], at http://www.supremecourt.ie/Judgments.nsf/1b0757edc371032e802572ea0061450e/2ca87fab5fd004ff8025824a00329063?OpenDocument.

of the United Nations, its treaty committees, or its specialized agencies.[25]

Based on these facts, the international campaign to persuade countries to limit their population growth or embrace a contraceptive mentality has been conducted, not through any lawful legislative powers of the United Nations, but by promotion of this mentality as a "consensus of the nations," or through the conditioning of foreign aid or other benefits upon acceptance of particular interpretations of human rights treaties or development goals. This is important to remember as we now examine the international campaign to limit fertility.

The International Campaign against Women's Fertility

In *Humanae vitae*, Pope Paul VI predicted that the use of artificial contraception would increase marital infidelity, lead to a general lowering of moral standards as well as a loss of respect for women, and intervention into citizens' private lives by governments seeking to control people's fertility.[26] Sadly, each of the predictions has proven correct.

During much of the past sixty years, Western intellectuals and philanthropists have aggressively promoted birth control as a moral response to a variety of real or perceived global problems.[27] The West, and more particularly the United States, United Kingdom, and Scandinavian countries, have actively engaged in what might fairly be called "ideological colonization" through their worldwide promotion of a contraceptive mentality. This mentality asserts that widely available contraception is morally good and a necessary condition for sexual equality and reduction of poverty. Arising from a unique blend of eugenics, concerns about global competition for resources, a self-defeating "feminist" response to male domination in the public sphere, and an inadequate view of human development, the contraceptive mentality promises healthier, happier, and more perfect (but fewer) people, who will live in a more prosperous, peaceful, and just world.

This view is captured by a 2010 World Bank report that contends, "[h]igh fertility poses health risks for children and their mothers, detracts from human capital investment, slows economic growth, and exacerbates environmental threats."[28] Cautionary notes abound throughout the report indicating an absence

25 This statement is true, unless a state voluntary joins a binding treaty on such domestic matters.

26 Pope Paul VI, *Humanae vitae*, 17.

27 "One can date the beginning of the modern family planning movement from various starting points: Sanger's opening of the first birth control clinic in 1916; the nearly simultaneous establishment in 1952 of the first national population policy in India, the International Planned Parenthood Federation, and Rockefeller's Population Council; or the beginning of significant transfers of financial and technical assistance for population programs from industrial to developing countries in the mid- to late 1960s." Warren C. Robinson and John A. Ross, eds., *The Global Family Planning Revolution: Three Decades of Population Policies and Programs* (Washington D.C.: World Bank, 2007), 3, http://siteresources.worldbank.org/INTPRH/Resources/GlobalFamilyPlanningRevolution.pdf.

28 World Bank, *Determinants and Consequences of High Fertility: A Synopsis of the Evidence* (Washington D.C.: World Bank, 2010), https://openknowledge.worldbank.org/handle/10986/27497.

of robust scientific support for these claims,[29] but the authors are not deterred from rendering their conclusions, nor the World Bank from relying upon them in promulgating policy.

American Leadership in Population Matters

In making these claims, the World Bank merely echoes the views of many American leaders in the 1970s. Statements by Phyllis Tilson Piotrow, a US government advisor to the 1974 World Population Conference in Bucharest and consultant to the United States Agency for International Development (USAID), illustrate their views.

> I believe that population growth threatens not only present values and institutions but also the opportunity for billions of people, born and unborn, to live with peace, prosperity, and dignity in years to come. I believe, therefore, that private and public, national and international programs to limit population growth are desirable, necessary and ultimately inevitable. I believe also that the more rapidly and effectively fertility control programs are undertaken on a voluntary basis, the more likely they are to succeed in reducing population growth without either coercion or substantial increases in mortality.[30]

Note that Dr. Piotrow does not foreswear coercive means of population control, nor does she acknowledge any limits on public initiatives to reduce population growth if voluntary acceptance is not forthcoming.

Voicing his agreement with these views, the future president of the United States of America, then US Representative to the United Nations, George H. W. Bush identified the architects of this contraceptive mentality. He wrote, "Certainly the private organizations, like the Population Crisis Committee, Planned Parenthood (national and international), the Population Council, the Population Reference Bureau, the Population Institute, Zero Population Growth,[31] and others, have played a major role in assisting government policy makers and in mobilizing the United States response to the world population challenge."[32] Each of the named organizations supported, and continues to support, both contraception and abortion as necessary components in their definition of the terms reproductive health, women's empowerment, population control, and economic development.

29 "Research designs that support valid identification of causal effects are generally infeasible." *Determinants and Consequences of High Fertility*, 4. "This topic is bedeviled by the likely endogeneity [personal preferences] of fertility decisions" *Determinants and Consequences of High Fertility*, 5. "[The environmental impact of high fertility is in the] relative infancy of systematic research on this issue." *Determinants and Consequences of High Fertility*, 8.

30 Phyllis Tilson Piotrow, *World Population Crisis: The United States Response* (New York: Praeger Publishers, 1973), xvi.

31 Renamed Population Connection in 2002, http://www.populationconnection.org/us/mission.

32 George H. W. Bush, foreword to Piotrow, *World Population Crisis*, vii.

Donald Critchlow has produced a comprehensive history of the family planning policies of the United States government from their inception in eugenic dreams of eliminating poverty (or at least the poor), through post-World War II concerns about overpopulation to contemporary debates about the role of the government in family planning and abortion.[33] He carefully documents the motivations, actions, and aspirations of those who effectively established the contraceptive mentality of America today, as well as the international aspirations of birth control advocates from the start—advocates that included some of the wealthiest Americans of the time. Oil tycoon John D. Rockefeller III; Katharine Dexter McCormick, heir to the International Harvester Company fortune; Hugh Moore, founder of Dixie Cup Corporation; Clarence Gamble, heir to the Proctor and Gamble fortune; and Mrs. Eleanor Pillsbury, wife of Philip Pillsbury, president of Pillsbury Corporation, were among the early leaders of the movement. All staunchly believed that population growth posed a threat to world peace and security, and hoped to convince the nations of Asia and most of the global South to undertake national initiatives to reduce what they saw as irresponsible, if not dangerous, population growth.

The early 1950s saw the creation of International Planned Parenthood Federation (IPPF) by Pillsbury and others,[34] with Moore serving as an officer.[35] The Population Council was founded the same year by Rockefeller.[36] IPPF was founded to promote and provide direct assistance to women and men seeking to limit family growth,[37] while the Population Council was charged with researching population growth, and providing technical assistance to countries attempting to reduce their growth.[38] Once established, these organizations received millions of dollars of grants from some of the largest charitable foundations in the world, including Ford Foundation, Millbank Fund, Carnegie Institute, Packard Foundation, MacArthur Foundation, and more recently, the Bill and Melinda Gates Foundation.[39]

Due to generous private and public funding, IPPF and the Population Council established a variety of educational programs both at home and abroad, as well as developed a growing network of local activists and providers throughout the world.[40] These programs, however, were limited in the services and advice they could offer since the primary methods of contraception available in the 1950s

33 Donald T. Critchlow, *Intended Consequences: Birth Control, Abortion, and the Federal Government in Modern America* (New York: Oxford University Press, 1999). See also chapter 1 in this volume which summarizes that history.

34 "Mrs. Philip W. Pillsbury Dies; Leader in Planned Parenthood," *New York Times* (August 28, 1971).

35 Glenn Fowler, "Hugh Moore, Industrialist, Dies; Birth-Control Crusader Was 85," *New York Times* (November 26, 1972).

36 Population Council, "Timeline," http://www.popcouncil.org/about/timeline.

37 See Critchlow, *Intended Consequences*, 26–27.

38 "Timeline," http://www.popcouncil.org/about/timeline.

39 Maria Sophia Aguirre and Cecilia A. Hadley, "Hindered Growth: The Ideology and Implications of Population Assistance," *International Journal of Social Economics* 32, no. 9 (September 2005): 783–813, notes 4 and 5.

40 Aguirre and Hadley, "Hindered Growth," note 4.

were condoms, diaphragms, and douching, all of which were messy and inconvenient. This changed dramatically in the 1960s with the invention of the oral contraceptive pill and the redesign of the pessary or what has become known as the modern intrauterine device (IUD). These technological developments changed the nature of the arguments used to advance a contraceptive mentality worldwide.

From Population Control and Eugenics to Women's Empowerment and Sustainable Development

Western fear of population growth and its potential to lead to widespread starvation, political turmoil, and worldwide conflict led to international efforts to persuade Asian and African nations to adopt government population policies.[41] While early efforts were largely pursued and funded by wealthy individuals and foundations, it was not long before national governments, the United Nations, and other international associations actively began promoting family planning as a component of economic development. National policies often aimed at "controlling population growth" in developed nations typically focusing on a eugenic form of control, using sterilization as a form of punishment for "habitual criminals,"[42] and incentivizing or mandating use of various forms of birth control (including sterilization) by the poor and "feeble-minded."

The 1927 US Supreme Court case of *Buck v. Bell* illustrates this mindset. Justice Oliver Wendell Holmes Jr., writing the majority opinion, approved mandatory sterilization for the mentally disabled. "It is better for all the world if, instead of waiting to execute degenerate offspring for crime or to let them starve for their imbecility, society can prevent those who are manifestly unfit from continuing their kind."[43] After the exposure of Third Reich eugenic experiments at the close of World War II, support for eugenic programs generally diminished but did not entirely disappear from public policy discussions. As an illustration of this point, I would note that *Buck v. Bell* has never been overruled.

Among developing nations, population control took a different course. While these policies too had a eugenic aspect, insofar as they rarely applied to what we would call the "elites" in a society, they were much more likely to be directed at reducing the total number of children born to women throughout the society.[44] The distinctions between the policies pursued by developed and developing nations become apparent when tracing the mutations of the population control movement over the past six decades.[45]

41 Wang, Gu, and Cai, "The End of China's One-Child Policy," 83–86.

42 Skinner v. Oklahoma, 316 U.S. 535 (1942).

43 Buck v. Bell, 274 U.S. 200, 207 (1927).

44 See Critchlow, chapter 1 of this book, p. 8, "[T]he belief that population control was for the masses and not for the elite remained an understood assumption as the Population Council launched efforts to organize and fund birth control clinics in Hong Kong, Japan, Korea, Pakistan, Taiwan, Thailand, Malaysia, Ceylon, Tunisia, and Egypt."

45 A more complete chronological listing of relevant events appears in Table 14–1 at the conclusion of this essay.

International Populations Conferences Become the Battleground

As part of her crusade for international acceptance of birth control, Margaret Sanger organized the first world conference dedicated to the issue of overpopulation, which was held in 1927. Gathering scientists from around the world, she hoped to engage the scientific community in her efforts to make contraception legal and accessible as a method to control world population. Ultimately, however, the only consensus to emerge from the conference was a call for governments to provide more statistical population data.[46]

It wasn't until 1954 that the United Nations sponsored its first World Population Conference in Rome. Heavily influenced by wealthy donors and the nascent work of Rockefeller's Population Council, the conference focused on methods to obtain accurate estimates of world population, as well as identifying population variables, their determinants, and their consequences. While national censuses have been conducted regularly throughout much of Western Europe since the 1700s (the United States has conducted a census every decade since 1790), many developing countries had no such practice. Even today, there are nations that do not have reliable birth and death registries or census data. To obtain more accurate information about world population, the United Nations sponsored technical assistance and coordination for large-scale population and housing censuses throughout the 1960s. Much of that assistance was provided through the United States Census Bureau and USAID.[47]

Eleven years later, the United Nations sponsored the Second World Population Conference held in Belgrade and, like the first conference, its participants were largely scientists, not diplomats. The focus was on the analysis of fertility as a component of economic development. This conference coincided with the start-up of population programs subsidized by USAID.

In 1974, the Third World Conference was held in Bucharest. Unlike the first two conferences, this conference was attended by representatives of 135 countries. Much had happened regarding population in the years between 1954 and 1974 and this meeting was intended to create a program for international action. In 1960, the United States Food and Drug Administration (FDA) approved Enovid as a hormonal birth control pill, and major changes were made in the design of the intrauterine device. In western countries, access to contraception was being recast from its historic characterization as a violation of law into a legal right. In the period of 1965 to 1973, the United States Supreme Court created a constitutional right in married couples to use contraception,[48] expanded that right to include unmarried adults,[49] and then pronounced abortion a fundamental right that could not be regulated in any manner during the first trimester, and even in

46 Matthew Connelly, *Fatal Misconception: The Struggle to Control World Population* (Cambridge, Mass: Belknap Press of Harvard University Press, 2008), 70.

47 John F. May, *World Population Policies: Their Origin, Evolution, and Impact* (New York: Springer, 2012).

48 Griswold v. Connecticut, 381 U.S. 479 (1965).

49 Eisenstadt v. Baird, 405 U.S. 438 (1972).

the final trimester, must be available when required to protect a woman's health, a term the Court defined so broadly as to be barely recognizable.[50]

Developed nations were increasingly promoting population control in high fertility countries through foreign aid. In 1962, Sweden became the first national government to provide development aid in support of family planning efforts in Ceylon (now Sri Lanka), India, and Pakistan.[51] In his 1965 State of the Union address, then President Lyndon Johnson referred to the world population as exploding and resources as scarce. During his administration it became US policy to condition foreign aid on governments "giv[ing] evidence of policies that would assure balance between food production and population growth." President Johnson also joined twenty-nine other heads of state in a Declaration on Population directed to United Nations Secretary General U Thant saying they believed "the opportunity to decide the number and spacing of children is a basic human right."[52]

During the same time, former US Secretary of Defense Robert McNamara became president of World Bank and announced that projects attempting to reduce fertility in developing countries would receive favorable review, and domestic population policies would be an element considered during review of loan applications.[53]

The Holy See was not exempt from debates surrounding population and birth control, and debates within the Church resulted in Pope John XXIII establishing a Pontifical Commission for the Study of Population, Family and Births in 1963.[54] Five years later, Paul VI issued *Humanae vitae*, affirming the right of married couples to determine the number and spacing of their children through periodic abstinence, but maintaining the prohibition on use of contraception.

During these tumultuous twenty years, arguments for international and domestic population policies were being recast again. Arguments connecting burgeoning populations and threats to world peace were giving way to arguments about large populations impeding economic development. Experience with national population policies in India, Sri Lanka, and Pakistan was mixed at best, leading to debates about the reasons for their lack of progress. Western nations continued to argue that widespread access to and use of contraception was the most promising path to controlling population growth, while much of Asia and Africa argued that economic development with improving education and social support were the only proven path to declines in fertility rates.

50 Roe v. Wade, 410 U.S. 113 (1973). In a companion case, Doe v. Bolton, 410 U.S. 179 (1973), "health" was defined as encompassing "physical, emotional, psychological, familial, and the woman's age."

51 Robinson and Ross, eds., *The Global Family Planning Revolution*, 3.

52 Susan Yoshihara, "Lost in Translation: The Failure of the International Reproductive Rights Norm," *Ave Maria Law Review* 11, no. 2 (Spring 2013): 371–372.

53 Robinson and Ross, eds., *The Global Family Planning Revolution*, 163–164.

54 The commission originally included six professionals but grew to ultimately include seventy members, including scientists, theologians, married couples, physicians, bishops, and cardinals. Richard J. Fehring, "An Analysis of the Majority Report 'Responsible Parenthood' and its Recommendations on Abortion, Sterilization and Contraception," *Life and Learning* 13 (2003): 122.

These competing world views defined the content of the Third World Population Conference. Developed countries resurrected Malthusian arguments about population and food supplies, arguing that world population growth was primarily due to a lack of effective fertility control measures and that growth threatened international food security. These arguments gained widespread public attention with the publication of the international best seller, *The Population Bomb* by Stanford University Professor Paul Ehrlich and his wife. "Public health professionals ascribed the early program disappointments to factors intrinsic to the programs themselves: poor planning, inadequate training of fieldworkers, inappropriate selection of field staff members, inadequate safeguards against fraudulent reporting, and so on. They believed that programs could be made more effective by revising and redesigning them."[55]

Developing nations argued that socioeconomic development was the key to reducing population pressures and that countries should focus on factors, such as high rates of infant mortality, low levels of education and economic opportunity for women, and reliance on family for old-age economic security. The view of the developing nations is best captured by Dr. Karan Singh, India's Minister of Health and Family Planning, who declared, "Development is the best contraceptive."[56]

In the end, neither side completely triumphed in the debates and the conference outcome document reflects a blend of both approaches. "The outcome of the Conference, the World Population Plan of Action, states, among other principles, that the essential aim is the social, economic and cultural development of countries, that population variables and development are interdependent and that population policies and objectives are an integral part (constituent elements) of socio-economic development policies."[57] Thus the dominant rationale for international population policies shifted from peace and security to economic development.

Ten years later, when the International Conference on Population convened in Mexico City, Paul VI's prediction that public authorities would use coercion to implement population policies had proven true. In 1976, the government of India modified its national population policy to include enormously enlarged targets for family planning, permitted local compulsory sterilization laws, increased monetary incentives for family planning "acceptors," and imposed significant financial penalties on those rejecting sterilization. Over ten million sterilizations, many coerced, were performed in the twenty months the policy was in effect.[58]

Three years later, in 1979, the People's Republic of China announced its draconian one-child policy imposing stiff financial penalties on couples having

55 Robinson and Ross, eds., *The Global Family Planning Revolution*, 3.

56 Robinson and Ross, eds., *The Global Family Planning Revolution*, 6.

57 United Nations, Key Conference "Outcomes on Population," United Nations, http://www.un.org/en/development/devagenda/population.shtml.

58 Lewis M. Simons, "Compulsory Sterilization Provokes Fear, Contempt," *Washington Post* (July 4, 1977).

more than one child, and permitting government officials to forcibly abort and sterilize women. During 1983, China recorded 21 million births, 14.4 million abortions, 20.7 million sterilizations (predominantly female), and 17.8 million IUD insertions. Many of these procedures were involuntary.[59]

Notwithstanding these horrific abuses, the United Nations awarded its first Population Award jointly to Indira Gandhi, prime minister of India, and Qian Xinzhong, minister-in-charge of the State Family Planning Commission of the People's Republic of China in recognition of their "outstanding contribution to the awareness of population questions or to their solutions." [60]

International media coverage of both the Indian and Chinese policies convinced President Ronald Regan to announce what has come to be called "The Mexico City Policy" at the 1984 International Conference on Population. This policy declares the United States to be neutral on population growth, but firmly opposed to the use of abortion as part of family planning efforts.[61] This was a major shift in US policy and resulted in a substantial reduction in US financial support for foreign population initiatives. This policy has been in place during every subsequent Republican presidential administration and withdrawn under every subsequent Democratic president.[62]

The outcome document of the 1984 conference continued to emphasize economic development as a means of reducing fertility rates and introduced provisions regarding respect for human rights of individuals and families, as well as noting correlations between high fertility with maternal mortality and morbidity.

The fifth and last UN-sponsored international conference on population was held in 1994 in Cairo. More than 180 nations participated, and a new programme of action for national and international action in the area of population and development was adopted. At this point, the idea that population control was a necessary component of world peace and security was largely repudiated, as were coercive means of achieving demographic goals. The claim that economic development advanced more rapidly through population plans centered on contraception, sterilization, and abortion, instead of education, promotion of infant and maternal health, as well as equal economic opportunities for men and women alike, was steadily being undermined by the evidence from three decades of population "control."[63] Notwithstanding the global experience, the

59 Wang, Gu, and Cai, "The End of China's One-Child Policy," 83–86.

60 Population Council, "United Nations Population Award to Indira Gandhi and Qian Xinzhong," *Population and Development Review* 9, no. 4 (1983): 747–753.

61 Kaiser Family Foundation, *The Mexico City Policy: An Explainer* (2017), https://www.kff.org/global-health-policy/fact-sheet/mexico-city-policy-explainer.

62 Kaiser Family Foundation, *UNFPA Funding & Kemp-Kasten: An Explainer* (May 4, 2018), https://www.kff.org/global-health-policy/fact-sheet/unfpa-funding-kemp-kasten-an-explainer. The policy and the events that lead to the Mexico City policy also resulted in passage of the Kemp-Kasten Amendment, an annual rider to the general appropriations bill, that prohibit US funding for any entity that "supports or participates in the management of a program of coercive abortion or involuntary sterilization," as determined by the president.

63 See Nicholas Eberstadt, "What You Won't Hear at Cairo," *Wall Street Journal*, Eastern ed. (September 6, 1994): A12.

United States delegation, led by President Bill Clinton's undersecretary of state for global affairs, Timothy Wirth, was firmly committed to worldwide promotion of contraception and availability of abortion.[64]

In support of their objectives, the US delegation along with delegations from Scandinavian and other Western European nations, continued to maintain that evidence from India, Sri Lanka, and Pakistan showing little economic impact from programs promoting contraception and sterilization was largely due to problems in the administration of those programs and not due to any intrinsic flaw in the strategy. These arguments were combined with three new justifications for the widespread promotion of contraception, and abortion when contraception failed: maternal health, women's empowerment, and sustainable development. Each of these justifications had been incubating in the United Nations' system for many years prior.

The idea that maternal health was dependent at least in part on the ability to avoid or terminate a pregnancy was increasingly a starting premise to any discussion of maternal health within the World Health Organization. The UN Commission on the Status of Women had been "studying" the link between family planning and the status of women since at least 1968;[65] while the concept of "sustainable development" was coming into its own as evidenced by the 1992 UN Conference on Environment and Development in Rio de Janeiro. Even if activists could not show a clear link between reduced fertility rates and economic growth, it was thought to be beyond dispute that increasing populations placed greater demands on natural resources and additional people would necessarily lead to increased environmental degradation.[66] Of course, this argument overlooked the fact that as people become more prosperous, they also consume more natural resources. The rural peasants of China's past did not produce the choking air pollution that exists in many Chinese cities today, and the sprawling farm families that lived in multigenerational households when agriculture was dominant consumed far less energy, water, and other natural resources than today's isolated urban households of one or two.[67]

In the end, a coalition of Asian, African, and Middle Eastern nations emerged, which, with the moral and rhetorical support of the Holy See, was able to defeat the worst propositions contained in the initial draft of a programme of action to emanate from the Conference. While far from ideal—for example, population "targets" continued to be recognized as a legitimate government policy—the outcome documents were far less radical than what had been presented to the delegates at the opening of the conference. "The final report now stated,

64 The machinations of the US delegation and other pro-contraception and abortion delegations at this conference is described by George Weigel in his lively and accurate, if somewhat intemperate article, "What Really Happened at Cairo," *First Things* 50 (February 1995) 24–31.

65 Final Act of the International Conference on Human Rights adopted by the International Conference on Human Rights at Teheran, United Nations, XVIII (1968): Section XVIII, 15.

66 A. de Sherbinin, D. Carr, S. Cassels, and L. Jiang, "Population and Environment," *Annual Review of Environment and Resources* 32 (November 21, 2007): 345–73.

67 Connelly, *Fatal Misconception*, 372.

unambiguously, that 'in no case should abortion be promoted as a method of family planning.'"[68] The traditional husband-wife-child form of family was the operative assumption of conference documents, and parental rights to direct the education of their children were reaffirmed. The concept of "reproductive health" was introduced as alternative and more inclusive language than "maternal and child health," but it too was defined in such a way as to exclude abortion. Overall, and in no small part due to the leadership and alliances formed by the Holy See, the Cairo documents, while far from ideal, were much more measured than what the organizers of the conference had hoped for and expected.

The Cairo conference was the last UN-sponsored worldwide conference on population, although many of the same topics are discussed and fought over at the annual meetings of the Commission of Population and Development. In some years, such as in 2017, the disagreements are so intense that no outcome document is issued at the end of the meeting. Other years, one side or the other gets the upper hand, and a document is issued that seems to create soft law implying that abortion is a legitimate form of "family planning" or, in the alternative, strictly limiting any international claim that a right to abortion exists. In short, like much of politics, the victory goes to the vigilant and persistent.

This historical review is not to provide a complete overview of international efforts to promote contraception. It is not even to provide a comprehensive discussion of the United Nations' advocacy for and distribution of pills and devices that prevent or terminate a pregnancy. Rather, this brief review illustrates the intellectual history and evolution of arguments surrounding the use of contraception, sterilization, and abortion, as tools of international ordering. Population policies were initially advanced as necessary for the maintenance of international peace and security, while simultaneously improving community composition by elimination of the "unfit." These arguments faded from public view as the coercive power of government was employed to achieve optimum fertility rates. In their place, new arguments regarding economic development and improving maternal health emerged, but these too are beginning to fade as evidence accumulates that high fertility rates are not inherent barriers to economic growth, and that increased prenatal care and delivery assistance by trained birth attendants are far more direct paths to better maternal health than hormonal contraception and abortion. This leaves only the two most recent claims advanced for comprehensive global access to contraception—women's empowerment and environmental sustainability. Both will be addressed in the following section exploring the teachings of *Humanae vitae* as a "humanely adequate" (dare I even say "sustainable") global ethic.

Humanae vitae as the Desirable Alternative

The Church was neither ignorant nor indifferent to these international efforts to interfere with couples' desires to bear and raise their children. In his important,

68 Weigel, "What Really Happened at Cairo," 25.

but deeply flawed, history of the global "population movement," *Fatal Misconception: The Struggle to Control World Population*, Matthew Connelly, professor of international history at Columbia University, characterizes the Church as "the most powerful force opposed to birth control and abortion worldwide,"[69] and on this point, he is correct. In 1930, Pope Pius XI promulgated his encyclical on Christian marriage, *Casti connubii*, carefully responding to arguments justifying the use of contraception within marriage, specifically addressing concerns about families living in extreme poverty and cases where pregnancy may threaten a woman's health.[70] In the 1940s, the Church was active in the drafting and promotion of the Universal Declaration of Human Rights, proclaimed as the aspirations of all nations by the United Nations General Assembly in 1948.[71] This document recognized the family as the fundamental unit of society, as well as the right of men and women to marry and found a family.[72] This language would seem a sure defense against the global designs of the population controllers and governments seeking to use coercion in the most intimate and personal decision a couple makes. But alas, this confidence proved to be misplaced as evidenced by the bestowal of the first UN Population Award to representatives of India and China, notwithstanding the fact that the two regimes had instituted the most shocking and coercive population policies since the close of World War II, when Nazi eugenic practices were uncovered.

The Holy See was not idle in the years between the proclamation of the Universal Declaration of Human Rights and the 1983 Population Award. As noted earlier in this essay, within three years of the FDA's approval of hormonal contraception, John XXIII established the Pontifical Commission for the Study of Population, Family and Births in 1963.[73] Five years later, after receiving both the majority and minority reports of the Pontifical Commission, Paul VI promulgated *Humanae vitae*, affirming the right of married couples to determine the number, spacing, and timing of children through periodic sexual abstinence, while remaining steadfastly opposed to the use of contraception.

This teaching was received by the faithful and Church hierarchy with varying degrees of enthusiasm, and on occasion, with outright rejection. A collection of statements from Church officials and theologians in a 1968 New Yorker magazine article, "Letter from Vatican City" illustrates this point.[74] Acceptance of the encyclical is evidenced by Cardinal Richard Cushing of Boston, who stated simply "Rome has spoken"; Cardinal James Francis McIntyre of Los

69 Connelly, *Fatal Misconception*, 14. Unfortunately, the major flaw in his work is his persistent misrepresentation of both the Church teaching on contraception and his unsubstantiated claim of illicit motives to that teaching was motivated by misogyny. See *Fatal Misconception*, 377.

70 Pope Pius XI, Encyclical Letter *Casti connubii* (December 31, 1930), 43–54, https://w2.vatican.va/content/pius-xi/en/encyclicals.index.html.

71 Glendon "Knowing the Universal Declaration of Human Rights," 1153.

72 *Universal Declaration of Human Rights*, art. 16, http://www.un.org/en/universal-declaration-human-rights.

73 See note 54 above.

74 Xavier Rynne, "Letter from Vatican City," *The New Yorker* XLIV (November 2, 1968): 131–147.

Angeles characterized the teaching as "refreshing"; while Archbishop Terence Cooke of New York showed humble obedience, "'Thou art Peter. Where Peter is, there is the Church.' . . . Be assured of our prayerful pastoral efforts in fulfilling this urgent responsibility." Archbishop John Murphy of Cardiff, Wales, was perhaps the most enthusiastic, "It will be hailed as the Magna Carta not merely of all women but of all men and all children."[75] Of the opposite opinion are Archbishop Denis Hurley of Durban, South Africa, "Acceptance [of the encyclical] is one of the most painful experiences of my life as a bishop" and Father Hans Küng, of Tübingen University in Germany, "The encyclical is not only not infallible, it is wrong."[76]

The dissenting clergy often echoed many of the secular arguments of the population controllers and their intellectual successors, "reproductive rights" activists. Their arguments included: denying married couples the right to employ the most reliable methods of preventing pregnancy was irresponsible and, in some cases, cruel given the personal and communal threats posed by extreme poverty or overpopulation; Natural Family Planning (NFP) failed more often than not; the sexual discipline required by NFP was unrealistic; NFP required the cooperation of husbands, who too often undervalued the health and well-being of their wives; and finally, denying couples the right to personally decide among the various methods of birth control denied their moral agency and infantilized the faithful. This litany, while incomplete, shows that neither Church officials nor theologians were immune to the cultural currents of the time.

What the record has subsequently shown is that most of these arguments were wrong and that the teaching of *Humanae vitae* and its theological progeny were, and are, correct. NFP is, in fact, the most responsible response to the challenges posed by a burgeoning world population—dramatic disparities in nations' economic development, abuse of our natural and human ecology, and a sinful failure to respect the unique gifts of women, accompanied by a debased conception of manhood.

Natural Family Planning and The Environment

Earlier in this essay, I noted the mounting body of evidence that population growth, while a factor, is not a consistent barrier to economic development, and in fact can propel it. I now turn to the growing body of evidence that NFP as an approach to family planning is the most protective of our natural environment.

"Teaching and Learning for a Sustainable Future," a multimedia teacher education program developed by the United Nations Educational, Scientific and Cultural Organization (UNESCO), contains a startling admission. Activity 4 of Module 13 is titled "A New Understanding of Population and Development," with the introductory paragraph captioned "Overpopulation: A Misguided Concern":

75 Rynne, "Letter from Vatican City," 138.

76 Rynne, "Letter from Vatican City," 140.

> From the 1950s onwards, some observers of development and environmental issues in developing countries concluded that rapid population growth or overpopulation was the underlying problem, and lower fertility the obvious answer. The urgency of the situation seemed to demand urgent programmes to promote contraception. *The analysis was mistaken and the strategy based on it was misguided.*[77]

The authors go on to observe that this mistaken analysis "laid stress on population numbers; the result was that numbers, rather than people, tended to become the object of population programmes." This, of course, was the central argument made by Paul VI in *Humanae vitae*—that a contraceptive mentality fails to place the well-being of the person at the center of each marital act.

The UNESCO module goes on to explain that human impact on the environment is not a straight-line correlation with the size of the population. Large populations do not invariably equal environmental degradation, nor do small populations invariably result in pristine environments. Rather, impact is determined by a combination of many factors, including but not limited to population, consumption, and technology, which in turn are determined by "gender issues, levels of inequality and poverty, freedom of markets, democracy, and rules about the use of commons like the oceans and atmosphere."[78] The significance of "[t]he new understanding on population and development is [that the international community now is] concerned first and foremost with impact on people, especially women, poor families and poor communities. Poverty, poor health, high fertility, inequality and lack of development opportunities for women intensify many types of environmental problems—and vice versa."[79]

Parts of this passage could have been written by Paul VI,[80] or any of his successors including Pope Francis. For example, in the recent encyclical, *Laudato si'*, Francis observes:

> Instead of resolving the problems of the poor and thinking of how the world can be different, some can only propose a reduction in the birth rate. At times, developing countries face forms of international pressure

77 UNESCO, T*eaching and Learning for a Sustainable Future* (2010), http://www.unesco.org/education/tlsf/mods/theme_c/popups/mod13t04s01.html; emphasis added.

78 UNESCO, *Teaching and Learning for a Sustainable Future* (2010), emphasis added.

79 UNESCO, *Teaching and Learning for a Sustainable Future* (2010), emphasis added.

80 See Pope Paul VI, Apostolic Letter *Octogesima adveniens* (May 14, 1971), 21, http://w2.vatican.va/content/paul-vi/en/apost_letters.index.3.html:

> Man is suddenly becoming aware that by an ill-considered exploitation of nature he risks destroying it and becoming in his turn the victim of this degradation. Not only is the material environment becoming a permanent menace—pollution and refuse, new illness and absolute destructive capacity—but the human framework is no longer under man's control, thus creating an environment for tomorrow which may well be intolerable. This is a wide-ranging social problem which concerns the entire human family.

See also Pope Paul VI, *Visit of Pope Paul VI to the FAO [Food and Agriculture Organization of the UN] on the 25th Anniversary of its Institution* (November 16, 1970), http://w2.vatican.va/content/paul-vi/en/speeches /1970.index.3.html.

> which make economic assistance contingent on certain policies of "reproductive health". Yet "while it is true that an unequal distribution of the population and of available resources creates obstacles to development and a sustainable use of the environment, it must nonetheless be recognized that demographic growth is fully compatible with an integral and shared development". To blame population growth instead of extreme and selective consumerism on the part of some, is one way of refusing to face the issues. It is an attempt to legitimize the present model of distribution, where a minority believes that it has the right to consume in a way which can never be universalized, since the planet could not even contain the waste products of such consumption.[81]

We see the Church's continued witness to the truth—neither the problem of poverty nor environmental degradation can be solved by putative "human rights" to artificial birth control, sterilization, or abortion.

And in fact, there is an increasing body of evidence that artificial birth control may exacerbate both poverty and environmental degradation. In the developing world where family is the only social "safety net" for the poor, the elimination of children often portends the absence of care and support during times of economic distress, illness, and old age. Even in the wealthy nations of the developed world where economic poverty is rarely life-threatening, we are discovering the absence of children and other family members results in acute social isolation and neglect of the elderly.

Simultaneously, we are learning that all means of birth control, other than the methods of NFP, contribute to environmental degradation to varying degrees. There is a growing body of evidence that women's use of hormonal contraception is unintentionally altering the aquatic environment of streams and rivers through the introduction of synthetic estrogen hormones into wastewater through a pill-user's urine. This, in turn, appears to reduce the fertility of fish and frogs, aquatic animals that have hormone receptors similar to humans. Of even greater concern is the possibility that in some locations, this unnecessary hormonal waste may be seeping into drinking water due to inadequate filtering technology, leading to lower sperm counts and greater susceptibility to prostate cancer in men.[82]

Condoms also pose environmental problems. Just last year, officials at the UNFPA noted that "male condoms remained UNFPA's least environmentally sustainable product due the quantities of water, chemicals and raw material

81 Pope Francis, Encyclical Letter *Laudato si'* (May 24, 2015), 50, http://w2.vatican.va/content/francesco/en/encyclicals.index.html.

82 Some of this research is summarized in a 2012 article in *Zenit* by Rebecca Oas, "Contraceptives and the Environment: What the Pill Is Doing to Our Water Supply" (May 16, 2012), https://zenit.org/articles/contraceptives-and-the-environment. A more complete review is provided in Albert Onzima, Gabriel Nuffield Kasozi, and Derek Muir, "Estrogenic Compounds in the Waste Water and Drinking Water Sources in Kampala, Uganda" (January 2016), at https://www.researchgate.net/publication/291350197_Estrogenic_compounds_in_the_waste_water_and_drinking_water_sources_in_Kampala_Uganda.

required for their production. Condoms also have a large environmental footprint due to the type and amount of resources used for packaging and shipping."[83] In addition to threats posed by the manufacturing and packaging of condoms, the environment suffers from the disposal of condoms. A 2014 article on "eco-friendly birth control" cites a study that reported "during a 2009 international coastal cleanup initiative, volunteers removed over 26,000 condoms worldwide. When they're in the ocean, condoms can cause problems for marine life, especially if they're ingested."[84] The adverse environmental impact of contraceptive disposal generally has been sufficiently established that in 2013 the UNFPA issued a guidance document entitled *Safe Disposal and Management of Unused and Unwanted Contraceptives*.[85]

None of these problems arise with the use of fertility awareness-based methods (namely, NFP). Yet, when this point is raised with advocates for contraception, the invariable response is that any adverse environmental impact of contraception, no matter the size, is outweighed by the adverse impact from the birth of another human being. And so, we return to the fundamental dispute between the Church and those who demand the world embrace contraception as a great good for humanity: Is public policy to be directed to the welcoming and flourishing of every human being, or is it to be directed to the benefit and pleasure of the present generation and, more particularly, members of this generation living in affluent societies? Between these two options, it is clear what justice requires.

Natural Family Planning and the "Liberation" of Women

As evidenced by my earlier outline of efforts to advance a global population policy, the dominant contemporary justification for widespread acceptance of contraception is a claim that sexual equality cannot be achieved without the suppression of human fertility, and most commonly, the suppression of women's fertility. This claim has been disproven, although at times awkwardly and unevenly, throughout Church history. As Sister Prudence Allen so masterfully demonstrates in her multivolume work, *The Concept of Woman*, the very idea of sexual equality is subject to a multitude of definitions and is deeply contested.[86] Does equality mean sameness or does it recognize and accommodate innate sexual differences, while affirming the equal dignity and value of both sexes? The Church resolutely defends the latter.

83 UNFPA, *Greening the Blue: Environmentally Friendly Male Condoms* (2017), http://www.greeningtheblue.org/news/unfpa-environmentally-friendly-male-condoms.

84 Alexandra Ossola, "Your Guide to Eco-friendly Birth Control," *Popular Science* (January 3, 2014), https://www.popsci.com/blog-network/ladybits/your-guide-eco-friendly-birth-control.

85 UNFPA, "Safe Disposal and Management of Unused, Unwanted Contraceptives" (2013), https://www.unfpa.org/sites/default/files/resource-pdf/Safe%20Disposal%20and%20Management%20of%20Unused%20Unwanted%20Contraceptives_2.pdf.

86 For readers wanting a brief introduction to Sr. Allen's work, see "Man-Woman Complementarity: The Catholic Inspiration," *Logos: A Journal of Catholic Thought and Culture* 9, no. 3 (2006): 87–108.

Without doubt, equality should be of central (but not exclusive) concern in any discussion of political rights. For example, the ability to participate in elections and seek public office should not be reserved to one sex alone. As John Paul II observed in his 1995 World Day of Peace message, "The growing presence of women in social, economic and political life at the local, national and international levels is thus a very positive development. Women have a full right to become actively involved in all areas of public life, and this right must be affirmed and guaranteed, also, where necessary, through appropriate legislation."[87] However, discerning the demands of equality when addressing questions that arise in the context of marriage, family, and human sexuality is far more difficult, particularly when trying to derive some legal principle or policy prescriptive from those demands.

Robert Rodes has written on how American law historically promoted chastity by means now thought repressive, but which, in fact, protected women, restrained men, and promoted the common good.[88] Among the examples he discusses are laws prohibiting fornication, adultery, pornography, and contraception. In his discussion of contraception, Rodes notes that *Griswold v. Connecticut* rested on the principle that the government had no authority to intervene in the private decisions of husbands and wives regarding sexual matters. The Church has little quarrel with this principle. *Eisenstadt v. Baird* extended this protection from government interference to sex by unmarried couples, a situation presenting much more complex public policy questions given the potential consequences of unmarried sexual intercourse—children and women abandoned by men who claim they are immune from responsibility since they did not consent to the creation of a child, and men deprived of access to their children by women who no longer wish to associate with the men. Justice William Brennan's argument in *Eisenstadt* was that, although it is desirable to deter nonmarital sex, using threat of pregnancy as a deterrent was much worse than permitting contracepted sex since the harm arising from the actions of those who were undeterred was an unwanted child and possibly an abandoned mother or excluded father. In the evaluation of each individual act, this reasoning seems persuasive, but after almost fifty years of lived experience with this standard, it is easy to see that Justice Brennan undervalued the deterrent effect of limiting access to contraception, as well as the pedagogical function of the law.

Courts and legislatures throughout the world followed the lead of the American court in decoupling sex and marriage, and we are now struggling with the aftermath—fatherless children, declining marriage rates, and elevated divorce statistics; skyrocketing rates of sexually transmitted disease and infections matched only by the rapidly increasing instances of sexual abuse and harassment; and widening income inequality between those who marry and those who

87 Pope John Paul II, *Message of His Holiness Pope John Paul II for the XXVIII World Day of Peace* (January 1, 1995), 9, http://w2.vatican.va/content/john-paul-ii/en/messages/peace.index.html.

88 Robert E. Rodes, "On Law and Chastity," *Notre Dame Law Review* 76, no. 2 (2001): 643.

cohabit or embrace other domestic arrangements.[89] Of course, Paul VI foretold many of the ill effects of widespread recourse to artificial contraception when he wrote that the use of artificial birth control "could open wide the way for marital infidelity and a general lowering of moral standards," and reduce women to mere instruments of male sexual satisfaction.[90]

It is interesting to note that only a few years prior to the promulgation of *Humanae vitae* in 1959, Dr. Alan Guttmacher, soon to be president of Planned Parenthood Federation[91] and a colleague of Margaret Sanger, published a survey of available contraceptive methods:

> If there were an infallible, simple, effortless method to pinpoint the hour of ovulation and one could make sure that the patient in question never ovulated more than once a month, the rhythm technique would immediately become the world's ideal contraceptive.[92]

The article does not explain why, if reliable in preventing pregnancy "the rhythm technique would immediately become the world's ideal contraceptive," but based on the authors' critique of other methods, we can speculate. Coitus interruptus is criticized as sexually unsatisfactory and "unsafe," although the authors appear to mean unreliable in preventing pregnancy. Post-coital douche is also rejected as unreliable. IUDs as they were available in the 1950s were described as "thoroughly condemned because of their ineffectiveness, their potential source for infection and irritation, as well as their carcinogenetic potentialities."[93] The devices were also believed to "function by causing very early abortions soon after the egg implants."[94] Condoms dulled men's sensation, were subject to leakage, and inhibited male sexual pleasure in some cases due to premarital experience with their use. Diaphragms were likely to be ill-fitted and required women insert them prior to sex-play and intercourse, an unlikely exercise at the end of a particularly tiring day. Over-the-counter contraceptive cream or jelly had only recently become available, so the authors could provide no clear evaluation of its

89 A detailed study of the American experience is provided in Charles Murray, *Coming Apart: The State of White America, 1960–2010*.

90 Pope Paul VI, *Humanae vitae*, 17.

91 In 1961, Dr. Guttmacher would assume leadership of Planned Parenthood Federation, and in 1964, he became chairman of the Medical Committee of the International Planned Parenthood Federation. Guttmacher also served in various leadership capacities of the Human Betterment Association of America, an association committed to advancing eugenic laws in the states. See Angela Franks, *Margaret Sanger's Eugenic Legacy: The Control of Female Fertility* (Jefferson, N.C.: MacFarland & Co., Inc., 2005), 55. The Guttmacher Institute, a leading research and policy organization committed to advancing use of contraception and access to abortion in the United States and globally, is named after him. Guttmacher Institute, Guttmacher Institute Strategic Plan 2016–2020 (2016), https://www.guttmacher.org/report/guttmacher-institute-strategic-plan-2016-2020.

92 Hilliard Dubrow and Alan F. Guttmacher, "The Present Status of Contraception," *Journal of the Mount Sinai Hospital, New York* 26, no. 2 (1959): 122–123.

93 Dubrow and Guttmacher, "The Present Status of Contraception," 119.

94 Dubrow and Guttmacher, "The Present Status of Contraception," 119.

merits. Vaginal suppositories had a relatively high pregnancy rate and required refrigeration in some climates. Cervical caps were difficult to fit, and patients often had difficulty applying and removing them.[95]

Some of these methods are no longer recommended or practiced, but many remain part of the contraceptive assortment available today and remain subject to most of the same complaints. It is little wonder that the an effective natural "rhythm technique" was identified as the ideal. The major reservation Guttmacher and his colleague expressed was the method's reliability, since at that time, the Rhythm Method had a pregnancy rate of 14 per one hundred years of coital exposure.[96] Today, the World Health Organization reports that the Symptom-Thermal Method (STM) of periodic sexual abstinence as commonly used is 98% effective in preventing pregnancy, which is 6% more effective than combined oral contraceptives (or "the pill") as commonly used.[97] Given this fact, effectiveness alone should make NFP the family planning methods of choice.

More importantly, as many others have noted, unlike all other methods of family planning, NFP is "cooperative." Each NFP method requires the engagement of both partners and therefore are less likely to be the method of choice when lust or domination factors into the sexual relationship. NFP encourages communication and development of multiple ways to show love and affection beyond the gift of marital intercourse. Finally, rather than infantilizing the laity as some theologians claimed after the promulgation of the *Humanae vitae*, NFP respects the couple's moral agency and capacity for mutual restraint. As currently taught and practiced, it is as Dubrow and Guttmacher said in 1958, probably the "world's ideal" approach to, and might I add "authentic" family planning.[98]

Conclusion

I have attempted to trace the development of the United Nations' commitment to contraception as a guarantor of world peace, an engine of economic development, a guardian of the natural environment, and an equalizer of men and women. Unfortunately, as UNESCO notes in its instruction regarding the connection between population and development, such analysis is mistaken and the policies misguided.

Only the methods of Natural Family Planning place the person at the heart of a couple's decisions about sex and childbearing. Only NFP instills the virtues of mutual restraint, communication, commitment, and respect—virtues that are instrumental to achieve the very goals that advocates of contraception desire.

95 Dubrow and Guttmacher, "The Present Status of Contraception," 119–123.

96 Condoms were reported to have a pregnancy rate of 6 to 16; the diaphragm ranged from 3.3 for constant use to 9.7 for irregular use; suppositories pregnancy rates ranged from 22 to 27; and cervical caps properly fitted produced a pregnancy rate of 8.

97 World Health Organization, Family planning/Contraception Fact Sheet (2018) 3, 7, at http://www.who.int/mediacentre/factsheets/fs351/en.

98 See Dubrow and Guttmacher, "The Present Status of Contraception," 123. And I would note, the methods of NFP are ideal as an intervention for couples who struggle to conceive.

World peace, economic development, protection of the environment, and authentic sexual equality require each of these virtues, both individually and communally.

It is no surprise that the teaching of *Humanae vitae* is despised and rejected by some (unfortunately, this is often the way with all truth). What could be surprising to those who do not share Catholic belief in divine guidance of the Church, is that one man, Paul VI, was wise enough to see the truth about marriage, sex, and procreation, and brave enough to proclaim it at a time when virtually the entire world was saying otherwise.

TABLE 14-1—Timeline of Family Planning and Population Control Movement

1927	The World Population Conference in Geneva is organized by Margaret Sanger.
1930	At the Lambeth Conference, the Anglican bishops pass Resolution 15 permitting the use of contraception "for serious reasons" within marriage.[99]
	Pius XI promulgates his papal encyclical, *Casti connubii*, reaffirming Catholic teaching on the purpose and nature of marriage, marital intercourse, and the immorality of contraception.[100]
1952	India adopts its first national population policy.[101]
	The International Planned Parenthood[102] and Population Council are created.
1954	The UN sponsors the first World Population Conference in Rome focused on scientific determination of world population given population variables, their determinants, and their consequences.
1959	In a comprehensive review of the state of available contraception, Alan Guttmacher, then Obstetrician and Gynecologist-In-Chief at Mount Sinai Hospital in New York, observes "If there were an infallible, simple, effortless method to pinpoint the hour of ovulation and one could make

99 The full text of the resolution states:

> Where there is [a] clearly felt moral obligation to limit or avoid parenthood, the method must be decided on Christian principles. The primary and obvious method is complete abstinence from intercourse (as far as may be necessary) in a life of discipline and self-control lived in the power of the Holy Spirit. Nevertheless in those cases where there is such a clearly felt moral obligation to limit or avoid parenthood, and where there is a morally sound reason for avoiding complete abstinence, the Conference agrees that other methods may be used, provided that this is done in the light of the same Christian principles. The Conference records its strong condemnation of the use of any methods of conception control from motives of selfishness, luxury, or mere convenience. See http://www.anglicancommunion.org/media/127734/1930.pdf

100 Pope Pius XI, *Casti connubii*, https://w2.vatican.va/content/pius-xi/en/encyclicals.index.html.

101 Warren C. Robinson and John A. Ross, eds., *The Global Family Planning Revolution: Three Decades of Population Policies and Programs* (Washington D.C.: World Bank, 2007), 2.

102 Donald T. Critchlow, *Intended Consequences: Birth Control, Abortion, and the Federal Government in Modern America* (New York: Oxford University Press, 1999), 31.

sure that the patient in question never ovulated more than once a month, the rhythm technique would immediately become the world's ideal contraceptive."[103] Three years later, Guttmacher would assume leadership of Planned Parenthood Federation, and in 1964 he became chairman of the Medical Committee of the International Planned Parenthood Federation.

1960 *Excerpta Medica* publishes a summary of a Japanese article discussing the utilization of IUDs in Japan in 32 different patterns, by 20,000 women, more than twenty years of usage, with few adverse long-term effects.[104]

The FDA announces its approval of Enovid as a hormonal birth control pill (almost half a million American women are already taking it as treatment for menstrual disorders and infertility).

1962 The Swedish government becomes the first nation to provide development aid in support of early family planning efforts in Ceylon (now Sri Lanka), India, and Pakistan.[105]

1963 The Pontifical Commission for the Study of Population, Family and Births is established by John XXIII to study the questions of population, birth control, and their effects on the family. The commission originally includes only six professionals but ultimately grows to include seventy members, including scientists, theologians, married couples, physicians, bishops, and cardinals.[106]

1965 The Second World Population Conference is held in Belgrade organized by the UN International Union for the Scientific Study of Population (IUSSP) and International Planned Parenthood Federation, with the topic of analysis of fertility as part of a policy for development planning. "This Conference was held at a time when expert studies on the population aspects of development coincided with the start-up of population programmes subsidized by the United States Agency for International Development (USAID)."[107]

During his State of the Union Address, President Lyndon B. Johnson declares the federal government would "seek new ways to use our knowledge to deal with the explosion in world population and the growing scarcity of world resources."[108]

103 Hilliard Dubrow and Alan F. Guttmacher, "The Present Status of Contraception," *Journal of the Mount Sinai Hospital, New York* 26, no. 2 (1959): 118.

104 Lazar Margulies, "History of Intrauterine Devices," *Bulletin of the New York Academy of Medicine* 51, no. 5 (June 1975): 662–667.

105 Robinson and Ross, *The Global Family Planning Revolution*, 3.

106 Richard J. Fehring, "An Analysis of the Majority Report 'Responsible Parenthood' and its Recommendations on Abortion, Sterilization, and Contraception," *Life and Learning* 13 (2003): 122.

107 United Nations, "Outcomes on Population," World Population Conference, Belgrade, August 30–September 10, 1965, http://www.un.org/en/development/devagenda/population.shtml.

108 Lyndon B. Johnson, "Annual Message to the Congress on the State of the Union," January 4, 1965, online by Gerhard Peters and John T. Woolley, The American Presidency Project, http://www.presidency.ucsb.edu/ws/?pid=26907.

1966 The Administrator of US Food for Peace Program "announced at a Planned Parenthood conference that the United States would insist that foreign governments 'give evidence of policies that would assure balance between food production and population growth.'"[109]

The US government conditions food aid to India on its adoption of a package of liberal reforms favoring private enterprise and foreign investment, as well as implementation of a national plan to limit population growth.[110]

1967 President Lyndon Johnson joins thirty heads of state who sign and present to UN Secretary General U Thant a Declaration on Population, saying they believe "the opportunity to decide the number and spacing of children is a basic human right."[111]

1968 Paul VI issues his encyclical *Humanae vitae*, which discusses the nature of married love and responsible parenthood, affirms the moral prohibition of contraception, and affirms the natural methods of family planning.

The International Conference on Human Rights is held in Teheran to review the progress made in the twenty years since the adoption of the Universal Declaration of Human Rights. Section XVIIII of the Final Declaration is dedicated to the "human rights aspects of family planning." It notes that the Commission on the Status of Women "has begun to study the relations of family planning to the status of women" and expressly embraces the idea that population control is a precondition to development. "[T]he the present rapid rate of population growth in some areas of the world hampers the struggle against hunger and poverty, and in particular reduces the possibilities of rapidly achieving adequate standards of living ."[112]

"The Population Bomb" is published by Stanford University Professor Paul R. Ehrlich, warning of mass starvation in the 1970s due to overpopulation, arguing that there were few immediate actions that could forestall the disaster in most of the world.

USAID begins purchasing contraceptives to distribute in developing countries.[113]

109 Robert Marshall and Charles Donovan, *Blessed are the Barren* (San Francisco: Ignatius Press, 1991), 38.

110 Marshall and Donovan, *Blessed are the Barren*, 38.

111 Susan Yoshihara, "Lost in Translation: The Failure of the International Reproductive Rights Norm," *Ave Maria Law Review* 11, no. 2 (Spring 2013): 371–72.

112 *Final Act of the International Conference on Human Rights*, adopted by the International Conference on Human Rights at Teheran, UN, XVIII (1968), http://legal.un.org/avl/pdf/ha/fatchr/Final_Act_of_TehranConf.pdf

113 Kaiser Family Foundation, *The U.S. Government and International Family Planning & Reproductive Health Efforts* (2017), https://www.kff.org/global-health-policy/fact-sheet/the-u-s-government-and-international-family-planning-reproductive-health-efforts.

Robert McNamara, as president of World Bank, announces that population control will be an element of review of loans.[114]

1974 The World Population Conference is held in Bucharest sponsored by the United Nations. This is the first conference that focuses on population policy and is attended by representatives of 135 countries. "The outcome of the Conference, the World Population Plan of Action, states, among other principles, that the essential aim is the social, economic and cultural development of countries, that population variables and development are interdependent and that population policies and objectives are an integral part (constituent elements) of socio-economic development policies."[115]

1976 India announces a National Population Policy (NPP) that includes enormously enlarged targets for family planning (including sterilizations), permits states to enact compulsory sterilization laws, increases monetary incentives for family planning "acceptors," and disincentives for large families. This results in the performance of over ten million sterilizations in the twenty months the policy was in effect.[116]

1979 The UN Convention on the Elimination of All Forms of Discrimination against Women (CEDAW) is the first binding international treaty in which "family planning" was mentioned, and it was in the context of nondiscrimination, not in creating a right.

China adopts the one-child policy, known as the Family Planning Policy.

1981 The UN General Assembly adopts a resolution on the "Establishment of the United Nations Population Award," an annual award "to an individual, to individuals or to an institution for the most outstanding contribution to the awareness of population questions or to their solutions."[117]

Pope John Paul II issues his apostolic exhortation, *Familiaris consortio*, which discusses the role of the Christian family in the modern world, affirms moral prohibition of contraception, and supports Natural Family Planning methods.

1983 The first UN Population Award is given to Indira Gandhi, prime minister of India, and Qian Xinzhong, minister-in-charge of the State Family Planning Commission of the People's Republic of China.

114 Andrew M. Essig, "The World Bank: How it Compromises Economic Development by Promoting a Population Control Agenda," *White Paper Series* no. 7 (New York: International Organizations Research Group, 2007). John F. May, a lead demographer at the World Bank, notes that "after the publication of the *1984 World Development Report* (WDR) devoted to population issues, the Bank did not push the population agenda as forcefully." John F. May, *World Population Policies: Their Origins, Evolution, and Impact* (New York: Springer, 2012), 103.

115 United Nations, "Outcomes on Population," http://www.un.org/en/development/devagenda/population.shtml.

116 Lewis M. Simons, "Compulsory Sterilization Provokes Fear, Contempt," *Washington Post* (July 4, 1977).

117 United Nations Population Fund, Information Note on the United Nations Population Award (2017), https://www.unfpa.org/resources/information-note-united-nations-population-award.

Steven Mosher publishes *The Broken Earth: The Rural Chinese*, exposing the widespread use of force abortion as part of the family planning policy in China.

China records an estimated 21 million births, 14.4 million abortions, 20.7 million sterilizations (predominantly female), and 17.8 million IUD insertions. A large proportion of these procedures were involuntary.[118]

1984 Pope John Paul II writes a letter to Dr. Rafael M. Salas, secretary-general of the 1984 International Conference on Population and Executive Director of the United Nations Fund for Population Activities; the pope notes that development should extend beyond mere material benefits and include consideration of the spiritual development of the family and individuals.[119]

The UN International Conference on Population is held at Mexico City. The Reagan Administration announces US neutrality as far as population growth and opposition to abortion as means of family planning.

1985 The Kemp-Kasten Amendment prohibits US funding for any entity that "supports or participates in the management of a program of coercive abortion or involuntary sterilization," as determined by the president.[120]

1987 Pope John Paul II issues his encyclical *Solicitudo rei socialis*, which repudiates population "control" as a concept.

1988 Pope John Paul II issues *Mulieris dignitatem*, an apostolic letter that discusses the dignity and vocation of women.

1992 The UN Conference on Environment and Development in Rio de Janeiro introduces the concept of "Demographic Dynamics and Sustainability." "[P]olicies should be designed to address the consequences of population growth built into population momentum, while at the same time incorporating measures to bring about demographic transition."[121] Thus population control, a concept that had been sullied by the coercive government

118 Feng, W., Gu, B. and Cai, Y. "The End of China's One-Child Policy," *Studies in Family Planning* 47 (2016): 83–86.

119 Pope John Paul II, *Message of Pope John Paul II to Rafael M. Salas, Secretary General of the 1984 International Conference on Population* (June 7, 1984), http://w2.vatican.va/content/john-paul-ii/en/letters/1984.index.html.

120 Starting with Ronald Reagan, every Republican administration (including that of President Trump) has used the provision to defund the United Nations Population Fund (UNFPA) for supporting coercion in China. See Human Life Action, *2017 Legislative Report* Sec. 11, https://www.humanlifeaction.org/field-collection/field-report-section/445. For a critical view of the funding cut, see Sneha Barot, "Governmental Coercion in Reproductive Decision Making: Seeing it Both Ways," *Guttmacher Policy Review* 15 no. 4 (2012): 7, 15, https://www.guttmacher.org/gpr/2012/10/governmental-coercion-reproductive-decision-making-see-it-both-ways.

121 *Report of the United Nations Conference on Environment and Development*, prepared by United Nations Division for Sustainable Development, United Nations (1992), http://sedac.ciesin.columbia.edu/entri/texts/a21/a21-05-demographics.html.

programs, is incorporated into the idea of "sustainable development" while avoiding negative implications of Western imperialism and coercion.[122]

1994 Pope John Paul II issues his letter to Mrs. Nafis Sadik, secretary-general of the 1994 International Conference on Population and Development and executive director of the United Nations Population Fund, noting that "In defense of the human person, the Church stands opposed to the imposition of limits on family size, and to the promotion of methods of limiting births which separate the unitive and procreative dimensions of marital intercourse, which are contrary to the moral law inscribed on the human heart, or which constitute an assault on the sacredness of life. Thus, sterilization, which is more and more promoted as a method of family planning, because of its finality and its potential for the violation of human rights, especially of women, is clearly unacceptable; it poses a most grave threat to human dignity and liberty when promoted as part of a population policy. Abortion, which destroys existing human life, is a heinous evil, and it is never an acceptable method of family planning, as was recognized by consensus at the Mexico City United Nations International Conference on Population (1984)."[123]

The International Conference on Population and Development at Cairo Program of Action explicitly calls for dropping demographic and family planning program targets in favor of a broader policy agenda that includes a range of reproductive health measures, including family planning, as well as a series of social and economic policy measures designed to achieve sustainable development and empower women and to strengthen their rights. "[A]ccess to and promotion of contraceptives became the measure advocated both for the empowerment of women and also as a necessity if population growth is to slow and eventually stop."[124]

1995 Pope John Paul II issues the 1995 World Day of Peace message with the theme of "Women: Teachers of Peace."[125]

122 Maria Sophia Aguirre and Cecilia A. Hadley, "Hindered Growth: The Ideology and Implications of Population Assistance," *International Journal of Social Economics* 32, no. 9 (September 2005): 783–813.

123 Pope John Paul II, *Letter of His Holiness Pope John Paul II to the Secretary General of the International Conference on Population and Development* (March 18, 1994), http://w2.vatican.va/content/john-paul-ii/en/letters/1994.index.2.html.

124 Aguirre and Hadley, "Hindered Growth," 787. A United Nations website summarizes the resulting Programme of Action as "a guide for national and international action in population and development for the next 20 years" which "places emphasis on the indissoluble relationship between population and development and focuses on meeting the needs of individuals within the framework of universally recognized Human Rights standards instead of merely meeting demographic goals." United Nations, Key Conference "Outcomes on Population," United Nations, at http://www.un.org/en/development/devagenda/population.shtml.

125 Pope John Paul II, *Women: Teachers of Peace.* Message for World Day of Peace (January 1, 1995), at http://w2.vatican.va/content/john-paul-ii/en/messages/peace.index.html.

Pope John Paul II issues his letter of welcome to Gertrude Mongella, secretary-general of the Fourth World Conference on Women of the United Nations upon her visit to the Holy See.[126]

Pope John Paul II issues his Letter to Women "on the eve of" the Fourth World Conference on Women in Beijing.[127]

Pope John Paul II addresses members of the Delegation of the Holy See to the Fourth World Conference on Women emphasizing the Church's commitment to a concerted and priority strategy directed to girls and young women, especially to the poorest, in education and care.[128]

Mary Ann Glendon, appointed by Pope John Paul II as the first woman to head a Holy See delegation, addresses the 4th UN Conference on Women in Beijing.

2000 The UN General Assembly adopts the Millennium Declaration containing eight Millennium Development Goals, the fifth being to improve maternal health. This is to be achieved by "a reduction in maternal mortality by one half of the 1990 levels by the year 2000 and a further one half by 2015." As adopted by the General Assembly, the goal does not include any mention of population growth or reproductive health or family planning.

2007 Family planning, a controversial target rejected by Member States in the negotiations of the MDGs, is added as indicator MDG 5b in the annex of a report by the UN secretary-general.

2010 The United Nations General Assembly establishes UN Women, a super-agency that encompasses four previously existing UN entities: the Division for the Advancement of Women, the International Research and Training Institute for the Advancement of Women, the Office of the Special Adviser on Gender Issues and Advancement of Women, and the United Nations Development Fund for Women.

2015 The US government, the fourth largest voluntary donor to the UNFPA, gives $75 million.

2017 US federal funding to UNFPA is diverted to US State Department's Global Health Programs funding programs that do not promote or provide abortion.[129]

126 Pope John Paul II, *Letter of His Holiness Pope John Paul II to Mrs. Gertrude Mongella Secretary General of the Fourth World Conference on Women of the United Nations* (1995), at http://w2.vatican.va/content/john-paul-ii/en/letters/1995.index.2.html.

127 Pope John Paul II, *Letter to Women* (June 29, 1995), http://w2.vatican.va/content/john-paul-ii/en/letters/1995.index.1.html.

128 Pope John Paul II, *Address of His Holiness Pope John Paul II to Members of the Delegation of the Holy See to the Fourth World Conference on Women* (August 29, 1995), http://w2.vatican.va/content/john-paul-ii/en/speeches/1995/august.index.html.

129 See Human Life Action, *2017 Legislative Reports*, Sec. 9, https://www.humanlifeaction.org/legislative-reports/439.

15

Contraception

US Law and Messaging

Helen M. Alvaré

TECHNOLOGY, CULTURE, AND SOCIAL MORES have all played significant roles in connection with the use, promotion, and effects of contraception in the United States. What is less clearly understood is how the law has also played an outsize role. By means of statutes, regulations, and cases, the law has "spoken," explicitly and implicitly, about the meaning of sex and marriage, norms of male/female relations, and the value of different categories of children—especially rich as distinguished from poor, planned as distinguished from unplanned (or even feared), and black as distinguished from white.

There are several ways one could try to represent over 100 years of US contraception law. One could perform a chronological march through all the relevant laws. Or one could adopt a thematic approach highlighting the leading goals and messages communicated by such laws. The second approach is both more interesting and more revealing of the state's interests. In what follows, therefore, I will address three themes concerning US law on contraception. The first theme is the most important; consequently, this essay devotes substantial space to understanding it. The foundational theme concerns the shift in US policy from a concern generally to promote the physical and economic health and welfare of women and children to the valorization of sex without children and with indifference to marriage as the *sine qua non* of women's freedom. Throughout this shift, however, there has remained a state interest in reducing the number of children born to teenage and poor women.

The two other themes are more concisely discussed. One concerns the role of the law that constitutionalized contraception in constitutionalizing abortion, constitutionalizing nonmarital sex, and constitutionalizing same-sex marriage. The other is the role played by contraception in the failure of United States legislators to pass laws accommodating working mothers and their wish for more time and flexibility to care for their children.

Shifts in US Policy Over Time

Below is a very brief tour of the history of US laws concerning contraception, sufficient only to allow the reader to perceive its changing goals within the limited space available. Beginning in 1873 with a few federal laws, and then followed by laws in about half the states, there emerged the so-called "Comstock laws" (named after Anthony Comstock, a politician and postal inspector).[1] These banned, for example, use of the postal service to transact articles of "immoral use," contraception included. Different states' laws might ban importing, buying, selling, advertising, distributing, or manufacturing one or more of the "immoral articles." Some scholars hold that the primary target of the laws was pornography, but it is also agreed that the laws were further intended to curb premarital sex and what were at the time called "illegitimate children."[2]

Comstock laws began to be ridiculed in influential books and law review articles beginning in the 1920s. Many of the stricter forms of the law were already gone when, in 1965, the Supreme Court held in *Griswold v. Connecticut* that married couples had a constitutional right to obtain and use contraception.[3]

I will return to *Griswold* in a moment, but it should be noted that even before *Griswold*, the federal government was deploying contraception as a tool for achieving certain ends. The Centers for Disease Control and Prevention (CDC) credits the movement to make contraception part of government policy to Margaret Sanger, the foundress of Planned Parenthood Federation of America, who in the 1920s and 1930s wrote about the claimed health advantages of contraception: spacing childbirth, limiting family size, and avoiding abortion.[4]

Also, according to the CDC, contraception was actually first federally funded in the early 1940s when Margaret Sanger persuaded First Lady Eleanor Roosevelt that it could combat venereal disease and help prevent pregnancies among women working to supply the war effort.[5]

The shape of contemporary contraception law, however, most directly traces its origins to the *Griswold* case, wherein a Planned Parenthood director successfully asserted a right to supply contraception to married couples as against a state law banning that activity. In *Griswold*, the Supreme Court authored a new constitutional right of married couples to obtain and use contraception. It reasoned that, although the US Constitution does not have textual protection for contraception, it protects some *non*textual rights suggested by the "penumbras and emanations" of various other recognized constitutional rights. These nontextual rights were sufficient to protect married couples' relationships and bedrooms from law enforcement concerning contraception. For complicated reasons having to do with prior, unpopular uses of a doctrine known as "substantive due process,"[6] the Supreme Court did not then state that the right to

1 See Comstock Act, 17 Stat. 599 (1873).

2 See Rochelle Gurstein, *The Repeal of Reticence: A History of America's Cultural and Legal Struggles Over Free Speech, Obscenity, Sexual Liberation, and Modern Art* (New York: Hill & Wang, 1996).

3 Griswold v. Connecticut, 381 U.S. 479 (1965).

4 US Centers for Disease Control, "Achievements in Public Health, 1900–1999: Family Planning," *Morbidity and Mortality Weekly Report* 48, no. 47 (December 3, 1999): 1073–1080.

5 William L. Davis, "Family Planning Services: A History of U.S. Federal Legislation," *Journal of Family History* 16, no. 4 (1991): 381–400, cited at 385.

6 See generally David Bernstein, *Rehabilitating Lochner: Defending Individual Rights against Progressive Reform* (Chicago: University of Chicago Press, 2012).

use contraception was a "substantive due process" right. But today, *Griswold* is understood as a substantive due process case. The notion of substantive due process is so significant as a means by which contraception is today valorized, that it merits additional explanation.

Since *Mugler v. Kansas* in 1887, the Due Process Clause of the Fourteenth Amendment ("nor shall any State deprive any person of life, liberty, or property, without due process of law") has been understood to contain a "substantive" component and not simply a guarantee of procedural fairness.[7] The modern inquiry by which an interest is assessed to determine whether it qualifies as a substantive due process right indicates why a positive conclusion carries so much cultural significance.

The plurality opinion in the 1992 abortion decision in *Planned Parenthood v. Casey* wrote that substantive due process adjudication, "has represented the balance which our Nation, built upon postulates of respect for the liberty of the individual, has struck between that liberty and the demands of organized society."[8] A later iteration of the manner in which the Court discerns a substantive due process right appeared in the 1998 assisted suicide decision *Washington v. Glucksberg* (refusing to find a constitutional right to assisted suicide) when the Court said:

> Our established method of substantive-due-process analysis has two primary features: First, we have regularly observed that the Due Process Clause specially protects those fundamental rights and liberties which are, objectively, "deeply rooted in this Nation's history and tradition," . . . ("so rooted in the traditions and conscience of our people as to be ranked as fundamental"), and "implicit in the concept of ordered liberty," such that "neither liberty nor justice would exist if they were sacrificed," . . . . Second, we have required in substantive-due-process cases a "careful description" of the asserted fundamental liberty interest. . . . Our Nation's history, legal traditions, and practices thus provide the crucial "guideposts for responsible decision making," . . . that direct and restrain our exposition of the Due Process Clause.[9]

In short, to denominate a right as a substantive due process right is to grant it enormous legal and even cultural significance. This is what contraception enjoys.

In 1972, following *Griswold*, the Supreme Court extended to single persons the right of use of contraception, in the case of *Eisenstadt v. Baird*.[10] It thereafter extended the right to minors (albeit subject to some states' parental involvement laws[11]) in the case of *Carey v. Population Services*.[12] These set the framework against which legislation could proceed to carry out particular governmental

7 Mugler v. Kansas, 123 U.S. 623 (1887).

8 Planned Parenthood v. Casey, 505 U.S. 833, 850 (1992).

9 Washington v. Glucksberg, 521 U.S. 702 (1997), cited at 720, 721 (citations omitted).

10 Eisenstadt v. Baird, 405 U.S. 438 (1972).

11 Guttmacher Institute, *State Laws and Policies: An Overview of Minors' Consent Law* (February 1, 2018), https://www.guttmacher.org/state-policy/explore/overview-minors-consent-law.

12 Carey v. Population Services, 431 U.S. 678 (1977).

objectives for contraception. I will shortly discuss these cases further insofar as they also set the stage for same-sex marriage.

While the Court was legalizing contraception in the 1960s and 1970s, Congress and federal agencies were stepping up their birth control funding in response to fears about overpopulation and to worries about early and frequent childbearing, especially among the poor, creating suspicion even then about their intentions regarding African Americans.[13] The Johnson administration expanded federal family planning funding especially on a platform of poverty reduction in the 1960s and created family planning centers within the National Institutes of Health (NIH), and what is now called the Department of Health and Human Services (HHS).[14]

Under the Nixon Administration, family planning subsidies were explicitly targeted toward reducing childbearing by lower-income Americans. It was plainly proposed that a family with fewer children could invest more in each one, and thereby achieve better outcomes.[15]

In 1970, with significant support from both Republicans and Democrats, Congress passed Title X of the Public Health Service Act.[16] To this day, Title X provides enormous amounts of federal funding to states for contraception, as will be described further below.

Currently, the federal government spends nearly $2.1 billion annually on birth control, with the lion's share allocated to programs serving lower-income Americans. About 75 percent of all federal spending is through Medicaid—the federal health insurance program for poor and lower-income Americans—and 10 percent is through Title X. Annually, states spend approximately $225 million more, also targeting lower-income Americans.[17] The sheer amount of funding available showcases the degree of state interest. Below is a brief description of each of the major programs.

Medicaid

Medicaid insurance covers all Food and Drug Administration-approved drugs and devices for women and girls of childbearing age. The federal Medicaid program reimburses doctors providing contraception at a 90% rate, while the reimbursement rate for other Medicaid services is considerably less, ranging from 50% to 70%. States often supply the last 10% of the cost for low-income women.[18]

Contraception also receives favored treatment with respect to a Medicaid patient's choice of providers. While Medicaid managed-care enrollees are usually

13 Davis, "Family Planning Services: A History of U.S. Federal Legislation," 386. See also Donald Critchlow's chapter 1 in this volume and his work, *Intended Consequences: Birth Control, Abortion, and the Federal Government in Modern America* (New York: Oxford University Press, 1999).

14 Davis, "Family Planning Services," 387.

15 Martha J. Bailey, "Fifty Years of Family Planning: New Evidence on the Long-Run Effects of Increasing Access to Contraception," *Brookings Paper Econ Act* (Spring 2013): 341–409.

16 42 U.S.C. 300, et seq.

17 Guttmacher Institute, *Publicly Funded Family Planning Services in the United States: Fact Sheet* (September 2016), https://www.guttmacher.org/sites/default/files/factsheet/ fb_ contraceptive_serv_0.pdf.

18 Guttmacher Institute, *Publicly Funded Family Planning Services in the United States: Fact Sheet* (September 2016).

restricted to network providers, for contraception, a woman can go to the provider of her choice, even if he or she is not "in network."

The federal Affordable Care Act,[19] of 2010 established a new optional Medicaid eligibility group for family planning services, consisting of individuals with incomes at or below the highest income eligibility level established by the state for pregnant women. This new eligibility group entitles members *only* to family planning services and supplies and related diagnoses and treatment. Providers must give services for free.[20]

In 2016, Medicaid officials strongly recommended that providers step up their efforts to deliver more, and more effective, contraception to the poor. Medicaid guidelines to states and providers encourage the latter to "optimize" the use of long acting reversible contraceptives (hereafter "LARCs") by encouraging patients to consider them at every visit, by stocking a substantial amount and variety of contraception in order to make same-day access possible, and by recommending the insertion of an intrauterine device (IUD) or another long-acting contraceptive immediately after a woman has completed her labor and delivery. Medicaid also amended its reimbursement policies to facilitate doctors' adoption of each of these recommendations.[21] LARCs are not without controversy given not only their potential side effects, but also given the enthusiasm with which they are promoted in minority communities,[22] the fact that women are essentially sterilized for three to ten years, potential impacts upon sexual partnering, and their failure to protect against sexually transmitted infections.[23]

Title X

The Title X family planning program was created in 1970 as part of the Public Health Service Act. It provides grants to public and nonprofit agencies for contraception services, and research and training for both adults and adolescents. Contraception is by far the largest element of Title X expenditures.

Today, Title X receives $260 million per year and serves about four million clients, 88 percent of whom received contraception free or highly subsidized. The program currently covers, in addition to contraception, preconception care, natural family planning, and infertility services.[24]

19 Patient Protection and Affordable Care Act, 42 U.S.C. § 18001 et seq. (2010).

20 Alison Mitchell, Evelyne P. Baumrucker, and Elicia J. Herz, "Medicaid: An Overview," *A Congressional Research Service Report* [Report R43357] (January 10, 2014).

21 US Department of Health and Human Services, *Letter from Centers for Medicaid and Medicaid Services, to State Health Officials,* June 14, 2016 (SHO #16-008), https://www.medicaid.gov/federal-policy-guidance/downloads/sho16008.pdf.

22 Jenny A. Higgins, "Celebration Meets Cautions, LARC's Boons, Potential Busts and the Benefits of a Reproductive Justice Approach," *Contraception* 89, no. 4 (2014): 237–241.

23 See generally Women Speak for Themselves, *Fact Sheet: Teens and Long Acting Reversible Contraception (LARCs)* (September 2017), https://womenspeakforthemselves.com/fact-sheets-2/.

24 HHS Press Release, "HHS announces the availability of $260 million to fund the Title X family planning program" (February 23, 2018), https://www.hhs.gov/about/news/2018/02/23/hhs-announces-availability-260-million-fund-title-x-family-planning-program.html.

About nine out of every ten Title X users are female, 67 percent are under 30 years of age and 66 percent have family incomes at or below the poverty level. Clients are disproportionately black and Hispanic. Five-sixths of clients are 20 years and older.[25]

Community Health Centers

Contraception is also supplied through the Federal Health Center Program, through outlets called Community Health Centers ("CHCs"). These provide outpatient health services, including contraception, to underserved areas, which are disproportionately poor and minority.[26]

Maternal and Child Health Block Grants

HHS administers Maternal and Child Health Block Grants, which provide funds to states, territories and the District of Columbia to support a wide range of health and social service activities, including contraception, especially to low-income Americans. In 2016, it served almost fifty-four million women, infants and children.[27]

Emergency Contraception

In 2013, the US Food and Drug Administration (FDA) made certain forms of emergency contraception (ECs)—drugs taken after sex either to avoid conception or to avoid an embryo embedding into the womb—available over the counter without a prescription to women over the age of 17.[28]

The Contraception Mandate

The above programs demonstrate the state's longtime focus on distributing contraceptives to the poor. More recently, the state speaks a great deal about the role of contraception in aiding woman to achieve their "will," regarding childbearing, that is, about reducing "unintended" pregnancy. Reducing unintended pregnancy is the first and last goal noted in the CDC's 1999 summary of the country's

25 Congressional Research Service, "Title X (Public Health Service Act) Family Planning Program," by Angela Napili [Report RL 33644], last modified August 31, 2017, https://fas.org/sgp/crs/misc/RL33644.pdf.

26 Congressional Research Service Report, "Federal Health Centers: An Overview," by Elayne J. Heisler, [Report R43937], last modified May 19, 2017, https://fas.org/sgp/crs/misc/R43937.pdf and Congressional Research Service Report, "Factors Related to the Use of Planned Parenthood Affiliated Health Centers (PPAHCs) and Federally Qualified Health Centers (FQHCs)," by Elayne J. Heisler and Victoria L. Elliott, [Report R44295], last modified May 18, 2017, https://fas.org/sgp/crs/misc/R44295.pdf.

27 See Health Resources & Services Administration, "Title V Maternal and Child Health Services Block Grant Program," https://mchb.hrsa.gov/maternal-child-health-initiatives/title-v-maternal-and-child-health-services-block-grant-program.

28 See Food and Drug Administration Press Release, "FDA Approves Plan B One-Step Emergency Contraceptive for Use Without a Prescription for All Women of Child-bearing Potential," (June 20, 2013).

progress in family planning.[29] The Institute of Medicine (IOM), which is the scientific body upon which HHS often relies for expert advice, also continually states that family planning's *first* goal is the reduction of "unintended pregnancy."[30]

There is a correspondingly large focus on the role of contraception in empowering women's freedom not only to avoid procreation when they will but also to have sex unlinked to children and indifferent to marriage and to achieve social and economic equality with men. As the CDC claimed in its 1999 account of major achievements in public health, contraception has "improved the social and economic role of women."[31]

It is not always clear what the state means by this last claim, but, depending upon the source in which this observation appears, it seems to refer either to achieving identical sexual outcomes with men (no pregnancy), or to sexually active women's remaining unencumbered by children to more easily perform paid work.

The very best evidence concerning the state's current intentions regarding contraception, however, emerged during the struggle over the so-called "contraception mandate." There, the state did not offer a well-substantiated "health" argument about contraception.[32] It did not speak much about preventing poverty—as the mandate involved benefits for employees enjoying a health insurance benefit. It did not speak much about the good of children. When it did mention any of these arguments, they were brief and very weakly supported.[33] Rather, the state's argument dwelt upon women's right to attain their "will" regarding pregnancy and the role of contraception in women's attaining freedom and equality.

The mandate's history can be briefly recounted due to space limitations. The HHS issued the mandate in 2012 in order to fulfill the "preventive health care" provision of the Affordable Care Act.[34] As it has done on prior occasions, HHS turned to the IOM for a recommendation. Continually referred to by the president and HHS and even the Supreme Court as a "nonpartisan," "expert" group, in reality the IOM empaneled a committee composed in the majority of medical personnel associated with Planned Parenthood and other contraception and abortion advocates.[35] This committee issued a report recommending that all

29 CDC, "Achievements in Public Health, 1900–1999."

30 Institute of Medicine Committee on a Comprehensive Review of the HHS Office of Family Planning Title X Program, "A Review of the HHS Family Planning Program: Mission, Management, and Measurement of Results," ed. Adrienne Stith Butler and Ellen Wright Clayton (Washington, D.C.: National Academies Press, 2009), https://www.ncbi.nlm.nih.gov/books/NBK215219/.

31 CDC, "Achievements in Public Health, 1900–1999."

32 For a complete review of the federal government's attempted "health" argument for the mandate, see Helen M. Alvaré, "No Compelling Interest: The 'Birth Control" Mandate and Religious Freedom," *Villanova University Law Review* 58, no. 3 (2012): 379–436, 396–430.

33 Alvaré, "No Compelling Interest," 392–395, 428–440.

34 Anna Franzonello, staff counsel at the Americans United for Life, to the Centers for Medicare and Medicaid Services, Department of Health and Human Services, September 29, 2011, https://www.scribd.com/document/67496629/AUL-Comment-to-HHS-on-Preventive-Services.

35 Anna Franzonello to the Centers for Medicare and Medicaid Services.

health insurance policies be required to cover all FDA-approved contraceptives without any co-pay.[36] HHS freely acknowledged that the language of "contraceptives" included drugs and devices that could act to destroy an already developing human embryo.[37] HHS then adopted the IOM's recommendation, which became known as the "contraception mandate."[38] It claimed, among other things, to solve the problem of women's higher health-care costs and to promote women's and children's health by lowering unintended pregnancy. It was also regularly and forcefully advanced as securing women's freedom and equality with men in contemporary society.

The mandate exempted churches, but religious institutions such as hospitals, schools and charities were required to file paperwork with the government triggering governmental action attaching contraception coverage to the employer's insurance plan.

In defense of the mandate, the Obama administration weathered over one hundred lawsuits by three hundred plaintiffs and litigated twice all the way up to the US Supreme Court. In the first action, *Burwell v. Hobby Lobby Stores, Inc.*, the Court held that the federal government had not satisfied the relevant constitutional test by employing the "least restrictive means" to deliver to Hobby Lobby's employees the relevant drugs and devices, over the religious objections of the owners of this closely held corporation.[39] (Hobby Lobby corporation objected only to the drugs and devices with abortifacient potential.) In the second action, *Zubik v. Burwell*, the Court (now only eight justices because of the death of Associate Justice Antonin Scalia) requested that government and religious complainants try to agree upon a "less restrictive means" to deliver contraception and abortifacients to the employees of various religious institutions, without requiring the cooperation of the religious employers.[40] As of Spring 2018, it appears that the Trump administration will continue to work to reverse the contraception mandate. While it issued a rule rolling back the mandate in October 2017,[41] as of the date of this writing, its new rule has thus far twice been enjoined by federal judges.[42]

For the moment, it appears that religious institutions are protected against being forced to distribute certain contraceptives and abortifacients to their employees. As will be described below, however, given the Obama administration's

36 Institute of Medicine, Clinical Preventive Services for Women: Closing the Gaps (2011) [hereinafter IOM report].

37 26 Code of Federal Regulations 54.9815-2713(a)(1)(iv)(2013); 29 Code of Federal Regulations 2590.715-2713(a)(1)(iv)(2013); 26 Code of Federal Regulations 54.9815-2713(a)(1)(iv)(2013).

38 Final Rules for Group Health Plans and Health Insurance Issuers Relating to Coverage of Preventive Services Under the Patient Protection and Affordable Care Act, 77 Fed. Reg. 8725, 8725 (February 15, 2012).

39 Burwell v. Hobby Lobby Stores, Inc., 134 S. Ct. 2751 (2014).

40 Zubik v. Burwell, 136 S. Ct. 1557 (2016).

41 See 82 Fed. Reg. 47792, and 82 Fed. Reg. 47838 (October 6, 2017).

42 See Pennsylvania v. Trump, No. 17-4540 (E.D. Pa., December 15, 2017). See also Final Rules for Group Health Plans and Health Insurance Issuers Relating to Coverage of Preventive Services Under the Patient Protection and Affordable Care Act, 77 Fed. Reg. 8725, 8725 (February 15, 2012).

near-hyperbolic "women's rights" arguments for the mandate, it is more than likely that a later federal administration will again pursue similar policy. Certainly, some states have and continue to mandate including contraception in health insurance plans.[43] To better grasp the state's messaging on contraception therefore, it is important to consider the mandate in some detail.

At bottom, the mandate showcased the strength of the federal commitment to contraception as a blunt proxy or symbol for women's freedom—particularly their freedom to have sexual expression unlinked to children and indifferent to marriage. I claim this for the following reasons. First, the government forcefully pressed for the mandate despite contraception's decades-long failure to actually reduce unintended pregnancies among women. Neither federal nor state programs have succeeded on this count. Rather, unintended pregnancy rates have increased or stayed the same since the growth of federal and state funding for contraception beginning in the 1970s, precisely among the groups (low-income women) receiving it free or at very low cost. Women without free contraception actually experienced lower rates of unintended pregnancy.[44] Furthermore, according to sociologist Michael New, who investigated abortion and unintended pregnancy rates in twenty-six states with contraception mandates, at the end of several years, these states had similar rates of unintended pregnancies as states without mandates, and slightly higher abortion rates.[45]

Second, it is not clear that women themselves are as enthusiastic about contraception as the government that uses support for contraception as a symbol of its pro-woman bona fides. An NIH "request for proposal" concerning research about new contraceptive methods showcases women's difficulties and ambivalence:

> [H]ormonal contraceptives have the disadvantage of having many undesirable side effects. In addition, hormonal contraceptives are associated with adverse events, and obese women are at higher risk for serious complications such as deep venous thrombosis. The oral contraceptive pill's failure rate among American women ranges from 9–30%. The reason for such a high failure rate is the requirement for daily compliance. Furthermore, a recent report found that 40% of women were not satisfied with their current contraceptive method. . . . Long-acting reversible contraception, which does not require daily compliance, has a much lower typical use failure rate. . . . However, most of these methods are either devices, such as the IUD, or contain hormones. Use of intrauterine devices has only slowly gained acceptance in the US (from 0.8% in 1995 to 5.6% in

43 Guttmacher Institute, *State Laws and Policies: Insurance Coverage of Contraceptives* (February 1, 2018), https://www.guttmacher.org/state-policy/explore/insurance-coverage-contraceptives.

44 Guttmacher Institute, *Unintended Pregnancy in the United States: Fact Sheet* (September 2016), https://www.guttmacher.org/fact-sheet/unintended-pregnancy-united-states. See also Michael J. New, "Analyzing the Impact of State Level Contraception Mandates on Public Health Outcomes," *Ave Maria Law Review* 13, no. 2 (Summer 2015): 345–369.

45 New, "Analyzing the Impact of State Level Contraception Mandates," 363, 366, and 368.

> 2006–2010), and IUDs are unlikely to be used by the majority of women desiring contraception.[46]

Exploring women's dissatisfaction with contraception further, a 2013 Centers for Disease Control report stated

> Of the 45 million women who have ever used the pill, 30% discontinued use because of dissatisfaction. Nearly one-half of the 12.5 million women who had used Depo-Provera (46%) and the 5.6 million women who had used the contraceptive patch (49%) discontinued use due to dissatisfaction.[47]

Third, the federal government insists that women's economic health would be boosted by the mandate despite the absence of evidence. The government continually asserted that contraception was the most important source of women's higher health-care costs when in fact its own sources showed that health-care cost differentials between men and women arose not from contraception, but due to costs that the mandate did not reimburse. To wit: women's longevity, their greater predisposition to visit doctors, and their childbearing, cause women's overall higher lifetime costs.[48]

Fourth, while the government spoke in "panicked" tones about the need to force religious employers to fund birth control,[49] there was no actual shortfall in the availability or use of birth control by women prior to or after the mandate. The government acknowledged that over 89% of sexually active women were using birth control already.[50] The Guttmacher Institute's own sources showed that only a tiny percent of women reported that they could not afford contraception pre-mandate.[51] These women were likely eligible for government programs and benefits already providing contraception free or on a sliding-scale (see Medicaid discussion, above). The employed, more middle-class women targeted by the mandate to receive free contraception were not complaining about its cost.

46 US Department of Health and Human Services, *Female Contraceptive Development Program* (U01) (November 5, 2013), https://grants.nih.gov/grants/guide/rfa-files/RFA-HD-14-024.html.

47 Kimberly Daniels, William Mosher, and Jo Jones, "Contraceptive Methods Women Have Ever Used: United States, 1982–2010," *National Health Statistics Reports* 62 (February 14, 2013): 8, https://www.cdc.gov/nchs/data/nhsr/nhsr062.pdf.

48 Centers for Medicare & Medicaid Services, *National Health Care Spending by Gender and Age, 2004 Highlights* (2004); US Centers for Disease Control, *Visits to Physician Offices, Hospital Outpatient Departments, and Hospital Emergency Departments by Age, Sex, and Race: United States, Selected Years 1995–2011* (2012); US Centers for Disease Control, *Expenses for Health Care and Prescribed Medicine, by Selected Population Characteristics: United States, Selected Years 1987–2010* (2012).

49 Helen M. Alvaré, "Meanwhile, Outside the Panic Room: Contraception, Hobby Lobby, and Women's Rights," *Public Discourse* (July 10, 2014).

50 William D. Mosher and Jo Jones, "Use of Contraception in the United States: 1982–2008," *Vital and Health Statistics* 23, no. 29 (August 2010): 5, 9.

51 See Helen M. Alvaré, "No Compelling Interest," 427–430.

Most were already insured for it.[52] And, four years after the mandate, one of the most strenuous contraception champions in the country, the Guttmacher Institute, reported that there was no change in the amount or type of contraception usage among sexually active women.[53]

Fifth, although it claimed a "health" rationale for the mandate, the federal government could never cobble together a sound health-care argument. As noted above, the government claimed but could not prove that contraception could benefit women's health by reducing unintended pregnancies. Its argument about a relationship between unintended pregnancy and women's health proved very incomplete. Most of the studies it relied upon spoke only of "correlation" not "causation," and also noted the possibility of reverse causation between claimed health "effects" of unintended pregnancy—violence, drinking, smoking, depression, and unintended pregnancy. Some sources suggested that a third factor—a higher taste for risk—could account both for the unintended pregnancy and the named health conditions. Furthermore, the government's health argument never fully reflected the widely-acknowledged health risks of hormonal contraception, or the reality that women with health conditions strongly contraindicating for pregnancy are usually advised to avoid hormonal contraceptives.[54] And finally, it is significant that the US Preventive Services Task Force (the highest governmental medical expertise in the United States respecting necessary "preventive care") has not, even to this day, recommended contraception as preventive health care for women.[55]

There is one final way in which the mandate showcased the state's preoccupation with linking contraception to women's freedom for sex unlinked to children and indifferent to marriage. It was the visibility of single women leading the charge for the mandate on the argument that they had a right to nonmarital sex without fear of pregnancy. At the dawn of the mandate, a Planned Parenthood official published an editorial in the *New York Times* stating that the mandate would enable her divorced daughter to afford more expensive birth control.[56] On a National Public Radio program on which I appeared, a lawyer and representative of the National Women's Law Coalition praised the mandate because it could pay for her single daughter's long-acting contraception.[57]

Eventually, mandate supporters, including the White House, chose Sandra Fluke—a single woman and student attending Georgetown University Law

52 Institute of Medicine, *Clinical Preventive Services for Women*, 108–109; see also Alvaré, "No Compelling Interest," 424–426.

53 Guttmacher Institute, "News Release: New Study Finds Little Change in Patterns of US Contraceptive Use From 2012-2015" (March 13, 2017), https://www.guttmacher.org/news-release/2017/new-study-finds-little-change-patterns-us-contraceptive-use-2012-2015.

54 See Alvaré, "No Compelling Interest," 411–420.

55 US Preventive Services Task Force, *Published Recommendations*, http://www.uspreventiveservicestaskforce.org.

56 Vanessa Cullins, "Make Birth Control Affordable," *The New York Times* (July 18, 2011): A23.

57 The Diane Rehm Show, "New Debate Over Contraceptives and Women's Health," National Public Radio, July 21, 2011, http://thedianerehmshow.org/shows/2011-07-21/new-debate-over-contraceptives-and-womens-health.

School—to be the public face of the mandate. Fluke argued at a specially convened congressional hearing, and later in the news media, that her dignity and freedom as a woman obligated her religiously affiliated law school to buy her contraception in order for her to have sex with her boyfriend without the risk of pregnancy. After Rush Limbaugh called her a "slut" on his radio program, President Barack Obama publicized that he had telephoned her to express his personal gratitude for her statements,[58] and his assurances that her parents would be proud of her. Thereafter, she was the face of women's freedom at "women's night" at the Democratic National Convention that re-nominated Barack Obama for president. Fluke thereafter transitioned into full-time work within the Obama campaign, speaking continually about the mandate.

Another public face closely associated with the Obama administration's message on contraception was Hollywood actress Lena Dunham. On behalf of the Obama candidacy, Dunham filmed a re-election advertisement, promoting the mandate and comparing voting for Obama to a first-time sexual experience. She closed with the suggestion that it's "super uncool to be out and about and someone says, 'Did you…' and you say, 'No I wasn't ready'"—oddly appearing to advocate nonmarital sex for even a conflicted woman or girl.[59]

In addition to these efforts, the Obama campaign, the secretary of HHS, and various members of Congress began to refer to conscientious objectors or critics of Planned Parenthood as waging a "war on women."[60] In other words, advocacy for sex unlinked to children, became a proxy for supporting women. A White House-employed, evangelical consultant to President Obama, Michael Wear, wrote in his memoirs that a senior political advisor urged Obama to continue the "path of most resistance" regarding the mandate—even against fierce opposition from very sympathetic charities (i.e., the Little Sisters of the Poor)—in order to broadcast his pro-woman bona fides as against conservative religious males like Republican presidential candidate Mitt Romney.[61] Obama presidential campaign postcards thereafter urged women to "vote like your lady parts depend on it . . . because they kinda do,"[62] and invented a "letter to home" from a young, single adult, asking her parents for "$18,000 to help pay for my birth control?"[63]—referring to the claim that Mitt Romney would repeal the health-care law and the mandate. The political use of the "war on women" extended into the 2014 campaigns as well.

Federal and state governments also express their opinions about the purpose of contraception at law by the partners they choose to fund and ally with. Two

58 Lucy Madison, "Obama Calls Sandra Fluke to Offer Support over Limbaugh Comments," *CBS News*, (March 12, 2012).

59 See Lena Dunham, *Youtube*: *Your First Time*, http://www.youtube.com/watch?v=o6G3nwhPuR4.

60 Emily Schultheis, "Why Democrats Are Ditching the 'War on Women,'" *The Atlantic* (July 31, 2014).

61 See Jim Geraghty, "An Obama Insider's Lament," review of *Reclaiming Hope*, by Michael Wear, *National Review*, (January 2017).

62 Daniel Halper, "Obama Campaign: 'Vote Like Your Lady Parts Depend on It. Because They Kinda Do,'" *The Weekly Standard* (October 2, 2012).

63 Josh Hicks, "Misleading Messages from the Obama Campaign on the Contraceptive Mandate," *The Washington Post* (October 5, 2012).

important partners of many federal and state administrations are the Planned Parenthood Federation of America and Power to Decide (formerly the National Campaign to Prevent Teen and Unplanned Pregnancy, or NCTUP). Both organizations are vocal, straightforward advocates of contraception and regularly link it with women's ability to live, as Planned Parenthood writes, "strong healthy lives and fulfill their dreams—no ceilings, no limits."[64]

Since the *Griswold* case in 1965, Planned Parenthood is regularly the complainant in lawsuits seeking to overturn substantive or funding restrictions on birth control or abortion at any time during pregnancy, for any reason, and by any method.

Power to Decide/NCTUP is an important federal and state partner. It receives significant grants from HHS. Its spokespersons and resources have been offered to the public on federal websites. During the Obama Administration, on HHS' website womenshealth.gov, (then) NCTUP's Bedsider ("online birth control support") materials were promoted as a good guide to sexual relationships.[65] And an HHS Blog on talking to your kids about sex quotes a representative of a Bronx sex education program suggesting: "It's important to validate all different kinds of consensual sexual and romantic experiences."[66]

Power to Decide's mission, in addition to reducing teen pregnancies, is to reduce "unplanned" pregnancies among young adults. Its nearly entire approach is contraception. It takes no position on abortion.

The Bedsider campaign freely encourages casual sex for singles so long as contraception is used. It's "Frisky Friday" series, for example, offers recipes for "aphrodisiac food," or "heat[ing] up your weekends with our best sex tips." It offers consolation for girls depressed after sex with a virtual stranger saying, "[s]ome of the most modern, empowered, secure, sexylicious women among us have had at least one walk of shame."[67]

Power to Decide's e-cards and graphics have included invitations for casual sex, photos of natural objects resembling genitalia, or bondage equipment and other soft pornography.[68] Its "About Us" section touts a woman's right to "a healthy, happy sex life without having to worry about unplanned pregnancy." And it offers members a "Booty Log" app that encourages anonymous sharing of one's sexcapades in an online database. A Frisky Friday blog urged readers to cohabit and/or to have nonmarital babies if this is what they want. It advises:

64 Planned Parenthood, *Considering Pregnancy: Parenting Without a Partner*, https://www.plannedparenthood.org/learn/pregnancy/considering-pregnancy#sthash.L7uUJMbb.dpuf.

65 "Spotlight on Women's Health: An Interview About Talking to Teens About Healthy Relationships and Sex: Kayla Smith (peer health educator at Bedsider)," June 22, 2016, https://www.womenshealth.gov/blog/spotlight-kayla-smith.

66 "Spotlight on Women's Health: Talking to Your Kids About Sex: Lena Solow," July 5, 2015, https://www.womenshealth.gov/blog/spotlight-lena-solow.

67 See Meg McDonnell, "All Sex All the Time," *National Review* (March 6, 2014), https://www.nationalreview.com/2014/03/all-sex-all-time-meg-t-mcdonnell/.

68 National Campaign to Prevent Teen and Unplanned Pregnancy, *Bedsider Photos*, https://www.facebook.com/bedsider/photos/pb.131611470215125.-2207520000.1393271176./549424618433806/?type=3&theater.

"Just don't ever feel bad about your choice if you choose not to marry. If it's right for you, it's right."[69]

No doubt federal and state governments will, from time to time, continue to make arguments contending that contraception is essential to women's and children's health and to the autonomy of the poor. Likely, they will continue to lack nuance and neglect to refer to the health risks especially of hormonal contraception. They will neglect to consider the "sexual marketplace" into which they have thrust poor women and all women—a marketplace in which sex has become the "price" of dating or entry into the marriage market, as against women's stronger preferences.[70] It seems certain, however, that for the near future, state advocacy for contraception and contraception mandates will rely most strenuously on the claimed self-evident argument that contraception levels the playing field for women by empowering them, like men, to have sex without pregnancy, and to be unencumbered employees.

The Role of the Law Constitutionalizing Contraception, Abortion, Nonmarital Sex, and Same-Sex Marriage

This is a familiar story—how the law constitutionalizing contraception set the stage for the law constitutionalizing not only abortion, but also nonmarital sexual expression and eventually same-sex marriage. In the year following the Supreme Court's opinion legalizing same-sex marriage (*Obergefell v. Hodges*)[71] I participated on a panel at Yale Law School on the subject of this opinion. A same-sex-attracted professor arguing on behalf of Justice Kennedy's majority opinion in *Obergefell* opined strenuously that it was *opposite*-sex couples, and the law about *their* sexual behaviors and procreation that had opened wide the doors to the Court's opinion in *Obergefell,* which concluded that the ability or wish to procreate could not be a barrier to marriage recognition. I could not disagree.

The trajectory from *Eisenstadt* to *Obergefell* can be briefly summarized. The mediating factors linking contraception law to what came after are as follows: first, the *Eisenstadt* Court's description of the constitutional right at issue, as the right of *individuals* to make important decisions about matters "so fundamentally affecting a person" as the right whether or not to bear or beget a child. The right of privacy was thus removed from the relationship between husband and wife and put in-between the ears of a single individual. The right was also continuously linked, by virtue of *Eisenstadt,* to sexual expression without procreation, and to decisions subjectively important to the individual, even if *not* linked with any particular social good. While *Roe* was argued before *Eisenstadt,* it was also reargued *after*

69 The National Campaign to Prevent Teen and Unplanned Pregnancy, "The Real Housewives of Not In This Lifetime: What If Marriage Isn't Your Thing?" *Frisky Fridays* (March 15, 2013), https://www.bedsider.org/features/512-the-real-housewives-of-not-in-this-lifetime-what-if-marriage-isn-t-your-thing.

70 See generally, George A. Akerlof, Janet L. Yellen, and Michael L. Katz, "An Analysis of Out-of-Wedlock Childbearing in the United States," *The Quarterly Journal of Economics* 111, no. 2 (May 1996): 309; Timothy Reichert, "Bitter Pill," *First Things* 203 (May 2010), 25–34.

71 Obergefell v. Hodges 135 S. Ct. 2584 Ct. (2015).

that case, and therefore able to rely explicitly upon the just-quoted language from *Eisenstadt* about a right of decision making concerning procreation.

Later, in *Lawrence v. Texas—the* case constitutionalizing same-sex sexual acts—and in the *Obergefell* opinion constitutionalizing same-sex marriage, both cases focused upon individual sexual decisions, cut off from procreation, and relied on *Eisenstadt* among other cases. In *Obergefell*, for example, the Court cited *Eisenstadt* for the proposition that "[t]he fundamental liberties protected by the Fourteenth Amendment's Due Process Clause extend to certain personal choices central to individual dignity and autonomy, including intimate choices defining personal identity and beliefs."[72]

That *avoiding* children was already linked with achieving important human goods (substantive-due-process-level goods), made it all the easier for the *Obergefell* Court to conclude that states could not credibly argue any longer that they *especially* favored procreation or procreative relationships.

Second, *Eisenstadt*'s granting of contraception rights to single persons de facto made it more possible to participate in nonmarital sex without fear. Nonmarital sex was less frequent and more often linked with some relational commitment (e.g. engagement) prior to the widespread normalization of contraception. *Eisenstadt* was thereafter relied upon in the *Lawrence* case which, while technically about same-sex sex, is understood to constitutionalize virtually all consensual non-marital sex (with limited exceptions, for example, likely incest or statutory rape).

The Role of Contraception in the Continuing Absence of Laws Granting Flexibility or Leave to Mothers

The contraception cases communicated the message that being without children is a good that many wish to achieve. This is true not only of *Griswold* and *Eisenstadt*, but also of the *Hobby Lobby* and *Zubik* cases. In these latter cases, a majority of the Court did not push back on the state's claim that women had a "compelling need" for *free* contraception as an essential part of their human freedom, and their opportunity for equality with men.

Contraception law has also reinforced the idea that freedom in connection with sex and children is attainable via *individual* choices, once contraception is available. *Eisenstadt* claimed that women achieve freedom by making decisions alone, apart from the sexual partner. Justices Kennedy, Sotomayor, Ginsburg, Kagan, and Breyer agreed in *Hobby Lobby* that contraception is a "compelling" interest of women, with the latter four, in dissent, agreed that contraception is crucial to allowing women to participate "equally in the economic and social life of the nation."[73]

Once lawmakers and a wide swath of citizens have imbibed the notion that one of women's chief rights involves the power to avoid children, this erodes the notion that other citizens have duties to women who make private choices to *have* (versus avoid) children.

72 *Obergefell*, 2589.

73 *Hobby Lobby* at 2787, citing Planned Parenthood of Southeastern Pa. v. Casey, 505 U.S. 833, 856 (1992).

Practically speaking, too, if groups claiming to embody women's interests press continually for contraception and abortion, they communicate that other issues—such as paid leave and job flexibility for parents—are more "negotiable" if important at all. A brief look at the website of the leading feminist organization in the US, the National Organization for Women, reveals, for example, that it considers women's right to avoid childbearing as her *most* important right, followed by economic justice and ending violence.[74] It is more than likely that a concerted effort to champion women's interests in having children and caring for them—versus their claimed interests in avoiding them—would have resulted in more progress toward employment policies allowing women to manage the demands imposed when women have both children and work outside the home.

Conclusion

As discussed here, the law has played a strong role in effecting change in the meanings of sex and marriage. It has also changed societal norms respecting male/female relations. The law has pronounced on the value of different children (wanted v. unwanted, poor v. rich). This shift represents a move from governmental concern to promote the physical and economic health and welfare of women and children to the valorization of sex itself without children. It also speaks of an indifference to the marriage between a man and a woman who provide significant gifts to the building up of society through the bearing and nurturing of children.

Thoughtful citizens ought to ask if these changes have been ultimately good for men, women, children, and society itself. A wealth of sociological evidence responds in the negative. Commentators on both the left and right have even come together to mourn the loss of marriage, and the rise of nonmarital sex and nonmarital parenting; they agree on many ways to move forward to restore these norms.[75] The next question we may want to ask as a society is, how to move forward, how can law be a defender of men, women, children while also preserving equality and justice? At the very least, this requires adults to take more responsibility for the children they create. It requires the law at least to insist upon this, versus pursuing its current path of valorizing adult sexual expression without any thought to the well-being of children. It requires that we work strenuously to extend the benefits and blessings of stable family life to every person of every race and national origin, and every socioeconomic background. A full-length treatment of this subject comprises at least a book, and is indeed the subject of my book *Putting Children's Interests First in US Family Law and Policy: With Power Comes Responsibility*.[76] Whether or not we move in this direction will largely determine the future welfare of our country.

74 "Issues," National Organization for Women, https://now.org/issues.

75 Brookings Institution and American Enterprise Institute, *Opportunity, Responsibility and Security: A Consensus Plan for Reducing Poverty and Restoring the American Dream* (July 2016), at https://www.brookings.edu/wp-content/uploads/2016/07/Full-Report.pdf.

76 New York: Cambridge University Press, 2017.

PART V

Humanae vitae Contemporary Challenges

16

New Challenges to Humanae vitae

Conscience and Discernment

Janet E. Smith

THIS ESSAY REVIEWS THE PROJECT of contemporary revisionists in Catholic moral theology and argues that some moral theologians interpret Pope Francis's apostolic exhortation *Amoris laetitia* as promoting a view of conscience and discernment that undermines, if not abandons, the constant teaching of the Church that there are universal, absolute, and immutable moral norms.[1] This essay also shows that this interpretation of *Amoris laetitia* conflicts with Church teaching on the nature of conscience and its relationship to the moral law as set out in key magisterial documents. These challenges are especially problematic in light of Church teaching that is represented in Pope Paul VI's 1968 encyclical, *Humanae vitae*.[2] Indeed, the new challenges to *Humanae vitae* deny essential principles that the Church has understood and accepted for centuries. The challenges require an analysis and a response. Before taking up that task, it is important to briefly review the arguments of revisionists in the recent past.

Some Historical Context

Rejection of the Manuals

For centuries between the Council of Trent and the Second Vatican Council, moral theology was taught primarily to seminarians through textbooks known as "manuals," which were often heavy on arguments from authority and concrete case studies but light on fundamental principles and truncated the true breadth and depth of the Church's moral tradition, especially the teaching of St. Thomas Aquinas.[3] Revisionists were reacting against this manualist approach, which they saw as fundamentally legalistic, not personalist enough, and not Christocentric. They did not seek the renewal of better contact with its sources,

1 Pope Francis, Apostolic Exhortation *Amoris laetitia* (April 8, 2016), http://w2.vatican.va/content/francesco/en/apost_exhortations.index.html.

2 See Pope Paul VI, Encyclical Letter *Humanae vitae* (July 25, 1968), http://w2.vatican.va/content/paul-vi/en/encyclicals.index.html.

3 Servais Pinckaers, OP, *The Sources of Christian Ethics*, trans. Sr. Mary Thomas Noble, OP (Washington, D.C.: The Catholic University of America Press, 1995).

as envisioned (for example) by the influential Thomist Servais Pinckaers, but rather, they rejected many of the key principles and conclusions of the tradition. The prohibition of contraception was, to them, a prime example of "manualist morality," and the revisionists pushed for a change in the teaching both before and after *Humanae vitae* was published. James Keenan, in his *A History of Catholic Moral Theology in the Twentieth Century: From Confessing Sins to Liberating Conscience*, claims *Humanae vitae* "stymied" the progress over the manualists that was being made by the revisionists and neo-manualists before the encyclical was promulgated.[4]

Authoritative Teacher: Moral Theologian or the Magisterium?

There were two features of the manualist tradition that revisionists did approve: the manualists considered theologians to be the authoritative teachers of morality and among those teachers, a fair degree of diversity was tolerated. Manuals often reported which theologians held one position or another and, based on the stature of the theologians or their number as well as the strength of the arguments, would pronounce which position was "safer" to hold than others. But over time, the popes and curial offices began to assume the role of authoritative teachers and eventually the phrase "the Church teaches" no longer referred to the teaching of reliable theologians but to teachings expounded on in magisterial documents or curial decisions. In response, many moral theologians began to think of themselves as prophets, those who discern the direction in which Church teaching will or should develop,[5] and perhaps nowhere more so than in the area of sexual ethics. The notion of the moral theologian "ahead of the Church" began in earnest in the debate about contraception in the mid-twentieth century.

Proportionalism as a Method

Revisionists in the mid-twentieth century put forward a theory—called proportionalism—to replace the legalism of the manuals. There are several versions of proportionalism but a basic description would be that it involves weighing the "premoral" goods and evils that would result from two alternative courses of action. The only moral evil would be acting in a way that failed to choose the course whose benefits outweighed the harms. This was already an accepted procedure in the moral manuals in cases where a course of action was considered intrinsically immoral, but in proportionalism this procedure of decision-making was not used only for matters of prudence, but it became the foundational principle of all moral choices. Keenan observes, "In trying to establish a method for moral judgment as an alternative to the moral manuals, proportionalism was simply the logic of the moral manuals without the overriding absolute moral norms."[6]

4 James F. Keenan, *A History of Catholic Moral Theology in the Twentieth Century: From Confessing Sins to Liberating Consciences* (New York: Continuum International Publishing Group, 2010), 1.

5 Keenan, *A History of Catholic Moral Theology in the Twentieth Century*, 132.

6 Keenan, *A History of Catholic Moral Theology in the Twentieth Century*, 158.

Proportionalism became the key tool for those who mounted an attack on the Church's teaching on contraception. This attack developed just prior to and during the discussion of contraception that took place during the drafting of *Gaudium et spes* and as part of the work of the Special Commission on Family, Marriage and Birth Rate formed by Pope John XXIII and expanded by Pope Paul VI, which advised the pope that the Church could and should change its teaching on contraception.[7] Proportionalists seemed to want, in some sense, to honor the judgment that there were negative values in contraception—indicated by their coining of such terms as *premoral evil*, *ontic evil*, and *disvalue*—while at the same time, holding that there were circumstances where contraception was morally permissible, the benefits outweighing the negative aspects. Those moralists who rejected the Church's teaching on contraception also claimed that the natural law arguments used to defend it placed undue emphasis on the ordination of sexual intercourse to reproduction and did not take into account the higher human or spiritual values of the marital act. Henceforth, they spoke of the Church's teaching as being "biologistic" or "physicalistic."

Rejection of Absolute Norms

Those opposing proportionalism claimed it was at base relativistic. If individuals could morally choose to do something that the Church teaches to be an "intrinsic evil" because greater good than evil would result, this would mean that there are no actions that qualify as intrinsically evil, actions that can never be done, no matter the intention, the circumstances, or the consequences. Proportionalists denied they were relativists or that they rejected the existence of absolute objective evils. Proportionalists claimed that there is an objectively moral action that each individual should do in each particular instance but that it could not be determined ahead of time by appealing to some universal norm without reference to intention, circumstances, and consequences. Some even denied that proportionalism meant a rejection of universal objective absolute moral norms; Fr. Bernard Häring, for instance, allowed that there are abiding truths, such as the wrongness of slavery, but that is a truth, in his view, that came to be known through a historical process.[8] One cannot, according to proportionalists, derive moral norms through an analysis of human nature or the human essence and, in general, they were opposed to absolute moral norms consistently held by the Church through the centuries. That position effectively guts the traditional understanding of objective norms as norms that apply at all times *and* all places.

7 For a recounting of the history of *Gaudium et spes* with respect to contraception and the work of the pontifical commission, see Roberto de Mattei, "The Encyclical *Humanae vitae* in the Context of its Time," *l'ubica*, posted November 18, 2017, https://gloria.tv/article/nwBDLPVPh1Dj67cMAAo21aAhV; see also Robert McClory, *Turning Point* (New York: Crossroad, 1995) and Francis W. Swift, "An Analysis of the American Theological Reaction to Janssens' Stand on the Pill," *Louvain Studies* 1 (1966–1967): 19–54.

8 Bernard Häring, *Free and Faithful in Christ: Moral Theology for Clergy and Laity*, vol. 1, *General Moral Theology* (New York: The Seabury Press, 1978), 323.

Proportionalism remained a force in Catholic moral theology until the promulgation of Pope John Paul II's 1993 encyclical letter *Veritatis splendor,* which vigorously reasserted the reality of absolute moral norms.[9] It now seems to be largely defunct as a moral theory.[10] Modern revisionists now regard proportionalism as "a transitional phase in Catholic theological ethics,"[11] between manualist moral theology and current emphases on particular contexts, virtue, and self-determination. Modern revisionists certainly continue to challenge claims that there are absolute moral norms based on an *a priori* human essence and the correlative claim that some actions are intrinsically evil, all the while protesting that they are not relativists.[12] Nonetheless, the question of intrinsic evils does not greatly interest them. The fact is that, even if there were intrinsic evils, revisionists would still allow a freedom of conscience that does not give high priority to the role of universal objective absolute moral norms in individual decision-making. What they are primarily interested in is helping individuals become fully self-realizing by helping them make moral decisions according to the moral values they claim as their own. They seek to liberate Catholics from the authority of the Church's magisterium and argue that instead, "[W]e must help persons develop morally mature personalities through becoming self-governing moral subjects. Whereas earlier moralists decided what was right or wrong in every area of life, contemporary moralists are interested *in helping subjects rightly realize their moral truth*"[13] (my emphasis). This is the process they now call "discernment."[14] This approach now forms the basis of the new challenges to *Humanae vitae.*

Standard Challenges to *Humanae vitae* Re-emerge

Some current challenges to *Humanae vitae* are not much different from what they were twenty-five or even fifty years ago. For instance, alive and well is the claim that the teaching of *Humanae vitae* has not been "received" by the faithful, that the *sensus fidelium* has rejected the teaching of *Humanae vitae.*[15] Since the

9 Pope John Paul II, Encyclical Letter *Veritatis splendor* (August 6, 1993), http://w2.vatican.va/content/john-paul-ii/en/encyclicals.index.html.

10 See Charles E. Curran, *Catholic Moral Theology in the United States: A History* (Washington, D.C.: Georgetown University Press, 2008), 109.

11 Keenan, *A History of Catholic Moral Theology in the Twentieth Century*, 158.

12 Edward Pentin, "Pontifical Academy for Life Member: Term 'Intrinsically Evil' Too Restricting," (blog) *National Catholic Register*, January 29, 2018, http://www.ncregister.com/blog/edward-pentin/pontifical-academy-for-life-member-term-intrinsically-evil-too-restricting.

13 James F. Keenan, SJ and Thomas R. Kopfensteiner, "Moral Theology out of Western Europe," *Theological Studies* 59, no. 1 (February 1, 1998): 107–135.

14 For a pre-*Amoris laetitia* recounting of a similar position, see Keenan and Kopfensteiner, "Moral Theology out of Western Europe," 108. Pope Francis has given several seminal speeches on the importance of discernment: see, for instance, Cindy Wooden, "Pope Francis asks Jesuits to Teach Diocesan Priests the Art of Discernment," *America Magazine* (August 25, 2016). See also "Pope's Full Address to Newly Appointed Bishops," *Zenit* (September 14, 2018), https://zenit.org/articles/popes-address-to-newly-appointed-bishops.

15 Massimo Faggioli, "*Humanae Vitae*, A Half-Century On: How Different Catholics Read It," *Commonweal* (January 9, 2018). See also Albert Gelpi and Barbara Charlesworth Gelpi, "Epilogue: *Sensus fidelium*"

vast majority of sexually active Catholics have used contraception and since all the polls show the vast majority do not think it is wrong to use contraception, this shows that the faithful do not find the use of contraception to be incompatible with Christian discipleship.[16]

Certainly, revisionists insisted then, and insist now, that the teaching of *Humanae vitae* was not infallible and thus, not binding on the consciences of individuals.[17] Indeed, revisionists claim that the teachings of the Church based on natural law were subject to the same limitations revisionists understand to be true of natural law itself—that is, norms said to be true by natural law are shaped by cultures and cannot necessarily be said to have universal validity.[18] The Church must allow its teaching to be shaped by historical development in cultures. Nor is Scripture a reliable source of universal moral truths since it is a historical document that needs to be interpreted. If the Church is not infallible or even reliable, then it is important to respect the freedom and creativity of the conscience. But in recent reports of conferences held in Rome[19] and in the text *Amoris laetitia Un punto di svolta per la teologia morale?*,[20] most of the "challenges" to the Church's teaching on contraception noted above receive little mention and certainly do not take central place. The focus is no longer on the objective morality of acts but on the subjective state of the agent. Whether or not contraception is objectively moral or not is virtually not addressed. Rather, questions of conscience reign supreme, and many of these questions are answered in a way that owes a great deal to the generation of theologians who had opposed *Humanae vitae* under the banner of proportionalism.

Amoris laetitia as a Development in Moral Theology

The new challenges to *Humanae vitae* are associated with interpretations of *Amoris laetitia* that claim that it accomplishes a development in moral theology.

---

in *From Vatican II to Pope Francis: Charting A Catholic Future*, ed. Paul Crowley, SJ (Maryknoll, N.Y.: Orbis Books, 2014), 170–180.

16 For an explanation of the proper role of the *sensus fidelium*, see International Theological Commission "*Sensus Fidei* in the Life of the Church" (2014), http://www.vatican.va/roman_curia/congregations/cfaith/cti_documents/rc_cti_20140610_sensus-fidei_en.html. See also Janet E. Smith, "The *Sensus Fidelium* and *Humanae vitae*," *Angelicum* 83 (2006): 271–297, also published in *Called to Holiness and Communion: Vatican II on the Church*, ed. Rev. Stephen Boguslawski, OP and Robert Fastiggi (Scranton: University of Scranton Press, 2009), 291–318.

17 Interestingly, Revs. John C. Ford, SJ and Gerald Kelly, SJ provide strong reasons to consider the teaching infallible at the time of *Casti connubii;* see *Contemporary Moral Theology,* Vol. II, *Marriage Questions* (Westminster, MD: The Newman Press, 1964), 263–278. Arguments for the infallibility of *Humanae vitae* can be found in John C. Ford, SJ, Germain Grisez, Joseph Boyle, John Finnis, and William E. May, *The Teaching of* Humanae Vitae*: A Defense* (San Francisco: Ignatius Press, 1988).

18 Häring, *Free and Faithful in Christ,* 319–333.

19 For example, see Edward Pentin, "Pontifical Gregorian University Hosts Series of Talks to Take New Look at *Humanae Vitae*," (blog) *National Catholic Register,* October 21, 2017 and Edward Pentin, "Cardinal Parolin: *Amoris Laetitia* Represents New Paradigm, Spirit and Approach," (blog) *National Catholic Register,* January 11, 2018.

20 Stephan Goertz and Caroline Witting, Amoris laetitia: *Un punto di svolta per la teologia morale?* (Milan: San Paolo, 2017).

Here I am not going to attempt to establish whether *Amoris laetitia* either accomplishes or sets out to accomplish a development in moral theology or whether it correctly utilizes texts cited.[21] Those, of course, are crucial questions, yet ones not likely to be definitively answered for some time. In the meantime, those who find a development of moral theology in *Amoris laetitia* will not hesitate to use their interpretation to address moral issues. While it is necessary to challenge their interpretation of *Amoris laetitia* as legitimate, here I am only going to attempt to demonstrate that the purported development is not compatible with established Church teaching primarily with respect to its understanding of what the conscience is.

Pastoral Understanding of Conscience and Moral Law

This development involves, among other things, the role of the individual conscience in decision-making. Certainly, from the time *Humanae vitae* was promulgated, not only theologians but also bishops' conferences claimed that individuals who found a conflict of duties between honoring the procreative good of the sexual act and the unitive good were to follow their consciences in this regard rather than submit to the teachings *of Humanae vitae*. Some of the bishops' conferences that made this claim in their initial response to *Humanae vitae* eventually clarified that claim in a way that amounted to a retraction.[22] What concept of conscience guided that claim was, I believe, not very clear at the time. It has become clearer since.

It must be noted, however, that the development purportedly advanced by *Amoris laetitia* is said not to be doctrinal but to be pastoral in nature. The pastoral method that some claim *Amoris laetitia* promotes is one that honors the decision of the individual conscience over conformity to Church teaching. A decision made in accord with the values the individual has discerned to have priority in his/her decision-making should have greater force in making the choice than the "rules" of the Church.[23] *Amoris laetitia* laments, "We also find it hard to make room for the consciences of the faithful, who very often respond as best they can to the Gospel amid their limitations, and are capable of carrying out their own discernment in complex situations. We have been called to form consciences, not to replace them."[24]

21 For a strong argument that *Amoris laetitia* does not properly use Thomistic texts see, Rev. Kevin Flannery, SJ and Rev. Thomas Berg, "*Amoris Laetitia*, 'Pastoral Discernment' and Thomas Aquinas," *Nova et Vetera* (English edition) 15, no. 2 (Summer 2017): 81–111.

22 See, for instance, the statements of the Canadian bishops (as well as others) in *The Birth Control Debate*, ed. Robert G. Hoyt (Kansas City, Mo.: National Catholic Reporter: 1968), 169–170; and their clarification "Statement on the Formation of Conscience" (December 1, 1973), http://www.consciencelaws.org/religion/religion040.aspx.

23 It is imprecise that the English translation of *Amoris laetitia* speaks of "rules"—which are generally what govern games and are not always equivalent to a "law," whereas the Latin text uses the term "*norma*" which certainly can mean "law." Still, here I use "rules" since it seems to correspond better with the understanding of discerners.

24 Pope Francis, *Amoris laetitia*, 37.

Few would argue that anything should "replace" consciences, but there is significant disagreement about what it means to "form" consciences, particularly in respect to the role of "norms" or "moral laws" in that formation.

Those who find a development in moral theology in *Amoris laetitia* (for convenience, I will refer to them as the "discerners"), look to passages that portray insistence on rules as an act that threatens to "replace" consciences, rather than form them.[25] In *Amoris laetitia* we read, "It is reductive simply to consider whether or not an individual's actions correspond to a general law or rule, because that is not enough to discern and ensure full fidelity to God in the concrete life of a human being."[26]

Section 305 speaks of the "simple" application of moral laws to objectively sinful situations as "throwing stones," as being a kind of violence:

> For this reason, a pastor cannot feel that it is enough simply to apply moral laws to those living in "irregular" situations, as if they were stones to throw at people's lives. This would bespeak the closed heart of one used to hiding behind the Church's teachings, "sitting on the chair of Moses and judging at times with superiority and superficiality difficult cases and wounded families." ... By thinking that everything is black and white, we sometimes close off the way of grace and of growth, and discourage paths of sanctification which give glory to God. Let us remember that "a small step, in the midst of great human limitations, can be more pleasing to God than a life which appears outwardly in order, but moves through the day without confronting great difficulties."[27]

Several themes of the discerners can be found in the above passage, notably the following: insisting on moral laws is exercising unfair judgment over the wounded; insisting on moral laws does not acknowledge the complexities of life—it is to see things as black and white; and that to insist on moral laws is to close off important avenues of growth. These themes grow out of the discerners' understanding of conscience which they find present in section 303:

> Recognizing the influence of such concrete factors, we can add that individual conscience needs to be better incorporated into the Church's praxis in certain situations which do not objectively embody our understanding of marriage. Naturally, every effort should be made to encourage the development of an enlightened conscience, formed and guided by the responsible and serious discernment of one's pastor, and to encourage an ever greater trust in God's grace. Yet conscience can do more than recognize that a given situation does not correspond objectively to the overall demands of the Gospel. It can also recognize with sincerity and honesty

25 The fullest statement of what I am calling the "discerners'" interpretation of *Amoris laetitia* is expressed by Cardinal Blaise Cupich, "Pope Francis's Revolution of Mercy: *Amoris Laetitia* as a New Paradigm of Catholicity," *Vatican Insider Documents* (February 9, 2018).

26 Pope Francis *Amoris laetitia*, 304.

27 Pope Francis, *Amoris laetitia*, 305.

> what for now is the most generous response which can be given to God, and come to see with a certain moral security that it is what God himself is asking amid the concrete complexity of one's limits, while yet not fully the objective ideal. In any event, let us recall that this discernment is dynamic; it must remain ever open to new stages of growth and to new decisions which can enable the ideal [28] to be more fully realized.

The disceners find in the above passage their view that conscience is not a repository of the natural law or even a trustworthy guide for how to live out the demands of the Gospel. Rather, the conscience enables a "dynamic" discernment that helps a moral agent to determine what is the best he/she can do at this moment. Moral decisions are not to be judged for the correspondence to natural law or the Gospel but as indicators of personal growth towards the "ideal."

What I hope to establish here is that there is a radical difference between the understanding of conscience employed by the Church in its magisterial documents (to be described below)[29] based largely on the thought of Saint Thomas Aquinas (which I will call the "traditional" position) and the discerners' interpretation of *Amoris laetitia*.[30]

Traditional View of Conscience

Strangely, both traditionalists and revisionists find support for their positions in the description of conscience given in *Gaudium et spes*:[31]

> In the depths of his conscience, man detects a law which he does not impose upon himself, but which holds him to obedience. Always summoning him

28 The translation of the Latin "exemplar" by "ideal" is not unproblematic: the term "ideal" can suggest something rarely attained or even unattainable; "exemplar" does not have that connotation. See Robert Fastiggi and Dawn Eden Goldstein, "Does *Amoris laetitia* 303 Really Undermine Catholic Moral Teaching?," *Vatican Insider Documents* (September 26, 2017). For a response by Christian Brugger see Pete Baklinski, "Yes, *Amoris Laetitia* 303 Really Undermines Catholic Moral Teaching: Scholar," *Life Site News* (September 28, 2017).

29 A succinct and basic presentation of the Church's view on conscience can be found in the *Catechism of the Catholic Church*, in sections 1776–1794 and on natural law in sections 1950–1960.

30 A worthy comparison of the difference between the traditional view and revisionist view of conscience can be found in Robert J. Smith, *Conscience and Catholicism: The Nature and Function of Conscience in Contemporary Roman Catholic Moral Theology* (Lanham, Md.: University Press of America, 1998). Smith compares the understandings of conscience of Germain Grisez and Bernard Häring. The selection of Grisez as representative of the traditionalist view is perhaps unfortunate because he was not a traditional Thomist nor did he incorporate a personalist perspective into his work. Nonetheless, Smith's is a valuable study. See also David E. DeCosse, "The Primacy of Conscience, Vatican II, and Pope Francis: The Opportunity to Renew a Tradition," in *From Vatican II to Pope Francis: Charting A Catholic Future*, ed. Paul Crowley, SJ (Maryknoll, N.Y.: Orbis Books, 2014), 156–169.

31 Indeed, both Karol Wojtyła and Bernard Häring were involved in the drafting of *Gaudium et spes*, and that might account for the diversity of interpretations. A description of the two views of *Gaudium et spes* is found in Richard Spinello, "Pope John Paul II on Conscience," *Homiletic and Pastoral Review* (August 1, 2009) at http://www.hprweb.com/2009/08/pope-john-paul-ii-on-conscience; see also Linda Hogan, *Confronting the Truth: Conscience in the Catholic Tradition* (Mahwah, N.J.: Paulist Press, 2001).

> to love good and avoid evil, the voice of conscience when necessary speaks to his heart: do this, shun that. For man has in his heart a law written by God; to obey it is the very dignity of man; according to it he will be judged. Conscience is the most secret core and sanctuary of a man. There he is alone with God, Whose voice echoes in his depths.[32]

Traditionalists point to the claims of this passage that there is within the conscience a law that man "does not impose on himself, but which holds him to obedience" and that "man has in his heart a law written by God" and that "to obey it is the very dignity of man" to confirm the view of *synderesis* as the repository of natural law moral truths that should guide moral decisions.[33] In the traditional view, man's actual acts of conscience are to evaluate the morality of the possible choices before him in light of the universal principles (and their derivatives) that *synderesis* discloses to him. When there is a conflict between the agent's own will and what he understands to be the will of God, man's dignity lies not in abiding by his own judgment but in submitting to God's will. It is foundational to Christianity that God's will is always superior in goodness to man's. But submission to God's will does not mean that one is violating one's deepest self; rather one is conforming to the deepest truths of one's being. God's laws are laws that help persons perfect themselves. In fact, the ability to know those laws and to be able to act freely in accord with them, is considered to be the defining and the most noble features of the human person.

God has gifted mankind with the ability to discern the order He has established in the world and to know that living in accord with that order is beneficial for him. Indeed, man's essence is a part of that order and for man to live in accord with his essence is the very challenge of human life, an essence partially known through reason and more fully known through revelation. Indeed, moral truths are true because they are based on human nature, or the essence of the human person. Since all persons everywhere and at all times share the same human nature, the fundamental truths of morality are universally true.

The Church is, moreover, in the view of traditionalists, as John Henry Newman stated, the answer to "an urgent demand."[34] Since we and our cultures are so flawed, we can easily become confused about natural law truths. Thus, Christ gave the power of rightly interpreting natural law to the Church. Obeying the Church is not an act of surrendering one's dignity to an external authority but is responding generously to Christ Himself. Since "Christ . . . fully reveals man to

32 Vatican Council II, *Gaudium et spes* (December 7, 1965), 16, http://www.vatican.va/archive/hist_councils/ii_vatican_council/index.htm.

33 Häring cites this passage at the beginning of his treatment of conscience in *Free and Faithful in Christ*, 224. He does not immediately comment on it, but it seems to be the portion of this passage that has man "speaking with God" that suggests a "creative" element of acts of conscience and also the larger portion of his passage that speaks about the necessity of man obeying an erroneous conscience that is most appealing to him.

34 John Henry Newman, "A Letter Addressed to His Grace the Duke of Norfolk," 254, http://www.newmanreader.org/works/anglicans/volume2/gladstone/index.html.

man himself,"[35] we can become more fully one with Christ and the Father if we conform our actions to the Father's will.

Revisionist View of Conscience

The contemporary revisionist view of conscience is certainly not new, although I am not certain that traditionalists have altogether accurately understood it.[36] Now that it is linked with the practice of "discernment" some elements of the revisionist view of conscience, not always or fully recognized in the past, are coming into high relief. Here, I will largely be following the views of Häring, the Redemptorist, whose thinking on moral theology has been foundational for revisionists and remains so. Indeed, Keenan identifies Häring's work as the culminating achievement of the revisionist movement.[37] Keenan also notes that "Universally, conscience becomes the point of departure for revisionists."[38]

I will make four major points about the discerners' view of conscience, shaped, I believe, by the thought of Häring:

1. Häring's view of conscience was formed much more by insights in developmental psychology, among others, that of Erik Erikson, than it was rooted in the Thomistic philosophical view of conscience.[39]
2. The view of conscience rejected by Häring was a caricature of the Thomistic understanding of conscience.
3. The view developed by Häring was soundly rejected in *Veritatis splendor* which advanced a personalistic view of conscience that overcomes the legalistic view of conscience Häring found in the manuals. (Here, John Paul II's views on "participated theonomy" and "consciousness" are of key importance.)
4. The discerners' understanding of conscience yields an understanding of discernment and formation at odds with that advanced in magisterial documents.

Reading Häring's *Free and Faithful in Christ* is a dizzying and almost breathtaking experience. He sweeps the reader up in a torrent of enthusiasm for what is "free" and "creative" and "prophetic" with nods to fidelity and responsibility as well. He has an almost infectious confidence in the ability of Christians to put aside sin and boldly and prophetically create a new world. He works very hard to

35 *Gaudium et spes*, 22.

36 Claims that the revisionist view of conscience has been misunderstood by traditionalists can be found in Michael E. Allsopp and John J. O'Keefe, eds., *Veritatis Splendor: American Responses* (New York: Sheed and Ward, 2001).

37 Keenan, *A History of Catholic Moral Theology in the Twentieth Century*, 59, 95. Häring served on the Special Commission that advised Paul VI on contraception. He was one of the earliest dissenters from *Humanae vitae*, see "The Encyclical Crisis," *Commonweal* (September 6, 1968).

38 Keenan, *A History of Catholic Moral Theology in the Twentieth Century*, 97.

39 Häring, *Free and Faithful in Christ*, 87, 168–177.

free Christians from legalism and from obedience to any authority whose commands are accepted simply because they are laid down by authority.[40] Christ was freely faithful to His Father and so should we be. Christ came to set us free and to enable us to do creative work.

Häring had a view of the conscience that seems to equate conscience with the very self of the person: "Conscience has to do with man's total selfhood as a moral agent. The intellectual, volitional and emotional dynamics are not separated; they mutually compenetrate in the very depth where the person is person to himself."[41] That self (also called the "heart"), is constituted most basically by the moral values to which one has committed one's self through one's life choices.[42]

Häring describes Erikson's view of moral maturation as being one where an individual works to become autonomous from his superego and to establish interiorly a set of commitments to moral values that give him a fundamental orientation to life. The story of each individual's conscience is the story of how his choices shape him, choices made in "mutual reciprocity" with others. He is always to be seeking his own good and the good of others and to be willing to learn from his community. To grow morally, he must be true to his past and attempt to move forward, which would mean acting out of his deep fundamental orientation. What is more important than adherence to objective moral norms is that the individual preserve his authenticity. The self can be challenged, to be sure, but there should be no violence to the self in the form of reluctant adherence to norms not sincerely embraced by the moral agent since it would be a diminution of freedom and would inhibit future growth. It is wrong to try to persuade someone to perform or not perform an action out of obedience to some authority since that would be an imposition of external morality and thus would disqualify the act as being truly moral since, in this view, for an act to be truly moral it must stem from choices made in accord with the person's own values. Some choices not in accord with objective moral norms might have something of what Häring speaks of as a "prophetic" element because they can reveal hitherto unknown ethical possibilities.

In short, Häring's view of following one's conscience means being true to the values that have guided one's life whereas submitting to external norms would be to abdicate the freedom and responsibility that defines the Christian life. Perhaps this description explains why revisionists deny that they are rejecting absolute objective norms. It is not that such norms don't exist, it is that it is more important that one act in accord with one's own values.

Clearly, *synderesis* as a repository of natural law precepts is not a part of Häring's view of conscience. He rejected understandings of *synderesis* as the ready understanding of natural law, or universal absolute moral norms, from which other binding norms might be derived and which serve to guide a person

40 One reason for this is said to be his disappointment in the ready obedience of his fellow Catholics to the Nazi regime.

41 Häring, *Free and Faithful in Christ*, 235.

42 Häring, *Free and Faithful in Christ*, 90, 93, 259.

in making judgments of conscience in respect to particular acts. Conscience for him was the repository of the values to which one has committed one's self.

It is, thus not surprising that revisionists read *Gaudium et spes* and understand natural law very differently from traditionalists. They find it has a very personalist cast in speaking of the "voice of God within." The "law of God" that one finds within is not a set of universal moral values or norms but rather the natural striving for truth that each person finds within. Indeed, revisionists hold that *Gaudium et spes* advances a new paradigm of the conscience:

> [T]he actions and choices of the individual are a reflection of the kind of person one is and one will become. Actions are not considered in isolation from the person performing them. Furthermore, the person at the center of morality is 'part of the material world, interrelational with other persons, a social and historical being.' As a result the relationships and circumstances which go to make up the subject's experience do have real and enduring moral significance. *Gaudium et spes* puts forward a model of morality in which the person is the source of ethical discernment and action. In so doing it initiates a move toward a new paradigm, one that emphasizes personal responsibility rather than obedience.[43]

Again, the outcome of the discerner's view of conscience is that the job of the conscience is not to try to access the moral norms one knows by virtue of natural law, but it is to identify the values one has adopted through fruitful relationships with others.

Häring thinks natural law is something shaped by the community and that it changes over time as communities change. He uses the by now well-known categories of a classicist static morality and a historically conscious, dynamic morality.[44] The contrast he draws between two approaches to natural law is stark: "One mentality is closed minded, unresponsive, anthropocentric in the bad sense. This can be described as a rationalistic approach where there is no place left for new insights, no appreciation of the values and experiences of other cultures and subcultures." [45] And later, he describes the approach he advocates: "The other approach is "marked by the capacity to listen and to learn in dialogue with others with a vivid sense of the continuity of life. This attitude fits easily in the great dimensions of the history of salvation and revelation.... In this vision, natural law cannot be conceived as a closed system."[46]

In other passages, Häring identified natural law with the person's own striving to know the truth, not with the truths that can be naturally known by every person (the traditional view) or by the community over time (his earlier view):

43 Linda Hogan, *Confronting the Truth*, 108, footnote 19; Kevin Kelly, *New Directions in Moral Theology* (London: Sheed & Ward, 1987), 30.

44 Häring, *Free and Faithful in Christ*, 319.

45 Häring, *Free and Faithful in Christ*, 325.

46 Häring, *Free and Faithful in Christ*, 325.

> It is unthinkable to tell people in the Church or outside the Church to ignore their own conscience in favor of certain formulations of the "natural law," since natural law is not the legislation of any human authority but the sincerity of man searching the truth, the inner impulse to follow one's own sincere conviction.[47]

This view seems very compatible with the discerners' view of conscience, which considers sincerity, or being true to one's own values, as being the most important feature of a moral choice.

While there are many points of disagreement between the discerners' view of conscience and the traditional view that deserve attention, here I am going to focus on their claim that to try to lead someone to follow norms from an exterior source, is to do violence to the self, is to try to reestablish a childish dependence upon the superego, rather than to honor the person as a free and responsible adult. That claim is based on an erroneous view of the traditional view of conscience, and seriously conflicts with the understanding of conscience developed by John Paul II in his philosophical works and in the seminal encyclical *Veritatis splendor*.[48] Contemporary revisionists seem to have little awareness of how John Paul II's views of conscience—and consciousness—are very much personalist, although, of course, they differ in radical ways from the views of the discerners.

Conscience in *Veritatis splendor*

Veritatis splendor was written explicitly to demonstrate that many of the principles of revisionist theologians were not compatible with the moral theology taught and utilized by the Church, most particularly, that proportionalism was not a legitimate development of Church teaching.[49] The terminology favored by revisionists is throughout the document, such as "discernment," "creative," "freedom of conscience," and "fundamental option"; clearly an attempt was made to confront head on the claims of revisionists.

Veritatis splendor rejects a view of conscience that gives sovereignty to the autonomy of the reason of the individual person over the sovereignty of God.[50] That might not be quite what the revisionist view of conscience does, for their view of conscience does not focus exclusively upon reason and reason's attempt to discover objective truth. The autonomy revisionists promote is the autonomy of the "self" which is a mix of many factors, not just reason—discerners like to speak of the conscience as a person's individual "story." Nor do they necessarily

47 Robert Smith, *Conscience and Catholicism*, 94n103 citing, Bernard Häring, *Morality is for Persons* (New York: Farrar, Straus and Giroux, 1971), 171.

48 Pope John Paul II, *Veritatis splendor*, 75.

49 For a traditionalist interpretation of *Veritatis splendor*, see *Veritatis Splendor and the Renewal of Moral Theology: Studies by Ten Outstanding Scholars*, ed. J. A. DiNoia, OP and Romanus Cessario, OP (Chicago: Midwest Theological Forum, 1999).

50 See Pope John Paul II, *Veritatis splendor*, 65.

reject the sovereignty of God: what they reject is not God's sovereignty but the value of insisting on His sovereignty and even more so they reject viewing the Magisterium as a reliable, let alone, infallible interpreter of God's law. Both are rejected as being disrespectful to the individual conscience and as being a wrong-headed way to accompany people in their discernment of moral choices.

What contemporary revisionists fail to see is how important personal appropriation of moral norms is to the Church's understanding of conscience, especially as described by John Paul II. Because of his work in phenomenology which puts great emphasis on the person and consciousness, John Paul II developed a personalistic Thomism that emphasized the importance of the interiority of the human person and especially his consciousness of himself as a moral agent, as an entity capable of knowing the truth and living in accord with it. In *Veritatis splendor* he hits head on some of the key concerns of contemporary revisionists:

> Man's *genuine moral autonomy* in no way means the rejection but rather the acceptance of the moral law, of God's command: "The Lord God gave this command to the man. . ." (Gen 2:16). *Human freedom and God's law meet and are called to intersect*, in the sense of man's free obedience to God and of God's completely gratuitous benevolence towards man. Hence obedience to God is not, as some would believe, a *heteronomy*, as if the moral life were subject to the will of something all-powerful, absolute, extraneous to man and intolerant of his freedom. If in fact a heteronomy of morality were to mean a denial of man's self-determination or the imposition of norms unrelated to his good, this would be in contradiction to the Revelation of the Covenant and of the redemptive Incarnation. Such a heteronomy would be nothing but a form of alienation, contrary to divine wisdom and to the dignity of the human person.[51]

Does not John Paul II manifest a keen appreciation of the concerns of contemporary revisionists here? He holds that it would in fact be a violation of man's nature and of the necessity that man be self-determining if the Christian life were to demand of the human person that he submit himself to "the will of something all-powerful, absolute, extraneous to man and intolerant of his freedom."[52] John Paul II does not counsel a robotic obedience to externally imposed laws; rather he speaks of a "participated theonomy"[53] wherein "man's free obedience to God's law effectively implies that human reason and human will participate in God's wisdom and providence."[54]

John Paul II's concept of participation is a very rich one; it is based on the ability of man to know the truth and freely choose it, an ability at the very core of man's nature. The human person and God are not at odds on that level. God's will

51 Pope John Paul II, *Veritatis splendor*, 41. Emphasis in the original.

52 Pope John Paul II, *Veritatis splendor*, 41.

53 Pope John Paul II, *Veritatis splendor*, 41.

54 Pope John Paul II, *Veritatis splendor*, 41.

is that man should never commit adultery; man's will should be that he never commit adultery and he should accept that, again, as a "law" friendly to his being. He is capable of seeing things as God sees things and valuing them as God does because he is made in the image and likeness of God.

John Paul II also had a very refined understanding of the terms "conscious" and "consciousness," developed in his days as a philosopher (these words and the concepts conveyed by them play a major role in his works), and even began preferring the term "self-conscious" to "rational" when speaking of man's essential nature (as he spoke of "self-determining" in place of "free," of "self-mastery" in place of "virtue," of "self-giving" in place of "social").[55] The words "conscious" and "consciousness" refer to the interiority of man, to his subjective appropriation of objective truths.

In *Love and Responsibility*, John Paul II coined the phrase "conscious parenthood" (akin to "responsible parenthood" but different in extremely important ways).[56] The term meant that the human being striving to live in accord with his dignity, with his nature as a truth-seeking, free, and responsible entity, would be conscious that sex leads to being a parent and that, thus, one should only have sex with someone with whom one is willing to be a parent—which, of course, means, with a spouse. That realization would not be one that makes a person morose or rebellious but one he would recognize as fully compatible with his own dignity and the dignity of others and, thus, he would embrace it as such a truth.

This view of man's relationship to God's moral truths is succinctly expressed in *Veritatis splendor*, quoting *Gaudium et spes*:

> Patterned on God's freedom, man's freedom is not negated by his obedience to the divine law; indeed, only through this obedience does it abide in the truth and conform to human dignity. This is clearly stated by the Council: "Human dignity requires man to act through conscious and free choice, as motivated and prompted personally from within, and not through blind internal impulse or merely external pressure. Man achieves such dignity when he frees himself from all subservience to his feelings, and in a free choice of the good, pursues his own end by effectively and assiduously marshalling the appropriate means."[57]

And further it states, "These universal and permanent laws correspond to things known by the practical reason and are applied to particular acts through the judgment of conscience. The acting subject personally assimilates the truth contained in the law. He appropriates this truth of his being and makes it his own by his acts and the corresponding virtues."[58]

55 Janet E. Smith, "The University of Natural Law and the Irreducibility of Personalism," *Nova et Vetera* (English edition) 11, no. 4 (Fall 2013): 1229–1248.

56 Janet E. Smith, "Conscious Parenthood," *Nova et Vetera* (English edition) 6, no. 4 (Fall 2008): 927–950.

57 Pope John Paul II, *Veritatis splendor*, 42, quoting *Gaudium et spes*, 17.

58 Pope John Paul II, *Veritatis splendor*, 52.

In the tradition, the act of discernment for a person making a difficult choice is not at all robotic but it involves the sincere attempt to discover what is God's will in respect to one's choice. There are several discussions in *Veritatis splendor* that demonstrate that such a view of conscience and discernment is not an abrogation of man's freedom or a violation of his self. Section 55 seems to be a direct response to Häring and the revisionist view of conscience. It speaks of those who:

> …stress the *complexity* typical of the phenomenon of conscience, a complexity profoundly related to the whole sphere of psychology and the emotions, and to the numerous influences exerted by the individual's social and cultural environment. On the other hand, they give maximum attention to the value of conscience, which the Council itself defined as "the sanctuary of man, where he is alone with God whose voice echoes within him." This voice, it is said, leads man not so much to a meticulous observance of universal norms as to a creative and responsible acceptance of the personal tasks entrusted to him by God.
>
> In their desire to emphasize the "creative" character of conscience, certain authors no longer call its actions "judgments" but "decisions": only by making these decisions "autonomously" would man be able to attain moral maturity. Some even hold that this process of maturing is inhibited by the excessively categorical position adopted by the Church's Magisterium in many moral questions; for them, the Church's interventions are the cause of unnecessary *conflicts of conscience.*[59]

Veritatis splendor goes on to say that the erroneous view of conscience it is rejecting leads to permitting persons "to do in practice and in good conscience what is qualified as intrinsically evil by the moral law. A separation, or even an opposition, is thus established in some cases between the teaching of the precept, which is valid in general, and the norm of the individual conscience, which would in fact make the final decision about what is good and what is evil."[60]

Revisionists would likely protest that they are not approving the choice to do intrinsically evil actions, since the agent does not consider the action to be intrinsically evil. In their view an action can be wrong and moral at the same time.[61]

Not only is the revisionists' and discerners' view of conscience very different from the tradition, the discerners' view does not conform to the way that Jesus welcomed and accompanied those who approached Him in respect to moral matters. *Veritatis splendor* gives primacy of place to the encounter of the rich young man with Jesus. He asks what *Veritatis splendor* depicts as "an essential

59 Pope John Paul II, *Veritatis splendor*, 55. Emphasis in the original.

60 Pope John Paul II, *Veritatis splendor*, 56.

61 For a good review of possible positions on the meaning of "erroneous conscience," see Brian V. Johnstone, "Erroneous Conscience in *Veritatis Splendor* and the Theological Tradition," in *The Splendor of Accuracy*, ed. Joseph A. Selling and Jan Jans (Grand Rapids, Mich.: Eerdmans, 1995), 115–135, especially 128–129.

and unavoidable question for the life of every man": "What must I do to gain eternal life?"[62] Jesus does not seek to discover what moral commitments the young man has made. Instead, without hesitation, He tells him he must follow the commandments, a rather black-and-white approach to matters, an approach that, in the eyes of some, it seems, could be portrayed as somewhat harsh. The young man asks for specificity and Jesus recites some of the commandments to him. When the young man states he has done these, Jesus does not try to discover if the young man has been following these in a robotic way, in blind obedience to authority—though according to *Veritatis splendor*, he has not been. *Veritatis splendor* states that the young man "has followed the moral ideal seriously and generously from childhood."[63] Jesus makes a challenge that it would be hard for anyone to embrace, especially a rich young man. He states, "If you wish to be perfect, go, sell your possessions and give the money to the poor, and you will have treasure in heaven; then come, follow me" (Mt 19:21).[64]

It could be said that features of Jesus' approach do not conform to some of the advice given in *Amoris laetitia* which states:

> Moral education entails asking of a child or a young person only those things that do not involve a disproportionate sacrifice, and demanding only a degree of effort that will not lead to resentment or coercion. Ordinarily this is done by proposing small steps that can be understood, accepted and appreciated, while including a proportionate sacrifice. Otherwise, by demanding too much, we gain nothing.[65]

The young man does not accept Jesus' challenge to give away all his possessions and follow Jesus. Rather, he walks away, just as many walked away when Jesus explained the Eucharist to them. Jesus does not run after him and counsel him to do the best that he can. The challenge remains.

Veritatis splendor speaks of this encounter as portraying the kind of growth in moral maturity that we must all go through.

> *Perfection demands that maturity in self-giving to which human freedom is called.* Jesus points out to the young man that the commandments are the first and indispensable condition for having eternal life . . . [Jesus' invitation to the young man] reveal[s] the particular dynamic of freedom's growth towards maturity, and at the same time *they bear witness to the fundamental relationship between freedom and divine law.* Human freedom and God's law are not in opposition; on the contrary, they appeal one to the other. The follower of Christ knows that his vocation is to freedom.[66]

62 Pope John Paul II, *Veritatis splendor*, 8.

63 Pope John Paul II, *Veritatis splendor*, 16.

64 Pope John Paul II, *Veritatis splendor*, 16.

65 Pope Francis, *Amoris laetitia*, 271.

66 Pope John Paul II, *Veritatis splendor*, 17.

As *Veritatis splendor* states, freedom begins with obedience to the commandments. Being obedient to the commandments is the foundation for a more radical adventure, the adventure of partaking in the life and destiny of Jesus, "sharing in his free and loving obedience to the will of the Father."[67]

A thoughtful reading of Scripture should lead the reader to ask, "Is there anything in Jesus' words or behavior that suggest that He would share the discerner's view of conscience?" Of the view that it is more important to be sincere and act in accord with one's own values than to be obedient to the objective norms of the Gospel? Jesus clearly believed His greatest achievement was being obedient to the Father in all things, something that came with enormous price. Of nothing was He more determined; in His view, nothing He said or did glorified God more. Jesus called His disciples to become one with Him and a means and a result of becoming one with Him would be the submission of their wills to God in all things. In His encounters with sinners, He admonished them to "go and sin no more" not to be true to their "selves."

Legitimate Pastoral Techniques

It is important to note that some of the techniques of moral formation and "accompanying" mentioned in *Amoris laetitia* have legitimate uses in educating youth, especially in preparation for reception of the sacraments, in spiritual direction or the confessional, and in pastoral counseling. *Amoris laetitia* speaks of such techniques as showing young people how behaving morally is to their advantage[68] and of the use of the principle of the law of gradualness.[69]

There are certainly times when the pastor may follow the principle of the law of gradualness and postpone pressing the force of an objective absolute universal norm. For instance, often in marriage preparation when a pastor learns that the couple he is preparing for marriage is already engaging in sexual intercourse, he may wait until a later meeting, after he has established a relationship with them, to help them to understand that they are not living in accord with God's plan for sexuality. Initially, he may find it helpful to stress that scientific studies show that marriages preceded by cohabitation are more likely to end in divorce rather than trying to get them to fully understand the Church's full view of marriage. He may wait until after the couple decide to separate before marriage to discuss with them the immorality of contraception, again, possibly stressing the bad health effects for the woman and its effectiveness more than its incompatibility with the procreative and unitive meanings of marriage.

Discerning the morality about attending the weddings of Catholics living in irregular situations or getting married outside of the Church requires great prudence. One of my friends told her brother that she could not attend his wedding unless he stopped cohabiting with his fiancée before the wedding. He was not happy with her "threat" but he and his fiancée reconsidered, stopped cohabiting,

67 Pope John Paul II, *Veritatis splendor*, 19.

68 See Pope Francis, *Amoris laetitia*, 265.

69 See Pope Francis, *Amoris laetitia*, 295.

and eventually become devout Catholics who were grateful to his sister. Other friends of mine, arguably overly strict Catholics, after much prayer and consultation, decided, against powerful "instincts," to attend the out-of-the-Church wedding of their oldest son because they believed their younger children would interpret them as being hateful and rebel should they not attend. That son eventually came back to the Church and the parents maintained a decent relationship with their younger children. I have even known devout Catholic parents with younger children in the house, who allowed an older son to live with his girlfriend in their home. They were confident they could convey to the son and the younger children that they disapproved of his behavior. Their intent was to remain close to him and to have multiple opportunities to persuade their son to marry his girlfriend. Surely that is a technique to be used rarely but within the realm of prudent strategy.

Discernment about prudential matters is no easy task but one sure rule is that one never does evil to achieve good. The laws of the Gospel, the Church, and natural law that are universal and absolute cannot be set aside in pursuit of other goods.

As legitimate as some of the pastoral techniques are in *Amoris laetitia*, unfortunately, the discerners might find some support in Section 7, on the education of children for their understanding of the place of "norms" in moral formation and judgment. Indeed, comparing some of those principles with others found in *The Truth and Meaning of Human Sexuality,*[70] a document of the former Pontifical Council for the Family,[71] will demonstrate how different views of conscience yield different principles for formation and discernment.

Amoris laetitia states that "[moral formation] should ... take place inductively, so that children can learn for themselves the importance of certain values, principles and norms, rather than by imposing these as absolute and unquestionable truths."[72] Revisionists may find in this passage a reflection of their aversion to "deduction" as a method that somehow is not open to the dynamism of experience. While there is no denying that a heavy-handed education in absolutes is inadvisable and while "induction" is a means for discovering truth, the tradition certainly holds that deduction has its place. Our minds are naturally logical, so deductive argument can be very effective; for instance, it works quite well to teach the immorality of abortion by moving from the naturally known absolute moral truth that it is wrong deliberately and willingly to take an innocent human life, to providing a demonstration of the humanity of the unborn and moving to a recognition that abortion is always wrong. The same could be done for many truths, such as the denial of fundamental human rights to those who differ from

70 Pontifical Council for the Family, *The Truth and Meaning of Human Sexuality: Guidelines for Education within the Family* (December 8, 1995), http://www.vatican.va/roman_curia/pontifical_councils / family/index.htm.

71 On August 15, 2016, Pope Francis issued the *Motu Proprio* which merged the Pontifical Council for the Family with the Pontifical Council for the Laity. The *Motu Proprio* instituted the Dicastery for The Laity, The Family, and Life; see http://w2.vatican.va/content/francesco/en/motu_proprio.index.html.

72 Pope Francis, *Amoris laetitia*, 264.

us in ethnicity or race: once we realize all human beings, no matter what race or ethnicity, share the same essence and that our rights are rooted in our essence, certain important truths can be readily deduced.

As noted above, in paragraph 271 *Amoris laetitia* seems to counsel against challenging people to submit themselves to a morality that they find to be demanding. The advice given in *Amoris laetitia* may not have universal application: while, by definition, demands for unreasonable sacrifices are unwise, many a parent has found that the only way for some children to make progress in the moral life is to put up with resentment and to have recourse to the coercion of punishment. The major difference between the advice given on moral formation in *Amoris laetitia* and that in *The Truth and Meaning of Human Sexuality* is that the latter speaks many times of the need to learn to sacrifice, to gain self-control[73] and self-mastery[74] and also of the appeal of universal absolute moral norms. *The Truth and Meaning of Human Sexuality* is confident that young people can grasp and dedicate themselves to challenging moral truths because, as *Veritas splendor* repeatedly maintains, they are written on our consciences. Moreover, we have access to grace that will make up for our weaknesses. *The Truth and Meaning of Human Sexuality* states:

> As its departure point, the formation of conscience requires being enlightened about: God's project of love for every single person, the positive and liberating value of the moral law, and awareness both of the weakness caused by sin and the means of grace which strengthen us on our path towards the good and towards salvation. . . .[75]
>
> [T]he formation of conscience requires being enlightened about the truth and God's plan and must not be confused with a vague subjective feeling or with personal opinion. In answering children's questions, parents should offer well-reasoned arguments about the great value of chastity and show the intellectual and human weakness of theories that inspire permissive and hedonistic behaviour.[76]

Whereas *The Truth and Meaning of Human Sexuality* speaks of God's law repeatedly,[77] in section 271 through section 286 of *Amoris laetitia,* there is no explicit mention of God as lawgiver. If all law given to us from God is ultimately for our flourishing, it would be important to reflect on that truth when considering moral education.

Conclusion

This essay has focused on the radically different understanding of conscience held by the discerners and the tradition of the Church. But, of course, the divide

73 See Pontifical Council for the Family, *Truth and Meaning of Human Sexuality*, 5, 31, 55, and 58.

74 See Pontifical Council for the Family, *Truth and Meaning of Human Sexuality*, 8, 18, 55, and 58.

75 Pontifical Council for the Family, *The Truth and Meaning of Human Sexuality*, 95.

76 Pontifical Council for the Family, *The Truth and Meaning of Human Sexuality*, 95–96.

77 Pontifical Council for the Family, *The Truth and Meaning of Human Sexuality*, 29, 54, 73, 95, 140.

goes deeper. Ultimately, the question is what criteria are to be used to determine the rightness or wrongness of an action.[78] Discerners are primarily concerned that an action should be representative of the moral agent's highest values. They talk about accompanying a person in the moral life but give no indication where that accompanying should take them. They reject the traditional understanding of natural law, Scripture, and the magisterium as authorities because all of them, in their view, are historically and culturally conditioned. As noted, the discerners also allow for the possibility that the decision of the moral agent in conflict with the moral teaching of the Church may, in fact, be the result of the guidance of the Holy Spirit and, thus, be prophetic. Yet how is it to be determined which decisions are guided by the Holy Spirit and which are prophetic? Won't all those decisions also be historically or culturally conditioned? Do the discerners hope to return to the time when moral theologians were the ones who decide which actions are moral and which not? What guarantees that those judgments are not historically and culturally determined? Or in the end, is that all we have? Do we merely have historically and culturally conditioned "truths" and thus, relativism with all its inherent problems and incompatibility with Church teaching?

The application of this reasoning to *Humanae vitae* is clear. Indeed, we do not need to speculate how it will be applied by discerners. Rev. Maurizio Chiodi, a member of the Pontifical Academy for Life, basing his reasoning on *Amoris laetitia*, tells us that there are circumstances that make the use of contraception obligatory.[79] A popular e-magazine reports on an address that he gave:

> The Italian moral theologian explained that "normally, the objective is identified with the moral norm known by reason and the subjective is identified with the conscience enlightened by the law." But he rejected this idea, arguing instead that "the relationship between objective and subjective is not a relationship between the norm known by reason and the conscience" but "between the act . . . and conscience." The task for philosophers and theologians, Chiodi said, is to "rethink a theory of conscience" that recovers "the original link between conscience and the moral act."[80]

The assumptions behind Chiodi's understanding of how *Humanae vitae* should be read in light of *Amoris laetitia* are precisely those identified in the course of this essay. The conscience is the self and it is the job of the conscience to discern the best that it can do in light of one's personal circumstances; there is no necessity to try to conform one's behavior to external norms both because abiding by

78 In truth, the ultimate questions are metaphysical—are there enduring essences and natures of things and actions that dictate how they are to be used and treated? If so, the traditional morality of the Church has a strong claim to truth and the historicist view of revisionists is very much threatened. But few revisionists even allude to the metaphysical presuppositions of their claims, let alone labor to justify them.

79 *LifeSiteNews*, "New Academy of Life Member uses *Amoris* to say some circumstances 'require' use of contraception" (January 8, 2018), https://www.lifesitenews.com/news/new-academy-for-life-member-uses-amoris-to-say-some-circumstances-require-c.

80 *LifeSiteNews*, "New Academy of Life Member."

external norms reduces the authenticity of an action and because the norms are social constructs.

Those who would defend *Humanae vitae* in the face of modern challenges to it must understand how radically the view of conscience (and moral norms, natural law, authority, etc.) diverges from that of the magisterium and shape their arguments accordingly.

17

Humanae vitae *and The Cross of Infertility*

Elizabeth R. Kirk

HUMANAE VITAE IS MOST OFTEN considered in the context of married couples who wish to avoid pregnancy, and much of the controversy surrounding its initial reception and continued relevance involves the deep divisions within our culture and within the Church regarding the practices of contraception, sterilization, and abortion, as well as pastoral concerns for those wounded by these practices and by the hardships related to child-bearing that many couples experience. The breach between the Church's clear teaching on contraception and the widespread acceptance and practice of it by Catholics presents an enormous pastoral challenge and a special task for theologians to account faithfully for the teaching in a way that touches the human heart.

Many focus on these "hard teachings" of *Humanae vitae* while its teachings on "conjugal love" and "the good of procreation" are considered primarily in scholarship and in pastoral application in relation to such practices and concerns. In this essay, I hope to offer some reflections from the perspective of infertility that demonstrate the beauty and consolation of its message.[1] Specifically, the purpose of this essay is to establish, from the perspective of infertility, that all married couples are called to live deeply and intentionally the vocation of marital fruitfulness.

I will reflect first on the cross of infertility itself, focusing on its role in Scripture and on the particular ways it affects a husband and wife in marriage. Then I will briefly summarize the teaching of *Humanae vitae* on the relationship between unity and fecundity in the conjugal union and reflect on how the cross of infertility remains an occasion for couples to experience marital fecundity, and to surrender to the way in which God plans for them to manifest His creative love. Finally, I will offer a few pastoral reflections and suggest that couples who carry the cross of

* Special thanks are extended to Rev. Kevin Flannery, SJ, Janet Smith, and Rev. Alessandro Borraccia, AVI, for their generous reading of this manuscript in draft, and for their helpful interventions.

1 There is ample room in theological scholarship to take into account more fully the experience of infertility. Examples of this include Michael Brummond, "Toward a Theology of Infertility: The Trinity in Richard of St. Victor," *Homiletic & Pastoral Review* (January 16, 2014); Kathryn Lilla Cox, "Toward a Theology of Infertility and the Role of *Donum Vitae*," *Horizons* 40, no. 1 (June 2013): 28–52; Timothy O'Malley, "Editorial Musings: The Charism of Infertility," *Church Life Journal* (April 4, 2017); Maura Ryan, "Faith and Infertility," in *Cloning*, Christian Reflection: A Series in Faith and Ethics 16 (Waco: The Center for Christian Ethics at Baylor University, 2005): 65–74. https://www.baylor.edu/ifl/index.php?id=937582.

infertility and in particular, who obey God's plan for procreation, can be witnesses for those who struggle with the "hard teachings" of *Humanae vitae*.

In this essay, I am not concerned with applying the principles of *Humanae vitae* to evaluate various technological and medical responses (assisted reproductive technologies, or ART) to infertility. *Donum vitae*, the instruction on respect for human life in its origin and on the dignity of procreation, promulgated by the Congregation for the Doctrine of the Faith (CDF), and its successor, *Dignitatis personae*, address those matters. There is also a great deal of associated scholarship, especially in the field of moral theology, on ART. In any case, according to those CDF documents, the principles articulated in *Humanae vitae* inform the standard that the Church has enunciated for evaluating the morality of ART,[2] and provide direction to infertile couples seeking to conceive a child. In *Donum vitae*, "the community of believers is called to shed light upon and support the suffering of those who are unable to fulfill their legitimate aspiration to motherhood and fatherhood."[3] In the spirit of that call, it is my intent to focus on the implications of *Humanae vitae* for those who carry this cross, whether temporarily or throughout their lives.

The Cross of Infertility

In Scripture, fruitfulness is both a command ("Be fruitful and multiply"[4]) and a blessing,[5] and it contains ample evidence of the deep sorrow that attends the cross of infertility. There is no doubt that infertility goes against nature—it is privation: a consequence of original sin, like death, and there are significant physiological, emotional, psychological, and even social aspects to the cross of infertility.[6] The words of Rachel capture the depth of the grief so well—"Give me children or I shall die!"[7] The barren womb is often depicted in Scripture as

2 Congregation for the Doctrine of the Faith (CDF), *Donum vitae* (February 22, 1987), 7, http://www.vatican.va/roman_curia/congregations/cfaith/doc_doc_index.htm. *Donum vitae* states that "a medical intervention respects the dignity of persons when it seeks to assist the conjugal act either in order to facilitate its performance or in order to enable it to achieve its objective once it has been normally performed. On the other hand, it sometimes happens that a medical procedure technologically replaces the conjugal act in order to obtain a procreation which is neither its result nor its fruit. In this case the medical act is not, as it should be, at the service of conjugal union but rather appropriates to itself the procreative function and thus contradicts the dignity and the inalienable rights of the spouses and of the child to be born."

3 CDF, *Donum vitae*, 8.

4 Gn 1:28. Scripture quotes in this chapter are taken from the Revised Standard Version, 2nd Catholic edition (San Francisco: Ignatius Press, 2006).

5 See Gn 49:25, when Jacob blesses his son Joseph, he asks God to bless him with "blessings of heaven above, blessings of the deep that lies beneath, blessings of the breasts and of the womb." See also Dt 7:14, Moses tells the Jewish people that one of the blessings for obedience to God is "you shall be blessed above all peoples; there shall not be male or female barren among you, or among your cattle."

6 See, for example, A. D. Domar, P. C. Zuttermeister, and R. Friedman, "The Psychological Impact of Infertility: A Comparison with Patients with Other Medical Conditions," supplement, *Journal of Psychosomatic Obstetrics and Gynecology* 14 (January 1993): 45–52, finding that infertile women report equivalent levels of anxiety and depression as women with cancer, hypertension, and heart disease and recommending that standard psychosocial interventions used for serious medical illness should also be applied in infertility treatment.

7 Gn 30:1.

a curse.[8] However, upon scrutiny, barrenness as curse or punishment is not the primary role of infertility in Scripture; most of the barren women of Scripture were virtuous women. Rather, infertility, especially in the cases of women past menopause, provides the occasion for God's purposeful intervention in perpetuating His people, in difficult or even impossible circumstances, and demonstrates His faithfulness to his covenant and the plan He has for them (which will culminate in the miraculous conception and birth of Jesus). Indeed, the repeated theme of the childless couple and God's purposeful, miraculous intervention permeates the entire narrative history of the Jewish people. In each of the cases of Abraham and Sarah,[9] Isaac and Rebekah,[10] Jacob and Rachel,[11] Manoah and his wife,[12] Elkanah and Hannah,[13] the Shunammite couple,[14] and Zechariah and Elizabeth,[15] God opened and closed the womb to accomplish His divine plan or to show forth His mercy and omnipotence—for "nothing is impossible with God."[16]

All of the barren women described in Scripture, save one, conceive and bear a child. And, although that one incident is in some sense a personal punishment or curse, it too demonstrates God's purposeful intervention in the plan of salvation for His people. When Saul disobeyed God by offering an unlawful sacrifice, Samuel pronounced God's judgment upon him:

> You have not kept the commandment of the Lord your God, which he commanded you; for now the Lord would have established your kingdom over Israel forever. But now your kingdom shall not continue; the Lord has sought out a man after his own heart.[17]

This new king, David, whose kingdom God promised would never end, took as his first wife Saul's daughter, Michal. When David brought the Ark to Jerusalem, Michal observed him dancing before the Ark, and "despising him in her heart," she mocked him. The passage concludes, "Michal the daughter of Saul had no child to the day of her death."[18] Perhaps her barrenness was a personal curse, but the more important aspect of the story is that her sterility demonstrated the fulfillment of God's providential plan. Because she and David had no offspring,

8 See, for example, Gn 20:18, the Lord closed the wombs of the house of Abimelech because he had taken Sarah for his own, and Hos 9:11–14, "Give them, O Lord—what will you give? Give them a miscarrying womb and dry breasts."

9 See Gn 17:15–21.

10 See Gn 25:21.

11 And Leah; see Gn 29 and 30.

12 See Jgs 13:2–3.

13 See 1 Sm 1:1–20.

14 See 2 Kgs 4:14–17.

15 See Lk 1:5–24.

16 Lk 1:36–37.

17 1 Sm 13:13–14.

18 2 Sm 6:23.

Saul's descendants (through her) would never be part of the eternal house of David, as Samuel had prophesied. God closes and opens the womb for His own purpose.

Couples who struggle with infertility might find solace in meditating on these scriptural passages. Indeed, what a privilege it is to carry the cross that played such a role in salvation history! On the other hand, these stories can be discouraging because, except for Michal, all of the women *do* conceive and bear children eventually. Sadly, many couples are never able to conceive or carry to term a child and this cross weighs heavily on the man, the woman, and on them both as a couple.

Because our bodies carry within them the potential for motherhood and fatherhood, infertility damages one's understanding of one's own femininity or masculinity. A man stands outside the biological processes of pregnancy and childbirth and, in many ways, learns his own fatherhood from the child's mother.[19] Nevertheless, men too suffer deeply from the cross of infertility. Abraham cried aloud in lamentation to God, "What will you give, for I continue childless?"[20] When it is the case that infertility is caused by the man's particular physiological difficulty, his own sterility may cause him feelings of insecurity as he suffers deeply not because he is unable to provide for his family but because he is literally unable to provide a family.

And yet, the cross of infertility necessarily plays out on the woman in a particular way. The absence of pregnancy, or the inability to conceive, never shows on a man in the way that it is repeatedly visited upon the woman, whose belly is never swollen with new life and who is reminded by her body that she is, for yet another month, not pregnant. According to Pope John Paul II, the ability to conceive and bear children gives rise to woman's particular "feminine genius," that is, her special ability to give and receive the human person in love. Although John Paul II is careful to say that this "is not limited to an exclusively bio-physiological interpretation of women,"[21] this physical capacity does reveal an important dimension of the female vocation, that is, motherhood. "This unique contact with the new human being developing within her gives rise to an attitude towards human beings—not only towards her own child, but every human being—which profoundly marks the woman's personality."[22] Therefore, for a woman to be unable to conceive and give birth is the occasion not only for deep emotional sadness, but also a more fundamental anguish regarding her worth *as a woman*.

Infertility can affect women in another very particular way. John Paul II cautioned that the woman must take care that her sensitivity to others "does not succumb to the temptation to possessive selfishness."[23] This tendency toward

19 See Pope John Paul II, Apostolic Letter *Mulieris dignitatem* (August 15, 1988), 18, http://w2.vatican.va/content/john-paul-ii/en/apost_letters/1988.index.html.

20 Gn 15:2.

21 Pope John Paul II, *Mulieris dignitatem*, 18.

22 Pope John Paul II, *Mulieris dignitatem*, 18.

23 Pope John Paul II, "Society and Church Need Genius of Woman" (July 23, 1995), http://www.ewtn.com/library/PAPALDOC/JP95723B.htm.

possessive selfishness, in the context of infertility, can become a possessive desire to *have* children—to think of a child as an object rather than as a gift, a unique other person. Indeed, according to Proverbs, the barren womb is never satisfied.[24] A literary story will illustrate the point. In C. S. Lewis's *The Great Divorce*, a mother expects to encounter her son as a guide as she makes her way on a purgatorial journey to heaven. To her great dismay, someone else greets her. She cries out,

> No one has the right to come between me and my son. Not even God. Tell Him that to his face. I want my boy, and I mean to have him. He is mine, do you understand? Mine, mine, mine for ever and ever.[25]

The narrator concludes, observing how the mother perverted a natural, noble relationship:

> No natural feelings are high or low, holy or unholy, in themselves. They are all holy when God's hand is on the rein. They all go bad when they set upon their own will and make themselves into false gods. . . . Everything . . . is good when it looks to Him and bad when it turns from Him. And the higher and mightier it is in the natural order, the more demoniac it will be if it rebels.[26]

The lure of assisted reproductive technologies reinforces this temptation to view the child as object and to idolize parenthood and treats the man and the woman as instruments toward the production of that child. In vitro fertilization, for example, involves the creation of embryos outside the woman's body, the screening of embryos for optimal implantation and survival, possible "reduction" in the event that multiple embryos implant, and the storage or destruction of "excess" embryos. The child produced through this process is treated from her conception as an interchangeable, fungible, and ultimately disposable commodity, rather than as a unique and beloved human person. Such a method combines the worst aspects of technological proficiency and a consumerist mentality and preys on the very natural (and good) desire for children while doing nothing to identify or treat the underlying causes of infertility.

In addition to its effect on men and on women, the cross of infertility strikes to the very heart of the vocation to married life. Because children are the visible sign of a married couple's union and love (i.e., the two are made one literally),[27] the

24 See Prv 30:16.

25 C. S. Lewis, *The Great Divorce* (New York: Simon & Schuster, 1996), 93–94.

26 Lewis, *The Great Divorce*, 92, 96.

27 Pope John Paul II, Apostolic Exhortation *Familiaris consortio* (November 22, 1981), 14, "[T]he couple, while giving themselves to one another, give not just themselves but also the reality of children, who are a living reflection of their love, a permanent sign of conjugal unity and a living and inseparable synthesis of their being a father and a mother." http://w2.vatican.va/content/john-paul-ii/en/apost_exhortations.index.html.

very act that is ordered toward new life can come to feel sterile, selfish, or even pointless. Just as *Humanae vitae* predicted that contraception and pornography risk reducing one's spouse to an object of pleasure,[28] a hyper-focus on fertility can reduce one's spouse to a means to have children. In *Love and Responsibility*, Karol Wojtyła reflected on the deeply rooted inclination toward motherhood and fatherhood in woman and man—the longing for a child. In parenthood, he observes, men and women "find a confirmation not only of their physical but also of their spiritual maturity and a foreshadowing of extending their existence."[29] This longing, written into human biology, also occurs on the spiritual plane—a longing for the fruit of "the flesh of my flesh," for one made in our image, for love made incarnate as a person, for immortality—and this longing is satisfied in a concrete way in a biological child. The fulfillment of this longing is best expressed through parenthood within marriage, in light of the other goods of marriage, fidelity and indissolubility. Indeed, without the supernatural perspective of the meaning of marriage, biological generation loses its transcendent meaning. As Mr. Blue exclaims when he expresses gratitude for the incarnate Christ, "Without Christ we would be little more than bacteria breeding on a pebble in space. . . . Only for him, I would be confounded before the awful fertility and intricacy of all life."[30] To be deprived, then, of the child that explains the radical self-gift and permanence of marriage is to feel cheated of one of the chief goods of marriage. Marriage is meant to create a space for others, specifically for a child, and the *emptiness* of that space can threaten to define or destroy the marriage itself.

Finally, differences in modes of communication can pose a challenge for husbands and wives in these circumstances. Again, Scripture provides us with glimpses into these aspects of the cross of infertility. For example, infertility causes Rachel and Jacob to turn on each other. Out of envy at her sister Leah's fertility, Rachel cries out to her husband, demanding that he give her children. Jacob responds to her in anger, "Am I in the place of God, who has withheld from you the fruit of the womb?"[31] In another case, infertility creates a gulf of misunderstanding and loneliness between spouses. Elkanah had two wives—Peninnah, who had children, and Hannah, who had none. Hannah grieved her infertility bitterly and her husband, although he loved her deeply, could not understand the depth of her sorrow. He said, "Hannah, why do you weep? And why do you not eat? And why is your heart sad? Am I not more to you than ten sons?"[32] The answer was clearly, "no," as she went—alone—to the temple, "deeply distressed and prayed to the Lord, and wept bitterly."[33]

28 See Pope Paul VI, Encyclical Letter *Humanae vitae* (July 25, 1968), 17, https://w2.vatican.va/content/paul-vi/en/encyclicals.index.html.

29 Karol Wojtyła, *Love and Responsibility: A New Translation*, trans. Grzegorz Ignatik (Boston: Pauline Books & Media, 2013), 245.

30 Myles Connolly, *Mr. Blue* (Cluny Media, 2015), 34–35.

31 Gn 30:1–2.

32 1 Sm 1:8.

33 1 Sm 1:10.

In light of the suffering of infertility, I turn now to *Humanae vitae* and the message it holds for those who carry this cross.

Humanae vitae and Its Implications for the Cross of Infertility

The teachings articulated in *Humanae vitae* arose in the context of questions about contraception but are not narrowly restricted to that subject. Rather, the questions were examined through a "deeper reflection on the principles of the moral teaching on marriage—a teaching which is based on the natural law as illuminated and enriched by divine Revelation."[34] The problems under consideration, notably concerns about rapid demographic development, the dignity of women, and the proper role of technology in alleviating human suffering, were analyzed, like every other problem that touches upon human life, "in the light of an integral vision of man," which takes into account his supernatural, eternal vocation.[35] Marriage is a natural reality, not a mere human construct, and has a supernatural dimension. "It is in reality the wise and provident institution of God the Creator, whose purpose was to effect in man His loving design."[36] The heart of *Humanae vitae*'s teaching about marriage is that: "husband and wife, through that mutual gift of themselves, which is specific and exclusive to them alone, develop that union of two persons in which they perfect one another, cooperating with God in the generation and rearing of new lives."[37]

Fundamental to a proper understanding of the institution of marriage is that it is a communion of persons (a "unity") that gives life (is "procreative"). It is especially important to appreciate the authentic meaning of Christian marriage for it signifies the covenant between Christ and His Church.[38] In light of this understanding of the human person and of the dignity of marriage, Pope Paul VI considered the particular questions about the transmission of human life.

The characteristic marks of such a union are that it is fully human, that it is total, that it is faithful and exclusive until death, and that it is fecund.[39] Conjugal love requires an awareness of "responsible parenthood," which Paul VI states includes a knowledge and respect of biological processes, an understanding that reason and will have dominion over tendencies of passion, and a profound relationship to the objective moral order established by God.[40] The exercise of responsible parenthood—either to receive or avoid new life—must be conformed "to the will of God the Creator. The very nature of marriage and its use

34 Pope Paul VI, *Humanae vitae*, 4.

35 Pope Paul VI, *Humanae vitae*, 7.

36 Pope Paul VI, *Humanae vitae*, 8.

37 Pope Paul VI, *Humanae vitae*, 8.

38 "For this reason, a man shall leave his father and mother and be joined to his wife, and the two shall become one flesh. This is a great mystery, and I mean in reference to Christ and the Church" (Eph 5:31–32).

39 Pope Paul VI, *Humanae vitae*, 9.

40 Pope Paul VI, *Humanae vitae*, 10.

makes His will clear, while the constant teaching of the Church spells it out."[41] Applying these precepts, Paul VI concludes: "The Church, nevertheless, in urging men to the observance of the precepts of the natural law, which it interprets by its constant doctrine, teaches that each and every marital act must of necessity retain its intrinsic relationship to the procreation of human life."[42]

That teaching, Paul VI stated, is based upon the "inseparable connection" between the two meanings of the conjugal act: union and procreation.[43] The conjugal act manifests that the reality of conjugal love exists, and it does not represent merely an idea, or an ideal. And this reality of conjugal love is this: any act of human sexual intercourse can be affective (rather than unitive) and/or generative (rather than procreative), but only a conjugal act expresses the full meaning of marriage and is therefore uniquely unitive *and* procreative. It is *unitive*, marked by faithfulness and indissolubility.

> The married couple forms "the intimate partnership of life and love established by the Creator and governed by his laws; it is rooted in the conjugal covenant, that is, in their irrevocable personal consent" (*Gaudium et spes*, 48). Both give themselves definitively and totally to one another. They are no longer two; from now on they form one flesh. The covenant they freely contracted imposes on the spouses the obligation to preserve it as unique and indissoluble.[44]

Conjugal love is *procreative* because, as the Catechism states, it "naturally tends to be fruitful. A child does not come from outside as something added on to the mutual love of the spouses, but springs from the very heart of that mutual giving, as its fruit and fulfillment."[45]

These two meanings of the conjugal act (unity and fecundity)[46] flow from the marital bond and are inseparable or so interdependent such that damage to one by necessity harms the other.[47] A conjugal act expresses *both* the unitive

41 Pope Paul VI, *Humanae vitae*, 10.

42 Pope Paul VI, *Humanae vitae*, 11. See also *Catechism of the Catholic Church*, 2366, "This particular doctrine, expounded on numerous occasions by the Magisterium, is based on the inseparable connection, established by God, which man on his own initiative may not break, between the unitive significance and the procreative significance which are both inherent to the marriage act." Hereinafter cited as CCC.

43 Pope Paul VI, *Humanae vitae*, 12. See also Pope Pius XI, Encyclical Letter *Casti connubii* (December 31, 1930), 72, "[E]very sin committed as regards the offspring becomes in some way a sin against conjugal faith, since both these blessings are essentially connected." https://w2.vatican.va/content/pius-xi/en/encyclicals.index.html.

44 CCC, 2364, quoting *Gaudium et spes*, 48.

45 CCC, 2366.

46 Sources speak of unity and fecundity as meanings or significations (as in *Humanae vitae*), as goods (e.g., the *bonum prolis*, as used by St. Augustine), as values, as properties, or as ends. It is not my purpose to analyze or resolve the proper terminology. For a helpful treatment of these discussions, see Janet Smith, "The Universality of Natural Law and the Irreducibility of Personalism," *Nova et Vetera* (English edition) 11, no. 4 (Fall 2013): 1229–1247.

47 It is not the purpose of this essay to establish the inseparability thesis of the conjugal act, although I take this as a received part of the Church's tradition. The observations I wish to make about marriage from the perspective of infertility apply, I believe, whether unity and procreation are considered to be

and procreative meanings of marriage because it is the *only* sort of act that joins together a man and a woman in a union marked by fidelity and indissolubility and creates a space within that union marked by fecundity. Therefore, when a married couple engages in contraception, the sexual act may express intimacy and be affective, but it is neither unitive nor can it be procreative in the conjugal sense. John Paul II explains it in this way: "when the conjugal act is *deprived of its inner truth* because it is deprived artificially of its procreative capacity, it also *ceases to be an act of love*" (italics in the original).[48] The contraceptive act does not signify the relationship between Christ and His Church. The creation of a child in a petri dish through in vitro fertilization does not signify the relationship between Christ and His Church. These acts might be affective or generative, but they are not unitive and procreative.

In *Gaudium et spes*, the Council fathers considered the interrelatedness of the two meanings of marriage in the case of married couples who "find themselves in circumstances where at least temporarily the size of their families should not be increased."[49] They warned that "where the intimacy of married life is broken off, its faithfulness can sometimes be imperiled and its quality of fruitfulness ruined, for then the upbringing of the children and the courage to accept new ones are both endangered."[50] Implicit in this remark is the truth that genuine intimacy (unity) is integrally connected with procreation (fruitfulness). Because, as further explained below, fruitfulness involves both the conception *and* the upbringing of children, to endanger the quality of fruitfulness (through an attack on unity, even due to prolonged abstinence) is not simply to foreclose the possibility of conceiving new children but implicates the upbringing of *existing* children who are part of the conjugal union. Similarly, in *Familiaris consortio*, John Paul II considered the case of divorced persons who have remarried but who cannot separate for a serious reason, such as the upbringing of children. In such cases, he stated that they must "take on themselves the duty to live in complete continence."[51] Far from being contradictory, these two passages make sense when one recalls that the first involves a conjugal union and the second does not. The obligation to abstain from the act which is proper only to marriage, in the context of a second marriage *with children*, demonstrates that such unions, although they may be affective and loving, are not unitive or procreative and

inseparable from one another or whether they are so interrelated as to be amplified or diminished by the presence or absence of the other. The clear teaching of the Church is that *both* unity and procreation must be present in the marital act. See CCC, 2363, "The spouses' union achieves the twofold end of marriage: the good of the spouses themselves and the transmission of life. These two meanings or values of marriage cannot be separated without altering the couple's spiritual life and compromising the goods of marriage and the future of the family. The conjugal love of man and woman thus stands under the twofold obligation of fidelity and fecundity."

48 Pope John Paul II, *Man and Woman He Created Them: A Theology of the Body*, trans. Michael Waldstein (Boston: Pauline Books & Media, 2006), 123:6. Hereafter cited as TOB.

49 Vatican Council II, *Gaudium et spes* (December 7, 1965), 51, http://www.vatican.va/archive/hist_councils/ii_vatican_council/index.htm.

50 *Gaudium et spes*, 51.

51 Pope John Paul II, *Familiaris consortio*, 84.

therefore refraining from intimacy does not, and indeed cannot, ruin the quality of fruitfulness, for such a meaning does not exist in such irregular unions.

As the passage in *Gaudium et spes* makes clear, procreation has always signified the conception *and* upbringing of children. Indeed, the Church teaches that the conjugal union is the only one that adequately safeguards the dignity of the child, in terms of her origin *and* her upbringing.[52] Only marriage is ordered *of itself* to the welcoming of children. Indeed, it is on account of children that "the exclusive and indissoluble union between a man and a woman has a plenary role to play in society as a stable commitment that bears fruit in new life."[53] Pope Francis states, "The family is the foundation of co-existence and a remedy against social fragmentation. Children have a right to grow up in a family with a father and a mother capable of creating a suitable environment for the child's development and emotional maturity."[54] Thus, marriage forms the foundation of society not only because it is the best place for a child to be born, but also because it is the best place for a child to grow up. Parents' participation in God's creative love continues beyond birth to raising children and providing for their moral and spiritual development. That is, "[P]hysical generation also fully corresponds to its meaning only if it is completed by fatherhood and motherhood *in the spirit*, whose expression and fruit is the whole educational work of the parents in regard to the children born of their bodily conjugal union."[55] Therefore, procreation (the expansive term, as opposed to mere biological generation) only exists within the conjugal union and is inseparable from conjugal unity. If a husband rapes his wife, it is not a conjugal act; the act is not unitive, but it also lacks fruitfulness, though it may constitute an act of generation in the strict biological sense if a child results. The child so conceived is not the fruit of her parents' conjugal love, though certainly she ought to have been. Indeed, it offends

52 See Pontifical Council for the Family, "Family, Marriage, and 'De Facto' Unions" (2000), http://www.vatican.va/roman_curia/pontifical_councils/family/index.htm. "On the one hand, the dignity of human persons requires their origin to be from parents joined in marriage, from the necessary intimate, integral, mutual and permanent union that comes from being spouses. This then is a good *for the children*. This is the only origin that adequately safeguards the principle of the children's identity not only from the genetic or biological viewpoint, but also from the biographical and historical perspective. On the other hand, marriage itself constitutes the most human and humanizing context for welcoming children, the context which most readily provides emotional security and guarantees greater unity and continuity in the process of social integration and education. The union between a mother and a conceived child and the irreplaceable function of the father require the child to be welcomed into a family which will guarantee it if possible the presence of both parents." (internal quotations omitted).

53 Pope Francis, Apostolic Exhortation *Amoris laetitia* (March 19, 2016), 52, http://w2.vatican.va/content/francesco/en/apost_exhortations.index.html.

54 Pope Francis, *Address to Humanum Conference* (November 17, 2014), http://www.catholicherald.co.uk/news/2014/11/17/full-text-pope-franciss-opening-address-to-humanum-conference.

55 TOB 78:5. See also Pope John Paul II, *Familiaris consortio*, 28: "The fruitfulness of conjugal love is not restricted solely to the procreation of children, even understood in its specifically human dimension: it is enlarged and enriched by all those fruits of moral, spiritual and supernatural life which the father and mother are called to hand on to their children, and through the children to the Church and to the world." See also CCC, 2367: "Married couples should regard it as their proper mission to transmit human life and to educate their children."

the dignity of the child to come to be in some other fashion than the conjugal act, such as through a rape.[56] Recall the story of Abraham and Sarah, who were promised descendants as numerous as the stars.[57] When the promise was not immediately fulfilled after waiting for ten long years, Sarah and Abraham took the matter of the promise into their own hands, seeking to fulfill it by their own actions. Without the benefit of modern reproductive technologies, Sarah gave Abraham her slave woman, Hagar, and by her, he had a son, Ishmael.[58] And yet, this child was not deemed to fulfill the covenantal promise,[59] in his (or in God's) eyes, demonstrating that procreation is not simply a matter of generation of biological children but rather has a more capacious meaning, involving cooperation with God's plan.[60]

To summarize, then, procreation *and* union express the whole warp and weft of the act of conjugal love. Any act that damages one aspect of conjugal love, whether unity or fecundity, diminishes or destroys the other. There are those who argue that the two meanings are not inseparable or interdependent and that the teachings of *Humanae vitae*, while prophetic and ideal, are difficult and that objective rules cannot govern all of the broken circumstances of human relationships. Although falling short of the ideal, contraceptive sex within marriage, according to some, might be permitted for the sake of the marital union, especially if the marital union on the whole is "open to life."[61] Such a view might suggest that even where procreation is foreclosed intentionally, the unitive significance of marriage may be preserved so that even this admittedly fallen situation has constructive elements. This line of thinking might continue by analogy: the conjugal acts of infertile couples (or of the elderly, or of fertile couples during infertile periods) demonstrate that spouses can still experience the full unitive meaning of the conjugal act, without possibility of procreation. Such an analogy requires the conclusion that the unitive and procreative meanings of marriage can be separated without harm to the other, and that the conjugal acts of infertile couples, although unitive, are not "procreative" merely because they are not generative of biological children.

The beauty of *Humanae vitae*, for the infertile couple, is that conjugal love expressed fully and faithfully carries with it *both* of its meanings: it is unifying *and* fruitful. The conjugal acts of infertile couples are not empty or meaningless, or even "just unitive." The *Catechism* states, "Spouses to whom God has not

56 See CDF, *Donum vitae*, 5 (relying upon *Gaudium et spes*, 51): "the gift of human life must be actualized in marriage through the specific and exclusive acts of husband and wife, in accordance with the laws inscribed in their persons and in their union."

57 See Gn 15:5.

58 See Gn 16:1–16.

59 See Gn 17:19–21.

60 In his letter to the Galatians 4:21–31, Paul expounds upon the allegory of Hagar and Sarah, contrasting the children of slavery with the children of the promise. The children of the conjugal union are children of the promise.

61 Of course, this argument was explicitly rejected in *Humanae vitae* itself (see 14). This teaching has been continually repeated and reinforced since the promulgation of *Humanae vitae*.

granted children can nevertheless have a conjugal life full of meaning, in both human and Christian terms. Their marriage can radiate a fruitfulness of charity, of hospitality, and of sacrifice."[62] Despite the heaviness and special suffering associated with the cross of infertility, this reality provides great comfort and consolation for infertile couples because it affirms that their conjugal acts are not only unitive but remain procreative, whether or not they result in that outcome in each and every case, or in *any* case. Indeed, *Humanae vitae* clearly states that the conjugal act "does not … cease to be legitimate even when, for reasons independent of their will, it is foreseen to be infertile. For it is natural adaptation to the expression and strengthening of the union of husband and wife is not thereby suppressed."[63] The prophet Isaiah offers comfort to the barren, beautifully describing the fruitfulness that is possible with faithfulness to God:

> Sing, O barren one, who did not bear; break forth into singing and cry aloud, you who have not had labor pains! … Enlarge the place of your tent, and let the curtains of your habitations be stretched out … For you will spread abroad to the right and to the left, and your descendants will possess the nations and will people the desolate cities.[64]

The Church, in her maternal wisdom, affirms repeatedly that the conjugal union of infertile couples remains fruitful and gives concrete suggestions for ways in which fecundity might manifest itself within an individual marriage. For example, John Paul II states,

> It must not be forgotten however that, even when procreation is not possible, conjugal life does not for this reason lose its value. Physical sterility in fact can be for spouses the occasion for other important services to the life of the human person, for example, adoption, various forms of educational work, and assistance to other families and to poor or handicapped children.[65]

At times, this is framed in terms of "spiritual parenthood," a concept perhaps most commonly used in the context of religious and priests.[66] We must go further,

62 CCC, 1654. See also *Gaudium et spes*, 50: "Therefore, marriage persists as a whole manner and communion of life, and maintains its value and indissolubility, even when despite the often intense desire of the couple, offspring are lacking."

63 Pope Paul VI, *Humanae vitae*, 11.

64 Is 54:1–3.

65 Pope John Paul II, *Familiaris consortio*, 28. See CCC, 2379: "The Gospel shows that physical sterility is not an absolute evil. Spouses who still suffer from infertility after exhausting legitimate medical procedures should unite themselves with the Lord's Cross, the source of all spiritual fecundity. They can give expression to their generosity by adopting abandoned children or performing demanding services for others." See also CDF, *Donum vitae*, 8, and Pope John Paul II, *Letter to Families* (February 2, 1994), 22, https://w2.vatican.va/content/john-paul-ii/en/letters/1994.index.3.html.

66 For example, in an address to adoptive families, John Paul II said that "seeing Mother Teresa's manner, attitudes, way of being, helps us understand what it meant to her, beyond the purely physical dimension, to

however, with the case of married men and women. While husbands and wives may exercise a sort of "spiritual parenthood" together or individually (for example, in the case of serving as a godparent), *marital fruitfulness* is something qualitatively different from spiritual parenthood. Indeed, children are not merely entitled to the individual love of each parent, of a mother and of a father, but to their mutual love for one another.

> Every child has a right to receive love from a mother and a father; both are necessary for a child's integral and harmonious development. As the Australian Bishops have observed, each of the spouses "contributes in a distinct way to the upbringing of a child. Respecting a child's dignity means affirming his or her need and natural right to have a mother and a father." We are speaking not simply of the love of father and mother as individuals, but also of their mutual love, perceived as the source of one's life and the solid foundation of the family. Without this, a child could become a mere plaything. Husband and wife, father and mother, both "cooperate with the love of God the Creator, and are, in a certain sense, his interpreters." They show their children the maternal and paternal face of the Lord. Together they teach the value of reciprocity, of respect for differences and of being able to give and take. If for some inevitable reason one parent should be lacking, it is important to compensate for this loss, for the sake of the child's healthy growth to maturity.[67]

Therefore, the fruitfulness of marriage is something inherent in the conjugal union itself and that can be said truly to be the product of their "mutual love."

Marital fruitfulness in the context of infertility is not a "second best" sort of parenthood. The understanding of marriage elucidated in *Humanae vitae* allows infertile couples to understand that their marriages are ordered toward union *and* fecundity in a very real sense. To be sure, fecundity is realized in its fullest sense through a biological child. But, as we have seen, even in that case, fruitfulness does not end with the conception of a child through the conjugal act but extends to her upbringing and education. Far from being a materialist concept, then, marital fruitfulness is expansive. So, for example, we can say that when a couple welcomes into their home and raises a child through adoption, this child is genuinely the fruit of his adoptive parents' conjugal love. As Pope Francis stated, "the choice of adoption and foster care expresses a particular kind of fruitfulness in the marriage experience."[68] He urges even those with biological children to find "other expressions of fruitfulness that in some way prolong the love that sustains them. . . . Families should not see themselves as a refuge from society, but instead go forth from their homes in a spirit of solidarity with

be a mother; it helped her to go to the spiritual root of motherhood." Pope John Paul II, *Address to the Meeting of the Adoptive Families Organized by the Missionaries of Charity* (September 5, 2000), http://w2.vatican.va/content/john-paul-ii/en/speeches/2000/jul-sep.index.2.html.

67 Pope Francis, *Amoris laetitia*, 172.

68 Pope Francis, *Amoris laetitia*, 180.

others."[69] Christian marriages are fruitful, he exhorts, "by their witness of fraternity their social concern, their outspokenness on behalf of the underprivileged, their luminous faith and their active hope."[70]

In some important and real sense, conjugal love is always fecund, "[i]t is not confined wholly to the loving interchange of husband and wife; it also contrives to go beyond this to bring new life into being"[71] and therefore spouses should look beyond the particular experience of the suffering of infertility to discern how their particular marriage is called to bear fruit. The fundamental good of marriage is

> [E]njoyed by the married couple, even if they are childless, who with their bodies do honour to one another's humanity, by never acting in a way which denies the permanence, exclusivity and generative nature of the marriage, but by maintaining its dignity as the sort of relationship through which people come to be. The marriage acts of such a couple express their unity in the flesh, their shared reproductive future, whatever that may be.[72]

This perspective of the infertile couple helps us to understand why it is so important to uphold the fullness of the teachings in *Humanae vitae* and to resist temptations to pick apart the wholeness and integrity of its teaching on conjugal love and the good of procreation.

Some Pastoral Reflections

Finally, there is much that could be said about the pastoral response to the suffering of couples who struggle with infertility, and there are many resources and worthy initiatives that seek to address it.[73] One limitation is that many initiatives focus largely on supporting couples who arc going through infertility treatments, or who have turned to adoption. More could be done for those couples who are and who will remain childless. I have tried to suggest that a faithful interpretation of *Humanae vitae,* especially a robust appreciation for the fruitfulness of all marriages, provides great consolation to couples who struggle with this cross. Three additional observations will have to suffice.

First, special attention should be paid to infertility as an occasion for husband and wife to grow closer together through shared suffering, especially because it goes to the heart of the marital vocation and involves marital intimacy. *Humanae*

69 Pope Francis, *Amoris laetitia*, 181.

70 Pope Francis, *Amoris laetitia*, 184.

71 Pope Paul VI, *Humanae vitae*, 9.

72 Mary Catherine Geach, "Lying with the Body," *The Monist* 91, nos. 3–4 (October 2008): 523–557.

73 See The Apostolate of Hannah's Tears at https://hannahstears.org; Marie Meaney, *Embracing the Cross of Infertility* (Front Royal, Va.: Human Life International, 2012), available at https://www.academia.edu/30111723/Embracing_the_Cross_of_Infertility_2012, containing excellent recommendations for carrying the cross of infertility and for supporting others who carry it; and Elizabeth Kirk, "10 Things Other than IVF that Could Help a Couple Suffering with Infertility," *Aleteia* (April 16, 2014).

vitae teaches that marriage involves "mutual gift of themselves."[74] Further, conjugal love is "total—that very special form of personal friendship in which husband and wife generously share everything, allowing no unreasonable exceptions and not thinking solely of their own convenience."[75] Infertility is a particular opportunity to show this mutual self-gift and friendship to one's spouse with all of his or her weaknesses and defects (including physical infertility), and to share together their suffering with Christ, the source of all spiritual fruitfulness.[76] Couples should be especially encouraged to know that "it is not by sidestepping or fleeing from suffering that we are healed, but rather by our capacity for accepting it, maturing through it and finding meaning through union with Christ, who suffered with infinite love."[77] Couples should be encouraged to seek refuge and strength together in the sacraments. As Pope Francis states,

> If this love is to overcome all trials and remain faithful in the face of everything, it needs the gift of grace to strengthen and elevate it. In the words of Saint Robert Bellarmine, "the fact that one man unites with one woman in an indissoluble bond, and that they remain inseparable despite every kind of difficulty, even when there is no longer hope for children, can only be the sign of a great mystery."[78]

Second, pastors should encourage couples that acceptance of this suffering does not negate hope. This is particularly difficult in the context of infertility because the structure of the reproductive cycle means that each month the couples' hopes are raised and dashed anew. Josef Pieper said hope was not the "presumptuous anticipation of fulfillment,"[79] but rather "the power to wait patiently for a 'not yet' that is the more immeasurably distant from us the more closely we approach it."[80] But what if "not yet" is "not ever"? Benedict XVI goes a bit further to say that, "it is, however, hope—not yet fulfillment; hope that gives us the courage to place ourselves on the side of good even in seemingly hopeless situations."[81] Here again, a biblical story is illustrative. When Hannah went to the temple, she was weeping so bitterly, moving her lips silently in prayer, that the priest Eli thought she was drunk. When she told him, without detail, that she had been imploring God in her sorrow, he replied, "Go in peace, and the God of Israel grant your petition which you have made to him." Remarkably, she "went her way and ate, and her countenance was no longer sad."[82] Without any sure evi-

74 Pope Paul VI, *Humanae vitae*, 8.

75 Pope Paul VI, *Humanae vitae*, 9.

76 CDF, *Donum vitae*, 8.

77 Pope Benedict XVI, Encyclical Letter *Spe salvi* (November 30, 2007), 37, http://w2.vatican.va/content/benedict-xvi/en/encyclicals.index.html.

78 Pope Francis, *Amoris laetitia*, 124.

79 Josef Pieper, *Faith, Hope, Love* (San Francisco, Ignatius Press, 2012), 138.

80 Pieper, *Faith, Hope, Love*, 110.

81 Pope Benedict XVI, *Spe salvi*, 37.

82 1 Sm 1:17–18.

dence, she had hope that her prayer had been heard and would be answered—although she knew not how. Not every infertile couple will have their prayers answered in the way that Hannah did with the birth of a son. But, when Hannah went away in peace, she did not know this would be her outcome. When a husband and wife place themselves on the side of good even in the hopeless case of infertility, they express a hope that fruitfulness may come in many ways. The emptiness that they may feel is present in their conjugal life can be transformed by hope to a space "which can only be filled by God and which God is even now waiting to fill."[83] In the case of conjugal love centered on God as the author of human life, trusting in His plan for creative love bears much fruit.

Third, pastors should consider that couples who carry the painful cross of infertility serve as silent witnesses against the culture of contraception and in support of the "hard teachings" of *Humanae vitae*. An ironic aspect of the pain of infertility is that many people assume infertile couples are childless by choice—even that childlessness is a desirable good. Moreover, some pastors often praise large families for their obedience to God's providential plan and their fidelity to Church teaching—inadvertently implying that those with small families or with no children are unfaithful. They should consider that couples who carry the cross of infertility, and in particular, obey God's plan for procreation in seeking to remedy the infertility, are also witnesses to such fidelity. Throughout salvation history, God has preferred to provide for His glory to be revealed through the weak and the insignificant. In today's culture of contraception, abortion, sexual expressionism, and the objectification of children, who better to reveal the glory of God's fruitfulness than the barren husband and wife? "Better than this [unrighteousness] is childlessness with virtue, for in the memory of virtue is immortality, because it is known both by God and by men."[84]

Ultimately, the teachings of *Humanae vitae* represent the teachings of Christianity regarding suffering—and also hope and joy—in the specific context of marriage. The task of fruitfulness belongs to every Christian, and infertility is simply one example of the way in which our human suffering can bear spiritual fruit. Truly, we can say that the paradox of the "barren bearing fruit" is the story of salvation itself. In the closing passage of Habakkuk, the prophet looks forward to the day when the oppressor of the Jewish people will be destroyed. He praises God, though nothing has yet happened and though all looks barren and desolate, because he trusts the One who is faithful to His promises: "though the fig tree does not blossom, nor fruit be on the vines, the produce of the olive fail and the fields yield no food . . . yet I will rejoice in the Lord, I will joy in the God of my salvation."[85]

83 Caryll Houselander, *The Reed of God* (Notre Dame, Ind.: Ave Maria Press, 2006), 30.

84 Wis 4:1.

85 Hab 3:17–18.

18

God's Plan, Married Love, and the Gift of Children

Christopher Kaczor

✸ God's plan, in one sense, is the same for us all: the universal vocation of every human being from Adam and Eve to the most recently procreated human being is the shared call to know, to love, and to serve God and other people. In fulfilling this vocation, we find happiness.

In a second sense, God's plan involves different states in life. The vocation as a state in life varies from person to person. Some are called to know, love, and serve God and other people as priests or as religious sisters or brothers. Some are called to know, love, and serve as husband and wife. Marriage is a true vocation. Some are called to know, love, and serve as single people, and this is their true vocation.

Finally, there is a third sense of vocation, personal vocation.[1] A particular man may be called to serve as a Jesuit priest teaching a class on Kant's *Critique of Pure Reason* at Boston College. A particular woman may be called to serve as a Carmelite sister taking care of the infirm elderly at Marycrest Manor. And a particular man may be called to marry a particular woman and to be the father of their children. A personal vocation is utterly unique to that particular individual and to no other. Just as Mary alone was called to be the mother of Jesus, and Joseph alone was called to be the husband of Mary, so each of us is called to some task specific to us alone. As Blessed John Henry Cardinal Newman put it,

> I am created to do something or to be something for which no one else is created. . . . God has created me to do Him some definite service; He has committed some work to me which He has not committed to another. I have my mission. . . . Somehow I am necessary for His purposes, as necessary in my place as an Archangel in his. . . . He has not created me for naught. I shall do good, I shall do His work; I shall be an angel of peace, a preacher of truth in my own place.[2]

1 Germain Grisez and Russell Shaw, *Personal Vocation: God Calls Everyone by Name* (Huntington, Ind: Our Sunday Visitor, Inc., 2003).

2 John Henry Newman, *Prayers, Verses and Devotions* (San Francisco: Ignatius Press, 2002), 338–339.

A personal vocation is to be husband or wife to *this* spouse, to be father or mother to *this* child, to respond to the specific needs, weaknesses, desires, proclivities, and strengths of those whom God has placed in our lives. The universal vocation of every human person is the vocation to love, and this love is to be carried out by each individual in a specific way in his or her unique and personal circumstances. God has made us for love.

God's plan helps us to find an answer to one of the most important questions a person can ask, "What makes for a good life?" We find an interesting convergence of philosophical, theological, and psychological insight on this question. Though they disagreed about many matters, Aristotle and Epicurus agreed that without loving friendships no human being could be happy.[3] In the theological realm, Augustine of Hippo summarized the teaching of Jesus for having a blessed life: "Love, and do what you will" (*dilige, et fac quod vis*).[4] In his *Summa Theologiae*, Thomas Aquinas, like countless Christian theologians before and after, linked loving rightly with living happily.[5] Contemporary psychology also reinforces the centrality of love for human flourishing. The lead researcher of the Harvard Study of Human Development, George Vaillant, said, "Happiness is love, full stop."[6] Likewise, Martin Seligman, the founder of "positive psychology," emphasized loving relationships as the single most important element of his understanding of human flourishing.[7]

But if living a good life cannot be had without loving, Sigmund Freud was also surely right in saying, "We are never so defenseless against suffering as when we love."[8] C. S. Lewis, though a radical critic of Freud, agreed with him about this matter. Lewis wrote,

> To love at all is to be vulnerable. Love anything and your heart will be wrung and possibly broken. If you want to make sure of keeping it intact you must give it to no one, not even an animal. Wrap it carefully round with hobbies and little luxuries; avoid all entanglements. Lock it up safe in the casket or coffin of your selfishness. But in that casket—safe, dark, motionless, airless—it will change. It will not be broken; it will become unbreakable, impenetrable, irredeemable. The alternative to tragedy, or at least to risk of tragedy, is damnation. The only place outside Heaven

3 Aristotle, *Nicomachean Ethics* (Indianapolis: Hackett Publishing Company, 1999); Epicurus, *The Art of Happiness* (New York: Penguin, 2012).

4 Augustine, *Homilies on the Gospel of St. John*, trans. Paul A Boer Sr. (n.p.: Veritatis Splendor Publications, 2012).

5 Thomas Aquinas, *Summa Theologiae, Prima Secundae*, questions 1–5, http://www.newadvent.org/summa/2001.htm.

6 Scott Stossel, "What Makes Us Happy, Revisited," *The Atlantic* (May 2013); George E. Vaillant, *Triumphs of Experience: The Men of the Harvard Grant Study* (Cambridge, Mass.: Harvard University Press, 2015).

7 Martin Seligman, *Flourish: A Visionary New Understanding of Happiness and Well-Being* (New York: Free Press, 2011), 20.

8 Sigmund Freud, *Civilization and its Discontents* (New York: W. W. Norton & Company, 1989), 33.

where you can be perfectly safe from all the dangers and perturbations of love is Hell.[9]

Not only does loving expose a person to suffering, but suffering for someone can augment love. The "IKEA effect" is the psychological finding that people value their IKEA furniture (which they had to toil to construct) more than furniture that did not require assembly.[10] We love what we have worked for, toiled over, and suffered for. If these insights are correct, suffering and enjoying a good human life are not antonyms, but necessarily coexisting variables. Through their connection in love, to live well and to suffer are not mutually exclusive but mutually implicative.

We can perhaps better see the connection between flourishing and suffering by considering the nature of love. In his book *One Body*, Alexander Pruss proposed that love involves willing the good of the other person as other, appreciating the good of the one who is loved, and seeking unity with the one who is loved.[11] Love's first characteristic, then, is to will the good of other persons as other, to desire the good for them for their own sake. Thus, love of enemies is a paradigm case of authentic love, for in loving one's enemies there is no reasonable expectation that they will give us something back in return.

The second characteristic of love, according to Pruss, is appreciation. Willing the good of the other as other is not sufficient for the fullness of love. As the founder of L'Arche, Jean Vanier wrote, "To love someone is not first of all to do things *for* them, but to reveal to them their beauty and value, to say to them through our attitude: 'You are beautiful. You are important. I trust you. You can trust yourself.' To love someone is to reveal to them their capacities for life, the light that is shining in them."[12] Love involves appreciation of the reality of what is good about an individual. If we "do good" for others, but hold them in contempt as human garbage, we fail to love them. To love people is to choose an intentional focus in appraising them. "Whatever is true, whatever is honorable, whatever is just, whatever is pure, whatever is lovely, whatever is gracious, if there is any excellence and if there is anything worthy of praise, think about these things."[13] This focus is compatible with, indeed demands, a responsiveness to reality. I am not really loving my mother if I appreciate her as Prince George of England.

Love's appreciation of others is not blindness to their faults, failings, and foibles, but mindfulness that everyone is more than their faults, failings, and foibles. As Alexandr Solzhenitsyn wrote in his *Gulag Archipelago*, "The line separating good and evil passes not through states, nor between classes, nor between political parties either—but right through every human heart—and through all human hearts. This line shifts. Inside us, it oscillates with the years.

9 C. S. Lewis, *The Four Loves* (New York: Houghton Mifflin Harcourt, 1991), 121.

10 Dan Ariely, *The Upside of Irrationality: The Unexpected Benefits of Defying Logic* (New York: Harper Perennial, 2011), 83.

11 Alexander Pruss, *One Body* (South Bend, Ind.: University of Notre Dame Press, 2012), Chapter 2.

12 Jean Vanier, *From Brokenness to Community* (New York, Paulist Press, 1992), 16.

13 Phil 4:8 (New American Bible Revised Edition).

And even within hearts overwhelmed by evil, one small bridgehead of good is retained."[14]

Every human person on earth is a shifting mixture of the good and the bad, in both moral and nonmoral terms. We can choose to focus on what is bad. But to love someone is to choose to focus on what is good.

The third characteristic of love, according to Pruss, is that it seeks unity with the beloved. Erotic love, friendship love, parental love, and other types of love differ, in part, by virtue of the kinds of unity they seek. Erotic lovers desire sexual union. Loving friends desire to share activities together, like walking, chatting, and working. Loving parents desire to raise their children and watch them in their activities. Lovers of God desire to be unified with the Lord in prayer, service, and theology.

If we understand love in this threefold way, and if love is needed for a good human life, then we have reason to hold that the good life for a human being will involve suffering. To will the good for another person often involves a sacrificial cost to the one who so chooses. To care for the sick, to bear wrongs patiently, and to change for the beloved involve sacrifice.

The fragility of human goodness in all dimensions makes the one who appreciates the good of the beloved vulnerable to loss and disappointment. The goodness of health fades into decrepitude, intelligence into dementia, and human life ends always in death. Human beauty, of body or soul, does not endure, as the Bard noted, "every fair from fair sometime declines, / By chance or nature's changing course untrimm'd."[15]

Finally, suffering arises because our unity with others makes us suffer in compassion when they suffer. When we love our friend, we suffer when our friend is sad, sick, or silenced. Since suffering is virtually ubiquitous in the human experience, our unity with those we love leads us to suffer when they suffer. In sum, human flourishing and human suffering are linked by love which seeks at some personal cost to give to the beloved, which appreciates the fragile good of the beloved, and which is unified with the beloved in times of sorrow.

We find this mutual implication of suffering and flourishing vividly in the lived reality of married love. Even those in happy marriages can appreciate the grain of truth in the joke: "First, the engagement ring, then, the wedding ring, and then, the suffering." Willing the good of one's spouse often involves sacrifice, sometimes heroic sacrifice. Married love appreciates the reality of the spouse, but that reality can disappoint. What makes married love distinctive is not so much willing the good or appreciating the other, but the kind of unity that is promised in married love. In Catholic marriage, the couple is asked,

> Have you come here to enter into Marriage without coercion, freely and wholeheartedly? Are you prepared, as you follow the path of Marriage, to

14 Alexandr Solzhenitsyn, *Gulag Archipelago* (New York: Harper Perennial Modern Classics, 2007), 312.

15 William Shakespeare, Sonnet 18, lines 7–8, at http://shakespeare.mit.edu/Poetry/sonnet.XVIII.html.

> love and honor each other for as long as you both shall live? Are you prepared to accept children lovingly from God and to bring them up according to the law of Christ and his Church?[16]

Unless the couple promises a love that is free, faithful, and fruitful, the couple is not free to marry in the Catholic Church. This unity as husband and wife, for as long as they both shall live, can cause suffering. As J. R. R. Tolkien observed in a letter to his son, "Nearly all marriages, even happy ones, are mistakes: in the sense that almost certainly (in a more perfect world, or even with a little more care in this very imperfect one) both partners might be found more suitable mates. But the 'real soul-mate' is the one you are actually married to."[17] It is important to remember, lest we have an unbalanced picture, that every alternative to marriage also involves suffering. For most people, marriage, despite its difficulties, characteristically leads to greater flourishing than the alternatives.[18]

And how do children relate to marital flourishing? Some people view the procreation and education of children as, at best, one option among many for married couples and at worst a negative drain on the well-being of the couple. A hedonistic philosophy of life regards marriage with suspicion and children with even greater suspicion. Human flourishing, according to this view, involves lots of sex, drugs, drinking, and ease of life. Contraception is not just an option but an obligation.

Perhaps no one more notoriously embodied this philosophy than *Playboy* magazine founder Hugh Hefner. He celebrated abortion, premarital sexual behavior, a pro-contraceptive mentality, and an emphasis on self-satisfaction. Yet, even Hugh Hefner eventually realized that what he was looking for could not be found in sexual escapades with casual partners. At 63, Hefner married and fathered two children in rapid succession. The *New York Times* reported that Hefner said:

> "Having this marriage now and these children, seeing toys in the mansion, I get teary-eyed." Indeed, his eyes fill and he presses his fingers to his mouth punishingly hard. "I spent so much of my life looking for love in all the wrong places," he says, wiping his eyes. Though it should sound trite, it doesn't. The weariness in his voice and the weight in his face suggest the toll of decades of grueling work, of nursing the impossible image of himself as the life of every party.[19]

16 International Commission on English in the Liturgy, *The Order of Celebrating Matrimony*, 2nd edition (Washington, D.C.: United States Conference of Catholic Bishops, 2016).

17 "Letter to Michael Tolkien" (March 1941) in J. R. R. Tolkien, *The Letters of J. R. R. Tolkien* (New York: Houghton Mifflin Harcourt, 2014), 51.

18 W. Bradford Wilcox et al., *Why Marriage Matters, Third Edition: Thirty Conclusions from the Social Sciences* (New York: Broadway Publications, 2011).

19 Alex Witchel, "Father Rabbit," *The New York Times* (November 22, 1992).

The life of the party is now dead, but we can learn from Hefner's missteps. Despite his love for his children, expressed in the passage above, his decades of habituation in lack of commitment led to his marriage falling apart before a decade was done. The goods of marriage, like all human goods, are fragile. Given the failure of the hedonistic view, even admitted by its most notorious advocate, let's consider a radically different answer to the question, how do children relate to marital flourishing?

Classic Christian belief emphasizes, in accordance with its Jewish roots, the goodness of having children. According to the Second Vatican Council, "Marriage and conjugal love are by their nature ordained toward the begetting and educating of children. Children are really the supreme gift of marriage and contribute very substantially to the welfare of their parents."[20]

I would suggest that children contribute to the flourishing of their parents in three dimensions: friendship, erotic love, and helping the parents get to heaven.

Realizing Erotic Love

We can think about erotic love in a variety of ways. One of the most memorable and influential views is proposed in Plato's *Symposium*. In the *Symposium*, the Platonic Aristophanes tells a story about the origins of erotic love. Once, human beings had four arms, four legs, and two faces. We were liked conjoined twins joined back to back. We were so powerful, in our original creation, that we rebelled against the gods. Our punishment for this unsuccessful rebellion was to be split in two in order to weaken us. This punishment both gave us the form we now have (two arms, two legs, one face) and gave rise to erotic love, the desire to be as united as possible with the beloved.

Modern ways of speaking about love echo the Platonic Aristophanes. Jerry Maguire says to his beloved, "You complete me." Couples speak of "my better half" and "my other half." When a relationship fails, we "break up." Erotic love might be defined as seeking to be as united as possible with the beloved, especially in a bodily, sexual way.

To be as united as possible involves being united with the beloved in terms of exclusivity as well as permanence. Love songs speak of "you alone" and "forever." When in the madness of erotic love, one feels as if love will last forever and one wishes for this love to last forever. The beloved of erotic love is utterly irreplaceable, a singularity that cannot be replicated. Moreover, erotic love is a love of the whole person, rather than just love of the other as (potential) sexual partner. If the Platonic Aristophanes is right in his conception of erotic love, it makes sense that erotic love prompts couples to vow to be husband and wife in good times and in bad, in sickness and in health, until death do us part. Erotic love is the desire to be together forever.

Procreation is a way of realizing the goals of erotic love, to be together forever, united to this one alone until death. Every child is a living and lasting

20 Vatican Council II, *Gaudium et spes*, 50, http://www.vatican.va/archive/hist_councils/ii_vatican_council/index.htm.

sign of the unity that once existed between the mother and the father. Every child forever unites the mother to the child's father alone, and the father to the child's mother alone.[21] Normally, the unity is not merely physical, as if it were a mere matter of shared DNA, but emotional and psychological. Loving parents, whatever their differences, share in having good will, appreciation, and desired unity with their children. Even after divorce, many couples still share a love and devotion to their children.

Enhancing Friendship

In *The Seven Principles of Making Marriage Work*, psychologist John Gottman wrote that the determining factor in whether a wife or husband feels satisfied with the sex, romance, and passion of their relationship is the quality of the couple's friendship.[22] Friendship could be defined in terms of mutual good will, shared activity, and shared emotional life.[23] Having children together fosters marital friendship because shared children give the parents an extra reason to have good will for each other. This person is not just my wife but also the mother of my children. In virtue of loving the children, I have an extra reason for loving her. When difficulties arise, as they inevitably do, children provide an extra motivation to make things work. Couples who know that the kids will suffer if a marriage falls apart have an extra reason to seek reconciliation.

The activity of raising children, as well as accompanying them as adults, gives the couple a shared emotional life. Mother and father are united in joy at First Holy Communion, graduation from high school, celebration of a wedding, or the birth of a grandchild. Mother and father are united in sorrow at school-yard bullying, high school hazing, an arrest of a child for drunk driving, or the unemployment of an adult son or daughter. A child inevitably brings to his or her parents times of frustration and desolation and at other times elation and exhilaration. The rollercoaster ride of parenthood goes from panic, rage, and stress to serenity, tranquility, and exhilaration, and then back again. Whatever their emotional ups and downs, children benefit parents by providing them resources for a shared emotional life, enhancing their friendship.

Aristotle famously distinguished between friendships of pleasure, utility, and virtue. We love in friends what is pleasurable, useful, or excellent, and so from a focus on these three things different kinds of friendships arise. Children do not aid a friendship of pleasure, that which is based on having fun and hedonistic experiences; friendships of pleasure, however, tend not to last anyway. Children also do not much aid a friendship of utility, since children usually need our help

21 I should add a word about people who become parents via adoption. Although they do not have a bond of DNA with their child, people who become parents via adoption are *truly* parents. A couple who adopts a child may say in truth, "This child is truly ours."

22 John Gottman, *The Seven Principles of Making Marriage Work* (New York: Random House, 2015), 19.

23 Christopher Kaczor and Jennifer Kaczor, *The Seven Big Myths about Marriage: What Science, Faith, and Philosophy Teach Us About Love and Happiness* (San Francisco: Ignatius Press, 2014), 39–40.

rather than offer it. Our spouse, moreover, is less likely to be useful to us if he or she is focused on helping the children. But a friendship of utility is, by its nature, a second-rate kind of friendship. In a friendship of utility, I don't really care about my friend as much as the benefits that friend gives to me. But what about a friendship of virtue? In this friendship, friends care about each other not simply because they give one another pleasure or utility, but because of the excellence of the other person.

How do we gain virtue? At least for the acquired virtues, we gain an excellent character by repeatedly doing excellent acts. When a couple has a child, that vulnerable baby needs round-the-clock help. In performing caring, gentle, kind, and loving acts for their baby, their toddler, their grade-schooler, their teenager, and their young adult child, parents grow into more caring, gentle, kind, and loving people.[24] Inasmuch as the couple has more children, they have further opportunity for growth in virtue. Inasmuch as they grow in virtue, they establish or strengthen the basis for a friendship of virtue.[25]

Helping Parents Go to Heaven

Having children helps a couple go to heaven,[26] I think, in part by providing an opportunity for deepening faith. Faith is a gift that grows when exercised and atrophies, or even dies, when not exercised. Responsible parenthood can be an act of faith in God's guidance of the Church and God's providential care for each family. Blessed John Henry Cardinal Newman wrote:

> Let every one who hears me ask himself the question, what stake has *he* in the truth of Christ's promise? How would he be a whit the worse off, supposing (which is impossible), but, supposing it to fail? . . . What have *we* ventured? I really fear, when we come to examine, it will be found that there is nothing we resolve, nothing we do, nothing we do not do, nothing we avoid, nothing we choose, nothing we give up, nothing we

24 Of course, raising children does not automatically make a person virtuous. To become virtuous requires a difficult task, but not one that completely overwhelms. For this reason, the Church encourages *responsible parenthood* rather than maximal reproduction. Responsible parenthood involves practical wisdom about the strengths and weaknesses of the couple, their economic situation, and all the relevant circumstances. To have children contrary to what practical wisdom would warrant is not conducive to virtue, but rather to vice. All people are called to be generous to the poor in giving donations, but it would, for most people, be contrary to practical wisdom to give away 90 percent of the family's income. So too, married couples are called to be generous in giving life, but it would be contrary to practical wisdom, for most people, to have as many children as biologically possible.

25 From a psychological perspective, the following article makes a similar point. Roy F. Baumeister, Kathleen D. Vohs, Jennifer Aaker, Emily N. Garbinsky, "Some Key Differences between a Happy Life and a Meaningful Life," *Journal of Positive Psychology* 8, no. 6 (2013): 505–516.

26 I do not mean to imply "going to heaven" as an extrinsic reward essentially unrelated to one's earthly life. Heaven and Hell, loving God and neighbor or not loving God and neighbor, begins here on earth. The state of being alienated from God here and now comes to its ultimate conclusion at death in the state of continuing to be alienated from God for all eternity. So also, loving God and neighbor in this life can continue and be brought to perfection after death in what we call Heaven.

> pursue, which we should not resolve, and do, and not do, and avoid, and choose, and give up, and pursue, if Christ had not died, and heaven were not promised us.[27]

Those who accept and live the call to responsible parenthood can say that they ventured living in accordance with what they believed God wanted from them. How many people with three, five, seven, or more children, would have had only one or two but for their venture of faith? I know I am one.

If a couple follows the Church's teaching, it is likely that the couple will have a larger family than they would have had if they had not followed the Church's teaching. The reason is fairly simple. If a couple is not using contraception but rather is using Natural Family Planning (NFP) to delay births, then in each woman's cycle a decision must be made to abstain from sexual intercourse during the fertile time of the cycle, during which time she is characteristically more interested in having sex. So, at each cycle, the urges of nature prompt a couple to reconsider their decision to postpone having a child. If the couple has a healthy sex drive, the couple has an ongoing incentive for making love rather than periodically abstaining. Of course, many couples forgo entirely using NFP, as well as contraceptive methods, so for them (again assuming normal fertility and sex drive) it is likely that their family size will be greater than the contemporary average.

If a couple has a larger family, they will almost certainly have a larger share of the emotional highs and lows that accompany having any children. At least for good parents, having children adds something radically new to one's life, an unconditional commitment of love to this particular person until death. So, each child a couple has reaffirms in a new way the vows made in marriage: to love in good times and in bad, in sickness and in health, until death. Although no explicit vow is made to the child, there can be no question that good parents have an unbreakable commitment to each child that reflects the unconditional commitment of the marriage vow, in its turn a visible sign of the invisible reality of God's irrevocable love for each of us.[28]

The suffering that teenage and adult children can cause their parents can tempt their parents to waver in their duty of unconditional love. For example, it can cause immense pain and sadness to raise a child to be a good Catholic, and to see the child turn away from the practice of faith. Elie Wiesel's son, Elisha Wiesel, speaks of his Jewish experience on this point:

> There is a chasidic story of the Baal Shem Tov, who was once approached by a chasid, bemoaning how far his son had strayed. The rebbe's surprising answer: "Love your son more." . . . My father must have heard this story

27 John Henry Newman, "Sermon 20. The Ventures of Faith," in *Parochial and Plain Sermons* (San Francisco: Ignatius Press, 1987), 925–926.

28 I should add that good parents may, with great regret, come to the conclusion that physical contact with a violent or mentally ill child is no longer possible. This lack of physical contact is compatible with unconditional love. Such sad cases are similar to situations in which a spouse may and should separate from a violent or mentally ill spouse. The marital or parental love remains but is sadly imperfect.

> because he lived it. He believed in me even when I did not believe in myself. He believed in me as I set out on a journey that would take me very far from Judaism and from him. And he believed in me even as I shouted at him that I wanted nothing to do with his religion, that I wanted to be an X factor in every equation he and my mother had used to project my life, that I would be an atheist or a Buddhist, anything but what he told me I had to be. My father kept telling me to be a good student, a good son, a good Jew. But he said it more quietly.[29]

After his father's death, the son felt the presence, love, and guidance of his father in ways even more powerful than when his father was alive. Elie Wiesel must have surely been tempted to stop loving his son, but his fidelity—with God's help—paid off.

Christian spouses can help other people to be open to the gift of faith. In their very mode of living, Christian spouses with larger families can provide testimony by forgoing the vacations and other material perks enjoyed by the typical "two income-two children" family. A martyr is a "witness," a public sign to others of the Kingdom. A priest or nun in distinctive religious garb silently prompts a question in those who see them, "What if they are right about the importance of God? They seem awfully committed to it."[30] A large family communicates a similar message to the world. Life is not primarily about bodily pleasure, increasing riches, or possessing power.

Divine Commandments

Jesus taught that the greatest commandment is, "Thou shalt love the Lord thy God with all thy heart, and with all thy soul, and with all thy mind."[31] Love and knowledge are connected, inasmuch as we cannot love what we do not know and the more we know about the goodness of the one we love, the more we can appreciate the one we love. We are helped to heaven by deepening our knowledge of God.

According to Aquinas, one path to deeper knowledge of God is apophatic theology, the way of remotion. Apophatic theology proceeds by denial of characteristics to God. We have a less inaccurate understanding of God when we clear

29 Elisha Wiesel, "Lessons From My Father: Elie Wiesel's Son On His Rebellion, And His Father's Love," *The New York Jewish Week* (June 7, 2017). http://jewishweek.timesofisrael.com/lessons-from-my-father.

30 Before becoming Pope Benedict XVI, Joseph Cardinal Ratzinger had this to say about the meaning of religious celibacy: "The renunciation of marriage and family is thus to be understood in terms of this vision: I renounce what, humanly speaking, is not only the most normal but also the most important thing. I forgo bringing forth further life on the tree of life, and I live in the faith that my land is really God—and so I make it easier for others, also, to believe that there is a kingdom of Heaven. I bear witness to Jesus Christ, to the Gospel, not only with words, but also with a specific mode of existence, and I place my life in this form at his disposal. . . . The point is really an existence that stakes everything on God and leaves out precisely the one thing that normally makes a human existence fulfilled with a promising Future." Joseph Ratzinger, *Salt of the Earth: Christianity and the Catholic Church at the End of the Millennium; An Interview with Peter Seewald* (San Francisco: Ignatius Press, 1997), 195.

31 Mt 22:37.

away misconceptions about God. Negative theology is a way of denial: God is not composed of parts. God has no beginning. God is not a body.

All parents come to realize quickly that their parenthood is not like the parenthood of God. God is not impatient. God is not overwhelmed. God is not at a complete loss about what to do. In coming to know who God is not, in coming to see ever more clearly that we are not God, parents come closer to the true God.

Indeed, children teach parents humility. As young children, we know we are not God. Someone else determines when we get out of bed, what we wear, what we eat, and where we go. When we become adults, it is easier to get the feeling that we are the ultimate arbiters of our universe. As adults, it is easier to fall into the illusion that we are in complete control. We decide when we get out of bed, what we wear, what we eat, and where we go. One might even come to believe that one has "the right to define one's own concept of existence, of meaning, of the universe, and of the mystery of human life."[32]

Children shatter the illusion that we are God. The philosopher Jean-Paul Sartre held that all human beings have the "desire to be God." This desire to be God is thwarted by children. We do not choose their looks, their native intelligence, their athletic ability, their temperament as introverted or extraverted, their slowness or rapidity to react.[33] We cannot, despite efforts to discipline them, make our children as we might like.

We are also *vulnerable* in our children. Even if we are healthy, their sicknesses afflict us. For parents, the good of the child is constitutive of their own good, so when this good is undermined the parents are also undermined. The social and educational traumas of children impinge upon parents regardless of social class or educational achievement. Children make the parents feel helplessness. When our children suffer, we parents suffer because we are the ones who are supposed to care and protect but we cannot do it. This can open the parents to call on God whose care and protection can ultimately save even the most hopeless situation.

According to Aquinas, another path to deeper knowledge of God is analogy, an understanding of how God is not exactly like but nevertheless similar to created things. Parents are like God in that they cooperate in giving life. Aside from God, parents have the most power over the lives of their young children, determining virtually every aspect of their lives. In experiencing the powerful, unconditional love that parents have for children, parents can come to realize, in a limited sense, something more about the powerful, unconditional love of God for them and for their children. In understanding the fragility of their children, parents can better understand their own fragility and dependence upon God, their Heavenly Father.

When Jesus was asked by the rich young man about how to get to heaven, our Lord replied, "If you wish to enter into life, keep the commandments."[34]

32 Planned Parenthood v. Casey, 505 U.S. 833, 851 (1992).

33 See Michael Sandel, *The Case against Perfection: Ethics in the Age of Genetic Engineering* (Cambridge, Mass.: Belknap Press, 2009).

34 Mt 19:17 (New American Standard Bible). This translation is used for subsequent citations from Scripture.

Jesus specifically mentioned the fourth commandment, "Honor your father and mother."[35] Having children helps parents to fulfill this commandment.

It is easy to be critical of one's own parents. They fail at this and at that. But when people have children of their own, they realize how very difficult it is to be a good parent. The stresses and strains of raising children tax our patience, our gentleness, and can overwhelm our best intentions. When we have children of our own, we realize that despite our great love for our kids, we often fail them. In realizing our own imperfections, it becomes easier to forgive the imperfections of our own parents.

Moreover, in having children, we can come to a deeper understanding of what our own parents gave to us. We can appreciate the enormous time, energy, and efforts it takes to raise children. When we have babies, we realize how much our parents did for us as infants. When we have teenagers, we can perhaps better recall the difficulties we were to our parents as teenagers. The suffering of raising children can lead to greater gratitude to our own parents for having suffered for us. When we are grateful to our own parents, it is easier to give them the honor that God commands us to give.

In the Gospel according to Matthew, Christ talks about the final judgment. In separating those who are entering heaven from those going to hell, Jesus says to those entering heaven, "I was hungry, and you gave Me something to eat, I was thirsty, and you gave Me something to drink; I was a stranger, and you invited Me in; naked, and you clothed Me; I was sick, and you visited Me."[36] I remember hearing this passage in church as a child and thinking, "Oh no. Everybody is going to go to Hell. After all, who does this? Mother Teresa and her sisters in the Missionaries of Charity will be fine, but everyone else is in big trouble."

Only after I had children did I understand this teaching of Jesus in a new way. After all, every good mother and every good father do these things on a daily basis. The baby is hungry, and good parents give the child something to eat. The child is thirsty, and good mothers and fathers give their child something to drink. Their son or daughter is naked, and they clothe him or her. How many times do parents bring their sick children to the doctor or hold their hand when they have a fever. And every child comes into the family as a stranger, but good parents welcome the child anyway. So perhaps, on the Judgment Day, the good Lord, having watched our daily toils as mothers and fathers, will say to us, "Come, you who are blessed by my Father. Inherit the kingdom prepared for you from the foundation of the world."[37]

35 Mt 19:19.

36 Mt 25:35–36.

37 Mt 25:34. I should add that fulfilling parental duties does not exhaust the call of Matthew 25. If I am a good father, but do not reach out to those outside my family in need whom I can help, I have not fulfilled this commandment. Indeed, part of being good parents is to teach one's children that the circle of love is not limited to family and friends. There is no better way to teach this lesson than by showing them by example and drawing them into the practice of caring for those in need outside the family. For many people, caring deeply for one's own child can loosen the grip of selfishness and open the door to seeing others in need as worthy of care.

For good reasons then did the Second Vatican Council echo classic Christian teaching, "Marriage and conjugal love are by their nature ordained toward the begetting and educating of children. Children are really the supreme gift of marriage and contribute very substantially to the welfare of their parents."[38]

38 *Gaudium et spes*, 50.

PART VI

Signs of Growth and Healing

19

Signs of Hope and Healing in Theology

A Tale of Two Statements

John S. Grabowski

✷ On September 20, 2016, a group of scholars presented a statement at an event sponsored by the United Nations Interagency Task Force on Religion and Development. The statement offered a resume of a report which had been commissioned and produced earlier by the UK-based Winjgaards Institute and was signed by some 150 scholars, most of them Catholic.[1] The statement was clearly launched as a preemptive "first strike" against the upcoming fiftieth anniversary of Pope Paul VI's encyclical, *Humanae vitae.* It also aimed to provide grist for the United Nations population control mill and to bring pressure to bear on the Church to change her teaching. To achieve these aims, the statement dusted off arguments leveled against the document at its promulgation and in its immediate aftermath: the Church's teaching articulated by Paul VI was physicalist (i.e., it derived moral norms from biological laws), there is no discernible moral difference between natural and artificial means of birth regulation, it was neither supported in Scripture nor definitively taught by the Church, and was unsubstantiated by modern sciences.

The same day at a news conference on the campus of The Catholic University of America, a different group of Catholic scholars presented a counter statement, supporting the encyclical and its teaching and refuting the claims recycled from the past by the Winjgaards writers. Though pulled together at the eleventh hour (when news of the Winjgaards effort came to light) and without funding or political sponsorship, the statement when presented was signed by some 590 Catholic scholars. Of these, signatures from medical doctors and scientists alone outnumbered the total Winjgaards signers—which might raise questions about the accuracy of some of the statement's scientific claims. Within a week, the number of scholars who had signed the statement had nearly doubled.[2] Clearly, it was no longer 1968.

1 The statement is entitled "Catholic Scholars' Statement on the Ethics of Using Contraceptives." It, along with a list of signatories, can be found at: http://www.wijngaardsinstitute.com/statement-on-contraceptives/. As of March 18, 2018, the statement had 178 signatories.

2 For a copy of the statement "Affirmation of the Church's Teaching on the Gift of Sexuality" and a list of signatories, see: https://trs.cua.edu/humanae-vitae.

While not insignificant, the numbers do not tell the real story. To point to the larger number of academics willing to put their names and expertise on the line in publicly supporting the teaching than those willing to oppose it and hail it as a "sign of the times" would be to miss the biblical roots and recent history of that phrase in recent Catholic theology.

The appeal to the "sign of the times" is found in Pope John XXIII's apostolic constitution convening the Second Vatican Council, *Humanae salutis*.[3] It was incorporated into early drafts of what became the pastoral constitution *Gaudium et spes*. However, there the drafters equated "the signs of the times" with the Roman proverb *vox temporis, vox Dei*[4]—a sense at odds with the Christological and eschatological overtones of Jesus' challenge to the Pharisees and Sadducees request for a sign in the Gospel: "In the evening you say, 'Tomorrow will be fair, for the sky is red'; and, in the morning, 'Today will be stormy, for the sky is red and threatening.' You know how to judge the appearance of the sky, but you cannot judge the signs of the times.[5] The final conciliar text does not cite the Gospel passage directly but retains its sense: "To carry out such a task, the Church has always had the duty of scrutinizing the signs of the times and of interpreting them in the light of the Gospel."[6] Reading the signs of the times is not simply a survey of public opinion at a given moment; it is discernment carried out in the light of Christ and the Gospel. Such a view is buttressed by the later Christological anthropology articulated in the document: "Christ, the final Adam, by the revelation of the mystery of the Father and His love, fully reveals man to man himself and makes his supreme calling clear."[7] That statement has been rightly hailed by scholars as "the standard and short formula of the Pastoral Constitution."[8]

The real problem with the Winjgaards statement is that it ignores the developments of the last fifty years. This is not just true of the sciences which have documented the havoc contraceptives have wreaked on women's health, on relationships between women and men, and on the wider culture. It is also true in theology, where there have been significant developments in explicating the basis of the teaching. This brief essay will argue that there are biblical and

3 Pope John XXXIII, Apostolic Constitution *Humanae salutis* (December 25, 1961), 4. For the Latin text, see the Vatican website at: https://w2.vatican.va/content/john-xxiii/la/apost_constitutions/1961.index.html. All citations of magisterial texts (both in original and in translation) are from those available on the Holy See's website unless otherwise noted.

4 See Joseph Ratzinger, "Part I: The Church and Man's Calling, Introductory Article and Chapter I," in *Commentary on the Documents of Vatican II*, vol. 5, ed., Herbert Vorgrimler, trans. W. J. O'Hara (New York: Herder and Herder, 1969), 115.

5 Mt 16:2b–3. Biblical citations in this chapter are from the New American Bible Revised Edition unless otherwise noted.

6 Vatican Council II, *Gaudium et spes* (December 7, 1965), 4. The Latin reads: "Ad tale munus exsequendum, per omne tempus Ecclesiae officium incumbit signa temporum perscrutandi et sub Evangelii luce interpretandi."

7 *Gaudium et spes*, 22.

8 The phrase is that of Walter Kasper, "The Theological Anthropology of *Gaudium et Spes*," *Communio: International Catholic Review* 23 (Spring 1996): 129–40; cited at 137.

anthropological developments articulated in magisterial teaching and Catholic theology, showing the rich and deep basis in the tradition for the teaching of the encyclical, and that these constitute the real "signs of the times" to which we must attend in our day.

In what follows, I will present a brief overview of some of the principal lines of theological development which emerged before and in the decades since the encyclical. I will focus particularly on those arguments that highlight the moral difference between natural and artificial means of birth regulation.[9] These can be gathered together under the following headings: the idea of sexual intercourse as an embodied language (i.e., "linguistic"); the dignity of the person (i.e., personalist); the anthropological status of fertility (i.e., anthropological); contraception and human ecology (i.e., ecological); Natural Family Planning as a practice formative of conjugal chastity (i.e., virtue ethics); and the biblical basis for the "inseparable connection" between the unitive and procreative meanings of conjugal love (i.e., biblical).[10] Reasons of space prevent any more than a cursory overview of these trends. Many of them have been more fully developed in other essays in this volume.

Linguistic

One of the recurring ideas of the catechesis on the body given by Pope John Paul II is the basic communicability of the human body—the body expresses and "excarnates" the person.[11] Bodily activity communicates the subjectivity and freedom of the person. This basic communicability of the body in its masculinity or femininity extends to sexual activity. To give one's body is to give oneself in totality.[12] A hermeneutical key for reading and interpreting this embodied

9 There certainly have also been further developments in philosophical scholarship which are supportive of the teaching in areas such as natural law and action theory. Such developments are outside of the scope of this brief essay and will not be treated here except insofar as they impinge on the theological ideas considered. For an overview of the whole spectrum of arguments which have been put forward in defense of the encyclical, see Janet E. Smith, John S. Grabowski, J. Budziszewski, and Maria Fedoryka, "Self-Gift: The Heart of *Humanae vitae*," *National Catholic Bioethics Quarterly* 16, no. 3 (Autumn 2016): 449–474. For an earlier but more extended analysis, see Janet E. Smith, Humanae Vitae: *A Generation Later* (Washington, D.C.: The Catholic University of America Press, 1991).

10 The category headings are mine, but they refer to ideas discernible in the literature.

11 See Pope John Paul II, *General Audience* (October 24, 1979), which explores the meaning of the body in light of the human person's "original solitude." See also the general audiences of October 10, 1979; November 21, 1979; and February 20, 1980. These audiences are available on the Vatican website at https://w2.vatican.va/content/john-paul-ii/en/audiences.index.html. However, for the best available English translation of the catechesis, see Pope John Paul II, *Man and Woman He Created Them: A Theology of the Body*, trans. Michael Waldstein (Boston: Pauline Books and Media, 2006). English citations of the Theology of the Body catechesis will refer to this edition and use Waldstein's numeration for audience number as well as page numbers.

12 The commonly heard objection that the idea of "total self-giving" is unrealistic misses the key point that the claim is one concerning the objective meaning of sexual self-gift—not a claim about the subjective experience of couples. For an example of such a claim, see Florence Caffrey Bourg, "Multi-Dimensional Marriage Vocations and Responsible Parenthood," in *Leaving and Coming Home: New Wineskins for Catholic Sexual Ethics*, ed. David Cloutier (Eugene, Ore.: Cascade Books, 2010), 147–72, and especially 166–70.

language is found in the vows by which husband and wife unite themselves in the sacrament of marriage. These vows encompass not just a couple's sexual relationship, but the whole of their life together.[13] The task of the couple in their sexual relationship is to "reread" the language of the body in light of the truth of their wedding vows. It is their mutual gift of self that the wedding vows articulate and intercourse expresses. The problem with contraception is that it imposes a contradictory language of withholding, rejection, and refusal. John Paul II wrote in *Familiaris consortio*: "Thus the innate language that expresses the total reciprocal self-giving of husband and wife is overlaid, through contraception, by an objectively contradictory language, namely, that of not giving oneself totally to the other."[14] It is as if the contracepting couple says to one another, "I give myself wholly to you, but not my fertility" and "I accept you unconditionally, but not your fertility."

Insofar as John Paul II derives his understanding of the communicability of the body in action not simply from philosophical analysis but from the opening chapters of Genesis, it is apparent that his expression of the Church's teaching is not based on a physicalist understanding of natural law or on reason alone.

This understanding of the linguistic nature of sexuality has been carried forward in the teaching of Pope Francis. In his apostolic exhortation *Amoris laetitia,* he wrote:

> Sexuality is not a means of gratification or entertainment; it is an interpersonal language wherein the other is taken seriously, in his or her sacred and inviolable dignity. As such, "the human heart comes to participate, so to speak, in another kind of spontaneity." In this context, the erotic appears as a specifically human manifestation of sexuality. It enables us to discover "the nuptial meaning of the body and the authentic dignity of the gift." In his catechesis on the theology of the body, Saint John Paul II taught that sexual differentiation not only is "a source of fruitfulness and procreation," but also possesses "the capacity of expressing love: that love precisely in which the human person becomes a gift."[15]

For both John Paul II and Francis, the communicability of the body in its masculinity or femininity is ordered to self-donative love expressed in the couple's sexual relationship.

Personalist

A second strand of argument, closely related to the first, might be termed "personalist" as it locates the evil of contracepted sex in the violation of the dignity of the person. One of the objections raised against *Humanae vitae* by those who purported to be sympathetic to its teaching was that the beautiful personalist

13 See Pope John Paul II, *General Audience* (July 4, 1984).

14 Pope John Paul II, Apostolic Exhortation *Familiaris consortio* (November 22, 1981), 32.

15 Pope Francis, Apostolic Exhortation *Amoris laetitia* (March 19, 2016), 151.

analysis of married love in the early sections of the document (e.g., 8–9) is not carried forward in its moral analysis of contraception in marriage (e.g., 11–12).[16] But, is such a compartmentalized reading of the document accurate? There are reasons to think it is not.

The use of the term "unitive" by Paul VI in section 12 of the document to describe the interpersonal dimension of conjugal love and its "inseparable connection" to procreation was not invented out of whole cloth, as some theologians subsequently complained;[17] rather it had both remote and proximate antecedents in the tradition. There had long been awareness of the interpersonal dimensions of marital sexual expression in the tradition even in the face of patristic and medieval insistence on procreation as the primary good or end of marriage. Though stronger in the Christian East, the growth of sacramental theology in the medieval West gave new prominence to friendship, love, and even pleasure within marital sexuality.[18] These ideas, which continued to grow in the face of rigorist reactions, flowered in the phenomenological personalism of the twentieth century in the work of scholars such as Dietrich von Hildebrand.

This rich vein of Catholic thought was deeply mined by Karol Wojtyła in his philosophical defense of Catholic sexual ethics in *Love and Responsibility*—undoubtedly an important proximate source for the teaching of Paul VI in *Humanae vitae*.[19] In the face of modern culture and its ethical instantiations in utilitarianism, Wojtyła rejects the idea that the person can be reduced to a mere object of enjoyment.[20] Rather, the person is the kind of good who cannot be used as a means to an end but instead must be accepted in love.[21] This "personalistic norm" is a hybrid of Kantian personalism and the New Testament's injunctions to love of neighbor. It gives Wojtyła an ethical tool to evaluate sexual self-donation. That is, sexual self-gift is good to the degree that the person is given and received in his or her totality and utilitarian to the degree that the person is treated as an object for use. Drawing on previous personalist analysis, Wojtyła describes sexual intercourse as an act of complete self-giving between

16 See Walter Kasper, *Theology of Christian Marriage*, trans. David Smith (New York: Crossroad, 1986), 13.

17 See Michael Barbieri and Joseph Selling, "The Origin of *Humanae Vitae* and the Impasse in Fundamental Theological Ethics," *Louvain Studies* 37, no. 4 (2013): 365–375, especially 375.

18 For a historical overview of (especially western) Catholic thought on the ends of marriage, see Casmir Onyegwara, "'Be Fruitful and Multiply:' Catholic Teaching on the Ends of Marriage with Reference to Questions Posed by Igbo Culture," (PhD diss., The Catholic University of America, 2015), at https://cuislandora.wrlc.org/islandora/object/cuislandora%3A28298. For a more concise overview of shifts in Catholic sexual teaching, see William E. May, Ronald Lawler, and Joseph Boyle, Jr., *Catholic Sexual Ethics: A Summary, Explanation and Defense*, 3rd ed. (Huntington, Ind.: Our Sunday Visitor, 2011), 77–111.

19 Michael Barbieri and Joseph Selling attribute not only significant influence but the substance of *Humanae vitae*'s teaching to Wojtyła. For them, this makes it clear that the encyclical was not the teaching of the whole Church but rather a reflection of the idiosyncratic ideas of a single Polish cardinal in 1968. See "The Origin of *Humanae Vitae*," 364–389.

20 See Karol Wojtyła, *Miłość i Odpowiedzialność* [*Love and Responsibility*] (Kraków, Wydawnicto, Znak, 1960), English translation by H. T. Willetts (New York: Farrar, Straus, and Giroux, 1981), 25–39.

21 Wojtyła, *Love and Responsibility*, 41.

spouses.[22] If the person is not given and received unreservedly, then he or she is "used" rather than loved—a basic offense against human dignity.[23] This personalist insight into human dignity and its bearing on conjugal love serves to connect the rich analysis of divine and married love in *Humanae vitae* to its use of the "unitive signification" of conjugal love and its connection to procreation.

The "personalist argument" also has continued to inform magisterial teaching and scholarly reflection. Thus, in *Familiaris consortio*, John Paul II writes that contraception, "leads not only to a positive refusal to be open to life but also to a falsification of the inner truth of conjugal love, which is called upon to give itself in personal totality."[24] Catholic sacramental theology which flowered in twentieth century personalism, has yielded a rich insight into human dignity and has created a an ethical framework capable of addressing new questions raised by the ongoing adaption of contraceptive technologies insofar as it does not rest its arguments on adherence to a set of biologically-derived norms.

Anthropological

The underpinning of the previous two sets of arguments is anthropological. That is, they rest on an understanding of the existential depth of fertility within the makeup of the person. In *Love and Responsibility*, Wojtyła had drawn on the insights of earlier phenomenological personalists (such as von Hildebrand and Edith Stein) to argue that the complementary differences between the sexes are not merely biological, but pertain to the person as a whole.[25] So too, for Wojtyła, sexual difference and "the sexual urge" to which it gives rise, while embracing

22 Wojtyła, *Love and Responsibility*, 66–68. Wojtyła actually argues that there are three ends of marriage: *procreation, mutuum adiutorium*, and *remedium concupiscentiae*. While procreation is primary, all depend on love for their proper realization. For an analysis of the relationship of Wojtyła's personalism to other strands of twentieth century personalist thought, see John S. Grabowski, "Person or Nature: Rival Personalisms in 20th Century Catholic Sexual Ethics," *Studia Moralia* 35 (1997): 283–312.

23 Interestingly, Wojtyła holds that this is the case whether the other is "used" simply for pleasure as in contraception or for procreation. See *Love and Responsibility*, 58–59, 61–63, 233.

24 *Familiaris consortio*, 32. For an extended analysis of this idea in the teaching of John Paul II, see Smith, Humanae Vitae: *A Generation Later*, 250–58. For a wider consideration of modern magisterial teaching, see Donald Asci, *The Conjugal Act as a Personal Act: A Study of the Catholic Concept of the Conjugal Act in Light of Christian Anthropology* (San Francisco: Ignatius Press, 2002).

25 In his ground-breaking treatment of love in marriage, Dietrich von Hildebrand stated, "it would be incredibly superficial to consider as a mere biological difference the distinction between man and woman, which really shows us two complementary types of the human species." See Dietrich von Hildebrand, *Die Ehe* (1929), trans. *Marriage: The Mystery of Faithful Love* (Manchester, N.H.: Sophia Institute Press, 1991), 13. Edith Stein used Thomistic ideas to argue for a similar position: "The insistence that the sexual differences are 'stipulated by the body alone' is questionable from various points of view. 1) If *anima = forma corpis*, then bodily differentiation constitutes an index of differentiation in the spirit. 2) Matter serves form, not the reverse. That strongly suggests that the difference in the psyche is the primary one." Edith Stein, "Letter to Sister Callista Kopf" in *Self Portrait in Letters 1916–1942*, eds. L Gelber and Romaeus Leuven, trans. Josephine Koeppel (Washington, D.C.: ICS Publications, 1993), 99. For a more complete examination of these thinkers and their influence on Karol Wojtyła/ John Paul II, see the excellent study by Prudence Allen, RSM, "Man-Woman Complementarity: The Catholic Inspiration," *Logos* 9, no. 3 (2006): 87–108.

the physical and psychological differences between the sexes, are deeper than them—reaching to the order of existence and thus impacting the person as a whole.[26] The impact of empiricism on modern thought and culture causes many people to presume that because sexuality can be studied biologically that it is merely biological instead of being rooted in human nature and its inclinations ("the order of existence" on Wojtyła's terms).[27]

Hence the Church's opposition to contraception and her concomitant promotion of natural means of fertility awareness and responsible parenthood are not based on an effort to derive moral laws from biological functions but on a fundamentally different view of the person. John Paul II teaches in *Familiaris consortio*:

> In the light of the experience of many couples and of the data provided by the different human sciences, theological reflection is able to perceive and is called to study further the difference, both anthropological and moral, between contraception and recourse to the rhythm of the cycle: it is a difference which is much wider and deeper than is usually thought, one which involves in the final analysis two irreconcilable concepts of the human person and of human sexuality. The choice of the natural rhythms involves accepting the cycle of the person, that is the woman, and thereby accepting dialogue, reciprocal respect, shared responsibility and self-control.[28]

In other words, natural means of fertility awareness see fertility as a gift given by God and an integral part of the person, while the various forms of artificial contraception or sterilization problematize fertility—ultimately treating it as a kind of disease which needs to be suppressed through chemical or surgical means.

Pope Francis has continued to defend the gift of fertility and its anthropological depth in his teaching ministry. He has encouraged the promotion of natural means of fertility awareness[29] and has spoken repeatedly of the importance of children and the witness of large families to the Church and to the world.[30] Regarding its anthropological ground, Pope Francis has been outspoken in pushing back against the encroachments of "gender ideology" and biotechnology on the family:

> The recent proposal to advance the dignity of a person by radically eliminating sexual difference and, as a result, our understanding of man and woman, is not right. . . . But the utopia of the "neuter" eliminates both human dignity in sexual distinctiveness and the personal nature of the generation of new life. The biological and psychological manipulation of sexual difference, which biomedical technology can now make appear as a simple matter of personal choice—which it is not!—runs the risk of dismantling the energy

26 See Wojtyła, *Love and Responsibility*, 52–53, 230; see also *The Acting Person*, ed. Anna-Teresa Tymieniecka, trans. Andrzej Potocki and Analecta Husserliana (Boston: D. Reidel, 1979), 215–218.

27 See Wojtyła, *Love and Responsibility*, 51–52.

28 Pope John Paul II, *Familiaris consortio*, 32.

29 See Pope Francis, *Amoris laetitia*, 222.

30 See Pope Francis, *Amoris laetitia*, 167.

> source that feeds the covenant between man and woman, making it creative and fruitful.... Henceforth, the mystery of human generation radiates a profound wisdom about life. Received as a gift, life is itself exalted. Generating life regenerates us; by giving of our lives, we are enriched.[31]

Furthermore, the gift of fertility and the inherent fruitfulness of love make definite ethical demands on conjugal life: "From the outset, love refuses every impulse to close in on itself; it is open to a fruitfulness that draws it beyond itself. Hence, no genital act of husband and wife can refuse this meaning, even when for various reasons it may not always in fact beget a new life."[32]

Given such clear and emphatic teaching by the Holy Father, one can only wonder at those who characterize Pope Francis as maintaining silence in regard to the central teaching of *Humanae vitae*.[33]

Perceiving fertility as a gift given by the Creator has implications not only for understanding the human person made in His image but for human stewardship of the body and the world.

Ecological

Responding to the call of Popes John Paul II and Francis for "a new feminism" and a better articulation of "the feminine genius,"[34] Catholic "new feminist" scholars have been at the forefront of those identifying the negative impact of contraceptives on the ecology of the human body—particularly women's bodies. Beyond the obvious health impacts of contraceptives which target women's fertility, there are deeper and more insidious impacts. Most contraceptives aim at suppressing the unique cyclical form of women's fertility in order to make them sexually available for men. In a sense, women internalize a kind of technological misogyny and our cultural "war on women" to better conform to male sexual demands. The Church's teaching conversely is powerfully pro-woman, rejecting this overriding of fertility in the name of sexual availability.[35] The Church places

31 See Pope Francis's address to the Participants in the General Assembly of the Pontifical Academy for Life (October 5, 2017), 3, https://w2.vatican.va/content/francesco/en/speeches/2017/october.index.2.html.

32 Pope Francis, *Amoris laetita*, 80 (referencing *Humanae vitae*, 11–12). The Latin text reads: "Non pervenit ille quasi sub finem alicuius processus, sed contra autem ab amoris initio tamquam essentiale quiddam adest, quod negari non potest nisi idem amor praecidatur. Inde a principio se in se ipse claudendi omnem impulsum refellit amor atque ad fecunditatem patet, quae eundem ultra propriam ipsius exsistentiam producit. Itaque nullus coniugum genitalis actus hanc significationem infitiari potest, quamvis varias ob causas haud semper novam vitam re generare possit."

33 See, for example, Walter Kasper, *Il messaggio di Amoris Laetitia: Una discussione fraternal* (Queriniana Editions, 2018).

34 Pope John Paul II issued his call for a "new feminism" in his 1995 encyclical letter *Evangelium vitae*, 99. One of his articulations of "the feminine genius can be found in his 1995 *Letter to Women*, 10–12. For Pope Francis's recognition of the feminine genius, see *Amoris laetitia*, 173. See also *Address to Consecrated Men and Women of the Diocese of Rome* (May 16, 2015).

35 The point is forcefully argued by Angela Franks, "The Gift of Female Fertility: Church Teaching on Contraception," in *Women, Sex and the Church: A Case for Catholic Teaching*, ed. Erika Bachiochi (Boston: Pauline: 2010), 97–120.

the couple's shared fertility at the center of her call to responsible parenthood. Because healthy men are generally always fertile, this means that a woman's unique pattern of fertility is placed at the center of the couple's sexual life and decision-making. Natural methods of fertility awareness, therefore, not only promote respect for the gift of fertility and the ecology of the body but promote a form of human ecology within the married relationship by fostering dialogue and shared decision-making about sex and openness to life.

The phrase "human ecology" was used by John Paul II in his encyclical celebrating the one hundredth anniversary of Pope Leo XIII's *Rerum novarum*: "The first and fundamental structure for 'human ecology' is the family, in which man receives his first formative ideas about truth and goodness, and learns what it means to love and to be loved, and thus what it actually means to be a person."[36] Building on this understanding, Pope Benedict XVI stressed the interdependence of "the human environment" with "the natural environment"[37] and argued that "openness to life" is central to authentic human development:

> When a society moves towards the denial or suppression of life, it ends up no longer finding the necessary motivation and energy to strive for man's true good. If personal and social sensitivity towards the acceptance of a new life is lost, then other forms of acceptance that are valuable for society also wither away. The acceptance of life strengthens moral fiber and makes people capable of mutual help. By cultivating openness to life, wealthy peoples can better understand the needs of poor ones, they can avoid employing huge economic and intellectual resources to satisfy the selfish desires of their own citizens, and instead, they can promote virtuous action within the perspective of production that is morally sound and marked by solidarity, respecting the fundamental right to life of every people and every individual.[38]

Pope Francis has pushed this idea of the interdependence of human ecology and care for "our common home" the earth, even further. In his encyclical on the environment, he states: "Human ecology also implies [a] profound reality: the relationship between human life and the moral law, which is inscribed in our nature and is necessary for the creation of a more dignified environment. Pope Benedict XVI spoke of an 'ecology of man,' based on the fact that 'man too has a nature that he must respect and that he cannot manipulate at will.'"[39] Yet like his predecessor, Pope Francis emphatically rejects abortion, sterilization, and contraception as means to limit human population in the name of care for the planet:

36 Pope John Paul II, Encyclical Letter *Centesimus annus* (May 1, 1991), 39.

37 See Pope Benedict XVI, Encyclical Letter *Caritas in veritate* (June 29, 2009), 48–50.

38 Pope Benedict XVI, *Caritas in veritate*, 28.

39 Pope Francis, Encyclical Letter *Laudato si'* (May 24, 2015), 155. For an overview of "integral ecology" in recent Church teaching and particular the teaching of Pope Francis, see the excellent study by Jennifer E. Miller, "The Virtue of Sobriety: Integral Human Ecology in its Full Flourishing," *Nova et Vetera* (English edition) 16, no. 1 (Winter 2018): 205–229.

> Instead of resolving the problems of the poor and thinking of how the world can be different, some can only propose a reduction in the birth rate. At times, developing countries face forms of international pressure which make economic assistance contingent on certain policies of "reproductive health." Yet "while it is true that an unequal distribution of the population and of available resources creates obstacles to development and a sustainable use of the environment, it must nonetheless be recognized that demographic growth is fully compatible with an integral and shared development." To blame population growth instead of extreme and selective consumerism on the part of some, is one way of refusing to face the issues.[40]

Both the natural world and human fertility are gifts which come from the Creator's loving design. One should not sacrifice the latter in the name of protecting the former.

Virtue

The fact that natural methods of fertility awareness have high rates of effectiveness at avoiding pregnancy can lead to the perception that they are simply one group of family planning methods among others. Reflecting on the fact that these same methods can help couples—even those with impaired fertility—to become pregnant can help to underscore the fact that they are genuine methods of *family planning* and not merely "contraception."[41]

Yet there is a deeper set of differences between natural and artificial means of birth regulation which reveal that, from another perspective, natural means are not "methods" at all—they are moral practices which help to form couples in virtue. In *Love and Responsibility* Karol Wojtyła offers this understanding of natural means of fertility awareness and family planning:

> . . .[T]he utilitarian interpretation distorts the true character of what we call the natural method, which is that it is based on continence as a virtue and this . . . is very closely connected with love of the person.
>
> Inherent in the essential character of continence as a virtue is the conviction that the *love of man and woman loses nothing as a result of temporary abstention from erotic experiences, but on the contrary gains*: the personal union takes deeper root, grounded as it is above all in the affirmation of the value of the person and not just in sexual attachment. *Continence as a virtue cannot be regarded as a 'contraceptive measure.'*[42]

40 Pope Francis, *Laudato si'*, 50.

41 This is especially true when fertility awareness is joined to targeted medical intervention designed to treat the underlying disease of which infertility is a symptom such as in NaProTECHNOLOGY ™. See Katie Elrod and Paul Carpentier, "The Church's Best Kept Secret: Church Teaching on Infertility Treatment," in *Women, Sex and the Church*, ed. Bachiochi, 121–41. For a general overview of Catholic teaching and pastoral practice in regard to infertility, see Carmen Santamaria and Angelique Ruhi-Lopez, *The Infertility Companion for Catholics: Spiritual and Practical Support for Couples* (Notre Dame, Ind.: Ave Maria Press, 2012).

42 Wojtyła, *Love and Responsibility*, 241 (emphasis in original).

> I will make one modification to Wojtyła's language here in light of more recent work in virtue ethics. Periodic continence (i.e., refraining from genital sex), is a moral *practice* productive of virtue in the life of a married couple. The idea is as old as the New Testament when St. Paul recommends temporary continence so that couples can devote themselves more fully to prayer.[43]

This practice does not just aid unhindered prayer—it helps couples develop other virtues integral to married life and love. Specifically, it forms couples in the self-mastery that is at the heart of conjugal chastity, enabling a couple's sexual relationship to communicate the free gift of self in love. In his catechesis on the Theology of the Body, John Paul II makes the following comment on the teaching of *Humanae vitae*:

> Although the "periodic" character of continence in this case is applied to the so-called "natural rhythms" (HV 16), still *continence* itself is a definite and permanent attitude, *it is a virtue*, and thus the whole mode of behavior guided by it becomes virtuous character. The encyclical underlines rather clearly that here it is *not* merely a matter of a certain "*technique*," but of *ethics* in the strict sense of the term as *the morality of a certain behavior*.[44]

It should be noted that periodic continence is part of every marriage. Couples have to abstain from sexual union during periods of illness, absence from one another, and recovery from childbirth. Mere necessity is not itself productive of virtue. However, when the practice of continence is freely chosen by the couple, it can become a practice which shapes their character over time. As John Paul II states later in the same audience: "In the case of a morally upright regulation of fertility brought about by periodic continence, the point is clearly to *practice conjugal chastity*, that is, of a certain ethical attitude."[45]

This way of looking at natural means of fertility awareness and methods of family planning based on them put forward by Karol Wojtyła (John Paul II) has been developed further by theologians.[46] It also connects this issue to the current retrieval of virtue ethics within both philosophy and theology which has begun in recent decades to be applied to issues of sexuality.[47]

43 See 1 Cor 7:3–5.

44 Pope John Paul II, *Man and Woman*, 635 (no. 124:4, emphasis in original).

45 Pope John Paul II, *Man and Woman*, 635 (no. 124:6, emphasis in original).

46 See, for example, John S. Grabowski, *Sex and Virtue: An Introduction to Sexual Ethics*, Catholic Moral Thought Series (Washington, D.C.: The Catholic University of America Press, 2003), 142–154. See also Michel Therrien, "The Practice of Responsible Parenthood, NFP, and the Covenantal Unity of Spouses," in *Leaving and Coming Home: New Wineskins for Catholic Sexual Ethics*, ed. David Cloutier (Eugene, Ore.: Wipf and Stock Publishers, 2010), 173–205.

47 Both *Sex and Virtue* and *Leaving and Coming Home* are devoted to virtue-based explorations of sexual ethics as a whole.

Biblical

The authors of the Wijngaards statement declare confidently: "The teaching that using 'artificial' contraception is an intrinsic wrong always and everywhere is not revealed, nor has it ever been shown to be essential for the truth of the Christian revelation."[48] While such a statement might have been defensible in 1968, it ignores counter arguments which have been put forward in both magisterial teaching and theological literature which seek to demonstrate that the teaching is indeed supported by and anchored in biblical revelation.

John Paul II's presentation of sexual union as a form of the language of the body which expresses and subsequently recalls the vows articulated in the wedding liturgy closely corresponds to biblical scholarship which has highlighted sexual intimacy as the embodied gesture which ratifies and expresses the covenant of marriage.[49] This line of biblical scholarship has also been employed in efforts to articulate a more biblical approach to questions of the theology of marriage and sexual ethics.[50]

It is certainly an overstatement to view the Theology of the Body catechesis as wholly focused on sex. The catechesis offers, as John Paul II repeatedly stated, "an adequate anthropology"[51]—adequate to many of the questions of the modern world. In the concluding audience of the Theology of the Body, he noted their application to a whole range of issues: "One must immediately observe, in fact, that the term 'theology of the body' goes far beyond the content of the reflections presented here. These reflections do not include many problems belonging, with regard to their object, to the theology of the body (e.g., the problem of suffering and death, so important in the biblical message)."[52] Scholars have thus begun to apply this anthropology to a variety of issues: suffering,[53] the

48 Catholic Scholars' Statement on the Ethics of Using Contraceptives, §6.3.

49 On the basic structure of a covenant and its distinction from contracts in biblical thought, see Gene M. Tucker, "Covenant Forms and Contract Forms," *Vetus Testamentum* 15, no. 4 (1965): 487–503. On the biblical depiction of marriage of covenant, see Paul F. Palmer, SJ, "Christian Marriage: Contract or Covenant?" *Theological Studies* 33, no. 4 (December 1972): 617–665, especially 617–619, 639–640. For a more comprehensive study of marriage as a covenant in scripture, see Gordon Paul Hugenberger, *Marriage as a Covenant: A Study of Biblical Law and Ethics Developed from the Perspective of Malachi*, Supplements to Vetus Testamentum 52 (Leiden: Brill, 1994). On the role of sexual union within this covenant see Hugenberger, 216–279; see also Maurice Gilbert, SJ, "'*Une seule chair*' (Gn 2, 24)," *Nouvelle revue théologique* 100, no. 1 (1978): 66–89.

50 See Grabowski, *Sex and Virtue*, 23–48.

51 In the index to his volume, Waldstein notes that this phrase is found six times in the catechesis (nos. 13:2, 14:3, 15:1, 23:3, 25:2, 26:2). He also observes that the Italian *adeguato* does not carry the connotation of meeting minimal requirements as it can in English. In no. 55:2 John Paul II defines the Italian as meaning "commensurate with its object." See *Man and Woman*, 678.

52 Pope John Paul II, *Man and Woman*, 660 (no. 133:1).

53 See José Granados, "Toward a Theology of the Suffering Body," *Communio: International Catholic Review* 33, no. 4 (Winter 2006): 540–563. See also Peter Harman, "Towards a Theology of Suffering: The Contribution of Karol Wojtyła/Pope John Paul II," (STD diss., The Catholic University of America, 2009), especially 303–415.

moral status and agency of the vulnerable,[54] and a range of other subjects such as technology, work, prayer, and eschatology.[55]

Nonetheless, John Paul II was clearly aware that among the pressing questions of the modern world were those concerning sexuality in general and the highly contested issue of birth regulation in particular. Therefore, it is not surprising that he concluded the catechesis with a series of audiences on *Humanae vitae* and its assertion of an "inseparable connection" between the unitive and procreative meanings of the conjugal act. John Paul II clearly saw his biblical anthropology as "adequate" to addressing that question. The whole of the Theology of the Body sheds light on the nature of the human person as male and female, the nature of love, and the ethical structure of action. Indeed, each of the preceding themes—the communicability of the body and the meaning of sexual self-gift, the dignity of the person, the existential weight of sexual difference and fertility, the interconnection of human stewardship of the body and the natural world, and the call to self-mastery and growth in love—are grounded in the sacred text and illumined by John Paul II's experiential reading of them. Thus, he writes: "Precisely on the background of such a full whole [i.e., the whole of the catecheses] it becomes evident the moral norms just mentioned [i.e., *Humanae vitae*, nos. 11–12] is not only part of the natural law, but also of the *moral order revealed by God*."[56]

For John Paul II, the teaching of *Humanae vitae* also finds attestation in particular biblical texts. For example, he points to Genesis 4:1 as a biblical articulation of the sexual form of "the language of the body": "The man had intercourse with his wife Eve, and she conceived and gave birth to Cain, saying, 'I have produced a male child with the help of the LORD.'" He points out that the original Hebrew text says that the man "knew" (Hebrew *yāḏa'*) his wife. This, he explains, is not a euphemism on the sacred writer's part, but a philosophically apt way to describe the knowledge which spouses gain in sexual self-gift.[57] And he notes that this knowledge is not just of each other as spouses (i.e., "man and wife") but of each other as potential mother and father.[58] If either of these dimensions is negated, the truth of the reciprocal gift is falsified and the language of the body is not spoken in truth. Thus, even the "inseparable connection" of *Humanae vitae* has biblical foundation.

Conclusion

In point of fact, every one of the criticisms of *Humanae vitae* advanced by the authors of the Wijngaards statement has been substantively addressed both by

54 See Jeffrey Tranzillo, *John Paul II on the Vulnerable* (Washington, D.C.: The Catholic University of America Press, 2012).

55 Mary Timothy Prokes, FSE, *Toward a Theology of the Body* (Grand Rapids, Mich.: Eerdmans, 1996). While not written as a direct commentary on John Paul II's catechesis, Prokes's work is clearly influenced and inspired by it. See also Susan Windley-Daoust. *Theology of the Body, Extended: The Spiritual Signs of Birth, Impairment and Dying*. Cincinnati: Lectio Publishing, 2014.

56 Pope John Paul II, *Man and Woman*, 621 (no. 119:4, emphasis in original).

57 See the weekly general audience of March 5, 1980 in Pope John Paul II, *Man and Woman*, no. 20.

58 See the weekly general audience of March 12, 1980 in Pope John Paul II, *Man and Woman*, no. 21.

magisterial teaching and theological scholarship. Certainly, one could contest some or all of these arguments and the conclusions they generate. However, the authors of that document do not take that route—they simply ignore them and, by so doing, seem to suggest that a significant part of the last fifty years of Catholic theology simply did not happen. Nothing has changed since 1968.

But that simply is not the case. Many of the doubts raised about the application of the Church's perennial opposition to contraception in light of the new context of the twentieth century and the development of oral contraception have been addressed and, indeed, largely dispelled. The teaching does not rest on conformity to moral rules "read off" of biological processes. There are a host of morally significant differences between natural means of fertility awareness and family planning and contraception. The teaching has a foundation in Scripture and not simply in the natural law and the constant tradition of the Church. Scientific study confirms the dangers posed by contraceptive technologies to the human body (particularly the bodies of women) and to the environment. Social science helps us understand the catastrophic impact of the modern sexual revolution which oral contraception supported. By every objective measure, the warnings of Pope Paul VI in *Humanae vitae*, no. 17, about the impact of widespread contraceptive use have proven to be prophetic.[59]

To heed the Second Vatican Council's call to scrutinize "the signs of the times" in the light of the Gospel, it is also worth noting that the lines of development identified here map on to the Council's own blueprint for the renewal of Catholic theology—particularly the Church's moral teaching. This blueprint included, first, "more living contact with the mystery of Christ,"[60] further elaborated in the Christological anthropology of *Gaudium et spes*, no. 22 noted above. Second, a renewed theology must be "more nourished on the teaching of the Bible"[61] which the Council elsewhere calls "the soul of sacred theology."[62] Third, this theology should "shed light on the loftiness of the calling of the faithful in Christ and the obligation that is theirs of bearing fruit in charity for the life of the world,"[63] language which recalls the universal call to holiness articulated elsewhere in the Council's documents.[64] The magisterial teaching and theological scholarship highlighted in the strands of development charted above follow the trajectory for renewal laid out by the Council.

The clarification of the teaching and the reasons for it outlined here are not simply a matter of academic interest. Nor is it aimed at "indoctrinating" the teaching in order to weaponize it or turn it into stones to hurl at others.[65] The

59 See Mary Eberstadt's brilliant analysis of "The Vindication of *Humanae vitae*" in chapter 8 of *Adam and Eve after the Pill: Paradoxes of the Sexual Revolution* (San Francisco: Ignatius, 2012), 134–58, and chapter 2 of this volume.

60 Vatican Council II, *Optatam totius* (October 28, 1965), 16.

61 *Optatam totius*, 16.

62 Vatican Council II, *Dei verbum* (November 18, 1965), 24.

63 *Optatam totius*, 16.

64 See Vatican Council II, *Lumen gentium* (November 21, 1964), 40.

65 See Pope Francis's warning in *Amoris laetitia*, 49.

truth of what the Church teaches is at the service of the human person, her own pastoral ministry, and ultimately the work of the New Evangelization. To a culture bloodied and scarred by the modern sexual revolution and its ongoing fallout, the Church offers an alternative vision of marriage, love, and life—their meaning and interconnection. By so doing, she acts as a field hospital in which the wounded can encounter Christ the great physician and His mercy, as well as charting a path toward living out the new life which He freely imparts.

20

Signs of Growth and Healing

Health Care and Science

Richard J. Fehring

✷ MY ESSAY ON THE HISTORY OF Catholic Natural Family Planning (NFP) scientists (chapter 8 in this volume) ended with discussing scientists who were active during the papacy of John Paul II (1979–2005). This present essay continues with the time period from approximately 2000 to 2018 and, indeed, into the future. My purpose here, however, is to delineate signs of growth and healing in health care and science related to NFP and not to focus on individual NFP scientists. Given that purpose, recent trends in NFP science and historical factors that influence NFP science can provide us with signs of growth regarding NFP and its application to medicine and health care. Here, I will cover five areas to demonstrate that hope. Before doing so, however, a word should first be said about a handful of hopeful trends that have also occurred in this time period. They are: US federal government funding of NFP research, a resurgence of NFP interest among Catholic health-care professionals, and efforts to publish NFP science.

Growth in NFP Support and Research

NFP and Federal Funding

In the United States during the presidency of George W. Bush (2001–2009), several conservative Catholic leaders were appointed to important government institutions. Among the federal appointments, those to the Office of Population Affairs (OPA), would prove helpful to NFP education and use.

OPA oversees the administration of Title X in the Department of Health and Human Services (HHS). Title X, which was created in 1970 as part of the Public Health Service Act, is the "only federal program dedicated solely to the provision of family planning and related preventive health care."[1] In its general

1 Title X is "designed to provide contraceptive supplies and information to all who want and need them, with priority given to persons from low-income families." In addition to providing voluntary family planning, Title X-funded centers provide family planning education and counseling, including information on the methods of Natural Family Planning; "breast and cervical cancer screening; sexually transmitted disease (STD) and human immunodeficiency virus (HIV) testing, referral, and prevention education; and pregnancy diagnosis and counseling. By law, Title X funds cannot be used in programs where abortion is a method of family planning." *Title X Family Planning Annual Report, 2017 National Summary*, 1, at https://www.hhs.gov/opa/sites/default/files/title-x-fpar-2017-national-summary.pdf.

requirements for grantee family planning programs, Title X includes NFP education and provision of services. In 2008, OPA issued a call for research proposals and programs that would help increase the use of NFP services in the Title X clinics and among other family planning providers. Research grants were awarded to Joseph Stanford, MD (University of Utah), Victoria Jennings, PhD (Georgetown University, Institute for Reproductive Health), and several other research organizations. One of the largest grants was provided to Marquette University's Institute for NFP which helped fund an online provision of NFP services and the first randomized comparison study of NFP methods since the early 1980s.[2]

The US federal government has been helpful in monitoring use of NFP and Fertility Awareness-Based Methods (or FABMs) through one of their major studies, the National Survey of Family Growth (NSFG).[3] The NSFG studies women from the age of 15–44 to determine family planning trends in the United States since 1977.[4] The latest study on contraceptive trends in the NSFG showed an increase of 4% in "rhythm" and NFP use among the 20–29 age group from 2008 to 2014.[5] This increase might reflect a rejection of hormonal steroids and a desire to use the newer fertility monitoring applications (apps), most of which are based on Rhythm. Information from this population-based data is useful for NFP researchers who often do not have access to large data sets.

Catholic Health-care Professionals

Interest in practicing medicine according to the Catholic faith has grown among Catholic health-care professionals over the last twenty years. This can be seen, for example, in the growth and interests of the members of the Catholic Medical Association (CMA). In the year 2000, for example, there were approximately three hundred CMA members. In 2018, the number rose to over 1,000.[6] In the past (late twentieth century), it was difficult to schedule NFP science on the CMA's annual meeting agenda. Today, NFP is often included as one of the plenary session presentations, preconference topics, and break-out sessions. The interest in supporting Church teaching, especially as it pertains to fertility and family planning, is now apparent in CMA leadership as well. For example, past

2 Richard J. Fehring, Mary Schneider, Kathleen Raviele, Dana Rodriguez, and Jessica E. Pruszynski, "Randomized Comparison of Two Internet-Supported Fertility Awareness Based Methods of Family Planning," *Contraception* 88, no. 1 (July 2013): 24–30.

3 The NSFG is a population-based survey produced by the National Center for Health Statistics, a division of the Center for Disease Control and Prevention (CDC).

4 And then every few years: 1982, 1988, 1995, 2002, 2008, 2010, 2011, and 2015. See, for example, M. L. Kavanaugh and J. Jerman, "Contraceptive Method Use in the United States: Trends and Characteristics Between 2008, 2012, and 2014," *Contraception* 97, no. 1 (January 2018): 14–21.

5 The NSFG includes an item for "rhythm" and another for "temp/mucus." The NSFG includes under the title "rhythm" calendar-based methods that are self-devised. The term "temp/mucus" is denoted for Natural Family Planning.

6 Catholic Medical Association Former President Dr. Peter Morrow, personal communication to the author (during the June 2018 CMA "boot camp").

CMA Presidents Dr. Kathleen Raviele and Dr. Lester Ruppersberger provide clear witness of offering NFP-only obstetrics/gynecology practices as well as regularly promote NFP and Church teaching among Catholic physicians. This was not typical in the past.

In addition to the above, CMA leaders integrate NFP information in their annual medical ethics "boot camp" for Catholic medical students. Finally, the CMA journal, *The Linacre Quarterly*, frequently offers peer-reviewed articles on NFP and related topics. And, it features the NFP science publication produced by the United States Conference of Catholic Bishops (USCCB) NFP Program, *Current Medical Research*.[7] Of note is that in 2014, *The Linacre Quarterly* featured a special issue entirely devoted to NFP. And the November 2018 is devoted to the fiftieth anniversary of *Humanae vitae*.

NFP Scientific Publications—Then and Now

Efforts to publish research on NFP science and methodology have mostly been reliant on individuals and their specific research. As discussed in my chapter 8 on the history of NFP scientists in this volume, many have had success with their efforts. In addition to those publications, there are two efforts that are worthy of note. In 1977, the inaugural issue of the journal, the *International Review of Natural Family Planning* was published. The journal was initiated and published by Fr. Paul Marx, OSB, PhD, through the Human Life Center at Saint John's University in Collegeville, Minnesota.[8] On the advisory board for the journal were thirty-two individuals including many of the "who's who" in NFP science at that time.[9] The articles from the journal were linked to the National Library of Medicine Indexes affording the articles wide readership. More recently, under the efforts of Dr. Joseph Stanford, NFP research is featured in the new open access journal, *Frontiers in Medicine*.

The examples above are just some positive movements in NFP science and applications to health care. This essay presents the signs of growth and healing for the science and medical application of NFP in the following five areas: (1) the application of the internet and cell phone apps, (2) fertility monitoring technology and precision medicine, (3) the integration of NFP with women's health, (4) globalization of science, and (5) the development of "big" data.

7 United States Conference of Catholic Bishops, *Natural Family Planning, Current Medical Research*, http://www.usccb.org/nfp/medical-research/index.cfm.

8 Paul Marx, "Foreword," *International Review of Natural Family Planning* 1 (1977): iv–vi. The journal contains classic articles about NFP science, methodology, and related Catholic teaching. Its last issue was Fall/Winter 1989.

9 For example, Drs. James Brown, Thomas Hilgers, Anna Flynn, Konald Prem, Rudolf Vollman, Claude Lanctot, and research and NFP pioneers Drs. Michelle and Francois Guy from France and a physician wife team that was on the 1960s papal birth control commission, Dr. Charles Rendu and his wife, Elizabeth.

The Internet and Mobile NFP Applications

In the twenty-first century, the widespread access to the internet and the development of mobile applications has made a significant contribution to NFP education. One of the first in the United States to use these formats is not a Catholic NFP leader but a secular fertility-awareness-based combined method leader,[10] Toni Weschler.

Weschler popularized NFP at the turn of the twenty-first century through her book, *Taking Charge of Your Fertility*.[11] Weschler's online charting system, example charts, and fertility consultation were designed for clients as a subscription membership (the first to charge fees for this type of service). Weschler's e-resources (including apps for iPhones and Androids), were among the very first electronic strategies in the fertility awareness and NFP community. Since then, there have been many other online systems of NFP, hundreds of new fertility-monitoring apps, and new social NFP/FABM networks for both achieving and avoiding pregnancy.[12] Social networking is one of the main communication modes for modern young women. Social networking that focuses on young women's health through the menstrual cycle can be a powerful tool to promote health and identify early symptoms that might indicate health problems. This tool can be especially useful when it is linked to health-care professionals, such as physicians and advanced practice professional nurses who specialize in understanding the menstrual cycle and the methods of NFP.

According to the National Center for Health Statistics, women of reproductive age access health information on the internet (in blogs and social networks) more than men.[13] The internet is the primary source of information on women's health, the menstrual cycle (e.g., unusual uterine bleeding), and other related problems.[14] According to the Pew Foundation, approximately 80% of US adults own a cell phone (the rate is about 87% among African Americans).[15] Menstrual cycle tracking apps are the fourth most used health apps among adults and the most frequent among adolescents.[16] There are, however, not many NFP

10 Fertility-awareness-based combined method refers to the educator's allowance of contraceptive barrier methods in the fertile time. Authentic NFP makes use of *periodic sexual abstinence* as the means to avoid pregnancy. With NFP, no barriers or chemicals are used to avoid pregnancy.

11 Toni Weschler, *Taking Charge of Your Fertility* (New York: Harpers Collins, 2002).

12 See Michelle L. Moglia, Henry V. Nguyen, Kathy Chyjek, Katherine T. Chen, and Paula M. Castaño, "Evaluation of Smartphone Menstrual Cycle Tracking Applications Using an Adapted Applications Scoring System," *Obstetrics & Gynecology* 127, no. 6 (May 2016): 1153–1160. See also Marguerite Duane, Alison Contreras, Elizabeth T. Jensen, and Amina White, "The Performance of Fertility Awareness-Based Method Apps Marketed to Avoid Pregnancy," *Journal of the American Board of Family Medicine* 29, no. 4 (July 2016): 508–511.

13 Robin A. Cohen and Barbara Stussman, "Health Information Technology Use Among Men and Women Aged 18–64: Early Release of Estimates from the National Health Interview Survey, January–June, 2009," *National Center for Health Statistics*, Health e-Stats (February 2010).

14 LeeAnn A. Kahlor and Michael Mackert, "Perception of Infertility Information and Support Sources among Female Patients who Access the Internet," *Fertility and Sterility* 91, no. 1 (January 2009): 83–90.

15 Kahlor and Mackert, "Perception of Infertility Information and Support Sources."

16 Cohen and Stussman, "Health Information Technology Use."

methods that have a web-based menstrual cycle monitoring system as well as a cell phone app that provides easy access to menstrual cycle monitoring, a social network, and professional support.

In 2008, a website program was launched (in English and Spanish) to teach couples the Marquette Model (MM) of NFP and provide online consultation (i.e., provide ease of access for couples across the United States).[17] The website included information on NFP, user forums, a menstrual cycle charting system, protocols for special reproductive circumstances (e.g., monitoring fertility during the postpartum breastfeeding transition), and online support from professional nurses and physicians.[18]

The website NFP system also facilitated studies to determine the effectiveness of special protocols for postpartum women,[19] effectiveness to avoid pregnancy among women transitioning through perimenopause,[20] and the effects of focused intercourse during the estimated fertile window with couples wishing to achieve pregnancy.[21] In addition, the website facilitated the provision of women's health care beyond family planning in that the professional nurses managing the website and their physician consultants (through the user forums) answer many related health questions (e.g., assessing and managing polycystic ovarian syndrome (PCOS), and unusual uterine bleeding), with over 35,000 posts.[22] In essence, these studies demonstrate that the online NFP website is a system of providing women's health care and the use of the menstrual cycle is a vital sign. There are many other websites and NFP learning systems that have some combination of online existence, consultation, charting systems, and fertility monitoring apps.[23] Below are several examples.

Among the more significant changes for NFP education in the last five years or so are those having to do with the mobile fertility monitoring application systems—especially those that are either very simple to use[24] or are linked to a

17 Richard J. Fehring, Mary Schneider, and Kathleen Raviele, "Pilot Evaluation of an Internet-Based Natural Family Planning Education and Service Program," *Journal of Obstetric, Gynecologic, and Neonatal Nursing* 40, no. 3 (May–June 2011): 281–291.

18 See Marquette University, "A Naturally Healthy Approach," http://nfp.marquette.edu. As of April 2018, the MM online system had over 10,600 women/couples registered on the site.

19 Thomas Bouchard, Mary Schneider, and Richard J. Fehring, "Efficacy of a New Postpartum Transition Protocol for Avoiding Pregnancy," *Journal of the American Board of Family Medicine* 26, no. 1 (January 2013): 35–44.

20 Qiyan Mu and Richard Fehring, "Efficacy of Achieving Pregnancy with Fertility-Focused Intercourse," *MCN: The American Journal of Maternal/Child Nursing* 39, no. 1 (January–February 2014): 35–40.

21 Richard Fehring and Qiyan Mu, "Cohort Efficacy Study of Natural Family Planning among Perimenopause Age Women," *Journal of Obstetric, Gynecologic, and Neonatal Nursing* 43, no. 3 (May–June 2014): 351–358.

22 As of February 2017.

23 An example is Sensiplan in Germany and Europe, a Sympto-Thermal system. See Elizabeth Raith-Paula, Petra Frank-Herrmann, Gunter Freundl, and Thomas Stowitzki, *Naturliche Familienplanung heute*, 4th edition (Heidelberg, Germany: Springer, 2008), 13.

24 For example, Dynamic Optimal Timing or DOT, developed by the staff of the IRH at Georgetown University, see https://www.dottheapp.com/news. This system is problematic for Catholics since it encourages barrier methods to be used during the fertile time.

Bluetooth for cell phones. Some are useful while others, unfortunately, are problematic for Catholics. Among the problematic ones are those that either include contraceptive barrier use[25] as part of the FABM system or are connected to fertility clinics that provide IVF should the user have difficulty becoming pregnant.[26]

Among the more helpful apps is Natural Cycles,[27] which was developed by Swedish researchers. This app includes the ability to record the basal body temperature (BBT) and results from luteinizing hormone (LH) urine test kits. The Natural Cycles app has a built-in algorithm that calculates an estimated fertile window based on the first day of menses and the BBT recordings and provides indicators regarding the woman's fertile window (a red color for potential fertile days and green color for estimated infertile days). Researchers and developers of this fertility monitoring application conducted a study to provide evidence for the accuracy of determining ovulation and the fertile window of the menstrual cycle with their fertility monitoring app.[28] They were able to obtain 317 women participants (mean age 30.1) who generated 1,501 cycles of data. The results showed no pregnancies recorded with intercourse on the green days and one pregnancy reported with intercourse on a red fertile day among the participants using this system to avoid pregnancy. The researchers subsequently conducted and published a study to determine the effectiveness of the app in helping women avoid pregnancy.[29]

The Natural Cycles app study was a retrospective analysis of data produced by 4,050 women aged 18 years or older who used the app for three months at a minimum and entered data for at least twenty days. The 4,050 women who purchased the app and agreed to the study produced 2,085 women-years of data. The participants had a total of 143 unintended pregnancies. These pregnancies and the 2,053 women-years of use yielded a perfect use Pearl Index of pregnancy rate of 0.5 and 7.0 (per 100 woman years) for typical use. Survival analysis produced a typical use pregnancy rate of 7.5. The authors concluded that their app improved the effectiveness of using a fertility awareness-based method of family

25 As in DOT. In addition to the conflict with Catholic moral teachings prohibiting use of contraception, it should be noted that barriers used during the estimated fertile phase also confound the results of established effectiveness studies, in that it is not known if the effectiveness is due to using fertility awareness, or the barrier, or both together. It can also be said that failure rates for the contraceptive barriers may be estimated as higher than known when used during the fertile time since typical studies do not test use exclusively during the fertile window.

26 See, for example, Glow fertility monitoring app, https://itunes.apple.com/us/app/glow-ovulation-period-tracker/id638021335?mt=8. To read about Glow First, a premium membership fund linked to the app that provides support for assisted reproductive technology treatments, see https://abcnews.go.com/Technology/glow-fertility-app-pregnant-give-money/story?id=19901626.

27 See https://www.naturalcycles.com/en. According to the website, the company has sold over 700,000 units in 200 countries.

28 Elina Berglund Scherwitzl, Angelica Lindén Hirschberg, and Raoul Scherwitzl, "Identification and Prediction of the Fertile Window Using NaturalCycles," *The European Journal of Contraception and Reproductive Health Care* 20, no. 5 (January 2015): 403–408.

29 Elina Berglund Scherwitzl, Kristina Gemzell Danielsson, Jonas A. Sellberg, and Raoul Sherwitzl, "Fertility Awareness-based Mobile Application for Contraception," *The European Journal of Contraception and Reproductive Health Care* 21, no. 3 (May 2016): 234–241.

planning. They indicated that the app is especially effective in preventing unintended pregnancy when couples consistently use contraceptive barrier methods on the estimated (red) fertile days. These conclusions remove Natural Cycles from the category of authentic NFP methods. Clearly the researchers speak of a combined FABM. At the same time, it can be said that Catholic NFP users could obtain supportive information from this app since it monitors the BBT and the results from luteinizing hormone (LH) urine test kits. When seeking to avoid pregnancy, Natural Cycles can provide support to the typical NFP user without the introduction of barriers during the fertile time.

Another innovative fertility app-based program called "Cycle Technologies" is interesting since it is promoted as being useful to both plan and avoid pregnancies. Founded in 2002 by a private company that partnered with governments, nonprofits, and nongovernment organizations (NGOs), Cycle Technologies states that its mission is to prevent unintended pregnancies and help people have the families that they want when they are ready to have them.[30] Its products are promoted as "free" and "safe" alternatives for women who are interested in effective, side-effect-free, family planning options. The company claims that its products have been used by six million people from sixty countries, helping to prevent 5.5 million pregnancies and to successfully plan 1.5 million pregnancies.

This age of fertility indicators, mobile apps for smartphones, and internet access also is thought to have been responsible for the increase in use of the Rhythm Method and NFP among younger women (i.e., age 20–24) in the United States as indicated in recent NSFG studies.[31] According to German researchers, knowledge of fertility indicators and symptoms in a woman's cycle has increased dramatically in recent decades.[32] If a woman wants to use this knowledge, it is all too understandable in the age of the personal computer and smartphone that she will use resources that make her daily work easier, especially regarding the daily charting of fertility symptoms. This new technology help make life as favorable and natural as possible for women.

The large numbers of apps that have been downloaded with the Cycle Technology and Natural Cycle systems demonstrate the interest and need for such easy and accessible menstrual cycle charting systems for using NFP. Now that access to these apps can be made through satellite cell towers and do not need additional infrastructure, anyone with a cell phone or other mobile device can take advantage of useful resources. This access was demonstrated in an article in *National Geographic* showing Samburu women in Nairobi, Africa, with handheld tablets connected to the internet by satellite and uploaded with educational programs.[33] Certainly, NFP education should be part of such global e-education.

30 See website https://www.cycletechnologies.com.

31 M. L. Kavanaugh, and J. Jerman, "Contraceptive Method Use in the United States: 2008, 2012, and 2014," 14–21.

32 Guenter Freundl, Christian Gnoth, and M. Krahlisch, "Zykluscomputer und-Apps," *Gynäkologische Endokrinologie* 14, no. 2 (April 2016): 1–11.

33 Robert Draper, "How Africa's Tech Generation is Changing the Continent," *National Geographic* 232 (December 2017): 96–117.

Fertility Monitoring and Precision Medicine

Since all classic NFP methods make use of careful monitoring of the woman's menstrual cycle through charting, the development of technologies to facilitate the process has contributed substantially to the practice of NFP. In addition, a more recent conceptualization in health care called "precision medicine and health" has significance for NFP use. Precision medicine means targeting medical interventions on an individual's genes, environment, and lifestyle for treatments. Precision health involves predicting and preventing health problems based on not just genes, the environment, and lifestyles but also population-based data to drive those decisions for personal and targeted health care. Applied to NFP, that would mean the following benefits: helping women be more precise in predicting the fertile phase of the menstrual cycle, targeting the best method of NFP for the individual and couple during particular phases of their reproductive life, assessing patterns of the woman's menstrual cycle parameters for potential health problems, and using parameters of the menstrual cycle for assessing medical treatments for women. Below, we will consider the contributions of electronic monitoring of fertility. Having more precision in estimating the fertile phase of the menstrual cycle and the levels of hormone will allow health professionals and scientists to better study the associations of lifestyle, (e.g., diet and exercise) on the menstrual cycle and general health.

Electronic Devices and Fertility Information

In the 1980s and 1990s, inexpensive microelectronics made available fast digital thermometers as an aid to using BBT methods. During that same time period, electronic BBT monitors were developed with small computers that were designed to track the menstrual cycle and to estimate the fertile time of the menstrual cycle.[34] The Bioself monitor is an example of such a monitor that has a built-in computer which tracks cycle length and temperature. The Bioself is based on BBT and calendar algorithms and provides the user with a red light for fertility and a green light for infertility.

The Baby-Comp (for achieving pregnancy) and the Lady-Comp (for avoiding pregnancy) are similar devices developed by Valley Electronics GmbH, a company based in Germany. In an effort to better serve the American market, Valley Electronics LLC was born in 2010. Another device, the L'Sophia, was developed and marketed in Japan. This Japanese fertility monitor has been miniaturized and

34 Richard J. Fehring, "New Technology in Natural Family Planning," *Journal of Obstetric, Gynecologic, and Neonatal Nursing* 20, no. 3 (May 1991): 199–205; Richard Fehring, "Evaluation of the Lady Free Biotester in Determining the Fertile Period," *Contraception* 57, no. 5 (May 1998): 325–328; Richard J. Fehring, and W. Schlaff, "Accuracy of the Ovulon Fertility Monitor to Predict and Detect Ovulation," *Journal of Nurse-Midwifery* 43, no. 2 (1998): 117–120; R. Fehring and N. Gaska, "A Comparison of the Ovulation Method with the CUE Ovulation Predictor in Determining the Fertile Period," *Journal of the American Academy of Nurse Practitioners*, 8, no. 10 (October 1996): 461–466; Richard J. Fehring, "New Low and High Tech Calendar Methods of Family Planning," *Journal of Nurse Midwifery and Women's Health* 50, no. 1 (January 2005): 31–38.

called the *Sophia* women's thermometer or the *Petite Sophia*. They are available through major online shopping sites.

Another computerized BBT device called the Cyclotest 2 (which is available and advertised on the internet) has been updated as microelectronics have developed. A group of researchers from the Academic Teaching Hospital of the University of Dusseldorf, Germany, tested the efficacy of the Cyclotest 2 Plus by comparing the fertile time in a woman's cycle as detected by the Cyclotest 2 Plus with the fertile time determined by the Sympto-Thermal Method (STM) of NFP.[35] Newer temperature measuring devices have recently been developed that offer continuous temperature measurement and are thought to be more accurate than a single temperature upon rising in the morning. One such device called the DuoFertility measures continuous temperature and movement by having the woman wear a sensor as an axillary patch. Researchers recently conducted a study to determine the accuracy of the device by comparing the continuous measure of body temperature with serial ultrasound of the developing follicle, that is, the gold standard of detecting the day of ovulation, and in comparison to luteinizing hormone.[36]

A number of fertility devices have been tested to see if salivary or vaginal electrical resistance can provide the user with information to determine the beginning and end of the fertile window. One such device, called the OvaCue fertility monitor, is sold and marketed in the United States[37] as a device to achieve pregnancy only and for use with NFP.[38] The OvaCue monitor provides a predictive marker (a peak in salivary resistance readings) about 5–7 days before ovulation and a vaginal electrical resistance nadir followed by a rise in vaginal electrical resistance readings as a confirmation of ovulation. Because the OvaCue both predicts and confirms ovulation, it can potentially be used as a method to avoid or achieve pregnancy, that is, as a means of or an assistive device for NFP. Consumers like the device since it is a one-time purchase and does not require test strips. However, the salivary and vaginal electrical resistance is an inaccurate estimator of fertility and has never been tested for use in avoiding pregnancy.

Progesterone (and Estrogen) Tests

A recent study showed that the serum threshold of 5–7 μg/mL of progesterone past the LH surge or cervical mucus peak, confirms ovulation in close to 100%

35 G. Freundl, P. Frank-Hermann, and M. Bremme, "Results of an Efficacy-Finding study (EFS) with the Computer-Thermometer Cyclotest 2 Plus Containing 207 Cycles," *Advances in Contraception* 14, no. 4 (December 1998): 201–207; G. Freundl, P. Frank-Hermann, and E. Godehardt, et al., "Retrospective Clinical Trial of Contraceptive Effectiveness of the Electronic Fertility Indicator Ladycomp/Babycomp," *Advances in Contraception* 14, no. 2 (June 1998): 97–108.

36 Jennie C. B. Rollason, Joanne G. Outtrim, and Raj S. Mathur, "A Pilot Study Comparing the DuoFertility® Monitor with Ultrasound in Infertile Women," *International Journal of Women's Health* 6 (July 2014): 657–662.

37 The device is marketed and developed by Zetek Corp. in Aurora, Colorado.

38 R. Fehring and N. Gaska, "A Comparison of the Ovulation Method with the CUE Ovulation Predictor."

of ovulatory menstrual cycles.[39] Based on the results of this study, a simple home urine progesterone (P) dip test was developed by Amy Beckley, PhD, that is designed to confirm ovulation when a threshold level of progesterone has been reached post a peak day of mucus or a positive LH test.[40] Currently, the only way to self-confirm ovulation is to take daily first morning body temperatures and track a significant rise in the body temperature from baseline. This temperature method is time-consuming and often inaccurate. Women who wish to confirm ovulation with a progesterone test currently need to have a physician order a serum test and have a laboratory measure the progesterone level (which is expensive and time-consuming). The P tests are now commercially available through MFB Fertility, and many women are already using the P tests for various reasons.

There are a number of independent ongoing studies to confirm the accuracy of the P test. The P test could be useful for women who: suffer from PCOS; are in the postpartum breastfeeding transition; have serious reasons to avoid pregnancy; or in the event that the usual indicators for the end of the fertile phase are not conclusive. This urine P test recently received US Food and Drug Administration (FDA) approval. The urine P test has not yet been validated with independently published studies that compare the urine results with serum progesterone levels. Ideally, a study that compared the urine P test with ultrasound-detected day of ovulation would provide the best evidence.

In addition to the P test, two professors of biochemistry at the University of Wisconsin, Madison, Drs. Katie Brenner and Doug Weibel, co-founded, along with Jodi Schroll, MBA, bluDiagnostics to develop a quick, saliva-based method for measuring not only progesterone but also estrogen.[41] They indicated that variations and ratios in estrogen and progesterone levels are closely related to ovulation and could be very helpful for timing of conception. The co-founders of bluDiagnostics aim to obtain FDA approval and reach the market in the near future.

The approach of bluDiagnostics is to utilize a wet paper saliva test that connects to a cell phone app system through Bluetooth technology and provide the user with daily probabilities of fertility. The co-founders are also thinking beyond fertility and considering how they can provide data that will contribute to women's overall health.

Seamless systems that integrate fitness indicators, health indicators, and information from the menstrual cycle are the directions for the future to assist in NFP education and method use.

39 Rene Ecochard, Rene Leiva, Thomas Bouchard, H. Boehringer, A. Direito, R. Mariani, and R. Fehring, "Use of Urinary Pregnanediol 3-Glucuronide to Confirm Ovulation," *Steroids* 78, no. 10 (July 2013): 1035–1040.

40 Brian Fraga, "At-home Ovulation Test a 'Breakthrough' for NFP: Company Hopes to Release Progesterone Test This Summer That Will Help Couples Pinpoint Ovulation," *Our Sunday Visitor Newsweekly* (May 22, 2016): 4.

41 See https://www.bludiagnostics.com.

NFP and Women's Health

NFP educators are well aware of the usefulness of the practice of charting a couple's fertility—especially as it pertains to the woman. Since the early part of the twenty-first century, a number of developments occurred that support NFP use and education. They are: monitoring the menstrual cycle as a vital sign, the importance of fertility literacy, and integrating women's health with NFP.

Monitoring the Menstrual Cycle as a Vital Sign

The subcommittees of both the American Academy of Pediatrics and American College of Obstetricians and Gynecologists (and other health-care professionals) have recommended monitoring the menstrual cycle as vital signs for female adolescents and young adults.[42] This is due to the reality that significant health problems are manifested as changes in the parameters of a woman's menstrual cycle and/or lack of ovulation.

Others have recommended that women of all reproductive ages monitor their menstrual cycle for potential health problems.[43] The National Institute of Child Health and Human Development and the Office of Women's Health (an Office of the National Institutes of Health, or NIH, and the Institute of Child Health and Human Development) have sponsored conferences on the menstrual cycle and synchronizing women's health. The conferences promote empowerment of women through ensuring a healthy menstrual cycle. They also include the study of PCOS, infertility, anorexia, and premature ovarian failure. The evidence from presentations at these conferences demonstrate the usefulness of women (of all reproductive ages) charting their menstrual cycles. The presentations were based on research but the presentations were not published.

Among the findings, it is clear that charting can help to identify early hints of menstrual cycle pathologies and could be useful as an aid to early warning signs for a number of health problems.[44] Menstrual cycle charting systems

42 American Academy of Pediatrics and American College of Obstetricians and Gynecologists, "Menstruation in Girls and Adolescents: Using the Menstrual Cycle as a Vital Sign," *Pediatrics* 118, no. 5 (November 2006): 2245–2250.

43 Petra Frank-Herrmann, C. Gnoth, S. Baur, T. Strowitzki, G. Freundl, "Determination of the Fertile Window: Reproductive Competence of Women—European Cycle Databases," *Gynecological Endocrinology* 20, no. 6 (2005): 305–312; Pilar Vigil, Francisco Ceric, Manuel E. Cortés, and Hanna Klaus, "Usefulness of Monitoring Fertility From Menarche," *Journal of Pediatric Adolescent Gynecology* 19, no. 3 (June 2006):173–179; Pilar Vigil, Carolina Lyon, Betsi Flores, Hernán Rioseco, and Felipe Serrano, "Ovulation, a Sign of Health," *The Linacre Quarterly* 84, no. 4 (November 2017): 343–355.

44 Michal Dishi, Daniel A. Enquobahrie, Dejene F. Abetew, Chunfang Qiu, Carole B. Rudra, and Michelle A. Williams, "Age at Menarche, Menstrual Cycle Characteristics and Risk of Gestational Diabetes." *Diabetes Research and Clinical Practice* 93, no. 3 (September 2011): 437–442; John A. Morrison, Charles J. Glueck, Stephen Daniels, Ping Wang, and Davis Stroop, "Ramifications of Adolescent Menstrual Cycles ≥ 42 Days in Young Adults," *Fertility and Sterility* 96, no. 1 (July 2011): 236–240; Jacqueline Chung, Symphorosa S. C. Chan, Ka Wah Yiu, Terence T. Lao, and Tony Kwon Chung, "Menstrual Disorders in a Paediatric and Adolescent Gynaecology Clinic: Patient Presentations and Longitudinal Outcomes," *Hong Kong Medical Journal* 17, no. 5 (October 2011): 391–397; Lina Michala and Aris Antsaklis, "Anorexia Nervosa: A Psychiatric Illness with Gynecological Manifestations. A Survey of Knowledge and Practice among

that include information on menses, ovulation, phases of the cycle, and unusual uterine bleeding are useful in the detection, prediction, diagnoses, and treatment of women's health problems. In addition, women who effectively monitor their menstrual cycles and related symptoms are able to identify problematic lifestyle characteristics and health issues in their early phases which may predispose them to serious pathologies in the future. The more information gathered about normal and abnormal parameters of a woman's menstrual cycle and related symptoms, the better health professionals can use this information to inform women about potential and actual health problems. Although studies have described normal parameters of the menstrual cycle, few of them have provided information on patterns of menstrual parameters especially among young women and the association of these parameters with lifestyle and other signs of health problems.[45] There is need for more research in this area.

Fertility Literacy

Fertility health knowledge, or "literacy," is a sub-concept of health knowledge. It includes education about information related to men and women's fertility throughout their lives.[46] Fertility knowledge has been increasingly recognized as a critical component that may impact people's sexual and reproductive behavior and outcomes.[47] However, multiple studies have shown that fertility knowledge is lacking among diverse populations from different countries.[48] The following example demonstrates this problem.

Primary care physicians from Australia conducted a study among women seeking pregnancy with artificial reproductive technologies. They found that after twelve months of treatments, only 12.7% had fertility awareness knowledge.

Greek Gynecologists," *European Journal of Obstetrics, Gynecology, and Reproductive Biology* 153 (December 2010): 170–172.

45 Laurence A. Cole, Donald G. Ladner, and Francis. W. Byrn, "The Normal Variabilities of the Menstrual Cycle," *Fertility and Sterility* 91, no. 2 (February 2009): 522–527; Richard J. Fehring, Mary M. Schneider, and Kathleen Raviele, "Variability in the Phases of the Menstrual Cycle," *Journal of Obstetric, Gynecologic, and Neonatal Nursing* 35, no. 3 (May–June 2006): 376–384.

46 Mary Lee Barron, "Fertility Literacy for Men in Primary Care Settings," *The Journal for Nurse Practitioners* 9, no. 3 (March 2013): 155–160; Jacki Witt, Kimberly McEvers, and Patricia J. Kelly, "Knowledge and Experiences of Low-Income Patients with Natural Family Planning," *The Journal for Nurse Practitioners* 9, no. 2 (February 2013): 99–104.

47 Kirstin MacDougall, Yewoubdar Beyene, and Robert D. Nachtigall, "Age Shock: Misperceptions of the Impact of Age on Fertility Before and After IVF in Women Who Conceived after Age 40," *Human Reproduction* 28, no. 2 (February 2013): 350–356.

48 C. H. Y. Chan, T. H. Y. Chan, B. D. Peterson, C. Lampic, and M. Y. J. Tam, "Intentions and Attitudes towards Parenthood and Fertility Awareness among Chinese University Students in Hong Kong: A Comparison with Western Samples," *Human Reproduction* 30, no. 2 (February 2015): 364–372; C. Lampic, C., A. Skoog Svanberg, P. Karlström, and T. Tydén. "Fertility Awareness, Intentions Concerning Childbearing, and Attitudes Towards Parenthood Among Female and Male Academics," *Human Reproduction* 21, no. 2 (February 2006): 558–564; Tanja Tydén, Agneta Skoog Svanberg, Per-Olof Karlström, Lina Lihoff, and Claudia Lampic, "Female University Students' Attitudes to Future Motherhood and their Understanding About Fertility," *The European Journal of Contraception and Reproductive Health Care* 11, no. 3 (October 2006): 181–189.

This was up from 2.1% at the beginning of treatment.[49] These same physicians were interested in the fertility knowledge among women that were of reproductive age, who attended a general medical practice, and were not seeking infertility services.[50] The researchers found that only 4.3% of the respondents were using fertility awareness-based methods for family planning, 9.8% were seeking pregnancy, 37.1% actively sought to improve their knowledge of fertility, and 76.6% strongly agreed or agreed that having intercourse during the fertile time of the menstrual cycle would aid couples in achieving a pregnancy. However, only 2.1% of the participants were able to correctly identify the fertile phase of the menstrual cycle. They concluded that most women who attend general medical clinics express interest in fertility awareness education. They also mentioned that those women who indicate that they use FABMs be assessed as to their actual knowledge of these methods. The authors mentioned that there is a need for further research as to how best to provide information to women on fertility awareness-based methods and fertility knowledge. The authors did not express familiarity with newer methods of NFP that used hormonal monitoring nor the use of fertility monitoring apps. That said, their work supports the need for the type of education which most NFP methods provide.

Some researchers are investigating strategies to promote fertility literacy. For example, researchers Mary Lee Barron, PhD, APRN and Qiyan Mu, PhD, RN are currently developing fertility knowledge and fertility risk assessment tools to be used by health-care professionals.[51] These fertility knowledge survey tools can also be used to assess interventions designed to increase fertility knowledge among men and women.

Integrating Women's Health with NFP

Since the mid-1990s, there has been an increase of private medical practices and clinics that offer women's health care without providing contraception. Many also offer one or more methods of NFP. This is due to the realization among some health-care professionals (mostly Catholics) that: (1) there is a lack of fertility knowledge among women and men, (2) the menstrual cycle is a vital sign of women's health, (3) use of hormonal contraception for women can mask

49 Kerry D. Hampton, Danielle Mazza, and Jennifer M. Newton, "Fertility-Awareness Knowledge, Attitudes, and Practices of Women Seeking Fertility Assistance," *Journal of Advanced Nursing* 69, no. 5 (July 2012): 1076–1084.

50 Kerry D. Hampton and Danielle Mazza, "Fertility-Awareness Knowledge, Attitudes and Practices of Women Attending General Practice," *Australian Family Physician* 44, no. 11 (November 2015): 840–845.

51 See Mary Lee Barron, "Fertility Literacy for Women in Primary Care Settings," *JNP: The Journal for Nurse Practitioners* 9, no. 3 (March 2013): 161–165; Mary Lee Barron, "Fertility Literacy for Men in Primary Care Settings," *JNP: The Journal for Nurse Practitioners* 9, no. 3 (March 2013): 155–160; Qiyan Mu, "Under the Microscope: In-Depth Review of Research on Fertility-Knowledge Education Programs: Can Education Be the Right Approach to Improve Fertility Knowledge among Young Men and Women? An Evaluation of the Published Fertility-Knowledge Education Programs." *Natural Family Planning, Current Medical Research* 27, nos. 3 & 4 (Summer/Fall 2016), reprinted in *The Linacre Quarterly* 84, no. 1 (2017): 85–92.

important health symptoms in a woman, and (4) use of hormonal contraceptives to manage female health problems by suppressing the menstrual cycle rather than treating the root causes is bad medicine. Examples of these efforts include what is commonly referred to as "NFP-only" medical practices that individual physicians offer.[52] Other national and international efforts have also been established. Among those, the Fertility*Care*™ Centers of America, which offer NaProTECHNOLOGY™ and Creighton Model Fertility*Care* to patients, is noteworthy. Founded in Omaha, Nebraska, by Dr. Thomas Hilgers, this network is the first of its kind established in the United States and with international reach.[53]

A second relatively new development of a national FABM system is that of Fertility Education and Medical Management (FEMM) clinics and health-care providers.[54] FEMM is a comprehensive women's health program that involves teaching women to understand their bodies, to recognize vital signs of health (including their signs of fertility), and to provide evidence-based and ethical medical protocols. FEMM offers a training program for health-care professionals and others so that they can teach the FEMM menstrual cycle tracking system. Training for health-care professionals in the FEMM medical protocols is also provided.

Supporting the above and with a view to target the lack of FABM knowledge among health-care professionals is Fertility Appreciation Collaborative to Teach the Science (FACTS). This organization is comprised of physicians, health-care professionals, and educators who work to provide information about NFP and FABMs for the medical community.[55] Their mission is to share the best evidence available for health-care colleagues and students so they can: "educate women and men about their fertility, empower them to make more informed choices about family planning, and enable women to collaborate with medical professionals to better monitor and manage their reproductive health."[56] FACTS leaders accomplish this by holding webinars, making presentations at conferences for health-care professionals, conducting research, and promoting NFP and FABM among health-care professionals.

Globalization of NFP Science

As noted in chapter 8 of this volume, since the 1930s, NFP scientists and physicians were able to network with each other to promote and develop NFP science and methodology. Since 1968, the year *Humanae vitae* was promulgated, the international NFP scientific community was able to network more easily in international conferences sponsored, in part, by funds from the World

52 For example, Dr. Kathy Raviele, whose essay is chapter 10 of this volume, has an NFP-only Ob/GYN practice in Georgia.

53 This network has approximately 150 physicians and advanced practice nurses listed as providing these services. See Fertility*Care*™ Centers of America at https://fertilitycare.org.

54 See the FEMM website at https://femmhealth.org.

55 See www.factsaboutfertility.org.

56 https://www.factsaboutfertility.org/about.

Health Organization (WHO), the United States Aid to International Development (USAID), and other organizations. This series of meetings spanned the 1970s–2000s. The leading organizations in the 1970s–1980s were the International Federation for Family Life Promotion (IFFLP), the Human Life Foundation (later "Human Life and NFP Foundation"), and the Human Life Center. These national and international organizations were notable for the development and promotion of NFP science and methodology.

The IFFLP, in particular, was an important global organization. It was incorporated in 1974 and dissolved in 1997 (due to lack of financial support).[57] The IFFLP was formally incorporated for the purpose of providing leadership, guidance, and education in the fields of family life education and NFP. The IFFLP grew into an international organization comprised of more than one hundred organizational members from seventy-two countries. The IFFLP provided consultation and technical assistance and guidance in training areas for members, international scientific congresses, and workshops. Programs included NFP demonstration and development, family life education, breastfeeding promotion, and technical assistance in the Third World.

Another NFP organization with international outreach is the Institute for Reproductive Health (IRH). The IRH was founded in 1985 as part of Georgetown University's School of Medicine with funding from USAID.[58] As mentioned earlier, the IRH was primarily established to conduct NFP research and effective programming in developing countries to identify "gaps" in family planning. The work of the institute included research on the development, implementation, and testing of new, easy-to-use FABM[59] and provide leadership in international collaboration and with international programs. IRH has made significant contributions to furthering FABM science and viability globally to health-care providers, especially those in public health.

The use of the internet to promote international cooperation in research by means of voice and video communications online has progressed both informally (i.e., small research groups that work on specific projects) and formally with defined organizations. The International Institute for Restorative Reproductive Medicine (IIRRM), is one such formal group.

IIRRM was formed in the early 2000s as an online network to unite NFP providers and researchers who promote evidence-based reproductive health-care services that cooperate with and restore reproductive function.[60] The IIRRM focuses investigations and treatments on identifying and correcting

57 Information on the International Federation for Family Life Promotion (IFFLP) can still be found online at https://uia.org/s/or/en/1100047235. It should be noted that some former members of IFFLP formed their own organizations and continue to meet annually in Europe to share information and promote research. See for example, http://www.ieef.eu.

58 Institute for Reproductive Health at http://irh.org.

59 Such as the Standard Days Method (SDM) and the Two-Day Method discussed in my essay on the history of NFP scientists, chapter 8 of this volume.

60 The International Institute for Restorative Reproductive Medicine at https://restorative-reproductive-medicine.com.

abnormalities and restoring or optimizing normal reproductive function. The IIRRM sponsors and endorses research that cooperates with and restores normal reproductive function or anatomy. Some of the IIRRM features online are Grand Rounds, Research Update Webinar series, Journal Club, and an annual in-person meeting.[61]

Development of Big Data

The term "big data" has a wide range of definitions depending on the area of science that is involved; for example, environmental and meteorology science uses extremely high-volume data sets to predict future weather occurrences. For health research "big data" encompasses "high volume, high diversity biological, clinical, environmental, and lifestyle information collected from single individuals to large cohorts, in relation to their health and wellness status, at one or several time points."[62] Big data involves a strong governance model and best practices of new technologies that are compliant with community-based quality standards, shared data storage, data integration, and advanced analytics. The US government mandated health-care data and health-care data-based systems are examples of systems that develop big data.

Another example of "big data" as gathered through a strong government model is the data that was collected from the mandated governmental health records in Denmark. These government-mandated health records that represent the people of Denmark as a population, showed that there was a significant 20% risk of breast cancer among women using hormonal contraception and a risk of 38% among those who were using hormonal contraception for ten years or more.[63] Another study in Denmark using government-regulated health registries showed an association between the use of progesterone-type birth control methods and depression.[64] Large data sets like these are considered population based and thus findings can represent what is happening to members of that population.

Regarding NFP and women's health, the use of mobile fertility monitoring apps that reflect the menstrual cycle and the parameters of the menstrual cycle have the potential to produce large data sets of menstrual cycles (i.e., millions).

61 Of note was a by-invitation-only meeting held in September 2016 which brought together key NFP scientists in Cranbrook, Canada. The scientists were from Australia, Canada, Chile, England, France, Germany, Italy, New Zealand, and the United States.

62 Wullianallur Raghupathi and Viju Raghupathi, "Big Data Analytics in Healthcare: Promise and Potential," *Health Information Science and Systems* 2, no. 3 (February 2014) https://doi.org/10.1186/2047-2501-2-3; Emilie Baro, Samuel Degoul, Régis Beuscart, and Emmanuel Chazard, "Toward a Literature-Driven, Definition of Big Data in Healthcare," *BioMed Research International* vol. 2015 (February 2015), Article ID 639021, 9 pages, http://dx.doi.org/10.1155/2015/639021

63 Lina S. Mørch, Charlotte W. Skovlund, Philip C. Hannaford, Lisa Iversen, Shona Fielding, and Øjvind Lidegaard, "Contemporary Hormonal Contraception and the Risk of Breast Cancer," *New England Journal of Medicine* 377, no. 3 (December 2017): 2228–2239.

64 Charlotte Wessel Skovlund, Lina Steinrud Mørch, Lars Kessing, and Øjvind Lidegaard, "Association of Hormonal Contraception with Depression," *JAMA Psychiatry* 73, no. 11 (September 2016): 1154–1162.

Examples of this can be seen in the data from Cycle Technologies and Natural Cycles that have sold millions of fertility monitoring apps. The best scenario would be to have these fertility monitoring apps synced to an online site that health professionals can access and contribute to. This would allow health-care professionals to see patterns of the menstrual cycle for women with regular cycles but also those with special circumstances (e.g., postpartum transition to fertility). Such menstrual cycle charting systems could be sold and used by multiple health-care professionals and health systems that are linked to one another and thus result in the ability to generate large data sets. The usefulness of this can be demonstrated by the Marquette Model's recent research.

The Marquette Model's online charting system yielded multiple studies from the data that was collected from the MM online charting system, user registration, and online forums. The recent extended use-effectiveness studies included women/couples from all fifty states and five foreign countries.[65] The data set of the MM online system provides more generalizable evidence that applies to middle-class educated Catholic women and couples. The online forums also provided further information into the marital dynamics and the struggles of couples using the MM system.[66] Furthermore, the online charting system provides researchers with thousands of fertility monitoring charts and cycles that provide information and patterns of use. Menstrual cycle charting from women going through fertility transitions, such as from postpartum amenorrhea to regular menstrual cycles, the transition from regular cycles through peri-menopause and into menopause, and the transition off hormonal contraception to regular menstrual cycles, would provide important information on the menstrual cycle and menstrual cycle patterns. Knowledge of these patterns could be used to develop better NFP protocols for women and couples in these transitions. Furthermore, this information could be provided to these couples so that they can have a better understanding of their special situation.

Useful research can also be done using existing data sets such as the NSFG that continue to be developed though US federal funds. These data sets also provide population-based data. NFP researchers need to take more advantage of the rich information in these data sets related to contraception, NFP, and women's health. Recent studies using the NSFG have not only shown an increase in use of NFP but also the differences in divorce rates among NFP users and users of contraception, and the association of contraceptive use with abortion and sexually transmitted diseases.[67] Researchers also need to be active in helping to shape

65 Richard J. Fehring and Mary Schneider, "Effectiveness of an Online Natural Family Planning Service Program," *MCN: The American Journal of Maternal Child Nursing* 42, no. 1 (January/February 2017): 43–49; Richard J. Fehring, Mary Schneider, and Thomas Bouchard, "Effectiveness of an Online Natural Family Planning Program for Breastfeeding Women," *Journal of Obstetric, Gynecologic, and Neonatal Nursing* 46, no. 4 (July–August 2017): e129–137.

66 Richard J. Fehring and Dana Rodriguez, "Spiritual Care of Couples Using Natural Family Planning," *The Linacre Quarterly* 80, no. 3 (August 2013): 225–238.

67 Richard J. Fehring, "The Influence of Contraception, Abortion and Natural Family Planning on Divorce Rates as Found in the 2006–2010 National Survey of Family Growth," *The Linacre Quarterly* 82, no. 3 (August 2015): 273–282; Richard J. Fehring, "The Influence of Contraception, Abortion and Natural

these data sets and the questions used in these data sets so that they yield a better picture of use of NFP methods.

Despite the advantages, there are also unique disadvantages with big data and the internet systems that produce the sets. The problem concerns data security and access to the data systems that generate the data. The maintenance of internet security is a daily problem that includes the use of secure virtual servers, the obtaining and maintaining of security certification, constant updating of software, the utilizing of software and software developers who are knowledgeable with online security, the hiring of online security specialists, and the need for funds to cover the cost for these expensive systems and necessary security. A positive of this need for security is the constant updating of websites, charting systems, and mobile apps. In today's internet-connected world, websites and mobile apps can become old very quickly. It was different in the 1970s–1990s when systems of NFP could be developed and the graphics and literature for it lasted for years. That no longer can happen in order to remain relevant, attractive, and cyber-secure for new users.

Conclusion

The growth and development of internet, mobile apps, and social networks have changed society and, as a result, have had a profound effect on NFP science and NFP education. There is a revolution in online charting systems, more refined biological indicators, NFP social networking groups, and integrative health care that includes NFP. The globalization of health care, research, and the ability to gather large data sets have provided evidence that confirms the predictions and truths exposed in *Humanae vitae*. The evidence shows more interest in use of NFP and FABMs for avoiding and achieving pregnancy and the integration into women's health care.

On April 4, 2018, NFP scientists from Europe, South America, the United States, and Canada gathered to discuss the current evidence for NFP methods, newer fertility monitoring technology, and NFP and marital dynamics, and to make recommendations for future research in NFP. These scientists consisted of those who are near the end of their scientific career, mid-career scientists, and scientists who have just completed their doctoral programs. Although a relatively small group, the energy, knowledge, and creativity that these scientists generated provide hope and a sense of a continuation of the research that Popes Paul VI, Pius XII, and John Paul II requested in this important sector of human life.

Family Planning on Divorce Rates as Found in the 2006–2010 National Survey of Family Growth," *Life and Learning XXIV*, in *Proceedings of the Twenty Fourth (2014) Conference of University Faculty for Life*, ed. J. Koterski (2017), 199–213; Richard Fehring, Thomas Bouchard, and Maria Meyers, "Influence of Contraception Use on the Reproductive Health of Adolescents and Young Adults," *The Linacre Quarterly* 85, no. 2 (May 2018): 167–177.

21

Signs of Hope

Diocesan Natural Family Planning Ministry in the United States

Theresa Notare

✷ In the United States, Natural Family Planning (NFP) education is formally offered by many Catholic dioceses because of the Church's teaching on God's design of the human person, sexuality (including fertility), marriage, conjugal love and responsible parenthood, the good of children, and the family. In fact, NFP education is understood as a ministry in Catholic dioceses since it is part of the Church's total pastoral care of married couples.[1] Indeed, because of Catholic teaching, it can be said that the Church has a responsibility to offer "practical help to those who wish to live out their parenthood in a truly responsible way."[2]

The task of reflecting upon the pastoral signs of hope regarding diocesan NFP ministry in the United States is both simple and complex. The simple approach would be to discuss the number of advances that have had an impact on diocesan NFP ministry. This inventory includes advances such as the rise of education in the Theology of the Body whose teachers and speakers have seeded the dioceses with strong education in how God made men, women, human sexuality, and the nature of marriage.[3] Theology of the Body education has also taken place in seminaries and Catholic universities in conjunction with classes on the Church's moral teachings on sexuality and Christian anthropology. Due to this advance, many current diocesan Marriage and Family directors have graduated

1 See Administrative Committee, United States Conference of Catholic Bishops, *Standards for Diocesan NFP Ministry*, 3rd ed. (Washington, D.C.: USCCB, 1990; 2010), 1.

2 Pope John Paul II, Apostolic Exhortation *Familiaris consortio* (November 22, 1981), 35, w2.vatican.va/content/john-paul-ii/en/apost_exhortations.index.html. See also Pope John Paul II, Encyclical Letter *Evangelium vitae* (March 25, 1995), 88, w2.vatican.va/content/john-paul-ii/en/encyclicals.index.html.

3 Some examples include: Theology of the Body Institute, http://tobinstitute.org; Theology of the Body Evangelization Team (TOBET), https://tobet.org; and Ruah Woods (https://www.ruahwoods.org). Notable speakers who have traveled the United States include Christopher West (http://www.christopherwest.com) who greatly popularized Theology of the Body (sometimes not without attracting criticism); Monica Ashour (https://tobet.org/about/speakers); Katrina Zeno (http://katrinazeno.com); and Damon Owens (Joy To Be, https://joytob.org/about).

from Catholic theologates where this education has been prominent.[4] This is notable because there was a time, especially in the 1970s and 1980s, when a higher degree in the social sciences rather than Catholic theology dominated the resumes of diocesan Marriage and Family Life directors.

Regarding NFP science and methods, there has been significant improvement over the years. For example, some NFP leaders have simplified their systems through evidence based research and others have developed new methods altogether.[5] A cervical mucus method with a companion medical system which provides ethical health care for women was developed by another NFP leader.[6] And, it should be emphasized that over the years, the American NFP providers have grown as professional teacher training and client education programs.[7] This can be seen especially in the development of NFP internet education programs among many of these providers demonstrating a willingness to meet people through a popular virtual medium. Although somewhat controversial, the introduction of fertility apps can also be cited as a sign of hope since some are helpful to NFP education.[8] Fertility apps push the frontier of where NFP education ought to move given the interests and habits of modern people. In addition, and although not yet in the market place, there is exciting work being conducted by several scientists to help couples more accurately pinpoint their window of fertility through the development of ovulation testing devices. Examples include the work of Drs. James Brown (Australia) and Len Blackwell (New Zealand) and the progesterone tests from Amy Beckley (Denver, Colorado).[9]

Among Catholic physicians and nurses, there has been a slow but steady movement of those who have taken up the banner of supporting Church teaching in *Humanae vitae* in a variety of ways, especially through establishing

4 Currently, the most commonly attended schools among diocesan Marriage and Family Life directors include: The Catholic University of America; the Pontifical John Paul II Institute for Studies on Marriage and Family at The Catholic University of America (a program largely independent from the university, with a separate faculty); the Franciscan University in Steubenville, Ohio; and the University of Dallas in Texas.

5 For example, the Marquette Model's Sympto-Hormonal Method makes use of a fertility monitor to help the woman more accurately identify her time of fertility. See hps://nfp.marquette.edu.

6 Thomas Hilgers, MD, developed the Creighton Model Fertility*Care* ™ Method and the ethical women's health-care system of NaProTECHNOLOGY ™ (Natural Procreative Technology).

7 Historically, these providers in the United States include the pioneers: Billings Ovulation Method® represented first by the Family of the Americas and later by the Billings Ovulation Method® Association—USA (BOMA-USA); the Sympto-Thermal Method as provided by Couple to Couple League International (CCL); and the Creighton Model Fertility*Care* ™ System (CrM). The second wave of NFP providers include Northwest Family Services' Sympto-Pro method (Sympto-Pro) and the Marquette Model (MM), a Sympto-Hormonal method.

8 For a review of fertility apps, see Marguerite Duane, Alison Contreras, Elizabeth T. Jensen, and Amina White, "The Performance of Fertility Awareness-Based Method Apps Marketed to Avoid Pregnancy," *Journal of the American Board of Family Medicine* 29, no. 4 (July 2016): 508–511. See also Richard J. Fehring's essay "Signs of Growth and Healing: Health Care and Science," chapter 20 in this volume.

9 See a brief review of the work of these scientists in *Current Medical Research* 28, nos. 3 and 4 (Summer/Fall 2017): 28–30 at http://www.usccb.org/nfp/medical-research/upload/CMR-Summer-Fall-2017.pdf. See also Richard J. Fehring's chapter 20 in this volume.

"NFP-Only" medical practices.[10] As mentioned above, there is the pioneering work of: Thomas Hilgers, MD, with his development of both the Creighton Model Fertility*Care*™ system, and NaProTECHNOLOGY™, and the respective educational programs that are tailored for physicians;[11] Richard J. Fehring, PhD, RN, with the development of the Marquette Model Sympto-Hormonal Method[12] and his general education programs for health-care professionals; and Dr. Marguerite Duane, who helped to co-found FACTS, an organization devoted to the general NFP education of physicians on the science and methodology of NFP.[13] These examples, and many more have had an impact on diocesan NFP ministry—they are all "signs of hope." That said, the question of what comprises the signs of hope in diocesan NFP ministry is more complex than citing these examples of advances. That is because NFP services and education in the dioceses are a *ministry*.

As with all ministries in the Church, diocesan NFP ministry is an expression of God's call regarding a particular task: "Whom shall I send?"[14] In this case, God's request is to ask specific people to help others embrace His plan for married love through NFP education. The most important sign of hope, therefore, is the faithful response of the diocesan NFP leader: "Here I am, . . . send me."[15]

Mindful of this context, this reflection is organized in two parts. First, I will consider current diocesan NFP ministry, attempting to highlight its growth by moving back and forth between what was and what is and attempting to tease out examples of the work of diocesan NFP leaders. And second, I would like to consider the importance of the characteristic of perseverance as an essential element of the diocesan NFP leader in the face of ongoing challenges. I'll use the example of NFP and marriage preparation to demonstrate that point. My message is this: the people who have generously answered yes to God's call are the signs of hope in diocesan NFP ministry.

Overview of Diocesan NFP Ministry in the USA

Today, as in the past, diocesan NFP ministry provides education on NFP and the Church's teachings on human sexuality, marriage, conjugal love, responsible parenthood, and related topics. This ministry is most commonly "integrated into the structure of the diocese with an NFP coordinator appointed by the bishop."[16] The diocesan NFP coordinator is typically paid (full- or part-time) and is usually an NFP user or a teacher. Most diocesan NFP services can be found under the

10 An "NFP-Only" medical practice integrates Catholic teaching on the morality of certain health-care protocols and does not provide contraception, elective sterilization, or abortion for patients. These practices will either refer patients to NFP providers when needed or offer NFP methods as part of the services of their practices.

11 See https://www.popepaulvi.com and https://www.naprotechnology.com.

12 See https://nfp.marquette.edu.

13 See www.FactsAboutFertility.org.

14 Is 6:8. Scripture quotes in this chapter are taken from the New American Bible Revised Version.

15 Is 6:8.

16 *Standards for Diocesan NFP Ministry*, 1.

Office of Marriage and Family Life.[17] Typically, the components of diocesan NFP ministry include volunteer teachers of different NFP methods—both cervical mucus based methods and multi-indexed method (such as Sympto-Thermal and Sympto-Hormonal); a variety of NFP classes that are provided throughout the diocese; a presence in marriage preparation programs; and outreach education to a variety of audiences (engaged or married couples, clergy, and health-care professionals, young adults, and so on). They are also often engaged in fertility appreciation and chastity education. Why do I begin with something that sounds so mundane—that NFP ministry is part of the diocesan structure? The fact that we can say this today is a sign of hope.

In the past, NFP was not typically integrated into the structure of diocesan ministry. Diocesan NFP ministry exists today because of the faith, vision, creativity, courage, perseverance, and sacrifice of NFP leaders—clergy, religious, and lay men and women, married and single. For a deeper understanding of this point, the discussion that follows talks about two aspects of diocesan NFP ministry: (1) that NFP exists in the diocese as a valid ministry; and (2) that the NFP teacher is part of a well-prepared diocesan team.

The Process of Integrating NFP Ministry into the Diocesan Structure

Some thirty years ago in most dioceses, NFP ministry was not formally recognized. In fact, it was often debated as to whether it was appropriate for a diocese to offer NFP education. This was mostly because of the "medical" look of NFP education. It was argued that a Catholic hospital or physician ought to provide NFP education, not the Church.

Adding further complexity to this picture is the problem of obtaining a precise understanding of an individual diocese's NFP assets which include a budget, knowledgeable staff, certified teachers, medical support for referrals, and, in the diocese, the will of the bishop and support of the clergy. In the past, diocesan budgets were notoriously "tight," and bishops did not easily fund "new" ministries. Access to NFP teacher training sessions for the teacher candidate was also difficult in the early years. It often meant that candidates had to search for classes and travel far to participate. Then there was the question of how to pay for expensive NFP teacher training, especially given the fact that most diocesan budgets were already committed to established ministries.[18] These obstacles contributed to the lack of NFP teachers in many dioceses.[19] Related to teaching NFP was the need to develop a referral list that included physicians who

17 NFP ministry in some dioceses is structured differently and can be found under offices such as Faith Formation or Respect Life Activities. It can also be located under Catholic Charities or in a Catholic hospital.

18 When I would receive requests for help to fund an NFP teacher candidate, I would advise the person to contact a pastor of a well-funded parish or the local Knights of Columbus. These were reliable sources of support for emerging NFP teachers.

19 The lack of local teachers was one reason why many national NFP providers developed distance learning education. It also explains why some dioceses eventually developed their own teacher training programs (e.g., the Diocese of Cleveland).

were at least "NFP friendly." In the early years, it was rare for physicians to know about NFP methods. In general, medical professionals were largely ignorant of NFP science and exclusively promoted contraception. Regarding the support of the clergy, unfortunately, the general topic of NFP was not easily accepted by many (including bishops). For tradition-minded clergy, NFP had an "appearance" of "birth control," which they did not want to promote. To the more progressive, ready-to-change-Church-teaching clergy, they didn't see the difference between NFP and contraception. "Follow your conscience" was a commonly quoted response of clergy when couples sought pastoral guidance. Given these obstacles, it is remarkable that in the late 1970s–early 1980s there were a handful of dioceses that proved to be the exception to the rule and developed vibrant NFP ministry.[20]

With regard to the majority of dioceses, in the late 1980s, it was common for the diocesan NFP coordinator to be a volunteer and an NFP teacher (not necessarily "certified" by a national NFP provider—there were many local NFP service delivery systems at the time). The volunteer NFP coordinator only provided NFP education and had no other ministry responsibilities.[21] The coordinator was usually a married woman with small children who worked out of her home. These hearty souls were often asked to be the diocesan contact for NFP by someone in the chancery. Whether they were asked by the bishop's office or a marriage and family life director, in practice, whenever they had a project to move forward, they typically would face interference from chancery staff. In the early 1980s, when I began my work in the bishops' NFP Program, I would consult with these coordinators who told me that they would have to beg a diocesan staff person to support the NFP efforts by allowing such administrative tasks as publishing NFP information in the diocesan newspaper, approving inclusion of NFP information in a diocesan priest mailing, allowing access to engaged couples in marriage preparation programs, and supporting efforts to provide NFP lectures or seminars. In those years, I spent many an hour advising an NFP coordinator who worked out of her kitchen, often with babies and children vying for her attention. It is not an exaggeration to say that most of our consultations had to do with helping to devise a strategy to "win over" a particular diocesan staff person. In the 1980s and 1990s, there was, unfortunately, hostility to NFP ministry in many dioceses. Thankfully, that is no longer common.

On this point, it is inspiring to note that some NFP coordinators made a conscious decision to love the staff who were especially opposed to NFP ministry. This approach led them to volunteer for team projects that had nothing to do with NFP, an approach that went the distance in establishing good relationships that helped diffuse ignorance and prejudice. When an NFP coordinator would report back to me, a typically positive remark was "and now they know Church teaching is good, NFP works, and I'm not crazy!" A beautiful example of this can

20 Among these diocesan pioneers are the Archdioceses of Boston, New York, Portland (Oregon), and St. Louis and the Dioceses of Cleveland, Memphis, Phoenix, Wichita, and St. Cloud.

21 Today, the coordinator is usually the director of Marriage and Family Life who often has responsibility for several ministries besides NFP.

be seen in the Diocese of Springfield in Illinois. The first NFP coordinator there began her work as a volunteer teacher of chastity in a Catholic high school in the 1980s. At the same time, she volunteered to provide Billings Method classes to couples. She also took her chastity and NFP message on the road to various parishes in the diocese and people noticed. In due time, the bishop asked her to become the diocesan NFP coordinator—with a salary and office in the chancery. It only took about twenty years. Eventually, she was appointed Family Life director and retired with confidence that the diocese would continue the NFP ministry that she helped to build.

On the national level, supportive activities from the bishops' NFP Program contributed to the promotion of Church teaching and NFP in a way that sought to mitigate opposition in the local church.[22] The founder of the bishops' NFP Program, Bishop James T. McHugh (1932–2000),[23] consistently reached out to the diocesan bishops to understand their needs in marriage ministry, especially regarding NFP. Before he was ordained a bishop, then Msgr. McHugh traveled the nation giving talks about Church teaching and NFP, met with priests to answer their questions, wrote articles, and organized meetings with NFP teachers, diocesan leaders, and NFP scientists. Bishop McHugh created many strategies by which both Church teaching and the NFP message could be moved into the heart of the local church's marriage ministry. One simple strategy, for example, was an annual task to personally phone the appropriate staff in each diocese to request the contact information of the diocesan NFP coordinator. This request was made "on behalf of the bishops' conference." Not only was this a needed and practical task, but it communicated the message that the National Conference of Catholic Bishops was interested in NFP ministry.[24]

A second example of an administrative but effective project that promoted diocesan NFP ministry was Bishop McHugh's creation of a national survey of diocesan NFP ministry. This survey asked basic questions about the dioceses' NFP ministry structure and services (which methods were taught in the diocese, whether NFP was included in marriage preparation, and so on). In the annual report that it generated, a note of gratitude which listed the participating dioceses was included. The report was sent to all bishops. That simple strategy

22 Then called, the Diocesan Development Program for NFP.

23 Ordained a priest of the Archdiocese of Newark in 1957, Bishop McHugh spent much of his early priesthood working for the bishops' conference in Washington, D.C. He was first assigned to the Family Life Bureau, later becoming its executive director (1965–1975). Once the abortion issue emerged, he became the first executive director of the Secretariat of Pro-Life Activities (1972–1978). In fact, Bishop McHugh is credited as the "father of the pro-life movement" in the United States since he was responsible for not only writing and implementing the Catholic bishops' *Pastoral Plan for Pro-Life Activities* but also for founding the National Right to Life. See Robert N. Karrer, "The National Right to Life Committee: Its Founding, Its History, and the Emergence of the Pro-life Movement prior to Roe v. Wade," *Catholic Historical Review* 97, no. 3 (July 2011): 527–557. McHugh was ordained an auxiliary bishop of Newark (1988), then headed the Diocese of Camden (1989–1998), and later, spent the last year of his life as bishop of Rockville Centre in New York (1999–2000).

24 The bishops' conference changed names over the years to the current United States Conference of Catholic Bishops.

caused many a diocesan staff person to contact the bishops' NFP Program to pledge the participation of their diocese in the future so that "something would be done" about NFP ministry. This project continues today and over half of the 197 dioceses typically participate in the annual survey.[25]

Although there is much more to say about the contributions of Bishop McHugh to diocesan NFP ministry, constraints of space will allow for only one critical example of his pastoral vision. In the past, there was fierce rivalry among NFP teachers. Bishop McHugh saw this as an obstacle to the acceptance and growth of diocesan NFP ministry. He sought to resolve the tensions by seeking a means to integrate them into diocesan marriage ministry as a team—a major strategy was to create program standards.

Diocesan NFP Teachers and the Standards for Diocesan NFP Ministry

In the dioceses today, when NFP teachers join the diocesan team, they primarily provide classes in their NFP method of certification. They also present NFP as the skills by which married couples can healthfully and morally live God's design for married love. Regardless of the method they teach, when NFP teachers are part of the diocesan NFP team, they "are accountable to and work in cooperation with the NFP coordinator."[26] They respect their colleagues and the other NFP methods that are offered in the diocese, and they are engaged in various diocesan educational events such as marriage preparation. To this picture, it can be said that when diocesan NFP ministry is strong, there is another layer of teachers. There are those who are trained in the Church's teaching and the general information about NFP. They are often called "promoters" or even fall into the category of a type of catechist.

Currently, the majority of dioceses have different NFP teachers who are certified in various methods of NFP by different NFP providers. With regard to the NFP methods they offer, the most common are a version of the cervical mucus method (with the Billings Ovulation Method® and the Creighton Model being most prevalent) and versions of the Sympto-Thermal Method (with the Couple to Couple League instruction being most prevalent).[27] In recent years, there has also been growth in the Sympto-Hormonal Method (notably that of the Marquette Model). It should also be mentioned that some NFP teachers have become more flexible in recent years regarding obtaining more than one certification in an NFP method. They do this in the interest of helping their couples, especially those with difficulties in understanding their signs of fertility. This was rarely desired nor easily achieved in the past. In any case, this picture of the current-day diocesan NFP teacher may seem ordinary and even "expected."

25 Entitled the National Survey of Diocesan NFP Programs (or "Profile"), this annual survey generates findings compiled in reports that are available at http://www.usccb.org/nfp/diocesan-ministry/national-survey-profile.cfm.

26 *Standards for Diocesan NFP Ministry*, 7.

27 This information can be found in each of the annual diocesan NFP program surveys available at http://www.usccb.org/nfp/diocesan-ministry/national-survey-profile.cfm.

After all, in a world that is saturated with contraception, shouldn't NFP teachers band together to "fight the good fight?" One would hope. That was not the case in the past.

In the past, we can generally say that NFP teachers shared a common vision to oppose the contraceptive wave that swept the world. They did so under the rubric of promoting Church teaching. They greatly differed, however, on a number of serious points which caused bitter rivalry. Among the topics which engendered tensions were the following: which NFP method was the most effective,[28] which subjects ought to be standard in the curriculum of the NFP teacher candidates (including whether a supervised practicum was necessary), the basic elements of couple follow-up and record keeping, how to ensure couple autonomy, breastfeeding protocols and whether breastfeeding information ought to be treated in standard NFP classes, if NFP education should be insured over possible liability, and whether it was moral to teach single women. The list was so extensive and the in-fighting was so common that diocesan NFP coordinators consistently lobbied Bishop McHugh to intervene.

Part of the landscape in the early years that added fuel to the NFP teaching fire was the woefully inconsistent way in which NFP was taught to both teachers and couples. On the one hand, there were the dioceses and regional NFP associations that had developed since 1968. Some of these were quite strong. The Diocese of Cleveland, for example, created its own versions of the Sympto-Thermal Method and cervical mucus method. The Cleveland NFP methods and curricula are not only based on solid NFP research and are well designed but are also consistently updated. This commitment and approach continues to this day. In fact, the faculty of Cleveland's NFP teacher training program trains teachers not only for their diocese but also for other dioceses. Many diocesan NFP education programs, however, were not as well designed as Cleveland's. Unfortunately, problems of teaching nonevidence-based, anecdotal, or even false information were rampant among some diocesan programs. And the pedagogical education of the teachers themselves was mostly neglected. For example, in many diocesan NFP teacher training programs, there was little study of the principles of adult learners and how NFP ought to be taught to them. Various aspects of professional conduct, administration, and accountability were also neglected. Understandably, this situation did not inspire confidence among the couples who attended the NFP classes or the clergy who were supposed to refer their parishioners to them. Some couples also complained to their parish priests, the bishop, and even the bishops' national NFP Program leaders about this situation.

Against the inconsistencies of diocesan NFP education, the national NFP providers emerged as signs of hope. They contributed to the viability of NFP in their individual work in the development of formal teacher training and couple/client curricula. They were not without their problems in the beginning, but in general, they were striving for professionalism.

28 For Sympto-Thermal Method teachers this often touched upon arguments over the accuracy of the basal body temperature and the cervical self-check.

A summary of the national NFP pioneers would include the following: The Billings community was first represented in the United States by the Family of the Americas which was headed by Mercedes Wilson. Nearly at the same time as Wilson worked, Dr. Hanna Klaus (St. Louis, Missouri) and Mrs. Kay Ek (St. Cloud, Minnesota) also promoted the Billings Ovulation Method®. Today, although Family of the Americas continues its work, the Billings Method is officially represented by the Billings Ovulation Method® Association—USA (BOMA-USA), headed by Sue Ek (Kay's daughter). The Creighton Model Fertility*Care*™ System, developed by Dr. Thomas Hilgers and colleagues, represents a medical approach to the observation of the cervical mucus sign. Along with the teacher education programs, Hilgers formed the American Academy of NFP (now American Academy of Fertility*Care*™ Professionals) to accredit Creighton Model education centers and certify teachers.[29] The Couple to Couple League (CCL) co-founded by John and Sheila Kippley with Dr. Konald Prem, promoted the Sympto-Thermal Method. These were the three main providers. Later, Northwest Family Services, led by Rose Fuller and Fr. Richard Huneger and others developed the Sympto-Pro Method. And, Marquette University's Sympto-Hormonal Method created by Richard J. Fehring, PhD, RN, would take their place besides the original providers.

This is a long story to say that within the dioceses there was such great diversity in NFP education and teacher training that the in-fighting and inconsistently trained teachers caused a type of ministerial chaos. In the late 1980s, requests for standards were sent to Bishop McHugh from many diocesan NFP coordinators. They argued that they needed help to create an integrated team. They wanted to evaluate their NFP teachers, validate their ministry, and therefore, prove the competency of the NFP services that they provided in their dioceses.

Bishop McHugh understood the importance of the issues. In 1987, he formed a Certification Committee comprised of NFP experts, some national providers, and diocesan NFP coordinators representing the main national methods and providers as well as regional providers. By 1990, this committee wrote the *Standards for Diocesan NFP Ministry* (hereafter, *Standards*)[30] which was published by the Administrative Committee of the bishops' conference. The *Standards* provide a blueprint for diocesan NFP ministry. They also articulate the role and responsibilities of diocesan NFP teachers and how they should be integrated into the diocesan NFP ministry.

Since 1990, a tremendous amount of painstaking work has gone into establishing competence and fostering harmony in diocesan NFP ministry. The bishops' NFP Program facilitates the implementation of the *Standards* with a mentoring process that assigns a master diocesan NFP coordinator to consult with the individual diocesan NFP coordinator whose program is under evaluation. Those diocesan NFP teacher training programs that applied to the bishops' conference for evaluation (Approval) and were found to be inadequate were asked to either

29 See https://aafcp.net/.

30 See http://www.usccb.org/nfp/diocesan-ministry/standards.cfm.

change their programs or to dissolve and adopt a national provider program. Diocesan NFP coordinators were able to invite their NFP teachers to meet these ministerial standards (Certification) in order to join the diocesan NFP team. They could use the *Standards* to create a professional and respectful NFP team as well as to require accountability from their teachers. The bishops' NFP *Standards* are a sign of hope in diocesan NFP ministry and have contributed to its institutionalization. It is an ongoing project of the bishops' NFP Program that was initiated by Bishop McHugh who responded to the needs of the diocesan NFP leaders he served.

Persistence: A Central Trait of the NFP Leader

A consistent sign of hope within diocesan NFP ministry is the ability of its leaders to persevere. They typically recognize a challenge and respond with solutions. Sometimes their solutions to challenges are not entirely successful, but that does not stop them. These servants of God are resilient. When they face a challenge, they pray, think, and act, and if it does not work, they try something different. In other words, they do not give up. This persistent pastoral action is almost a requirement in diocesan NFP ministry. Its effect gives the appearance that NFP ministry does not progress in a straight line. The ministry tends to zig and zag, sometimes taking a circular route, or to even "stop," giving the impression of no movement at all. This is where the story gets complicated because the diocesan NFP leader's response to challenges happens within a larger context. Part of the context is that NFP ministry has grown up in an environment which opposes its fundamental nature and values. NFP leaders have had to continuously respond to this opposition, which is mostly due to a specific modern perspective, especially in the United States.

From the modern perspective, factors that work against NFP include the following: a universal preference for all things technological; an appetite for fast-paced experiences that yield instant results; little patience or interest in anything that takes great effort or causes discomfort, especially with regard to satisfying human desires; widespread acceptance of nonmarital sexual activity; a belief that it is not immoral to separate procreation from sexual intercourse; a belief that children are a personal "choice" in marriage, not essential to the nature of marriage; acceptance of contraception and elective sterilization; general ignorance about the viability of NFP methods, especially among health-care providers who also tend to view fertility as a problem to solve; and, among many Catholics, an inconsistent theologically mature understanding of Church teaching which supports NFP use in marriage. To complicate this scenario, there has also been political and legal action over the years that work against the nature of marriage and the family,[31] including the decriminalization of contraception, the promotion of no-fault divorce, the legalization of abortion, the redefinition of marriage to include same-sex couples, and government action such as the HHS contraceptive mandate. Such legal actions have stacked the deck against marriage and the

31 Note the essays by Helen Alvaré (chapter 15) and Teresa Stanton Collett (chapter 14) in this volume.

family and, therefore, NFP which supports both. Add to this dire picture the fact that dioceses often have few resources available to those who would build NFP ministry, and the enormity of the challenge can easily be seen.

As can be imagined, trying to cover all these points and demonstrate how NFP educators have faced each challenge would be the stuff of a book and beyond the scope of this essay. Here we will focus upon one challenge: the integration of NFP in marriage preparation.

NFP and Marriage Preparation

In the early years of diocesan NFP ministry, it was rare to include NFP education in marriage preparation. It was also rare to receive instruction about the Church's moral prohibition of contraception in marriage preparation. There was a culture of silence in the dioceses. For example, a constant refrain from NFP leaders was how to have clergy talk and preach about the teachings in *Humanae vitae*, especially in marriage preparation. Another complaint had to do with trying to find ways to catch the attention of the marriage and family life director so that NFP could be included in diocesan marriage preparation programs. NFP leaders struggled to find multiple ways to break this silence.

Through the perseverance of diocesan NFP leaders, today, the majority of dioceses have marriage preparation guidelines that include NFP education.[32] This is a marked improvement compared to the past where most dioceses did not even have marriage preparation guidelines, let alone include NFP education in them. Consequently, the majority of diocesan marriage preparation programs provide basic NFP information.[33]

Although this last point is an advancement, it also presents an example of diocesan NFP ministry's meandering style of growth. Despite this improvement, there continues to be great variety among marriage preparation programs, especially regarding the quality of NFP education.[34] Enter the diocesan NFP leader with the single-minded intention to persevere. At one end of the spectrum, we may find that only NFP resources such as booklets or fact sheets comprise the NFP education in marriage preparation. In such dioceses, it is common that an NFP leader may be the one who has provided those resources and more than likely is hard at work trying to strategize how to improve the situation.[35] At the

32 The annual diocesan NFP survey for 2016 records 90% of the 100 respondents as having NFP in their marriage guidelines. The *Diocesan NFP Ministry National 2016 Profile Report*, Natural Family Planning Program, United States Conference of Catholic Bishops, 3, http://www.usccb.org/issues-and-action/marriage-and-family/natural-family-planning/diocesan-ministry/upload/2016-Diocesan-NFP-Profile-Report.pdf.

33 The *Diocesan NFP Ministry National 2016 Profile Report*, 2.

34 The *Diocesan NFP Ministry National 2016 Profile Report*, 4.

35 On this note, in the days before email and the Internet, I would receive letters from a lone CCL teacher in one of the dioceses in Alaska. She would plead for help to acquire brochures for her diocese which I happily sent her. And, for years we had a grandmother in Montana who although not a teacher and despite the great distances, acted like an NFP missionary as she met with various diocesan staff to urge the establishment of NFP ministry in their two dioceses.

other end of the spectrum, we can find dioceses that offer substantial NFP education in marriage preparation. This may take the form of lectures complete with witness couples or even day-long seminars. For example, when he was bishop of Rapid City, South Dakota, Archbishop Charles Chaput had implemented an all-day "Human Sexuality Workshop" that was considered an "innovation" at the time since no other diocese offered anything like it as part of marriage preparation.[36]

Added to this picture is the extremely hopeful sign in the movement among the diocesan NFP leaders toward establishing a requirement for a full course of NFP instruction in marriage preparation. In the past, many diocesan NFP teachers and coordinators would dream of this solution to the problem of spreading the word about Church teaching and NFP. Currently, twelve dioceses have this requirement and over twenty more have reported that they are considering implementing the requirement.[37] According to the 2016 survey of diocesan NFP programs, only "several years ago very few dioceses required a full course of NFP instruction as part of marriage preparation efforts."[38] In the diocesan NFP annual survey, this "number has increased threefold in the last decade. And, anecdotally, it seems that more and more individual priests are encouraging couples to take a full course of NFP as part of marriage preparation, even if not required by their diocese."[39]

Conclusion

It is clear that the signs of hope in diocesan NFP ministry are the people who have generously answered God's call to help His people understand and embrace His plan for married marriage. They embody the generosity and hopefulness of married love and life.

In conclusion, it is appropriate to turn our attention to the last section of *Humanae vitae,* in which Pope Paul VI makes an appeal to the bishops of the Church noting their urgent responsibility and requesting "concerted pastoral action" to help married couples in this area of ministry.[40] The Holy Father's plea can easily be applied to diocesan NFP leaders. They are cognizant of God's call for their assistance and, when they join the diocesan NFP ministry team, they are critically aware of their assistance to their bishops. The words of Paul VI therefore, take on a poignant beauty:

36 Chaput is currently the archbishop of the Archdiocese of Philadelphia and chairman of the bishops' Committee for Laity, Marriage, Family Life and Youth.

37 As of the writing of this essay, the twelve dioceses that require NFP are Bismarck, Colorado Springs, Covington, Denver, Fargo, La Crosse, Laredo, Lexington, Little Rock, Phoenix, St. Augustine, and Wichita.

38 *2016 National Survey of Diocesan NFP Ministry Report*, 3. See also Natural Family Planning Program, United States Conference of Catholic Bishops, *Requiring a Full Course of NFP Instruction in Marriage Preparation: A Report* (September 2008); note, updates from 2014 and 2016 are available at www.usccb.org/nfp/diocesan-ministry/nfp-topics-and-resources.cfm.

39 *2016 National Survey of Diocesan NFP Ministry Report*, 3–4.

40 See Pope Paul VI, Encyclical Letter *Humanae vitae* (July 25, 1968), 30, at https://w2.vatican.va/content/paul-vi/en/encyclicals.index.html.

> [G]reat indeed is the work of education, of progress and of charity to which We now summon all of you. And this We do relying on the unshakable teaching of the Church .... And We are convinced that this truly great work will bring blessings both on the world and on the Church. For man cannot attain that true happiness for which he yearns with all the strength of his spirit, unless he keeps the laws which the Most High God has engraved in his very nature. These laws must be wisely and lovingly observed.[41]

41 Pope Paul VI, *Humanae vitae*, 31.

Selected Bibliography

Akerlof, George A., Janet L. Yellen, and Michael L. Katz. "An Analysis of Out-of-Wedlock Childbearing in the United States." *The Quarterly Journal of Economics* 111, no. 2 (May 1996): 277–317.

Allen, Prudence. "Man-Woman Complementarity: The Catholic Inspiration." *Logos: A Journal of Catholic Thought and Culture* 9, no. 3 (2006): 87–108.

———. "Gender Reality vs. Gender Ideology." *Solidarity: The Journal of Catholic Social Thought and Secular Ethics* 4, no. 1, art. 1 (2014): 1–36.

Alvaré, Helen M. "No Compelling Interest: The 'Birth Control' Mandate and Religious Freedom." *Villanova University Law Review* 58, no. 3 (2012): 379–436.

———. *Putting Children's Interests First in US Law and Policy: With Power Comes Responsibility.* New York: Cambridge University Press, 2017.

Anderson, Carl, and José Granados. *Called to Love: Approaching John Paul II's Theology of the Body.* New York: Doubleday, 2009.

Anscombe, Elizabeth. *Contraception and Chastity.* London: Catholic Truth Society, 1975.

Anscombe, G. E. M., Mary Geach, and Luke Gormally. *Faith in a Hard Ground: Essays on Religion, Philosophy, and Ethics.* Exeter, UK: Imprint Academic, 2008.

Aquinas, Thomas. *Summa Theologiae.* Translated by the Dominican Fathers. http://www.newadvent.org/summa/.

Arendt, Hannah. *The Human Condition.* 2nd ed. Chicago: University of Chicago Press, 1958.

Arjonillo, Roland B. *Conjugal Love and the Ends of Marriage: A Study of Dietrich von Hildebrand and Herbert Doms in the Light of the Pastoral Constitution* Gaudium et Spes. New York: Peter Lang Publishing, Inc., 1998.

Asbell, Bernard. *The Pill: A Biography of the Drug that Changed the World.* New York: Random House, 1995.

Asci, Donald. *The Conjugal Act as a Personal Act.* San Francisco: Ignatius Press, 2002.

Bachiochi, Erika, ed. *The Church and Women: A Case for Catholic Teaching.* Boston: Pauline Books and Media, 2010.

Bartel, Sarah, and John S. Grabowski. *A Catechism for Family Life: Insights from Church Teaching on Love, Marriage, Sex, and Parenting.* Washington, D.C.: The Catholic University of America Press, 2018.

Barron, Mary Lee, and Richard J. Fehring. "Basal Body Temperature Recording: A Useful Recommendation to Couples Seeking Pregnancy?" *Journal of Maternal Child Nursing* 30, no. 5 (2005): 290–296.

Billings, Evelyn, and Ann Westmore. *The Billings Method: Controlling Fertility without Drugs or Devices*, rev. ed. Lewiston, N.Y.: Life Cycle Books, 2000. First published 1980 by Random House.

Billings, E. L., J. J. Billings, J. B. Brown, and H. G. Burger. "Symptoms and Hormonal Changes Accompanying Ovulation." *The Lancet* 299, no. 7745 (February 5, 1972): 282–284.

Bonomi, Gabriele. *Nuovo Metodo Natural per il Controlle delle Nascite: D'uovo.* Brescia, Italy: Bailetti, La Chiara, 1968.

Booth, Alan, and Ann Crouter, eds. *Men in Families.* Mahwah, N.J.: Lawrence Erlbaum Press, 1998.

Bouchard, Thomas P., Mary Schneider, and Richard J. Fehring. "Efficacy of a New Postpartum Transition Protocol for Avoiding Pregnancy." *Journal of the American Board of Family Medicine* 26, no. 1 (January 2013): 35–44.

———. "Achieving Pregnancy Using Primary Care Interventions to Identify the Fertile Window." *Frontiers in Medicine* 4, art. 250 (January 9, 2018): 1-7.

Boyle, John, ed. *Creative Love: The Ethics of Human Reproduction.* Front Royal, Va.: Christendom Press, 1989.

Bransfield, J. Brian. *The Human Person According to John Paul II.* Boston: Pauline, 2009.

Budziszewski, J. *The Nearest Coast of Darkness: A Vindication of the Politics of Virtues.* New York: Cornell, 1988.

———. *Written on the Heart: The Case for Natural Law.* Downers Grove, Ill.: InterVarsity, 1997.

———. *The Line Through the Heart: Natural Law as Fact, Theory, and Sign of Contradiction.* Wilmington, Del.: Intercollegiate Studies Institute, 2009.

———. *On the Meaning of Sex.* Wilmington, Del.: Intercollegiate Studies Institute, 2012.

———. *Commentary on Thomas Aquinas's Virtue Ethics.* New York: Cambridge, 2017.

Burke, Cormac. "Saint Augustine and Conjugal Chastity." *Communio: International Catholic Review* 17, no. 4 (1990): 545-565.

———. *Covenanted Happiness: Love and Commitment in Marriage.* Princeton: Scepter Publishers, 1999. First published 1990 by Ignatius Press.

———. "Marriage: A Personalist or an Institutional Understanding?" *Communio: International Catholic Review* 19 (Summer 1992): 278–304.

———. *The Theology of Marriage: Personalism, Doctrine, and Canon Law.* Washington, D.C.: The Catholic University of America Press, 2015.

Caffarra, Carlo. "Who is Like the Lord, Our God?" In *Why* Humanae vitae *was Right: A Reader*, edited by Janet E. Smith, chapter 10. San Francisco: Ignatius Press, 1993.

Cahall, Perry J. *The Mystery of Marriage: A Theology of the Body and the Sacrament.* Chicago: Hillenbrand Books, 2016.

Catechism of the Catholic Church. Washington, D.C.: United States Catholic Conference, Inc.—Libreria Editrice Vaticana, 1994.

Chesterton, G. K. *Brave New Family: G. K. Chesterton on Men and Women, Children, Sex, Divorce, Marriage and the Family.* Edited by Alvaro de Silva. San Francisco: Ignatius, 1990.

Cloutier, David. *Love, Reason, and God's Story: An Introduction to Catholic Sexual Ethics.* Winona, Minn.: Saint Mary's Press, 2008.

———, ed. *Leaving and Coming Home: New Wineskins for Catholic Sexual Ethics.* Eugene, Ore.: Cascade Books/Wipf & Stock, 2010.

Coleman, Gerald D. *Human Sexuality: An All-Embracing Gift.* Staten Island, N.Y.: Alba House, 1992.

Collins, Raymond F. *Sexual Ethics and the New Testament: Behavior and Belief.* New York: Crossroad, 2000.

Congregation for the Doctrine of the Faith (CDF). *Persona humana* [Declaration on Certain Questions Concerning Sexual Ethics]. December 29, 1975.

———. *Donum vitae.* Instruction. February 22, 1987.

———. *Dignitas personae.* Instruction. December 8, 2008.

———. *Placuit Deo, To the Bishops of the Catholic Church on Certain Aspects of Christian Salvation.* Letter. Febrary 22, 2018. http://www.vatican.va/roman_curia/congregations/cfaith/doc_doc_index.htm

Cornish, J. A., E. Tan, C. Simillis, S. K. Clark, J. Teare, and P. P. Tekkis. "The Risk of Oral Contraceptives in the Etiology of Inflammatory Bowel Disease: A Meta-Analysis." *American Journal of Gastroenterology* 103, no. 9 (2008): 2394–2400.

Cortés, Manuel E., and Andrea A. Alfaro. "The Effects of Hormonal Contraceptives on Glycemic Regulation." *The Linacre Quarterly* 81, no. 3 (2014): 209–218.

Cox, Kathryn Lilla. "Toward a Theology of Infertility and the Role of *Donum Vitae.*" *Horizons* 40, no. 1 (June 2013): 28–52.

Crawford, David S. "*Humanae Vitae* and the Perfection of Love." *Communio: International Catholic Review* 25 (Fall 1998): 414–438.

Critchlow, Donald T. *Intended Consequences: Birth Control, Abortion, and the Federal Government in Modern America.* New York: Oxford University Press, 1999.

Davis, William L. "Family Planning Services: A History of U.S. Federal Legislation." *Journal of Family History* 16, no. 4 (1991): 381–400.

Depew, David J., and Bruce H. Weber. *Darwinism Evolving: Systems Dynamics and the Genealogy of Natural Selection.* Cambridge, Mass.: MIT Press, 1997.

Donati, Pierpaolo, and Paul Sullins. *The Conjugal Family: An Irreplaceable Resource for Society.* Rome, Italy: Libreria Editrice Vaticana, 2015.

Döring, Gerhard K. "Uber die zuverlassigkeit der temperaturmethode zur empfangnisverhutung" [*Reliability of the Temperature Method as a Means of Contraception*], *Deutsche Medizinische Wochenschrift* 92 (1967):1055–1061. [English abstract: *The Yearbook of Obstetrics and Gynecology*, (Yearbook Medical Publisher), 354–355].

———. "Detection of Ovulation by the Basal Body Temperature Method." In *Proceedings of a Research Conference on Natural Family Planning,* edited by William A. Uricchio and Mary Kay Williams, 171–180. Washington, D.C.: The Human Life Foundation, 1973.

Duane, Marguerite, Alison Contreras, Elizabeth T. Jensen, and Amina White. "The Performance of Fertility Awareness-Based Method Apps Marketed to Avoid Pregnancy." *Journal of the American Board of Family Medicine* 29, no. 4 (July 2016): 508–511.

Eberstadt, Mary. "The Vindication of *Humanae Vitae*." *First Things* (August/September 2008), https://www.firstthings.com/article/2008/08/002-the-vindication-of-ihumanae-vitaei.

———. *Adam and Eve after the Pill: Paradoxes of the Sexual Revolution*. San Francisco: Ignatius Press, 2013.

———. "The Prophetic Power of *Humanae Vitae*." *First Things* (April 2018), at https://www.firstthings.com/article/2018/04/the-prophetic-power-of-humanae-vitae

Echeverria, Eduardo J. *"In the Beginning…": A Theology of the Body*. Eugene, Ore.: Wipf and Stock, 2011.

Ecochard, Rene, R. Leiva, Thomas Bouchard, H. Boehringer, A. Direito, R. Mariani, and Richard J. Fehring."Use of Urinary Pregnanediol 3-Glucuronide to Confirm Ovulation." *Steroids* 78, no. 10 (July 2013): 1035–1040.

Elliott, Peter. *What God Has Joined: The Sacramentality of Marriage*. Eugene, Ore.: Wipf and Stock, 2010.

Evans-Hoeker, Emily, David A. Pritchard, D. Leann Long, Amy H. Herring, Joseph B. Stanford, and Anne Z. Steiner. "Cervical Mucus Monitoring Prevalence and Associated Fecundability in Women Trying to Conceive." *Fertility and Sterility* 100, no. 4 (2013): 1033–1038.

Fastiggi, Robert L. *What the Church Teaches about Sex: God's Plan for Human Happiness*. Huntington, Ind.: Our Sunday Visitor Press, 2009.

Fedoryka, Maria. "Metaphysics of The Person: Love as Foundation and Fulfillment." In *The Many Facets of Love: Philosophical Explorations*, edited by Thomas Jay Oord, 96–103. Cambridge: Cambridge Scholars Press, 2006.

———. "'Finis superabundant operis': Refining an Ancient Cause for Explaining the Conjugal Act." *American Catholic Philosophical Quarterly* 90, no. 3 (2016): 477–498.

Fehring, Richard J."New Technology in Natural Family Planning." *Journal of Obstetric, Gynecologic, and Neonatal Nursing* 20, no. 3 (May 1991): 199–205.

———. "Physician and Nurses' Knowledge and Use of Natural Family Planning." *The Linacre Quarterly* 62 (November 1995): 22–28.

———. "Evaluation of the Lady Free Biotester in Determining the Fertile Period." *Contraception* 57, no. 5 (May 1998): 325–328.

———. "An Analysis of the Majority Report 'Responsible Parenthood' and its Recommendations on Abortion, Sterilization, and Contraception." *Life and Learning* 13 (2003): 121–146.

———. "The Future of Professional Education in Natural Family Planning." *Journal of Obstetric, Gynecologic, and Neonatal Nursing* 33 (January–February 2004): 34–43.

———. "New Low and High Tech Calendar Methods of Family Planning." *Journal of Nurse Midwifery and Women's Health* 50, no. 1 (January 2005): 31–38.

———. "Under the Microscope: A Brief History of Natural Family Planning." *Natural Family Planning Current Medical Research* 25, nos. 3 and 4 (Summer/Fall 2014): 12–19.

———. "The Influence of Contraception, Abortion, and Natural Family Planning on Divorce Rates as Found in the 2006–2010 National Survey of Family Growth." *The Linacre Quarterly* 82, no. 3 (July 1, 2015): 273–282.

Fehring, Richard J., Thomas Bouchard, and Maria Meyer. "Influence of Contraception Use on the Reproductive Health of Adolescents and Young Adults." *The Linacre Quarterly* 85, no. 2 (May 2018): 167–177.

Fehring, Richard J. and N. Gaska. "A Comparison of the Ovulation Method with the CUE Ovulation Predictor in Determining the Fertile Period." *Journal of the American Academy of Nurse Practitioners*, 8, no. 10 (October 1996): 461–466.

Fehring, Richard J., and Donna M. Lawrence. "Spiritual Well-Being, Self-Esteem and Intimacy among Couples Using Natural Family Planning." *The Linacre Quarterly* 61, no. 3 (August 1994): 18–29.

Fehring, Richard J., D. Lawrence, and C. Philpot. "Use-Effectiveness of the Creighton Model Ovulation Method of Natural Family Planning." *Journal of Obstetric, Gynecologic, and Neonatal Nursing* 23, no. 4 (1994): 303–309.

Fehring, Richard J., and Elizabeth McGraw. "Spiritual Responses to the Regulation of Birth: A Historical Comparison." *Life and Learning* 12 (December 2003): 265–283.

Fehring, Richard J., and Qiyan Mu. "Cohort Efficacy Study of Natural Family Planning among Perimenopause Age Women." *Journal of Obstetric, Gynecologic, and Neonatal Nursing* 43, no. 3 (May–June 2014): 351–358.

Fehring, Richard J., and Theresa Notare, eds. *Human Fertility: Where Faith and Science Meet. Proceedings of an Interdisciplinary Conference.* Milwaukee: Marquette University Press, 2008.

———. *Integrating Faith and Science through Natural Family Planning. Proceedings of an Interdisciplinary Conference.* Milwaukee: Marquette University Press, 2004.

———. *Science, Faith, and Human Fertility: The Third Conference on Ethical Fertility Health Management. Proceedings of an Interdisciplinary Conference.* Milwaukee: Marquette University Press, 2012.

Fehring, Richard J., and Dana Rodriguez. "Spiritual Care of Couples Using Natural Family Planning." *The Linacre Quarterly* 80, no. 3 (August 2013): 225–238.

Fehring, Richard J., and W. Schlaff. "Accuracy of the Ovulon Fertility Monitor to Predict and Detect Ovulation." *Journal of Nurse-Midwifery* 43, no. 2 (1998): 117–120.

Fehring, Richard J., and Mary Schneider. "Effectiveness of an Online Natural Family Planning Service Program." *MCN: The American Journal of Maternal Child Nursing* 42, no. 1 (January/February 2017): 43–49.

Fehring, Richard J., Mary M. Schneider, and Mary Lee Barron. "Protocol for Determining Fertility while Breastfeeding." *Fertility and Sterility* 84, no. 3 (2005): 805–807.

Fehring, Richard J., Mary M. Schneider, and Thomas Bouchard. "Effectiveness of an Online Natural Family Planning Program for Breastfeeding Women." *Journal of Obstetric, Gynecologic, and Neonatal Nursing* 46, no. 4 (July–August 2017): e129–137.

Fehring, Richard J., Mary M. Schneider, and Kathleen Raviele. "Variability in the Phases of the Menstrual Cycle." *Journal of Obstetric, Gynecologic, and Neonatal Nursing* 35, no. 3 (May–June 2006): 376–384.

———. "Efficacy of Hormonal Fertility Monitoring as a Method of Natural Family Planning." *Journal of Obstetric, Gynecologic, and Neonatal Nursing* 36, no. 2 (2007): 152–160.

Fehring, Richard J., Mary M. Schneider, Kathleen Raviele, and Mary Lee Barron. "Efficacy of Cervical Mucus Observations Plus Electronic Hormonal Fertility Monitoring as a Method of Natural Family Planning." *Journal of Obstetric, Gynecologic, and Neonatal Nursing* 36, no. 2 (March–April 2007):152–160.

Fehring, Richard J., Mary M. Schneider, Kathleen Raviele, Dana Rodriguez, and Jessica E. Pruszynski. "Randomized Comparison of Two Internet-Supported Fertility Awareness Based Methods of Family Planning." *Contraception* 88, no. 1 (July 2013): 24–30.

Fehring, Richard J., and Patrick Yeung, Jr., eds. "Special Issue on Natural Family Planning: Rhythm, NFP, and Human Fertility from Popes Pius XI through Benedict XVI." *The Linacre Quarterly* 79, no. 4 (November 1, 2012): 389–392.

Finnis, John M. *Natural Law and Natural Rights*. New York: Oxford University Press, 1980.

———. "Personal Integrity, Sexual Morality, and Responsible Parenthood." In *Why* Humanae Vitae *Was Right: A Reader*, edited by Janet E. Smith, chapter 7. San Francisco: Ignatius Press, 1993.

———. "The Good of Marriage and the Morality of Sexual Relations: Some Philosophical and Historical Observations." *American Journal of Jurisprudence* 42 (1997): 97–134.

Flannery, Kevin. "Philosophical Arguments against and for *Humanae Vitae.*" *Anthropotes* 10 (1994): 189–204.

Ford, John C., and Germain Grisez. "Contraception and the Infallibility of the Ordinary Magisterium." *Theological Studies* 39, no. 2 (1978): 258–312.

Ford, John C., SJ, Germain Grisez, Joseph Boyle, John Finnis, and William E. May. *The Teaching of* Humanae Vitae: *A Defense*. San Francisco: Ignatius Press, 1988.

Frank-Herrmann, P., J. Heil, C. Gnoth, E. Toledo, S. Baur, C. Pyper, E. Jenetzky, T. Strowitzki, and G. Freundl. "The Effectiveness of a Fertility Awareness Based Method to Avoid Pregnancy in Relation to a Couple's Sexual Behaviour during the Fertile Time: A Prospective Longitudinal Study." *Human Reproduction* 22, no. 5 (May 2007): 1310–1319.

Franks, Angela. *Margaret Sanger's Eugenic Legacy: The Control of Female Fertility*. Jefferson, N.C.: MacFarland & Co., Inc., 2005.

———. *Contraception and Catholicism: What the Church Teaches and Why.* Boston: Pauline Books and Media, 2013.

Freundel, G., A. Flynn, P. Frank-Herrmann, and C. Gnoth. "European Multicenter Study of Natural Family Planning (1989–1995): Efficacy and Drop-Out." The European Natural Family Planning Study Groups. *Advances in Contraception* 15, no. 1 (1999): 69–83.

Freitas, Donna. *The End of Sex: How Hookup Culture Is Leaving a Generation Unhappy, Sexually Unfulfilled, and Confused About Intimacy.* New York: Basic Books, 2013.

García de Haro, Ramón. *Marriage and the Family in the Documents of the Magisterium: A Course in the Theology of Marriage.* Translated by William E. May. San Francisco: Ignatius Press, 1993.

Garrow, David. *Liberty and Sexuality: The Right to Privacy and the Making of Roe v. Wade.* New York: Macmillan, 1998.

George, Robert P., and Jean Bethke Elshtain, eds. *The Meaning of Marriage, Family, State, Market, & Morals.* McLean, Va.: Spence Publishing Company, 2006.

Godet, P. G., G. R. May, and L. R. Sutherland. "Meta-Analysis of the Role of Oral Contraceptive Agents in Inflammatory Bowel Disease." *Gut, An International Journal of Gastroenterology and Hepatology* 37, no. 5 (1995): 668–673.

Gondreau, Paul. "The 'Inseparable Connection' between Procreation and Unitive Love (*Humanae Vitae*, §12) and Thomistic Hylemorphic Anthropology." *Nova et Vetera* (English edition) 6, no. 4 (2008): 731–764.

Gordon, Linda. *Woman's Body, Woman's Right: Birth Control in America.* New York: Viking, 1976.

Grabowski, John S. "*Evangelium Vitae* and *Humanae Vitae*: A Tale of Two Encyclicals." *Homiletic and Pastoral Review* 97, no. 2 (November 1996): 7–15.

———. "Rival Personalisms in 20th Century Catholic Sexual Ethics." *Studia Moralia* 35 (1997): 283-312.

———. *Sex and Virtue: An Introduction to Catholic Sexual Ethics.* Washington, D.C.: The Catholic University of America Press, 2003.

———. "Contraception, Sterilization, and Abortion and the Ethical and Religious Directives." In *Moral Issues in Catholic Health Care*, edited by Kevin T. McMahon, , 68–92. Wynnewood, Pa.: St. Charles Borromeo Seminary, 2004.

———. "Natural Family Planning and Marital Spirituality." In *Integrating Faith and Science through Natural Family Planning*, edited by Richard J. Fehring and Theresa Notare, 29-45. Milwaukee: Marquette University Press, 2004.

———. "Marriage as a Unitive and Procreative Partnership." Washington, D.C.: United States Conference of Catholic Bishops, November 2005. http://www.usccb.org/laity/marriage/npim.shtml.

Greely, Henry T. *The End of Sex and the Future of Human Reproduction.* Cambridge, Mass.: Harvard University Press, 2016.

Grigg-Spall, Holly. *Sweetening the Pill: Or How We Got Hooked on Hormonal Birth Control.* Alresford, UK: John Hunt Publishing, 2013.

Grisez, Germain. *Contraception and the Natural Law.* Milwaukee: Bruce, 1964.

———. "Marriage, Sexual Acts, and Family Life." In *The Way of the Lord Jesus, Vol. 2: Living a Christian Life*. Quincy, Ill.: Franciscan Press, 1993.

Grisez, Germain, Joseph Boyle, John Finnis, and William E. May. "'Every Marital Act Ought to be Open to New Life': Toward a Clearer Understanding." *The Thomist* 52, no. 3 (July 1988): 365–426.

Grondelski, John. "Fruitfulness as an Essential Dimension of Acts of Conjugal Love: An Interpretive Study of the Pre-Pontifical Thought of John Paul II." PhD diss., Fordham University, 1985. Available through University Microfilms International, Ann Arbor, MI, #86-12858.

Guevin, Benedict. *Christian Anthropology and Sexual Ethics*. Lanham, Md.: University Press of America, 2002.

Guevin, Benedict, and Jozef D. Zalot. *Catholic Ethics in Today's World.* Winona, Minn.: St. Mary's Press, 2008.

Gurstein, Rochelle. *The Repeal of Reticence: A History of America's Cultural and Legal Struggles Over Free Speech, Obscenity, Sexual Liberation and Modern Art.* New York: Hill & Wang, 1996.

Haas, John. "The Inseparability of the Two Meanings of the Marriage Act." In *Reproductive Technologies, Marriage and the Church*, edited by the National Catholic Bioethics Center, 89–106. Braintree, Mass.: The Pope John Center, 1988.

Hanby, Michael. "Re-Conceiving the Organism: Why American Catholic Bioethics Needs a Better Theory of Human Life." *Communio: International Catholic Review* 41, no. 3 (Fall 2014): 615–631.

———. "The Gospel of Creation and the Technocratic Paradigm: Reflections on a Central Teaching of *Laudato Si'*." *Communio: International Catholic Review* 42, no. 4 (Winter 2015): 724–747.

———. *No God, No Science?: Theology, Cosmology, Biology*. Malden, Mass.: Wiley Blackwell, 2017.

Harper, Kyle. *From Shame to Sin: The Christian Transformation of Sexual Morality in Late Antiquity*. Cambridge, Mass.: Harvard University Press, 2013.

Hasson, Mary Rice, and Michele M. Hill. "What Catholic Women Think about Faith, Conscience, and Contraception." In *Exploring What Catholic Women Think*. The Women, Faith, and Culture Project, Inc., 2011.

Hilgers, Thomas W. "Human Reproduction: Three Issues for the Moral Theologian." *Theological Studies* 38, no. 1 (March 1977):136–152.

———. *The Medical Applications of Natural Family Planning.* Omaha: Pope Paul VI Institute Press, 1991.

———. *The Scientific Foundations of the Ovulation Method.* Omaha, Neb.: Pope Paul VI Institute Press, 1995.

———. *The Medical & Surgical Practice of NaProTECHNOLOGY.* Omaha: Pope Paul VI Institute Press, 2004.

———. "The New Women's Health Science of NaProTECHNOLOGY." *Archives of Perinatal Medicine* 17, no. 4 (2011): 191–198.

Hilgers, Thomas W., G. E. Abraham, and D. Cavanagh. "Natural Family Planning I. The Peak Symptom and Estimated Time of Ovulation." *Obstetrics and Gynecology* 52, no. 5 (November 1, 1978): 575–582.

Hilgers, Thomas W., K. Diane Daly, Ann M. Prebil, and Sue K. Hilgers. "Cumulative Pregnancy Rates in Patients With Apparently Normal Fertility and Fertility-Focused Intercourse." *The Journal of Reproductive Medicine* 37, no. 10 (October 1992): 864–866.

Hilgers, Thomas W., and Joseph B. Stanford. "Creighton Model NaProEducation Technology for Avoiding Pregnancy: Use Effectiveness." *The Journal of Reproductive Medicine* 43, no. 6 (June 1998): 495–502.

Hofstadter, Richard. *Social Darwinism in American Thought.* New York: Braziller, 1959.

Hogan, Richard. *The Theology of the Body in John Paul II: What It Means, Why It Matters.* Frederick, Md.: The Word Among Us Press, 2006.

Hogan, Richard, and John M. LeVoir. *Covenant of Love: Pope John Paul II on Sexuality, Marriage, and the Family in the Modern World.* 2nd ed. San Francisco: Ignatius Press, 1992.

Holy See. *Submission of the Catholic Church to the XXII Council for the International Organizations of Medical Sciences Conference on Ethics and Human Values in Family Planning: An International Dialogue on Rights and Responsibilities of Individuals and Societies.* June 19–24, 1988. Reprinted in *The International Review of Natural Family Planning* 12, no. 2 (Summer 1988): 87–105.

Institute of Medicine Committee on a Comprehensive Review of the HHS Office of Family Planning Title X Program. *A Review of the HHS Family Planning Program: Mission, Management, and Measurement of Results.* Edited by Adrienne Stith Butler and Ellen Wright Clayton. Washington, D.C.: National Academies Press, 2009.

Janssens, Louis. "Considerations on *Humanae Vitae*." *Louvain Studies* 2, no. 3 (1969): 231-253.

Jonas, Hans. *The Phenomenon of Life: Toward a Philosophical Biology.* Evanston, Ill.: Northwestern University Press, 2001.

Joyce, George Hayward. *Christian Marriage: An Historical and Doctrinal Study.* 2nd ed. London: Sheed and Ward, 1948.

Kaczor, Christopher, and Jennifer Kaczor. *The Seven Big Myths about Marriage: What Science, Faith, and Philosophy Teach Us about Love and Happiness.* San Francisco: Ignatius Press, 2014.

Kahlenborn, C. F., Modugno, D. M. Potter, and W. B. Severs. "Oral Contraceptive Use as a Risk Factor for Premenopausal Breast Cancer: A Meta-Analysis." *Mayo Clinic Proceedings* 81, no. 10 (October 2006): 1290–1302.

Kambic, Robert T., and Virginia Lamprecht. "Calendar Rhythm Efficacy: A Review." *Advances in Contraception* 12, no. 2 (1996):123–128.

Kambic, Robert T., and Theresa Notare. "Roman Catholic Church-Sponsored Natural Family Planning Services in the United States." *Advances in Contraception* 10, no. 2 (1994): 85-92.

Keefe, Edward. "Self-Examination of the Cervix as a Guide in Fertility Control." *International Review of Natural Family Planning* 10, no. 4 (Winter 1986): 333–338.

Keenan, James F. *A History of Catholic Moral Theology in the Twentieth Century: From Confessing Sins to Liberating Conscience.* New York: Continuum International Publishing Group, 2010.

Kevles, Daniel. *In the Name of Eugenics: Genetics and the Uses of Human Heredity.* New York: Knopf, 1985.

Kiely, Bartholomew. "Contraception, In Vitro Fertilization and the Principle of Inseparability." *The Linacre Quarterly* 56, no. 2 (1989): 68–75.

Kippley, John. *Sex and the Marriage Covenant.* San Francisco: Ignatius Press, 2005. First published 1991 by The Couple to Couple League International, Inc. (Cincinnati).

Kippley, John, and Sheila Kippley. *The Art of Natural Family Planning.* 4th ed. Cincinnati: Couple to Couple League, 1996.

Klaus, H., J. M. Goebel, B. Muraski, M. T. Egizio, D. Weitzel, R. S. Taylor, M. U. Fagan K. Ek, and K. Hobday. "Use Effectiveness and Client Satisfaction in Six Centers Teaching the Billings Ovulation Method." *Contraception* 19, no. 6 (1978): 613–629.

Knaus, Herman. *Periodic Fertility and Sterility in Woman: A Natural Method of Birth Control.* Vienna: Wilhelm Maudrich Publisher, 1934.

Kupczak, Jaroslaw. *Gift and Communion: John Paul II's Theology of the Body.* Washington, D.C.: The Catholic University of America Press, 2014.

Kwasniewski, Peter. "St. Thomas on the Grandeur and Limitations of Marriage." *Nova et Vetera* (English edition) 10, no. 2 (Spring 2012): 415–436.

Lasnoski, Kent. *Vocation to Virtue: Christian Marriage as a Consecrated Life.* Washington, D.C.: The Catholic University of America Press, 2014.

Latkovic, Mark S. "God and True Christian Love: The Church on Openness to Life." *Ethics & Medics* 32, no. 7 (August 2007): 3–4.

———. "Is the Teaching of *Humanae Vitae* Physicalist? A Critique of the View of Joseph A. Selling." *The Linacre Quarterly* 62, no. 4 (November 1, 1995): 39–58.

———. "Pope John Paul II's 'Theology of the Body' and the Significance of Sexual Shame in Light of the Body's 'Nuptial' Meaning: Some Implications for Bioethics and Sexual Ethics." *Nova et Vetera* (English edition) 2, no. 2 (Fall 2004): 305–336.

Latz, Leo. *The Rhythm of Sterility and Fertility in Women: A Discussion of the Physiological, Practical, and Ethical Aspects of the Discoveries of Drs. K. Ogino (Japan) and H. Knaus (Austria) regarding the Periods when Conception is Impossible and when Possible.* Chicago: Latz Foundation, 1932.

Latz, Leo J., and E. Reiner. "Natural Conception Control." *Journal of the American Medical Association* 105, no. 16 (October 19, 1935): 1241–1246.

Lee, Patrick. *Abortion and Human Life.* 2nd ed. Washington, D.C.: The Catholic University of America Press, 2010.

Lee, Patrick, and Robert P. George. "What Sex Can Be: Self-Alienation, Illusion, or One-Flesh Union." *American Journal of Jurisprudence* 42, no. 1, art. 5 (1997): 135–157.

———. *Body-Self Dualism in Contemporary Ethics and Politics*. New York: Cambridge University Press, 2008.

———. *Conjugal Union: What Marriage Is and Why It Matters*. New York: Cambridge University Press, 2014.

Lewis, C. S. *The Abolition of Man*. New York: Harper Collins Publishers, 2001.

———. *The Great Divorce*. New York: Simon & Schuster, 1996.

———. *The Four Loves*. New York: Houghton Mifflin Harcourt, 1991.

Manhart, Michael, Marguerite Duane, April Lind, Irit Sinai, and Jean Golden-Tevald. "Fertility Awareness-Based Methods of Family Planning: A Review of Effectiveness for Avoiding Pregnancy Using SORT." *Osteopathic Family Physician* 5, no. 1 (2013): 2–8.

Marshall, John. "A Field Trial of the Basal-Body-Temperature Method of Regulating Births." *Lancet* 292, no. 7558 (July 6, 1968): 8–10.

Marshall, Robert, and Charles Donovan. *Blessed are the Barren*. San Francisco: Ignatius Press, 1991.

Martin, Francis. "Male and Female He Created Them: A Summary of Genesis Chapter One." *Communio: International Catholic Review* 20, no. 2 (1993): 240-265.

Masek, Lawrence. "Improving the Analogies in Contralife Arguments: The Consistency of Catholic Teachings about Regulating Births." *The Heythrop Journal* 49, no. 3 (2008): 442–452.

May, William E. *Sex, Marriage, and Chastity: Reflections of a Catholic Layman, Spouse, and Parent*. Chicago: Franciscan Herald Press, 1981.

———. *Sex and the Sanctity of Human Life*. Front Royal, Va.: Christendom Press, 1985.

———. "Sexual Ethics and Human Dignity." In *Persona Verita E Morale, Atti del Congresso Internazionale di Teologia Morale*, 477–495. Roma, 7–12 Aprile 1986. Vatican City: Citta Nuova Editrice, 1986.

———. "The Moral Methodology of Vatican II and the Teaching of *Humanae Vitae* and *Persona Humana*." *Anthropotes* 8 (1992): 41–60.

———. *Marriage: The Rock on Which the Family Is Built*. 2nd ed. San Francisco: Ignatius Press, 2009.

———. *Theology of the Body in Context: Genesis and Growth*. Boston: Pauline Books & Media, 2010.

May, William E., Ronald Lawler, OFM, and Joseph Boyle, Jr. *Catholic Sexual Ethics: A Summary, Explanation, and Defense*. 3rd ed. Huntington, Ind.: Our Sunday Visitor Press, 2011.

McCarthy, Donald, and Edward Bayer, eds. *Handbook on Critical Sexual Issues*. Revised ed. Philadelphia: The Pope John Center, 1989.

McCarthy, Margaret Harper, ed. *Torn Asunder: Children, The Myth of the Good Divorce and the Recovery of Origins*. Grand Rapids, Mich.: Eerdmans Publishing, 2016.

McClory, Robert. *Turning Point.* New York: Crossroad, 1995.

McLanahan, Sara, Laura Tach, and Daniel Schneider. "The Causal Effects of Father Absence." *Annual Review of Sociology* 39 (2013): 399–427.

Melina, Livio. *Learning to Love at the School of John Paul II and Benedict XVI.* Translated by Joel Wallace. Leominster, UK: Gracewing, 2011.

Miller, Jennifer E. "The Virtue of Sobriety: Integral Human Ecology in its Full Flourishing." *Nova et Vetera* (English edition) 16, no. 1 (Winter 2018): 205–229.

Mørch, Lina S., Charlotte W. Skovlund, Philip C. Hannaford, Lisa Iversen, Shona Fielding, and Øjvind Lidegaard. "Contemporary Hormonal Contraception and the Risk of Breast Cancer." *New England Journal of Medicine* 377 (Dec. 7, 2017): 2228–2239.

Morse, Jennifer Roback. *Smart Sex: Finding Life-Long Love in a Hook-Up World.* Dallas: Spence Publishing Company, 2005.

Mosher, Steven W. *Population Control: Real Costs, Illusory Benefits.* Piscataway, N.J.: Transaction Publishers, 2008.

Mu, Qiyan, and Richard J. Fehring. "Efficacy of Achieving Pregnancy with Fertility-Focused Intercourse." *MCN: The American Journal of Maternal/Child Nursing* 39, no. 1 (January–February 2014): 35–40.

Murphy, William F. "Revisiting Contraception: An Integrated Approach in Light of the Renewal of Thomistic Virtue Ethics." *Theological Studies* 72, no. 4 (December 1, 2011): 812–847.

New, Michael J. "Analyzing the Impact of State Level Contraception Mandates on Public Health Outcomes." *Ave Maria Law Review* 13, no. 2 (2015): 345–369.

Noonan, Jr., John T. *Contraception: A History of its Treatment by the Catholic Theologians and Canonists*. Cambridge, Mass.: Belknap Press, 1965.

———. *The Morality of Abortion: Legal and Historical Perspectives.* Cambridge, Mass.: Harvard University Press, 1970.

Notare, Theresa. "A Revolution in Christian Morals." Resolution No. 15 of Lambeth 1930." *Revue d'Histoire Ecclésiastique*. "Part I, Resolution No. 15, The Story." 94, no. 1 (1999): 54–75; "Part II, The Public Debate." 94, no. 2 (1999): 471–501.

———. *"A Revolution in Christian Morals." Lambeth 1930-Resolution #15, History & Reception.* PhD diss., The Catholic University of America, 2008.

Notare, Theresa, Alice Heinzen, and Cindy Leonard. "Diocesan NFP Ministry: Failures and Successes–Lessons Learned." *Anthropotes* 34, nos. 1–2 (2018): 375–388.

Odeblad, Erik. "Cervical Mucus and their Functions." *Journal of the Irish Colleges of Physicians and Surgeons* 26, no. 1 (1997): 27–32.

Ogino, Kyusaku. *Conception Period of Women.* Harrisburg, Pa.: Medical Arts Publishing Company, 1934.

Ouellet, Marc Cardinal. *Mystery and Sacrament of Love: A Theology of Marriage and the Family for the New Evangelization.* Translated by Michelle K. Borras and Adrian J. Walker. Grand Rapids, Mich.: Eerdmans Publishing, 2015.

Parenteau-Carreau, Suzanne. "The Sympto-Thermal Methods." *International Journal of Fertility* 26, no. 3 (1981): 170–181.

Petri, Thomas, OP. *Aquinas and the Theology of the Body: The Thomistic Foundations of John Paul II's Anthropology*. Washington, D.C.: The Catholic University of America Press, 2016.

Piderit, John J. *Sexual Morality: A Natural Law Approach to Intimate Relationships*. Oxford: Oxford University Press, 2012.

Pieper, Josef. *On Love*. San Francisco: Ignatius Press, 1997.

———. *Faith, Hope, Love*. San Francisco: Ignatius Press, 2012.

Pinckaers, Servais, OP. *The Sources of Christian Ethics*. Translated by Sr. Mary Thomas Noble, OP. Washington, D.C.: The Catholic University of America Press, 1995.

Pontifical Council for the Family. *The Truth and Meaning of Human Sexuality: Guidelines for Education within the Family*. December 8, 1995.

———. *Vademecum for Confessors Concerning Some Aspects of the Morality of Conjugal Life*. February 12, 1997.

Pope Benedict XVI. *Deus caritas est*. Encyclical Letter. December 5, 2005.

———. *Spe salvi*. Encyclical Letter. November 30, 2007.

———. *Caritas in veritate*. Encyclical Letter. June 29, 2009.

———. *Address on the Occasion of Christmas Greetings to the Roman Curia*. December 21, 2012.

Pope Francis. *Evangelii gaudium*. Apostolic Exhortation. November 24, 2013.

———. *Laudato si'*. Encyclical Letter. May 24, 2015.

———. *Amoris laetitia*. Apostolic Exhortation. April 8, 2016.

Pope John Paul II. *Redemptor hominis*. Encyclical Letter. March 4, 1979.

———. *Familiaris consortio*. Apostolic Exhortation. November 22, 1981.

———. *Mulieris dignitatem*. Apostolic Letter. August 15, 1988.

———. *Veritatis splendor*. Encyclical Letter. August 6, 1993.

———. *Gratissimam sane*. Letter to Families. February 2, 1994.

———. *Women: Teachers of Peace*. Message for World Day of Peace. January 1, 1995.

———. *Evangelium vitae*. Encyclical Letter. March 25, 1995.

———. *Man and Woman He Created Them—A Theology of the Body*. Translated by Michael Waldstein. Boston: Pauline Books and Media, 2006.

———. *Pope John Paul II Speaks on Women*. Edited by Brooke Williams Deely. Washington, D.C.: The Catholic University of America Press, 2014.

Pope Paul VI. *Humanae vitae*. Encyclical Letter. July 25, 1968.

———. *Octogesima adveniens*. Apostolic Letter. May 14, 1971.

———. *25th Allocution to the General Assembly of Pharmacology*. September 7, 1974.

Pope Pius XI. *Casti connubii*. Encyclical Letter. December 31, 1930.

———. *Address to Physicians*. 1932.

Pope Pius XII. *Allocution to Midwives*. October 29, 1951.

———. *Address to the National Congress of the Family Front and the Association of Large Families*. November 26, 1951.

———. *The Moral Limits of Medical Research and Treatment: Address to the First International Congress on the Histopathology of the Nervous System*. September 14, 1952.

Pruss, Alexander. *One Body: An Essay in Christian Sexual Ethics*. Notre Dame, Ind.: University of Notre Dame Press, 2013.

Putnam, Robert D. *Our Kids: The Dream in Crisis*. New York: Simon & Schuster, 2016.

Quay, Paul M. *The Christian Meaning of Human Sexuality*. San Francisco: Ignatius Press, 1985.

Queenan, John T., Victoria H. Jennings, Jeffery M Spieler, and Helena von Hertzen, eds. *Natural Family Planning: Current Knowledge and New Strategies for the 1990s. Proceedings of a conference, Part II, Georgetown University, Washington, DC, December 10–14, 1990*. Washington, D.C.: Georgetown University Institute for International Studies in Natural Family Planning, 1991.

Ratzinger, Joseph. "Concerning the Notion of Person in Theology." *Communio: International Catholic Review* 17 (Fall 1990): 439–454.

———. "Truth and Freedom." *Communio: International Catholic Review* 23 (Spring 1996): 16–35.

———."Difficulties Confronting the Faith in Europe Today." *Communio: International Catholic Review* 38 (Winter 2011): 728–737.

Regnerus, Mark. *Cheap Sex: The Transformation of Men, Marriage, and Monogamy*. New York: Oxford University Press, 2017.

Regnerus, Mark, and Jeremy Uecker. *Premarital Sex in America: How Young Americans Meet, Mate, and Think about Marrying*. New York: Oxford University Press, 2011.

Reed, James W. *The Birth Control Movement and American Society: From Private Vice to Public Virtue*. Princeton: Princeton University Press, 1993.

Rhonheimer, Martin. "Contraception, Sexual Behavior, and Natural Law: Philosophical Foundation of the Norm of *Humanae Vitae*." *The Linacre Quarterly* 56, no. 2 (May 1, 1989): 20–57.

———. *Ethics of Procreation and the Defense of Human Life: Contraception, Artificial Fertilization, and Abortion*. Washington, D.C.: The Catholic University of America Press, 2010.

Ribar, David C. "Why Marriage Matters for Child Wellbeing." In *Marriage and Child Wellbeing Revisited*, edited by Sara McLanahan and Isabel Sawhill. Special Issue. *The Future of Children:* 25, no. 2 (Fall 2015): 11–27.

Rice, F. J., C. A. Lanctot, and D. Garcia-Devesa. "Effectiveness of the Sympto-Thermal Method of Natural Family Planning: An International Study." *International Journal of Fertility* 26, no. 3 (1981): 222–230.

Riley, Patrick. *Civilizing Sex: On Chastity and the Common Good*. Edinburgh: T & T Clark, 2000.

Robinson, Warren C. and John A. Ross, eds. *The Global Family Planning Revolution: Three Decades of Population Policies and Programs*. Washington D.C.: World Bank, 2007.

Roos, J. Sarah Weddell, Erhard Godehardt, Julia Schiffner, Günter Freundl, and Christian Gnoth. "Monitoring the Menstrual Cycle: Comparison of Urinary and Serum Reproductive Hormones Referenced to True Ovulation." *The European Journal of Contraception and Reproductive Health Care* 20, no. 6 (2015): 438–450.

Rosen, Christine. *Preaching Eugenics: Religious Leaders and the American Eugenics Movement*. Oxford. Oxford University Press, 2004.

Rötzer, Josef. "Further Evolution of the Sympto-Thermal Methods." *International Review of Natural Family Planning* 1, no. 2 (Summer 1977): 139–150.

———. *Family Planning the Natural Way: A Complete Guide to the Symptom-Thermal Method—Including Questionnaires, Charts, and Reliable Procedures.* Old Tappan, N.J.: Fleming H. Revell Co., 1981.

Santamaria, Carmen, and Angelique Ruhi-Lopez, *The Infertility Companion for Catholics: Spiritual and Practical Support for Couples*. Notre Dame, Ind.: Ave Maria Press, 2012.

Schemenauer, Kevin. *Conjugal Love and Procreation: Dietrich von Hildebrand's Superabundant Integration*. Lanham, Md.: Lexington Books, 2011.

Schneider, A. P., C. M. Zainer, C. K. Kubat, N. K. Mullen, and A. K. Windisch. "The Breast Cancer Epidemic: 10 Facts." *The Linacre Quarterly* 81, no. 3 (August 2014): 244–277.

Schindler, D. C. "Perfect Difference: Gender and the Analogy of Being." *Communio: International Catholic Review* 43 (Summer 2016): 194–231.

Schu, Walter J. *The Splendor of Love: John Paul II's Vision for Marriage and Family.* New Hope, Ky.: New Hope Publications, 2003.

Seaman, Barbara. *The Doctor's Case Against the Pill.* Alameda: Peter Wyden, 1969.

Shivanandan, Mary. *Crossing the Threshold of Love, A New Vision of Marriage in the Light of John Paul II's Anthropology*. Washington, D.C.: The Catholic University Press, 1999.

Smith, Janet E. "The *Munus* of Transmitting Human Life: A New Approach to *Humanae Vitae*." *The Thomist* 54, no. 3 (July 1990): 385–427.

———. Humanae Vitae*: A Generation Later.* Washington, D.C.: The Catholic University of America Press, 1991.

———, ed. *Why* Humanae Vitae *was Right: A Reader.* San Francisco: Ignatius Press, 1993.

———. "The Error of Proportionalism." *Ethics and Medics* 19, no. 6 (June 1994): 1–3.

———. "Moral Terminology and Proportionalism." In *Recovering Nature: Essays in Natural Philosophy, Ethics, and Metaphysics in Honor of Ralph McInerny,* edited by Thomas Hibbs and John O'Callaghan, 127–146. Notre Dame, Ind.: University of Notre Dame Press, 1999.

———. "The Morality of Condom Use by HIV-Infected Spouses." *The Thomist* 70, no. 1 (January 2006): 27–69.

———. "The *Sensus Fidelium* and *Humanae Vitae*." *Angelicum* 83 (2006): 271–297.

———. "Conscious Parenthood." *Nova et Vetera* (English edition) 6, no. 4 (2008): 927–950.

———. "Conscience, Contraception, and Catholic Health-Care Professionals." *The Linacre Quarterly* 77, no. 2 (May 1, 2010): 204–228.

———. "The Kraków Document." *Nova et Vetera* 10, no. 2 (Spring 2012): 361–381.

———. "The Universality of Natural Law and the Irreducibility of Personalism." *Nova et Vetera* (English edition) 11, no. 4 (Fall 2013): 1229–1247

———, ed. *Why* Humanae Vitae *is Still Right*. San Francisco: Ignatius Press, 2018.

Smith, Janet E., and Christopher Kaczor. *Life Issues, Medical Choices: Questions and Answers for Catholics*. 2nd ed. Cincinnati: Servant, 2016.

Smith, Janet E., John S. Grabowski, J. Budziszewski, and Maria Fedoryka. "Self-Gift: The Heart of *Humanae vitae*." *National Catholic Bioethics Quarterly* 16, no. 3 (Autumn 2016): 449–474.

Smith, Russell E., ed. *Trust the Truth, A Symposium on the Twentieth Anniversary of the Encyclical* Humanae vitae. Braintree, Mass.: The Pope John Center, 1991.

Spaemann, Robert. *Persons: The Difference between 'Someone' and 'Something.'* Oxford: Oxford University Press, 2006.

Sri, Edward. *Men, Women and the Mystery of Love: Practical Insights from John Paul II's Love and Responsibility*. Ann Arbor, Mich.: Servant, 2007.

Stanford, Joseph B. "Population, Reproductive, and Sexual Health: Data are Essential Where Disciplines Meet and Ideologies Conflict." *Frontiers in Public Health* 4 (March 7, 2016): 27.

Stanford, Joseph B., A. G. Hutchinson, and J. G. Payne. "Utah Couples' Potential Use of Natural Family Planning." *Utah's Health: An Annual Review* 9, no. 1, (2003): 40–45.

Stanford, Joseph B., J. C. Lemaire, and P. B. Thurman. "Women's Interest in Natural Family Planning." *The Journal of Family Practice* 46, no. 1 (January 1998): 65–71

Stanford, Joseph B., Tracey A. Parnell, and Phil C. Boyle. "Outcomes from Treatment with Natural Procreative Technology in an Irish General Practice." *Journal of the American Board of Family Medicine* 21, no. 5 (November–December 2008): 375–384.

Stanford, Joseph B., and C. A. Porucznik. "Enrollment, Childbearing Motivations, and Intentions of Couples in the Creighton Model Effectiveness, Intentions, and Behaviors Assessment (CEIBA) Study." *Frontiers in Medicine (Lausanne)* 4 (2017): 147.

Stanford, Joseph B., S. E. Simonsen, and L. Baksh. "Fertility Treatments and Adverse Perinatal Outcomes in a Population-based Sampling of Births in Florida, Maryland, and Utah: A Cross-Sectional Study." *British Journal of Obstetrics and Gynaecology* 123, no. 5 (April 2016): 718–729.

Stanford, Joseph B., and K. R. Smith. "Characteristics of Women Associated with Continuing Instruction in the Creighton Model Fertility Care System." *Contraception* 61, no. 2 (2000): 121–129.

Stanford, Joseph B., Ken R. Smith, and Michael W. Varner. "Impact of Instruction in the Creighton Model Fertility*Care*™ System on Time to Pregnancy in Couples of Proven Fecundity: Results of a Randomized Trial." *Paediatric Perinatal Epidemiology* 28, no. 5 (September 2014): 391–399.

Stanford, Joseph B., P. B. Thurman, and J. C. Lemaire. "Physicians' Knowledge and Practices regarding Natural Family Planning." *Obstetrics and Gynecology* 94 (November 1999): 672–678.

Svendal, Gjertrud, Michael Berk, Julie A. Pasco, Felice N. Jacka, Anders Lund, and Lana J. Williams. "The Use of Hormonal Contraceptive Agents and Mood Disorders in Women." *Journal of Affective Disorders* 140, no. 1 (September 2012): 92–96.

Synod of Bishops. *Instrumentum Laboris* [*The Pastoral Challenges of the Family in the Context of Evangelization*]. June 26, 2014. http://www.vatican.va/roman_curia/synod/index.htm.

Tentler, Leslie. *Catholics and Contraception: An American History*. Ithaca, N.Y.: Cornell University Press, 2004.

Tham, Elizabeth, Karen Schliep, and Joseph B. Stanford. "Natural Procreative Technology for Infertility and Recurrent Miscarriage: Outcomes in a Canadian Family Practice." *Canadian Family Physician* 58, no. 5 (2012): e267–274.

Tiger, Lionel. *The Decline of Males*. New York: St. Martin's Griffin, 1999.

Tranzillo, Jeffrey. *John Paul II on the Vulnerable*. Washington, D.C.: The Catholic University of America Press, 2012.

Travaline, John M., and Louise A. Mitchell, eds. *Catholic Witness in Health Care: Practicing Medicine in Truth and Love*. Washington, D.C.: The Catholic University of America Press, 2017.

Trussell, J., B. Vaughan, and J. B. Stanford. "Are All Contraceptive Failures Unintended Pregnancies? Evidence from the 1995 National Survey of Family Growth." *Family Planning Perspectives* 31, no. 5 (1999): 246–247, 260.

Twomey, D. Vincent. *Moral Theology after* Humanae Vitae*: Fundamental Issues in Moral Theory and Sexual Ethics*. Portland, Ore.: Four Courts Press, 2010.

United State Catholic Conference. *Human Sexuality: A Catholic Perspective for Education and Lifelong Learning*. Washington, D.C.: United States Catholic Conference,1991.

United States Conference of Catholic Bishops. *Married Love and the Gift of Life*. Washington, D.C.: United States Conference of Catholic Bishops, November 2006.

———. *Ethical Directives for Catholic Hospitals*. 5th ed. Washington, D.C.: United States Conference of Catholic Bishops, November, 2009.

———. *Life-Giving Love in an Age of Technology*. Washington, D.C.: United States Conference of Catholic Bishops, November 17, 2009.

———. *Marriage: Love and Life in the Divine Plan*. Pastoral Letter. Washington, D.C.: United States Conference of Catholic Bishops, November 17, 2009.

United States Conference of Catholic Bishops Committee for Pro-Life Activities. *Human Sexuality from God's Perspective,* Humanae Vitae *25 Years Later*. Statement. 1993.

Uricchio, William A., and Mary Kay Williams, eds. *Proceedings of a Research Conference on Natural Family Planning*. Washington, D.C.: The Human Life Foundation, 1973.

Vande Vusse, L., L. Hanson, R. J. Fehring, A. Newman, and J. Fox. "Couples' Views of the Effects of Natural Family Planning on Marital Dynamics." *Journal of Nursing Scholarship* 35, no. 2 (April 2003): 171–176.

Vatican Council II. *Lumen gentium*. Dogmatic Constitution on the Church. November 21, 1964.

———. *Optatam totius*. Decree on Priestly Training. October 28, 1965.

———. *Dei verbum*. Dogmatic Constitution on Divine Revelation. November 18, 1965.

———. *Gaudium et spes*. Pastoral Constitution on the Church in the Modern World. December 7, 1965.

Vigil, Pilar, Leonard F. Blackwell, and Manuel E. Cortés. "The Importance of Fertility Awareness in the Assessment of a Woman's Health: A Review." *The Linacre Quarterly* 79, no. 4 (2012): 426–450.

Vollman, Rudolf F. "Assessment of the Fertile and Sterile Phases of the Menstrual Cycle." *International Review of Natural Family Planning* 1, no. 1 (Spring 1977): 40–47.

———. *The Menstrual Cycle*. Philadelphia: W. B. Saunders, 1977.

Von Hildebrand, Dietrich. *Purity: The Mystery of Christian Sexuality*. Steubenville, Ohio: Franciscan University, 1989. First printed in English as *In Defense of Purity: An Analysis of the Catholic Ideals of Purity and Virginity*. New York: Sheed and Ward, 1927.

———. *Marriage: The Mystery of Faithful Love.* Manchester, N.H.: Sophia Institute Press, 1991. First printed in English as *Marriage*. London: Longman & Todd, 1942.

———. *Man, Woman, and the Meaning of Love.* Manchester, N.H.: Sophia Institute Press, 2002. First printed in English as Man and Woman: *Love and the Meaning of Intimacy*. Chicago: Franciscan Herald Press, 1966.

———. *The Encyclical* Humanae Vitae*: A Sign of Contradiction.* Chicago: Franciscan Herald Press, 1968.

Wade, M. E., P. McCarthy, G. D., Barunstein, J. R. Abernathy, C. M. Suchindran, G. S. Harris, H. C. Danzer, and W. A. Uricchio. "A Randomized Prospective Study of the Use Effectiveness of Two Methods of Natural Family Planning." *American Journal of Obstetrics and Gynecology* 141, no. 4 (October 15, 1981): 368–376.

Waite, Linda, and Maggie Gallagher. *The Case for Marriage: Why Married People Are Happier, Healthier, and Better Off Financially.* New York: Broadway Books, 2000.

Watkins, Elizabeth Siegel. *On the Pill: A Social History of Oral Contraceptives, 1950–1970.* Baltimore: Johns Hopkins University Press, 1998.

Watt, Helen, ed. *Fertility & Gender: Issues in Reproductive and Sexual Ethics.* London: The Anscombe Bioethics Center, 2011.

Westoff, Charles F., and Elsie F. Jones. "The Secularization of U.S. Catholic Birth Control Practices." *Family Planning Perspectives* 9, no. 5 (September/October 1977): 203–207.

Wilcox, W. Bradford, Jared R. Anderson, William Doherty, David Eggbeen, Christopher G. Ellison, William Galston, Neil Gilbert, John Gottman, and Ron Haskins. *Why Marriage Matters, Third Edition: Thirty Conclusions from the Social Sciences.* New York: Broadway Publications, 2011.

Williams, Daniel K. *Defenders of the Unborn: The Pro-Life Movement before Roe v. Wade.* New York: Oxford University Press, 2016.

Williams, William V. "Hormonal Contraception and the Development of Autoimmunity: A Review of the Literature." *The Linacre Quarterly* 84, no. 3 (2017): 275–295.

Windley-Daoust, Susan. *Theology of the Body, Extended: The Spiritual Signs of Birth, Impairment and Dying.* Cincinnati: Lectio Publishing, 2014.

Wojtyła, Karol. *Love and Responsibility.* Translated by H. T. Willetts. New York: Farrar, Straus, Giroux, 1981. A New Translation, translated by Grzegorz Ignatik. Boston: Pauline Books & Media, 2013.

———. "The Anthropological Vision of *Humanae Vitae.*" Translated by William May. *Nova et Vetera* (English edition) 7, no. 3 (2009): 731–750. First published in Italian in *Lateranum* 44 (1978): 125–145.

Wojtyła, Karol, Stanislas Smolenski, Thadeus Slipko, Jules Turowicz, Georges Bajda, and Charles Meissner. "The Foundations of the Church's Doctrine Concerning the Principles of Conjugal Life: A Memorandum Composed by a Group of Moral Theologians from Kraków." English title, "Concerning the Principles of Conjugal Life." Translated by Thérèse Scarpelli Cory and Janet E. Smith. *Nova et Vetera* (English edition) 10, no. 2 (Spring 2012): 321–359.

World Health Organization. "A Prospective Multicentre Trial of the Ovulation Method of Natural Family Planning, II: The Effectiveness Phase." *Fertility and Sterility* 36, no. 5 (November 1981): 591–598.

About the Authors

Erin Adams, MD, Cornell University Resident Physician

Helen M. Alvaré, JD, Professor of Law, Antonin Scalia Law School, George Mason University

J. Budziszewski, PhD, Professor of Government and Philosophy, The University of Texas at Austin

Most Rev. Charles J. Chaput, OFM Cap., Archbishop of Philadelphia and Chairman, Committee on Laity, Marriage, Family Life and Youth, United States Conference of Catholic Bishops (2017–2019)

Teresa Stanton Collett, JD, Professor of Law, University of St. Thomas School of Law, and Director, University of St. Thomas Prolife Center

Donald T. Critchlow, PhD, Katzin Family Professor of History, Arizona State University, and Director, Center for Political Thought and Leadership (CPTL)

Marguerite R. Duane, MD, Adjunct Associate Professor, Georgetown University, School of Medicine, and Executive Director, FACTS (Fertility Appreciation Collaborative to Teach the Science), an organization dedicated to educating health-care professionals and medical students about the scientifically valid natural or fertility awareness-based methods of family planning

Mary Eberstadt, Senior Research Fellow, the Faith & Reason Institute, Washington, D.C.

Maria Fedoryka, PhD, Chair, Department of Philosophy, and Associate Professor of Philosophy, Ave Maria University

Richard J. Fehring, PhD, RN, FAAN, Professor Emeritus of Nursing, and Director of the Marquette University College of Nursing Institute for Natural Family Planning, Marquette University

John S. Grabowski, PhD, Associate Professor of Moral Theology, The Catholic University of America, Washington, D.C.

Michael Hanby, PhD, Associate Professor of Religion and Philosophy of Science, The Pontifical John Paul II Institute for Studies on Marriage and Family at The Catholic University of America, Washington, D.C.

Suzanne Nortier Hollman, PsyD, MSc, Associate Professor, Co-director, Institute for Psychological Sciences Training Clinic (Virginia)

Christopher Kaczor, PhD, Professor of Philosophy, Loyola Marymount University (California)

Elizabeth R. Kirk, JD, Associate Scholar, Charlotte Lozier Institute, and Kowalski Chair of Catholic Thought and Director of the Institute for Faith and Culture at St. Lawrence Campus Center, University of Kansas

Patrick Lee, PhD, Professor of Philosophy, the John N. and Jamie D. McAleer Chair in Bioethics, and Director of The Center for Bioethics, Franciscan University of Steubenville

Margaret Harper McCarthy, STD, Assistant Professor of Theological Anthropology, and Director of the Center for Cultural and Pastoral Research, Pope John Paul II Pontifical Institute for Studies on Marriage and the Family at The Catholic University of America

Theresa Notare, PhD, Assistant Director, Natural Family Planning Program, Secretariat for Laity, Marriage, Family Life and Youth, United States Conference of Catholic Bishops, Washington, D.C.

Kathleen M. Raviele, MD, Medical Consultant, Marquette University School of Nursing Institute for Natural Family Planning

Janet E. Smith, PhD, Professor of Moral Theology, Father Michael J. McGivney Chair of Life Ethics, Sacred Heart Major Seminary, Archdiocese of Detroit

Joseph B. Stanford, MD, MSPH, CFCMC, Professor, Department of Obstetrics and Gynecology; Adjunct Professor, Department of Pediatrics; Director, Office of Cooperative Reproductive Health, University of Utah School of Medicine

Deacon William V. Williams, MD, President and CEO, BriaCell Therapeutics Corporation